Exam Pro
Property

What is *Exam Pro*?

Exam Pro is a study aid that helps law students prepare to take their Property exams. Taking the sample exams and using the corresponding answers and analysis provides students with a more thorough understanding of Property and a better understanding of how to take exams.

What *Exam Pro* offers you:

- *Exam Pro* contains 8 comprehensive Property exams.

- Each *Exam Pro* contains 25 detailed problems.

- Detailed **Answer Keys** explain the best possible answer choice, why the other answers are not the best ones, and identify "red herring" answers designed to lure you toward incorrect responses.

Why *Exam Pro* will work for you:

- *Exam Pro* answers provide detailed analysis to help you recognize similar issues on your exam and provide complete and accurate responses.

- A **Table of Problems** helps you to locate specific topic areas and/or rules being tested by the different problems in the exams, which allows you to focus on the knowledge you know you need to improve.

- *Exam Pro* expands your scope of learning and understanding beyond the sample questions by providing citations to the leading Property Hornbooks and Treatises for each answer and explanation.

- *Exam Pro* was written by Peter T. Wendel, a respected and experienced law professor at the Pepperdine University School of Law. Professor Wendel has taught Property for over 20 years and has published a number of books in the Property area.

Exam Pro
from Thomson West

PROPERTY
Second Edition

By

PETER T. WENDEL
Professor of Law
Pepperdine University School of Law

Exam Pro

Mat #40603048

© West, a Thomson business, 2000
© 2007 Thomson/West
     610 Opperman Drive
     St. Paul, MN 55123
     1–800–313–9378
Printed in the United States of America

ISBN: 978–0–314–18070–4

 TEXT IS PRINTED ON 10% POST CONSUMER RECYCLED PAPER

*To all the students from whom
I've learned so much; especially Zean,
for teaching us how to handle
the real tests life inevitably presents.*

TO THE STUDENT:

This book is the Property contribution to West Group's new *Exam Pro* series. It is based on, and closely follows in presentation, the excellent Civil Procedure *Exam Pro* by Professor Linda S. Mullenix at the University of Texas School of Law.

The book consists of eight examinations in property, containing a total of 200 OBJECTIVE QUESTIONS. Virtually all of these questions are *actual, final exam questions* (some originally in essay form) which are being released for the first time. The questions will give you a real sense of the quality and type of questions you should be prepared to answer on an exam. Admittedly, a handful of these questions may be better suited for essay questions than objective, multiple choice questions, but exposing you to these questions will better prepare you for whatever questions you get on your final - be it multiple choice or essay. Moreover, a handful of these questions may be close calls. Reasonable people could disagree over which is the "best" answer. Nevertheless, by exposing you to tough, challenging problems, and by forcing you to wrestle with the different answers, you will be better prepared for whatever you encounter on your exam.

Each exam consists of twenty-five objective problems, followed by four to five multiple-choice answers. In the back of this book are tear-out answer sheets to allow you to take each exam under simulated examination conditions. Each exam is intended to take approximately one hour. If your professor permits you to use other materials during your exam, then use these as well.

Each exam has an answer key with a thorough discussion of the relevant rules and a step-by-step, detailed explanation of the analysis for the problem. The answer key explains why the *best* answer is the best choice, and it explains why the other proposed answers are incorrect, or not the best possible choice. The answer key also identifies "red herring" answers that are intended to lure you into appropriate-sounding, but incorrect, responses.

The primary purpose of this book is to assist first-year property students in preparing for objective, multiple choice examination questions. The questions, however, can also be used to help students prepare for essay questions. Many of the problems are essay quality fact patterns. The answer key explanations are well written, exam quality answers. Students can take the questions as objective, multiple choice examinations, or students can write out essay answers for the questions and compare their essays to the answer key explanations.

The answer key explanations set forth the relevant Property rules and take you step-by-step through the analysis. By the end of each answer explanation, you should not only understand the relevant Property rule better, you should also have a better understanding of how to apply the rule.

In addition to the thorough answer key explanations, for each answer the text provides up-to-date citations to some of the leading Property resources, including: the Stoebuck & Whitman Hornbook, PROPERTY (WEST 3D ED 2000), and the classic, multi-volume treatises POWELL ON REAL PROPERTY and THOMPSON ON REAL PROPERTY. Students are referred to the appropriate sections of these works for additional explanations of the rules, rationale, and analysis which went into the answer for each problem.

Each first-year Property course is taught differently at each law school, and each professor teaches selected topics in different sequences. This is becoming increasingly true as law schools cut the basic Property course from 6 credit hours, to 5, 4 or even 3 credit hours. And while law schools are looking to reduce the credit hours for the basic Property class, professors are looking for new topics to incorporate into the course. Writing a study aid under such conditions is a challenge. To facilitate your use of this book, and to maximize the benefit you can take from this book, following this PREFACE is an ORGANIZATION OF MATERIAL section which is designed to assist you: (1) in understanding the organization of the subject matter coverage in this book, and (2) in locating particular property topics as they appear in the problems in the exams. No matter how many credit hours your Property course has, which textbook book you use, or who your professor is, the problems in this book will help you understand Property better and help prepare you for your exam.

This book could not have been written without the assistance of a number of students who spent long hours proofing earlier drafts of the different exams and answer keys. I wish to offer my sincerest thanks and gratitude to Julie Trotter, Kerri Weiss, Tony Guthrie, Steve Mikhov, Jay Spagnola, Kelly Donegan, Daniel Gura, Jennifer Hume and Leslie Polizzotto for their painstaking attention to detail. Moreover, I could not have produced the final manuscript without the expert word processing assistance of Candace Warren and Sheila McDonald. I am forever indebted.

I hope you enjoy this book as much as I enjoy teaching Property. If you wish to discuss any of the questions in further detail, feel free to e-mail me at <pwendel@pepperdine.edu>.

PROFESSOR PETER T. WENDEL
PEPPERDINE UNIVERSITY SCHOOL OF LAW
AUGUST 2007

[Professor Wendel is a respected classroom teacher who has received several teaching awards. He has had the privilege of being a visiting professor at a number of different law schools, including UCLA, Washington University, Loyola, Santa Clara, and the University of Augsburg, Germany. His research and scholarship are primarily in the areas of Property and Wills & Trusts.]

PROPERTY
TABLE OF PROBLEMS

I. ORGANIZATION BY EXAMS

The Exams are organized according to the material typically covered in a 3, 4, or 5-6 credit Property course. Exams I, II and III focus on the material typically covered in a 3 credit Property course (or the first semester of a two semester Property course.). Exam IV focuses on the added material typically covered in a 4 credit property course. Exams V and VI focus on the added material typically covered in a 5-6 credit course. Exam 7 contains additional questions from all of the above, plus challenging overlapping questions. Exam 8 focuses on those "fringe" Property topics which some professors cover, which are important, but typically are covered in greater detail in other law school courses.

II. TABLE OF EXAM TOPICS

    CREATION/STATUTE OF FRAUDS ......
                          Exam V .... Problems 10, 25
                          Exam VI .... Problem 19
                          Exam VIII ..... Problem 22

    COVENANTS .... Exam V .... Problems 8, 14, 15-19
                          Exam VI .... Problems 1, 24
                          Exam VII ...... Problems 5, 6, 16

    DELIVERY .... Exam V .... Problems 2, 22, 23
                          Exam VI .... Problems 5, 6, 16
                          Exam VII ...... Problem 7

    ESTOPPEL BY DEED ...... Exam V .... Problem 11
                          Exam VI .... Problems 18, 22, 23
                          Exam VII ...... Problems 2, 3, 4

    TYPES
        General Warranty .... Exam V .... Problems 15-19
                          Exam VII ...... Problems 5, 6, 16, 21
        Special Warranty ..... Exam V .... Problems 15-19
                          Exam VII ...... Problems 5, 6, 16, 21
        Quitclaim .... Exam VI .... Problems 3, 4
                          Exam VII ...... Problems 5, 6, 21

DOWER/CURTESY................ Exam I .... Problem 14

EASEMENTS/LICENSES/PROFITS

    CREATION .... Exam IV .... Problems 1, 7, 12, 14, 18, 20, 24
                          Exam V .... Problem 5
                          Exam VII ...... Problems 12, 17
                          Exam VIII ..... Problems 11, 12

    EASEMENTS:
        Express/Implied/Prescriptive........
                          Exam IV .... Problems 12, 14, 18, 24
                          Exam V .... Problem 5
                          Exam VII ...... Problem 17
                          Exam VIII ..... Problems 11, 12

    REGULATORY TAKINGS ....
                              Exam VIII .....Problems 6, 13, 23

    EXACTIONS ....Exam VIII .....Problem 24

PROPERTY

TABLE OF CONTENTS

EXAM I

PROPERTY
MULTIPLE CHOICE OBJECTIVE QUESTIONS

EXAM I

Questions 1 and 2 are based upon the following fact pattern:

L orally leases Blackacre to T, from month to month, beginning January 1st, for $500 a month. In June, T stops paying rent. On July 1st, L gives T notice that L is terminating the lease on August 15th. T refuses to move out on August 15th. On August 20th, L physically evicts T from Blackacre. T sues L for wrongful eviction.

QUESTIONS:

1. **Assuming traditional common law principles apply, what is the most likely outcome?**

    (A)   L is liable for wrongful eviction.
    (B)   L is not liable as long as L used only as much force as is reasonably necessary.
    (C)   L is not liable as long as L's means of eviction are peaceful.
    (D)   L is not liable, because failure to pay rent constitutes a substantial breach of the lease.

2. **Assuming modern trend principles apply, what is the most likely outcome?**

    (A)   L is liable for wrongful eviction.
    (B)   L is not liable as long as L used only as much force as is reasonably necessary.
    (C)   L is not liable as long as L's means of eviction are peaceful.
    (D)   L is not liable, because failure to pay rent constitutes a substantial breach of the lease.

3. Olivia owns Demacres. She conveys Demacres as follows: "To Bill for life, then to Hillary and her heirs, but if Brock is ever elected president, then to Brock and his heirs."

Thereafter Bill dies, but Hillary and Brock are still alive. **Applying traditional common law principles, state the title to Demacres:**

(A) Hillary has a fee simple absolute.
(B) Hillary has a fee simple determinable, and Brock a possibility of reverter in fee simple.
(C) Hillary has a fee simple subject to condition subsequent, and Brock has a right of entry in fee simple.
(D) Hillary has a fee simple subject to an executory limitation, and Brock has a shifting executory interest in fee simple.
(E) Hillary has a fee simple subject to divestment, and Brock has a shifting executory interest in fee simple.

Questions 4 and 5 are based upon the following fact pattern:

O properly conveys Blackacre "to A and B and C and their heirs." Thereafter, A properly executes a deed which purports to convey her interest to D and her heirs. Then B dies testate (with a will). B's last will and testament devises all of her property to E and her heirs.

QUESTIONS:

4. **Applying traditional common law presumptions, what is the state of the title?**

(A) D holds an undivided 1/3 interest, and C holds an undivided 2/3 interest, as tenants in common.
(B) C, D and E hold undivided 1/3 interests as tenants in common.
(C) C holds fee simple absolute.
(D) C and D hold undivided 1/2 interests as tenants in common.

5. Applying modern trend presumptions, what is the state of the title?

   (A)   D holds an undivided 1/3 interest, and C holds an undivided 2/3 interest, as tenants in common.
   (B)   C, D and E hold undivided 1/3 interests as tenants in common.
   (C)   C holds fee simple absolute.
   (D)   C and D hold undivided 1/2 interests as tenants in common.

6. During a storm, a Himalayan tiger escapes from the Santa Barbara Zoo and is captured several days later by A on B's land. **Who has the superior claim to the tiger?**

   (A)   the Zoo, based on occupancy.
   (B)   the Zoo, based on animus revertendi.
   (C)   A, based on occupancy.
   (D)   B, based on rationi soli.

7. L, by written instrument, leases Blackacre to T. The lease is for a stated term of ten years, at an annual rent of $120,000 payable $10,000 per month on the first of each month. Just before the expiration of the term, L writes a letter to T telling T that he may remain in possession of Blackacre so long as he pays the rent and continues to use Blackacre as a farm. Three years after the expiration of the original lease, L wants to terminate the lease. **Assuming the jurisdiction follows the common law approach, the most likely result is:**

   (A)   L can terminate, but L must give one year's notice because T holds a periodic tenancy from year to year.
   (B)   L can terminate, but L must give six months notice because T holds a periodic tenancy from year to year.
   (C)   L can terminate, but L must give thirty days notice because T holds a periodic tenancy from month to month.
   (D)   L can terminate because T holds a tenancy at will.

Questions 8 and 9 are based upon the following fact pattern:

L leases Greenacres to T, in writing, for a term of 3 years. One year into the lease, T "assigns, subleases and transfers" all of her interest to T1. The agreement between T and T1 provides that T1 "assumes all the obligations" in the lease between L and T. Thereafter, T1 "assigns, subleases and transfers" all of his interest to T2 in an instrument which provides that T2 "assumes all the obligations" in the lease between L and T and that if T2 violates the agreement, T1 has a right to terminate and re-enter the property. Thereafter T2 fails to pay rent to L.

QUESTIONS:

8. **Who is liable to L, and on what grounds, under the traditional common law approach?**

    (A)   T (because L is in privity of contract with T) and T1 (because L is in privity of estate with T1).
    (B)   T and T1 (because L is in privity of contract with T and T1) and T2 (because L is in privity of estate with T2).
    (C)   T, T1 and T2 (because L is in privity of contract with T, T1 and T2, and privity of estate with T1).
    (D)   T, T1 and T2 (because L is in privity of contract with T, T1 and T2, and privity of estate with T2).
    (E)   T, T1 and T2 (because L is in privity of contract with T, T1 and T2, and privity of estate with T1 and T2).

9. **Who is liable to L, and on what grounds, under the modern trend approach?**

    (A)   T (because L is in privity of contract with T) and T1 (because L is in privity of estate with T1).
    (B)   T and T1 (because L is in privity of contract with T and T1) and T2 (because L is in privity of estate with T2).
    (C)   T, T1 and T2 (because L is in privity of contract with T, T1 and T2, and privity of estate with T1).
    (D)   T, T1 and T2 (because L is in privity of contract with T, T1 and T2, and privity of estate with T2).
    (E)   T, T1 and T2 (because L is in privity of contract with T, T1 and T2, and privity of estate with T1 and T2).

10.

Lot 1	Lot 2

Lots 1 and 2 are adjoining lots. They are both farms, but they are owned by different individuals. A owns lot 1, and B owns lot 2, though at no time relevant to this question is either A or B in actual possession of either lot. X, who has no interest in either lot, executes a deed purporting to convey both lots to C. C enters and actually occupies lot 1 in an open and notorious manner for the statutory period required for adverse possession.

At the end of this period, C brings suit to quiet title to lots 1 and 2, claiming both lots under X's deed. **The most likely result is:**

(A) C is entitled to lot 1 only.
(B) C is entitled to lot 2 only.
(C) C is entitled to neither lot.
(D) C is entitled to both lots.

11. O → To A for life, then to A's children who survive A and their heirs, but if A dies without being survived by children, then to C's children and their heirs.

Assume A and C are alive. A has no children, and C has one child, Z. **State the future interests:**

(A) A's children have a vested remainder in fee simple subject to divestment, and C's children have a shifting executory interest in fee simple.
(B) A's children who survive A have a contingent remainder in fee simple subject to an executory limitation, and C's children have a vested remainder in fee simple.
(C) A's children who survive A have a contingent remainder in fee simple, and C's children have an alternative contingent remainder in fee simple.
(D) A's children who survive A have a contingent remainder in fee simple, C's children have an alternative contingent remainder in fee simple, and O has a reversion in fee simple.

12. O → To A for life, then to A's children who survive A and their heirs, but if A dies without being survived by children, then to C's children and their heirs.

Assume A has a child X, C has a child Z, and both A and C are still alive. **State the future interests:**

(A)   X has a vested remainder in fee simple absolute.

(B)   X has a vested remainder, subject to open, in fee simple.

(C)   X has a contingent remainder, subject to open, in fee simple absolute, Y has an alternative contingent remainder, subject to open, in fee simple absolute, and O has a reversion in fee simple.

(D)   A's children who survive A have a contingent remainder in fee simple, C's children have an alternative contingent remainder in fee simple, and O has a reversion in fee simple.

13. O → To A for life, then to B and her heirs.

Thereafter in 1990, AP enters adversely and possesses and improves the property in a manner necessary to satisfy the requirements of adverse possession. In 1998, however, A transfers her interest to X. **Assuming the period prescribed by the statute of limitations is 10 years, state the title** <u>**in 2004**</u>**:**

(A)   AP holds fee simple absolute.

(B)   AP holds a life estate for the life of A, and B holds a vested remainder in fee simple.

(C)   AP holds a life estate for the life of X, and B holds a vested remainder in fee simple.

(D)   AP holds a life estate for the life of AP, and B holds a vested remainder in fee simple.

(E)   X holds a life estate for the life of A, B holds a vested remainder in fee simple, and AP's interest will not vest until 2008.

14. H and W are husband and wife. H and his brother, B, hold Malibuacres in joint tenancy. Thereafter B conveys his interest in Malibuacres to W. Thereafter, H dies and devises all of his property to UCLA. **Applying traditional common law principles,**

    (A)   W has a dower interest in H's property, which entitles her to all of H's interest in Malibuacres.

    (B)   W has a dower interest in H's property, which entitles her to a life estate in H's interest in Malibuacres.

    (C)   W has a dower interest in H's property, which entitles her to a life estate in 1/3 of H's interest in Malibuacres.

    (D)   W has no dower interest in Malibuacres because dower does not attach to property held in joint tenancy, but W ends up with all of it because of the right of survivorship.

15. Landlord leased an apartment to Tenant, and the lease imposed no express covenants on the landlord. Shortly after the lease began, rioting broke out in the area. Although the apartment was not directly damaged during the rioting, for almost two weeks now the apartment has been without electricity because arsonists burned the local power transformer. **If Tenant sues Landlord for an abatement of the rent:**

    (A)   Tenant would prevail under the covenant of quiet enjoyment.

    (B)   Tenant would prevail under the illegal lease doctrine.

    (C)   Tenant would prevail under the implied warranty of habitability.

    (D)   Tenant would prevail under both the illegal lease doctrine and the implied warranty of habitability.

    (E)   Tenant would prevail under the covenant of quiet enjoyment, the illegal lease doctrine, and the implied warranty of habitability.

16. O owns Greenacre. In 1980, A enters adversely upon Greenacre. In 1995, B fraudulently tells A that B owns Greenacre and that A has to go. A leaves and B immediately enters the property and uses it in a manner which satisfies the requirements for adverse possession. Assume the statute of limitations for adverse possession is 20 years. **In 2005, who most likely owns the land?**

    (A)   B, regardless of whether the jurisdiction applies the statute of limitations/penalty approach or the earnings/expectations approach.

    (B)   B, only if the jurisdiction applies the statute of limitations/penalty approach.

    (C)   B, only if the jurisdiction applies the earnings/expectations approach.

    (D)   O, regardless of whether the jurisdiction applies the statute of limitations/penalty approach or the earnings/expectations approach theory.

17. O →   To A for life, then to B as long as B does not sell alcoholic beverages on the land, then to C and her heirs

Applying traditional common law principles, state the future interests:

    (A)   B has a contingent remainder in fee simple subject to an executory limitation, and C has a shifting executory interest in fee simple.

    (B)   B has a vested remainder in fee simple subject to an executory limitation, and C has a shifting executory interest in fee simple.

    (C)   B has a vested remainder in life estate subject to an executory limitation, C has a shifting executory interest in fee simple, and O has a reversion in fee simple.

    (D)   B has a vested remainder in life estate determinable, and C has a vested remainder in fee simple.

18. Racquel owns the Arts Theater, a majestic old building built in the classic theater style. In 2000, the Valley Arts Association, a group of local artists, approached Racquel about renting the theater on a long term basis to use as a home for their local theater productions. The parties agreed to a five year term, with an option to extend the lease for another five years. When 2005 rolled around, all was well, and both parties agreed to extend the lease for another five years. In early 2007, however, a large portion of the plaster ceiling above the auditorium portion of the theater began to sag away from the ceiling joists. The Arts Association feared for the safety of the audience and canceled all shows until the ceiling could be fixed. Fixing the ceiling will be quite expensive since the auditorium ceiling is over six floors high. When the Arts Association approached Racquel, however, she refused to fix the ceiling, claiming that it was the tenant's problem. The lease contains a clause which obligates the tenant "to make any repairs which may become necessary to the interior of the theater." An initial investigation indicates that the problem may be the result of a latent defect in the roof, although there is no evidence Racquel knew of it before now. **Assuming the court applies the common law approach:**

(A) The Arts Association is responsible for fixing the ceiling under the tenant's duty to perform repairs.

(B) The Arts Association is not responsible for fixing the ceiling because the repair is beyond the scope of an ordinary repair.

(C) The Arts Association is not responsible for fixing the ceiling because the condition was caused by a latent defect.

(D) The Arts Association is not responsible for fixing the ceiling because the landlord is obligated to insure that the premises are fit for their intended purposes.

Questions 19 and 20 are based upon the following fact pattern:

Arnold owns the GoodBody Medical Building. The building has a good mix of doctors and medical specialists. In an attempt to diversify the tenant make-up, Arnold rents one of the offices to Debbie, a dentist. The lease is a term of years lease for 5 years, with an approval clause requiring Debbie to get Arnold's permission before assigning or subletting the office. One year after entering into the lease, Debbie decides that she is tired of staring down people's throats and quits the business. She has a good friend, Pamela, who is big in the cosmetic surgery business. Pamela would love to be in the Goodbody Medical Building. Arnold, however, is opposed to people using surgery to alter their appearances and refuses to consent. Debbie vacates the office, and it remains empty for 3 years before Arnold rents it to Doug (a young doctor who has just finished a stint in ER medicine and is looking to set up practice in pediatrics).

QUESTIONS:

19. Arnold sues Debbie for the rents due since she vacated. **The most likely result under the common law is:**

    (A)   Arnold can recover from Debbie, because he was free to reject Pamela as an assignee and he was free to let the office remain vacant.

    (B)   Arnold cannot recover from Debbie, because although he had no duty to mitigate, he had no right reject Pamela as an assignee.

    (C)   Arnold cannot recover from Debbie, because although he had no duty to accept Pamela as an assignee, he had a duty to mitigate.

    (D)   Arnold cannot recover from Debbie, because he had no right to reject Pamela as an assignee and he had a duty to mitigate.

20. **The most likely result under the modern trend is:**

    (A)   Arnold can recover from Debbie, because he was free to reject Pamela as an assignee and he was free to let the office remain vacant.

    (B)   Arnold cannot recover from Debbie, because although he had no duty to mitigate, he had no right reject Pamela as an assignee.

    (C)   Arnold cannot recover from Debbie, because although he had no duty to accept Pamela as an assignee, he had a duty to mitigate.

    (D)   Arnold cannot recover from Debbie, because he had no right to reject Pamela as an assignee and he had a duty to mitigate.

21. **<u>Assume the following statute applies to the following fact pattern</u>:**

An action to recover the title to or possession of real property shall be brought within twenty-one (21) years after the cause of action thereof accrued, but if a person entitled to bring such action, at the time the cause thereof accrues, is within the age of minority (i.e., under the age of eighteen (18) years), of unsound mind, or imprisoned, such person, after the expiration of twenty-one (21) years from the time the cause of action accrues, may bring such action within ten (10) years after such disability is removed.

Olivia owns Malibuacres. Anna enters Malibuacres adversely on January 1, 1985 and begins farming the land. When Anna entered, Olivia was only ten (10) years old. In 1992, Olivia is convicted of a felony and sentenced to prison until 2002. Olivia dies in prison on January 1, 2000. Olivia dies intestate, and all of her property passes to Olivia's only heir, Harold, who is 10 years old on January 1, 2000.

Assuming Anna's conduct otherwise satisfies the requirements for adverse possession, on what date did (or will) Anna acquire title through adverse possession?

    (A)   2003.
    (B)   2006.
    (C)   2010.
    (D)   2018.

22. On November 30, 1999, L leases Blackacre in writing "to T-1 for a term of five years, beginning January 1, 2000, at an annual rent of $120,000 payable $10,000 a month." On December 15, 2004, L leases Blackacre in writing "to T-2 for five years, beginning January 1, 2005." Both leases are without any express covenant as to delivery of possession. When T-2 arrives on January 1, 2005 to take possession of Blackacre, T-1 refuses to give possession of the premises to T-2. T-2 sues L for breach of duty to deliver legal and actual possession. **In a jurisdiction which applies the American approach to L's duty to deliver possession:**

    (A)   L is liable for breaching L's implied covenant to provide actual possession.

    (B)   L is liable for breaching L's implied covenant to provide legal possession.

    (C)   L is liable for breaching both the implied covenant to provide actual possession and the implied covenant to provide legal possession.

    (D)   L has not breached any implied duties as to delivery of possession.

23. O →   To A for life, then to B and her heirs, but if B fails to survive A, then to C and her heirs.

State the future interests:

    (A)   B has a contingent remainder in fee simple, and C has a shifting executory interest in fee simple.

    (B)   B has a contingent remainder in fee simple, C has an alternative contingent remainder in fee simple, and O has a reversion.

    (C)   B has a vested remainder in fee simple subject to divestment, and C has a shifting executory interest in fee simple.

    (D)   B has a vested remainder in fee simple subject to an executory limitation, and C has a shifting executory interest in fee simple.

24. O →   To A for life, then to O's heirs and the heirs of their bodies.

   Applying common law principles, state the title:

   (A)   A has a life estate, and O holds a reversion in fee simple absolute.
   (B)   A has a life estate, O's heirs have a contingent remainder in fee simple absolute, and O has a reversion.
   (C)   A has a life estate, O's heirs have a contingent remainder in fee tail, and O has a reversion.
   (D)   A has a life estate, O has a contingent remainder in fee tail, and O has a reversion.
   (E)   A has a life estate, O has a vested remainder in fee tail, and O has a reversion.

25. On December 31, 1996, L leases Blackacre in writing "to T-1 for residential purposes for a term of five years, beginning January 1, 1997, at an annual rent of $120,000 payable $10,000 a month." After the initial term is up, T-1 stays in possession and keeps making monthly payments, and L accepts the payments. On October 31, 2004, L agrees to lease Blackacre in writing "to T-2 for five years, beginning January 1, 2005." That same day (October 31st) L writes T-1 and informs T-1 that L is terminating the lease and T-1 needs to be out at the end of term, December 31, 2004. Both leases are without any express covenant as to delivery of possession. When T-2 arrives on January 1, 2005 to take possession of Blackacre, T-1 refuses to give possession of the premises to T-2. T-2 sues L for breach of duty to deliver legal and actual possession. **In a jurisdiction which follows the modern trend and applies the English approach as to L's duty to deliver possession:**

   (A)   L is liable for breaching L's implied covenant to provide actual possession.
   (B)   L is liable for breaching L's implied covenant to provide legal possession.
   (C)   L is liable for breaching both the implied covenant to provide actual possession and the implied covenant to provide legal possession.
   (D)   L has not breached any implied duties as to delivery of possession.

END OF EXAMINATION QUESTIONS

EXAM II

PROPERTY
MULTIPLE CHOICE OBJECTIVE QUESTIONS

EXAM II

1. O → To A for life, then to B and her heirs if B gives A a proper funeral.

    State the title:

    (A) A has a life estate, and B has a vested remainder in fee simple.
    (B) A has a life estate, and B has a contingent remainder in fee simple.
    (C) A has a life estate, B has a contingent remainder in fee simple, and O has a reversion in fee simple.
    (D) A has a life estate, O has a reversion in fee simple subject to an executory limitation, and B has a springing executory interest in fee simple.

2. Decedent, who is on his death bed, calls in his faithful servant Paul. In the presence of decedent's whole family, decedent points to his locked desk in the corner of his bedroom and says: "Paul, I want you to have my desk and the money in the top drawer of my desk." Decedent died the next day. **To what is Paul entitled under traditional common law principles?**

    (A) nothing.
    (B) the desk, but not the money.
    (C) the money, but not the desk.
    (D) both the money and the desk.

3. O →   To A for life, then to the then Dean of Res Ipsa Law School and
           his or her heirs.

    **A transfers A's interest to Dean Loquitor, the current dean of the
    Res Ipsa Law School. State the title:**

    (A) Dean Loquitor has fee simple absolute.
    (B) Dean Loquitor has a life estate, and the Dean of the Res Ipsa
         Law School at the time of A's death has a vested remainder in
         fee simple absolute.
    (C) Dean Loquitor has a life estate, the Dean of the Res Ipsa Law
         School at the time of A's death has a contingent remainder in fee
         simple, and O has a reversion in fee simple.
    (D) Dean Loquitor has a life estate pur autre vie, the Dean of the
         Res Ipsa Law School at the time of A's death has a contingent
         remainder in fee simple, and O has a reversion in fee simple.

4. L leases to T for a term of 10 years. The lease is silent with respect to
    assignment and subleases. One year later, T executes an instrument
    which "subleases, transfers and assigns" to T-1 "for a period of two
    years." During T-1's possession, T executes yet another instrument
    which "subleases, transfers and assigns" his "entire interest" to T-2.
    Thereafter, T-1 defaults on the rent payments to L. **Who is liable to L,
    and on what grounds?**

    (A) only T on privity of contract.
    (B) T on privity of contract, and T-2 on privity of estate.
    (C) T-1 on privity of contract, and T-2 on privity of estate.
    (D) T and T-1 on privity of contract, and T-2 on privity of estate.

5. Ali was eating lunch at an outside picnic table at "Bob's Lobster Shack" on the Boardwalk. The lobster claw had too much butter on it and slipped out of her hands. When she reached down to pick up it up, she found a ring on the Boardwalk under her table. The waitress told Bob, the owner of the lobster shack. Bob ran up and down the Boardwalk until he found Ali exiting the public restroom of the Trumpet Casino. Bob demanded the ring, but Ali cannot find it. Two hours later, Kristin, a maintenance employee of the Casino, finds the ring on the sink in the restroom while cleaning the restroom. **Assuming all the parties claim the ring, and applying traditional common law rules, who has the superior claim?**

   (A)   Ali, because a finder has superior rights over all but the true owner.
   (B)   Bob, to maximize the chances of returning the ring to the true owner.
   (C)   Kristin, because a finder has superior rights over all but the true owner.
   (D)   the Trumpet Casino owners, since it was found on their property by Kristin in the course of her duties as their employee.

6. O → To A for life, then to B and her heirs as long as B farms the land.

   State the title:

   (A)   A has a life estate, B has a contingent remainder in fee simple, and O has a reversion in fee simple.
   (B)   A has a life estate, B has a vested remainder in fee simple determinable, and O has a possibility of reverter in fee simple.
   (C)   A has a life estate, B has a vested remainder in fee simple determinable, and O has a right of re-entry in fee simple.
   (D)   A has a life estate, B has a vested remainder in fee simple subject to a condition subsequent, and O has a possibility of reversion in fee simple.

7. A invites B over to A's for an old fashioned country style barbecue. During the barbecue, a flock of geese fly over A's property. B runs to her car, grabs her shotgun, and shoots one of the geese, killing it. B then goes back to the barbecue to finish her meal. The goose, however, falls into a fast moving stream and is washed downstream where F, who is fishing in public waters, sees it floating by and grabs it. F takes it to a taxidermist, T, to have it stuffed. F tells T how F acquired the bird. When F comes back to claim the bird, T refuses to return it. **If all of the parties hear that T has the bird and claim it, who is most likely to prevail:**

   (A)   A, based on rationi soli.
   (B)   B, based on occupancy.
   (C)   F, based on occupancy.
   (D)   T, because T is rightfully in possession.

8. A, B and C own Blackacre as co-tenants. A builds a home on Blackacre. **What rights does A have against B and C with respect to the improvement?**

   (A)   A is entitled to contribution from B and C for the cost of the improvement.
   (B)   A is entitled to contribution from B and C for the value the improvement has added to Blackacre.
   (C)   If the land is partitioned and sold, A is entitled to the cost of the improvement before the proceeds from the partition sale are divided among the co-tenants.
   (D)   If the land is partitioned and sold, A is entitled to the value the improvement has added to the jointly held property before the proceeds from the partition sale are divided among the co-tenants.

9. With reference to problem 8, assume C moves into exclusive possession of Blackacre for 5 years, and then rents Blackacre to X for five years at full market value. **Under the general rule, what rights do A and B have against C, assuming A and B cannot show ouster?**

    (A) C has no liability.
    (B) C is liable to A and B for the actual rents received from X in excess of C's share.
    (C) C is liable to A and B for the reasonable rental value for the five years C was in exclusive possession.
    (D) C is liable to A and B for the reasonable rental value for the five years C was in possession, and C must account to A and B for the actual rents received from X in excess of C's share.

10. O takes a trip to Miami Beach. She brings along her most valuable ring to fit in with the jet set crowd. After arriving at the hotel, she notices that one of the prongs on the ring holding the diamond is broken. Fearing the diamond may fall out if knocked, O arranges to have J, a jeweler, fix it. O takes the ring to the hotel desk and asks the clerk to deliver the ring to J when J comes by and asks for it. Thereafter, X comes by the hotel to pick up a different package. X tells the clerk, "I'm here to pick up the package." The hotel clerk assumes that X is J and that "the package" refers to the ring. The clerk gives the ring to X. X and the ring are never seen again.

    What is O's best claim against the hotel under the traditional common law approach?

    (A) The bailment was for the benefit of both the bailor and the bailee, and the hotel breached its duty of ordinary care.
    (B) The bailment was for the sole benefit of the bailor, and the hotel breached its duty of slight care.
    (C) The bailment was for the sole benefit of the bailor, and the hotel breached its duty of ordinary care.
    (D) The bailment was for the sole benefit of the bailor, and the hotel breached its duty of extraordinary care.
    (E) The hotel is strictly liable for misdelivery.

Problems 11 through 17 are based upon the following fact pattern:

O conveys Malibuacres "to X in fee simple absolute." Thereafter in 1990 X takes a job in Europe. Immediately after X leaves, X's neighbor, Y builds a fence which encloses the back half of Malibuacres with Y's property. In addition, Y gardens the back half of Malibacres for over 15 years before anyone notices. In 2005, when X finally hears what Y has done, X jumps on the first plane back, only to have the plane crash, killing all on board. X's will, which was properly executed in 1999, leaves all of his property to Z, her 1 year old niece at the time (Z is 6 when X died).

Assume the jurisdiction has adopted the following statute:

An action to recover the title to or possession of real property shall be brought within 10 years after the cause of action thereof accrued, but if a person entitled to bring such action, at the time the cause thereof accrues, is within the age of minority (i.e., under the age of 18 years), of unsound mind, or imprisoned, such person, after the expiration of 10 years from the time the cause of action accrues, may bring such action within 5 years after such disability is removed.

QUESTIONS:

11. **Immediately after the conveyance from O to X, what is X's interest in the back half of Malibuacres?**

    (A) X owns it in fee simple absolute under both the common law and the modern trend approach.

    (B) X owns it in fee simple absolute under the common law approach, but he holds only a life estate under the modern trend.

    (C) X holds a life estate under the common law approach, but he owns it in fee simple absolute under the modern trend.

    (D) X holds only a life estate under both the common law and the modern trend.

12. Under *traditional common law principles*, what is the most likely state of the title to the back half of Malibuacres immediately *before* X's death?

   (A)   X owns it in fee simple absolute.
   (B)   Y owns it in fee simple absolute.
   (C)   Y holds a life estate, and O holds a reversion in fee simple.
   (D)   Y holds a life estate pur autre vie, and O holds a reversion in fee simple.

13. Under *the modern trend approach*, what is the most likely state of the title to the back half of Malibuacres immediately *before* X's death?

   (A)   X owns it in fee simple absolute.
   (B)   Y owns it in fee simple absolute.
   (C)   Y holds a life estate.
   (D)   Y holds a life estate pur autre vie.

14. Under *traditional common law principles*, what is the most likely state of the title to the back half of Malibuacres immediately *after* X's death?

   (A)   O owns it in fee simple absolute.
   (B)   Z owns it in fee simple absolute.
   (C)   Y owns it in fee simple absolute.
   (D)   Y holds a life estate, and O holds a reversion in fee simple.
   (E)   Y holds a life estate, and Z holds a remainder in fee simple.

15. Under *the modern trend approach*, what is the most likely state of the title to the back half of Malibuacres immediately *after* X's death?

   (A)   O owns it in fee simple absolute.
   (B)   Z owns it in fee simple absolute.
   (C)   Y owns it in fee simple absolute.
   (D)   Y holds a life estate, and O holds a reversion in fee simple.
   (E)   Y holds a life estate, and Z holds a remainder in fee simple.

16. Under *traditional common law principles*, the earliest Y can successfully claim fee simple absolute in the back half of Malibuacres is:

    (A)   2000.
    (B)   2005.
    (C)   2009
    (D)   2015.
    (E)   2022.

17. Under the *modern trend approach*, the earliest Y can successfully claim fee simple absolute in the back half of Malibuacres is:

    (A)   2000.
    (B)   2005.
    (C)   2009.
    (D)   2015.
    (E)   2022.

18. In 1980, A purchases a house for $100,000, $20,000 down. In 1990, A decides to marry B. Between 1980 and 1990, A had paid an additional $20,000 in principal against the $100,000 purchase price. After A and B marry, all payments are made with earnings from one or the other. In 2005, A and B make the final payment on the house. In 2007, A and B sell the house for $1,000,000, and A immediately dies thereafter. **Assume all of these events occurred in a community property jurisdiction, and the jurisdiction applies the time of vesting rule. What is the extent of A's interest in the proceeds?**

    (A)   all of the $1,000,000.
    (B) $540,000.
    (C) $520,000.
    (D) $500,000.
    (E) $400,000.

19. A and B own Blackacre as true joint tenants. B leases Blackacre in writing to X for ten years. After 5 years, B dies, devising all of his interest to C. **Which of the following describes the most likely state of the title under traditional common law principles?**

    (A)   A holds fee simple absolute.
    (B)   A holds fee simple, subject to X's remaining 5 years on the term of years lease.
    (C)   A and C hold Blackacre as tenants in common in fee simple absolute.
    (D)   A and C hold Blackacre as tenants in common in fee simple, subject to X's remaining 5 years on the lease.

20. A and B own Blackacre as true joint tenants. B leases Blackacre in writing to X for ten years. After 5 years, B dies, devising all of his interest to C. **Which of the following describes the most likely state of the title under the modern trend?**

    (A)   A holds fee simple absolute.
    (B)   A holds fee simple, subject to X's remaining 5 years on the term of years lease.
    (C)   A and C hold Blackacre as tenants in common in fee simple absolute.
    (D)   A and C hold Blackacre as tenants in common in fee simple, subject to X's remaining 5 years on the lease.

21. O → To A for life, then to A's first child and his or her heirs, but if none of A's children survive A, then to B and her heirs.

    Assume A has a child, C, and A is still alive. State the future interests:

    (A)   C has a contingent remainder in fee simple, B has an alternative contingent remainder in fee simple, and O has a reversion in fee simple.
    (B)   C has a vested remainder in fee simple subject to an executory limitation, and B has a shifting executory interest in fee simple.
    (C)   C has a vested remainder in fee simple, subject to divestment, and B has a shifting executory interest in fee simple.
    (D)   C has a contingent remainder in fee simple subject to divestment, and B has a shifting executory interest in fee simple.

Questions 22 through 25 are based upon the following fact pattern:

Oscar is the rightful owner of Malibuacres in fee simple absolute. In 1990, Oscar properly executes a deed conveying Malibuacres "to A and B and their heirs jointly." A and B built a small restaurant on the property and began operating "Pete's Diner" on the spot. In 1995, A dies with a properly executed will which gives all of A's property to C.

In 1999, B executes a written lease which "conveys the exclusive right of possession to X for a term of twenty years commencing on January 1, 2000, at a rate of $120,000 a year, payable $10,000 a month." The lease also contains an approval clause requiring "X to get B's consent before assigning the property."

In 2005, without B's knowledge or consent, X executes a written instrument which "assigns, subleases and conveys" all of X's interest to Y. The agreement also contains a right of re-entry clause in the event Y breaches any provision of the agreement.

In July of 2006, C shows up, takes possession of Malibuacres and locks out everybody else. Y attempts to take possession but is rebuffed by C. Y stops paying rent to X, who in turn stops paying rent to B. Assume it is December of 2006. C is still in exclusive possession of Malibuacres, and nobody is paying rent to anybody.

QUESTIONS:

22. **Under the traditional common law approach, state the title to Malibuacres:**

   (A) B alone holds Malibuacres, subject to X's leasehold interest, but Y's leasehold interest is voidable since the transfer to Y breached the lease.

   (B) B and C hold Malibuacres as tenants in common, subject to X's leasehold interest and subject to Y's interest.

   (C) B and C hold Malibuacres as tenants in common, subject to X's leasehold interest but Y's leasehold interest is voidable since the transfer to Y breached the lease.

   (D) B and C hold Malibuacres as joint tenants, subject to X's leasehold interest but Y's leasehold interest is voidable since the transfer to Y breached the lease.

   (E) B alone holds Malibuacres, subject to X's leasehold interest and subject to Y's interest.

23. **Under a traditional common law approach, when C comes and takes possession of Malibuacres:**

    (A)   C is a trespasser who does not affect X and Y's duty to pay rent.

    (B)   C is a co-tenant who has ousted X and Y.

    (C)   C is a trespasser and X and Y can sue for breach of the implied covenant of quiet enjoyment.

    (D)   C is a trespasser which affects B's duty to provide actual possession.

24. **Under the modern trend approach, state the title to Malibuacres:**

    (A)   B alone holds Malibuacres, subject to X's leasehold interest, but Y's leasehold interest is voidable since the transfer to Y breached the lease.

    (B)   B and C hold Malibuacres as tenants in common, subject to X's leasehold interest and subject to Y's interest.

    (C)   B and C hold Malibuacres as tenants in common, subject to X's leasehold interest but Y's leasehold interest is voidable since the transfer to Y breached the lease.

    (D)   B and C hold Malibuacres as joint tenants, subject to X's leasehold interest but Y's leasehold interest is voidable since the transfer to Y breached the lease.

    (E)   B alone holds Malibuacres, subject to X's leasehold interest and subject to Y's interest.

25. **Under the modern trend approach, when C comes and takes possession of Malibuacres:**

    (A)   C is a trespasser who does not affect X and Y's duty to pay rent.

    (B)   C is a co-tenant who has ousted X and Y.

    (C)   C is a trespasser and X and Y can sue for breach of the implied covenant of quiet enjoyment.

    (D)   C is a trespasser which affects B's duty to provide actual possession.

END OF EXAMINATION QUESTIONS

EXAM III

PROPERTY
MULTIPLE CHOICE OBJECTIVE QUESTIONS

EXAM III

Questions 1 and 2 are based upon the following fact pattern:

Louie owns an apartment building. It is a beautiful 30 story building on South Shore Drive overlooking Lake Michigan. Gerri leases the penthouse apartment. Two months after moving in, the only elevator in the building breaks. When Gerri complains to Louie, his response is "a little exercise would do you some good - take the stairs!" Gerri waits another three weeks and then moves out.

1. **Under the common law approach, the most likely result is:**

    (A) Gerri is still obligated to pay full rent. Louie has not breached any duty he owes her.
    (B) Gerri is still obligated to pay full rent. She has not been evicted from her apartment.
    (C) Gerri is entitled to a pro rata reduction in rent.
    (D) Gerri is relieved of all liability for rent.

2. **Under the modern trend, the most likely result is:**

    (A) Gerri is still obligated to pay full rent. Louie has not breached any duty he owes her.
    (B) Gerri is still obligated to pay full rent. She has not been evicted from her apartment.
    (C) Gerri is entitled to a pro rata reduction in rent.
    (D) Gerri is relieved of all liability for rent, though she has been only partially evicted.

Questions 3, 4, 5, 6 and 7 are based upon the following fact pattern:

O is the owner of Blackacre, a rolling estate with a beautiful home on it. In 2000, O properly executes and delivers a deed which conveys Blackacre "to A and B and their heirs as joint tenants and not as tenants in common."

On January 1, 2002, B announces his marriage to C. As a wedding gift, B properly executes and gives C a deed at their rehearsal dinner conveying his interest in Blackacre "to B and C as tenants by the entirety." B and C marry shortly thereafter.

On January 1, 2005, B leases Blackacre to X, his sister, for 5 years at $8,000 a month, even though the fair market value is $10,000 a month. The lease provides that (1) "X has the duty to repair the premises;" (2) "that B may use self-help eviction as long as the means of re-entry are peaceable;" and (3) "that X may not assign without B's consent."

QUESTIONS:

3. **State the title to Blackacre applying the traditional common law approach:**

   (A)   A and B hold as joint tenants, and because A did not agree to any of the subsequent transfers, C has no interest and X is an adverse possessor.

   (B)   A holds a half interest as a tenant in common with B and C, who hold a half interest as tenants by the entirety, and X is an adverse possessor because C did not agree to the lease to X.

   (C)   A holds a half interest as a tenant in common with B and C, who hold a half interest as joint tenants, and B's lease to X, which is valid, did not break the joint tenancy.

   (D)   A holds a half interest as a tenant in common with B and C, who held a half interest as joint tenants, but B's lease to X, which is valid, broke the joint tenancy and turned it into a tenancy in common.

   (E)   A holds a half interest as a tenant in common with B and C, who hold a half interest as tenants in common, and B's lease to X, which is valid, had no affect upon the tenancy in common.

4. State the title to Blackacre applying the modern trend approach:

    (A) A and B hold as joint tenants, and because A did not agree to any of the subsequent transfers, C has no interest and X is an adverse possessor.

    (B) A holds a half interest as a tenant in common with B and C, who hold a half interest as tenants by the entirety, and X is an adverse possessor because C did not agree to the lease to X.

    (C) A holds a half interest as a tenant in common with B and C, who hold a half interest as joint tenants, and B's lease to X, which is valid, did not break the joint tenancy.

    (D) A holds a half interest as a tenant in common with B and C, who held a half interest as joint tenants, but B's lease to X, which is valid, broke the joint tenancy and turned it into a tenancy in common.

    (E) A holds a half interest as a tenant in common with B and C, who hold a half interest as tenants in common, and B's lease to X, which is valid, had no affect upon the tenancy in common.

5. Assume, *arguendo*, that the lease to X is valid. Thereafter, X changes the locks to Blackacre. When C hears of this, C writes a letter to X demanding rent from X. The most likely result is:

    (A) X has ousted C, and X is liable to C for rent, but C would be better off suing B for an accounting to receive C's share of the rent X is paying to B.

    (B) X has ousted C, and X is liable to C for rent (which is better for C than if C had sued B for an accounting to receive C's share of the rent X is paying to B).

    (C) X has not ousted C, X is not liable for rent to C, but C can sue B for an accounting to receive C's share of the rent X is paying to B (which is worth more than if C sued X for rent).

    (D) X has not ousted C, X is not liable for rent to C, but C can sue B for an accounting to receive C's share of the rent X is paying to B (but C will not receive as much as C would have received if X had ousted C).

6. In addition to the fact pattern for questions 3-7 set forth above, assume further that on July 1, 2007, an earthquake hits Blackacre, breaking windows and water-pipes. X stops paying rent and refuses to repair the damage. B sues X to make X pay for the repairs. **The most likely result is that:**

    (A) B should prevail, regardless of whether the jurisdiction applies the common law or modern trend approach.
    (B) B should prevail if the jurisdiction applies the common law approach, but not if the jurisdiction applies the modern trend approach.
    (C) B should prevail if the jurisdiction applies the modern trend approach, but not if the jurisdiction applies the common law approach.
    (D) B should not prevail, regardless of whether the jurisdiction applies the common law or modern trend approach.

7. In addition to the fact pattern for questions 3-7 set forth above, assume further that on November 1, 2006, without B's consent, X executed an agreement "to assign" her interest in Blackacre to Y, commencing January 1, 2007, and terminating December 29, 2009. When B heard about the pending transfer to Y, B re-took possession of the premises while X was out shopping for the holidays. B changed the locks so that no one but B could use Blackacre. **If X sues B for wrongful eviction, the most likely result under the traditional common law approach is:**

    (A) X will prevail, because B had no right to possession.
    (B) X will prevail, because B used too much force in retaking possession.
    (C) B will prevail, because X's behavior breached the terms of the lease.
    (D) B will prevail, because B used only as much force as necessary in retaking possession.

8. Alice owns Greenacres. She rents Greenacres to Betsy. The lease provides that "Betsy has the right to possession from January 1, 2002 to December 31, 2006, at a rent of $60,000 a year to be paid $5,000 a month on the first of each month." Betsy goes into possession. On December 29, 2006, Betsy is in a bad car accident and requires surgery. She is heavily sedated for several days thereafter, and is not released from the hospital until January 3. She is unable to move out of Greenacres until January 5, 2007. Alice decides to hold Betsy liable to the fullest extent possible. **The most likely result under the modern trend is:**

   (A) Betsy is not liable for the delay in moving out because it was not her fault.
   (B) Betsy is liable, pro rata, for the three extra days she stayed over, but that is all.
   (C) Betsy is liable for an extra month.
   (D) Betsy is liable for an extra year.
   (E) Betsy is liable for a new five year term.

9. Officials from the Idaho Department of Fish & Game observed Conrad harvesting wild rice on land jointly owned by the state and the National Forest Service. The officials notified the local prosecutor who obtained a search warrant to search Conrad's residence. The prosecutor found 180 bags of wild rice which the state seized and sold (for $21,000) to keep it from perishing. Conrad was convicted of trespass. Nevertheless, Conrad has sued the state for conversion for recovery of the $21,000 from the sale of the wild rice. **In an action between Conrad and the state over the money, the most likely result is:**

   (A) Conrad will receive all $21,000, because he was first in time, first in right with respect to the wild rice.
   (B) Conrad will receive none of the money, because one who steals or converts property to his own use does not thereby acquire title to it.
   (C) The state will receive all $21,000, because concurrent owners have the right to assert the rights of other joint owners.
   (D) The state will receive $10,500, and Conrad will receive $10,500, because Conrad's right to possession, though wrongfully obtained, is superior to all but the true owner's right to possession.
   (E) The state will receive $10,500, and the court will order the other $10,500 distributed to the National Forest Service as the rightful owners of the property in question.

10. Olivia conveyed Paparaziacres as follows: "To Nicole for life, then to Paris as long as she does not go to jail again, but if she does, then to Lindsay and her heirs."

State the title under the common law approach:

(A)   Nicole has a life estate, Paris has a vested remainder in fee simple determinable, and Lindsay has a reversion in fee simple absolute.

(B)   Nicole has a life estate, Paris has a vested remainder in fee simple subject to an executory limitation, and Lindsay has a reversion in fee simple absolute.

(C)   Nicole has a life estate, Paris has a vested remainder in fee simple subject to an executory limitation, and Lindsay has a shifting executory interest in fee simple absolute.

(D)   Nicole has a life estate, Paris has a vested remainder in life estate determinable, and Lindsay has a vested remainder in fee simple absolute.

(E)   Nicole has a life estate, Paris has a vested remainder in life estate subject to an executory limitation, Lindsay has a shifting executory interest in fee simple, and Olivia has a reversion in fee simple.

11. L has a room to rent in her 2 bedroom private home. She puts the following advertisement in the local newspaper.

> *For Rent:*   African-American female seeks same to share private home, separate bedroom, all utilities shared 50-50. Monthly rent $500. Call 555-1212.

L has violated:

(A)   The Fair Housing Act of 1968.
(B)   The Civil Rights Act of 1866.
(C)   The Civil Rights Acts of 1866 and the Fair Housing Act of 1968.
(D)   No federal law, but possibly state anti-discrimination laws.

12. Landlord leases an aircraft hanger space to Tenant 1. The lease provides that written consent by Landlord is required before Tenant 1 can assign or sublet his interest. Tenant 1 wants to assign the lease to Tenant 2. Tenant 2 is a more suitable tenant (in better financial condition than Tenant 1), but Landlord refuses to give his consent simply because he wants higher rents than provided in the original lease between Landlord and Tenant 1.

Can Landlord lawfully withhold his consent?

(A) Landlord can lawfully withhold consent under both the common law and modern trend approaches.
(B) Landlord can lawfully withhold consent under the common law approach, but not under the modern trend approach.
(C) Landlord can lawfully withhold consent under the modern trend approach, but not under the common law approach.
(D) Landlord cannot lawfully withhold consent under either the common law approach or the modern trend approach.

13. Tenant entered into a commercial lease with Landlord to rent a store in Landlord's strip shopping center. The lease expressly required Tenant to use the premises solely for the sale of eyeglasses, lenses and other optical merchandise and for no other use. The lease provided for rent based on a percentage of gross sales, with a fixed minimum annual rental. Lastly, the lease obligated Tenant to maintain the premises in a manner consistent with the general character of the shopping mall and to refrain from any action that may damage the premises or any other part of the mall. Although Tenant has paid the fixed minimum annual rent under the lease, Tenant has never occupied the leased premises. **Landlord sues seeking an injunction requiring tenant to occupy and use the premises. The most likely result is:**

(A) Tenant is paying the obligated rent and is free to use the property as Tenant wishes. Tenant should prevail.
(B) Tenant is paying the obligated rent and is not breaching the restriction on how Tenant may use the premises. Tenant should prevail.
(C) There is no express provision in the lease obligating Tenant to occupy the premises and there is no ambiguity. Tenant should prevail.
(D) There is an implied obligation of Tenant to occupy the premises. Landlord prevails.

14. Zoe decides to rent an apartment in an upscale section of downtown which is going through gentrification. Older buildings are being bought, gutted, and turned into swank loft apartments. Because of the age of the building, it has an old-fashioned fire escape along one side of the building. The landlord checks to make sure the fire escape is safe, but otherwise takes no steps to secure it or the windows which abut it. Not too long after Zoe moves in, an intruder gains access to her apartment via the window off the fire escape and sexually assaults her.

If Zoe sues her landlord for her injuries sustained during the sexual assault, the most likely result under the modern trend is:

   (A)   The landlord will be liable because it breached its duty to make the premises reasonably safe in light of the foreseeable risk that entry could be gained via the fire escape and window.
   (B)   The landlord will be liable because landlords are strictly liable for injuries to tenants sustained on the premises.
   (C)   The landlord will not be liable because landlords have no duty to protect tenants from criminal acts of third parties.
   (D)   The landlord will not be liable because landlords are liable for injuries to tenants only if the condition which caused the injury constitutes a breach of the implied warranty of habitability.

15. While out on a Sunday afternoon, B loses his watch. C, while walking through the park on Monday, spots the watch and, seeing no one around, claims it. After wearing the watch for about a week, C is robbed at gunpoint by X, who takes the watch from him. A month later, X loses the watch, and D finds it.

Please list who has a claim to the watch, from strongest to weakest:

   (A)   B, C, X, D.
   (B)   B, C, D.
   (C)   B, D, C.
   (D)   D, B, C.

16. Pete wanted to purchase a boat. He went to 1st State Bank and borrowed $40,000 towards the purchase price. The Bank recorded a lien against the title to the boat. Pete leased a boat slip from the San Diego Boat Dock, docked the boat there, and used the boat to make a number of trips back and forth between California and Mexico. Pete unexpectedly disappeared from sight and failed to make a number of payments to either the Bank or the Boat Dock. The boat fell into disrepair. The Bank took possession of the boat and took it to Gerri's Boat Repair Shop for repairs. While working on the boat, an employee, Juan, found $100,000 in unmarked bills stashed under the floorboards of the boat. Pete has never been located, despite the fact that certain government officials have looked long and hard for him.

Applying traditional common law principles, who is entitled to the $100,000?

- (A) Juan, because a finder has superior rights against all but the true owner.
- (B) Juan, because the money is treasure trove.
- (C) Gerri's Boat Repair Shop, since Juan found the money in the course of his duties for the shop.
- (D) The San Diego Boat Dock, since Pete left his boat there and did not make all of his lease payments.
- (E) 1st State Bank, since Pete defaulted on his loan to the bank, and the money is mislaid property.
- (F) Gerri's Boat Repair Shop, since that is where the money was found.

17. Olivia conveys Greenacres as follows: "To Sammy for life, then to Mark and his heirs, but if the record for home runs in a single season is broken, then to the baseball player who breaks the record and his heirs."

Applying traditional common law principles, state the title to Greenacres:

   (A)   Sammy has a life estate, and Mark has a vested remainder in fee simple absolute.
   (B)   Sammy has a life estate, Mark has a vested remainder in fee simple determinable, and the player who breaks the record has a possibility of reverter in fee simple.
   (C)   Sammy has a life estate, Mark has a vested remainder in fee simple subject to condition subsequent, and the player who breaks the record has a right of entry in fee simple.
   (D)   Sammy has a life estate, Mark has a vested remainder in fee simple subject to an executory limitation, and the player who breaks the record has a shifting executory interest in fee simple.
   (E)   Sammy has a life estate subject to an executory limitation, Mark has a vested remainder in fee simple subject to divestment, and the player who breaks the record has a shifting executory interest in fee simple.

18. Sylvia pulls up to Pierre's in her brand new Mercedes. Pierre's is an exclusive restaurant in the city with no readily available parking but it offers valet parking. When she arrives, the valet asks to take her car. Sylvia, however, has seen those news reports on how valets treat their cars. She says "no way" and instead requests to park the car herself in the valet lot. The valet says "Suit yourself." After dinner, when Sylvia returns to the lot to get her car, she discovers a huge scratch along the length of the driver's side. She sues the restaurant.

The most likely result under the modern trend is:

   (A)   The restaurant is liable because the car was on its property.
   (B)   The restaurant is liable because the valet created safety expectations in Sylvia.
   (C)   The restaurant is not liable because it did not have custody of Sylvia's car.
   (D)   The restaurant is not liable because Sylvia parked her car herself.

19. Beth owns an apartment building. Thereafter, Beth acquires a nearby commercial building. Beth leases out the first floor of the commercial building to a group wishing to operate a nightclub on the location. The lease agreement covering the first floor provides that the entertainment is to be performed so that it cannot be heard outside of the building. To catch the trendy "clubbing" crowd, however, the bar operators decide to bring in local bands to entertain the patrons and to have the band start playing rather late in the evening and to play until the early morning hours. As is typical of contemporary music, the band thinks its music sounds best when played at a volume approaching that of departing jet engines. The residential tenants in Beth's nearby apartment building complain of the noise. When informed of the situation, Beth talks to the operators of the bar. They assure her they will correct the situation, but each time, after a few nights, the volume returns to its original level. After several weeks of this, the tenants decide they have had enough and vacate their apartments. Beth sues for rent. The tenants raise constructive eviction as their defense.

Under the common law approach, the most likely result is:

(A)   The tenants prevail, because the noise constitutes constructive eviction which breaches the implied warranty of habitability.

(B)   The tenants prevail, because the noise constitutes constructive eviction which breaches the covenant of quiet enjoyment.

(C)   Beth prevails, because she did not intend to deprive the tenants of their quiet enjoyment.

(D)   Beth prevails, because the bar is not on the same premises as the tenants' apartments.

(E)   Beth prevails, because she is not responsible for the actions of the band and bar operators.

20. Alice owns Greenacres. Alice rents Greenacres to Betsy, who executes a written lease which provides that "Betsy has the right to possession from January 1, 2000 to December 31, 2004, at a rent of $12,000 a year to be paid $1,000 a month on the first of each month." Betsy goes into possession. On December 1, 2004, Alice leases the property to Cindy commencing January 1, 2005 for a term of 2 years. On December 29, 2004, when Cindy shows up, Betsy claims that she is entitled to remain in possession because Alice has not properly terminated the lease. Alice writes Betsy a letter asserting that Betsy has no right to remain on the premises and demanding that Betsy vacate immediately. Betsy disputes Alice's claim but says that she'll move out by the end of January. Betsy moves out January 30, 2005. Cindy got tired of waiting and has rented another place. Alice sues Cindy.

The most likely result under the traditional American approach is:

(A)   Betsy was not entitled to stay beyond December 31, but Cindy is entitled to terminate the lease with Alice because Alice could not provide possession on the first day of the lease.

(B)   Betsy was not entitled to stay beyond December 31, and Cindy is still liable to Alice under the terms of their lease.

(C)   Betsy was entitled to stay beyond December 31, because Alice did not properly terminate the lease, but Alice is not liable to Cindy for failing to provide possession on the first day of the lease.

(D)   Betsy was entitled to stay beyond December 31, because Alice did not properly terminate the lease, and Alice is liable to Cindy for breach of the covenant of quiet enjoyment.

Questions 21, 22 and 23 are based on the following fact pattern:

Olivia owns Homeacres, a nice three acre parcel of land with a small house on it where she lives alone. In 1990, her mother has a stroke and is disabled. Being the loving daughter that she is, Olivia quits her job and moves back home to care for her mother - but she decides not to sell Homeacres but to hold on to it with the idea of moving back when her mother eventually dies. While Olivia is away taking care of her mother, one of her old neighbors, Andy moves into Homeacres and farms acres one and two during his time of possession. Andy had heard about Olivia's mother and decided that it was inefficient to let Homeacres sit idle. Andy breaks in and lives there from 1992 to 1999. In 1999, Andy decides to sell Homeacres to Betty. Andy properly executes and delivers a deed to Betty in exchange for valuable consideration which purports to sell Homeacres to Betty. Betty promptly moves into Homeacres and gardens acre two during her possession, but does not really use the other acres. Olivia's mom dies on 2006. In 2007, Olivia returns to Homeacres, only to find Betty living there.

> Assume the jurisdiction has adopted the following statute:
> An action to recover the title to or possession of real property shall be brought within 10 years after the cause of action thereof accrued, but if a person entitled to bring such action, at the time the cause thereof accrues, is within the age of minority (i.e., under the age of 18 years), of unsound mind, or imprisoned, such person, after the expiration of 10 years from the time the cause of action accrues, may bring such action within 5 years after such disability is removed.

21. Betty claims Homeacres based on adverse possession. **Betty claims she is entitled to tack her period of possession to Andy's period of possession. The most likely result is:**

    (A)   Betty should be able to tack as long as the jurisdiction applies the English approach to privity.
    (B)   Betty should be able to as tack long as the jurisdiction applies the American approach to privity.
    (C)   Betty should be able to tack regardless of whether the jurisdiction applies the English or American approach to privity.
    (D)   Betty should *not* be able to tack regardless of whether the jurisdiction applies the English or American approach to privity.

22. Assuming, *arguendo*, Betty is permitted to tack, the most likely result with respect to her claim of adverse possession is:

   (A)   Olivia should prevail because of the disability doctrine.
   (B)   Betty should prevail as long as the jurisdiction takes the subjective approach to claim of right.
   (C)   Betty should prevail as long as the jurisdiction takes the objective approach to claim of right.
   (D)   Betty should prevail regardless of whether the jurisdiction takes the objective or subjective approach to claim of right.

23. Assuming, *arguendo*, Betty prevails on her claim of adverse possession, Betty is entitled to:

   (A)   All three acres because of color of title.
   (B)   All three acres even without the benefit of color of title.
   (C)   Only two of the three acres.
   (D)   Only one of the three acres.
   (E)   Only the house in which she lived.

Questions 24 and 25 are based on the following fact pattern:

H and W are married. They have one child, C, who lives out of town. H and W bought 2 parcels of property during their marriage, each with a house on it. The deeds to each conveyed the property "to H and W jointly." The parcels were known as the "big house" and "the little house." H and W lived in the big house and used the little house as a vacation home. H died without a will in 1995.

After H's death, W continued to live in the big house and rented out the little house. W paid all the taxes on the property and made improvements to the house. Neither W nor C ever discussed the situation until 2007, when W had a falling out with C over her new husband. Shortly thereafter, C learned that under the state's intestate distribution statute, when one spouse dies survived by spouse and children, the surviving spouse receives 2/3rds of the deceased spouse's property, and the children split the other 1/3. Upon learning of her rights, C sued W asserting C's rights to the property. W countered by claiming she owned each parcel outright under the deeds, and if not, under adverse possession. The statute of limitation for adverse possession in the jurisdiction is 10 years.

24. **Assuming the court applies the common law approach, what is the most likely result:**

   (A)   W owns each parcel outright under the terms of the deeds and right of survivorship, and hence W owes C nothing.

   (B)   W will prevail on her claim of adverse possession and owes C nothing.

   (C)   W will not prevail on her claim of adverse possession, but as a surviving spouse she will not have to account to C or pay rent for living in the big house.

   (D)   W will not prevail on her claim of adverse possession, W must account to C for the rents received from the little house, but W is not liable for rent for living in the big house.

   (E)   W will not prevail on her claim of adverse possession, and W must account to C for the rents received from the little house and is liable for rent for living in the big house

25. **Assuming the court applies the modern trend approach, what is the most likely result:**

   (A)   W owns each parcel outright under the terms of the deeds and right of survivorship, and hence W owes C nothing.

   (B)   W will prevail on her claim of adverse possession and owes C nothing.

   (C)   W will not prevail on her claim of adverse possession, but as a surviving spouse she will not have to account to C or pay rent for living in the big house.

   (D)   W will not prevail on her claim of adverse possession, and W must account to C for the rents received from the little house but is not liable for rent for living in the big house.

   (E)   W will not prevail on her claim of adverse possession, and W must account to C for the rents received from the little house and is liable for rent for living in the big house.

END OF EXAMINATION QUESTIONS

EXAM IV

PROPERTY
MULTIPLE CHOICE OBJECTIVE QUESTIONS

EXAM IV

Questions 1, 2, 3 and 4 are based on the following fact pattern:

Aman and Bill own a ranch, jointly. Aman writes Carrie, his fiancee, a signed note giving her "the right to come on the ranch and hike as long as I own the ranch." Carrie is so excited that she rushes right out and buys a new pair of hiking boots. When Bill hears about what Aman did, he writes Carrie a letter telling her that despite what Aman said, she is not to come on the ranch.

One day while Bill is out walking, he sees a deer grazing on the ranch. Bill runs to his pick-up truck and grabs his gun. As Bill is lining up the deer in his sights, a shot rings out from another part of the ranch. Hit, the deer drops dead. Bill runs up and stands over the deer. Out of the thicket, Carrie strolls up with her gun still smoking. Carrie takes the deer and sells it.

QUESTIONS:

1. When Aman tells Carrie she can come on the ranch and hike, he is granting her:

    (A) a license.
    (B) an irrevocable license.
    (C) a profit.
    (D) an easement.
    (E) nothing, because he did not get Bill to agree to it.

2. **When Bill writes Carrie and tells her that despite what Aman said, she is not to come on the ranch,**

    (A)   Carrie's right to come on the ranch and hike is not affected.
    (B)   Carrie's can still come on the ranch and hike, but Bill can charge her a fee or sue Aman for an accounting.
    (C)   Carrie never really had the right to come on the ranch and hike, because Bill did not consent to Aman's granting permission.
    (D)   Carrie's right to come on the ranch is revoked because Bill has the power to exclude as an owner of the ranch.

3. **If Bill sues Carrie to recover the money from the sale of the deer, who is entitled to the money?**

    (A)   Bill, based on first in time, first in right.
    (B)   Bill, based on rationi soli.
    (C)   Carrie, based on occupancy.
    (D)   Bill and Carrie will split the money 50-50.

4. Assume that Carrie executes a written instrument which purports to assign the right to enter and hike to Dottie. Bill is adamantly opposed to Dottie coming on the land and hiking because Dottie is Bill's ex-wife.

    Bill sues to invalidate Dottie's right to enter and hike on the property. The most likely result is:

    (A)   The assignment is valid.
    (B)   The assignment is valid under the common law, but invalid under the modern trend.
    (C)   The assignment is invalid under the common law, but valid under the modern trend.
    (D)   The assignment is invalid.

5.   BLACKACRES

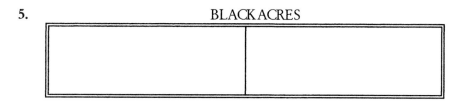

Blackacres is a 100 acre oasis in the middle of the desert with a fresh water spring-fed well on its eastern half. Owner subdivides Blackacres and sells the western half to Buyer. In the deed, which is recorded, Owner agrees, "for herself, her heirs and assigns, to provide spring water to the western half of Blackacres until the year 2025." Thereafter, Owner sells her interest to Professor, and Buyer leases her half to a Heavy Metal band as a summer residence. Professor can't stand the music, so she refuses to provide water to the western half and the band. **Heavy Metal band sues Professor to enforce the covenant. Under the original and prevailing Restatement of Property approach, the most likely result is:**

(A)   the band could obtain damages or equitable relief.
(B)   the band could obtain equitable relief only.
(C)   the band could obtain damages only.
(D)   the band is not entitled to any relief.

6.

BLACKACRE	WHITEACRE

A owns Blackacre. B owns Whiteacre, an adjoining parcel. A properly executes a writing which provides that "B has an easement to cross Blackacre." B properly records the instrument. Later A sells Blackacre to C. Then B sells Whiteacre to C. Later C sells Blackacre to D and Whiteacre to E. **E now wishes to use the easement to cross Blackacre. The most likely result is:**

(A)   E has no right to cross Blackacre.
(B)   E's right to cross Blackacre depends upon whether the easement is found to be appurtenant or in gross.
(C)   E is entitled to cross Blackacre because the easement is an express easement.
(D)   E is entitled to cross Blackacre because the easement was recorded.

Questions 7 and 8 are based upon the following fact pattern:

For valuable consideration, Owner, a Malibu resident, validly executes an instrument in favor of Student, a law student residing in the dormitories. The instrument provides that Owner conveys "to Student a right to drive across Owner's property to get to the beach," that the right is "to run with the land" and that "Owner, his heirs and assigns, promise to maintain the road." Student records the instrument. Thereafter Owner conveys his property to Purchaser, and Student conveys his interest to Undergraduate. Purchaser blocks the road. Undergraduate sues.

QUESTIONS:

7. The right to drive across the property is most likely:

    (A)   a license and Undergraduate has no right to use it.
    (B)   a license and Undergraduate has the right to use it.
    (C)   an easement and Undergraduate has the right to use it.
    (D)   an easement, but Undergraduate has no right to use it.

8. If Student sues Purchaser to enforce the agreement to maintain the road, the most likely result under the original and prevailing Restatement of Property approach is:

    (A)   the agreement is enforceable as an equitable servitude.
    (B)   the agreement is enforceable as a real covenant.
    (C)   the agreement is enforceable as either an equitable servitude or a real covenant.
    (D)   the agreement is an invalid covenant.

9. O owns two adjacent lots, lot 1 and lot 2. She sells lot 1 to A. A records the deed. The deed contains an express covenant restricting the lot conveyed to residential use. The deed states that "the covenant is to run with the lot conveyed and the adjacent land which O retains, to all subsequent grantees." Thereafter O leases the land she retained to B for 10 years. A leases lot 1 to C for 10 years. C starts to use the lot commercially. **Under the original and prevailing Restatement of Property approach, if B were to sue C, the most likely result is:**

    (A)   B could successfully sue C for either damages or injunctive relief.
    (B)   B could not sue C successfully for either damages or injunctive relief.
    (C)   B could successfully sue C for injunctive relief, but not damages.
    (D)   B could successfully sue C for damages, but not injunctive relief.

10. Olivia owns farmland along the Mississippi River that is protected from flooding by levees along the riverbank. Olivia sells part of the land, including a narrow strip right on the river, to Alice. The deed from Olivia to Alice contains an express covenant requiring Alice "to maintain the part of the levee along Alice's riverbank to protect the surrounding land and crops from the Mississippi's regular flooding." The deed is recorded. Thereafter, Olivia sells the land Olivia retained to Betty. Alice lets the levee along her riverbank fall into disrepair. **If Betty were to sue Alice, the most likely result is:**

    (A)   Betty has no right to sue Alice, because the covenant between Olivia and Alice will most likely be deemed personal to Olivia.
    (B)   Betty has no right to enforce the covenant, because it fails to touch and concern the land.
    (C)   Betty will be able to successfully sue Alice for damages or injunctive relief.
    (D)   Betty will be able to successfully sue Alice for injunctive relief, but not damages.

11. University Heights subdivision has approximately 95 lots and about 85 residents. When the subdivision was initially developed in 1992, an express covenant was put in all of the deeds. The covenant provided that all poplar, cottonwood, and aspen trees were to be cut down and eradicated from each lot in the subdivision to insure that the spruce and a birch trees could flourish. By 2006, none of the property owners were in full compliance, and only 18 owners had taken substantial steps toward compliance. **One of the property owners sues to require all of the owners to achieve full compliance. The most likely result is:**

   (A)   The court will enforce the covenant as an equitable servitude.
   (B)   The court will enforce the covenant as a real covenant.
   (C)   The court will not enforce the covenant because it has been abandoned (waived).
   (D)   The court will not enforce the covenant because of the changed conditions.

Questions 12 and 13 are based upon the following fact pattern:

O is the owner of two lots, both of which front on the Pacific Coast Highway ("PCH"). O has a house in the upper left corner of the western lot. He uses a paved road which starts in the lower right corner of the eastern lot, heads due north to the back of the lots, and then runs across the back of both lots over to the back left corner of the western lot. This is the easiest way to the house since there is a very steep hill along the front of the western lot along PCH. Thereafter O sells the eastern lot to X by deed which makes no reference to the road. X erects a barricade across the road to stop O from using it.

12. **If O sues for the right to continue to use the road to access the house on the western lot, the most likely result is:**

    (A)   X will prevail based on the Statute of Frauds.
    (B)   O will prevail, and his strongest claim is an implied easement by necessity.
    (C)   O will prevail, and his strongest claim is an implied easement by prior existing use if the jurisdiction applies the common law.
    (D)   O will prevail, and his strongest claim is an implied easement by prior existing use if the jurisdiction applies the modern trend.
    (E)   O will prevail, and his strongest claim is a license coupled with estoppel.

13. Assume, arguendo, that in problem 12 the court grants O the right to cross the eastern lot to reach the western lot. Thereafter O buys the lot to the *west* of the western lot and builds a road across the new lot to access the western lot. **O's building the new road most likely will:**

    (A)   terminate the right to cross the eastern lot, because it is no longer necessary to access the western lot.
    (B)   constitute abandonment and will terminate the right to cross the eastern lot.
    (C)   have no effect on the right to cross the eastern lot.
    (D)   have no effect on the right to cross the eastern lot, but if O uses the right to cross the eastern lot to access the new lot O just bought, X will be entitled to injunctive relief to stop O from trespassing on the right to cross the eastern lot.

14. George and Jesse finally decide to retire from politics. George owns a nice little compound right on the coast. Jesse buys the lot right across the street. Although George and Jesse were rivals in politics, Jesse assumes that bygones are bygones and walks across the edge of George's property every day to get to the beach. George is busy jumping out of airplanes and giving speeches, so he does not notice Jesse at first. Three years after Jesse started walking across George's property, George finally notices him one day. George comes out on his porch, looks Jesse in the eyes, and yells "Read my lips! No more walking across my property." Jesse thinks George is kidding (just like the other time) and continues walking across George's property. Jesse keeps walking across George's property every day for the next three years. The statute of limitations is 5 years.

George sues to stop Jesse from walking across his property, the most likely result is:

    (A)   George will prevail since he interrupted Jesse's use.
    (B)   Jesse will prevail if the jurisdiction does not apply the lost grant theory.
    (C)   Jesse will prevail if the jurisdiction applies the lost grant theory.
    (D)   Jesse will prevail under a claim of license coupled with estoppel.

15. O owns 10 lots which she plans to subdivide into Greenacres Subdivision. Between January 1, 2000, and December 31, 2004, O conveys 6 of the lots. Each of the 6 deeds contains a covenant that the purchaser, her heirs and assigns, will use the land as a single-family dwelling. On February 1, 2005, O conveys lot 7 to X, in exchange for valuable consideration, and X promptly records the deed. The conveyance contains no restrictions on X's use of lot 7. X begins construction of a multiple-family dwelling. **A, the purchaser of lot 3, sues to enjoin X. Assume the jurisdiction strictly interprets and applies the Statute of Frauds. The most likely result is:**

    (A)   X will prevail because there is no express restriction on lot 7.
    (B)   A will prevail because there is a common scheme.
    (C)   A will prevail because a multiple-family dwelling in the midst of single family homes constitutes a nuisance.
    (D)   X will prevail because A has no standing to enforce the restriction.

Questions 16 and 17 are based upon the following fact pattern:

Treehugger and Sunshine are neighbors. They each live in small cabins on 10 acre lots. They live way out in the country, far from the crowds, noise and pollution of city life. With suburban sprawl being what it is, however, they agree that the best thing to do is to restrict their lots to residential use only. They sign an agreement which provides that the respective lots will be used for residential purposes only, and that the only structure on each lot is to be the existing cabin. The agreement expressly binds their "heirs and assigns." They each properly record a copy of the agreement. Thereafter, Treehugger grants an easement to Andy to come on the land and fish, and Sunshine sells her land to Betty and moves to Montana. One day Treehugger falls out of a tree, hits his head and falls into a coma. Betty decides to take advantage of the situation and begins to build a bar on her property.

Andy sues Betty seeking damages for breach of the covenant.

QUESTIONS:

16. **Under the original and prevailing Restatement of Property approach, the most likely result is:**

    (A)   Andy is entitled to recover damages.
    (B)   Andy is not entitled to recover damages because the requisite vertical privity is lacking.
    (C)   Andy is not entitled to recover damages because the requisite horizontal privity is lacking.
    (D)   Andy is not entitled to recover damages because the requisite vertical and horizontal privity is lacking.

17. **Under the new Restatement (Third) of Property approach, the most likely result is:**

    (A)   Andy is entitled to recover damages.
    (B)   Andy is not entitled to recover damages because the requisite vertical privity is lacking.
    (C)   Andy is not entitled to recover damages because the requisite horizontal privity is lacking.
    (D)   Andy is not entitled to recover damages because the requisite vertical and horizontal privity is lacking.

18. Alice and Betty live across the street from each other. Alice owns Malibuacres, beachfront property on the ocean side of Pacific Coast Highway. Betty owns Gullsway, a large estate on the mountainside of Pacific Coast Highway. They are good friends. Alice once told Betty that Betty could walk across Malibuacres anytime Betty wanted to get to the beach. Betty decides to sell Gullsway. Kristin, a co-worker, hears about Betty's plans and inquires about buying Gullsway. When Kristin stops by Gullsway to check out the property, Betty takes her across the street to the beach to watch the sunset. Kristin falls in love with the property and purchases it. One day shortly after purchasing Gullsway, Kristin decides to walk over to the beach and catch the sunset. As she starts to cross Malibuacres, Alice comes running out of her house and yells at Kristin to get off Alice's property. **Kristin claims she has a right to cross Malibuacres to get to the beach. The most likely result is:**

(A) Kristin is out of luck.

(B) Kristin has an express easement appurtenant which grants her the right to continue to cross Malibuacres.

(C) Under license coupled with estoppel, Kristin is entitled to continue to cross Malibuacres.

(D) Under implied easements based on prior existing use, Kristin is entitled to continue to cross Malibuacres.

(E) Kristin has a prescriptive easement which entitles her to continue to cross Malibuacres.

19. O owns 50 acres. Five years ago, she subdivided and platted it into 50 lots. O recorded the plat, which contains no restrictions. Over the course of the next couple of years, O sold all 50 lots. The deeds to 45 of the lots contain express covenants restricting the lots to residential use. For totally unexplained reasons, 5 lots were sold with no express restrictions. A, the owner of the 10th lot sold (which has an express restriction on it) brings suit to enjoin B, the owner of the 30th lot sold, from building a gas station on lot 30 (which has no express restriction on it). **The most likely result is:**

   (A)   The court will not enjoin B's use of lot 30 because the courts do not imply real covenants.

   (B)   The court will find that a common scheme exists and grant A's request for an injunction against using lot 30 for anything other than residential use.

   (C)   The court will find that a common scheme exists but deny A's request for an injunction against using lot 30 for anything other than residential use on the grounds that as a prior purchaser A lacks standing.

   (D)   The court will deny A's request on the grounds that there is insufficient evidence of a common scheme.

Questions 20, 21, 22, and 23 are based upon the following fact pattern:

In 1896, Charlton owned Deliveranceacres, a four hundred acre parcel of land which surrounds a lake. The Rifleman Hunting Club purchased, in a signed writing which they recorded, "the exclusive right to all fishing and shooting privileges to Deliveranceacres, and the perpetual right to enter upon and fully and exclusively enjoy and use the same for its current and future stockholders." By 2000, The Rifleman Hunting Club had acquired complete title to approximately three hundred of the four hundred acres. In 2006, PETA purchased, from a successor to the original grantor, Charlton, 42.28 acres of the land to which the earlier grant of hunting and fishing rights applies. The seller informed PETA that The Rifleman Hunting Club possessed some type of hunting rights. Presently one single family home sits on the 42.28 acres. At one time the property also contained a barn and several small outbuildings.

PETA now wishes to build a four building, twenty-six unit condominium complex on the northeast corner of the property, an area farthest from the land The Rifleman Hunting Club owns and close to several other residences. Each unit would have two bedrooms and a single car garage. An architect's plans indicate that the area around the condominiums would contain a manicured lawn and a playground, along with walking paths and bridle paths in the undeveloped areas. Boat slips and a deck would be built on the shoreline. The condominium owners would be prohibited from hunting or fishing on the property.

During hunting season in late fall and early winter, 19 club members still hunt deer, pheasant, ducks and geese on the Club's property and PETA's property. At trial, the hunting club president indicated on maps the areas where the club hunts. These areas included the area that PETA plans to develop. The hunting club president asserted that the increased human activity and reduced cover for animals would interfere with their hunting activities.

After obtaining the necessary government permits for the development, PETA filed a declaratory judgment action to ascertain how the hunting club's hunting and fishing rights affect their property.

QUESTIONS:

20. As to the Rifleman's hunting and fishing rights, the most likely result is:

  (A) They hold a license.
  (B) They hold an easement.
  (C) They hold a profit.
  (D) They hold a leasehold interest.

21. As to how the Rifleman's hunting and fishing rights affect PETA's development plans, the most likely result is:

  (A) The Rifleman Hunting Club rights will prevail because the proposed development would substantially and unreasonably interfere with the club's rights.
  (B) PETA will prevail because any adverse impact upon the club's rights will be minimal in light of the additional land still available for hunting and fishing.
  (C) PETA will prevail because the original hunting and fishing rights were not transferable to the current club members.
  (D) PETA will prevail because the proposed development is within the reasonably foreseeable development of the land.

22. Assume that PETA could show that due to the intensive development of the surrounding lands and pollution of the water on the land, no animals or fish had been captured, killed or even seen in years on PETA's land. PETA's best argument would be that the hunting club's rights should be terminated:

  (A) because the specific purpose has been accomplished.
  (B) under abandonment.
  (C) because the specific purposes had become impossible.
  (D) under the changed conditions doctrine.

23. Assume Trapper sneaks onto PETA's land during hunting season and captures a fox. When PETA hears of it, PETA sneaks onto Trapper's property and takes it from Trapper's cage. If Trapper sues PETA for return of the fox, who has the superior claim under the modern trend?

  (A) Trapper, based on occupancy.
  (B) PETA, based on rationi soli.
  (C) The Rifleman Hunting Club, based on rationi soli.
  (D) The Rifleman Hunting Club, based on its exclusive right to hunt.

24. Olivia is the owner of lot 1. Nellie is the owner of lot 2.

Lot 1	Lot 2

Olivia lives on lot 1. Lot 2 is vacant. Olivia builds a driveway on lot 2. The driveway runs the length of the western boundary line of lot 2, from the southern edge where both lots border a roadway, up to the upper northwest corner where the driveway turns west and crosses the boundary between lots 1 and 2. Olivia uses the driveway to haul in lumber and materials to build a house in the upper northeastern corner of lot 1. Thereafter, Nellie sells lot 2 to Betty. Betty plans to build a house on lot 2 and has it surveyed to determine the exact boundaries. At that time she learns that the driveway, which she assumed was on lot 1, is actually on lot 2. Betty sues to stop Olivia's continued use of the driveway. **Olivia's best claim is:**

(A)   adverse possession.
(B)   prescriptive easement.
(C)   license coupled with estoppel.
(D)   implied easement by necessity.
(E)   implied easement based on prior existing use.

25.

Lot 1	Lot 2	Lot 3	Lot 4	Lot 5	Lot 6	Lot 7

Main Street

Lots 1 through 7 front on Main Street. In 1980, the local public utility obtained an express easement from each property owner to install water mains and connecting pipes. The easement expressly provides that the easement is to be "five feet in width, from the southern boundary of the lot." In 2000, a cable company obtained permission from each property owner to install, and did install, cable lines in the same five foot strip of each lot. In 2006, the public utility learns of the cable lines.

The public utility sues for damages and to have the cables lines removed. The most likely result is:

(A)   The public utility should prevail under first in time, first in right.
(B)   The public utility should prevail because it has the exclusive right to occupy the five foot strip.
(C)   The public utility should prevail because the cable installation substantially interferes with the utility's present partial occupation and/or with its possible future use.
(D)   The cable company should prevail because the property owners granted it an easement.

END OF EXAMINATION QUESTIONS

EXAM V

PROPERTY
MULTIPLE CHOICE OBJECTIVE QUESTIONS

EXAM V

1. Owner, Olivia Owen, and Purchaser, Paul Paige, agree that Paul will buy Olivia's house for $300,000. They draft the following memo:

   > I agree to buy Olivia Owen's house on Elm Street for $100 and other good and valuable consideration.
   >
   > signed/*Paul Paige/*

   Does the writing constitute an enforceable contract?

   (A) No, because it fails to comply with the Statute of Frauds.
   (B) Yes, but only against Paul.
   (C) Yes, but only against Olivia.
   (D) Yes, against both Paul and Olivia.

2. Othello, who owns Veniceacre, decides to give it to Duke as a gift. Othello properly executes a deed and gives it to Duke for Duke's attorney to review. While Duke's attorney is reviewing the instrument, Othello dies suddenly and unexpectedly. His Last Will and Testament gives all of his real property to Rod and all of his personal property to Iago. **Who owns Veniceacre?**

   (A) Duke.
   (B) Rod.
   (C) Iago.
   (D) Othello's heirs.

3. Purchaser executes a standard contract for the purchase of Whiteacre, a beautiful one-story home. The contract provides that "the property shall be free and clear of all encumbrances except all restrictions and easements of record." Prior to closing, Purchaser finds a recorded covenant which restricts all homes in the subdivision to one-story, thereby frustrating Purchaser's plans of adding a two story addition off the back of the house. Purchaser repudiates the contract.

If Owner sues for specific performance, the most likely outcome is:

(A)   Purchaser can repudiate the contract, because the covenant makes title unmarketable.

(B)   Purchaser can repudiate the contract, because of the unrecorded encumbrance.

(C)   Purchaser can repudiate the contract, because the covenant frustrates Purchaser's plans.

(D)   Owner is entitled to specific performance.

Questions 4, 5 and 6 are based upon the following fact pattern:

Owner conveys a one-half interest in the mineral rights underlying Greenacre to Miner, who fails to record the deed. Owner then sells Greenacre to Gullible by general warranty deed without any exceptions in the deed. Gullible fails to record the deed. Gullible then sells Greenacre to Naive by special warranty deed without any exceptions in the deed. Naive records the deed immediately. When Miner shows up to begin mining, Naive refuses to recognize Miner's interest.

Assume the jurisdiction has a grantor-grantee recording index and has adopted the following recording act:

Every conveyance of real property or an estate for years therein, other than a lease for a term not exceeding one year, is void against any subsequent purchaser or mortgagee of the same property, or any part thereof, in good faith and for valuable consideration, whose conveyance is first duly recorded, and as against any judgment affecting the title, unless the conveyance shall have been duly recorded prior to the record of notice of action.

QUESTIONS:

4. The statute sets forth which approach to the recording acts?

    (A)   a race recording act.
    (B)   a notice recording act.
    (C)   a race-notice recording act.

5. What is the extent of Miner's interest, if any?

    (A)   Miner has no interest in Greenacre because Gullible was a subsequent bona fide purchaser without notice.
    (B)   Miner has no interest in Greenacre because Naive is a subsequent bona fide purchaser who recorded first.
    (C)   Miner has a one-half interest in the mineral rights in Greenacre, but no right to enter Greenacre.
    (D)   Miner has a one-half interest in the mineral rights in Greenacre and an implied easement by necessity to permit him to enter Greenacre to mine.

6. After Miner shows up demanding entry to start mining, Naive contacts Gullible and persuades Gullible to record the Owner to Gullible deed. Is Naive entitled to protection under the recording act? The most likely result is:

    (A)   Naive is entitled to protection.
    (B)   Naive is not entitled to protection because Naive had notice of the Owner to Miner conveyance before her chain of title was properly recorded.
    (C)   Naive is not entitled to protection because Naive's chain of title is still not properly recorded since Gullible recorded after Naive.
    (D)   Naive is entitled to protection only if the jurisdiction applies an expanded scope of the search of the grantor index at the front end, requiring grantees to search under each grantor's name even before the date of the deed purporting to transfer title to the grantor.

7. Purchaser executes a standard contract to purchase Greenacre, a lush farm. Purchaser plans to build a huge shopping mall. When local residents hear of Purchaser's plans, prior to closing they persuade the city to rezone the property from commercial to residential, an unexpected change which greatly reduces the value of the land to Purchaser. Purchaser repudiates the contract to purchase.

If Owner sues for specific performance, the most likely result is:

(A)   Owner is entitled to specific performance under both traditional common law principles and the modern trend approach.
(B)   Owner is entitled to specific performance under traditional common law principles but not under the modern trend approach.
(C)   Owner is entitled to specific performance under the modern trend approach but not under traditional common law principles.
(D)   Owner is not entitled to specific performance under either traditional common law principles or the modern trend approach.

8. Patty properly executes a standard contract to purchase Greenacre from Oscar. Oscar properly executes and delivers a general warranty deed which purports to transfer Greenacre to Patty. Patty does not check the chain of title to Greenacre prior to closing. Patty never takes possession. Forty years later, when Patty goes to sell Greenacre to Gerri, Patty discovers that Oscar never had title to Greenacre.

Patty decides to sue Oscar. Applying traditional common law principles and a typical statute of limitations, the most likely result is:

(A)   Patty can successfully sue Oscar for breach of contract and breach of the present and future covenants.
(B)   Patty can successfully sue Oscar for breach of the present and future covenants only.
(C)   Patty can successfully sue Oscar for breach of the present covenants only.
(D)   Patty can successfully sue Oscar for breach of the future covenants only.
(E)   Patty can successfully sue Oscar only in her dreams.

9. Owner sold Greenacre to Purchaser. Owner financed the sale and had Purchaser execute a promissory note and mortgage (which did not contain a due on sale clause). Owner recorded the mortgage. Thereafter Purchaser sold Greenacre to Buyer. The contract and deed expressly provided that Buyer purchased Greenacre "subject to the mortgage."

Which of the following statements best describes Owner's legal rights as against Purchaser, Buyer and Greenacre:

(A) Both Purchaser and Buyer are personally liable for the mortgage debt, and in the event Buyer defaults on the payments, Owner can foreclose on the mortgage, sell Greenacre, and satisfy the debt out of the proceeds.

(B) Only Purchaser is personally liable for the mortgage debt, but Buyer agrees that in the event Buyer defaults on the payments, Owner can foreclose on the mortgage, sell Greenacre, and satisfy the debt out of the proceeds.

(C) Only Buyer is personally liable for the mortgage debt, and Buyer agrees that in the event Buyer defaults on the payments, Owner can foreclose on the mortgage, sell Greenacre, and satisfy the debt out of the proceeds.

(D) Only Purchaser is personally liable for the mortgage debt, and since Purchaser has sold Greenacre, Owner cannot sell Greenacre to satisfy the debt in the event Purchaser defaults on the payments.

10. John Doe agreed to sell his house to Nancy Roe. John executed the following deed and gave it to Nancy in exchange for her paying the agreed upon purchase price:

> I, John Doe, hereby grant to Nancy Roe the real estate situated at 123 Maple St. in Orange County, California.
>
> signed/*John Doe*/

The deed was not attested or acknowledged, or recorded.

Which of the following statements best describes the validity of the deed under the general rule:

(A)   The deed is valid as between the parties.

(B)   The deed is invalid because it does not contain the essential element of consideration.

(C)   The deed is invalid because it does not contain the essential element of attestation or acknowledgment.

(D)   The deed is invalid because it was not recorded.

(E)   The deed is invalid because (1) it was not recorded, and (2) it does not contain the essential elements of (a) consideration and (b) attestation or acknowledgment.

11. O owns Whiteacre. A properly executes and delivers a deed which purports to sell Whiteacre to B, who fails to record or go into possession. O properly executes and delivers a deed which purports to sell Whiteacre to A, who records. A properly executes and delivers a deed which purports to sell Whiteacre to C, who records.

Assuming the jurisdiction applies estoppel by deed, has a notice recording act, and a grantor-grantee recording index, the most likely result is:

(A)   C owns the property if the jurisdiction requires a grantee to perform a standard scope of the search of the recording system.

(B)   C owns the property if the jurisdiction requires a grantee to perform an expanded scope of the search of the recording system.

(C)   C owns the property if the jurisdiction requires a grantee to perform either a standard scope or an expanded scope of the search of the recording system.

(D)   B owns the property if the jurisdiction requires a grantee to perform a standard scope of the search of the recording system.

(E)   B owns the property if the jurisdiction requires a grantee to perform an expanded scope of the search of the recording system.

Questions 12 and 13 are based upon the following fact pattern:

O properly conveys Blackacre to A, an out-of-town investor who fails to record. O subsequently sells Blackacre to B, who has actual notice of the O to A deed. B records. A moves onto Blackacre. Thereafter B sells Blackacre to C, who records. A then records the O to A deed. The jurisdiction has a grantor-grantee recording index.

12. Assume the jurisdiction adopts the following recording act. Who owns the property?

No conveyance, transfer or mortgage of real property, or any interest therein, . . . shall be good and effectual in law or equity against creditors or subsequent purchasers for a valuable consideration and without notice, unless the same be recorded according to law.

   (A) A owns Blackacre.
   (B) A owns the property only if the jurisdiction requires an extended scope of search of the grantor-grantee index at the back end of the search - requiring each grantee to continue to search under each grantor's name after the date of the recording of the first deed purporting to transfer the grantor's title.
   (C) A owns the property if the jurisdiction requires an extended scope of search of the grantor-grantee index at the front end of the search - requiring each grantee to search under each grantor's name before the date of the deed purporting to convey title to the grantor.
   (D) C owns Blackacre.

13. Assume the jurisdiction adopts the following recording act.   No conveyance shall be valid, as against purchasers for valuable consideration, until it is recorded. **Who owns the property?**

    (A)   A owns Blackacre.
    (B)   A owns the property only if the jurisdiction requires an extended scope of search of the grantor-grantee index at the back end of the search - requiring each grantee to continue to search under each grantor's name after the date of the recording of the first deed purporting to transfer the grantor's title.
    (C)   A owns the property if the jurisdiction requires an extended scope of search of the grantor-grantee index at the front end of the search - requiring each grantee to search under each grantor's name before the date of the deed purporting to convey title to the grantor.
    (D)   C owns Blackacre.

14. Buyer and Owner enter into a standard contract of sale with respect to Greenacre. Unbeknownst to either party, all of the electrical wiring in the house was installed in violation of the local housing code. The parties close on the deal, and Owner properly executes and delivers a general warranty deed to Buyer.

    Which of the following statements best describes the probable legal significance of the code violation pre- and post-closing?

    (A)   Pre-closing the violation constituted an encumbrance which would have permitted Buyer to rescind the contract, and post-closing it constitutes a breach of the covenant against encumbrances.
    (B)   Pre-closing the violation did **not** constitute an encumbrance which would have permitted Buyer to rescind the contract, but post-closing it constitutes a breach of the covenant against encumbrances.
    (C)   Pre-closing the violation constituted an encumbrance which would have permitted Buyer to rescind the contract, but post-closing it does **not** constitute a breach of the covenant against encumbrances.
    (D)   Pre-closing the violation did **not** constitute an encumbrance which would have permitted Buyer to rescind the contract, and likewise post-closing it does **not** constitute a breach of the covenant against encumbrances.

Questions 15, 16, 17, 18, and 19 are based upon the following fact pattern:

In 1995, Slick properly executed a special warranty deed which purports to convey Getawayacre, vacation property located thousands of miles away, to Bertha for $200,000. After a number of years, Bertha realized that she was never going to be able to get out to Getawayacre. In 2003, Bertha properly executed a general warranty deed which purports to convey Getawayacre to Chris for $150,000. Before Chris can get out to Getawayacre, Oscar takes possession in 2004 and refuses to relinquish possession. After investigating the situation, Chris learns that Oscar is the true owner and that Slick never had any interest in Getawayacre.

Assume a 5 year statute of limitations for causes of action based on breaches of the covenants in a deed. Assume Chris sues shortly after learning that Oscar is the true owner.

QUESTIONS:

15. Under the general common law approach, who can successfully sue whom for breach of the present covenants?

    (A)   Chris can sue Bertha, and if Chris recovers from Bertha, Bertha can sue Slick.

    (B)   Chris can sue Bertha, and even if Chris recovers from Bertha, Bertha cannot sue Slick.

    (C)   Chris can sue Bertha or Slick, and if Chris recovers from Bertha, Bertha can sue Slick.

    (D)   Chris can sue Slick only.

    (E)   Chris cannot sue anyone.

16. Under the general common law approach, who can successfully sue whom for breach of the future covenants?

    (A)   Chris can sue Bertha, and if Chris recovers from Bertha, Bertha can sue Slick.

    (B)   Chris can sue Bertha, and even if Chris recovers from Bertha, Bertha cannot sue Slick.

    (C)   Chris can sue Bertha or Slick, and if Chris recovers from Bertha, Bertha can sue Slick.

    (D)   Chris can sue Slick only.

    (E)   Chris cannot sue anyone.

17. Under the <u>modern trend</u> approach, who can successfully sue whom for breach of the <u>present</u> covenants?

   (A)   Chris can sue Bertha, and if Chris recovers from Bertha, Bertha can sue Slick.
   (B)   Chris can sue Bertha, and even if Chris recovers from Bertha, Bertha cannot sue Slick.
   (C)   ;Chris can sue Bertha or Slick, and if Chris recovers from Bertha, Bertha can sue Slick.
   (D)   Chris can sue Slick only.
   (E)   Chris cannot sue anyone.

18. Under the <u>modern trend</u> approach, who can successfully sue whom for breach of the <u>future</u> covenants?

   (A)   Chris can sue Bertha, and if Chris recovers from Bertha, Bertha can sue Slick.
   (B)   Chris can sue Bertha, and even if Chris recovers from Bertha, Bertha cannot sue Slick.
   (C)   Chris can sue Bertha or Slick, and if Chris recovers from Bertha, Bertha can sue Slick.
   (D)   Chris can sue Slick only.
   (E)   Chris cannot sue anyone.

19. Under the <u>modern trend</u> approach to the running of the covenants, who can successfully sue whom and for how much?

   (A)   Chris can sue Bertha only for $150,000.
   (B)   Chris can sue Slick only for $150,000.
   (C)   Chris can sue Bertha or Slick for $150,000, and if Chris recovers from Bertha, Bertha can sue Slick for $200,000 if the jurisdiction applies the rescissionary approach.
   (D)   Chris can sue Bertha or Slick for $150,000, and if Chris recovers from Bertha, Bertha can sue Slick for $150,000 if the jurisdiction applies the rescissionary approach.
   (A)   Chris cannot sue anyone.

Questions 20 and 21 are based upon the following fact pattern:

Owner and Buyer entered into a properly executed contract to sell the property situated at 123 Maple St. Prior to closing, a 7.8 earthquake hits the area, seriously damaging the house.

QUESTIONS:

20. **Which of the following statements best describes the parties' rights and obligations under the traditional <u>common law</u> American approach?**

    (A) If the damage is substantial, Buyer can rescind the contract.
    (B) If the damage is substantial, Owner can still get specific performance, though an abatement in purchase price will be necessary.
    (C) Regardless of the damage, Owner is entitled to specific performance for the full purchase price, but if Owner has insurance, Buyer is entitled to the insurance proceeds.
    (D) Regardless of the damage, Owner is entitled to specific performance for the full purchase price, and if Owner has insurance, Owner is entitled to the insurance proceeds too.

21. **Which of the following statements best describes the parties' rights and obligations under the <u>modern trend</u> American approach?**

    (A) If the damage is substantial, Buyer can rescind the contract.
    (B) If the damage is substantial, Owner can still get specific performance, though an abatement in purchase price will be necessary.
    (C) Regardless of the damage, Owner is entitled to specific performance for the full purchase price, but if Owner has insurance, Buyer is entitled to the insurance proceeds.
    (D) Regardless of the damage, Owner is entitled to specific performance for the full purchase price, and if Owner has insurance, Owner is entitled to the insurance proceeds too.

Questions 22 and 23 are based upon the following fact pattern:

Nelson's wife died in 1990. In 1995, Nelson executed his will, devising all his property to his four daughters. In 2000, Nelson properly executed and delivered a quitclaim deed which purported to convey Nelson's residence to Jonathan as a gift, reserving a "Life Estate in and to said property, with power to revoke, sell, rent, lease, mortgage or otherwise dispose of said property during Nelson's natural lifetime." Nelson continued to live in the residence until his death in 2005 and used none of his reserved powers.

QUESTIONS:

22. **Under the traditional common law approach, who is entitled to the residence upon Nelson's death?**

    (A)   The four daughters are entitled to the residence, because the power to revoke makes the transfer testamentary.
    (B)   The four daughters are entitled to the residence, because the quitclaim deed was ineffective to transfer property previously devised.
    (C)   Jonathan, because the deed created a defeasible fee subject to a life estate, and the life estate has terminated without the power to revoke being exercised.
    (D)   Jonathan, because as long as a document substantially complies with the requirements for a will, it is effective to transfer property at time of death.

23. **Under the modern trend approach, who is entitled to the residence upon Nelson's death?**

    (A)   The four daughters are entitled to the residence, because the power to revoke makes the transfer testamentary.
    (B)   The four daughters are entitled to the residence, because the quitclaim deed was ineffective to transfer property previously devised.
    (C)   Jonathan, because the deed created a defeasible fee subject to a life estate, and the life estate has terminated without the power to revoke being exercised.
    (D)   Jonathan, because as long as a document substantially complies with the requirements for a will, it is effective to transfer property at time of death.

24. Bluto, who owns Canadacres, decides to attend law school. Bluto borrows $40,000 from A to pay for his first year expenses. Bluto executes a note and mortgage on Canadacres, but A fails to record the mortgage. Bluto borrows $40,000 from B to pay for his second year expenses. Bluto tells B about A's note and mortgage. Bluto executes a note and mortgage on Canadacres in favor of B. B records his mortgage. Bluto borrows $50,000 from C to pay for his third year expenses (the extra money is necessary to cover the toga party graduation bash). Bluto executes a note and mortgage on Canadacres in favor of C. Unfortunately, Bluto defaults on the payments to A, who forecloses. Canadacres is sold for only $70,000.

Assuming the jurisdiction has a notice recording act, how will the proceeds most likely be distributed under the "parties' expectations" theory?

(A)   A is entitled to $40,000, B is entitled to $30,000, and C will receive nothing.

(B)   A is entitled to nothing, B is entitled to $20,000, and C will receive $50,000.

(C)   A is entitled to $10,000, B is entitled to $30,000, and C will receive $30,000.

(D)   The proceeds will be split evenly.

(E)   Who cares, they should have known that any land named Canadacres is worthless!

25. Ron owns Creightonacres, a vast wasteland in the middle of Nebraska (redundant?). Ron accepts an offer to teach for a semester in California, the land of milk and honey. While Ron is away visiting, Darth drafts a deed which purports to convey Creightonacres from Ron to Darth. Darth signs Ron's name to the deed. Darth does not record the deed. Darth then offers to sell Creightonacres to Lea. Lea searches the chain of title prior to purchasing and sees that Ron is the record owner. When she questions Darth about that, Darth shows her the deed which purports to convey title from Ron to Darth. Lea requires Darth to record the deed, which he does. Darth executes and delivers a special warranty deed to Lea in exchange for valuable consideration. Lea in turns sells Creightonacres to Luke, giving Luke a general warranty deed. When Ron returns from the land of milk and honey, he senses a disturbance in his title. Ron sues Luke to quiet title.

Who owns the land assuming the jurisdiction has a notice recording act?

- (A) Ron, because the deed from Darth to Lea was a fraudulent deed.
- (B) Ron, because the deed from Darth to Lea was a forged deed.
- (C) Ron, because Lea did not qualify as a subsequent bona fide purchaser without notice.
- (D) Luke, because the force (of the recording act) is with him (i.e., he qualifies for protection).

END OF EXAMINATION QUESTIONS

EXAM VI

PROPERTY
MULTIPLE CHOICE OBJECTIVE QUESTIONS

EXAM VI

1. O orally agrees to sell Farmland to B. B gives O a down payment, takes possession, and begins to plant crops on the farm. O, however, repudiates the agreement. **If B sues for specific performance, B's best argument would be:**

    (A) the Statute of Frauds.
    (B) the doctrine of estoppel.
    (C) the doctrine of part performance.
    (D) the doctrine of equitable conversion.

2. After years of operation, O agrees to sell his store to P. The contract provides that O will convey insurable title. Before closing, P discovers that the local zoning ordinance prohibits commercial operations at that location. O assures P it has not been a problem in the past. P decides the price is too high in light of this unexpected risk. **P repudiates the contract, and O sues for specific performance. The most likely result is judgment for:**

    (A) P, because the zoning ordinance frustrates P's intent to operate a store making the contract unenforceable.
    (B) P, because the present violation of the zoning ordinance makes the contract unenforceable.
    (C) O, if O can obtain title insurance on the property.
    (D) O, if the chances of anyone suing to enforce the zoning ordinance are slim.

Questions 3 and 4 are based upon the following fact pattern:

O, who owns Blackacre, executes a mortgage creating a security interest in Blackacre in favor of A. A, however, does not record the mortgage. O then sells Blackacre to B, for value, by special warranty deed which does not mention the mortgage. B does not record. B conveys to C by quitclaim deed. C gives value and records the quitclaim deed. A records the mortgage. B records the special warranty deed.

QUESTIONS:

3. Assuming none of the parties had actual notice of the prior transactions and the jurisdiction has a grantor-grantee recording index. Who owns Blackacre in a notice recording act jurisdiction?

    (A)   B, free and clear of the mortgage.
    (B)   B, subject to the mortgage.
    (C)   C, free and clear of the mortgage.
    (D)   C, subject to the mortgage.

4. Assuming none of the parties had actual notice of the prior transactions and the jurisdiction has a grantor-grantee recording index. Who owns Blackacre in a race-notice recording act jurisdiction?

    (A)   B, free and clear of the mortgage.
    (B)   B, subject to the mortgage.
    (C)   C, free and clear of the mortgage.
    (D)   C, subject to the mortgage.

Questions 5 and 6 are based upon the following fact pattern:

O learns that she has cancer, but the doctors inform her they caught the disease in its early stages and her chances for successful treatment are very high. Nevertheless, O properly executes a deed to Blackacre conveying it to her son, S. She hands the deed to him and orally tells him to keep it just in case she dies so the property will not have to go through probate. O remains in possession of Blackacre. 5 years later, after successfully beating the cancer, O asks for the deed back. S refuses to give it back.

QUESTIONS:

5. **O sues to quiet title, claiming she never transferred the property to S. What is the best statement of the burden of proof and likely outcome under the modern trend?**

   (A)   S has the burden of proving a valid delivery and should be able to prove it under these facts.
   (B)   S has the burden of proving a valid delivery and should NOT be able to prove it under these facts.
   (C)   O has the burden of proving there was NOT a valid delivery and should prevail under these facts.
   (D)   O has the burden of proving there was NOT a valid delivery and should NOT prevail under these facts.

6. Assume that instead of O giving the properly executed deed to her son, she gave the deed to her attorney, with the instructions to give it to her son, S, one year from then, if she did not change her mind and ask for it back. Six months later, the hospital seeks to attach the property to pay for her medical bills.

   Should the hospital be able to attach the property?

   (A)   The hospital should not be able to attach the property because O has no interest in it while it is in escrow.
   (B)   The hospital should not be able to attach the property because such oral conditions on delivery are enforceable.
   (C)   The hospital should be able to attach the property because the attorney has not delivered the deed to S yet.
   (D)   The hospital should be able to attach the property because such conditions on an escrow render the delivery to the escrow ineffective.

7. O sells Redacre to P, an out of town buyer. O failed to tell P that Redacre had been the sight of a bloody murder several years before, a fact well known to O and to the community which has made it difficult for P to resell the property.

If P sues O, P's best chance of prevailing is:

   (A) on an implied warranty of habitability theory.
   (B) on a duty to disclose theory, if the jurisdiction applies the traditional common law approach.
   (C) on a duty to disclose theory, if the jurisdiction applies the modern trend approach.
   (D) on a duty to disclose theory under either the traditional common law approach or the modern trend approach.

8. O, the rightful owner of Blackacre, grants X an easement to walk across Blackacre to get to the beach. X fails to record. O then conveys Blackacre for valuable consideration to A by warranty deed with no mention of X's easement. A then conveys Blackacre for valuable consideration to B by quitclaim deed with no mention of X's easement. X records, then B records, and then A records. B takes possession and finds X regularly walking across Blackacre. B sues to quiet title.

Assuming neither A nor B had actual or inquiry notice of X's easement,

   (A) B prevails over X's easement under both a notice and a race-notice recording act approach.
   (B) B prevails over X's easement under a notice recording act but not under a race-notice recording act.
   (C) B prevails over X's easement under a race-notice recording act but not under a notice recording act.
   (D) B does NOT prevail over X's easement under either a notice or a race-notice recording act approach.

9. O, the rightful owner of Legaland, conveys Legaland to A by warranty
    deed as a gift for graduating from law school. Thereafter, O executes a
    quitclaim deed giving Legaland to B and gives the deed to B as a wedding
    gift. B has no notice of A's deed. B records, and then A records.

    B sues to quiet title. The most likely result is B prevails:

    (A)   if the jurisdiction has a race recording statute.
    (B)   if the jurisdiction has a notice recording statute.
    (C)   if the jurisdiction has a race-notice recording statute.
    (D)   if the jurisdiction has either a race or a race-notice statute.
    (E)   only in his dreams.

10. O defaulted on O's mortgage with 1st National Bank, which foreclosed
    on the property pursuant to a power of sale clause in the mortgage. 1st
    National accidentally did not advertise the foreclosure sale, as required by
    law, but it told all of its executives and best clients. The bidding was
    heavy, and the top bid exceeded the outstanding balance on the
    mortgage.

    **If O sues the bank anyway, the most likely result under the modern
    trend approach is:**

    (A)   The Bank failed to exercise due diligence, and O is entitled to
          the difference between a fair price and the sale price.
    (B)   The Bank failed to exercise due diligence, and O is entitled to
          the difference between the fair market value and the sale price.
    (C)   The Bank failed to exercise good faith, and O is entitled to the
          difference between a fair price and the sale price.
    (D)   The Bank failed to exercise good faith, and O is entitled to the
          difference between the fair market value and the sale price.
    (E)   The Bank's failure to advertise constitutes harmless error
          because the top bid exceeded the outstanding mortgage.

Questions 11 and 12 are based upon the following fact pattern:

O conveys Greenacre to A, who does not record. O conveys Greenacre to B, who gives valuable consideration, has no actual notice of A's deed, and records the O-B deed. The O-B deed, however, has a patent defect in the acknowledgment (the jurisdiction follows the majority rule with respect to whether recorded defective deeds provide constructive notice). B conveys Greenacre to C, who performs an actual search of the jurisdiction's grantor-grantee recording index, gives valuable consideration, and records properly. Then A records.

11. Who owns Greenacre under a notice recording statute?

    (A)   A.
    (B)   B.
    (C)   C.
    (D)   O.

12. Who owns Greenacre under a race-notice recording statute?

    (A)   A.
    (B)   B.
    (C)   C.
    (D)   O.

13. S contracted to sell Whiteacre to P. The contract provided that S would provide marketable title and recited 7 recorded encumbrances which P agreed to waive. The contract did not recite, however, an eighth recorded encumbrance for an easement for the public utility's above ground electrical poles and lines which ran across a corner of the property. When P conducted the title search and discovered the electrical line easement, P repudiated the contract. S sued for specific performance. **Under the modern trend:**

    (A)   S should prevail because easements do not constitute an encumbrance.
    (B)   S should prevail because the easement is an open and notorious public easement.
    (C)   P should prevail because the easement is an encumbrance.
    (D)   P should prevail because the easement breaches his quiet enjoyment of the property.

Questions 14 and 15 are based upon the following fact pattern:

O engages B, a real estate broker, to help O sell Blueacre. B produces X, who signs a standard contract for sale. Upon further investigation, X discovers that X's contemplated use would violate the zoning laws covering Blueacre. O knew about X's intended use, and both parties assumed that the use would be permissible under the zoning laws. X repudiates the contract. B sues O to collect B's real estate commission. O sues X for specific performance.

QUESTIONS:

14. The most likely outcome under the traditional <u>common law</u> approach is:

   (A)   O is entitled to specific performance, and B is entitled to B's commission.
   (B)   O is not entitled to specific performance, but B is entitled to B's commission.
   (C)   O is not entitled to specific performance, and B is not entitled to B's commission.
   (D)   O is entitled to specific performance, but B is not entitled to B's commission.

15. The most likely outcome under the <u>modern trend</u> approach is:

   (A)   O is entitled to specific performance, and B is entitled to B's commission.
   (B)   O is not entitled to specific performance, but B is entitled to B's commission.
   (C)   O is not entitled to specific performance and B is not entitled to B's commission.
   (D)   O is entitled to specific performance, but B is not entitled to B's commission.

16. O, owner of Greenacre which is located in California, properly executes a deed granting "all my land in California to my favorite niece, Carolyn." O then gives the deed to Edward, telling him to give the deed to Carolyn only if she survives O. The deed was not recorded. O subsequently dies, devising all of her property to X. **Under the modern trend, the most likely outcome is that:**

   (A)   Carolyn is entitled to Greenacre.
   (B)   Carolyn is not entitled to Greenacre because the deed's description of the property and/or the recipient is defective.
   (C)   Carolyn is not entitled to Greenacre because of the oral condition.
   (D)   Carolyn is not entitled to Greenacre because the conveyance is testamentary and failed to comply with the Wills Act formalities (2 witnesses).

17. A agrees to buy some land from O, the rightful owner. They enter into the following contract concerning Blackacre, a 500 acre farm and farmhouse:

   "I, O, hereby agree to sell to A my farmhouse and a sufficient amount of land for a garden. Price: As determined by an independent appraiser to be selected by our mutual friend, F. Received, $1,000 down payment."

   Signed: "O"
   "A"

   A subsequently changes her mind and refuses to close on the contract. **O sues for specific performance. Judgment for:**

   (A)   O, because he has an enforceable contract.
   (B)   A, because the contract fails to describe the parties adequately.
   (C)   A, because the contract fails to describe the price adequately.
   (D)   A, because the contract fails to describe the property adequately.

18. O owns Greenacre. Nevertheless, A purports to convey Greenacre to B in exchange for valuable consideration. B records. A then purports to convey Greenacre to C in exchange for valuable consideration. C records. O then purports to convey Greenacre to A, who fails to record.

Who owns Greenacre? Assume the jurisdiction has 1) a notice recording act, 2) applies the doctrine of estoppel by deed, and 3) requires a standard scope of search of the grantor-grantee recording index.

(A)   A.
(B)   B.
(C)   C.
(D)   O.

19. State the township grid pattern description for the following piece of property:

Principal Meridian

(A)   Range 2 South, Township 2 East.
(B)   Township 2 South, Range 2 West.
(C)   Township 2 North, Range 2 East.
(D)   Range 2 North, Township 2 East.

20. S contracted to sell Whiteacre to P. The contract provided that S would provide marketable record title. A title search prior to the close of escrow reveals that a portion of the land S is purporting to convey is on record as belonging to X. S assures P that S has established title by adverse possession to this portion of the property.

If P refuses to go through with the deal, will S be able to successfully sue P for specific performance?

(A)   No, because damages are an adequate remedy for S's injury.

(B)   No, because S cannot convey marketable record title.

(C)   Yes, as long as the court determines that if X were to sue, it is unlikely X would prevail.

(D)   Yes, as long as the court determines that damages are not an adequate remedy for S, and S is able to prove to the court that S would prevail as against X.

(E)   Yes, as long as the court determines that if X were to sue, it is unlikely X would prevail and that it is unlikely that X will ever assert a claim against P.

21. Ace Homes purchased a tract of land, subdivided it into lots, and constructed single-family homes on the subdivided lots. Those homes were sold to purchasers, and in some cases, resold to subsequent purchasers. Three years after the homes were originally sold, cracks developed in the foundations, walls, and ceilings.

Assuming the statute of limitations has not run, under the modern trend:

(A)   Only homeowners who were the original purchasers of the home may sue the builder for breach of the implied warranty of marketable title.

(B)   Only homeowners who were the original purchasers of the home may sue the builder for breach of the implied warranty of quality.

(C)   The owner of any home, whether original or subsequent purchaser, may sue the builder for breach of the implied warranty of quality.

(D)   No suit may be brought since all contractual duties merged into the deed and no collateral promises for separate consideration were made.

Questions 22 and 23 are based upon the following fact pattern:

O owns Blackacre. Nevertheless, A purports to convey Blackacre to B in exchange for valuable consideration. B records. O then conveys Blackacre to A, who records. A then conveys to C in exchange for valuable consideration. C records. Assume the jurisdiction has 1) a notice recording act, and 2) applies the doctrine of estoppel by deed.

QUESTIONS:

22. If the jurisdiction requires a standard scope of search of the grantor-grantee index, who owns Blackacre?

   (A)   A.
   (B)   B.
   (C)   C.
   (D)   O.

23. If the jurisdiction requires an expanded scope of search of the grantor-grantee index, who owns Blackacre?

   (A)   A.
   (B)   B.
   (C)   C.
   (D)   O.

24. O agrees to sell Whiteacre, including the 3 story house on Whiteacre, to P for $1,000,000. Before the parties close on the contract, however, the house sustains $300,000 in damages during a storm. Neither party had insurance on the property.

Under the modern trend approach, the most likely result will be that:

(A) O can obtain specific performance for the full amount of the purchase price.

(B) O can obtain specific performance, even though the damage is substantial, but O must agree to an abatement in the purchase price.

(C) O can obtain specific performance because the damage is not substantial, and O must agree to an abatement in the purchase price.

(D) O cannot obtain specific performance because the damage is substantial.

25. In 1910, O, owner of Blueacre, and X enter into, and record, a 99 year lease. In 1960, O conveys Blueacre to A by deed which states it is subject to X's lease. A records the deed. In 1970, A conveys Blueacre to B by deed which makes no reference to X's lease, but B has actual knowledge of the lease. B records the deed. In 1980, B conveys to C by deed which makes no reference to the lease, but C has actual knowledge of the lease. C records the deed.

Assuming X is not in possession and the jurisdiction has a 30 year marketable title act, in 2004:

(A) X's interest is valid since B had actual knowledge of the lease.

(B) X's interest is valid since C had actual knowledge of the lease.

(C) X's interest is valid because C's root of title references the lease.

(D) X's interest is not valid even though B and C had actual knowledge of the lease because C's root of title is the 1970 deed.

(E) X's interest is not valid even though B and C had actual knowledge of the lease because C's root of title is the 1980 deed.

END OF EXAMINATION QUESTIONS

EXAM VII

PROPERTY
MULTIPLE CHOICE OBJECTIVE QUESTIONS

EXAM VII

Questions 1, 2, 3, 4, 5 and 6 are based upon the following fact pattern:

Olivia is the owner of Greenacre. Nevertheless, for $30,000 Andy properly executes and delivers to Barb a special warranty deed which purports to transfer title of Greenacre from Andy to Barb. Barb properly records the deed, which has a patent defect in the acknowledgment.

Thereafter, for $50,000 Olivia properly executes and delivers to Andy a general warranty deed which purports to transfer title to Greenacre from Olivia to Andy. Andy records the deed but does not take possession.

Thereafter, Andy properly executes and delivers to Carl a special warranty deed which purports to transfer title to Greenacre from Andy to Carl. Carl knows about the prior deed from Andy to Barb. Carl paid Andy $40,000 for the property, but the deed recites that the consideration was $60,000. Carl records the deed which he received from Andy but does not take possession.

Thereafter, Barb realizes that her deed has a defective acknowledgment. Andy and Barb re-execute the deed, this time with a proper acknowledgment. Barb takes it down and asks the recorder to record it, but the recorder mistakenly records it under the name of the notary public, Noel.

Thereafter, for $75,000 Carl properly executes and delivers to Deb a quitclaim deed which purports to transfer title to Greenacre from Carl to Deb. Deb records the deed but does not take possession. Shortly thereafter, Barb comes forward and asserts her claim to Greenacre.

Assume the jurisdiction has adopted the following recording act statute:

No conveyance, transfer or mortgage of real property, or of any interest therein, nor any lease for a term of one year or longer, shall be good and effective in law or equity against creditors or subsequent purchasers for valuable consideration and without notice, unless the same be recorded according to the law.

QUESTIONS:

1. **The statute sets forth which approach to the recording acts?**

   (A)   a race recording act.
   (B)   a notice recording act.
   (C)   a race-notice recording act.

2. Assume the jurisdiction applies estoppel by deed and requires a standard scope of the search of the grantor-grantee index.

   Who has the superior claim to the property under the jurisdiction's recording act?

   (A)   Andy.
   (B)   Barb.
   (C)   Carl.
   (D)   Deb.
   (E)   Olivia.

3. Assume the jurisdiction applies estoppel by deed and requires an **expanded** scope of the search of the grantor-grantee index requiring each grantee to search the grantor index under each grantor's name **prior** to the date each grantor purportedly received title.

   Who has the superior claim to the property under the jurisdiction's recording act?

   (A)   Deb, because the deed from Andy to Barb was defective and did not pass any interest to Barb.
   (B)   Deb, because she qualifies for protection under the notice recording act.
   (C)   Deb, but only if she did not actually search the grantor-grantee recording indexes.
   (D)   Barb.

4. Assume the jurisdiction applies estoppel by deed and requires an **expanded** scope of the search of the grantor-grantee index requiring each grantee to search the grantor index under each grantor's name **after** the date of the recording of the first deed which purports to convey title out from the grantor to another party.

    Who has the superior claim to the property under the jurisdiction's recording act?

    (A) Deb, because the deed from Andy to Barb was defective and did not pass any interest to Barb.
    (B) Deb, because she qualifies for protection under the notice recording act.
    (C) Deb, only if she did not actually search the grantor-grantee indexes.
    (D) Deb, because Barb's re-recording was mistakenly recorded.
    (E) Barb.

5. Assume, *arguendo*, that Barb prevails.

    Under the modern trend, whom can Deb sue and on what grounds?

    (A) Only Carl, for breach of both the present and the future covenants in the deed.
    (B) Carl and Andy, for breach of both the present and the future covenants in the deed.
    (C) Only Andy, for breach of both the present and the future covenants in the deed, and for breach of the express terms of the contract promising to convey title.
    (D) Only Andy, for breach of the present covenants in the deed, but only if the statute of limitations has not run.
    (E) Only Andy, for breach of the future covenants only.

6.   Assume, *arguendo*, that Deb prevails.

      Whom can Barb sue and on what grounds?

      (A)   Carl and Andy, for breach of both the present and the future covenants in the deed.
      (B)   Only Andy, for breach of both the present and the future covenants in the deed, and for breach of the express terms of the contract promising to convey title.
      (C)   Only Andy, for breach of both the present and the future covenants in the deed.
      (D)   Only Andy, for breach of the present covenants, but only if the statute of limitations has not run.
      (E)   Only Andy, for breach of the future covenants only.

7.   Fred properly executes a quitclaim deed conveying Blackacre to his daughter, Doris, and hands the deed to her. Doris does not know what to do with the deed. Instead of recording it, she asks her father to keep it for safekeeping. She hands the deed back to her father. He puts it in his safe deposit box, to which only he has access.

      Who owns Blackacre?

      (A)   Doris, because the deed transferred Blackacre to her, and she has not transferred any property interest in Blackacre.
      (B)   Fred, because the deed transferred nothing to Doris because it was not recorded.
      (C)   Fred, because the deed transferred nothing to Doris because it was not properly delivered.
      (D)   Fred, because although the deed transferred Blackacre to Doris, she effectively transferred the interest back to her father.

Questions 8, 9, 10 and 11 are based upon the following fact pattern:

Olivia owns two tracts of land, one on the ocean side of Pacific Coast Highway ("PCH") and the other just across the street on the mountain side of PCH. On the mountain side, Olivia builds a 4 unit apartment building. Each unit has an extensive balcony with gorgeous views of the ocean. Ali is interested in leasing the upper north apartment. The rent is steep, but the views are awesome. Ali enters into a written lease with Olivia to rent apartment 2 North "for a term of years, to commence each year on January 1, and to end December 31, at a rent of $18,000 a year, payable $1,500 a month."

Olivia has trouble renting the other apartments. Faced with mounting bills, she decides to sell to her sister, Doris, part interest in the lot on the other side of PCH (the ocean side). Olivia properly executes and records a deed which provides that Olivia conveys title to "Olivia and Doris and their heirs and assigns as joint tenants with right of survivorship and not as tenants in common." Thereafter, Doris properly executes a deed which provides that Doris conveys her interest in the property "to my nephew Kile for life, remainder to Kile's children."

Doris put the deed in a safe deposit box at her local bank. The safe deposit boxes are in a separate part of the bank. Entrance to the area is guarded by a security guard. Only persons leasing a safe deposit box or having authorized access to one are permitted beyond the security guard. Within this secure area, there is a special viewing area where there are enclosed cubicles so the parties can open their safe deposit boxes in privacy. When Doris entered one such cubicle to put the deed in her safe deposit box, she found a wad of $100 bills on the chair in the cubicle. The bills total $10,000. Doris reported her find to the bank. The bank contacted all the people who were listed as having been in that area that week, but no one came forward to claim the money.

Doris and Olivia obtain the necessary permits and approvals and begin to construct a high rise apartment building which shortly will block most of Ali's view of the ocean. Ali thought the noise and traffic jams caused by the construction across the street were bad enough, but then Olivia lowered the rents on all the other apartments in an effort to lease them. Olivia was able to lease 1 North, the unit directly below Ali's, to Bert. Unfortunately, Bert is a chain smoker, and Ali hates the smell of cigarette smoke. Ali complains that the common areas reek of smoke. Moreover, when Bert smokes on his balcony, the coastal breeze pushes the smoke up to Ali's balcony, making it unbearable for Ali to be on the balcony when Bert is smoking. If Ali's balcony door is open (to take advantage of the coastal breeze), the smoke comes into Ali=s apartment. Even when the balcony door is closed, Ali complains that some of the smoke seeps into her unit. Ali complained to Olivia some time ago about the noise from the construction, that the new building is going to block her view, and about Bert's smoking, but to date Olivia has done nothing.

QUESTIONS:

8. Applying the traditional common law approach, state the most likely state of the title to the parcel of land on the ocean side of PCH:

    (A)   Olivia and Doris own it as tenants in common in fee simple absolute.

    (B)   Olivia and Doris own it in joint tenancy in fee simple absolute.

    (C)   Olivia owns half interest as tenant in common, and the other half is owned by Kile for life, then to Kile's children as tenants in common in fee simple.

    (D)   Olivia owns half interest as tenant in common, and the other half is owned by Kile for life, then to Kile's children in joint tenancy in fee simple.

    (E)   Olivia owns half interest as tenant in common, and the other half is owned by Kile for life, then to Kile's children as tenants in common for life, and Doris retains a reversion in fee simple.

9. Ali's lease is most likely a:

    (A)   term of years.
    (B)   periodic tenancy from year-to-year.
    (C)   periodic tenancy from month-to-month.
    (D)   tenancy at will.
    (E)   holdover tenancy.

10. If Ali were to sue Olivia for the conditions surrounding her apartment (the smoke from her neighbor, the noise from the construction, and the blocked view), her best chances of prevailing on any of these claims would be:

   (A)   under covenant of quiet enjoyment.
   (B)   under the illegal lease doctrine.
   (C)   under the implied warranty of habitability.
   (D)   under frustration of purpose.

11. Assume the true owner never returns to claim the $10,000 Doris found. Under the modern trend approach, who is entitled to the money? The most likely result is:

   (A)   Doris, because the finder of lost property has superior title over all but the true owner.
   (B)   The Bank, because mislaid property goes to the owner of the land where it is mislaid.
   (C)   The Bank, to protect the expectations of the Bank.
   (D)   Doris, to reward the finder.

Questions 12, 13, 14, 15 and 16 are based on the following fact pattern:

Ollie is the rightful owner of 3 rustic wooded lots, 10 acres each, situated just south of Yosemite near the Sierra Mountains:

Lot 1	Lot 2	Lot 3

In January of 1998, Zack properly executes and delivers a deed which purports to transfer title to lots 1-3 to Alice, an avid camper and hiker. Whenever Alice can get away (she lives in Los Angeles - approximately 7 hours away), she drives up to the area and hikes into the lots. Being the environmentalist that she is, instead of building a house, she constructs a small "hut" of branches (10 feet by 10 feet by 7 feet with a sloped thatched straw roof) on the southern part of lot 2 which she uses as her base when she visits the area. Alice also harvests the wild berries which grow on the lots.

In 1999, Alice conveys to Bob, in exchange for $12,000 a year, to be paid monthly, the right to enter lot 1 for 5 years, commencing January 1, 2000, to cut trees in an environmentally friendly manner and haul them away." In 2000, Ollie properly executes and delivers a deed which purports to transfer title to lot 3 to Cindy. Cindy goes into actual possession of lot 3.

In January of 2002, after a long weekend hiking, Alice falls asleep at the wheel while driving home and is involved in a head on collision in which she sustains severe head trauma. As a result of her injuries, she falls into a deep coma. Bob, who reads about the accident in the paper, decides to take advantage of the situation. Bob builds a log cabin on lot 1 and begins living there.

In January of 2006, Alice awakens from her coma. To help her physical and spiritual recovery, she resumes camping on lot 2, but lacks the strength to begin hiking again. By May of 2007, Alice has regained enough strength to begin hiking again. Last week she came upon Cindy on lot 3 and Bob on lot 1. Although Alice asserted her rights to the property, both parties claimed they had rights to the respective lots. Coincidentally, Ollie has just learned about Alice and Bob's claims, and

Ollie has asserted his rights to lots 1 and 2. Alice and Bob countered by claiming they had rights to the lots.

QUESTIONS:

12. **In 1999, when Alice and Bob enter into their agreement, what is the extent of Bob's interest in Lot 1? The most likely result is:**

    (A)   Bob holds no interest since Alice is not the rightful owner.
    (B)   Bob holds a license.
    (C)   Bob holds an easement.
    (D)   Bob holds a profit.

13. Assume the following statute of limitations applies to the problem:

    An action to recover the title to or possession of real property shall be brought within **five (5)** years after the cause of action thereof accrued, but if a person entitled to bring such action, at the time the cause thereof accrues, is within the age of minority (i.e., under the age of eighteen (18) years), of unsound mind, or imprisoned, such person, after the expiration of **five** years from the time the cause of action accrues, may bring such action within **two (2)** years after such disability is removed.

    In May of 2007, when Ollie and Alice assert their claims to lot 2, who has the superior claim? The most likely result is:

    (A)   Ollie, because Alice's possession is not sufficiently open and notorious.
    (B)   Ollie, because Alice's possession is not continuous enough.
    (C)   Ollie, because Alice's injury interrupted her possession and she had to start over.
    (D)   Alice, since she never relinquished her claim to the property.

14. Assume, *arguendo*, that Alice successfully claims adverse possession to part of lot 2.

    Keeping in mind the state's statute of limitations and disability doctrine set forth above, in May of 2007, when Alice and Cindy assert their claims to <u>lot 3</u>, who has the superior claim?

    (A)   Cindy, because her actual possession trumps Alice's constructive possession.
    (B)   Cindy, if the jurisdiction applies a notice recording act.
    (C)   Alice, under color of title.
    (D)   Alice, under first in time, first in right.

15. Assume, *arguendo*, that Alice successfully claims adverse possession of part of lot 2. **Keeping in mind the state's statute of limitations and disability doctrine set forth above, in May of 2007, when Ollie, Alice and Bob assert their claims to <u>lot 1</u>, who has the superior claim?**

    (A)   Ollie, under first in time, first in right.
    (B)   Alice, but Bob is entitled to either remove his improvements or he is entitled to compensation for them.
    (C)   Alice, and Bob is not entitled to remove his improvements or to compensation for them.
    (D)   Alice, because Bob entered with Alice's permission and thus is not adverse.
    (E)   Bob, under adverse possession.

16. Assuming, *arguendo*, that Alice learned in 1999 that Zack did not have good title to pass to her when he purported to sell the land, Alice can successfully sue Zack:

    (A) For breach of the present covenants if Zack gave her a general or special warranty deed.

    (B) For breach of the present and future covenants if Zack gave her a general warranty deed.

    (C) For breach of the present and future covenants if Zack gave her a special warranty deed.

    (D) For breach of the future covenants if Zack gave her a general or special warranty deed.

    (E) Alice cannot successfully sue Zack yet because she has no damages yet.

Questions 17, 18, and 19 are based upon the following fact pattern:

O is the rightful owner of four lots. The following is an aerial view of the lots. Lots 1 and 3 are bounded on the east by Pacific Coast Highway ("PCH"). Lots 2 and 4 are bounded on the west by the ocean:

Lot 2	Lot 1
Lot 4	Lot 3

O properly executes a deed conveying lot 1 to A. The deed expressly provides that "O retains a right of way across lot 1 to access lots 2 and 4." The deed is not recorded. Thereafter, A properly executes a deed conveying lot 1 to B for valuable consideration. There is no mention of O's right of way in the deed between A and B. There is no evidence on lot 1 of O's right to cross lot 1 because O has continued to cross lot 3 to access lots 2 and 4 despite the right to cross lot 1.

Thereafter, O properly and validly conveys lot 3 to C. The deed expressly provides that "the following provisions run with the land conveyed: O retains an express easement; and no structure taller than 20 feet may be erected on the property, so as to maintain, to the extent reasonably possible, the beautiful views of the ocean and mountains that run along the shoreline." The deed is recorded.

Thereafter, C properly and validly contracts to sell lot 3 to D. The contract provides that C "will provide good merchantable title, free and clear of all encumbrances except special taxes subject, however, to all restrictions and easements of record applying to the property."

Assume the jurisdiction has a grantor-grantee recording index and a notice recording act.

QUESTIONS:

17. **What right, if any, does O have to cross lots 1 and/or 3 to access lots 2 and 4?**

   (A)   O has no right to cross either lot 1 or 3 because O has access via the ocean.
   (B)   O still has an express easement to cross lot 1.
   (C)   O's express easement to cross lot is extinguished because it was not recorded, but O has an implied easement by necessity to cross lot 3.
   (D)   O's express easement to cross lot is extinguished because it was not recorded, but O has an implied easement based on prior existing use to cross lot 3.

18. Assume D has not yet closed on the contract with C. **Assuming the reason D wants to buy lot 3 is to build a four story apartment complex on lot 3, if D wants to get out of the contract, can D get out of the contract?**

   (A)   No, because the height restriction is not enforceable against D.
   (B)   No, because D is getting what D contracted for.
   (C)   Yes, because of the contract doctrine of mutual mistake.
   (D)   Yes, because the restriction constitutes a recorded encumbrance which makes the title unmarketable.

19. Assume D closes on the contract with C and starts building a four story apartment complex on lot 3. **Does B have standing to enforce the restrictive covenant and enjoin D from building the apartment complex?**

   (A)   No, under any approach.
   (B)   Only if the jurisdiction takes the common law approach to who has standing to enforce a restrictive covenant.
   (C)   Only if the jurisdiction takes the common scheme approach to who has standing to enforce a restrictive covenant.
   (D)   Only if the jurisdiction takes the third party beneficiary approach to who has standing to enforce a restrictive covenant.
   (E)   Yes, under any approach.

Questions 20, 21, and 22 are based upon the following fact pattern.

GREENACRES

Owner conveyed the eastern half of Greenacres (a 100 acre estate) to Purchaser. Purchaser immediately recorded the deed from Owner to Purchaser. In addition, Purchaser obtained a standard title insurance policy on the half he bought. Unknown to Purchaser, the half retained by Owner was landlocked following the transaction. Thereafter Owner sold the half she had retained to Grantee. Grantee fails to record her deed but claims a right to an easement across the half of Greenacres bought by Purchaser.

QUESTIONS:

20. If Purchaser files a claim with his title insurance company in a jurisdiction which also recognizes the duty to search and disclose, the most likely result is:

   (A)   Purchaser is not entitled to recover.
   (B)   Purchaser is entitled to recover in tort.
   (C)   Purchaser is entitled to recover under the policy.
   (D)   Purchaser is entitled to recover both under the policy and in tort.

21. Thereafter Purchaser conveys the eastern half of Greenacres by quitclaim deed to Fran. Grantee announces plans to subdivide his half into 50 lots for a subdivision for single family homes with access to the lots being provided by a road which Grantee will build running across Fran's half of Greenacres.

    Fran sues Grantee to enjoin the use of the easement across Fran's land. Fran claims protection under the jurisdiction's recording act. The most likely result is:

    (A)   Fran will prevail if the jurisdiction has a notice recording act.
    (B)   Fran will prevail if the jurisdiction has a race recording act.
    (C)   Fran will prevail if the jurisdiction has a race-notice recording act.
    (D)   Fran will prevail if the jurisdiction has a notice or race-notice recording act.
    (E)   Fran will not prevail.

22. **Assume Fran sues in the alternative, claiming that under the law of easements Grantee's new use of the easement is illegal. The most likely result is:**

    (A)   Fran is entitled to a complete injunction against any use of the road, even by Grantee.
    (B)   Fran is entitled to an injunction against any use of the road by anyone other than Grantee.
    (C)   Fran is entitled to damages but not injunctive relief.
    (D)   Fran is not entitled to any relief.

For questions 23, 24 and 25, assume at the beginning of each problem that O is the true owner of Malibuacres, and that O owns it in fee simple. Anyone described as a "BFP" is a good faith purchaser for valuable consideration without actual or inquiry notice of any outstanding deeds; anyone not so described is not. In analyzing the problems, analyze who will prevail in a (1) race; (2) notice; and (3) race-notice recording act system unless the directions indicate otherwise. Assume a standard scope of the search of the grantor-grantee indexes.

23. On January 1, 2007, O conveys Malibuacres to A who does not record. On March 1, 2007, O conveys Malibuacres to B, a BFP. On April 1, 2007, B learns of the deed from O to A. On May 1, 2007, B records the O to B deed. **Choose the best answer:**

    (A) A prevails over B under all three approaches: race; notice; and race-notice.

    (B) B prevails over A under all three approaches: race; notice; and race-notice.

    (C) A prevails under the notice and race-notice approaches, but B prevails under the race approach.

    (D) B prevails under race and race-notice approaches, but A prevails under the notice approach.

24. On January 1, 2007, O conveys Malibuacres to A. On February 1, 2007, O conveys Malibuacres to B, a BFP. On March 1, 2007, A records the O to A deed. On April 1, 2007, B records the O to B deed. **Choose the best answer:**

    (A) B prevails over A under all three approaches.

    (B) B prevails under notice, but A prevails under race and race-notice.

    (C) A prevails under notice and race-notice, but B prevails under race.

    (D) A prevails over B under all three approaches.

25. On January 1, 2007, O conveys Malibuacres to A, who does not record. On February 1, 2007, O conveys Malibuacres to B, a BFP. On March 1, 2007, A records the O to A deed. On April 1, 2007, B conveys Malibuacres to C who records the B to C deed. **Under a notice recording act approach, the likely result in a contest between A and C is:**

(A)   C should prevail, because C is a BFP without notice.
(B)   C should prevail, because B was a BFP without notice.
(C)   A should prevail, because B did not record.
(D)   A should prevail, because A recorded before C.

END OF EXAMINATION QUESTIONS

EXAM VIII

PROPERTY
MULTIPLE CHOICE OBJECTIVE QUESTIONS

EXAM VIII

1. ACME Housing, a non-profit corporation, wants to build a federally subsidized low-income housing project in Valleytown, an affluent, nearly-all-white suburb. Valleytown refuses to rezone the site of the proposed project from single-family residential to multi-family, mainly because the property values near the project would drop sharply. A majority of the families who would qualify for the housing project are African-American.

    If the zoning scheme is attacked in federal court as being exclusionary and in violation of the Equal Protection Clause of the 14th Amendment to the United States Constitution, who will prevail?

    (A)   ACME Housing, because the exclusionary zoning and refusal to rezone has a racially discriminatory effect.
    (B)   ACME Housing, because the exclusionary zoning and refusal to rezone is sufficient evidence of a racially discriminatory intent.
    (C)   Valleytown, because there is insufficient evidence of racially discriminatory intent, and discriminatory effect alone is not sufficient.
    (D)   ACME Housing, because the exclusionary zoning and refusal to rezone does not substantially advance a legitimate public interest.

Questions 2 and 3 are based upon the following fact pattern:

Roger and Anita love dogs, Dalmatians in particular. After their dogs gives birth to a litter, the puppies are stolen. Fortunately, the police rescue the puppies. In fact, the police rescue a total of 99 dogs from a group intent on selling the dogs for use in scientific research. Roger and Anita are so grateful, they agree to take in all the rescued dogs. They move out to the country where they enter into a standard, 25 year term of years lease to lease Pongoacres from Mickey. They build a kennel to care for the dogs. Although the country kennel works well for a decade or so, suburban sprawl finally catches up to Roger and Anita. Slowly but surely, the land around them is sold for subdivision development. The closest homes are approximately 200 yards from the kennel. Within a couple of years of the first subdivision being built, Roger and Anita begin receiving complaints about incessant barking, foul odors and a plague of flies and ticks. Although Roger and Anita do their best to control the situation, nothing appears to satisfy their new neighbors.

2.   **Kruela and a few other neighbors sue, claiming the dog kennel constitutes a nuisance; but other neighbors testify that the dogs are no problem. The most likely result is:**

     (A)   Roger and Anita should prevail because they and the dogs were there first.
     (B)   Roger and Anita should prevail because their use of the land is not unreasonable and any interference with the surrounding property is not substantial. The plaintiffs are being hyper-sensitive when it comes to the dogs.
     (C)   Roger and Anita should prevail as long as the local zoning permits dog kennels at that location.
     (D)   Kruela should prevail, because the kennel constitutes a nuisance *per se.*
     (E)   Kruela should prevail, because the kennel constitutes a nuisance in fact.

3. Assume, *arguendo*, that the court determines that the kennel constitutes a nuisance and permanently enjoins its operation. **Can Roger and Anita prematurely terminate their lease with Mickey to avoid further liability under the lease? The most likely result is:**

    (A) No, regardless of whether the jurisdiction takes the common law or modern trend approach to the issue.
    (B) Not if the jurisdiction takes the common law approach to the issue, but yes if the jurisdiction takes the modern trend approach.
    (C) Not if the jurisdiction takes the modern trend approach to the issue, but yes if the jurisdiction takes the common law approach.
    (D) Yes, regardless of whether the jurisdiction takes the common law or modern trend approach to the issue.

4. Gerri wishes to purchase Greenacres, but doesn't have enough money to purchase it outright. She borrows $300,000 from Stagecoach Lenders, executing the appropriate promissory note and mortgage documents. Stagecoach Lenders properly records the necessary documents. Thereafter, Gerri receives a great job offer out of town. She sells Greenacres to Carolyn. As part of the transaction, Carolyn agrees in writing to "assume the mortgage." Thereafter, Carolyn decides that she wants to move closer to home, and sells Greenacres to Kristin "subject to the mortgage." Kristin in turn, sells Greenacres to Paul who agrees to "assume the mortgage." Thereafter, the mortgage goes into default, and Stagecoach Lenders sues.

    Assuming the jurisdiction does not have an anti-deficiency statute, who, if anyone, is personally liable to Stagecoach Lenders following the default? The most likely result is:

    (A) Only Gerri.
    (B) Gerri and Carolyn.
    (C) Gerri, Carolyn, and Kristin.
    (D) Gerri, Carolyn, Kristin, and Paul.
    (E) Gerri, Carolyn, and Paul.

Questions 5 and 6 are based on the following fact pattern:

Jessie owns a popular restaurant. Its major attraction is that it has a lovely patio with an unobstructed view of the Japanese Gardens located in the nearby park. The mayor decides that the public would benefit from, and traffic congestion might be lessened be, a footpath connecting the Gardens to the public library located on the opposite side of Jessie's restaurant. The path is developed immediately in front of Jessie's patio, with only about one yard crossing onto a section of her unoccupied property. Very few people end up using the pathway. Because the intrusion was so minimal, the government offers no compensation.

5. **Jessie sues to enjoin use of the section of the pathway which crosses her property, or in the alternative, for damages under inverse condemnation. The most likely result is:**

    (A)   The court will enjoin the use of the pathway. So few people use the pathway it fails to qualify as "public use" as required under the power of eminent domain.

    (B)   The court will enjoin the use of the pathway. Its claimed public purpose is questionable, and it unconstitutionally infringes on her reasonable, investment backed expectations.

    (C)   The court will not enjoin the use of the pathway as long as the city agrees to compensate Jessie for the city's taking.

    (D)   The court will not enjoin the use of the pathway, nor will it require the city to compensate Jessie because the claimed "takings" is not significant enough to warrant compensation.

6. Assume that the path does *not* encroach onto Jessie's property. Instead the path runs along the border of Jessie's property, butting up to it but at no point crossing it. Although the foot traffic along the pathway is sparse and sporadic, it intermittently blocks the view from Jessie's patio and infringes on its sense of privacy. As a result of the foot traffic by the patio, customers are no longer drawn to the patio and Jessie's profits have fallen by 1/3. **If Jessie sues for damages under inverse condemnation, what is the most likely result?**

  (A) Jessie will prevail, because she is unfairly being singled out to bear a burden that should be born by the public as a whole.

  (B) Jessie will prevail, because the city's action substantially and unreasonably interferes with her reasonable, investment backed expectations.

  (C) The city will prevail, because Jessie's 1/3 drop in profits does not constitute a substantial interference with her reasonable, investment backed expectations.

  (D) The city will prevail, because the city's action neither regulates nor invades Jessie's property so there is no possible "takings" - either trespassory or regulatory.

7. Chelsea is a new town which has just incorporated, breaking off from an unincorporated section of New London, State of Nirvana. One of the first orders of business for the new town is to establish a planning department and zoning scheme. After much research and analysis, the city council votes to zone the western half of Chelsea as a residential-apartment building zoning district which allows cumulative uses. Thereafter, A, B, C, D and E each purchase and develop lots in the western half of Chelsea. A builds a single-family home. B builds a two-family duplex. C builds a small apartment complex. D builds a convenience shop down the street. E opens a used car lot across the street.

Who is in compliance with the zoning ordinance?

  (A) A and B.
  (B) A, B and C.
  (C) C only.
  (D) C and D.
  (E) A, B, C, D and E.

8. Oscar, the owner of Greenacres, decides to sell Greenacres to Alice. Alice cannot afford to purchase Greenacres outright, so she borrows the necessary money from Bank of Finance. Alice executes a promissory note and mortgage, which Bank properly records. Thereafter Alice rents Greenacres to Betsy, who executes a lease which provides that "Betsy has the right to possession from January 1, 2003 to December 31, 2007, at a rent of $12,000 a year to be paid $1,000 a month on the first of each month." Betsy goes into possession. Two years later, Alice defaults, and Bank forecloses on the property. The Bank properly joins Betsy as a party to the foreclosure action. Assume the jurisdiction has a notice recording act and grantor-grantee recording index.

State the rights of the respective parties:

(A)   When Bank forecloses, Betsy's lease is wiped out, terminating the lease; and Betsy has no rights as against Alice.

(B)   When Bank forecloses, Betsy's lease is wiped out, terminating the lease; but Betsy has a cause of action against Alice for breach of the covenant of quiet enjoyment.

(C)   When Bank forecloses, if Betsy recorded the lease it is unaffected by the foreclosure; and the purchaser at foreclosure takes subject to the remaining term of Betsy's lease.

(D)   When Bank forecloses, Betsy's lease is unaffected by the foreclosure even if she did not record (because Betsy is in possession of the property, the purchaser at foreclosure cannot qualify for protection under the jurisdiction's recording act).

9. Ron and Mary plan to open a halfway house for parolees from a state prison in a residential neighborhood. The halfway house residents will include individuals who are completing their sentences for crimes involving alcohol abuse, sexual abuse, drug abuse and drug dealing. The halfway house is consistent with the zoning for the proposed location. Local residents fear an increase in crime and depreciation in property values. Local residents bring suit to prevent the halfway house's opening, claiming that the halfway house would constitute a nuisance. **The most likely outcome is:**

    (A)   The residents should prevail, because the presence of the halfway house would probably depreciate the value of the surrounding properties substantially.
    (B)   The residents should prevail, because their fear of harm outweighs the social value of the halfway house.
    (C)   Ron and Mary should prevail, because the resident's fear of harm is too speculative and the halfway house's social value is high.
    (D)   Ron and Mary should prevail, because the halfway house's use is consistent with the local zoning ordinance.

10. H and W marry and live in California, a community property state. From W's earnings during marriage, W accumulates $600,000, all of which W holds in her name alone. In 2000, H and W move to Missouri, a non-community property state, where W accumulates an additional $300,000 from W's earnings in Missouri which she again holds in her name alone. On December 1, 2007, W dies and leaves a will which devises all of her property to UCLA. Assume Missouri law provides that upon W's death, H is entitled to an elective share of ONE-THIRD (1/3) of W's probate estate.

    Of the $900,000 total which W accumulated, how much can H successfully claim following W's death? (Assume, *arguendo*, that Missouri has not adopted the Uniform Disposition of Community Property Rights at Death Act.)

    (A) $200,000
    (B) $300,000
    (C) $400,000
    (D) $500,000
    (E) $600,000

Questions 11 and 12 are based upon the following fact pattern:

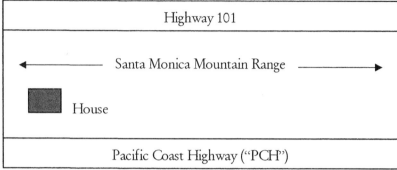

Pacific Ocean

Owner owns Malibuacres, a sprawling estate which runs from the ocean inland to Highway 101 (almost 20 miles). Owner's home is nestled two miles in from PCH on top of the first mountain ridge overlooking the ocean. Owner's only access to her house is by a road branching off PCH (it is virtually impossible to reach the house from Highway 101 due to the mountains). Developer purchases all of Owner's acreage running along PCH up to just shy of the house. Developer orally assures Owner that after the transaction Owner may continue to use the road forever to access her house. The deed from Owner to Developer, however, contains no reference to the road.

11. After Developer purchases the land over which the road runs, Owner's interest in the road under the modern trend is most likely:

    (A)   a profit.
    (B)   an express easement.
    (C)   an implied easement by necessity.
    (D)   an implied easement by prior existing use.
    (E)   a license.

12. Thereafter, Developer sells her property to the Santa Monica Conservancy. The Conservancy decides to return the land to its natural condition. The Conservancy blocks off the road at the point where it intersects PCH, barring Owner from using the road to access her house.

Assuming the jurisdiction has a notice recording act, the most likely result is that:

(A)   Owner should <u>not</u> be entitled to use the road because the Santa Monica Conservancy qualifies as a subsequent bona fide purchaser without notice.

(B)   Owner should be entitled to use the road if the jurisdiction recognizes license coupled with estoppel.

(C)   Owner should <u>not</u> be entitled to use the road because easements cannot be reserved in a stranger to the deed.

(D)   Owner should be entitled to use the road even if the Santa Monica Conservancy were to qualify as a subsequent bona fide purchaser without notice.

13. Tiger owns a 150 acre tract of land in the Town of Nicky which has been used as a private golf course since 1931. The part of town where the golf course is located has been zoned for residential use, single family detached homes only, since the turn of the century. In the 1970s, the Town of Nicky became concerned about its diminishing open spaces. Between 1976 and 1996, a number of planning studies recommended that the golf course remain a golf course to preserve open space and to help control flooding. In 1996, the Town adopted a Comprehensive Planning Scheme which recommended that the golf course remain undeveloped. In 2004, the Town rezoned the golf course from residential use to solely recreational use. **Tiger sues, claiming that the rezoning constitutes a regulatory taking. The most likely result is:**

(A)   The Town should prevail. The ordinance properly advances legitimate state goals.

(B)   Tiger should prevail. The ordinance deprives him of all economically beneficial or productive use of the land.

(C)   Tiger should prevail, because the ordinance is tantamount to a physical invasion

(D)   Tiger should prevail, because the ordinance does not have a sufficiently close nexus to its purported legitimate state goals.

Questions 14 and 15 are based upon the following fact pattern:

Oak Park Avenue is located in a quiet part of Pleasantville. The street has 10 lots on each side of the street. All twenty lots are of identical size, perfect for single family homes. The block is in the middle of an zoning district with an ordinance which provides that the area is zoned "exclusively and solely for single family residential use and no other" under Pleasantville's master plan. The local YMCA organization has recently purchased lot 10 at the end of the block. The YMCA hopes to construct a swimming pool and gym complex on the property. There are other available lots within Pleasantville where the complex would be in compliance with the local zoning requirements, but the YMCA likes lot 10's location because of its proximity to the residential sections of Pleasantville. The YMCA believes that its proximity will make it easier and safer for young families and children to use the facilities. Some of the local residents, however, have expressed concerns over the proposal. They fear the increased noise will disrupt the quiet neighborhood and the increased traffic will be a safety hazard for the children on the block.

QUESTIONS:

14. **In assessing the YMCA's plans in light of the zoning ordinance, the YMCA's best chance is to:**

    (A)   seek to have the zoning ordinance amended and the lot rezoned.
    (B)   seek a special exception/special-use permit.
    (C)   seek a variance.
    (D)   seek to have the zoning ordinance declared unconstitutional.

15. Assume that the YMCA petitions to have the property rezoned, and the appropriate zoning body approves the request on the grounds that it is in the best interests of the community.

    Some of the local residents who live on Oak Park Avenue, including the owner of lot 9 next door, challenge the rezoning. The most likely result is:

    (A) The rezoning will be upheld because the plaintiffs lack standing.
    (B) The rezoning will be upheld because the appropriate zoning body concluded that it would be in the best interests of the community.
    (C) The rezoning will be upheld as a valid exercise of the government's police powers.
    (D) The rezoning will be struck down as "spot zoning."

16. Martha and Howie are neighbors. Their houses are directly across the street from each other. Howie has a bright, almost neon, red front door. His house is gray. The red door is such a stark contrast to the rest of the house that Martha wonders how anyone could have such poor taste. Martha calls a neighborhood meeting and gets the Stewartsville city council to adopt an ordinance based on aesthetics which requires Howie to repaint his front door a more conforming color the next time it needs painting. Howie refuses to comply, so the city sues. **What is the likely result?**

    (A) The city prevails under either the traditional approach or the modern trend approach.
    (B) The city prevails under the traditional approach, but not under the modern trend approach.
    (C) The city prevails under the modern trend approach, but not under the traditional approach.
    (D) Howie prevails under either the modern trend approach or the traditional approach.

Questions 17 and 18 are based upon the following fact pattern:

Jake decided to go into the motorcycle business. He borrowed $100,000 from 1st State Bank to purchase Harleyacres, a vacant lot where he starts the business. Jake signed a promissory note and executed the necessary mortgage papers, which 1st State Bank recorded. Later, Jake decided to expand into the tatoo business. Jake borrowed $45,000 from National Trust & Loan to finance the expansion. Jake signed a promissory note and executed the necessary mortgage papers, which National Trust & Loan recorded. Recently, to keep up with the trends, Jake decided to expand into the body piercing business. Jake borrowed $25,000 from 1st Federal Bank and Trust. Jake signed a promissory note and executed the necessary mortgage papers, which 1st Federal Bank and Trust recorded. Business has dropped off, and Jake has defaulted on the loan payments to National Trust & Loan. National Trust & Loan forecloses on the loan. The foreclosure sale generates a total of $60,000.

17. **How is the $60,000 most likely to be distributed?**

   (A)   1st State Bank is entitled to all of it, because it holds the senior mortgage and its mortgage is greater than the sale proceeds.
   (B)   National Trust & Loan is entitled to be paid off first, since it is the foreclosing mortgagee, with the remaining balance going to 1st State Bank.
   (C)   National Trust & Loan is entitled to be paid off first, since it is the foreclosing mortgagee, with the remaining balance going to 1st Federal Bank and Trust.
   (D)   National Trust & Loan is entitled to be paid off first, since it is the foreclosing mortgagee, with the remaining balance going to Jake.
   (E)   Since there is not enough money to pay off all the creditors, the creditors will share pro rata in the foreclosure sale proceeds.

18. Following National Trust & Loan's foreclosure sale, what is the state of the title to Harleyacres - the title which the purchaser receives:

(A)   The purchaser takes subject to the mortgages held by National Trust & Loan and 1st Federal Bank and Trust.
(B)   The purchaser takes subject to 1st State Bank's mortgage, but otherwise free and clear of any and all mortgages and liens.
(C)   The purchaser takes subject to 1st State Bank's mortgage and subject to the remaining balance on 1st Federal Bank and Trust's mortgage.
(D)   The purchaser takes subject to the remaining pro rata balances on the mortgages held by 1st State Bank, National Trust & Loan, and 1st Federal Bank and Trust.
(E)   The purchaser takes free and clear of any and all mortgages and liens.

19. The State of Capitalism (its license plate motto is "The Greedy State!") plans to condemn a residential neighborhood, clear the land, and convey it to "Toys for You" to build and operate a toy assembly plant. The state's proposal includes a provision to offer each resident just compensation for their property. The thinking behind the state's plan is that it will reduce unemployment and boost the economy, two severe problems in the area. **Residents of the neighborhood sue to enjoin the project on the ground that Capitalism is illegally taking the property for a private use. What is the most likely result?**

(A)   Capitalism prevails, because the overall use will provide a public benefit.
(B)   Capitalism prevails, because the government can use its power of eminent domain for any purpose it deems reasonable, so long as it provides just compensation.
(C)   The residents prevail, because "Toys for You" can and should negotiate with the residents to purchase their land. Capitalism's action is an abuse of governmental power, an illegal taking for private use.
(D)   The residents prevail, because the government cannot condemn one person's property to convey it to another private person to boost the economy.

Questions 20 and 21 are based upon the following fact pattern:

O is going to Europe for the summer. O deposits $10,000 in a joint bank account with his closest friend, A, so that A can pay the bills on O's property while O is away. O dies intestate (without a will) while in Europe. O's only heir, H, is a distant relative O never met.

20. Under the common law approach, who is entitled to the funds in the account?

   (A) H, because the account is a convenience account.
   (B) A, because the account is a true joint tenancy account.
   (C) A, because O never intended the funds to go to H.
   (D) A, because the account is a payable on death account.
   (E) A, because the account is a convenience account.

21. Under the modern trend approach, who is entitled to the funds in the account?

   (A) H, because the account is a convenience account.
   (B) A, because the account is a true joint tenancy account.
   (C) A, because O never intended the funds to go to H.
   (D) A, because the account is a payable on death account.
   (E) A, because the account is a convenience account.

22. An otherwise properly drafted and executed deed, which describes the property to be conveyed as "all the grantor's property in a certain county (or similar designated area)" is:

   (A) a valid deed with a Peter Pumpkin clause.
   (B) a valid deed with a Mother Hubbard clause.
   (C) a valid deed with a Rapunzel clause.
   (D) a valid deed with a Cinderella clause.
   (E) an invalid deed because it fails to describe the property adequately as required by the Statute of Frauds.

23. Lake Tahoe is one of the clearest lakes in the world. Historically, the lake's clarity stems from the fact that the water is low in nutrients and it lacks a steep temperature gradient which prevents deep water circulation and mixing. Since the mid-1950s, however, the nutrient level in the lake has been increasing dramatically because of soil being washed into the lake. The soil is being washed into the lake because of increased development in the Lake Tahoe Basin surrounding the lake. The increase in nutrients will inevitably lead to increased algae growth, which will cause the lake to lose its clarity and color. In the late 1960s, Congress and the States of Nevada and California authorized the creation of the Tahoe Regional Planning Agency (TRPA). Between 1970 and 1980, the TRPA made numerous attempts at regulating development in the area which failed, all of which failed to protect the lake. In 1981, the TRPA adopted an ordinance which temporarily suspended virtually all development within the Lake Tahoe Basin to permit the TRPA to study the problem and possible solutions. The moratorium on development remained in effect until 1984, when the TRPA adopted a completely revised land-use plan.

Many of the landowners who live within the Lake Tahoe Basin sued, claiming that the temporary development ban constituted a "takings" under the Fifth Amendment. The most likely result is:

(A)   The landowners should prevail because the ordinance is tantamount to a physical invasion of the landowners' property.

(B)   The landowners should prevail because the ordinance deprived the landowners of all economically beneficial or productive use of the land.

(C)   The landowners should prevail because the ordinance took a "slice" of their property rights when viewed temporally: during the time the development moratorium was in effect, it deprived them of all economically beneficial or productive use of the land.

(D)   The TRPA should prevail because the temporary development moratorium properly advanced legitimate state goals.

24. Developer owns approximately 13.5 acres of undeveloped land in the Town of No-Growth. The Town of No-Growth has an ordinance which requires all proposed developments of more than 10 acres to retain a minimum of 30 percent of the site as open space. Developer submits a plan to develop the 13.5 acres into a subdivision. The 13.5 acres would be subdivided into 51 individual, residential lots. The only road leading into the subdivision would be Dead End Road, which currently ends at the boundary to the proposed subdivision. Dead End Road would enter at one corner of the subdivision, snake through the entire subdivision, and end at the other end. Local residents oppose the subdivision on the grounds that it will reduce open space within the city. They also complain that Dead End Road often becomes impassible in winter snow and ice, hindering emergency access, a situation which would only be compounded by the subdivision. The Fire Department testifies in support of the emergency access concerns, pointing out that the subdivision's proximity to "wild land fuels" and the steep grade slopes approaching the subdivision site will only heighten the emergency access difficulties. The Fire Department asks the Town to require a second access road. The Town conditions approval of the subdivision on Developer retaining 30 percent of the subdivision land as open space per the Town ordinance and on Developer providing a secondary access road for emergency purposes.

Developer sues the Town claiming the requirements constitute a takings. The most likely result is:

(A) Neither requirement constitutes a takings because both properly advance legitimate state interests.

(B) The requirement that Developer retain 30 percent of the subdivision land as open space constitutes a takings, but the requirement that Developer provide a secondary access road does not.

(C) The requirement that Developer provide a secondary access road constitutes a takings, but the requirement that Developer retain 30 percent of the subdivision land as open space does not.

(D) Both requirements constitute a takings because neither properly advances legitimate state interests.

25. Billie-Bob's Appliance Center has owned and operated an appliance store in Podunk, Missouri since 1973. Billie-Bob's sells televisions, stereos, and a variety of appliances. Prior to 2000, Billie-Bob had no trouble with the reception on his display televisions. In 2000, Thelma and Louis' Travel Service opened next door to Billie-Bob's. Thelma and Louis' Travel Services uses computers to make reservations and gather the latest rates and vacancies. Shortly after Thelma and Louis' opened for business, Billie-Bob's customers began to complain that the pictures on his display televisions were bad; on two of the three channels available in Podunk he had a difficult time "getting a picture that was fit to watch." After unsuccessfully attempting remedial measures, Billie-Bob traced the problem to interference from Thelma and Louis' operations. When Billie-Bob raised the problem with Thelma and Louis, they stated "if you don't like it, you can move." Thelma and Louis admit that Billie-Bob's problems are caused by radiation leaking from their computers. The computers are not defective or being improperly used, the radiation leak is simply a by-product of the design of those particular types of computers. Technology is available which would virtually eliminate the amount of radiation leak.

If Billie-Bob sues, claiming that Thelma and Louis' computers constitute a nuisance, the most likely result is:

(A) Billie-Bob should prevail because he was there first.

(B) Billie-Bob should prevail because the computers constitute a nuisance in fact.

(C) Thelma and Louis should prevail because Billie-Bob's Appliance Center constitutes a hyper-sensitive use of the property.

(D) Thelma and Louis should prevail because they were not negligent in their operation of the computers.

(E) Thelma and Louis should prevail as long as their use complies with the local zoning ordinance.

END OF EXAMINATION QUESTIONS

ANSWER KEY
EXAM I

PROPERTY
ANSWER KEY AND EXPLANATIONS

EXAM I

1. **The best answer is (A).** Under the traditional common law approach, a landlord may rightfully use self-help to retake possession of leased premises from a tenant in possession without incurring liability for wrongful eviction as long as two conditions are met: (1) The landlord is legally entitled to possession, such as where a tenant holds over after the lease terminates or where a tenant breaches a lease which contains a forfeiture clause; and (2) the landlord uses no more force than reasonably necessary.

    Although the jurisdictions are somewhat at odds over what constitutes "peaceable" re-entry, the first requirement to using self-help in retaking possession is that the landlord is legally entitled to possession. At common law, the landlord's duty to provide legal possession is independent of the tenant's duty to pay rent. The tenant's failure to pay rent does not automatically terminate the lease. The failure gives the landlord the right to bring a cause of action for damages, but not to terminate the lease and retake possession. The landlord is entitled to legal possession only if the lease contains a forfeiture or right of reentry clause expressly authorizing the landlord to retake possession in the event the tenant breaches. Common law will not imply a forfeiture clause in a lease, it must be express. There is no evidence in the facts that the lease between L and T contained a forfeiture clause.

    Under the facts presented, the only way L could be entitled to legal possession is if L properly terminated the lease. The lease is a month to month periodic lease. At common law, a party wishing to terminate a month to month periodic lease had to give at least one month's notice, to terminate on the last day of the term. The facts indicate that the periodic term between L and T starts on the first of the month and implicitly ends on the last day of the month. To terminate properly, L must give at least one month's notice to terminate on the last day of the month. L gave T more than a month's notice, but the notice was not to terminate on the last day of the term. Because the notice is defective, L has not properly terminated the lease and is not entitled to legal possession.

Regardless of how peaceful L's re-entry was, L was not entitled to legal possession and hence is liable for wrongful eviction.

Answers (B) and (C) are incorrect because each assumes that the landlord is entitled to legal possession, a legal requirement not satisfied under the facts and the common law approach. **Answer (D) is incorrect** because at common law, failure to pay rent gave rise to a cause of action for damages, but it did not directly affect the tenant's right to possession. If the landlord is not entitled to legal possession, the eviction is wrongful.

- **Additional references**: *See* 2 RICHARD R. POWELL, POWELL ON REAL PROPERTY §§ 17.02[a][i], 16.04[3] (Michael Allan Wolf ed., 2000); 5 THOMPSON ON REAL PROPERTY, SECOND THOMAS EDITION §§ 40.09, 40.08(a) (1994 & Supp. 2006); 4 THOMPSON at § 39.05(b)(3); WILLIAM B. STOEBUCK & DALE A. WHITMAN, THE LAW OF PROPERTY §§ 6.78, 6.80 (3d ed. 2000); *see also* Berg v. Wiley, 264 N.W.2d 145 (Minn. 1978).

2. **The best answer is (A) [if you applied the 'modern trend' to the common law approach, the correct answer would be (C)].** The modern trend approach prohibits landlords from using self-help to re-take actual possession of the leased premises and requires the landlord to use the judicial system even where the landlord has the legal right to possession. The modern trend concern is that permitting the landlord to use self-help to evict the tenant runs the risk of a violent reaction. The tenant may resist, which could lead to injuries to either the tenant, the landlord, or innocent bystanders. To try to minimize the costs associated with requiring the landlord to use the judicial process, the modern trend offers the landlord summary eviction proceedings - but the landlord's only option is to use the judicial system. Any self-help eviction by the landlord constitutes wrongful eviction.

Many jurisdictions still follow the common law approach, which permits self-help, but a split has developed within the common law approach as to how much force the landlord may use in exercising self-help eviction. While not depriving the landlord of his or her right to use self-help eviction, increasingly the common law jurisdictions are taking the public policy against the potential for violence into consideration. Accordingly, while the 'traditional' common law approach permits the landlord to use self-help eviction as long as he or she uses only as much force as reasonably necessary to evict the tenant, there is a 'modern trend' within the common law approach which permits self-help eviction only as long as the landlord's means of re-entry are peaceable. Even under the common law approach, however, the landlord's right to use self-help eviction is conditioned upon the landlord being legally entitled to possession - that the landlord holds the superior legal right to possession.

The first requirement before a landlord can use self-help to evict a tenant is that the landlord must prove he or she is entitled to legal possession of the property. At common law, the covenants in a lease were deemed independent of each other. A tenant's breach of his or her duty to pay rent did not permit the landlord to breach his or her duty to provide legal possession. A tenant's breach of his or her duty to pay rent merely gave rise to a cause of action for damages by the landlord against the tenant. Under the modern trend, however, the general rule is that a serious breach of the tenant's duties under the lease, such as tenant's failure to pay rent, entitles the landlord to terminate the lease even in the absence of an express forfeiture clause. The steps the landlord must take to terminate the lease vary from jurisdiction to jurisdiction, but the tenant's breach entitles the landlord to terminate the lease and reclaim possession.

In the alternative, even if the tenant's failure to pay rent does not, in and of itself, entitle the landlord to terminate the lease, the landlord may still terminate the lease and regain legal possession to the property by giving proper notice of termination to the tenant. The lease in question is a month to month periodic lease. At common law, a party wishing to terminate a month to month periodic lease had to give at least one month's notice, to terminate on the last day of the term. Under the modern trend, the party wishing to terminate a month to month periodic lease has to give at least one month's notice, to terminate on any day after the 30 day notice. The facts indicate that the periodic term between L and T starts on the first of the month and ends on the last day of the month. To terminate properly under the modern trend, L must give at least one month's notice to terminate on any day thereafter. L gave T more than a month's notice, but the notice was not to terminate on the last day of the term. Under the modern trend, as long as the lease is a month-to-month periodic, the notice need not terminate on the last day of the term. L has properly terminated the lease and is entitled to legal possession of the premises.

Assuming the landlord is entitled to legal possession of the property, whether the landlord is entitled to use self-help to evict the tenant varies from jurisdiction to jurisdiction. The majority rule appears to be that the landlord may use self-help to evict the tenant as long as the means of eviction are peaceful. What constitutes peaceful means is yet another issue, with some jurisdictions construing the requirement so narrowly as to make it virtually impossible for the landlord to comply with the requirement. Nevertheless, the modern trend majority rule appears to be that the landlord may use self-help to evict the tenant as long as the means are peaceful.

Under the facts presented, L can argue that L is entitled to legal possession because of the serious nature of T's breach of the covenant in the lease (T's failure to pay rent), or on the basis of L's properly terminating the lease. Inasmuch as L holds the legal right to possess the property, under the modern trend L may use self-help eviction as long as the means of regaining actual possession are peaceful.

Answers (B) and (C) are incorrect because they misstate the landlord's right to use self-help eviction under the modern trend;. Under the modern trend the landlord may never use self-help. The landlord must resort to the judicial system. **Answer (D) is incorrect** because it is incomplete. Although failure to pay rent under the modern trend may cause the tenant to lose the legal right to possession, that in and of itself is not enough to determine whether the landlord is liable for wrongful eviction. Even if the landlord is entitled to legal possession, under the modern trend the landlord cannot use self-help to regain actual possession. [There is a 'modern trend' to the common law approach under which the landlord may still use self-help, but only if the self-help is 'peaceable.' If you applied the modern trend approach to the common law rule, the correct answer would be (C).]

- **Additional references**: *See* 2 RICHARD R. POWELL, POWELL ON REAL PROPERTY §§ 17.02[1], [2] (Michael Allan Wolf ed., 2000); 5 THOMPSON ON REAL PROPERTY, SECOND THOMAS EDITION §§ 40.08(a), 40.09(b)(1) (1994 & Supp. 2006); WILLIAM B. STOEBUCK & DALE A. WHITMAN, THE LAW OF PROPERTY §§ 6.78, 6.80 (3d ed. 2000); *see also* Berg v. Wiley, 264 N.W.2d 145 (Minn. 1978).

3. **The best answer is (D).** The key to analyzing possessory estate and future interest problems is to read and construe comma to comma, paying particular attention to the words of limitation used. It is usually best to analyze a conveyance first *as drafted*, and then re-analyze the conveyance in light of any additional facts which occurred to see if they make any difference in the analysis.

The first clause conveys the property "to Bill for life, ..." The words of purchase "to Bill" indicate that Bill holds the possessory estate. The words of limitation "for life" are the classic words used to create a life estate, one of the finite estates. Bill holds a life estate.

The second clause conveys the property "then to Hillary and her heirs, ..." The words of purchase "to Hillary" indicate that Hillary holds the future interest following Bill's possessory estate. Bill holds a finite estate. The future interest following a finite estate must be either a reversion (if the future interest is held by the grantor) or a remainder (if the future interest is held by someone other than the grantor). Since Hillary is not the grantor, Hillary holds a remainder.

A remainder is contingent unless it meets the test for being vested. To be vested, the party holding the remainder must be born, ascertainable, and there must be no express condition precedent in the same clause creating the remainder or the preceding clause. Hillary is born and ascertainable. The only issue is whether there is an express condition precedent, a condition which Hillary must satisfy before she can claim the right to possession. There is no express condition precedent in the clause creating the remainder or the preceding clause. The remainder is vested. Hillary holds a vested remainder, but of what duration?

The express words of limitation in the conveyance are the key to the duration of each estate. Here, the express words of limitation are "and her heirs, ..." Those are the classic words of limitation to create a fee simple absolute. At first blush, it looks like Hillary holds a vested remainder in fee simple absolute. Reading clause to clause, however, it is clear that the next clause contains language qualifying Hillary's right to possession.

In analyzing the qualifying language following a vested remainder in fee simple, the first key is whether the qualifying language sets forth a condition precedent or a condition subsequent. A condition precedent is a condition which *may* occur before the vested remainder becomes possessory. If the condition is a condition precedent, the vested remainder is subject to divestment. If, on the other hand, the condition is a condition subsequent, a condition which may occur only after the vested remainder becomes possessory, the key is who holds the future interest, the grantor or someone else. If the grantor, the remainder is a vested remainder in fee simple determinable or a vested remainder subject to a condition subsequent, depending on the express words of limitation introducing the condition. If someone other than the grantor holds the future interest, the remainder is a vested remainder subject to an executory limitation.

Looking carefully at the nature of the condition qualifying Hillary's fee simple, is the condition a condition precedent or a condition subsequent? Can the condition occur *before* the remainder becomes possessory, or only after? Is it possible that Brock could be elected president before Hillary's remainder becomes possessory? Notice, the question is "Is it *possible* . . ." - *not* is it likely. As long as the condition could occur before the remainder becomes possessory, the condition is a condition precedent. Hillary's vested remainder in fee simple is subject to divestment. (This also raises the issue of whether the express condition precedent would also cut short Bill's life estate the moment the condition occurs. This is a question of grantor's intent. If it would, Bill's life estate technically is a life estate subject to an executory limitation - but this wrinkle is beyond the scope of most first year Property courses and so the answers assume that your professor did not cover the material to this degree of detail.)

The future interest following a vested remainder subject to divestment is an executory interest. Since the future interest would be taking possession from someone other than the grantor, the interest is a shifting executory interest (as opposed to a springing executory interest - where the executory interest is taking possession from the grantor). The express words of limitation in the clause creating the executory interest are the key to its duration. Here, the express words of limitation are "and his heirs, ..." Those are the classic words of limitation to create a fee simple. Brock holds a shifting executory interest in fee simple absolute.

What difference, if any, do the additional facts make in the analysis? First, Bill is dead, so his life estate has ended. Hillary's vested remainder is no longer a future interest. The vested remainder became possessory the moment Bill died. It no longer is a vested remainder, it is the possessory estate. Since it is the possessory estate, it no longer is capable of divestment. Only vested remainders may be divested, not possessory estates. Hillary's vested remainder in fee simple is now simply a fee simple. But which fee simple?

The condition which qualifies Hillary's right to hold possession of the property still exists and is valid. Legally, it has changed from a condition precedent to a condition subsequent. Brock is still alive and still may be elected president. Hillary holds a fee simple which *may* be cut short. Hillary holds a fee simple defeasible. There are three fee simple defeasibles: a fee simple determinable, a fee simple subject to a condition subsequent, and a fee simple subject to an executory limitation. Which fee simple defeasible Hillary holds depends first on *who* holds the future interest following the fee simple defeasible and, if the grantor holds the future interest, on the words of limitation introducing the condition subsequent. Since Brock, someone other than the grantor, holds the future interest, Hillary holds a fee simple subject to an executory limitation, and Brock still holds a shifting executory interest in fee simple.

As initially drafted, is there a Rule Against Perpetuities problem? Executory interests are subject to the Rule Against Perpetuities. Under the Rule Against Perpetuities, the future interest must vest, if at all, within the lives in being (the lifetime of anyone alive at the time the interest was created) plus 21 years, or the interest is void from its attempted creation. For purposes of executory interests, the requirement that the interest must vest is equivalent to requiring that the interest become possessory. Notice that the Rule Against Perpetuities does not require that the executory interest vest within the lives in being plus 21 years, only that under no circumstances may the executory interest vest *after* the lives in being plus 21 years. If the court can conceive of one scenario where the condition could be satisfied but not until after the lives in being plus 21 years, the executory interest is void.

Is it possible that the Brock could be elected president, but not until 21 years after all the lives in being at the creation of the interest are dead? No. Brock counts as a "life in being" at the time the interest is created. Since the express condition is tied to a life in being, the future interest cannot violate the Rule Against Perpetuities. Brock's shifting executory interest in fee simple is valid.

Answer (A) is incorrect because it implicitly is based upon the legal conclusion that Brock's interest violates the Rule Against Perpetuities. Although executory interests are subject to the Rule Against Perpetuities, if the express condition is tied to a life in being at the time the interest was created, the condition must occur, if at all, during the life of one of the lives in being. There is no way to delay the condition from occurring until after all the lives in being have died plus another 21 years. Since the condition must occur (i.e., the executory interest must vest), if at all, within Brock's lifetime, his executory interest does not violate the Rule Against Perpetuities. **Answers (B) and (C) are incorrect** because they incorrectly analyze the fee simple defeasible. A fee simple determinable and a fee simple subject to condition subsequent require that the future interest be held by the grantor. Since the future interest is held by a third party, someone other than the grantor, the possessory estate cannot be either a fee simple determinable or a fee simple subject to condition subsequent. **Answer (E) is incorrect** because it fails to recognize the need to change the terminology to reflect the fact that Hillary's vested remainder has become possessory. Since the remainder has become possessory, it cannot be subject to divestment. The condition which qualifies Hillary's right to possession is no longer a condition precedent but has become a condition subsequent.

- **Additional references**: *See* CORNELIUS J. MOYNIHAN, INTRODUCTION TO THE LAW OF REAL PROPERTY 33-34, 126-129 (2d ed. 1988); PETER T. WENDEL, A POSSESSORY ESTATES AND FUTURE INTERESTS PRIMER 43-65, 17-32 (3rd ed. 2007); 2 THOMPSON ON REAL PROPERTY, SECOND THOMAS EDITION § 17.02 (2000 & Supp. 2006); 3 THOMPSON at §§ 23.03, 23.07.

4. **The best answer is (A).** Under the common law presumptions, if a conveyance to multiple grantees satisfies the unities of time, title, interest, and possession, the conveyance is presumed to create a joint tenancy as opposed to a tenancy in common. Here, O's conveyance to A, B and C satisfies the four unities. The respective interests vested at the same *time*; the respective interests were created by the same instrument (*title*); the respective 1/3 interests were of the same type and duration (*interest*), and each held an equal right to possess the whole (*possession*). Initially, A, B, and C held the property in joint tenancy.

A joint tenant can unilaterally sever his or her share *inter vivos*. Thus, when A conveyed her interest *inter vivos* to D, A's 1/3 was severed from the joint tenancy. The 4 unities of joint tenancy still exist, however, between B and C. They still hold undivided interests in joint tenancy as to the remaining 2/3. At that point in time, the state of the title is: D holds an undivided 1/3 interest in the property as a tenant in common with B and C, who hold an undivided 2/3 interest in the property as joint tenants.

The key characteristic of a joint tenancy is the right of survivorship. When one joint tenant dies, his or her interest is said to "expire" and the respective shares of the surviving joint tenants are recalculated. A joint tenant cannot sever the joint tenancy by virtue of a last will and testament. Although a will is executed inter vivos, it is not effective until death. The common law reasoned that the joint tenant's interest expired before the will severed it. A's conveyance did not affect the joint tenancy which continued to exist between B and C who held an undivided 2/3 interest in the property. Thus B's last will and testament devising all of her property to E does not sever the joint tenancy which exists between

B and C or pass any interest to E. When B died, B's interest expired and C held the 2/3 interest alone. D held D's 1/3 interest as tenant in common, so it is not affected by B's death. The final state of the title is: D holds an undivided 1/3 interest and C holds an undivided 2/3 interest in the property as tenants in common.

Answer (B) is incorrect because B's will does not sever the joint tenancy, so B's will transfers no interest in the joint tenancy to E. **Answer (C) is incorrect** because it fails to take into account that A severed her 1/3 interest in the property when she conveyed it to D, thereby converting it into a tenancy in common. **Answer (D) is incorrect** because it recalculates the shares of the parties when they should not be recalculated. If the property is held in joint tenancy, and one of the joint tenants dies, the shares of the surviving joint tenants are recalculated pursuant to the right of survivorship. There is no right of survivorship, however, with interests held in tenancy in common. Shares held in tenancy in common are not recalculated upon the death or transfer of one of the tenants in common (absent merger - where the same party holds more than 1 share). When B dies, B's interest in the joint tenancy property expires, and C's share is recalculated to 2/3. D's share does not change since D holds her interest in tenancy in common, not joint tenancy.

- **Additional references**: *See* 7 RICHARD R. POWELL, POWELL ON REAL PROPERTY ch. 51, ¶¶ 615[1], 618[1], 617[3] (Michael Allan Wolf ed., 2000); 4 THOMPSON ON REAL PROPERTY, SECOND THOMAS EDITION §§ 31.06(b), 31.07, 31.08(b) (2004 & Supp. 2006); WILLIAM B. STOEBUCK & DALE A. WHITMAN, THE LAW OF PROPERTY §§ 5.3-5.4 (3d ed. 2000).

5. **The best answer is (B).** Under modern trend presumptions, even if a conveyance to multiple grantees satisfies the unities of joint tenancy (time, title, interest, and possession), the conveyance is presumed to create a tenancy is common as opposed to a joint tenancy. The modern trend focuses more on the intent of the parties. Absent clear evidence in the instrument of conveyance of the intent to create a joint tenancy, the presumption is that the grantor intended a tenancy in common so each tenant's share is devisable and inheritable. Here, although O's conveyance to A, B and C satisfies the four unities of joint tenancy, there is no express intent to create a joint tenancy. Under the modern trend presumptions, A, B, and C hold the property initially as tenants in common, not as joint tenants.

Tenancy in common does **not** have a right of survivorship. Tenants in common can freely alienate their interests inter vivos (as can joint tenants), and in the event a tenant in common dies without transferring his or her interest inter vivos, the interest is devisable (can be transferred at time of death by a properly executed last will and testament) or inheritable (if not devised at time of death, it will pass to the tenant's heirs under the state's intestate distribution scheme). Here, there is no problem with A transferring A's 1/3 share inter vivos to D. When B dies, there is no problem with B devising B's 1/3 share to E. C, D and E each hold an undivided 1/3 interest as tenants in common.

Answer (A) is incorrect because it fails to take into account that tenancy in common interests are devisable. **Answer (C) is incorrect** because it fails to take into account that tenancy in common interests are transferable inter vivos and at time of death. **Answer (D) is incorrect** because it fails to take into account that tenancy in common shares are not recalculated upon the death of a tenant. The shares remain the same (absent merger—where the same party holds more than 1 share), the share is simply transferred to a different party. Answer (D) also fails to take into account that tenancy in common shares are devisable.

- **Additional references**: *See* 7 RICHARD R. POWELL, POWELL ON REAL PROPERTY ch. 51, ¶¶ 616[1], 601[2], 601[9] (Michael Allan Wolf ed., 2000); 4 THOMPSON ON REAL PROPERTY, SECOND THOMAS EDITION §§ 32.06(b)(2), 32.07 (2004 & Supp. 2006); WILLIAM B. STOEBUCK & DALE A. WHITMAN, THE LAW OF PROPERTY § 5.2 (3d ed. 2000).

6. **The best answer is (A).** There are several different ways one can establish property rights in a wild animal.

   The doctrine of rationi soli provides that the owner of the real property has constructive possession of all wild animals on one's property. B will claim the tiger based on rationi soli because the tiger was on B's land when it was captured.

   The doctrine of animus revertendi provides that one who tames a wild animal has constructive possession of the animal even when the animal is not in the person's actual possession or on the person's real property. There is no evidence that the tiger had been tamed to the point where it would naturally return to the Zoo.

Occupancy provides that one acquires a property interest in a wild animal when one (1) demonstrates an intent to appropriate the animal to individual use, (2) deprives the animal of its natural liberty, and (3) brings the animal under certain control. When the tiger was in its display at the Santa Barbara Zoo, the Zoo had occupancy of the tiger. A will argue that when the tiger escaped from the Zoo, the Zoo lost its occupancy of the tiger. A will claim superior title to the tiger based on A's current occupancy of the tiger.

The law, however, goes to greater lengths to protect a property interest once it is acquired than it does the initial efforts to acquire the property interest. When the tiger escaped from the Zoo, the Zoo appeared to no longer have occupancy of the tiger because it appeared as if the tiger was no longer deprived of its natural liberty and was not under the Zoo's certain control. Nevertheless, once a wild animal has been occupied, if the animal escapes, the party having occupancy of the animal does not lose his or her property claim to the animal until the animal returns to its natural habitat. Although the tiger appears to be a wild animal again, legally it is not because tigers are not native to Southern California. The Zoo has not lost its superior claim to the tiger. The Zoo's property interest based on occupancy attached to the tiger before it ever went on B's land. Under first in time, first in right, the Zoo's claim based on occupancy trumps B's rationi soli claim.

Answer (B) is incorrect because there is no evidence the tiger had been domesticated to the point where it would naturally return to the zoo, so animus revertendi is not applicable. **Answer (C) is incorrect** because as between B's rationi soli claim and A's occupancy claim, B will prevail. B's rationi soli interest in the tiger attached before A's occupancy (first in time, first in right), thereby deterring trespass. **Answer (D) is incorrect** because the zoo never lost its occupancy of the tiger, since the tiger never returned to its natural habitat, and the zoo's property interest under occupancy attached to the tiger before B's property claim based on rationi soli.

- **Additional references:** *See* 2 THOMPSON ON REAL PROPERTY, SECOND THOMAS EDITION § 13.03(c) (2000 & Supp. 2006); RALPH E. BOYER ET AL., THE LAW OF PROPERTY: AN INTRODUCTORY SURVEY §§ 1.1-1.2 (4th ed. 1991); RAY A. BROWN, THE LAW OF PERSONAL PROPERTY, 17-18 (Walter B. Raushenbush 3d ed. 1975).

7. **The best answer is (B).** When L and T first entered into the lease, the lease was a term of years. The lease had a fixed beginning and ending.

No notice was necessary to terminate it. Before the initial term of years lease ended, however, L and T agreed that T could remain in possession after the initial term expired. Although T remained in possession after the initial term of years lease had expired, T is not a holdover tenant. L expressly authorized T to remain in possession on condition that T paid rent. The issue is what type of estate was created. L's express offer to T that T may remain in possession so long as T pays the rent, and T's implicit acceptance of the offer by staying in possession and paying rent, constitutes an express agreement between the parties which gives rise to an inference that the parties intended a periodic tenancy. Even if one were to argue that the express terms of the new lease constitute a tenancy at will, once payments began and were accepted, the courts are likely to conclude that the parties entered into a periodic lease.

The notice required to terminate a periodic tenancy depends on the duration of the repeating period. Here, there is some ambiguity as to what should be considered the duration of the period. When L and T agreed to the new tenancy before the end of the initial tenancy, there was no mention of the new term. To the extent the parties incorporated the terms of the initial lease into their new agreement, in the initial lease, the rent was set forth as an annual rent to be paid monthly. Where the way the rent is reserved (the amount of rent over an express period of time set forth in the lease) is different from the way the rent is to be paid, the general rule is the way the rent is reserved controls. Here, since the rent was reserved on an annual basis, to be paid monthly, the new term would be a year to year lease. Moreover, where there is ambiguity as to duration of the periodic tenancy, the courts often look to the circumstances surrounding the lease to help ascertain the more likely intent of the parties as to the duration of the periodic tenancy. Here, the premises are to be used as a farm. The nature of the use is such that the more likely intent of the parties is that the rent should be year to year as opposed to month to month. A court is more likely to construe the new lease as a periodic year to year lease, which at common law required at least six months notice to terminate.

Answer (A) is incorrect because it misstates the notice required at common law to terminate a year to year periodic lease. **Answer (C) is incorrect** because it incorrectly analyzes the duration of the periodic lease in light of the general rule, the circumstances surrounding the lease, and the use of the land. **Answer (D) is incorrect** because generally the courts boot strap a tenancy at will into a periodic tenancy once a pattern of rental payments is established.

- **Additional references:** *See* 2 RICHARD R. POWELL, POWELL ON REAL PROPERTY ch. 16, §§ 16.04[2], 16.04[3] (Michael Allan Wolf ed., 2000); 4 THOMPSON ON REAL PROPERTY, SECOND THOMAS EDITION §§ 39.05(b) (2004 & Supp. 2006); WILLIAM B. STOEBUCK & DALE A. WHITMAN, THE LAW OF PROPERTY § 6.17 (3d ed. 2000); RESTATEMENT (SECOND) OF PROPERTY § 1.5 (1977).

8. **The best answer is (D).**   A tenant or subtenant may be liable to a landlord under either privity of contract or privity of estate.

A landlord is in privity of contract with a tenant or subtenant if the two are parties to an agreement or, under third party beneficiary principles, if the subtenant expressly assumes liability for the provision in the lease between the landlord and the tenant. Here, L is party to the same lease agreement as T, so they are in privity of contract. Both T1 and T2 expressly assumed all the obligations in the lease between L and T, thereby establishing privity of contract between L and T1 and T2 under third party beneficiary principles.

Although L can be in privity of contract with one or more tenants/subtenants, L can be in privity of estate with only one party (unless there are concurrent tenants). When L first leased to T, L and T were not only in privity of contract, they were also in privity of estate. Under common law principles, the landlord is in privity of estate with the party who has the right to possession on the last day of the lease prior to the landlord re-taking the right of possession. Under the initial lease, the party who had the right to possession on the last day of the lease was T. If, however, a tenant were to lease the right to possession to a subtenant, the issue becomes whether the tenant has conveyed *all* of his or her interest to the subtenant. If the tenant conveys *all* of his or her interest (i.e., the rest of his or her term), intrinsically that would mean that the subtenant would have the right to possession on the last day of the initial lease. Where the tenant conveys all of his or her interest, the conveyance is an assignment, and the landlord and the subtenant would now be in privity of estate. If, however, the tenant conveys *less than all of his or her interest*, that intrinsically would mean that the tenant would still have the right to possession on the last day of the initial lease. The conveyance is a sublease, and the landlord and the tenant remain in privity of estate.

While the issue of whether the tenant has conveyed all of his or her interest may appear rather straightforward, it is particularly troubling where the tenant conveys the rest of his or her term to a subtenant but retains the right to re-enter in the event the subtenant breaches. Under the traditional common law approach, the courts take a traditional property approach to the issue. At common law, a right of re-entry was considered not a property interest but merely a "chose in action." Thus, under the traditional common law approach, where the tenant conveys the rest of his or her term but retains a right of entry, the rule appears to be that the tenant was deemed to have assigned his or her interest (although not all the courts agreed with this conclusion).

Here, T conveyed all of T's interest to T1, thereby creating privity of estate between L and T1. When T1 conveyed T1's interest to T2, T1 retained a right to re-enter in the event T2 breached. Under the traditional common law approach, the right of re-entry does not constitute a property interest. T1 has not retained any reversionary interest, merely a chose in action. Because T1 has conveyed all of T1's interest, T2 is in privity of estate with L.

Answers (A) and (B) are incorrect because they fail to recognize that L is in privity of contract with both of the subtenants under the third party beneficiary theory because the subtenants expressly assumed the obligations in the lease between L and T. **Answer (C) is incorrect** because it fails to take into account the fact that, at traditional common law, a right of re-entry in the event the subtenant breached was not a property interest. T1 has conveyed *all* of T1's interest despite the right of entry. **Answer (E) is incorrect** because a landlord can be in privity of estate with only one tenant (absent concurrent tenants).

- **Additional references:** *See* 2 RICHARD R. POWELL, POWELL ON REAL PROPERTY §§ 17.04[1][b], 17.04[2] (Michael Allan Wolf ed., 2000); 5 THOMPSON ON REAL PROPERTY, SECOND THOMAS EDITION §§ 42.04(d), 42.04(e)(1)-(e)(3) (1994 & Supp. 2006); WILLIAM B. STOEBUCK & DALE A. WHITMAN, THE LAW OF PROPERTY §§ 6.67-6.70 (3d ed. 2000).

9. **The best answer is (C).** As discussed above, see answer to problem 8, a tenant or subtenant may be liable to a landlord under either privity of contract or privity of estate.

Privity of contract is the same under both the common law approach and the modern trend approach. A landlord is in privity of contract with a tenant or subtenant if the two are parties to an agreement or, under third party beneficiary principles, if the subtenant expressly assumes liability of one or more of the provisions in the lease between the landlord and the tenant. Here, L is party to the same lease agreement as T, so they are in privity of contract. Both T1 and T2 expressly assumed all the obligations in the lease between L and T, thereby establishing privity of contract between L and T1 and T2 under third party beneficiary principles.

Although privity of contract is the same under both the common law approach and the modern trend approach, privity of estate arguably is not. The landlord is in privity of estate with the party who has the right to possession on the last day of the lease prior to the landlord re-taking the right of possession. When a tenant leases the right to possession to a subtenant, the issue becomes whether the tenant has conveyed all of his or her interest to the subtenant. If the tenant conveys *all* of his or her interest, the conveyance is an assignment, and the landlord and the subtenant would now be in privity of estate. If, however, the tenant conveys *less than all of his or her interest*, the conveyance is a sublease, and the landlord and the tenant remain in privity of estate. Under the traditional common law approach, the courts take a traditional property approach to the issue of whether the tenant has conveyed *all* of his or her interest.

Under the modern trend, however, the courts look more at the intent of the parties in assessing whether the conveyance is an assignment or a sublease. One could argue that although the tenant retains a right of re-entry in the event of a breach, the parties never intended for the right of re-entry to be effective. For all practical purposes, the parties assumed that the tenant was conveying *all* of his or her interest. Despite this argument, however, the courts have reasoned under the intent based approach, the tenant must not have intended to convey all of his or her interest if the tenant expressly reserves a right to re-enter. As long as the tenant retains *any* interest, even just a right to re-enter in the event the subtenant breaches, the tenant has retained a reversionary interest and has not conveyed all of his or her interest.

Here, T conveyed all of T's interest to T1, thereby creating privity of estate between L and T1. When T1 conveyed T1's interest to T2, T1 retained a right to re-enter in the event T2 breached. Under the intent based approach, T1 intentionally withheld part of his or her interest by retaining the right to re-enter in the event T2 breaches. Thus, T1 did not intend to and has not conveyed all of T1's interest. Thus T1 remains in privity of estate with L.

Answers (A) and (B) are incorrect because they fail to recognize that L is in privity of contract with both of the subtenants under the third party beneficiary theory based on the subtenants' express assumption of the obligations in the lease between L and T. **Answer (D) is incorrect** because it fails to take into account the modern trend approach which focuses on the intent of the parties. Because T1 has retained a right of re-entry in the event T2 breaches, T1 must have intended to retain an interest in the property. **Answer (E) is incorrect** because a landlord can be in privity of estate with only one tenant (absent concurrent tenants).

- **Additional references**: *See* 2 RICHARD R. POWELL, POWELL ON REAL PROPERTY §§ 17.04[1][b], 17.04[2] (Michael Allan Wolf ed., 2000); 5 THOMPSON ON REAL PROPERTY, SECOND THOMAS EDITION §§ 42.04(d), 42.04(e)(1)-(e)(3) (1994 & Supp. 2006); WILLIAM B. STOEBUCK & DALE A. WHITMAN, THE LAW OF PROPERTY §§ 6.67-6.70 (3d ed. 2000).

10. **The best answer is (A).** X has no interest in either lot, so when X executes a deed purporting to convey both lots to C, C acquires no interest in either lot. C's interest in the lots depends upon C's claim under adverse possession.

Adverse possession requires actual entry which gives rise to possession which is exclusive, adverse, open and notorious, under claim of right and continuous for the statutory period. The facts state that C actually entered and occupied lot 1 in an open and notorious and continuous manner for the statutory period. C's possession appears to have been exclusive and adverse. The only element in doubt is claim of right. Claim of right focuses on the adverse possessor's actions and/or state of mind. Under the majority approach, the objective approach, the adverse possessor's state of mind is irrelevant. As long as the adverse possessor satisfies the other requirements, the adverse possessor owns the property. Under the minority approach, the subjective approach, the adverse possessor's state of mind is relevant. The jurisdictions which inquire into the adverse possessor's state of mind, however, are split over what is the requisite state of mind. Some require the adverse possessor to think he or she is rightfully entitled to the property in question (the "good faith" adverse possessor). Others require the adverse possessor to know that he or she is not entitled to the property but to claim it anyway (the "aggressive trespasser" adverse possessor). Assuming the jurisdiction follows the majority/objective approach to claim of right, or the good faith approach, C satisfies the claim of right requirement. There is no reason to believe that C knew or should have known that X was not the rightful owner of lots 1 and 2. The most likely result is that C satisfies the elements of adverse possession.

Having determined that C is entitled to claim title based on adverse possession, the issue becomes how much land is C entitled to? Absent color of title, an adverse possessor is entitled to only as much land as the adverse possessor actually possessed. Color of title is a claim of adverse possession based upon a faulty written instrument which purports to transfer title. X's deed to C permits C to claim adverse possession under color of title. Color of title ordinarily entitles the adverse possessor to not only the land actually possessed, but also the land constructively possessed under the terms of the written instrument. X's deed here purports to convey not only lot 1, which C has actually possessed, but also lot 2. The constructive possession scope of the doctrine of color of title, however, is limited to contiguous (side by side) lots which are owned by the same owner. Here, although lots 1 and 2 are contiguous, they are not owned by the same owner. C is entitled to lot 1 only.

Answer (B) is incorrect because C never actually possessed lot 2, and C cannot successfully claim lot 2 under color of title because lots 1 and 2 are not owned by the same owner. When C entered lot 1 adversely and under color of title, the owner of lot 1 had grounds to sue C for ejectment. One way to think of adverse possession is that it operates like a statute of limitations, cutting off the true owner's cause of action for ejectment. As to lot 2, however, when C entered lot 1 adversely and under color of title, the owner of lot 2 has no grounds to sue C for ejectment. C is not trespassing on lot 2. To permit C to claim lot 2 under color of title when lot 2 is owned by a different owner and C has not trespassed on lot 2 would raise serious questions as to how the owner of lot 2 should have known of C's claim to lot 2. Accordingly, color of title only applies to contiguous lots which are owned by the same owner. **Answer (C) is incorrect** because it fails to recognize that C has satisfied the requirements for adverse possession as to lot 1 and can claim all of lot 1 under color of title. **Answer (D) is incorrect** because it fails to recognize the limitation that color of title only applies to contiguous lots which are owned by the same owner. Since lot 2 is owned by a different party and C never entered lot 2, C cannot claim lot 2 under color of title.

• **Additional references**: *See* 16 RICHARD R. POWELL, POWELL ON REAL PROPERTY ch. 91, §§ 1012, 1013 (Michael Allan Wolf ed., 2000); 10 THOMPSON ON REAL PROPERTY, §§ 87.05, 87.07, 87.11, 87.12 (1998 & Supp. 2006); RALPH E. BOYER ET AL., THE LAW OF PROPERTY: AN INTRODUCTORY SURVEY §§ 4.3, 4.9 (4th ed. 1991).

11. **The best answer is (D).**   In construing a conveyance, remember to construe comma to comma, distinguishing the words of purchase (the words indicating who is to take the interest) from the words of limitation (the technical words which describe the duration of the estate the party takes). Reading comma to comma, the first clause is a classic example of a life estate. The words of purchase are "to A." The words of limitation are "for life." A has a life estate.

The next clause grants the future interest to A's children. A future interest following a life estate which is held by a third party (a party other than the grantor) is a remainder. A remainder is vested if the holder of the interest is (1) born, (2) ascertainable, and (3) there is no express condition precedent (an express condition which the party must satisfy before being entitled to claim the right to possession) in the clause creating the remainder or the preceding clause (reading comma to comma). A has no children, so the party holding the remainder is neither born nor ascertainable. Moreover, there is an express condition precedent in the clause creating the remainder. The gift of the remainder is to "A's children *who survive A*." Thus, the remainder is a contingent remainder. The words of limitation "and their heirs" at the end of the clause creating the remainder indicate that A's children who survive A hold a remainder in fee simple.

Reading clause to clause, the clause after the remainder to A's children purports to convey an interest to C's children. The interest in C's children will become possessory, if at all, after A's life estate ("if A dies without being survived by children"), so it too is a remainder. The words of limitation "and their heirs" indicate the remainder is of fee simple duration. The issue is whether the remainder is vested. At first glance, the remainder appears to be vested (at least vested subject to open). C's child Z is born, ascertainable, and there is no express condition precedent in the clause creating the remainder. But the clause preceding the clause creating the remainder expressly indicates that the interest in C's children is conditioned upon A not being survived by children. Thus, there is an express condition precedent qualifying the remainder in C's children in the clause preceding the clause creating the remainder. C's children hold an alternative contingent remainder in fee simple.

Lastly, although it would appear that either A's children or C's children must take the future interest following the life estate, that is not necessarily the case under the common law approach. If the life estate were to end prematurely (through forfeiture, merger or renunciation), at common law if the first contingent remainder has not vested by the premature termination of the life estate, both the contingent remainder and the alternative contingent remainder are destroyed. If both contingent remainders are destroyed, however, there has to be someone who will hold the right to possession. The default taker is always the grantor, O. Since the right to possession would default to O only if the life estate ended and both remainders were destroyed, O's right to possession would follow the life estate. When the future interest following a finite estate is held by the grantor, the interest is a reversion. O, the original grantor, holds a reversion in fee simple.

Answer (A) is incorrect because it incorrectly analyzes the remainder in A's children as a vested remainder. A vested remainder subject to divestment exists when the express condition precedent is in the clause *following* the clause creating the remainder (reading comma to comma). If the express condition precedent is in the *same* clause or the clause preceding the clause creating the remainder, the remainder is a contingent remainder. Here, reading comma to comma, the express condition that A's children must survive A is in the same clause as the clause granting the remainder to A's children, so the remainder is a contingent remainder. **Answer (B) is incorrect** because vested remainders are subject to executory limitations, not contingent remainders. A vested remainder is subject to an executory limitation when the clause following the clause which granted the vested remainder contains an express condition subsequent which may cut short the remainder after it becomes possessory. Here, the remainder is contingent, not vested, and the express condition is a condition precedent, not subsequent. **Answer (C) is incorrect** because it fails to take into account that both contingent remainders may be destroyed if the life estate were cut short by merger, forfeiture or renunciation and the first contingent remainder has not vested. In such a case, there has to be a default taker. The state of the title has to include that O has a reversion in fee simple.

- **Additional references:** *See* CORNELIUS J. MOYNIHAN, INTRODUCTION TO THE LAW OF REAL PROPERTY 117-123, 129-130, 135-137 (2d ed. 1988); PETER T. WENDEL, A POSSESSORY ESTATES AND FUTURE INTERESTS PRIMER 42-49, 58-79, 158-162 (3rd ed. 2007); 3 THOMPSON ON REAL PROPERTY, SECOND EDITION §§ 23.10, 23.11, 23.15, 22.01 (2001 & Supp. 2006).

12. **The best answer is (D).** The clause granting A's children their interest is a remainder. The interest is a future interest following a life estate, and it is held by a third party (someone other than the grantor).

A remainder is vested if the party holding the future interest is born, ascertainable, and there is no express condition precedent. When originally drafted, A had no children so the remainder was contingent because the party holding the remainder was neither born nor ascertainable. Once A has a child, X, the question is whether that changes the analysis. Applying the three step test for whether the remainder is vested or contingent, X is now born and ascertainable. The remainder looks vested, but subject to open since the gift is to a class (A's children) and A can still have more children (so the class is open). But the clause creating the remainder expressly provides that the remainder is held by A's children "who survive A." There is an express condition precedent in the same clause as the clause creating the remainder. So while X is born and ascertainable, there is still an express condition precedent which X has to meet to claim the right to possession. The express condition precedent means the remainder is still a contingent remainder even after the birth of A's first child. Contingent remainders are not subject to open, only vested remainders are subject to open. A's children who survive A still hold a contingent remainder in fee simple. C's children still hold an alternative contingent remainder in fee simple. And, as discussed in the answer to problem 11, O still has a reversion in fee simple.

Answers (A) and (B) are incorrect because they fail to take into account the express condition precedent, set forth in the same clause as the clause creating the remainder, that A's children have to survive A to claim the right to possession under the remainder. (Answer (A) also fails to take into account that the gift is to A's children, a class, and that even if the gift were now vested, it would be vested, subject to open, to reflect that the class is still open in that A could have more children.) **Answer (C) is incorrect** because it incorrectly mixes contingent remainders with class gifts subject to open. Vested remainders may be subject to open, to show that at least one member of the class holds a vested interest but that other members may still enter the class, but contingent remainders cannot be subject to open.

- **Additional references:** *See* CORNELIUS J. MOYNIHAN, INTRODUCTION TO THE LAW OF REAL PROPERTY 117-123, 129-130, 135-137 (2d ed. 1988); PETER T. WENDEL, A POSSESSORY ESTATES AND FUTURE INTERESTS PRIMER 42-49, 58-79, 158-162 (3rd ed. 2007); 3 THOMPSON ON REAL PROPERTY, SECOND THOMAS EDITION §§ 23.10, 23.11, 23.15, 22.01 (2001 & Supp. 2006).

13. **The best answer is (B).**   An adverse possessor adversely possesses against the possessory estate of the party who holds the right to possession when the adverse possession begins.   The first issue then is what is the state of the title when AP begins adversely possessing?

In construing a conveyance, remember to construe comma to comma, distinguishing the words of purchase (the words indicating who is to take the interest) from the words of limitation (the technical words which describe the duration of the estate the party takes).   Reading comma to comma, the first clause is a classic example of a life estate.   The words of purchase are "to A."   The words of limitation are "for life."   A has a life estate.

The next clause grants the future interest to B.   The future interest following a life estate which is held by a third party (a party other than the grantor) is a remainder.   A remainder is vested if the holder of the interest is born, ascertainable, and reading comma to comma, there is no express condition precedent (an express condition which the party must satisfy before being entitled to claim the right to possession) in the clause creating the remainder or the preceding clause.   Inasmuch as "B" stands for the personal name of the taker, B is born and ascertainable.   There is no express condition precedent in the clause creating the remainder or the preceding clause.   B's remainder is vested.   The words of limitation "and her heirs" following the grant to B indicate that B holds a vested remainder in fee simple absolute.

When AP begins adversely possessing, A holds the possessory estate.   Thus AP is adversely possessing against A's life estate.   Before AP's adverse possession vests, A transfers her life estate to X.   A cannot transfer more than A holds.   Therefore, X holds A's life estate - a life estate measured by A's life, or a life estate *pur autrie vie.*   Transfers of title after adverse possession has begun do not affect the running of the statute of limitations.   Thus A's transfer of A's life estate to X does not affect the running of AP's adverse possession claim.   AP's adverse possession claim vests in 2000.   AP now holds the possessory estate of the party who held the right to possession when the adverse possession began.   AP holds the life estate A held - the life estate measured by A's life.   The adverse possession claim has no affect on the future interest.   Thus B still holds a vested remainder in fee simple absolute.

Answer (A) is incorrect because it fails to take into consideration that the adverse possessor is adversely possessing against the possessory estate of the party who holds the right to possession when the adverse possession begins. Here, A held the right to possession when the adverse possession began. A held only a life estate, not a fee simple absolute. **Answer (C) is incorrect** because it fails to take into account that a life tenant cannot transfer more than he or she holds. When a life tenant transfers all of his or her interest, the grantee receives a life estate measured by the original life tenant. X did not receive a life estate measured by X's life, but rather a life estate measured by A's life. **Answer (D) is incorrect** for similar reasons. Adverse possession transfers the right to possession of the party who held the right to possession when the adverse possession began to the adverse possessor. AP acquired A's right to possession, a life estate measured by A's life. AP does not acquire a generic life estate to be measured by AP's life. **Answer (E) is incorrect** because it fails to take into account that transfers of the right to possession *after* the adverse possession has begun do not affect the running of the statute of limitations for adverse possession. Courts do not start the statute of limitations over just because the holder of the right to possession transfers his or her right to possession, either inter vivos or testamentary.

- **Additional references:** *See* 2 RICHARD R. POWELL, POWELL ON REAL PROPERTY ch. 15, ¶ 201 (Michael Allan Wolf ed., 2000); 3 POWELL ch. 20, § 20.04; 2 THOMPSON ON REAL PROPERTY, SECOND THOMAS EDITION §§ 19.01-19.03 (2000 & Supp. 2006); 3 THOMPSON § 23.01(a); 10 THOMPSON § 87.18; PETER T. WENDEL, A POSSESSORY ESTATES AND FUTURE INTERESTS PRIMER 42-44, 47-49, 58-65, 6-9 (3rd ed. 2007).

14. **The best answer is (C).** At traditional common law, a surviving wife was entitled to claim her dower rights. Dower granted the surviving wife a life estate interest in 1/3 of the deceased husband's qualifying real property. Qualifying real property was any interest in real property in which the husband was "seised" and the interest was inheritable. (One has "seisen" if he or she holds a freeholds estate: a fee simple, fee simple defeasible, or life estate interest in the land.)

Here, when H and his brother, B, first acquired Malibuacres in joint tenancy, no dower interest attached to the property because a joint tenant's interest in joint tenancy is not inheritable. When B conveyed his interest to W, however, the four unities necessary for a joint tenancy were severed, and the co-tenancy was transformed into a tenancy in common. W and H now hold Malibuacres as tenants in common. An interest held in tenancy in common is inheritable. Moreover, H was seised in his interest in tenancy in common. Despite H's attempt to devise his interest to UCLA, W's dower interest attached the moment the property was transformed into tenancy in common property. W holds a dower interest in H's half of the tenancy in common which entitles her to a life estate interest in 1/3 of H's 1/2 interest in Malibuacres.

Answer (A) is incorrect because it is based upon a mistaken statement of the dower doctrine. Dower gives the surviving spouse only a life estate interest and only in 1/3 of the qualifying real property. Although Malibuacres is qualifying real property, W is not entitled to all of the property, only to a life estate interest in 1/3 of the property. **Answer (B) is incorrect** because although it correctly limits W's dower interest in duration to a life estate, it fails to limit the interest to 1/3, as opposed to all, of H's qualifying real property. **Answer (D) is incorrect** because although dower does not attach to property held in joint tenancy, the answer fails to take into account that a joint tenant may unilaterally sever a joint tenancy by transferring his or her interest. When B transferred his interest to W, the conveyance severed the 4 unities of title necessary for joint tenancy at common law, creating a tenancy in common between H and W. There is no right of survivorship in a tenancy in common. H's interest in the tenancy in common property is subject to dower. W will not end up with all of Malibuacres since H may devise his tenancy in common interest in Malibuacres, subject to W's dower claim to H's 1/2 interest.

- **Additional references**: *See* 15 RICHARD R. POWELL, POWELL ON REAL PROPERTY ch. 85A, § 85A.04 (Michael Allan Wolf ed., 2000); 7 POWELL ch. 51, ¶ 618[1][a]; 3 THOMPSON ON REAL PROPERTY, SECOND THOMAS EDITION §§ 21.02(a) (2001 & Supp. 2006); 4 THOMPSON § 31.08(b); WILLIAM B. STOEBUCK & DALE A. WHITMAN, THE LAW OF PROPERTY §§ 2.13, 5.3-5.4 (3d ed. 2000).

15. **The best answer is (C).** Absent an express covenant in the lease to cover the issue, there are three principal doctrines which govern the landlord-tenant relationship: the covenant of quiet enjoyment, the illegal lease doctrine, and the implied warranty of habitability.

The implied warranty of habitability arguably gives a tenant the greatest protection. The tenant's duty to pay rent is contingent upon the landlord's duty to deliver and maintain habitable premises throughout the term of the lease. What constitutes "habitable" varies from jurisdiction to jurisdiction, but the general consensus appears to be what a reasonable person would consider acceptable. Conditions which do not amount to a nuisance or even a breach of local housing codes can render the premises "uninhabitable." Although the landlord's duty does not include conditions created by the tenant, it does include conditions created by third parties. Thus, even though the electrical problem was created by criminal acts of third parties off the premises, the tenant is still entitled to relief under the implied warranty of habitability.

Historically, the tenant's primary protection was the covenant of quiet enjoyment. The essence of the covenant is that the landlord will not disrupt the tenant's quiet enjoyment of the property during the term of the lease. The classic example of the landlord breaching the covenant of quiet enjoyment is where the landlord enters the property and physically evicts the tenant. By actually evicting the tenant, the landlord has breached the tenant's right to quiet enjoyment. Rarely, however, do landlords actually enter and evict a tenant. More often, a condition will arise which forces the tenant to vacate the premises. If the condition arose as a result of a breach of duty which the landlord owed the tenant, and if the condition was substantial and severe enough, the courts may find that the landlord constructively evicted the tenant, thereby breaching the covenant of quiet enjoyment.

Before the landlord will be liable for breaching the covenant of quiet enjoyment, however, the tenant must show that the constructive eviction was caused by a breach of a duty which the landlord owes the tenant. The duty can be either an express duty imposed upon the landlord by virtue of the lease agreement, or one of the few implied duties at common law: duty to disclose latent defects about which the landlord knew or should have known; duty to maintain common areas; duty to make any promised repairs or repairs the landlord voluntarily undertakes; duty not to fraudulently misrepresent the condition of the property; duty to maintain furnished dwellings leased for short terms; and duty to abate immoral conduct or nuisances which arise on property owned by the landlord.

Even assuming that the condition arose as a result of a breach of a duty which the landlord owes the tenant, the tenant must also prove that the condition was severe enough to constructively evict the tenant. The condition constitutes constructive eviction if it seriously interferes with the beneficial enjoyment of the property or renders the property substantially unsuitable for the purposes for which they were leased.

Even if the condition were severe enough to constitute a constructive eviction, before the tenant could successfully claim constructive eviction, the tenant has to give the landlord notice of the problem, give the landlord reasonable time to remedy the situation, and then, if the problem is not fixed, vacate in a timely manner.

Applying the implied covenant of quiet enjoyment to the facts of the problem, there are no express covenants or duties imposed on the landlord under the terms of the lease, and none of the implied common law duties cover the situation. The tenant cannot successfully invoke the implied covenant of quiet enjoyment. (Moreover, under the traditional, common law approach to the covenant of quiet enjoyment, the tenant could not use the doctrine affirmatively to recover damages, but only as a defense to a suit brought by the landlord. Under the modern trend, however, the tenant may use the doctrine affirmatively as a sword to recover damages.)

Under the illegal lease doctrine, if, on the first day of the lease, there is a violation of the local housing code which the landlord knew or should have known about and which constitutes a material threat to the safety or health of the tenant, the lease constitutes an illegal lease and the tenant is entitled to relief. Here, the condition impairing the habitability of the premises did not arise until after the lease had commenced. The tenant has no recourse under the illegal lease doctrine.

Answer (A) is incorrect because to prevail under the covenant of quiet enjoyment, the tenant must prove that the condition which constructively evicted the tenant was caused by a breach of a duty which the landlord owed the tenant. Here, the fact that the electricity is out is not the result of any breach of any duty which Landlord owed Tenant. **Answer (B) is incorrect** because to prevail under the illegal lease, the tenant must prove that the offending condition existed on the first day of the lease. Here, the condition (that the electricity is out) was not present on the first day of the lease. **Answer (D) is incorrect** because Tenant would not prevail under the illegal lease doctrine for the reasons set forth in explaining why answer (B) is incorrect. **Answer (E) is incorrect** because Tenant would not prevail under the covenant of quiet enjoyment for the reasons set forth in explaining why answer (A) is incorrect.

- **Additional references:** *See* 2 RICHARD R. POWELL, POWELL ON REAL PROPERTY ch. 16B, §§ 16B.03[2], 16B.04[2] (Michael Allan Wolf ed., 2000); 5 THOMPSON ON REAL PROPERTY, SECOND THOMAS EDITION §§ 40.22(c)(5), 40.23(c)(6), 40.23(c)(8) (1994 & Supp. 2006); RALPH E. BOYER ET AL., THE LAW OF PROPERTY: AN INTRODUCTORY SURVEY §§ 9.7-9.8 (4th ed. 1991).

16. **The best answer is (B).** B's claim to the property is based upon adverse possession. Adverse possession requires actual entry which gives rise to possession which is exclusive, adverse, open and notorious, under claim of right and continuous for the statutory period. Even assuming

that B's possession satisfies the requirements of adverse possession, as the fact pattern states it does, B has been in possession of the property for only 10 years. The statute of limitations requires the adverse possession to be 20 years. B's only hope is to claim that B can tack B's time of adverse possession onto A's time of adverse possession.

To tack, adverse possessors must be in privity. What constitutes privity? Under the American view, privity requires some type of reasonable connection between the adverse possessors - a voluntary transfer or some meeting of the minds - so as to justify permitting the latter adverse possessor to combine the periods of adverse possession. The focus is on the relationship between the adverse possessors. The adverse possessor has to *earn* the right to tack or reasonably be entitled to *expect* to tack. Privity exists where the transfer of possession is by agreement, gift, descent or devise (the right to possession is passed through intestacy or by will). The American view embodies the earnings/expectations theory of adverse possession.

Under the English approach to privity, however, as long as there is no significant temporal gap in possession between successive adverse possessors, the adverse possessors may tack their periods of adverse possession. As long as there is no gap, the true owner has notice of the claim of adverse possession. The English view focuses more on punishing the true owner for sleeping on his or her rights and not checking the property during the statutory period. Under the penalty approach, also known as the statute of limitations approach, the relationship between the adverse possessors does not matter as long as there is no significant gap in possession.

Inasmuch as B fraudulently induced A to leave the property, under the American approach B has not "earned" the right to tack B's time of possession onto A's time of possession, nor has B any reasonable expectation that B has the right to tack. The transfer was not by agreement, gift, descent or devise; the transfer was by deceit. As a matter of public policy, B's conduct is not the type which justifies permitting B to combine the periods of adverse possession. Under the "earnings/expectations approach," there has not been a truly voluntary transfer which would permit B to tack.

Under the English view, however, there was no gap in possession between A's leaving and B's entering. The true owner has had ample opportunity to discover the adverse possession, and O's failure to keep up with his property means that O should be punished. B may successfully tack under the penalty approach which is embodied in the

English approach to privity and tacking - but not under the earnings approach.

Answers (A) and (C) are incorrect because under the earnings/expectations approach, B is not entitled to tack. Inasmuch as B fraudulently induced A to vacate the premises, B has not earned the right to add A's period of adverse possession to B's. **Answer (D) is incorrect** because under the penalty/statute of limitations approach, B is entitled to tack. Inasmuch as there was not a significant temporal gap in possession between the adverse possessors, O had ample opportunity to discover the adverse possession and should be punished for sleeping on his or her rights.

- **Additional references**: *See* 16 RICHARD R. POWELL, POWELL ON REAL PROPERTY ch. 91, § 1014[2] (Michael Allan Wolf ed., 2000); 10 THOMPSON ON REAL PROPERTY, SECOND THOMAS EDITION § 87.13 (1998 & Supp. 2006); RALPH E. BOYER ET AL., THE LAW OF PROPERTY: AN INTRODUCTORY SURVEY §§ 4.3, 4.6-4.7 (4th ed. 1991).

17. **The best answer is (D). (If you applied the modern trend approach and assumed that O granted B fee simple absolute, answer B would be the correct answer—though the question specifically asked you to apply traditional common law principles.)** In construing a conveyance, remember to construe comma to comma, distinguishing the words of purchase (the words indicating who is to take the interest) from the words of limitation (the technical words which describe the duration of the estate the party takes). Reading comma to comma, the first clause is a classic example of a life estate. The words of purchase are "to A." The words of limitation are "for life." A has a life estate.
The future interest following a life estate is either a remainder (if the future interest is held by a third party - someone other than the grantor) or a reversion (if the future interest is held by the grantor). The clause after A's life estate grants the future interest to B, someone other than the grantor. B holds a remainder.

A remainder is a contingent remainder if it does not qualify as a vested remainder. A remainder is vested if the holder of the interest is (1) born, (2) ascertainable, and (3) there is no express condition precedent (an express condition which the party must satisfy before being entitled to claim the right to possession) in the clause creating the remainder or the preceding clause (reading comma to comma). Inasmuch as "B" stands for the personal name of the taker, B is born and ascertainable. Is there an express condition precedent in the clause creating the remainder or the preceding clause? There is language in the clause creating the remainder which qualifies B's interest, but does the express language set forth a condition precedent or a condition subsequent? A condition subsequent is an express condition which may occur *only after* the party holding the remainder takes possession. A condition precedent is an express condition which may occur *before* the party holding the remainder takes possession. In construing the condition, "as long as B does not sell alcohol on the land," the more reasonable construction is that it is intended as a condition which may occur *only after* B takes possession of the property. It is a condition subsequent which is intended to control how B uses the property after B takes possession. Since it is not a condition precedent, B holds a vested remainder. B is born, ascertainable, and there is no express condition precedent.

What is the duration of B's vested remainder? Under the modern trend, a grantor is presumed to convey all that he or she holds. Under the traditional common law approach, the proper words of limitation were necessary to convey a fee simple absolute. The proper words of limitation were "and her heirs" or "and his heirs." If the proper words of limitation were not used, the default estate at common law was the life estate. Here, there are no proper words of limitation, so by default, at common law, B holds a life estate; but B's life estate may be cut short if B sells alcohol on the land. The express condition is a condition subsequent - a condition which may cut short B's life estate.

The common law courts deemed the qualifying language "as long as" to indicate that the future interest is to go to the party holding the future interest whether the life estate ends naturally or prematurely. C will take the property either at the natural end of B's life or if the life estate ends prematurely if B sells alcohol on the land. Where a life estate may be cut short but the future interest is held by the same party regardless of how the life estate ends, the life estate is a life estate determinable and the future interest which follows it is a remainder. Accordingly, B holds a vested remainder in life estate determinable. C holds a remainder. The words of limitation "and her heirs" indicate that the duration of C's estate is a fee simple. C is born, ascertainable, and there is no express condition precedent, so C's remainder is vested. C holds a vested remainder in fee simple absolute.

Answer (A) is incorrect because it incorrectly analyzes the express condition as a condition precedent thereby classifying the remainder as contingent, and it incorrectly grants B a fee simple when under the common law approach B does not hold a fee simple because the words of limitation "and her heirs" are missing. **Answer (B) is incorrect** because it grants B a fee simple when under the common law approach B does not hold a fee simple since the words of limitation "and her heirs" are missing. [If you applied the modern trend approach and assumed that O granted B fee simple absolute, answer B would be the correct answer. But the call of the question specifically indicated that you were to apply traditional common law principles, so answer B is incorrect.] **Answer (C) is incorrect** because it mistakes the difference between a life estate determinable and a life estate subject to an executory limitation. In the latter, the express condition is introduced by the words "but if, . . ." which the common law deemed to indicate that the party granted the future interest was to get the future interest only if the express condition occurred, and if not, the property was to revert to the grantor. The express condition subsequent here is introduced by the phrase "as long as, . . ." indicating that the life estate is a life estate determinable, not subject to an executory limitation.

- **Additional references**: *See* 2 RICHARD R. POWELL, POWELL ON REAL PROPERTY ch. 15, ¶¶ 202[1], 203[6] (Michael Allan Wolf ed., 2000); 3 POWELL ch. 20, § 20.04[1]; 3 THOMPSON ON REAL PROPERTY, SECOND THOMAS EDITION §§ 23.01(a), 23.06 (2001 & Supp. 2006); 2 THOMPSON §§ 19.03, 19.06; PETER T. WENDEL, A POSSESSORY ESTATES AND FUTURE INTERESTS PRIMER 43-44, 47-48, 58-65, 138-39 (3rd ed. 2007).

18. **The best answer is (A).** The common law view of leases is that they are a conveyance of real property. The landlord conveys the right to possession to the tenant, no more and no less. Absent fraud, deceit or concealment, the tenant has the duty to inspect the premises to insure that they are fit for the tenant's intended purposes. The landlord's duty to disclose extends only to defects about which the landlord knows, and the landlord has no duty to fix them. The prevailing philosophy is caveat emptor - "buyer beware." The landlord does not warrant the fitness or safety of the premises. The lessee takes the premises as he or she finds them, and under the law of waste, is obligated to return the premises in the condition in which the tenant received them. The law of waste has the effect of imposing the duty to make most repairs on the tenant. Where the general duty to make repairs is augmented by an express contractual provision obligating the tenant to repair the premises, courts have been even more willing to impose the duty to repair (and even to rebuild in some cases) on the tenant.

There is a developing modern trend for commercial rentals that the landlord has a duty to maintain the premises and keep them fit for the purposes for which they were rented (a parallel doctrine to the residential implied warranty of habitability). The duty to keep the premises fit for the purposes for which they were rented arguably shifts the duty to repair from the tenant back to the landlord. Financially, the landlord arguably is in a better position to pay for the repairs, especially since the landlord will benefit in the long run more than the tenant typically.

Here, the call of the question specifically says to apply the common law rule. The law of waste and its implicit duty on the tenant to keep the premises repaired applies. Moreover, there is an express clause indicating that the tenant has the duty to repair the interior of the premises. Under the traditional common law approach, the Arts Association bears the duty to repair the ceiling.

Answer (B) is incorrect because under the common law approach, the tenant's duty to repair was rather extensive. Although the repair is quite extensive here, it still is simply a repair, not a complete rebuilding. Moreover, where there is an express and unqualified clause imposing a duty to repair, the courts are even more willing to hold the tenant responsible even where the repair is extensive and costly. **Answer (C) is incorrect** because absent an express clause otherwise, the landlord does not warrant the condition of the premises. Caveat emptor (or caveat lessee as applied to the landlord-tenant situation) is the rule. There is no evidence of fraud or concealment. The landlord's duty is limited to disclosing those latent defects about which the landlord knows or should know. There is no evidence that Racquel knew of the latent defect, and there is no duty to on the landlord to correct them. **Answer (D) is incorrect** because although the modern trend is to impose the duty to repair on the landlord (at least in the absence of an express clause), the call of the question expressly said to apply the common law approach.

- **Additional references:** *See* 5 THOMPSON ON REAL PROPERTY, SECOND THOMAS EDITION §§ 40.23(a), 40.23(a)(2)(ii), 40.23(b) (1994 & Supp. 2006), 8 THOMPSON ON REAL PROPERTY § 70.08(b)(3); WILLIAM B. STOEBUCK & DALE A. WHITMAN, THE LAW OF PROPERTY §§ 6.23, 6.36 (3d ed. 2000); Gehrke v. General Theatre Corp., 289 N.W.2d 773 (Neb. 1980).

19. **The best answer is (A).** Under the common law approach, the lease is considered a conveyance of the right to possession for the term of the lease. The tenant becomes the owner of the right to possession for the duration of the lease, and the landlord has minimal rights and responsibilities with respect to the property.

Although leaseholds are generally transferable without the landlord's permission, where there is an express approval clause requiring the tenant to get the landlord's approval, such clauses are valid (although construed narrowly). Moreover, under the common law approach, the landlord is free to deny the request to assign or sublease for any reason. When Arnold rejected Debbie's request to assign the lease to Pamela, Arnold was acting within his rights under the common law approach.

In addition, under the common law, conveyance approach to leases, the landlord has no duty to mitigate if a tenant abandons. The landlord may mitigate, but he or she is not required. Moreover, if the landlord attempts to mitigate, the landlord must be careful to make sure his or her efforts are not construed as an acceptance. Here, Arnold has made no efforts to mitigate, nor is he required to under the common law.

Answer (B) is incorrect because where there is an approval clause and no express requirement that the landlord act reasonably, under the common law approach the landlord is free to act unreasonably in withholding consent. Under the common law approach, Arnold is free to unreasonably withhold consent to Debbie's proposed assignment to Pamela. **Answer (C) is incorrect** because at common law, the landlord has no duty to mitigate when a tenant abandons. **Answer (D) is incorrect** because at common law the landlord can unreasonably withhold consent and has no duty to mitigate.

- **Additional references**: *See* 2 RICHARD R. POWELL, POWELL ON REAL PROPERTY ch. 17, §§ 17.04[1][b], 17.05[2] (Michael Allan Wolf ed., 2000); 5 THOMPSON ON REAL PROPERTY, SECOND THOMAS EDITION §§ 40.11(c), 40.11(c)(1) (1994 & Supp. 2006); WILLIAM B. STOEBUCK & DALE A. WHITMAN, THE LAW OF PROPERTY §§ 6.67, 6.71, 6.82 (3d ed. 2000).

20. **The best answer is (D).** While the common law takes a conveyance approach to the lease, the modern trend takes a contracts approach to the lease. Under the contracts approach, the parties are obligated to act in good faith and to mitigate damages. The obligation to act in good faith means that even where the lease contains an approval clause, and the clause is silent as to whether the landlord must act reasonably in withholding consent, the duty to act in good faith imposes a duty on the landlord to act reasonably. Arguably landlords are still adequately protected since they can still reject a proposed conveyance on commercially reasonable grounds. Factors which the landlord may consider when deciding whether to withhold consent to a proposed conveyance include the financial responsibility of the proposed assignee,

suitability of the premises for proposed use by the proposed assignee, nature of the occupancy, etc. Whether the landlord withheld consent on commercially reasonable grounds becomes a fact sensitive inquiry.

Here, Arnold's reason for refusing to permit the assignment appears to be entirely personal. Although there are no details as to Pamela's financial situation, the facts arguably indicate her financial situation is good when the facts describe her as "big" in the cosmetic surgery business. Moreover, the reason Arnold apparently denied permission had nothing to do with her financial responsibility or the suitability of her proposed use, but instead focused on Arnold's personal belief about the appropriateness of cosmetic surgery. Under the modern trend, Arnold appears to have breached his duty to act in a commercially reasonable manner in deciding whether to approve the proposed assignment.

In addition to requiring landlords to act in a commercially reasonable manner with respect to assignments, the modern trend also requires landlords to act in a commercially reasonable manner if a tenant abandons. While the common law views the lease as a conveyance of the right of possession, with the landlord having minimal rights and duties with respect to the property after the conveyance, the modern trend views the lease as an ongoing contractual relationship where the landlord and tenant have ongoing rights and duties even after the lease has been executed. In particular, under the modern trend, the courts reason that the landlord has a duty to mitigate damages if the tenant abandons. The new duty rests not only upon principles of fairness and the contract duty to act in good faith, but also on the inefficiency of letting the rented property lay vacant.

Under the modern trend, Arnold had a duty to mitigate damages upon Debbie's abandonment. The burden of proof is upon the landlord to prove reasonable attempts at mitigating damages since the landlord is in the best position to present evidence of mitigation. Here, Arnold took no steps to try and mitigate damages. His failure to try will bar any attempt he may make at recovering back rent from Debbie.

Answer (A) is incorrect because it implicitly applies the common law, conveyance based approach to the issues of (1) the landlord's ability to withhold consent unreasonably to a proposed assignment, and (2) the landlord's duty to mitigate. The call of the question specifically asks for the modern trend approach. Under the modern trend, the landlord can withhold consent to a proposed assignment only for commercially reasonable grounds, and a landlord has a duty to mitigate in the event the tenant vacates. **Answer (B) is incorrect** because although it applies the modern trend to the landlord's ability to withhold consent to a proposed assignment, it applies the common law to the landlord's duty to mitigate. **Answer (C) is incorrect** because although it applies the modern trend to the landlord's duty to mitigate, it applies the common law to the landlord's ability to unreasonably withhold consent to a proposed assignment.

- **Additional references:** *See* 2 RICHARD R. POWELL, POWELL ON REAL PROPERTY ch. 17, §§ 17.04[1][b], 17.05[2] (Michael Allan Wolf ed., 2000); 5 THOMPSON ON REAL PROPERTY, SECOND THOMAS EDITION §§ 40.11(c), 40.11(c)(1) (1994 & Supp. 2006); WILLIAM B. STOEBUCK & DALE A. WHITMAN, THE LAW OF PROPERTY §§ 6.67, 6.71, 6.82 (3d ed. 2000).

21. **Answer (B) is the best answer.** Anna's adverse possession began in 1985. The statute of limitations in the jurisdiction is 21 years unless the disability doctrine applies. If the disability doctrine does not apply, Anna gains title to the property in 2006.

The disability doctrine applies only to (1) qualifying disabilities which (2) the party who has the right to possession has (3) "at the time the cause thereof accrues," (at the time the adverse possession began). Qualifying disabilities which arise *after* the adverse possession began do not affect the running of the statute of limitations. Transfers of title which occur after the adverse possession began do not affect the statute of limitations, even if the new owner or new party with the right to possession suffers from a qualifying disability.

The party who had the right to possession on the day Anna's adverse possession began was Olivia, the true owner. The only qualifying disability which applied to Olivia on January 1, 1985, the day the adverse possession began, was that Olivia was within the age of minority. The legal effect of a qualifying disability is to toll the statute of limitations until the disability is removed, and then add ten years to that date. Olivia reached the age of majority in 1993. Adding ten years to that date, Anna would acquire adverse possession in 2003 under the disability approach.

Inasmuch as the disability doctrine is intended to provide extra protection to the party who has the right to possession and who suffers from a qualifying disability on the day the adverse possession begins, the disability doctrine can be used only to extend the time period within which the party may bring his or her cause of action for ejectment, not to shorten the time period. Since the statute of limitations without considering the disability gave Olivia until 2006 to file her cause of action, and the statute of limitations considering the disability doctrine gave Olivia only until 2003 to file her cause of action, the disability doctrine would not be applied to shorten the statute of limitations. Olivia had until 2006 to file her cause of action for ejectment.

Answer (A) is incorrect because it fails to take into account that the disability doctrine cannot be used to shorten the statute of limitations which would otherwise apply. **Answers (C) and (D) are incorrect** because they incorrectly take into consideration disabilities which arise after the day on which the adverse possession begins. Only qualifying disabilities which the party who has the right to possession has on the day the adverse possession begins count for purposes of the disability statute.

- **Additional references:** *See* 16 RICHARD R. POWELL, POWELL ON REAL PROPERTY ch. 91, § 91.10[3] (Michael Allan Wolf ed., 2000); 10 THOMPSON ON REAL PROPERTY, SECOND THOMAS EDITION §§ 87.18, 87.01 (1998 & Supp. 2006); RALPH E. BOYER ET AL., THE LAW OF PROPERTY: AN INTRODUCTORY SURVEY § 4.8 (4th ed. 1991).

22. **The best answer is (D).** Virtually all jurisdictions agree that a lease inherently includes the covenant of quiet enjoyment. The covenant of quiet enjoyment imposes a duty upon the landlord to provide legal possession to the tenant. If the landlord, one claiming through the landlord, or one holding superior title to the landlord, interferes with the tenant's possession, the landlord has breached the covenant of quiet enjoyment.

While the jurisdictions are in general agreement with respect to the landlord's duty to provide legal possession, the jurisdictions are split over the landlord's duty to provide actual possession on the first day of the lease where the lease is silent on the matter. Under the English approach, the landlord has a duty to provide actual possession on the first day of the lease. Thereafter the issue of actual possession of the premises is the tenant's responsibility, as long as the interloper is not the landlord, one claiming through the landlord, or one claiming superior title to the landlord. Under the American approach, the landlord has no duty to provide actual possession on the first day of the lease, only legal possession. The tenant bears the risk of a third party being in possession of the premises on the first day of the lease.

With respect to the landlord's duty to provide legal possession to the tenant, did L have legal possession to convey to T-2 on January 1, 2005, the first day of the lease between L and T-2? Was the lease between L and T-1 properly terminated? Whether the lease between L and T-1 was properly terminated depends upon which type of lease it was. The lease was a term of years lease because the last day of the lease between L and T-1 could be determined on the first day of the lease. No notice is necessary to terminate a term of years lease. The lease terminates automatically upon the set date, and the right to legal possession reverts to the landlord. T-1's right to possession terminated automatically December 31, 2004. L had legal possession to grant to T-2 beginning January 1, 2005.

Did L have an implied duty to provide T-2 with actual possession? Under the American approach, L has no such implied duty. The tenant bears the risk that actual possession will not be available. L has not breached any of the duties as to delivery of possession.

Answer (A) is incorrect because it confuses the American approach and the English approach to the issue. Under the English approach, the landlord *has* an implied duty to deliver actual possession on the first day of the lease under the English approach. Under the American approach, the landlord has *no* such duty. **Answer (B) is incorrect** because it incorrectly analyzes the nature of the lease between L and T-1. Since the lease is a term of years lease, it terminated automatically on December 31, 2004, and L had the legal right to possession to convey to L-2. **Answer (C) is incorrect** because as a general rule, two wrongs do not make a right. (Answer (C) simply combines the two wrong answers set forth in (A) and (B).)

- **Additional references**: *See* 2 RICHARD R. POWELL, POWELL ON REAL PROPERTY ch. 16B, § 16B.02[1] (Michael Allan Wolf ed., 2000); 4 THOMPSON ON REAL PROPERTY, SECOND THOMAS EDITION §§ 39.05(a), 39.06(b)(1) (2004 & Supp. 2006); 5 THOMPSON § 40.22(b); WILLIAM B. STOEBUCK & DALE A. WHITMAN, THE LAW OF PROPERTY §§ 6.14, 6.21, 6.73 (3d ed. 2000).

23. **The best answer is (C).** In construing a conveyance, remember to construe comma to comma, distinguishing the words of purchase (the words indicating who is to take the interest) from the words of limitation (the technical words which describe the duration of the estate the party takes). Reading comma to comma, the first clause is a classic example of a life estate. The words of purchase are "to A." The words of limitation are "for life." A has a life estate.

The next clause grants the future interest to B. The future interest following a life estate which is held by a third party (a party other than the grantor) is a remainder. A remainder is contingent unless it qualifies as vested. A remainder is vested if the holder of the interest is (1) born, (2) ascertainable, and (3) there is no express condition precedent (an express condition which the party must satisfy before being entitled to claim the right to possession) in the clause creating the remainder or the preceding clause (reading comma to comma). Inasmuch as "B" stands for the personal name of the taker, B is born and ascertainable. There is no express condition in the clause creating the remainder or the preceding clause which B must satisfy before B is entitled to claim possession. The remainder is vested. The words of limitation "and her heirs" following the grant to B indicate that B holds a vested remainder in fee simple, but the qualifying language which follows the fee simple words of limitation indicate that the fee simple is not absolute, but rather a fee simple defeasible.

The fee simple defeasible can either be a fee simple determinable, a fee simple subject to a condition subsequent, a fee simple subject to an executory limitation, or a fee simple subject to divestment. The first key is who holds the future interest following the fee simple: the grantor (in which case the fee simple must be one of the first two possible fee simple defeasibles) or someone other than the grantor (in which case the fee simple must be one of the latter two possible fee simple defeasibles). Since C, someone other than the grantor, holds the future interest following B's remainder, B's fee simple must be either a fee simple subject to an executory limitation or a fee simple subject to divestment. The determining factor is whether the condition which qualifies B's remainder is a condition precedent to B taking possession or a condition subsequent. Here, the condition, "if B fails to survive A," is a condition precedent in that it is a condition which B must satisfy before B can take possession. If B fails to survive A, B's vested remainder will never become possessory. Thus B holds a vested remainder in fee simple subject to divestment.

The future interest following a fee simple subject to divestment is an executory interest. An executory interest may be either springing (which means the party holding the executory interest takes the right to possession from the grantor) or shifting (which means the party holding the executory interest takes the right to possession from someone other than the grantor). Reading comma to comma, C holds the future interest following B's vested remainder subject to divestment. C holds an executory interest in fee simple. Inasmuch as C is taking the right to possession from B, not the grantor, C holds a shifting executory interest in fee simple.

Answers (A) and (B) are incorrect because they incorrectly analyze the remainder as a contingent remainder. Because the condition, that B must survive A, is a condition precedent, one might think that the remainder is a contingent remainder. The question is whether the condition precedent is expressed as a condition which B must satisfy before taking possession or as a condition which may divest B of B's right to take possession. Reading comma to comma, the express condition precedent is not in the same clause creating the remainder or the preceding clause, but rather the subsequent clause. The more reasonable construction is that the condition is not one which qualifies B's right to possession, the condition is one which may divest B of B's right to possession.

Answer (D) is incorrect because it incorrectly analyzes the difference between a vested remainder subject to divestment and a vested remainder subject to an executory limitation. In both cases, there is a clause creating a vested remainder in fee simple and then the next clause contains express language qualifying the remainder. The key is whether the qualifying language sets forth a condition precedent (a condition which may occur before the remainder becomes possessory) or a condition subsequent (a condition which may occur only after the remainder becomes possessory). If the express condition is a condition precedent, if the condition occurs, it may divest the vested remainder before it ever becomes possessory. Thus the vested remainder in fee simple is subject to divestment if the condition is a condition precedent. If, however, the condition is a condition subsequent, the condition qualifies how long the remainder may be possessory after becoming possessory. In such a case, the vested remainder in fee simple is subject to an executory limitation. The condition in question is a condition which must be tested before B takes possession, so it is a condition precedent. Since it is a condition precedent, B holds a vested remainder in fee simple subject to divestment, not subject to an executory limitation.

- **Additional references**: *See* CORNELIUS J. MOYNIHAN, INTRODUCTION TO THE LAW OF REAL PROPERTY 123-129, 190-198 (2d ed. 1988); PETER T. WENDEL, A POSSESSORY ESTATES AND FUTURE INTERESTS PRIMER 43-44, 47-48, 58-65, 17-34 (3rd ed. 2007); 3 THOMPSON ON REAL PROPERTY, SECOND THOMAS EDITION §§ 23.07, 23.10, 23.11, 26.01-26.03 (2001 & Supp. 2006).

24. The best answer is (A). In construing a conveyance, remember to construe comma to comma, distinguishing the words of purchase (the words indicating who is to take the interest) from the words of limitation (the technical words which describe the duration of the estate the party takes). Reading comma to comma, the first clause is a classic example of a life estate. The words of purchase are "to A." The words of limitation are "for life." A has a life estate.

The future interest following a life estate can only be a reversion (if the future interest is held by the grantor) or a remainder (if the future interest is held by a third party - someone other than the grantor). The express words of purchase in the conveyance indicate that the future interest is held by O's heirs, someone other than the grantor, so O's heirs hold a remainder.

A remainder is contingent unless it satisfies the requirements for vested remainders. A remainder is vested if the holder of the interest is (1) born, (2) ascertainable, and (3) there is no express condition precedent (an express condition which the party must satisfy before being entitled to claim the right to possession) in the clause creating the remainder or the preceding clause. Are O's heirs born and ascertainable? Because one must survive the decedent to qualify as an heir, a person who is alive has no heirs, only "heirs apparent." Since O is still alive, O's heirs are not ascertainable (they cannot be named). The remainder is contingent.

What is the duration of the remainder? The express words of limitation in the clause creating the interest are the key to determining the duration of the interest. Typically the words of limitation immediately follow the words of purchase. Here, the phrase "the heirs of their bodies" are the common law words of limitation to create a fee tail. O's heirs hold a contingent remainder in fee tail.

Since the last express interest of the conveyance does not convey a full fee simple, only a fee tail, there has to be a default taker who will take the right to possession when the fee tail ends. In addition, even if the last express interest of the conveyance were a fee simple, since the remainder is contingent, there has to be a default taker in the event the remainder fails to vest. The default taker is always the grantor. Since O, the grantor, would take the property only after a finite estate (either after the fee tail terminated or after A's life estate if the remainder failed to vest), the grantor holds the future interest following a finite estate. The future interest following a finite estate is a reversion if it is held by the grantor. Thus, O holds a reversion. Default reversions are in fee simple unless there is express language qualifying the reversion. O holds a reversion in fee simple.

The state of the title appears to be: A has a life estate, O's heirs have a contingent remainder in fee tail, and O has a reversion. Under the Doctrine of Worthier Title, however, anytime a single conveyance creates a future interest in O's heirs, by operation of law the future interest is given to O. Striking the reference to "O's heirs" in the conveyance and inserting "O," the state of the title would be that A has a life estate, O now holds a reversion (future interest following a life estate held by the grantor) in fee tail, and O holds a reversion in fee simple.

Under the merger doctrine, however, if the same party holds successive vested interests, merge the vested interests into the larger interest. Reversions are vested by nature. After applying the Doctrine of Worthier Title, O holds successive reversions. Under merger, O's reversion in fee tail merges into the larger estate: O's reversion in fee simple. Following merger, the state of the title is A holds a life estate, and O holds a reversion in fee simple.

Answer (B) is incorrect because it fails to take into account the Doctrine of Worthier Title and because it fails to note that the words of limitation grant O's heirs a fee tail, not a fee simple. **Answer (C) is incorrect** because it fails to take into account the Doctrine of Worthier Title. **Answer (D) is incorrect** because it fails to take into account that once the Doctrine of Worthier Title gives the contingent remainder O's heirs held to O, the interest is no longer a remainder. The future interest is held by O, the grantor, and since it follows a life estate, it is now a reversion. **Answer (E) is incorrect** because it fails to take into account the merger doctrine.

- **Additional references:** *See* CORNELIUS J. MOYNIHAN, INTRODUCTION TO THE LAW OF REAL PROPERTY 34-36, 44, 123-124, 104-105, 151-152, 136 (2d ed. 1988); PETER T. WENDEL, A POSSESSORY ESTATES AND FUTURE INTERESTS PRIMER 43-48, 58-65, 150-52 (3rd ed. 2007); 2 THOMPSON ON REAL PROPERTY, SECOND THOMAS EDITION ch. 18, § 18.03, ch. 19, § 19.03 (2000 & Supp. 2006); 3 THOMPSON ch.22, § 22.02, ch. 23, §§ 23.03, 23.10, ch. 30, §§ 30.23, 30.03.

25. The best answer is (A). Virtually all jurisdictions agree that a lease inherently includes the covenant of quiet enjoyment. The covenant of quiet enjoyment imposes a duty upon the landlord to provide legal possession to the tenant. If the landlord, one claiming through the landlord, or one holding paramount title to the landlord, interferes with the tenant's possession, the landlord has breached the covenant of quiet enjoyment.

While the jurisdictions are in general agreement with respect to the landlord's duty to provide legal possession, the jurisdictions are split over the landlord's duty to provide actual possession on the first day of the lease where the lease is silent on the matter. Under the English approach, the landlord has a duty to provide actual possession on the first day of the lease. Thereafter the issue of actual possession of the premises is the tenant's responsibility, as long as the interloper is not the landlord, one claiming through the landlord, or one claiming paramount title to the landlord. Under the American approach, the landlord has no duty to provide actual possession on the first day of the lease, only legal possession. The tenant bears the risk of a third party being in possession of the premises on the first day of the lease.

The first issue under the facts is whether L had legal possession to convey to T-2 on January 1, 2005, the first day of the lease between L and T-2. Was the lease between L and T-1 properly terminated? Whether the lease between L and T-1 was properly terminated depends upon which type of lease it was. Although the original lease between L and T-1 was a term of years, T-1 held over and L accepted T-1's holdover by accepting T's rent payments.

What type of lease then was created between L and T-1 when L accepted T's payments? The jurisdictions are split over the answer to this question. Some jurisdictions hold that when a term of years tenant for a year or longer holds over, a new one year term lease is created. To the extent T-1 has held over for several years running, under this approach each year a new one year term of years lease arose. No notice is necessary to terminate a term of years lease. The lease terminates automatically upon the set date, and the right to legal possession reverts to the landlord. Under this approach, L and T-1 held a term of years lease which terminated on December 31, 2004. L had legal possession to grant to T-2 on January 1, 2005.

Other jurisdictions hold that when a term of years tenant for a year or longer holds over, a new periodic tenancy is created. The issue then is whether the new periodic tenancy is a month to month or a year to year. To the extent that the term is ambiguous, most courts hold that residential tenancies, if ambiguous, should be construed as month to month periodic tenancies. Even if a jurisdiction were to construe the new tenancy as a year to year periodic tenancy, the issue arguably is moot since under the modern trend, all that is necessary to terminate a periodic lease up to a year to year term is 30 days notice, to terminate on the last day of the term (unless it is a month to month tenancy, in which case the notice may terminate on any day as long as there is 30 days notice). On October 31, L gave T-1 notice L was terminating the lease effective December 31, the last day of the period. L gave proper notice to terminate if the lease is construed as a periodic lease. Since L properly terminated the periodic lease, the legal right to possession reverted to L. L had legal possession to grant to T-2 on January 1, 2005.

Did L have an implied duty to provide T-2 with actual possession? Under the English approach, L has an implied duty to provide actual possession on the first day of the lease. The landlord bears the risk that actual possession will not be available. Since T-1 held over and is in actual possession of the property when T-2 arrives to take possession on the first day of the new lease, L has breached the duty to deliver actual possession under the English approach.

Answer (B) is incorrect because it implicitly incorrectly analyzes the nature of the lease between L and T-1. Whether the hold-over tenancy created a term of years lease or a periodic lease, on December 31, 2004, L had the legal right to possession to convey to L-2. **Answer (C) is incorrect** because although L has breached the duty to provide actual possession, L has not breached the duty to provide legal possession. **Answer (D) is incorrect** because under the English approach, L does have a duty to provide actual possession on the first day of the lease, and L has breached that duty here.

- **Additional references:** *See* 2 RICHARD R. POWELL, POWELL ON REAL PROPERTY ch. 16, §§16.04[3], 16.03[7], ch. 16B, § 16B.02[1], ch. 17, § 17.06 (Michael Allan Wolf ed., 2000); 4 THOMPSON ON REAL PROPERTY, SECOND THOMAS EDITION §§ 39.05(a), 39.06(b)(1) (2004 & Supp. 2006), 5 THOMPSON ON REAL PROPERTY §§ 40.10(a)-(c), 40.22(b), 43.06(a); WILLIAM B. STOEBUCK & DALE A. WHITMAN, THE LAW OF PROPERTY §§ 6.14, 6.20-6.21, 6.73-6.74 (3d ed. 2000).

ANSWER KEY
EXAM II

PROPERTY
ANSWER KEY AND EXPLANATIONS

EXAM II

1. **The best answer is (D).** In construing a conveyance, remember to construe comma to comma, distinguishing the words of purchase (the words indicating who is to take the interest) from the words of limitation (the technical words which describe the duration of the estate the party takes). Reading comma to comma, the first clause is a classic example of a life estate. The words of purchase are "to A." The words of limitation are "for life." A has a life estate.

The next clause grants a future interest to B. The future interest following a life estate is either a reversion (if held by the grantor) or a remainder (if held by a third party - a party other than the grantor). Since B is not the grantor, at first blush it appears as though B holds a remainder.

A remainder is vested if the holder of the interest is (1) born, (2) ascertainable, and (3) there is no express condition precedent (an express condition which the party must satisfy before being entitled to claim the right to possession) in the clause creating the remainder or the preceding clause (reading comma to comma). B is born and ascertainable. There is, however, qualifying language in the clause purporting to grant B a remainder. The express language sets forth a condition precedent, a condition which B must satisfy before B can take possession of the property. It appears as if B holds a contingent remainder, but closer examination of the condition reveals otherwise.

The key to understanding the future interest B holds is in the express language setting forth the condition precedent which B must satisfy before B can claim possession of the property. Where the express condition precedent is set forth in the same clause creating the future interest (which appears to be a remainder) or the preceding clause, the key is determining *when* the express condition precedent can be satisfied. As long as the express condition precedent can be satisfied before the preceding finite estate ends or at the moment the finite estate ends, the future interest will be a remainder (and contingent at that). Where, however, the express condition precedent is one which by nature *cannot* be satisfied during the preceding finite estate or at the moment the finite estate ends, the future interest is an executory interest.

Returning to the express condition precedent in the conveyance, there is no way B can give A a proper funeral before the end of A's life estate. By nature, the condition precedent cannot be satisfied before the expiration of the preceding life estate. B holds an executory interest. Notice, even if B is able to satisfy the express condition precedent, there is a "gap" between the end of the finite estate (the life estate here) and the time when the express condition can be satisfied.

Someone must have the right to possession during the gap between A's death and the time for B to fulfill or fail to fulfill the condition precedent. The default taker is always the grantor, here O. O holds the future interest which will immediately follows A's life estate. The future interest following a life estate which is held by the grantor is a reversion. The default estate is fee simple, but here O's fee simple can be cut short if B gives A a proper funeral. Since O's fee simple can be cut short, O holds a fee simple defeasible. Since the future interest following O's fee simple defeasible is held by a third party, B, O must hold a fee simple subject to an executory limitation. B holds an executory interest in fee simple. Since B's executory interest will take possession, if at all, from the grantor, it is a springing executory interest in fee simple.

Answer (A) is incorrect because it fails to recognize that there is an express condition precedent in the clause purporting to create the remainder in B. **Answers (B) and (C) are incorrect** because although they recognize that there is an express condition precedent in the clause purporting to create the remainder in B, which normally makes the remainder a contingent remainder, they fail to recognize that the express condition precedent is one which inherently cannot be satisfied prior to B taking possession. This constitutes the classic "gap" scenario: where there appears to be a life estate and remainder, but careful reading of the facts indicates that there is a "gap" between the end of the life estate and when the express condition precedent can be satisfied. When there is a "gap" scenario, the grantor takes a reversion in fee simple subject to an executory limitation, the limitation being that the grantor's right to possession will terminate if the party satisfies the express condition.

- **Additional references:** *See* CORNELIUS J. MOYNIHAN, INTRODUCTION TO THE LAW OF REAL PROPERTY 43-44, 104, 187-189 (2d ed. 1988); PETER T. WENDEL, A POSSESSORY ESTATES AND FUTURE INTERESTS PRIMER 43-44, 47-48, 58-65, 101-02 (3rd ed. 2007); 2 THOMPSON ON REAL PROPERTY, SECOND THOMAS

EDITION §§ 19.03, 17.01(c)(3) (2000 & Supp. 2006); 3 THOMPSON at §§ 22.02, 26.01.

2. **The best answer is (A).** At common law, for there to be a valid inter vivos gift: (1) the donor had to have the intent to make a present transfer of the property, (2) there had to be delivery, and (3) there had to be acceptance. Acceptance of the gift is presumed as long as the item in question is an item of value. Applied to the facts of the problem, the decedent clearly indicated his intent to transfer his desk and the money in the top drawer of the desk. The issue is one of delivery.

Common law required delivery so that the donor could experience the "wrench" of parting with the item, to bring home the finality of the donor's actions and for evidentiary purposes. As a general rule, if manual delivery of the item is possible, manual delivery is required. Where manual delivery is not possible, symbolic or constructive delivery is permitted. Constructive delivery is achieved by delivering something which gives control over the item in question, such as a key. Symbolic delivery is achieved by delivering something which symbolizes the item. The most common form of symbolic delivery is a piece of paper which expresses the intent to deliver the item which the donor cannot manually deliver. Common law was very strict about requiring manual delivery where possible, especially in death bed scenarios because of the courts' concerns about the Wills Act formalities which are required to transfer a property interest at time of death.

Here, the donor can manually deliver the money. The decedent should have requested that his servant take the money out of the desk drawer and put it in the decedent's hand so that the decedent could have manually delivered the money to the servant. There is no delivery of the money.

Although the donor arguably cannot manually deliver the desk, there is no evidence of either constructive or symbolic delivery. Pointing to the item in question is not sufficient to constitute delivery under the traditional common law approach.

Answers (B), (C) and (D) are incorrect because they fail to recognize that there was not an acceptable form of delivery for either the money (which the donor could manually deliver) or the desk (which arguably the donor could not manually deliver, but which was not properly delivered constructively or symbolically).

- **Additional references**: *See* 15 RICHARD R. POWELL, POWELL ON REAL PROPERTY ch. 85, §§ 85.21, 85.21[2] (Michael Allan Wolf ed., 2000); 2 THOMPSON ON REAL PROPERTY, SECOND THOMAS EDITION § 13.04(a)(2) (2000 & Supp. 2006); RALPH E. BOYER ET AL., THE LAW OF PROPERTY: AN INTRODUCTORY SURVEY §§ 3.2-3.4 (4th ed. 1991).

3. **The best answer is (D).** In construing a conveyance, remember to construe comma to comma, distinguishing the words of purchase (the words indicating who is to take the interest) from the words of limitation (the technical words which describe the duration of the estate the party takes). Reading comma to comma, the first clause is a classic example of a life estate. The words of purchase are "to A." The words of limitation are "for life." A has a life estate.

The future interest following a life estate can only be a reversion (if the future interest is held by the grantor) or a remainder (if the future interest is held by a third party - someone other than the grantor). The express words of purchase in the conveyance indicate that the future interest passes "then to the then Dean of Res Ipsa Law School," someone other than the grantor, so the then Dean holds a remainder.

A remainder is contingent unless it qualifies as vested. A remainder is vested if the holder of the interest is (1) born, (2) ascertainable, and (3) there is no express condition precedent (an express condition which the party must satisfy before being entitled to claim the right to possession) in the clause creating the remainder or the preceding clause (reading comma to comma). Is the party who holds the remainder born and ascertainable? Can you determine the day the conveyance is created who will be the Dean of the Law School when the life estate *ends*? Notice the express language of the conveyance indicates that the future interest is held by the *"then* Dean," indicating the Dean at the time the life estate ends, not the current Dean. Because it is impossible to ascertain at this moment who will be the Dean at that moment, the remainder is contingent.

What is the duration of the remainder? The express words of limitation in the clause creating the interest are the key to determining the duration of an interest. Typically the words of limitation immediately follow the words of purchase. Here, the phrase "and his or her heirs" are the common law words of limitation to create a fee simple. The *"then* Dean" holds a contingent remainder in fee simple.

Since the remainder is contingent, there has to be a default taker who will take the right to possession if the remainder fails to vest before the end of the life estate. The default taker is always the grantor. Since the grantor would take the property after the life estate if the remainder fails to vest, the grantor holds the future interest following a finite estate. The future interest following a finite estate is a reversion if it is held by the grantor. O holds a reversion. Default reversions are in fee simple unless there is express language qualifying the reversion. O holds a reversion in fee simple.

The state of the title as executed is: A has a life estate, the "*then* Dean of Res Ipsa Law School" has a contingent remainder in fee simple, and O has a reversion. A then transfers A's life estate to the current Dean of the Res Ipsa Law School, Dean Loquitor. Life estates are transferable, but the party cannot transfer more than he or she holds. A can only transfer A's life estate, a life estate measured by A's life. Dean Loquitor holds A's life estate - life estate measured by another's life (A's life). Dean Loquitor holds a life estate pur autre vie.

Under the merger doctrine, if the same party holds successive vested interests, the vested interests merge into the larger interest. Can the Dean's life estate pur autre vie be merged into the contingent remainder? No. First, the same party does not hold the interests since it is impossible to tell who will be the Dean when A dies. It may or may not be Dean Loquitor. Second, since the "*then* Dean" is not ascertainable, the remainder is contingent, not vested. Only vested interests may be merged. Merger does not apply to the life estate held by Dean Loquitor and the remainder held by the then Dean.

Answer (A) is incorrect because it mistakenly applies the merger doctrine. **Answer (B) is incorrect** because it fails to recognize that the life estate is measured by the life of A, not Dean Loquitor, and it mistakenly concludes that the remainder is vested. **Answer (C) is incorrect** because it fails to recognize that the life estate is measured by the life of A.

- **Additional references:**   *See* CORNELIUS J. MOYNIHAN, INTRODUCTION TO THE LAW OF REAL PROPERTY 43-44, 54, 104-105, 129-133, 136 (2d ed. 1988); PETER T. WENDEL, A POSSESSORY ESTATES AND FUTURE INTERESTS PRIMER 43-44, 47-48, 58-65, 49-50, 74-79 (3rd ed. 2007); 2 THOMPSON ON REAL PROPERTY, SECOND THOMAS EDITION §§ 19.03, 19.05 (2000 & Supp. 2006); 3 THOMPSON at §§ 22.03, 23.09, 30.03.

4. **The best answer is (B).** A tenant or subtenant may be liable to the landlord based upon either privity of contract or privity of estate.

Privity of contract may be established two ways. First, privity of contract exists between parties to an agreement. Since a landlord and tenant are parties to the original lease agreement, they are in privity of contract. A landlord, however, may or may not be in privity of contract with a subtenant. Assuming a landlord is not party to the agreement between the tenant and subtenant, a landlord may still be in privity of contract with a subtenant under a third party beneficiary analysis. A landlord is a third party beneficiary of the agreement between a tenant and subtenant if the subtenant expressly assumes one or more of the obligations which the tenant owes to the landlord.

Applying the principles of privity of contract to the facts, L and T are parties to the original lease. At a minimum, L is in privity of contract with T. L is not a party to either of the sub-agreements involving T-1 or T-2, so there is no direct privity of contract between L and T-1 or T-2. Moreover, there is no express assumption clause in the agreement between either T and T-1 or T and T-2 which would support a claim of third party beneficiary privity of contract between L and either of the subtenants. Accordingly, L is in privity of contract with T only.

Privity of contract continues to exist even after an assignment or sublease unless the landlord expressly releases the tenant in question from the privity of contract. Such a release is called a "novation." There is no evidence of a novation under the facts of the problem, so T remains in privity of contract with L despite the subsequent conveyances with T-1 and T-2. T is liable to L under privity of contract.

The party who is in privity of estate with the landlord is also liable to the landlord. Privity of estate exists between any two parties who will exchange the legal right to possession. As applied to the typical lease, the landlord is in privity of estate with the party who has the legal right to possession on the last day of the lease. Privity of estate exists originally between the landlord and the original tenant. Where the tenant conveys his or her right to possession, however, whether the tenant remains in privity of estate with the landlord depends on whether the tenant assigns or subleases his or her interest. An assignment is where the tenant transfers all of his or her interest to the subtenant. In such a case, the subtenant then will have the legal right to possession on the last day of the lease and hence will be in privity of estate with the landlord. A sublease is where the tenant transfers something less than all of his or her interest. In such a case, the tenant retains the legal right to possession on the last day of the original lease and hence remains in privity of estate with the landlord.

Under the facts of the problem, one year into the ten year term of years lease, T transferred the right to possession to T-1 for two years. Obviously, that is less than all of T's interest. The transfer from T to T-1 constitutes a sublease. T remains in privity of estate with L. Thereafter, T transfers his entire interest to T-2. At this point, T-2 assumes privity of estate with L. When T-1 defaults, L is in privity of contract with T and privity of estate with T-2. L can sue either or both of them to recover, and each of them in turn can sue T-1 under subrogation. (Subrogation permits one to step into the shoes of another and assert any and all claims that party could have asserted.)

Answer (A) is incorrect because it is incomplete. It fails to recognize that a landlord can sue whoever is in privity of estate with the landlord. **Answers (C) and (D) are incorrect** because there is no privity of contract between L and T-1. L is not a party to the agreement involving T-1, and there is no express assumption clause in the agreement between T and T-1 which would support a claim of privity of contract based on third party beneficiary.

- **Additional references**:   *See* 2 RICHARD R. POWELL, POWELL ON REAL PROPERTY §§ 17.04[1][b], 17.04[2] (Michael Allan Wolf ed., 2000); 5 THOMPSON ON REAL PROPERTY, SECOND THOMAS EDITION §§ 42.04(a), 42.04(d), 42.04(e)(1)-(e)(3) (1994 & Supp. 2006); WILLIAM B. STOEBUCK & DALE A. WHITMAN, THE LAW OF PROPERTY §§ 6.67-6.70 (3d ed. 2000).

5.   **The best answer is (A).**   Under the traditional common law rules regarding found tangible personal property, who has superior rights depends in large degree upon two key variables: (1) how the property is characterized (lost, mislaid, abandoned or treasure trove), and (2) where the object is found (private property vs. public property).

Whether the property is lost, mislaid, abandoned or treasure trove turns on the intent of the true owner at the time she or he relinquished possession of the item. An item is lost if the true owner unintentionally relinquished possession of the item. An item is mislaid if the true owner intentionally relinquished possession of the item with the intent of returning and repossessing it later, but then forgot to return and pick it up. An item is abandoned if the true owner intentionally relinquished possession of the item with no intent to ever repossess the item. And lastly, an item is treasure trove if the item is money, coin, gold, silver, plate or bullion and the owner intentionally hid the item underground intending to return later to reclaim it (modern trend, the item does not have to be buried underground to qualify as treasure trove).

A criticism of this common law classification scheme is that characterization of the item turns on the true owner's state of mind at the time he or she parts with the item, yet the court does not know who the true owner is. At best the evidence of the true owner's state of mind is circumstantial. Nevertheless, the common law approach presumes the owner's state of mind from the circumstances surrounding the location of the item at the time it is found. Assuming a reasonable true owner, which classification is most consistent with the most probable state of mind of the true owner in light of the facts surrounding where the item was found?

The ring is most probably lost property. Ali found the ring on the boardwalk under the outside picnic tables at Bob's Lobster Shack. The ring was not exactly hidden, nor was it below ground, so treasure trove is highly unlikely. Most people do not abandon rings, so absent evidence to support such an intent, the court will not presume that the true owner abandoned the ring (although it is easy to imagine such a scenario: where a young couple breaks up and neither party wants the ring anymore, so the party in possession simply throws it on the sidewalk to demonstrate his or her disdain for anything reminding him or her of the relationship!). So the issue is whether the ring was mislaid or lost. In light of the fact that the ring was found on the boardwalk under the picnic table, is it more likely that the owner placed it there intentionally or unintentionally? While one can imagine scenarios which support either, the more likely scenario is that the true owner unintentionally relinquished possession. Therefore, the ring is "lost" property.

The second key variable in determining who has the best claim to the found item is whether the item was found on private or public property. If found on private property, the common law granted the item to the owner of the private property generally to deter trespass and to protect landowners' expectations. Here, Ali found the ring on the boardwalk, presumably public property. Even if the boardwalk were actually private property designed to look like public property, private property which is open to the public generally is considered public property for purposes of the law of finders. The common law rule is that lost property found on public property belongs to the finder, who has superior rights over all but the true owner or one with a superior claim. Because the ring was found on the boardwalk, a public location, Ali prevails over Bob.

What about when Ali loses the ring and Kristin finds it? Who prevails as among Ali, Kristin, and the owners of the Trumpet Casino? Kristin will claim that she found the ring, and thus, as a finder of lost property she has superior rights to it over all but the true owner. The owners of the Trumpet Casino will claim that since Kristin is their employee, anything she finds in the course of her employment she finds for them, her employer. The courts are hopelessly split over how to treat cases of property found by employees in the course of their employment, but the employee has a better chance if the item is characterized as lost as opposed to mislaid. Under the relativity of property rights, however, even though a prior possessor is not the true owner, a prior possessor prevails against all subsequent possessors. Ali's claim will prevail against Kristin's and/or the owners' of the Trumpet Casino since Ali's rights to the ring arose prior to their rights.

Answer (B) is incorrect because the ring is most likely lost property found on public property. Bob cannot successfully claim that the ring was mislaid or that the ring was found on private property, either of which would be necessary for Bob to prevail. **Answers (C) and (D) are incorrect** because they fail to recognize the relativity to property rights. Once Ali's claim to the ring was established, she has superior rights over all but the true owner. Ali's claim was first in time, first in right over either Kristin's or the owner's of the Trumpet Casino.

- **Additional references**: *See* 2 THOMPSON ON REAL PROPERTY, SECOND THOMAS EDITION § 13.04(e) (2000 & Supp. 2006); RALPH E. BOYER ET AL., THE LAW OF PROPERTY: AN INTRODUCTORY SURVEY § 1.3 (4th ed. 1991); RAY A. BROWN, THE LAW OF PERSONAL PROPERTY, 24-26 (Walter B. Raushenbush 3d ed. 1975).

6. **The best answer is (B).** In construing a conveyance, remember to construe comma to comma, distinguishing the words of purchase (the words indicating who is to take the interest) from the words of limitation (the technical words which describe the duration of the estate the party takes). Reading comma to comma, the first clause is a classic example of a life estate. The words of purchase are "to A." The words of limitation are "for life." A has a life estate.

The next clause grants the future interest to B. The future interest following a life estate is either a reversion (if held by the grantor) or a remainder (if held by a third party - a party other than the grantor). Since B is not the grantor, the interest is a remainder.

A remainder is contingent unless it qualifies as vested. A remainder is vested if the holder of the interest is (1) born, (2) ascertainable, and (3) there is no express condition precedent (an express condition which the party must satisfy before being entitled to claim possession) in the clause creating the remainder or the preceding clause (reading comma to comma). Since one can name the person to whom the right to possession goes, B; B is therefore born and ascertainable. The issue is whether there is an express condition precedent in the words of the conveyance which B has to satisfy prior to taking possession.

There is an express condition in the clause creating the remainder. The question is whether this is a condition which the party holding the remainder has to satisfy *prior* to taking possession (a condition precedent), or whether this is a condition which the party holding the remainder has to satisfy *to keep possession after* taking possession (a condition subsequent). The more logical and reasonable construction is that the condition "as long as B farms the land" is a condition which B has to satisfy to keep possession of the property – a condition subsequent. B's remainder is vested.

What is the duration of B's vested remainder? The words of limitation "and her heirs" indicate that B holds a remainder in fee simple. The fee simple is qualified, however, by the express condition subsequent. Where a vested remainder in fee simple may be cut short by a condition subsequent, the critical question is who holds the future interest: a third party (someone other than the grantor) or the grantor? Here, the conveyance does not expressly indicate who holds the future interest. If there is not an express grantee to take a future interest, the default taker is the grantor. Thus, O, the grantor in our conveyance, holds the future interest following the qualified fee simple.

Since the fee simple may be cut short (if B stops farming the land), and the future interest is in the grantor, the remainder must be either a vested remainder in fee simple determinable (with O holding a possibility of reverter in fee simple absolute) or a vested remainder in fee simple subject to a condition subsequent (with O holding a right of re-entry in fee simple absolute). Which estate B holds depends upon the express words of limitation in the conveyance which indicate how B's fee simple may be cut short. Do the words indicate that the remainder will terminate *automatically* upon the condition occurring, or do the words indicate that upon the condition occurring O has a *right to re-enter* and re-claim the property? If the former, B holds a fee simple determinable; if the latter, B holds a fee simple subject to a condition subsequent. The words "as long as" are classic words of automatic termination indicating an intent that the estate is to end automatically the moment the condition occurs. Thus B holds a vested remainder in fee simple determinable, and O holds a possibility of reverter in fee simple absolute.

Answer (A) is incorrect because it incorrectly analyzes the remainder. The express condition that B farm the land is a condition subsequent, not a condition precedent. Therefore, B holds a vested remainder, not a contingent remainder. **Answer (C) is incorrect** because it incorrectly identifies the future interest O holds. The future interest which follows a fee simple determinable is a possibility of reverter, not a right of entry. **Answer (D) is incorrect** because it incorrectly identifies the future interest B holds. The words "as long as" are the classic words indicating that the estate is to be cut short immediately and automatically upon the condition occurring. Accordingly, B holds a fee simple determinable, not a fee simple subject to a condition subsequent, and O holds a possibility of reverter, not a possibility of reversion.

- **Additional references:** *See* CORNELIUS J. MOYNIHAN, INTRODUCTION TO THE LAW OF REAL PROPERTY 43-44, 123-125, 32-34 (2d ed. 1988); PETER T. WENDEL, A POSSESSORY ESTATES AND FUTURE INTERESTS PRIMER 43-44, 47-48, 58-65, 17-30 (3rd ed. 2007); 2 THOMPSON ON REAL PROPERTY, SECOND THOMAS EDITION §§ 19.03, 22.02 (2000 & Supp. 2006); 3 THOMPSON at §§ 23.03, 23.06, 24.01.

7. **The best answer is (C).** There are several different ways one can establish a property interest in a wild animal. Two of the most common are occupancy and rationi soli.

Occupancy occurs when one manifests an unequivocal intent to appropriate the animal to his or her personal use, deprives the animal of its natural liberty, and brings the animal under certain control. Rationi soli grants one who owns real property constructive possession over all wild animals on one's land so as to deter trespass.

B will claim the bird based on occupancy. By shooting and killing the bird, B deprived the animal of its natural liberty. It is questionable, however, whether B has brought the animal under certain control. Arguably not, since the bird is quickly floating away down the river to waste away. Nor is there any evidence that B was pursuing the bird as it floated away. Moreover, it is unclear whether B ever intended to appropriate the bird to her individual use. B did not immediately pursue the bird but rather returned to the barbecue to finish her meal.

Downstream, F spots the bird and grabs it. By grabbing it, F manifests an unequivocal intent to appropriate the bird to her personal use, deprives the animal of its natural liberty (to the extent one can argue the animal has any natural liberty left), and unlike B, brings the animal under certain control. F arguably has a stronger claim than B because if F did not grab the bird the facts indicate that the bird probably would have gone to waste. There doesn't appear to have been any way B could have tracked the bird down since it was floating downstream.

A will claim the bird based on rationi soli. A's claim of rationi soli would have trumped B's occupancy claim to the bird if B had prevailed. B was trespassing by exceeding the limited purpose for which B was granted permission to be on A's property (to attend the barbecue, not to hunt). Inasmuch as F trumps B, the question is whether A's claim of rationi soli should prevail over F's occupancy. Permitting A's claim to prevail would not promote the underlying public policy since F never trespassed on A's property. In addition, granting the bird to A would create a disincentive for parties like F to assert the effort necessary to capture the animal which otherwise would have gone to waste. F's claim of occupancy arguably should prevail over A's claim of rationi soli.

F has a superior claim to the bird over T. T will also claim the bird based on occupancy, but T will try to set up the jus tertii defense to F's claim. The jus tertii defense asserts that, inasmuch as someone else has superior rights to the item, the claimant has no right to have the item returned. F arguably has the superior claim to the bird, but even if F did not, as a prior possessor, F has superior rights over all but the true owner. At a minimum, F's rights to the bird based on occupancy arose prior to any claim T has to the bird. Even if F acquired possession of the bird wrongly, as the prior possessor, F is entitled to protection against T's claim. F trumps over T's claim based on first in time, first in right.

Answer (A) is incorrect because F was not trespassing when F grabbed the bird. The policy underlying rationi soli would not be served by applying it to F. **Answer (B) is incorrect** because B never brought the bird under certain control and may not have had the intent to appropriate it to B's individual use. Because the bird fell in the fast moving stream, the bird would have gone to waste if F had not grabbed it. Moreover, A's rationi soli claim would trump B's occupancy claim. B was exceeding the limited purpose for which B was invited onto the land, and thus was trespassing, when she shot the bird. **Answer (D) is incorrect** because F arguably is the rightful owner so any jus tercii defense T may assert is inapplicable, and under first in time, first in right, F has a stronger claim to the bird than does T.

- **Additional references**: *See* 2 THOMPSON ON REAL PROPERTY, SECOND THOMAS EDITION § 13.03(c) (2000 & Supp. 2006); RALPH E. BOYER ET AL., THE LAW OF PROPERTY: AN INTRODUCTORY SURVEY §§ 1.1-1.2 (4th ed. 1991); RAY A. BROWN, THE LAW OF PERSONAL PROPERTY, 17-18 (Walter B. Raushenbush 3d ed. 1975).

8. **The best answer is (D).** A co-tenant who improves jointly held property does so at his or her own risk. An improving co-tenant has no right to contribution from the other co-tenants for the costs of the improvement. The rationale is that it is unfair to permit one co-tenant to force another co-tenant to contribute toward an improvement that the other co-tenant may not think necessary. A is not entitled to contribution from the other co-tenants.

It is, however, equally unfair to permit co-tenants who do not contribute toward the cost of the improvement to benefit financially from the improvement. Therefore, if one co-tenant improves the jointly held property, and thereafter the property is partitioned, the co-tenants who did not contribute toward the cost of the improvement cannot benefit from the fact that the jointly held land had been improved. Only the co-tenant who contributed toward the improvement is entitled to the benefit of the improvement.

If the land is partitioned in kind, the part of the land with the improvement is awarded to the co-tenant who improved the land. If the nature of the improvement is such that the land cannot be divided so that all of the improvement is allocated to the improving co-tenant, the non-improving co-tenants can be forced to pay compensation (owelty) to the improving co-tenant.

If the partition is by sale, the improving co-tenant is entitled to credit for the improvement. The co-tenant who contributes to the improvement should receive the *added value* of the improvement at the time of the partition sale, *not the cost* of the improvement. Notice this approach places the risk of the effect of the improvement on the party who contribute towards it. If the improvement adds more value than it cost, the improving co-tenant gets the benefit; if the improvement loses value over time, the improving co-tenant absorbs the loss. Under the facts presented, A, the improving co-tenant, is entitled to the value the improvement added to the house, the extra proceeds generated at the time of the partition sale by virtue of the improvement.

Answers (A) and (B) are incorrect because an improving co-tenant is not entitled to contribution from the other co-tenants. **Answer (C) is incorrect** because an improving co-tenant is not entitled to the *cost* of the improvement before the proceeds from the partition sale are divided among the co-tenants, the improving co-tenant is entitled only to the *value the improvement has added* to the jointly held property.

- **Additional references:** *See* 7 RICHARD R. POWELL, POWELL ON REAL PROPERTY ch. 50, ¶¶ 604[2], 607[4], 607[6], 618[2] (Michael Allan Wolf ed., 2000); 4 THOMPSON ON REAL PROPERTY, SECOND THOMAS EDITION §§ 31.07(b), 32.07(b), 38.06 (2004 & Supp. 2006); 2 H. TIFFANY, REAL PROPERTY § 462 (3d ed. 1939).

9. **The best answer is (B).** Although a significant minority of states hold otherwise, the majority rule is that a co-tenant in exclusive possession of jointly owned property is not liable to other co-tenants absent a showing of ouster. What constitutes ouster varies from jurisdiction to jurisdiction. Under the traditional common law approach, ouster required proof that a co-tenant was physically denied access to the property. Under the modern trend approach, a demand to vacate or pay rent may be sufficient. Inasmuch as A and B cannot show ouster under either approach, pursuant to the general rule C is not liable to A and B for rent for the 5 years that C was in exclusive possession of Blackacre.

A co-tenant who receives rent or other payments from jointly owned property, however, generally must account to co-tenants for the payments received and is liable for proceeds in excess of his or her share. Thus C must account to A and B for the actual rents received from X which are in excess of C's share. Absent evidence of ouster, however, the co-tenant who received the monies must account only for the actual rents and payments received, not fair market value.

Answer (A) is incorrect because it fails to take into account the general rule that a co-tenant who receives rent or other payments from jointly owned property must account to co-tenants for the payments received and is liable for proceeds in excess of his or her share. **Answers (C) and (D) are incorrect** because they incorrectly impose on a co-tenant in exclusive possession of jointly owned property a duty to pay rent to other co-tenants even though there is no ouster. Although some jurisdictions impose such a duty, it is not the general rule.

- **Additional references:** *See* 7 RICHARD R. POWELL, POWELL ON REAL PROPERTY ch. 50, ¶¶ 603[a], 604[1] (Michael Allan Wolf ed.,

2000); 4 THOMPSON ON REAL PROPERTY, SECOND EDITION §§
31.07(c), 32.07(c) (2004 & Supp. 2006); WILLIAM B. STOEBUCK &
DALE A. WHITMAN, THE LAW OF PROPERTY § 5.8 (3d ed. 2000).

10. **The best answer is (E).** A bailment is created when one not rightfully
the owner of personal property is in possession of the personal property.
The rightful owner is the bailor, the party currently in rightful possession
is the bailee. The bailee has duty to care for the personal property while
in his or her possession and to deliver the property to the bailor on
demand or as agreed.

At common law, the degree of care which the bailee owed the bailor
depended on the nature of the bailment. If the bailment were primarily
for the benefit of the bailor, the bailee owed the bailor only slight care
and would not be liable for damage to the property unless the bailee was
grossly negligent. If the bailment were for the benefit of both the bailee
and the bailor, the bailee owed the bailor ordinary care and would be
liable for damage to the property if the bailee were negligent. If the
bailment were primarily for the benefit of the bailee, the bailee owed the
bailor extraordinary care and would be liable for damage to the property
even if the bailee were only slightly negligent.

Under the traditional common law approach, the initial step would be to
characterize which type of bailment was created. Obviously the bailment
was for the benefit of the bailor, O. Was the bailment also for the
benefit of the bailee, the hotel? Although at first blush it would appear
not, since the hotel received no direct benefit from the bailment, an
argument can be made that the service provided was part of the larger
service the hotel provides to its guests. Getting guests to stay at the hotel
is of benefit to the hotel, the bailee.

The issue of whether the bailment was primarily for the bailor's benefit
or for the benefit of both, however, is moot. Under the common law
analysis, whichever type of bailment was created, if the bailee
misdelivered the property, the bailee was strictly liable for the loss. Here,
the clerk misdelivered the ring. The hotel is strictly liable for misdelivery.

Answers (A), (B), (C) and (D) are incorrect because they fail to
recognize that a bailee is strictly liable for misdelivery of the bailor's
property. All the bailor has to prove is misdelivery, no negligence on the
bailee's part. O's best argument is to claim misdelivery since she avoids
the difficult issues of which form of bailment was created and which
degree of negligence, if any, the hotel committed.

- **Additional references**: *See* 2 THOMPSON ON REAL PROPERTY, SECOND THOMAS EDITION §§ 13.07(a)-13.07(d) (2000 & Supp. 2006); RALPH E. BOYER ET. AL., THE LAW OF PROPERTY: AN INTRODUCTORY SURVEY § 2.4 (4th ed. 1991); RAY A. BROWN, THE LAW OF PERSONAL PROPERTY, 282-283 (Walter B. Raushenbush 3d ed. 1975).

11. **The best answer is (C).** The problem raises the issue of what is necessary to convey a fee simple absolute under the common law approach versus the modern trend approach.

Under the traditional common law approach, use of the proper words of limitation were necessary to convey the intended possessory estate. The proper words of limitation to convey a fee simple absolute were the words "and his/her heirs." If the proper words of limitation were not used, the estate conveyed was the default estate. At common law the default estate was a life estate, with a reversion in fee simple absolute in the grantor.

The modern trend is more concerned with the grantor's intent. Moreover, the grantor is presumed to convey all that he or she owns unless the grantor properly expresses his or her intent to limit the estate being conveyed. Under the modern trend, the default estate is fee simple unless the grantor properly expresses a contrary intent.

Here, the deed from O to X expressly provided that O conveyed the property "to X in fee simple absolute." Under the common law approach, O did not use the proper words of limitation to convey a fee simple absolute. Despite O's apparent intent to convey a fee simple absolute to X, under the common law approach, X took only a life estate, and O retained a reversion in fee simple. Under the modern trend, O is presumed to convey all that O holds to X. Here, the intent expressed in the conveyance is consistent with the default presumption that O intended to convey a fee simple absolute to X.

Under the common law approach, X holds a life estate and O retained a reversion in fee simple absolue; under the modern trend X holds a fee simple absolute.

Answer (A) is incorrect because while X takes a fee simple under the modern trend, X does not under the common law approach. Because of the absence of the proper words of limitation, X takes only a life estate under the common law approach. **Answer (B) is incorrect** because it mixes up the common law and modern trend approaches. It is under the common law approach that X takes the life estate and it is under the modern trend that X takes the fee simple. **Answer (D) is incorrect** because it fails to recognize that the default under the modern trend is a fee simple. Under the modern trend, there are no words of limitation expressing a contrary intent, so X takes a fee simple absolute.

- **Additional references:** *See* 1 RICHARD R. POWELL, POWELL ON REAL PROPERTY ch. 13, §§ 13.01[3], 13.04[1] (Michael Allan Wolf ed., 2000); 2 THOMPSON ON REAL PROPERTY, SECOND THOMAS EDITION § 17.06 (2004 & Supp. 2006); PETER T. WENDEL, A POSSESSORY ESTATES AND FUTURE INTERESTS PRIMER 6-13, 43-44, 47-48 (3rd ed. 2007).

12. **The best answer is (D).** The problem raises the issue of what quality of title does a party acquire if his or her claim of adverse possession is successful.

Y will claim the back half of Malibuacres based on adverse possession. Adverse possession requires actual entry which gives rise to possession which is open and notorious, exclusive, adverse, under a claim of right, and continuous for the statutory period.

Actual entry, which starts the statute of limitations running on X's claim, is satisfied when the adverse possessor enters the property (assuming all of the elements are present upon entry). Y actually entered the property in 1990 immediately after X left for Europe.

Open and notorious, which requires possession that gives constructive notice to the true owner (if the true owner were to walk the property he or she would notice the adverse possessor) arguably is satisfied here because of the fence which encloses the back half of Malibuacres and the gardening of the enclosed portion. If X had checked the property, he would have noticed the fence and the gardening.

Exclusive possession, which requires the adverse possessor to regulate access to the property as a true owner would, appears satisfied here because Y built a fence around the portion of Malibuacres, which one would assume would keep others off of the enclosed portion, and there is no evidence that anyone else went on to the back half of Malibuacres after Y built the fence.

Adverse, which requires that the adverse possessor be on the property without the true owner's consent – not subservient to the true owner, is satisfied here because there is no evidence that X gave Y permission to X.

The jurisdictions are split as to what claim of right requires. Under the statute of limitation/penalty approach to adverse possession, which puts the spotlight on the adverse possessor and punishes him or her for sleeping on his or her rights, the jurisdictions take an objective approach to the claim of right element, focusing on the adverse possessor's actions. As long as the adverse possessor's actions satisfy the other requirements of the doctrine, the adverse possessor's actions will satisfy the claim of right requirement. Here, as demonstrated above, Y's actions have satisfied the other elements of adverse possession. Under the objective approach, Y has satisfied the claim of right element. Under the earnings/reward approach to adverse possession, which rewards the adverse possessor for putting the land to productive use, the jurisdictions take a subjective approach to the claim of right element, focusing on the adverse possessor's state of mind. The jurisdictions, however, are split between the good faith approach and the bad faith approach. The good faith approach requires the adverse possessor to have a good faith belief that he or she has a rightful claim of ownership to the property. Here, Y knew that he or she had no claim to the property but fenced it in nevertheless. Y would not satisfy the claim of right requirement if the jurisdiction applies the good faith approach. The bad faith approach requires the adverse possessor to know that the land is not his or hers yet intend to claim it anyway. Here, Y knew that the land in question is not hers yet she is claiming it anyway. Y would satisfy the bad faith approach. Y satisfies the claim of right element if the jurisdiction takes the objective approach (the majority approach) or if the jurisdiction takes the subjective bad faith approach (the minority of the minority approach), but not if the jurisdiction takes the good faith approach.

The continuous element requires that the adverse possessor occupy the land as continuously as an average of owner of similarly situated property. Here, Y is living on the land which is connected to the fenced in portion of X's property, and Y is gardening the land in question. It would appear as though Y is occupying the land as continuously as an ordinary owner would

All of the elements must be satisfied for the statutory period. Here, the jurisdiction requires that the elements be satisfied for 10 years. Y entered X's property in 1990, shortly after X left for Europe. All indications are that Y immediately satisfied all six elements (assuming the jurisdiction takes the objective or subjective bad faith to the claim of right element) and has done so for all 10 years. The most likely result is that Y can successfully assert a claim of adverse possession to the back half of Malibuacres. Y's claim vested in 2000, ten years after Y entered.

There is an issue, however, as to what title Y acquired when Y's adverse possession claim vested. A party who successfully establishes adverse possession acquires the quality of title of the party who had the right to possession when the adverse possession began. Here, X had the right to possess Malibuacres when Y began to adversely possess it. Under the traditional common law approach, X's right to possession, however, was only a life estate, not a fee simple absolute (see the answer to problem 11, above). Therefore, Y acquires only a life estate in the back half of Malibuacres, a life estate measured by X's life (a life estate pur autre vie). O still holds the reversion in fee simple absolute.

Answer (A) is incorrect because it fails to acknowledge that Y's claim of adverse possession has vested and that Y has acquired an interest in the back half of Malibuacres. **Answer (B) is incorrect** because it fails to acknowledge that X held only a life estate interest in Malibuacres under the traditional common law approach and that an adverse possessor acquires the quality of title of the party who had the right to possession when the adverse possession began. **Answer (C) is incorrect** because it fails to acknowledge that Y acquired X's life estate, so Y's interest is measured by X's life, not Y's life.

- **Additional references**: *See* 16 RICHARD R. POWELL, POWELL ON REAL PROPERTY ch. 91, §§ 19.01[2]-[7], [12] (Michael Allan Wolf ed., 2000); 10 THOMPSON ON REAL PROPERTY, SECOND THOMAS EDITION §§ 87.05-.11, 87.18 (1998 & Supp. 2006); RALPH E. BOYER ET AL., THE LAW OF PROPERTY: AN INTRODUCTORY SURVEY §§ 4.3, 4.6, 4.8 (4th ed. 1991).

13. **The best answer is (B).** The problem raises the issue of what quality of title does a party acquire if his or her claim of adverse possession is successful.

Y can successfully claim the back half of Malibuacres based on adverse possession (see the answer to problem 12 above). A party who successfully establishes adverse possession acquires the quality of title of the party who had the right to possession when the adverse possession began. Here, X had the right to possess Malibuacres when Y began to adversely possess it. Under *the modern trend approach*, X's right to possession is a fee simple absolute (see the answer to problem 11, above). Therefore, Y acquires fee simple to the back half of Malibuacres.

Answer (A) is incorrect because it fails to acknowledge that Y's claim to the property based on adverse possession has vested and title has been transferred to Y. **Answers (B) and (C) are incorrect** because they fail apply the traditional common law approach to what interest X had in Malibuacres as opposed to the modern trend.

- **Additional references:** *See* 16 RICHARD R. POWELL, POWELL ON REAL PROPERTY ch. 91, § 19.01[12] (Michael Allan Wolf ed., 2000); 10 THOMPSON ON REAL PROPERTY, SECOND THOMAS EDITION § 87.18 (1998 & Supp. 2006); RALPH E. BOYER ET AL., THE LAW OF PROPERTY: AN INTRODUCTORY SURVEY §§ 4.3, 4.6, 4.8 (4th ed. 1991).

14. **The best answer is (A).** Under the traditional common law approach, because the conveyance to X lacked the words of limitation to create a fee simple absolute, X took only a life estate and O retained a reversion in fee simple absolute (see the answer to problem 11 above). Accordingly, when Y's claim to the back half of Malibuacres vested, all Y took was a life estate pur autre vie (a life estate measured by X's life) (see the answer to problem 12 above).

When X died, X's life estate was extinguished. Because Y's interest in the back half of Malibuacres was dependent on X's life estate, when X died Y's interest in Malibuacres was also extinguished. O's reversion in fee simple absolute became possessory. O holds the property in fee simple absolute. Any claim Y has to the property based on adverse possession must start all over again.

Although transfers of title during a claim of adverse possession do not re-start the statutory period, the key here is that the transfer was split *before* the adverse possession began. Where a claim of adverse possession is successful, the adverse possessor acquires the right to possession of the party who has the right to possession on the day the adverse possession began. Here, under the traditional common law approach, Y acquired X's life estate only, so when X died, Y's interest in the property was extinguished and Y must start adversely possessing the property all over again to claim an interest in it.

Answer (B) is incorrect because it assumes that X owned the property in fee simple absolute when X died and had the right to devise it to Z. It fails to acknowledge that under the common law approach X never had a fee simple absolute and it fails to acknowledge that Y took X's interest under adverse possession so X had nothing to devise to Z. **Answer (C) is incorrect** because it fails to acknowledge that under the common law even though Y successfully adversely possessed the land, Y took X's life estate, not fee simple absolute. So when X died, Y's interest in the property was extinguished. **Answer (D) is incorrect** because it fails to recognize that the life estate Y acquired through adverse possession was a life estate pur autre vie based on the duration of X's life, not Y's life. Y acquired X's interest in the back half of Malibuacres, which was a life estate measured by X's life. **Answer (E) is incorrect** because it fails to recognize that under the common law approach X took only a life estate, so X had nothing to devise to Z and Y's interest extinguished when X died.

- **Additional references**: *See* 1 RICHARD R. POWELL, POWELL ON REAL PROPERTY ch. 13, §§ 13.01[3], 13.04[1] (Michael Allan Wolf ed., 2000); 16 POWELL ON REAL PROPERTY ch. 91, § 19.01; 2 THOMPSON ON REAL PROPERTY, SECOND THOMAS EDITION § 17.06 (2004 & Supp. 2006);10 THOMPSON ON REAL PROPERTY § 87.18; PETER T. WENDEL, A POSSESSORY ESTATES AND FUTURE INTERESTS PRIMER 6-13, 43-44, 47-48 (3rd ed. 2007).

15. **The best answer is (C).** Under the modern trend approach, when Y successfully claimed adverse possession of the back half of Malibucares, Y acquired fee simple absolute to the land in question. Accordingly, X had no interest in Malibuacres when he died. X had no interest to convey to Z, and X's death has no effect on Y's interest in Malibuacres. Y continues to hold the back half of Malibuacres in fee simple absolute.

Answer (A) is incorrect because it assumes O retained an interest in the property following the conveyance to X. Under the modern trend, O conveyed a fee simple absolute to X and retained no interest. **Answer (B) is incorrect** because it fails to recognize that Y's adverse possession claim is successful. Because Y's adverse possession is successful, X had no interest to devise to Z. **Answers (D) and (E) are incorrect** because they apply the common law approach and assume that Y acquired only a life estate when Y's adverse possession claim vested. The question calls for application of the modern trend approach which means that X held the land in fee simple absolute, and Y acquired X's fee simple absolute when Y's adverse possession claim vested.

- **Additional references**: *See* 1 RICHARD R. POWELL, POWELL ON REAL PROPERTY ch. 13, §§ 13.01[3], 13.04[1] (Michael Allan Wolf ed., 2000); 16 POWELL ON REAL PROPERTY ch. 91, § 19.01; 2 THOMPSON ON REAL PROPERTY, SECOND THOMAS EDITION § 17.06 (2004 & Supp. 2006);10 THOMPSON ON REAL PROPERTY §

87.18;   PETER T. WENDEL, A POSSESSORY ESTATES AND FUTURE
INTERESTS PRIMER 6-13, 43-44, 47-48 (3rd ed. 2007).

16. **The best answer is (D).**   Under the traditional common approach, X
acquired only a life estate in Malibuacres (see the answer to problem 11
above), so when Y successfully adversely possessed the property, Y
acquired X's life estate only (see the answer to problem 12 above).
Accordingly, when X's life estate terminates upon X's death, O's
reversion became possessory.   O holds the property in fee simple
absolute.   Y must start the adverse possession process all over again,
starting in 2005 when X died.   If Y can meet the requirements of adverse
possession for the statutory period (10 years here), the earliest Y can
successfully claim adverse possession of the back half of Malibuacres in
fee simple absolute is 2015.

Answer (A) is incorrect because it fails to acknowledge that under the
traditional common law approach all Y took when Y successfully
adversely possessed the land against X was X's life estate.   Y's claim to
the land must start all over again when the right to possession shifts to O
upon X's death.   **Answer (B) is incorrect** because it has nothing to
support it other than 2005 is the year X died.   The statute of limitation is
10 years.   Y's interest vested either in 2000 or 2015 depending on
whether X took a life estate or fee simple, respectively.   **Answer (C) is**
incorrect because it assumes the disability doctrine applies from the date
X executed his will.   The disability doctrine applies only if the party who
has the cause of action has a qualifying disability the day the adverse
possession began.   Here, X had no disability when Y began adversely
possessing the property and execution of the will does not re-start the
statutory period.   **Answer (E) is incorrect** because it assumes the
disability doctrine applies to Z's interest in the property.   The disability
doctrine does not apply to X's purported transfer to Z because (1) under
the common law approach X had only a life estate so X had no interest
to transfer to Z, and (2) assuming, *arguendo*, X had a fee simple absolute,
transfers of title after a claim of adverse possession has begun do not re-
start the statutory period.

•   **Additional references:**   *See* 1 RICHARD R. POWELL, POWELL ON
REAL PROPERTY ch. 13, §§ 13.01[3], 13.04[1] (Michael Allan Wolf
ed., 2000); 16 POWELL ON REAL PROPERTY ch. 91, § 19.01; 2
THOMPSON ON REAL PROPERTY, SECOND THOMAS EDITION §
17.06 (2004 & Supp. 2006);10 THOMPSON ON REAL PROPERTY §
87.18;   PETER T. WENDEL, A POSSESSORY ESTATES AND FUTURE
INTERESTS PRIMER 6-13, 43-44, 47-48 (3rd ed. 2007).

17. **The best answer is (A).** Under the modern trend approach, X acquired a fee simple in Malibuacres (see the answer to problem 11 above), so when Y successfully adversely possessed the property, Y acquired a fee simple absolute (see the answer to problem 13 above). Under the modern trend, Y successfully claimed adverse possession of the back half of Malibuacres in fee simple absolute in 2000.

Answer (B) is incorrect because it withholds recognizing Y's claim of adverse possession until X dies. The moment Y met the requirements of adverse possession for the statutory period, in 2000, Y acquired title by operation of law. X's death has no relevance to Y's claim under these facts and rules. **Answer (C) is incorrect** because it assumes that X's execution of a will devising his interest to Z has an effect on Y's claim of adverse possession. It does not because Y's claim had already vested and because execution of a will has no effect upon a testator's (the party who executed the will) property - a will has no effect until the testator dies. **Answer (D) is incorrect** because it assumes that Y's claim for adverse possession must start all over again when X dies. Y's claim would have to start all over again if X held only a life estate, but under the modern trend X held fee simple absolute so Y acquired fee simple absolute and X's death has no effect on Y's claim. **Answer (E) is incorrect** because it assumes the disability doctrine applies to Z's interest in the property. The disability doctrine does not apply to X's purported transfer to Z because (1) under the modern trend approach Y's interest in Malibuacres had already vested in fee simple absolute so X had no interest left when X died, and (2) even assuming, *arguendo*, that X still held title to the back half of Malibuacres, transfers of title after a claim of adverse possession has begun do not re-start the statutory period.

- **Additional references:** *See* 1 RICHARD R. POWELL, POWELL ON REAL PROPERTY ch. 13, §§ 13.01[3], 13.04[1] (Michael Allan Wolf ed., 2000); 16 POWELL ON REAL PROPERTY ch. 91, § 19.01; 2 THOMPSON ON REAL PROPERTY, SECOND THOMAS EDITION § 17.06 (2004 & Supp. 2006);10 THOMPSON ON REAL PROPERTY § 87.18; PETER T. WENDEL, A POSSESSORY ESTATES AND FUTURE INTERESTS PRIMER 6-13, 43-44, 47-48 (3rd ed. 2007).

18. **The best answer is (C).** The problem raises the issue of how an asset should be characterized when separate property and community property funds are commingled to purchase the asset.

There are several different approaches to how to characterize an asset when separate and community property funds are used to purchase the asset: (1) the time of inception approach; (2) the time of vesting approach; (3) the pro rata approach; and (4) the gift approach. The call of the question specifically asks for how the facts would come out under the time of vesting approach.

Under the time of vesting approach, the asset is characterized according to the nature of the funds which were used to "vest" the property interest in the purchasers. The property interest typically vests upon the final payment. Hence the key question is whether separate property funds or community property funds were used to make the final payment. If separate property funds were used, the asset is characterized as separate property. If community property funds were used, the asset is characterized as community property. Here, the final payment was made with community property funds, so under the time of vesting approach, the asset is characterized as a community property asset.

But what about the separate property funds which were contributed toward the purchase price? Under the time of vesting approach, whichever way the asset is characterized, the funds of the different characterization are treated as a loan which has to be paid back, with interest. Under these facts, since the asset is characterized as community property, A's separate property funds which were used to help purchase the asset are treated as a loan from A to the community. This loan has to be paid back first (with interest, but that is beyond the scope of the material), with the remaining balance being the community's interest.

Here, A used (or "loaned") a total of $40,000 of A's separate property. The "loan" is $40,000 because A put down $20,000 of A's separate property and paid an additional $20,000 in principal, for a total of $40,000, before A and B got married and started using community funds to pay off the house. Thus $40,000 is A's separate property, which is deducted from the $1,000,000 sale proceeds. The remaining $960,000 are community funds. As community property, however, upon A's death A is entitled to half of it - or $480,000. Combining A's separate property interest in the asset ($40,000) plus A's half of the community property ($480,000), A's total interest in the sale proceeds is $520,000.

Answer (A) is incorrect because it implicitly mischaracterizes the asset as A's separate property asset without acknowledging that community property funds were used to purchase the asset. Although the time of inception approach would characterize the asset as A's separate property, A would still not be entitled to all $1,000,000 since community funds were also used and need to be taken into consideration. **Answer (B) is incorrect** because although it properly applies the time of vesting approach, it miscalculates how to split the proceeds. Answer B simply splits the $1,000,000 in half as if it were all community property, and then makes B pay all of the $40,000 loan back. The loan was not to B but to the community. The community should pay the loan back. The loan should be paid back first, then the remaining proceeds are split 50-50. **Answer (D) is incorrect** because it implicitly characterizes the asset as community property and splits it half and half without taking into account that separate property funds were also used to purchase the asset. Answer (D) fails to take into account how the loan of separate property assets should be repaid. Answer (D) would be the correct answer if the gift approach were taken. The $40,000 in separate property funds which were used would be considered a "gift" by A to the community with no need to repay it. **Answer (E) is incorrect** because it takes something of the pro rata approach, splitting the asset 40-60 since 40% of the purchase price was paid with A's separate property funds. A, however, would still be entitled to half of the 60% which is characterized as community funds, so answer (E) is incorrect even under the pro rata approach.

- **Additional references:** *See* 7 RICHARD R. POWELL, POWELL ON REAL PROPERTY ch. 53, § 53.03[1] (Michael Allan Wolf ed., 2000); 4 THOMPSON ON REAL PROPERTY, SECOND THOMAS EDITION §§ 37.10(b), 37.14 (2004 & Supp. 2006); WILLIAM B. STOEBUCK & DALE A. WHITMAN, THE LAW OF PROPERTY § 5.15-5.16 (3d ed. 2000).

19. **The best answer is (D).** The first issue is what affect, if any, does a lease have upon property held in joint tenancy.

Traditional common law was very strict about the four unities necessary to create and maintain a joint tenancy: the unities of time, title, interest, and possession. The joint tenants must acquire their interests at the same time (time); they must acquire their interests through the same instrument or by joint adverse possession (title); they must hold equal undivided shares of the same duration (interest); and they must each have a right to possess the whole (possession). A joint tenant can transfer his or her right to possession to another joint tenant without it severing the joint tenancy. If, however, the joint tenant transfers his or her right to possession to someone other than one of the joint tenants, at common law the joint tenancy was severed as to that share.

As applied to the facts of the problem, under the common law approach, when B leased Blackacre to X, that terminated the joint tenancy and converted it into a tenancy in common between A and B, subject to X's ten year lease. Five years later, when B dies devising all of his interest to C, two issues arise. First, what is the effect of B's death, as landlord, upon the lease with X? Second, can a tenant in common devise his or her share?

As to the latter, unlike joint tenancy, which is characterized by its right of survivorship, there is no right of survivorship in a tenancy in common. A tenant in common can devise his or her share as he or she wishes, and in the absence of a will, the interest will pass through intestacy. Assuming B executed a valid will, there is no problem with B devising his interest to C.

Does C take subject to X's leasehold interest? If the lease is either a term of years or a periodic lease, death of either the landlord or the tenant generally is construed as having no affect upon the lease. If, however, the lease is a tenancy at will, death of either party terminates the lease. B leased Blackacre to C for ten years. By all appearances, the lease constitutes a term of years since the exact term of the lease can be calculated (the end date can be determined on the first day of the lease). Since the lease is a term of years, the landlord's death does not affect the lease, and C takes as a tenant in common with A, subject to X's term of years.

Answers (A) and (B) are incorrect because they fail to take into account the common law rule that a lease severs the joint tenancy and converts it into a tenancy in common. Once the joint tenancy is severed, the right of survivorship is destroyed and each tenant in common's interest is devisable and inheritable. Once B leased the property to X, the joint tenancy was severed, destroying the right of survivorship. **Answer (C) is incorrect** because it incorrectly terminates the term of years lease upon the death of the landlord. Neither the death of the landlord nor the death of the tenant generally affects a term of years lease.

- **Additional references**: *See* 7 RICHARD R. POWELL, POWELL ON REAL PROPERTY ch. 50, § 601[2], ch. 51, §§ 617[1], 618, 618[1] (Michael Allan Wolf ed., 2000); 2 POWELL ch. 16, § 16.03[7]; 4 THOMPSON ON REAL PROPERTY, SECOND THOMAS EDITION §§ 31.06(b), 31.08(b), 32.07, 39.06(b)(1) (2004 & Supp. 2006); WILLIAM B. STOEBUCK & DALE A. WHITMAN, THE LAW OF PROPERTY §§ 5.2-5.4, 6.85 (3d ed. 2000).

20. The best answer is (A). The first issue is what affect, if any, does a lease have upon property held in joint tenancy.

Under the modern trend, the key is the intent of the parties, not technical formalities or the unities of time, title, interest and possession. Assuming A and B held Blackacre as true joint tenants and not as tenants in common, under the modern trend the general rule is that one joint tenant's leasing his or her interest to a third party does not affect the joint tenancy. The right to survivorship between the joint tenants remains in effect even after the lease.

Under the facts of the problem, when B dies, under the joint tenancy's right of survivorship, A holds the property outright unless B's will severs the joint tenancy. A will is not effective until the testator dies. The will has no affect on the property while the joint tenant is alive. When the joint tenant dies, the joint tenant's interest is extinguished under the right of survivorship before the will becomes effective. The will does not affect the joint tenancy property and A holds it free of any interest in C.

The more difficult issue is what happens to X's lease. Under the traditional common law, the reasoning would be if X is B's tenant, and B's interest is extinguished, then X's interest must also be extinguished. That reasoning, however, is based upon a more mechanical, traditional property approach to the issue. Under the modern trend, the approach is to focus on the intent of the parties. Inasmuch as B entered into a 10 year term of years lease, B's intent was that X should be entitled to possession for the full term. Under the modern trend, the joint tenant who receives the benefit of the intent based approach (that the joint tenancy remains intact despite one tenant leasing his or her interest) arguably should also bear the burden of the intent based approach (that the leasing joint tenant intended for the tenant to have the right to possession for the term of the lease).

Despite the logic and consistency of this reasoning, however, the courts have applied the traditional right of survivorship view to the issue of whether the lease continues when the leasing co-tenant dies. Under the modern trend intent based approach, the courts reason that the key is the right of survivorship. The leasing co-tenant did not intend to terminate the right of survivorship when the co-tenant leased his or her share. The courts reason that since the right of survivorship remains intact, it must be given effect when the leasing co-tenant dies. A party cannot convey more than he or she owns. When a co-tenant's interest expires, any lease which depends upon that interest likewise is terminated. The co-tenant is deemed not to have intended to terminate the right of survivorship when leasing the jointly held property, but to have intended that the lease is subject to the right of survivorship despite the fact that the lease is a term of years.

Answer (B) is incorrect because it takes the intent based approach too far under current case law. Under the modern trend intent based approach, the intent of the deceased joint tenant saves the right of survivorship despite the lease but does not save the term of years lease from the effect of the right of survivorship. The lease is terminated when the joint tenant's interest is extinguished under the right of survivorship. **Answers (C) and (D) are incorrect** because they fail to take into account the modern trend approach that a lease does not sever the joint tenancy. Despite one joint tenant's leasing his or her right to possession, the joint tenancy and its right of survivorship remain intact.

- **Additional references**: *See* 7 RICHARD R. POWELL, POWELL ON REAL PROPERTY ch. 51, ¶ 617[3] (Michael Allan Wolf ed., 2000); 2 POWELL ch. 16, § 16.03[7][d]; 4 THOMPSON ON REAL PROPERTY, SECOND THOMAS EDITION § 31.08(b) (2004 & Supp. 2006); WILLIAM B. STOEBUCK & DALE A. WHITMAN, THE LAW OF PROPERTY: § 5.4 (3d ed. 2000).

21. **The best answer is (C).** In construing a conveyance, remember to construe comma to comma, distinguishing the words of purchase (the words indicating who is to take the interest) from the words of limitation (the technical words which describe the duration of the estate the party takes).

Reading comma to comma, the first clause is a classic example of a life estate. The words of purchase are "to A." The words of limitation are "for life." A has a life estate.

The future interest following a life estate can only be a reversion (if the future interest is held by the grantor) or a remainder (if the future interest is held by a third party—someone other than the grantor). The express words of purchase in the conveyance indicate that the future interest passes "to A's first child," someone other than the grantor. A's first child holds a remainder.

A remainder is contingent unless the remainder passes the test for being vested. A remainder is vested if the holder of the interest is: (1) born, (2) ascertainable, and (3) there is no express condition precedent (an express condition which the party must satisfy before being entitled to claim the right to possession) in the clause creating the remainder or the preceding clause (reading comma to comma). Is the party who holds the remainder born and ascertainable? At the time of the conveyance, A has a child C. C is born and ascertainable. The clause contains an express condition precedent, the child has to be A's first child. The facts imply that C is A's first child, and there is nothing which contradicts the assumption. Since C is born and ascertainable, and has satisfied the express condition precedent, the remainder is vested.

What is the duration of the remainder? To determine the duration of an interest, the words of limitation in the clause creating the interest are the key. Typically the words of limitation immediately follow the words of purchase. Here, the phrase "and his or her heirs" are the common law words of limitation to create a fee simple. Thus, reading comma to comma, C holds a vested remainder in fee simple – but not absolute since there is qualifying language in the rest of the conveyance. Reading comma to comma, the clause after the clause creating the remainder sets forth the condition that "if none of A's children survive A, then to B and her heirs." The issue is what effect, if any, does the express condition have on C's vested remainder in fee simple.

Wherever a vested remainder in fee simple is qualified, there are two variables to analyze: (1) who holds the future interest, the grantor or a third party (someone other than the original grantor); and (2) is the condition qualifying the remainder a condition which can occur before the remainder becomes possessory or only after the remainder becomes possessory? Here, the express language of the conveyance indicates that the future interest is held by a third party, B. Where the qualifying language in the clause following a vested remainder in fee simple grants the future interest to a third party, the remainder is either a vested remainder subject to divestment (if the qualifying condition is one which can occur *before* the remainder becomes possessory) or a vested remainder subject to an executory limitation (if the qualifying condition can occur *only after* the remainder becomes possessory).

Here, the condition, "but if A is not survived by any children," is a condition to be tested the moment A's dies. The condition must be satisfied *before* the remainder can become possessory. Thus, C's vested remainder in fee simple is a vested remainder in fee simple subject to divestment (in the event A is not survived by children), and the future interest following a vested remainder subject to divestment is an executory interest. B holds an executory interest in fee simple. Since B is taking possession from someone other than the grantor, B's executory interest is a shifting executory interest in fee simple. The future interests are: C has a vested remainder in fee simple, subject to divestment, and B has a shifting executory interest in fee simple.

Answer (A) is incorrect because it fails to take into account that A's first child, C, is born - making what would otherwise be a contingent remainder vested. **Answer (B) is incorrect** because it incorrectly analyzes the nature of the condition qualifying the vested remainder. The express condition in the clause following the clause creating the remainder is a condition precedent, not a condition subsequent. Thus, the remainder is a vested remainder subject to divestment, not subject to an executory limitation. **Answer (D) is incorrect** because it incorrectly analyzes the remainder. Reading comma to comma, the only express condition precedent is that the child has to be A's first child. C is A's first child. The remainder is contingent.

- **Additional references**: *See* CORNELIUS J. MOYNIHAN, INTRODUCTION TO THE LAW OF REAL PROPERTY 123-129 (2d ed. 1988); 3 THOMPSON ON REAL PROPERTY, SECOND THOMAS EDITION §§ 23.01(a), 23.07, 26.01 (2001 & Supp. 2006); PETER T. WENDEL, A POSSESSORY ESTATES AND FUTURE INTERESTS PRIMER 43-44, 47-48, 58-65, 17-31, 103-114 (3rd ed. 2007).

22. **The best answer is (A).** The first issue is which co-tenancy did O create when O conveyed Malibuacres to "to A and B and their heirs jointly." At traditional common law, as long as the four unities of time, title, interest, and possession were present, the default co-tenancy was joint tenancy. The joint tenants must acquire their interests at the same time (time); they must acquire their interests through the same instrument or by joint adverse possession (title); they must have equal undivided shares of the same duration (interest); and they must each have a right to possess the whole (possession). When the four unities are present plus the unity of marriage, the preferred default co-tenancy is tenancy by the entirety.

The conveyance from O to A and B satisfies the four unities necessary for a joint tenancy. A and B acquired their interest in Malibuacres at the same time and through the same instrument (the deed from O). Absent express language to the contrary, it is assumed they acquired equal interests and each had a right to possess the whole. The conveyance from O to A and B jointly created a joint tenancy. (There are no facts indicating whether A and B are married, and even if they were, one of the key characteristics of a tenancy of the entirety is the right of survivorship, so for purposes of this problem, the analysis would be the same.)

A joint tenant can convey his or her interest unilaterally, which terminates the joint tenancy as to that share. When A executed the will devising A's interest to C, what effect, if any, did that have on the joint tenancy? A will is not effective to convey a property interest until the testator's death. The mere execution of a will which purports to convey a property interest in property held in joint tenancy has no effect upon the joint tenancy. Moreover, the key characteristic of the joint tenancy is the right of survivorship which provides that upon the death of one joint tenant, his or her share expires and the interests of the remaining joint tenants are re-calculated.

When A died, A's interest in Malibuacres expired. The will did not sever the joint tenancy. B holds Malibuacres outright as sole owner. The property is no longer held in any co-tenancy. There is no problem then with B entering into a term of years lease with X.

A leasehold interest is freely alienable absent an express approval clause requiring the tenant to get the landlord's consent before transferring. Inasmuch as approval clauses contravene the general public policy favoring alienability of property interests, they are construed narrowly. Under the facts of the problem, although B included an approval clause in the lease with X, the clause only restricts assignments, not subleases.

The issue is whether X assigned or subleased when X transferred all of X's interest in Malibuacres but retained a right of entry clause in the event Y breached the agreement. Traditional common law took a rather mechanical, property based approach to distinguishing between an assignment and a sublease. An assignment is where the tenant transfers all of his or her interest to the subtenant. A sublease is where the tenant transfers something less than all of his or her interest. Here, X transferred all of X's interest but retained a right of re-entry in the event Y breached the agreement. At common law, a right of re-entry is not a property interest but merely a chose in action. Thus, under the traditional common law approach, although not all the courts were in agreement, X appears to have assigned X's interest.

Inasmuch as the agreement between B and X requires X to get B's consent before assigning the property, X has breached the terms of the lease with B. B did not know about the assignment and therefore should not be deemed to have waived B's right to object. B holds Malibuacres subject to X's leasehold interest, but Y's leasehold interest is voidable since the transfer to Y breached the lease.

Answers (B), (C) and (D) are incorrect because C took no interest in Malibuacres. Under the traditional common law analysis, A and B were joint tenants. A's will did not sever the joint tenancy, and upon A's death, A's interest expired before the will becomes effective. B alone owns Malibuacres. **Answer (E) is incorrect** because X's transfer to Y constitutes an assignment, not a sublease, under the traditional common law approach. At common law, a right of re-entry was considered merely a chose in action, not a property interest. Here, X conveyed all of X's interest but reserved a right to re-enter in the event Y breaches. X's conveyance constitutes an assignment, so it breaches the agreement between B and X that X would get B's consent before assigning the property. Since X's transfer to Y breached the lease with B, Y's interest is voidable.

- **Additional references**: *See* 7 RICHARD R. POWELL, POWELL ON REAL PROPERTY ch. 51, ¶¶ 615[1], 616[3] (Patrick J. Rohan ed. 1999); 2 POWELL ch. 16, § 16.03, ch. 17, §§ 17.04[1][b], 17.04[2][a]; 4 THOMPSON ON REAL PROPERTY, SECOND THOMAS EDITION §§ 31.02, 31.06(a)-(b), 39.05(a) (2004 & Supp. 2006); 5 THOMPSON § 42.04(a), (b)(2), (d); WILLIAM B. STOEBUCK & DALE A. WHITMAN, THE LAW OF PROPERTY: §§ 5.3, 6.68 (3d ed. 2000).

23. **The best answer is (A).** As established above (see the answer to question 22), C has no legal right to Malibuacres. C is not a co-tenant. C is a trespasser/adverse possessor.

While the jurisdictions are split over the landlord's duty to provide actual possession to the incoming tenant, even if the jurisdiction recognizes such a duty, the duty applies only to the first day of the lease. B provided X with actual possession on the first day of the lease, and X provided Y with actual possession on the first day of the sublease with Y.
A tenant can sue for breach of the implied covenant of quiet enjoyment if one with a superior right to legal possession disturbs the tenant's quiet enjoyment of the premises. Inasmuch as C has no legal right to possession, neither X nor Y can sue for breach of the covenant of quiet enjoyment. C is a trespasser who enters after the first day of the lease, which means C is the tenant's problem, not the landlord's, under traditional common law analysis.

Answer (B) is incorrect because under the common law approach, A and B were joint tenants with right of survivorship. Upon A's death, A's interest expires before A's will devises A's interest to C. C takes no interest under A's will. When C enters Malibuacres, C has no right to possession. **Answer (C) is incorrect** because a tenant can sue for breach of the covenant of quiet enjoyment if the landlord, or someone claiming through the landlord, or with superior title to the landlord's, evicts the tenant. Here, C has no right to possession, so B is not liable for C's actions. **Answer (D) is incorrect** because even assuming, arguendo, that the jurisdiction requires the landlord to provide actual possession to the tenant and not just legal possession, the duty to provide actual possession is limited to the first day of the lease. Since B provided actual possession to Malibuacres on the first day of the lease to X, B has fulfilled any duty B may have had to provide actual possession.

- **Additional references**: *See* 2 RICHARD R. POWELL, POWELL ON REAL PROPERTY ch. 16B, §§ 16B.02[1][a], 16B.03[2] (Patrick J. Rohan ed. 1999); 5 THOMPSON ON REAL PROPERTY, SECOND THOMAS EDITION § 40.22(b), (b)(1), (c)(5) (1994 & Supp. 2006); WILLIAM B. STOEBUCK & DALE A. WHITMAN, THE LAW OF PROPERTY §§ 6.21, 6.31, 6.34 (3d ed. 2000).

24. **The best answer is (B).** The first issue is which co-tenancy O created when O conveyed Malibuacres to "to A and B and their heirs jointly."

Under the modern trend approach, the default co-tenancy is a tenancy in common. Even if the conveyance satisfies the four unities of time, title, interest, and possession, the co-tenancy is presumed to be a tenancy in common. To opt out of tenancy in common, the deed must express precise language indicating an intent to create a joint tenancy. Such language would need to provide expressly that the conveyance was to "A and B as joint tenants with right of survivorship" or "to A and B as joint tenants with right of survivorship and not as tenants in common." There is no such express language in the conveyance from O to A and B. Under the modern trend approach, A and B would hold the property as tenants in common.

There is no right of survivorship associated with a tenancy in common. Moreover, each tenant in common has the right unilaterally to convey his or her interest, inter vivos or testamentary, to another. When A dies with a properly executed will which purports to convey A's interest in Malibuacres to C, the devise is valid and B and C now hold Malibuacres as tenants in common. Each co-tenant has the right to lease his or her share, but not to bind the share of other co-tenants.

When B enters into a lease with X, B is entitled to lease B's interest to X. B and C hold Malibuacres as tenants in common, subject to X's leasehold interest.

A leasehold interest is freely alienable absent an express approval clause requiring the tenant to get the landlord's consent before transferring. Inasmuch as approval clauses contravene the general public policy favoring alienability of property interests, they are construed narrowly. Under the facts of the problem, although B included an approval clause in the lease with X, the clause only restricts assignments, not subleases.

The issue is whether X assigned or subleased when X transferred all of X's interest in Malibuacres but retained a right of re-entry clause in the event Y breached the agreement. Under the modern trend, the courts look more at the intent of the parties in assessing whether the conveyance is an assignment or a sublease. One could argue that although the tenant retains a right of re-entry in the event of a breach, the parties never intended for the right of re-entry to be effective. For all practical purposes, the parties assumed that the tenant was conveying *all* of his or her interest. Despite this argument, however, the courts have reasoned under the intent based approach, the tenant must not have intended to convey all of his or her interest if the tenant expressly reserves a right to re-enter. As long as the tenant retains *any* interest, even just a right to re-enter in the event the subtenant breaches, the tenant has retained a reversionary interest and has not conveyed all of his or her interest.

Here, when X conveyed X's interest to Y, X retained a right to re-enter in the event Y breached. Under the intent based approach, X intentionally withheld part of his or her interest by retaining the right to re-enter in the event Y breaches. Thus, X did not intend to and has not conveyed all of X's interest. Under the modern trend, if the tenant conveys all of his or her interest but reserves a right of re-entry in the event of a breach, the conveyance is construed as a sublease. Since the modern trend would construe X's conveyance to Y as a sublease, X has not breached the terms of the lease with B, and the conveyance to Y is valid. B holds Malibuacres subject to X's leasehold interest and subject to Y's leasehold claim because X did not breach the terms of the lease with B in subleasing to Y.

Answers (A) and (E) are incorrect because under the modern trend, A and B took as tenants in common. A's devise to C is valid, so B and C hold as tenants in common. B alone does not own the property. **Answer (C) is incorrect** because it fails to reflect that X's transfer to Y did not breach of the terms of X's agreement with B. Under the modern trend, if a tenant conveys all of his or her interest save a right of re-entry in the event of breach, the courts reason that the conveying tenant must have intended to reserve an interest (the right of re-entry). Under the modern trend approach, because X expressly retained a right of re-entry, X must not have intended to convey all of X's interest, so X has not conveyed all of X's interest. Accordingly, X subleased X's interest to Y. Because X subleased X's interest to Y and did not assign the interest, X was not obligated to get B's approval. The conveyance to Y is valid. **Answer (D) is incorrect** because B and C do not hold Malibuacres as joint tenants. A and B held Malibuacres as tenants in common. A's devise to C neither expresses an intent to create a joint tenancy between B and C nor could it create a joint tenancy between B and C because they did not acquire their interests at the same time or through the same instrument. B and C hold as tenants in common. Moreover, B and C hold subject to X and Y's leasehold claims for the reasons set forth above.

- **Additional references**: *See* 7 RICHARD R. POWELL, POWELL ON REAL PROPERTY ch. 50, ¶ 601[2], ch. 51, ¶ 616[1] (Patrick J. Rohan ed. 1999); 2 POWELL ch. 17, §§ 17.04[1][b], 17.04[2]; 4 THOMPSON ON REAL PROPERTY, SECOND THOMAS EDITION §§ 32.06(b)(2), 32.07 (2004 & Supp. 2006); 5 THOMPSON § 42.04(b)-(d); WILLIAM B. STOEBUCK & DALE A. WHITMAN, THE LAW OF PROPERTY §§ 5.2, 6.68 (3d ed. 2000).

25. **The best answer is (B).** As established above (see the answer to question 24), under the modern trend approach, C is a tenant in common with a legal right to possess Malibuacres. As a tenant in common, C has a legal right to possess the whole. When C shows up and takes possession, C is entitled to possess Malibuacres, but not to the exclusion of other co-tenants. Inasmuch as X has leased B's right to possession and then transferred the right to possession to Y, Y stands in the shoes of the co-tenant B and has the same right to possession that C has. When Y attempts to possess Malibuacres but is rebuffed by C, C has ousted Y.

Answers (A), (C), and (D) are incorrect because each answer fails to recognize that C is a co-tenant. Under the modern trend, A's devise of A's interest in Malibuacres is valid. C takes A's share and becomes a tenant in common with B. Although B may lease B's share, B's actions do not bind C or affect C's right to possession. When C enters and excludes X and Y, however, C is committing ouster. X and Y have a legal right to possess Malibuacres since they hold B's right to possession.

- **Additional references**: *See* 7 RICHARD R. POWELL, POWELL ON REAL PROPERTY ch. 50, ¶¶ 601[1], 602[9], 603 (Patrick J. Rohan ed.

1999); 4 THOMPSON ON REAL PROPERTY, SECOND THOMAS EDITION §§ 32.06(a), 32.07(d) (2004 & Supp. 2006); WILLIAM B. STOEBUCK & DALE A. WHITMAN, THE LAW OF PROPERTY §§ 5.2, 5.8 (3d ed. 2000).

PROPERTY
ANSWER KEY AND EXPLANATIONS

EXAM III

1. **The best answer is (D).** At common law, a tenant's principal recourse against a landlord was to claim constructive eviction under the covenant of quiet enjoyment. If the landlord breached a duty which the landlord owed to the tenant, and the conditions which arose as a result of the breach were so egregious as to seriously interfere with the beneficial enjoyment of the property or render the property substantially unsuitable for the purposes for which they were leased, the tenant could claim constructive condition. Under constructive eviction, the tenant had to give the landlord notice of the problem, give the landlord reasonable time to remedy the situation, and then, if the problem was not fixed, vacate in a timely manner.

   A tenant could claim breach of the covenant of quiet enjoyment, however, only if the landlord was responsible for the condition - i.e., if the condition arose as a result of the landlord's breach of a duty which the landlord owed to the tenant. The duty could either be an express duty set forth in the lease, or one of the implied duties at common law: duty to disclose latent defects about which the landlord knew or should have known; duty to maintain common areas; duty to make any promised repairs or repairs the landlord voluntarily undertakes; duty not to fraudulently misrepresent the condition of the property; duty to maintain furnished dwellings leased for short terms; and duty to abate immoral conduct or nuisances which arise on property owned by the landlord.

   The first issue is whether the fact that the only elevator is broken seriously interferes with Gerri's beneficial enjoyment of her apartment and renders the apartment substantially unsuitable for the purposes for which it was leased - living in. On the one hand, the fact that the elevator is broken does not affect the conditions within the apartment at all. The problem is one of access. Should Gerri be forced to walk the full 30 floors each time she wants to enter and exit her apartment? Arguably not. The beneficial use and suitability of the apartment for the purposes for which it was leased should be construed as including reasonable access to the apartment. Having to walk up and down 30 flights of stairs each time she wants to enter and exit her apartment seriously interferes with Gerri's beneficial enjoyment of her apartment and renders the apartment substantially unsuitable for the purposes for which it was leased. Arguably, the broken elevator has constructively evicted Gerri. The facts indicate that Gerri gave Louie notice of the problem, gave him reasonable time to remedy the situation, and then, after the problem continued, vacated in a timely manner. The issue is whether the problem is a breach of a duty Louie owed Gerri.

Because the facts fail to indicate whether there are any express duties under the terms of the lease, Gerri's only option is to invoke one or more of the implied duties. Of the six implied duties, one appears to impose a legal duty on Louie which he breached under the facts. Louie has a duty to maintain the common areas. Clearly the elevator constitutes a critical common area which the tenants need to reach their apartments. Although an argument can be made that the tenants still have access via the stairs, inability to use an elevator arguably constitutes a breach of the duty to maintain the common areas. Permitting the landlord to pick and choose which common areas to maintain after the tenants entered into the lease would effectively be permitting the landlord to change the understanding of the parties after the lease has been executed.

Assuming that Gerri has been constructively evicted, the issue still remains whether the eviction is complete or partial. If the tenant is actually evicted, the tenant is relieved of all obligation to pay rent regardless of whether the eviction is partial or complete. But if the eviction is merely constructive, many courts hold that where the eviction is merely partial eviction, the tenant is not relieved of all duty to pay rent but rather the rent is merely abated. Inasmuch as Gerri has been evicted only from her use of the elevator, but not her penthouse apartment, at best Gerri has only been partially evicted.

This partial eviction, however, is different from the classic partial eviction scenario. Gerri has not been constructively evicted from one room of her apartment, or from a closet, she has been evicted from the only reasonable means of accessing her whole apartment. Denying her sole reasonable means of accessing her apartment effectively denies her use of the whole apartment. So while in one respect her eviction is merely partial, in terms of its affect upon her ability to use and enjoy the premises for the purposes for which they were leased, the eviction is tantamount to a complete eviction. Gerri should be relieved of her obligation to pay any rent, even though one can argue that her eviction is merely partial.

Answer (A) is incorrect because it overlooks the landlord's implied duty to maintain the common areas. Louie has a duty to maintain the elevator, and he has breached that duty. **Answer (B) is incorrect** because it fails to take into account that the common areas are part of the leased premises. The landlord's duty to the tenant under the covenant of quiet enjoyment extends beyond the physical boundaries of the apartment the tenant is leasing. **Answer (C) is incorrect** because although Gerri has been deprived only of her ability to use the elevator, her inability to use the elevator has effectively deprived her of her ability to use and enjoy her apartment for the purposes for which they were leased. To ask a tenant to walk up and down 30 flights of stairs each time the tenant wished to exit and enter the apartment is an unreasonable interference with the tenant's use of the leased premises.

- **Additional references**: *See* 2 RICHARD R. POWELL, POWELL ON REAL PROPERTY ch. 16B, §§ 16B.03, 16B.04[2] (Patrick J. Rohan ed. 1999); 5 THOMPSON ON REAL PROPERTY, SECOND THOMAS EDITION §§ 40.22(c)(1)-(3), 40.23(c)(8) (1994 & Supp. 2006); WILLIAM B. STOEBUCK & DALE A. WHITMAN, THE LAW OF PROPERTY §§ 6.30, 6.33 (3d ed. 2000).

2. **The best answer is (D).** (The answer is the same under the modern trend as it was under the common law, but the controlling doctrine and analysis is different.) Under the modern trend approach, the implied warranty of habitability provides that the landlord has the duty to provide and maintain habitable premises. What constitutes habitable premises varies from jurisdiction to jurisdiction, but the standard appears to be what a reasonable person would consider habitable.

Applying the reasonable person approach, there appears to be little doubt that a reasonable person would think that requiring a tenant to walk up and down 30 flights of stairs each time the time wished to go out is unreasonable. Louie, however, can counter that the purpose of the implied warranty of habitability is to insure that the premises are safe and healthy. The penthouse is still safe and healthy. The problem is that requiring tenants to walk up and down 30 flights of stairs to reach their apartments arguably is not safe and healthy.

On balance, under the modern trend the courts are more likely to find that a reasonable person would conclude that requiring Gerri to walk up and down 30 flights of stairs is unreasonable and in breach of the implied warranty of habitability. Although the exact scope of the implied warranty of habitability is unclear, under the circumstances use of the elevator to reach the apartment appears to be an essential part of the lease.

The remedies for breach of the implied warranty of habitability are the basic contract remedies of damages, rescission, and reformation. If Gerri wishes to rescind the lease, she should be entitled to walk away without any liability and she may be entitled to damages.

Answer (A) is incorrect because under the modern trend, the tenant's duty to pay rent is dependent upon the landlord's duty to provide habitable premises. Assuming that the elevator is considered an essential part of the premises, the landlord has a duty to maintain the elevator under the implied warranty. **Answer (B) is incorrect** because it fails to take into account that the common areas may be considered an essential part of the leased premises. The landlord's duty to the tenant under the implied warranty of habitability is to provide habitable premises, which may extend beyond the physical boundaries of the apartment the tenant is leasing depending on the circumstances. **Answer (C) is incorrect** because the remedies for breach of the implied warranty of habitability include the basic contract remedies, including rescission. Gerri is entitled to rescind the lease and walk away with no liability.

- **Additional references**: *See* 2 RICHARD R. POWELL, POWELL ON REAL PROPERTY ch. 16B, §§ 16B.03, 16B.04[2] (Patrick J. Rohan ed. 1999); 5 THOMPSON ON REAL PROPERTY, SECOND THOMAS EDITION §§ 40.22(c)(1)-(3), 40.23(c)(8)   (1994 & Supp. 2006); WILLIAM B. STOEBUCK & DALE A. WHITMAN, THE LAW OF PROPERTY §§ 6.38, 6.41, 6.42 (3d ed. 2000).

3. **The best answer is (E).** At common law, as long as the four unities of time, title, interest, and possession where satisfied, the default estate was joint tenancy. The unity of time required the parties to acquire their interests at the same time. The unity of title required the parties to acquire their interest through the same instrument. The unity of interest required the parties to hold equal shares of the same duration. The unity of possession required the parties to each hold the right to possess the whole.

When O conveyed to A and B, A and B acquired equal one half interests at the same time through the same instrument and each had an equal right to possess the whole. The express language of the deed, that A and B hold "as joint tenants and not as tenants in common" also supports the characterization that A and B hold as joint tenants. Joint tenants have the power unilaterally to transfer their interests inter vivos. If a joint tenant transfers his or her interest, however, the transfer breaks the unities as to the share transferred. B has the power to unilaterally transfer B's half interest to B and C. A will now hold A's share as tenant in common with the holder of B's share.

The issue is how to characterize the title to the one half interest B transferred to B and C. The express language of the deed from B to B and C indicates an intent to create a tenancy by the entirety. A tenancy by the entirety requires the 4 unities of a joint tenancy plus the fifth unity of marriage. The problem is that B conveyed B's share to B and C at the rehearsal dinner before they were married. Since delivery occurred prior to marriage, the fifth unity is lacking and B and C cannot hold a tenants by the entirety. Inasmuch as one of the key characteristics of the tenancy of the entirety is the right of survivorship, one might argue that B and C should be deemed to hold their interest as joint tenants so they can have the right of survivorship. The problem with that argument, as applied to the facts, is that B acquired B's interest through the O to A and B deed. At common law, if one wanted to create a joint tenancy in property which one already held, the owner had to use a straw party to satisfy the four unities (particularly the unities of time and title). Because B did not use a straw party, B's failure to meet the 4 unities means that when B conveyed to B and C, B and C took B's interest as tenants in common. Although joint tenancy is closer to the concurrent estate B wanted to create, tenancy by the entirety (because both have the right of survivorship), at common law the rules were strictly enforced. B's intent is irrelevant. B and C would hold as tenants in common.

Tenants in common can freely transfer their interest without affecting the tenancy in common. B can lease B's interest in Blackacre without it affecting the tenancy in common which B shares with C and with A.

Answer (A) is incorrect because joint tenants may unilaterally sever the joint tenancy. B severed the joint tenancy when B conveyed B's half interest to B and C. **Answer (B) is incorrect** because to create a tenancy by the entirety the unities of time, title, interest, possession and marriage must be present at the time of conveyance. B and C were not married, so they cannot hold the share as tenants by the entirety (in addition, since B's interest predated C's interest, to satisfy the unities of time and title, B needed to use a straw party under the common law approach). **Answers (C) and (D) are incorrect** because at common law, to create a joint tenancy the unities of time, title, interest and possession must be present at the time of conveyance. Since B's interest predated C's interest, to satisfy the unities of time and title, B needed to use a straw party under the common law approach.

• **Additional references**: *See* 7 RICHARD R. POWELL, POWELL ON REAL PROPERTY ch. 51, ¶¶ 615[1], 618[1][a], ch. 52, ¶ 621[1] (Patrick J. Rohan ed. 1999); 4 THOMPSON ON REAL PROPERTY, SECOND THOMAS EDITION §§ 31.06(a), 31.06(c), 31.07, 31.08(b), 32.06(a), 33.06(a) (2004 & Supp. 2006); ROGER A. CUNNINGHAM ET AL., THE LAW OF PROPERTY: AN INTRODUCTORY SURVEY §§ 5.2-5.5 (3d ed. 2000).

4. **The best answer is (C).** The modern trend focuses much more on the intent of the parties as opposed to the four unities. Under the modern trend, the default estate is tenancy in common unless the parties adequately express an intent to opt out of tenancy in common.

When O conveyed to A and B, the express language in the deed indicated the intent that A and B hold "as joint tenants and not as tenants in common." Although this language is not enough in some jurisdictions to opt out of tenancy in common (because it fails to refer expressly to the right of survivorship), in most jurisdictions it adequately expresses the intent to create a joint tenancy. Joint tenants have the power unilaterally to transfer their interests inter vivos. If a joint tenant transfers his or her interest, however, the transfer breaks the unities as to the share transferred. B has the power unilaterally to transfer B's interest to B and C. A now holds A's share as a tenant in common with the holders of B's share.

The issue is how to characterize B's share now that B and C hold it. The express language of deed from B to B and C indicates an intent to create a tenancy by the entirety. A tenancy by the entirety requires the 4 unities of a joint tenancy plus the fifth unity of marriage. Under the modern trend, many jurisdictions no longer recognize tenancy by the entirety, but assuming the jurisdiction still does, the problem is that B conveyed B's share to B and C at the rehearsal dinner before they were married. Since delivery occurred prior to marriage, the fifth unity is lacking and B and C cannot hold as tenants by the entirety. Inasmuch as one of the key characteristics of the tenancy of the entirety is the right of survivorship, a strong argument can be made that B and C should be deemed to hold their interest as joint tenants so they can have the right of survivorship. The joint tenancy is closest to B's intent. Moreover, although at common law, if one wanted to create a joint tenancy in property which one already held, the owner had to use a straw party to satisfy the four unities (particularly the unities of time and title), the modern trend no longer requires the "two to transfer" requirement. B could transfer from B to B and C as joint tenants.

Lastly, although at common law a lease was deemed to terminate the tenant's unity of possession, thus severing the joint tenancy, the modern trend is to assume that a joint tenant did not intend to sever a joint tenancy by entering into a lease. B can lease B's interest in Blackacre without affecting the joint tenancy which B shares with C. A holds a half interest in tenancy in common with B and C, who hold as joint tenants. B's lease to X is valid, and, under the modern trend, the lease does not affect the joint tenancy between B and C.

Answer (A) is incorrect because joint tenants may unilaterally sever the joint tenancy. B severed the joint tenancy when B conveyed B's half interest to B and C. **Answer (B) is incorrect** because to create a tenancy by the entirety, the unities of time, title, interest, possession and marriage must be present at the time of conveyance. B and C were not married, so they cannot hold the share as tenants by the entirety. **Answer (D) is incorrect** because it applies the common law rule as to the issue of what effect, if any, does one joint tenant's leasing his or her share have upon the joint tenancy. At common law, the lease severed the joint tenancy and turned it into a tenancy in common. The modern trend approach assumes that the joint tenant did not intend to break the joint tenancy, so it remains intact despite the lease. **Answer (E) is incorrect** because it applies the common law approach to B and C's failed attempt at a tenancy by the entirety. The modern trend looks more to the intent of the parties. Although B and C did not properly create a tenancy by the entirety, under the modern trend the joint tenancy is closer to their intent since both have the right of survivorship. The modern trend would hold B and C to be joint tenants.

- **Additional references**: *See* 7 RICHARD R. POWELL, POWELL ON REAL PROPERTY ch. 51, ¶¶ 615[1], 618[1][a], 618[1][b], ch. 52, ¶ 621[1] (Patrick J. Rohan ed. 1999); 4 THOMPSON ON REAL PROPERTY, SECOND THOMAS EDITION §§ 31.06(a), 31.06(c), 31.07, 31.08(b), 32.06(a), 33.06(a) (2004 & Supp. 2006); WILLIAM B. STOEBUCK & DALE A. WHITMAN, THE LAW OF PROPERTY §§ 5.2-5.5 (3d ed. 2000).

5. **The best answer is (D).** Each co-tenant has an equal right to possession. When one co-tenant enters into a lease with a non-co-tenant, the non-co-tenant receives only the leasing co-tenant's right to

possession, no more. The other co-tenants still have the right to enter and possess the property. If the leasee ousts the other co-tenants, the leasee is liable to the other co-tenants for rent (calculated as each co-tenant's share of the fair market value of the property). If the leasee does not oust the other co-tenants, the co-tenants are only entitled to seek an accounting from the leasing co-tenant to receive their share of the actual rent from the leasing co-tenant. If the leasing co-tenant has leased only his or her share of the property (as reflected by the actual rent under the lease versus the leasing co-tenant's share of the fair market rent), the non-leasing co-tenants are not entitled to any of the rent received.

Ouster occurs when a co-tenant not in possession attempts to enter and is barred from entering. The modern trend does not require the co-tenant out of possession to have to seek entry where it is clear that the party in possession will not permit it (so as to avoid the potential for violence). Under either the traditional rule or the modern trend, there arguably is not enough evidence that X would have barred C from entering if C had requested permission to enter. X may have changed the locks simply to protect X and his or her belongings. C never asked for permission to enter Blackacre. C simply assumed that X's changing the locks meant that X would not permit C to enter. C was not barred from entering, and even under the modern trend, there does not appear to be enough evidence to conclude that X would have barred C if C had attempted to enter.

X has not ousted C and therefore is not liable to C for rent. If X were liable to C for rent, C would receive C's share of the fair market value from X. The fair market value is $10,000 a month. C's share is half of B's share, which is half of Blackacre (A holds the other half). C owns a 25% share of Blackacre, so C would be entitled to $2,500 if C had been ousted. Although C was not ousted, C can seek an accounting from B and is entitled to C's share of the actual rents B is receiving. X pays B $8,000 a month. B's 25% of $8,000 is $2,000 a month. C will receive less than C would if X had ousted C.

Answers (A) and (B) are incorrect because X's conduct does not rise to the level of ouster. At common law, the co-tenant out of possession had to attempt physically to take possession of the property and be denied possession. There is no evidence C ever attempted to take possession and was denied. Although the modern trend does not require the co-tenant out of possession to attempt to take possession where it is clear such attempt would be denied, there is no such evidence here. X may have changed the locks not to exclude C, but merely for security purposes. **Answer (C) is incorrect** because ouster entitles the co-tenant to his or her share of the fair market rental value of the property. In an accounting, the co-tenant is entitled to only his or her share of the actual rents received if the leasing co-tenant has leased more than merely his or her share. Here, B has leased more than B's share, but at a rate below market. C will not be entitled to as much from an accounting as C would have received if C had been ousted.

- **Additional references:** *See* WILLIAM B. STOEBUCK & DALE A. WHITMAN, THE LAW OF PROPERTY § 5.8 (3d ed. 2000); 7 RICHARD R. POWELL, POWELL ON REAL PROPERTY ch. 50, ¶¶ 603[1], 604[1] (Patrick J. Rohan ed. 1999); 4 THOMPSON ON REAL PROPERTY, SECOND THOMAS EDITION §§ 31.07(c), 32.07(c) (2004 & Supp. 2006).

6. **The best answer is (B).** At common law, the law of waste provided that a tenant had the duty to return the property to the landlord in basically the same condition as the property was in when the tenant received it (except for reasonable wear and tear). Under affirmative waste, the tenant could not make substantial changes to the property, even if the changes arguably were improvements which increased the value of the property. Under permissive waste, the tenant could not stand by and let the property deteriorate even if the deterioration was due to natural causes. The effect of the doctrine of waste was to place the burden of repair on the tenant.

The contractual provision in the lease between B and X providing that X has the duty to repair the premises is consistent with the traditional common law doctrine of waste. Under the modern trend approach, however, the implied warranty of habitability provides that the landlord has the duty to provide and maintain habitable premises. The provision in the lease between B and X providing that X has the duty to repair the premises is inconsistent with the duty placed on the landlord under the implied warranty of habitability.

The issue is whether the parties can contract out of the implied duties under the implied warranty of habitability. Although the modern trend approach generally takes more of a contractual view of the landlord-tenant relationship, as opposed to the traditional common law property approach, the modern trend also takes a more pro-tenant status approach. At least in the residential context, the assumption is that the parties lack equal bargaining power - that the typical residential tenant has no real power to negotiate terms and conditions in a lease. Because of this, the general rule is that parties to a residential lease cannot shift the duty to repair under the implied warranty of habitability from the landlord to the tenant. (Although there is some authority that the parties can shift the duty to repair to the tenant in a commercial setting, the facts here support the conclusion that the lease is a residential lease.)

Answer (A) is incorrect because it implicitly represents that the tenant's duty to repair is the same under the common law and modern trend, which is not the case. Under the common law duty not to commit waste, the tenant has the duty to repair. Under the modern trend implied warranty of habitability, the landlord has the duty to repair, and the duty cannot be shifted contractually - at least not in residential leases. **Answer (C) is incorrect** because although it implicitly recognizes that the common law and modern trend are different, it confuses the two. The landlord prevails under the common law approach and not under the modern trend approach. **Answer (D) is incorrect** because it implicitly represents that the tenant's duty to repair is the same under the common law and modern trend, which is not the case.

- **Additional references:** *See* 2 RICHARD R. POWELL, POWELL ON REAL PROPERTY ch. 16B, §§ 16B.04[2], [2][d], [3][a][i] (Patrick J. Rohan ed. 1999); 5 THOMPSON ON REAL PROPERTY, SECOND THOMAS EDITION §§ 40.23(b), 40.23(c)(8) (1994 & Supp. 2006); 8 THOMPSON § 70.08(b)(3)(i)-(iii); WILLIAM B. STOEBUCK & DALE A. WHITMAN, THE LAW OF PROPERTY §§ 6.36, 6.38, 6.40 (3d ed. 2000).

7. **The best answer is (A).** Under the traditional common law approach, a landlord is entitled to use self-help in evicting a tenant only if the landlord is entitled to legal possession and the landlord uses no more force than reasonably necessary. A landlord is entitled to legal possession when the tenant holds over or if the lease has a right of re-entry clause in the event the tenant breaches the lease.

X is not holding over, so B is entitled to legal possession only if there is a right of re-entry clause and breach which permits B to retake legal possession. The lease expressly provides: "that B may use self-help eviction as long as the means of re-entry are peaceable;" and "that X may not assign without B's consent." A right of re-entry clause must be express. B's best argument is that the clause authorizing B to use self-help eviction should be construed as implicitly including the right to re-enter in the event of a breach. X's counter-arguments are: (1) that there is no express reference to any right to re-enter, (2) that the lease should be construed against the drafter (the landlord usually which would be B here), and (3) that the clause authorizing self-help was intended to apply only to holdover situations and not to include any right to re-enter.

Even assuming, *arguendo*, that B prevails and a court were prone to construe the clause authorizing the right to use self-help as including the right to re-enter upon a breach of the lease, there is still the question of whether X has breached the lease. The lease expressly provides that X may not assign without B's consent. Such approval clauses reduce the alienability of the property and generally are construed narrowly. Since the clause makes express reference to requiring consent only if the tenant wants to assign, the clause should be construed narrowly not to apply to subleasing.

An assignment is when the tenant transfers all of his or her interest. A sublease is when the tenant transfers something less than all of his or her interest. Here, X has not transferred all of X's interest but has retained the last two days of the original term. While this short reversion may appear to be a sham reversion simply to avoid the express restriction against assignments, the common law courts permitted such arrangements. Moreover, the fact that the parties called the agreement "an assignment" or used the word "assign" is not controlling under the mechanical, common law approach. Under a traditional property approach, an assignment required the tenant to transfer *all* of the tenant's interest. X has not transferred all of X's interest, so X has not assigned X's interest but rather has only subleased X's interest. Thus, there is no breach of the lease permitting B to exercise B's right to re-enter even assuming a court were to construe the lease as containing a right to re-enter.

Answer (B) is incorrect because even assuming a landlord is entitled to legal possession, a landlord is entitled to use self-help eviction only if the landlord uses no more force than reasonably necessary. Here, B used no more force than reasonably necessary. B merely changed the locks while X was away. B did not use too much force under the common law standard. **Answer (C) is incorrect** because X's agreement with Y did not breach the lease restriction against assignment. The lease provision does not apply to subleases. Under the common law approach, an assignment occurred if the tenant conveyed *all* of his or her interest. Since X retained the last two days of the original term, X did not give up all of X's interest in the lease. X did not assign X's interest. X merely subleased part of X's interest. **Answer (D) is incorrect** because even if B used only as much force as necessary in retaking possession, a landlord is only entitled to use self-help eviction if the landlord is legally entitled to possession. Here, since X's agreement with Y did not breach the lease, B is not legally entitled to possession.

- **Additional references:** *See* 2 RICHARD R. POWELL, POWELL ON REAL PROPERTY ch. 17, §§ 17.01, 17.02[1][a], 17.04[1][b], 17.04[2][a], 17.02 (Patrick J. Rohan ed. 1999); 5 THOMPSON ON REAL PROPERTY, SECOND THOMAS EDITION §§ 40.08(b)(3), 40.09, 42.04(b)-(d) (1994 & Supp. 2006); WILLIAM B. STOEBUCK & DALE A. WHITMAN, THE LAW OF PROPERTY §§ 6.67, 6.68, 6.78, 6.80 (3d ed. 2000).

8. **The best answer is (B).** If a tenant holds over after the proper termination of a lease, the landlord has the option of treating the tenant as a trespasser and ejecting the tenant, or the landlord may treat the tenant as a holdover tenant for a new term. At common law, the new term depended on the term of the original lease. If the original lease was a term of years, as a general rule the new term would be a tenancy from year to year.

Here, Betsy did not move out by December 31, 2006 as required under the terms of the original lease. A strict approach to the traditional common law holdover doctrine would conclude that Betsy is liable for a new year to year lease. Even at common law, however, some courts held that where the holdover is involuntary, the tenant should not be liable as a holdover tenant. Those courts took more of an intent based approach, reasoning that the tenant should not be liable as a holdover tenant unless the tenant was at fault to some degree. Inasmuch as the modern trend is for the courts to be more intent based, and pro-tenant, coupled with the general judicial dislike for the somewhat harsh consequences under the holdover doctrine, the most likely result is that Betsy will not be liable under the holdover doctrine. She did not intend to holdover. Her injury forced her to delay her departure. Under the circumstances, the most likely result is that Betsy will not be liable under the holdover doctrine.
Although Betsy most likely will not be liable under the holdover doctrine, she did remain in possession of the premises for an additional three days. She probably will be held liable under a quantum meruit theory for the three additional days that she was in possession of the premises. As a matter of fairness, the tenant should be liable for the days she remained in possession and the landlord was unable to collect rent for those days.

Answer (A) is incorrect because it fails to take into account that Betsy had the benefit of the premises for the three days she remained in possession unexpectedly. Although Betsy did not intend to remain in possession, it would seem only fair to permit the landlord to recover at least for the days which she actually held over. **Answers (C), (D) and (E) are incorrect** because they fail to take into account the modern trend, intent based approach which holds that the tenant is not liable under the holdover tenant doctrine if the tenant holds over involuntarily.

- **Additional references**: *See* 2 RICHARD R. POWELL, POWELL ON REAL PROPERTY ch. 17, § 17.06 (Patrick J. Rohan ed. 1999); 5 THOMPSON ON REAL PROPERTY, SECOND THOMAS EDITION § 40.10(d) (1994 & Supp. 2006); WILLIAM B. STOEBUCK & DALE A. WHITMAN, THE LAW OF PROPERTY § 6.20 (3d ed. 2000).

9. **The best answer is (D).** Property rights are relative. Although one who steals or converts property to his own use does not thereby acquire title to it but rather holds the property subject to the rights of the true owner, one who wrongfully holds possession will prevail against all but those with a superior claim.

Although Conrad obtained possession of the wild rice wrongfully, Conrad's right to possession is superior to all but the true owner's claim. The state of Idaho, as joint owner of the land from which the rice was taken, is part owner of the rice and therefore has a superior claim to half of the rice based on its joint ownership of the land in question. As to half of the money, the state has a superior claim and is entitled to half of the money. As to the other half, however, the true owner is the National Forest Service. The National Forest Service, however, has not stepped forward and asserted a claim to that half of the proceeds. Until the true owner asserts its rights, the party in possession has a superior claim.

Courts do not go out and look for true owners or notify them of potential claims. Absent a claim by the National Forest Service, as between the state and Conrad, Conrad prevails as to the National Forest Service's half under first in time, first in right.
Answer (A) is incorrect because Conrad was not first in time, first in right. The property is owned by the state of Idaho and the National Forest Service. They own the property jointly under first in time, first in right. Their rights to the property include the right to the crops growing on the property, which they constructively possess. Their rights, if properly asserted, are first in time, first in right over Conrad's claim.
Answer (B) is incorrect because it fails to recognize that property rights are relative. One who wrongfully obtains possession retains possession against all but the true owner. Conrad is entitled to keep the money

wrongfully obtained until those with a superior right to the money come forward and assert their rights. **Answer (C) is incorrect** because concurrent owners can only assert a claim to their share of the property in question. The state of Idaho has a half interest in the property. The state of Idaho can claim only half of the proceeds from the sale of the rice. The state cannot assert the claim of the other concurrent owner. **Answer (E) is incorrect** because courts do not decide the rights of parties not before the court, nor do courts go out and notify parties of their rights in matters currently pending before the court. If the party does not come into court and assert their rights, the courts resolve disputes based upon the relative rights of the parties before the court.

- **Additional references**: *See* 2 THOMPSON ON REAL PROPERTY, SECOND THOMAS EDITION § 13.03(b) (2000 & Supp. 2006); RALPH E. BOYER ET. AL., THE LAW OF PROPERTY: AN INTRODUCTORY SURVEY § 1.1 (4th ed. 1991); WILLIAM B. STOEBUCK & DALE A. WHITMAN, THE LAW OF PROPERTY § 1.3 (3d ed. 2000); Gissel v. State, 727 P.2d 1153 (Idaho 1986).

10. **The best answer is (E). (If you applied the modern trend and assumed that Paris received fee simple as opposed to merely a life estate, the best answer is (C).)** The key to analyzing possessory estate and future interest problems is to read and construe comma to comma, paying particular attention to the words of limitation used. The first clause conveys the property "to Nicole for life, ..." The words of purchase, "to Nicole" indicate that Nicole holds the possessory estate. The words of limitation, "for life," are the classic words used to create a life estate, one of the finite estates. Nicole holds a life estate.

The second clause conveys the property "then to Paris as long as she does not go to jail again, ..." The words of purchase "to Paris" indicate that Paris holds the future interest following Nicole's possessory estate. Nicole holds a finite estate. The future interest following a finite estate must be either a reversion (if the future interest is held by the grantor) or a remainder (if the future interest is held by someone other than the grantor). Since Paris is not the grantor, Paris holds a remainder.

A remainder is contingent unless it meets the test for vested. To be vested, the party holding the remainder must be (1) born, (2) ascertainable, and (3) there must be no express condition precedent in the same clause creating the remainder or the preceding clause (reading comma to comma). Paris is born and ascertainable. The only issue is whether there is an express condition precedent, a condition which Paris must satisfy before she can claim the right to possession. There is no express condition precedent in the clause preceding the clause creating the remainder in Paris. There is an express condition in the clause creating the remainder. Paris gets the property "as long as she does not go to jail again, ..." Careful analysis of the condition, however, indicates that it is not a condition precedent but a condition subsequent. The phrase "as long as" is classic condition subsequent introductory language. The condition subsequent controls how long Paris gets to keep the right to possession after she takes possession. Since Paris is born, ascertainable, and there is no condition precedent, Paris holds a vested remainder. But of what duration?

Looking for the express words of limitation to see how long Paris will get to keep possession once she takes it, the words are conspicuous by their absence. None of the classic words of limitation are present, only the phrase "to Paris . . . ." Under the modern trend, the grantor is presumed to convey all that the grantor holds, so a strong presumption would arise that Paris holds a fee simple, but subject to the express condition subsequent. At common law, however, the default estate (if the proper words of limitation are not used) is a life estate. The call of the question specifically asks for the state of the title at common law. Paris holds a life estate. The life estate may be cut short, however, if Paris goes to jail again.

In analyzing a life estate which may be cut short, the keys are (1) who is to take the right to possession in the event the finite estate is cut short, the grantor or someone else, and (2) the words of limitation used to introduce the condition subsequent. If the future interest following the finite estate being cut short goes to someone other than the grantor, the critical question is whether the third party is to take the future interest *only* if the life estate is cut short, or regardless of whether the life estate is cut short. If the former, then the grantor holds the future interest in the event the life estate is not cut short. If the latter, the third party is the only party holding a future interest.

Whether the identified party takes the future interest only if the condition occurs or regardless of whether the condition occurs turns on the intent of the grantor as expressed in the express words of limitation introducing the condition. The words "as long as" typically indicate that the party holding the future interest takes regardless of whether the finite estate ends early. The words of limitation "but if" typically indicate that the party holding the future interest takes *only* if the finite estate ends early. Here, the conveyance contains both clauses. The "but if" clause, however, arguably indicates that Lindsay is to take only if Paris goes to jail again. Therefore, if Paris does not go to jail again, the grantor, Olivia, holds the future interest following Paris's life estate.

Since the future interest is split depending on whether the condition subsequent occurs or not, this is reflected in the terminology for the estates. Paris holds a life estate subject to an executory limitation, Lindsay holds a shifting executory interest in fee simple, and Olivia holds a reversion in fee simple.

Answers (A), (B) and (C) are incorrect because they apply the modern trend to the question of Paris's possessory estate. The call of the question, however, specifically asks for the common law approach to the conveyance. At common law, the default estate is the life estate. Since the words of limitation necessary to create a fee simple ("and his heirs") are not present, Paris holds the default estate, a life estate. (Under the modern trend, answer (C) would be the correct answer since the fee simple is being cut short and the future interest is held by a third party.) **Answer (D) is incorrect** because the clause "but if" indicates that Lindsay is to take the right to possession *only* if Paris goes to jail again. If Paris does not go to jail again, the future interest is not expressly provided for, so it goes to the default taker: the grantor.

- **Additional references:** *See* CORNELIUS J. MOYNIHAN, INTRODUCTION TO THE LAW OF REAL PROPERTY 43-46, 108-110, 117-131 (2d ed. 1988); PETER T. WENDEL, A POSSESSORY ESTATES AND FUTURE INTERESTS PRIMER 43-44, 47-48, 58-65, 137-41 (3rd ed. 2007); 2 RICHARD R. POWELL, POWELL ON REAL PROPERTY ch. 15, ¶ 202[1] (Patrick J. Rohan ed. 1999); 3 POWELL ch. 20, §§ 20.04[1], 20.05[2], ch. 21 § 21.02[1][b]; 2 THOMPSON ON REAL PROPERTY, SECOND THOMAS EDITION §§ 17.02, 19.01,19.03 (2000 & Supp. 2006), 3 THOMPSON §§ 22.01, 23.01(a).

11. **The best answer is (A).** There are two federal statutes designed to combat discrimination in housing.
    The first was the Civil Rights Act of 1866, which prohibits discrimination on the basis of race, regardless of the race. The reference in the ad to the race of the landlord and the statement that she "seeks same" indicates that the landlord intends to discriminate on the basis of race. The Civil Rights Act of 1866, however, applies only to the actual rental or sale of real property, not to discriminatory advertising. The advertisement set forth above, in and of itself, does not violate the Civil Rights Act of 1866.

The Fair Housing Act of 1968 likewise prohibits discrimination on the basis of race. Like the Civil Rights Act of 1866, the coverage of the Fair Housing Act is critical to analyzing the problem. First, the Fair Housing Act of 1968 prohibits racial discrimination not just in the sale or rental of real property, but also with respect to advertisements for the sale or rental of real property. L's advertisement indicates that she is seeking another African-American to share the home with her. Inasmuch as the advertisement expresses an intent to discriminate on the basis of race, the advertisement appears to violate the Fair Housing Act of 1968. Most of the prohibitions of the Fair Housing Act of 1968, however, do not apply to landlords with less than 4 units if the landlord resides in one of the units. Since L is simply leasing out a bedroom in her house, L would appear to fall within this exemption. The exemption for landlords with less than 4 units, however, does not apply to advertisements with discriminatory provisions. Even though L could discriminate on the basis of race under the Fair Housing Act of 1968 in *renting* the bedroom in her private home, she cannot discriminate on the basis of race in *advertising* the bedroom for rent. L has violated the Fair Housing Act of 1968.

Answers (B) and (C) are incorrect because they fail to take into account the narrow scope of the Civil Rights Act of 1866. The 1866 Act does not cover discriminatory advertisements. **Answer (D) is incorrect** because it fails to recognize that the Fair Housing Act of 1968 does prohibit discriminatory advertisements by landlords, even if the landlord owns less than 4 units and resides in one of them.

- **Additional references**: *See* 2 RICHARD R. POWELL, POWELL ON REAL PROPERTY ch. 16B, § 16B.09[1][a]-[b] (Michael Allan Wolf ed., 2000); 5 THOMPSON ON REAL PROPERTY, SECOND THOMAS EDITION §§ 43.03(b)(1)(B)-(C), 43.03(e)(3) (1994 & Supp. 2006).

12. **The correct answer is (B)**. The general rule is that leasehold estates are freely alienable absent express provisions requiring the tenant to get the landlord's consent before transferring. Because such approval clauses restrict the alienability of the land, they are strictly construed. Here, the lease expressly requires the tenant to get the landlord's written approval before assigning or subleasing.

Where the lease contains an approval clause, the issue is whether the landlord may withhold consent for any reason or no reason whatsoever. Where the lease is silent on whether the landlord may arbitrarily withhold consent, the jurisdictions are split. Under the traditional common law approach, the courts deemed that the landlord-tenant relationship was personal and the tenant had no right to force the landlord to accept a new tenant. Pursuant to this reasoning, the common law approach is that the landlord may arbitrarily withhold consent under an approval clause where the clause is silent on the landlord's duty to act reasonably.

Under the modern trend, the courts take more of a contracts approach to the lease and to the landlord-tenant relationship. Under the contracts approach, the parties have a general duty to act reasonably and in good faith. Accordingly, under the modern trend approach, the landlord is entitled to withhold his consent under an approval clause only if he has a commercially reasonable objection to the assignment. A landlord can refuse to consent to the assignment based on commercially reasonable considerations, but he is not entitled to withhold consent merely because property values have increased and the lease value is now below market value.

If the lease had expressly provided that the landlord could withhold his consent unreasonably, the clause would probably be enforced under the modern trend approach and the landlord could refuse consent for any reason. Where the lease is silent as to whether the landlord can unreasonably withhold consent, under the modern trend approach the ambiguity is resolved against the landlord. In this case, the lease is silent as to the landlord's duty to act reasonably. Therefore, Landlord cannot withhold his consent in this situation because he does not have a commercially reasonable objection.

Answer (A) is incorrect because the contract does not provide expressly that the landlord may withhold consent arbitrarily. Therefore, although the landlord may arbitrarily withhold consent under the common law approach, under the modern trend the landlord must have a commercially reasonable objection to the assignment before he can refuse to consent. **Answer (C) is incorrect** because it confuses the common law and modern trend approaches. The landlord may arbitrarily withhold consent under the common law approach, but not under the modern trend approach. **Answer (D) is incorrect** because it fails to recognize that under the common law approach the landlord may arbitrarily withhold consent.

- **Additional references:** *See* 2 RICHARD R. POWELL, POWELL ON REAL PROPERTY chap. 17, § 17.04[1][b] (Michael Allan Wolf ed., 2000); 5 THOMPSON ON REAL PROPERTY, SECOND THOMAS EDITION § 42.04(b)(3)(ii) (1994 & Supp. 2006); WILLIAM B.

STOEBUCK & DALE A. WHITMAN, THE LAW OF PROPERTY § 6.71 (3d ed. 2000); Kendall v. Ernest Pestana, Inc., 709 P.2d 837 (Cal. 1985).

13. The best answer is (D). A tenant in a strip shopping mall is in a unique situation. The tenant's actions affect not only the landlord, they also affect the other tenants in the mall. To a degree, the economic health of each store depends on the mix and conduct of the other tenants. The courts have been cognizant of this unique economic interdependence in analyzing shopping mall landlord-tenant issues.

The general rule is that a "use clause" in a shopping mall lease is to be construed narrowly. Where a lease has a "use clause" setting forth the tenant's intended uses for the premises, and the clause goes on expressly to limit the tenant's use of the premises to those uses and no other, the tenant may change its business and reduce the scope of its use as long as the decision is made in good faith and in the exercise of legitimate business judgment. The "use clause" does not require the tenant to use the facilities for the precise permitted uses. This is true even if the lease charges rent based on a percentage of the gross sales. The fact that the change in use will decrease the rent payable is not controlling. The courts have even held that a temporary closure of a store for reasons beyond the tenant's control did not constitute a breach of the lease.

Under the contract doctrine of necessary implication, however, the courts will imply an agreement by the parties (a) that they will do whatever is necessary to carry out the purpose of the contract, and (b) to refrain from hurting the other party's right to the benefits of the contract. Under the terms of this lease, not only is there a "use clause," but there is also a percentage lease clause and a clause requiring each tenant in the shopping mall to perform affirmative acts to maintain the general character of the shopping mall.

Complete vacancy for an indefinite period of time is inconsistent with the purpose of the contract and the express clauses of the lease. Unlike a mere change of use, or a short term temporary closure for reasons beyond the tenant's control, a tenant's decision to not occupy and use the premises affects not only the landlord but the other tenants as well. Construing the lease as a whole and in light of the doctrine of necessary implications, the lease imposes an implied obligation on Tenant to occupy and use the premises.

Answer (A) is incorrect because it fails to take into account the interdependent nature of shopping mall tenants and the express provision of the lease requiring the tenant to take affirmative steps to maintain the general character of the mall. Paying rent but vacating the premises adversely affects the general character of the mall and economically hurts the other mall tenants. **Answer (B) is incorrect** because it fails to take into account the other express covenants in the lease. Although the "use clause" in and of itself is probably not enough to imply an obligation to occupy and use the premises, the lease, when construed as a whole and in light of the doctrine of necessary implications, warrants implying an obligation to occupy and use the premises. **Answer (C) is incorrect** because it fails to take into account the contract doctrine of necessary implications. If the express terms of the lease and the circumstances surrounding execution of the lease warrant it, the courts will imply an agreement by the parties that they will do whatever they should do to carry out the purpose of the contract and to refrain from hurting the other party's right to the benefits of the contract. The doctrine of necessary implications applies even if there is no ambiguity in the contract.

- **Additional references:** *See* 2 RICHARD R. POWELL, POWELL ON REAL PROPERTY ch. 17A, § 17A.02[3][b][ii] (Patrick J. Rohan ed. 1999); 5 THOMPSON ON REAL PROPERTY, SECOND THOMAS EDITION § 44.14(f)(2) (1994 & Supp. 2006); WILLIAM B. STOEBUCK & DALE A. WHITMAN, THE LAW OF PROPERTY § 6.25 (3d ed. 2000); Slater v. Pearle Vision Center, Inc., 546 A.2d 676 (Pa. Sup. 1988).

14. **The best answer is (A).** The issue of a landlord's tort liability is a complex issue, so complex that the jurisdictions are split as to the proper approach. The traditional common law rule was that landlords were immune from tort liability. The lease is a property conveyance, and as such, the tenant obtains the exclusive right of possession. The common law courts reasoned that it is anomalous to hold that the landlord owes the tenant any duty arising out the condition of the property since the tenant is in exclusive possession and control of those very premises.

Under the modern trend, however, the courts are increasingly imposing tort liability on the landlord for injuries to the tenant arising out of the condition of the premises. Some jurisdictions have expanded the landlord's tort liability by creating various exceptions to the traditional common law rule. Other jurisdictions have expanded the landlord's tort liability by making the landlord's duties for tort purposes commensurate with the tenant's duties under the implied warranty of habitability. Under either approach, however, the courts have expanded the landlord's tort liability to include liability for acts of third parties where the risk of injury is foreseeable and the landlord has failed to take reasonable steps to protect against the risk.

Here, the danger of crime, particularly urban crime, is all too common in today's society. Gaining access to the premises is a reasonably foreseeable risk, and one which arises from the condition of the premises. The fire escape provides easy access to an unsecured entry into the apartment. The landlord has a duty to take whatever reasonable steps were called for to secure the fire escape and/or window. The landlord's failure to do so exposed the tenant to an unreasonable and foreseeable risk of injury. The landlord should be liable.

Answer (B) is incorrect because although at one time the courts appeared to be moving towards a strict liability approach to landlord's liability, the leading decision adopting the strict liability approach has been overruled on the grounds that it unfairly burdened landlords. **Answer (C) is incorrect** because although it represents the traditional common law response to the issue, increasingly under the modern trend courts are holding landlord's liable for criminal acts of third parties where the criminal action was reasonably foreseeable either because repeated criminal acts in the area put the landlord on notice of the risk or the nature of the situation put the landlord on risk. Here, the easy access from the fire escape put the landlord on notice of the risk of criminal entry. **Answer (D) is incorrect** because courts have held that the landlord's duty to the tenant is not identical to the implied warranty of habitability. Special conditions and circumstances may justify imposing tort liability even in the absence of a breach of the implied warranty of habitability. Assuming, arguendo, that the standard were there had to be a breach of the implied warranty of habitability, one could still argue that the easy access to the apartment via the fire escape breached the requirement that the landlord provide premises that are reasonably safe.

- **Additional references:** *See* 2 RICHARD R. POWELL, POWELL ON REAL PROPERTY ch. 16B, § 16B.08[5][b]-[c] (Patrick J. Rohan ed. 1999); 5 THOMPSON ON REAL PROPERTY, SECOND THOMAS EDITION § 40.24(d)(1)-(2) (1994 & Supp. 2006); WILLIAM B. STOEBUCK & DALE A. WHITMAN, THE LAW OF PROPERTY § 6.47 (3d ed. 2000); Aaron v. Havens, 758 S.W.2d 446 (Mo. 1988).

15. **The best answer is (A).** There are two general rules governing the law of finders. First, the owner of property does not lose her title by losing her property (at least absent evidence of adverse possession or a subsequent bona fide purchaser without notice - neither of which is present under the current facts). Second, a finder has superior rights against all but the true owner. An important qualifier to the second rule is that prior possessors have superior rights to subsequent finders. It does not matter how the possessor came into possession.

Under the facts, B is the true owner of the watch. Since B holds title (which is not lost when he loses the watch), B has the strongest claim to the watch. As to all the other parties, their claims are based solely on possession. As to claims based solely on possession, the key principle is first in time, first in right. The first party to possess the watch after B was C. C is a finder, because he acquired physical control over the watch and intended to keep it. C then takes next in line after B. C has superior rights against all but the true owner, B. That right is similarly not lost when he loses possession of the watch, particularly here where C did not "lose" possession as much as possession was taken involuntarily.

Although X's possession was wrongful, having robbed C to get possession, X still has possession of the watch. Even wrongfully obtained possession is protected against subsequent possessors. Although X has no rights as against claims by B and C, X could sue D and successfully recover the watch as a prior possessor. Property rights are relative, not absolute. As a result, D has the lowest interest in the watch, even though he is the one currently in possession.

Answers (B), (C) and (D) are incorrect because they incorrectly fail to recognize that X has a claim to the watch even though X's possession of the watch was obtained wrongfully. **Answer (C) is also incorrect** because it incorrectly gives D priority over C. Even though D is the current possessor of the watch, C did not lose his claim when he lost the watch. **Answer (D) is also incorrect** because it incorrectly gives D, the current possessor, title. Although D is entitled to possession, he is not first in time, nor first in right. D is not entitled to title to the watch.

- **Additional references:** *See* RAY A. BROWN, THE LAW OF PERSONAL PROPERTY, 24-32 (Walter B. Raushenbush 3d ed. 1975); 2 THOMPSON ON REAL PROPERTY, SECOND THOMAS EDITION §§ 13.03(b), 13.04(c), 13.04(e)(1)-(2) (2000 & Supp. 2006); WILLIAM B. STOEBUCK & DALE A. WHITMAN, THE LAW OF PROPERTY § 1.3 (3d ed. 2000).

16. The best answer is (E). Under the traditional common law of finders, who has superior rights depends in large degree upon two key variables: (1) how the property is characterized (lost, mislaid, abandoned or treasure trove), and (2) where the object is found (private property vs. public property).

Whether the property is lost, mislaid, abandoned or treasure trove turns on the intent of the true owner at the time she or he relinquished possession of the item. An item is lost if the true owner unintentionally relinquished possession of the item. An item is mislaid if the true owner intentionally relinquished possession of the item intending to return later to repossess it, but then forgets to return and pick it up. An item is abandoned if the true owner intentionally relinquished possession of the item with no intent of repossessing the item. And lastly, an item is treasure trove if the item was gold or silver and the owner intentionally hid the item underground with the intention of returning later to reclaim it (modern trend - the item may be valuables other than gold or silver (including paper money), and the item does not have to be buried underground to qualify as treasure trove).

A criticism of the common law classification scheme is that it turns on the true owner's state of mind at the time he or she parts with the item, yet the court does not know who the true owner is. Evidence of the true owner's state if mind is circumstantial at best. Nevertheless, the common law approach presumes the owner's state of mind from the circumstances surrounding the location of the item at the time it is found. Assuming a reasonable true owner, which classification is most consistent with the most probable state of mind of the true owner in light of the facts surrounding where it was found?

Most people do not abandon $100,000, so absent evidence to support such an intent, the court will not presume that the true owner abandoned the money (although it is easy to imagine such a scenario - where the money is drug money and the party in possession simply decides it is too risky to come back to get the money!). In addition, at common law, to qualify as treasure trove, the item had to be made of gold or silver and hidden underground. Money hidden above ground did not qualify as treasure trove at common law.

The issue is whether the money was mislaid or lost. Since the money was found hidden in the floorboards, is it more likely that the owner placed it there intentionally or unintentionally? It is difficult to imagine a scenario where someone would drop $100,000 and the money would accidentally end up under the floorboards. The more likely scenario is that the true owner intentionally placed the money there with the intention of returning later to retrieve it. A court would probably construe the money as mislaid property.

At common law, mislaid property generally went to the owner of the locus where the item was found on the assumption that the true owner may retrace his or her steps to retrieve the item. To maximize the chances of the item being returned to the true owner, the owner of the locus where the item is found should get the item. Here, the item was found on the boat, not at the repair shop. The true owner would not know to retrace his or her steps to the repair shop, but would know to retrace his or her steps to the boat. The Bank, which has superior rights to possess the boat, is entitled to the money.

(In addition, the second key variable analyzed to determine who should get found property is whether the item was found on private or public property. If found on private property, the common law granted the item to the owner of the private property generally to deter trespass and to protect the property owner's expectations. Here, Juan found the money in the boat, presumably private property. Inasmuch as Pete has defaulted on the payments to the Bank, the Bank took possession of the boat and steps into the shoes of the true owner. The Bank can assert the public policy arguments of deterring trespass and protecting the expectations of property owners. Even if the court were to construe the money as lost, a strong argument can be made that the Bank would still get the money as the owner of the private property where the money was found.)

Answer (A) is incorrect because it is an overstatement. A finder of lost property does not always prevail against all but the true owner. A prior finder trumps a subsequent finder; and if the finder found the property on private property, at common law the owner of the private property usually prevails to protect the property owner's expectations and to deter trespass. **Answer (B) is incorrect** because at common law, treasure trove had to be buried below ground. Here, the money was hidden above ground. **Answer (C) is incorrect** because Gerri's Boat Repair Shop's claim to the money is a derivative claim based upon's Juan's claim to the ring. Gerri's Boat Repair Shop's claim to the money is based upon the law of agency-principal. Gerri's Boat Repair Shop's claim is that anything an agent (an employee) finds in the course of his or her employment belongs to the principal (the employer). To the extent Juan does not have a valid claim to the item found, however, Gerri's Boat

Repair Shop has no claim to the item. **Answer (D) is incorrect** because although Pete owed money to the San Diego Boat Dock, the Boat Dock did not make a claim against the boat. Even if the Boat Dock had, 1st State Bank had recorded a lien against the title to the boat, and under first in time, first in right, has a superior right to seize the boat as security for the money Pete owes the Bank. **Answer (F) is incorrect** because although it implicitly invokes the rule that mislaid property goes to the owner of the property where the item is found, the answer fails to distinguish the difference between the boat and the repair shop. The money was found on the boat, and so should go to the owner of the boat. The fact that the boat happens to be at the repair shop is irrelevant for purposes of the rule. If the true owner were to retrace his or her steps in an attempt to regain possession of the money, the true owner would know to retrace his or her steps to the boat. The true owner, however, would have no idea that the boat had been to the repair shop. Moreover, in terms of protecting property owners' expectations and deterring trespass, these public policy concerns apply to the boat, not to the repair shop.

- **Additional references:** *See* RAY A. BROWN, THE LAW OF PERSONAL PROPERTY, 24-32 (Walter B. Raushenbush 3d ed. 1975); 2 THOMPSON ON REAL PROPERTY, SECOND THOMAS EDITION § 13.04(e)(1)-(2) (2000 & Supp. 2006); RALPH E. BOYER ET. AL., THE LAW OF PROPERTY: AN INTRODUCTORY SURVEY § 1.3 (4th ed. 1991); Benjamin v. Lindner Aviation, 534 N.W.2d 400 (Iowa 1995).

17. **The best answer is (A). (The best answer is (E) if you did not apply the Rule Against Perpetuities.)** The key to analyzing possessory estate and future interest problems is to read and construe comma to comma, paying particular attention to the words of limitation used.

    The first clause conveys the property "to Sammy for life, ..." The words of purchase, "to Sammy" indicate that Sammy holds the possessory estate. The words of limitation, "for life," are the classic words used to create a life estate. Sammy holds a life estate.
    The second clause conveys the property "then to Mark and his heirs, ..." The words of purchase "to Mark" indicate that Mark holds the future interest following Sammy's possessory estate. Sammy holds a finite estate. The future interest following a finite estate must be either a reversion (if the future interest is held by the grantor) or a remainder (if the future interest is held by someone other than the grantor). Since Mark is not the grantor, Mark holds a remainder.

A remainder is contingent unless it meets the test for vested. To be vested, the party holding the remainder must be (1) born, (2) ascertainable, and (3) there must be no express condition precedent in the same clause creating the remainder or the preceding clause (reading comma to comma). Mark is born and ascertainable. The only issue is whether there is an express condition precedent, a condition which Mark must satisfy before he can claim the right to possession. There is no express condition precedent in the clause creating the remainder or the preceding clause. The remainder is vested. Mark holds a vested remainder, but of what duration?

The key to the duration of each estate are the words of limitation. Here, the express words of limitation are "and his heirs, ..." Those are the classic words of limitation to create a fee simple absolute. At first blush, it looks like Mark holds a vested remainder in fee simple absolute. Reading clause to clause, however, it is clear that the next clause contains language qualifying Mark's right to possession.

In analyzing the qualifying language following a vested remainder in fee simple, the first key is whether the qualifying language sets forth a condition precedent or a condition subsequent. A condition precedent is a condition which *may* occur before the vested remainder becomes possessory. If the condition is a condition precedent, the vested remainder is subject to divestment. If, on the other hand, the condition is a condition subsequent, a condition which must occur, if at all, after the vested remainder becomes possessory, the key to the analysis is who holds the future interest: the grantor or someone else. If the grantor, the remainder is a vested remainder in fee simple determinable or a vested remainder subject to a condition subsequent, depending on the express words of limitation introducing the condition. If someone other than the grantor holds the future interest, the remainder is a vested remainder subject to an executory limitation.

Looking carefully at the nature of the condition in the clause following the clause creating the remainder - is the condition a condition precedent or a condition subsequent? Can the condition occur *before* the remainder becomes possessory, or only afterwards? Is it possible that a baseball player could break the record for home runs before Mark's remainder becomes possessory? Notice, the question is "Is it *possible* . . ." - not is it likely. As long as the condition could occur before the remainder becomes possessory, the condition is a condition precedent. Mark's vested remainder in fee simple is subject to divestment. The "but if" language introducing the express condition precedent arguably also cuts short the life estate the moment the condition occurs. So Sammy's life estate is a life estate subject to an executory limitation.

The future interest following a vested remainder subject to divestment is an executory interest. Because the future interest would be taking possession from someone other than the grantor, the interest is a shifting executory interest (as opposed to a springing executory interest - where the executory interest is taking possession from the grantor). The key to the duration of the executory interest are the words of limitation. Here, the words of limitation are "and his or her heirs" – the classic words of limitation to create a fee simple. The player who breaks the home run record holds a shifting executory interest in fee simple absolute.

That would appear to be the end of the analysis, except that executory interests are subject to the Rule Against Perpetuities. Under the Rule Against Perpetuities, the future interest must vest, if at all, within the lives in being at the time the interest was created plus 21 years, or the interest is void from its attempted creation. For purposes of executory interests, the requirement that the interest must vest is equivalent to requiring that the interest become possessory. Notice that the Rule Against Perpetuities does not require that the executory interest vest within the lives in being plus 21 years, only that under no circumstances may the executory interest vest *after* the lives in being plus 21 years. If the court can conceive of one scenario where the condition could be satisfied but not until after the lives in being plus 21 years, the executory interest is void.

Is it possible that the current record for most home runs in a single season could stand unbroken for as long as the life of anyone currently alive, and then for another 21 years? Sure. Is it possible that thereafter some baseball player may hit more home runs in a single season, thereby setting a new record? Sure. As long as it is possible that the condition may be satisfied, but not until after all the lives in being at the time the interest is created plus 21 years, the interest violates the Rule Against Perpetuities and is void. The shifting executory interest in fee simple held by the baseball player who breaks the record for most home runs in a single season is void.

When an interest is void, the general rule is to strike the whole clause which creates the interest, and the clause which introduced the clause. Applying the general rule to the conveyance, strike the words starting with "but if . . ." and continuing until the end of the conveyance. All that is left is "To Sammy for life, then to Mark and his heirs." Re-analyzing the state of the title, Sammy holds a life estate, and Mark holds a vested remainder in fee simple absolute.

Answers (B) and (C) are incorrect because they incorrectly analyze the fee simple possessory estate in the vested remainder. A fee simple determinable and a fee simple subject to condition subsequent requires that the future interest be held by the grantor. Since the future interest is held by a third party, someone other than the grantor, the possessory estate cannot be either a fee simple determinable or a fee simple subject to condition subsequent. Moreover, the express condition is not a condition subsequent but rather a condition precedent. **Answer (D) is incorrect** because it misconstrues the nature of the condition qualifying how long Mark and his heirs can keep possession of the property. If the condition were a condition subsequent, answer (D) would be correct. But since the condition is one which *may* occur before the vested remainder becomes possessory, the condition is a condition precedent, which makes the vested remainder subject to divestment if the condition occurs before the remainder becomes possessory. **Answer (E) is incorrect** because it fails to recognize that the executory interest in question violates the Rule Against Perpetuities because it is possible that the condition may occur, but not until after 21 years after all of the lives in being at the time the interest is created are dead.

- **Additional references:** *See* CORNELIUS J. MOYNIHAN, INTRODUCTION TO THE LAW OF REAL PROPERTY 43-46, 117-129 (2d ed. 1988); PETER T. WENDEL, A POSSESSORY ESTATES AND FUTURE INTERESTS PRIMER 43-44, 47-48, 58-65,17-31, 103-14, 172-76, 188-96 (3rd ed. 2007); WILLIAM B. STOEBUCK & DALE A. WHITMAN, THE LAW OF PROPERTY §§ 2.11, 3.2, 3.7, 3.11, 3.17 (3d ed. 2000).

18. **The best answer is (B).** A bailment arises when the bailor (the true owner of the personal property) relinquishes possession of her personal property to another, the bailee. The bailee assumes a duty to care for the property and to return it to the bailor per their agreement.

The basic requirements of a bailment are that the bailee must (1) take actual physical control of the personal property (2) with the intent to possess it. The definitions of "physical control" and "intent to possess" are fairly flexible in the eyes of the court. The standards are rather soft and fact sensitive. If the court does not think imposing liability would be expected or fair, the courts often declare that the defendant did not have one or the other of the two requirements. Because of the frequency with which these types of cases have come up, however, the courts inclined to impose liability have created exceptions to the requirements to facilitate finding liability.

In an attended lot such as this, there are two possibilities grounds for finding a valid bailment. The first is a true bailment. If a driver leaves the keys with the valet and receives a claim check to present upon its return, a true bailment would have been created. There is, however, no evidence that Sylvia left her keys or received a claim check. The second possible basis for finding a bailment is under the doctrine of "constructive bailment." If the bailor leaves the item within the general possession and control of the bailee, by leaving the item among other bailed items, the bailee is deemed to have physical control over the item and intent to possess it. The bailor may reasonably expect that the bailee will exercise some care in watching the item. Here, even though Sylvia did not leave her keys, she parked her car with permission in a lot where there were attendants present parking other cars and exercising surveillance, and she expected that her car would be safe. Under these facts, a "constructive bailment" arguably has arisen and the bailee will be liable if the bailee does not exercise a reasonable degree of care to protect the bailed item.

Answer (A) is incorrect because it is not the controlling issue. If Sylvia had simply parked her car in the restaurant's lot without an attendant being present, the courts disagree over whether a bailment has been created. Some cases hold no, others yes. The discrepancy renders the answer too iffy. **Answer (C) is incorrect** because the court will most likely impose constructive custody in this situation. **Answer (D) is incorrect** because the fact that Sylvia parked the car herself is not controlling. The valet gave Sylvia permission to use the lot, thereby creating an expectation in Sylvia that her car would be safe. This expectation will be of great importance in a court's decision.

- **Additional references:** *See* RAY A. BROWN, THE LAW OF PERSONAL PROPERTY, 213-222 (Walter B. Raushenbush 3d ed. 1975); 2 THOMPSON ON REAL PROPERTY, SECOND THOMAS EDITION §§ 13.07, 13.07(a) (2000 & Supp. 2006); RALPH E. BOYER ET. AL., THE LAW OF PROPERTY: AN INTRODUCTORY SURVEY § 2.1 (4th ed. 1991); McGlynn v. Parking Authority of City of Newark, 432 A.2d 99 (N.J. 1981).

19. **The best answer is (B).** At common law, a tenant's principal recourse against a landlord was to claim constructive eviction under the covenant

of quiet enjoyment. If the landlord breached a duty which the landlord owed to the tenant, and the conditions which arose as a result of the breach were so egregious as to seriously interfere with the beneficial enjoyment of the property or render the property substantially unsuitable for the purposes for which they were leased, the tenant could claim constructive eviction. Under constructive eviction, the tenant had to give the landlord notice of the problem, give the landlord reasonable time to remedy the situation, and then, if the problem were not fixed, vacate in a timely manner.

A tenant could claim breach of the covenant of quiet enjoyment, however, only if the landlord was responsible for the condition - i.e., if the condition arose as a result of the landlord's breach of a duty which the landlord owed to the tenant. The duty could either be an express duty set forth in the lease, or one of the implied duties at common law: duty to disclose latent defects about which the landlord knew or should have known; duty to maintain common areas; duty to make any promised repairs or repairs the landlord voluntarily undertakes; duty not to fraudulently misrepresent the condition of the property; duty to maintain furnished dwellings leased for short terms; and duty to abate immoral conduct or nuisances which arise on property owned by the landlord.

There is little doubt that the volume of the music at that time of the night seriously interfered with the tenants' beneficial enjoyment of their apartments and rendered the apartments substantially unsuitable for the purposes for which they were leased - sleeping in. The noise constructively evicted the tenants. The facts indicate that the tenants gave Beth notice of the problem, gave her reasonable time to remedy the situation, and then, after the problem continued, vacated in a timely manner. The issue is whether the problem is a breach of a duty Beth owed the tenants.

The facts fail to indicate whether there are any express duties under the terms of the lease, so the tenants only option is to invoke one or more of the implied duties. Of the six implied duties, two appear to impose a legal duty on Beth which she breached under the facts. First, the landlord has a duty to abate immoral conduct or nuisances which arise on property owned by the landlord. Although the volume of the music arguably does not constitute immoral conduct, it arguably does constitute a private nuisance. The volume of the music at that time of the night substantially and unreasonably interferes with the use and enjoyment of the surrounding residential apartments. Moreover, the landlord has an implied duty to make any promised repairs or repairs the landlord voluntarily undertakes. Beth promised to look into the situation and made attempts at correcting the situation. Having promised and undertaken corrective action, Beth had an implied duty to follow through and rectify the situation. Her failure to do so constitutes a breach of her duty to the tenants.

Answer (A) is incorrect because the tenants are claiming constructive eviction. Constructive eviction is a breach of the covenant of quiet enjoyment, which at common law was the tenant's principal recourse against the landlord. The tenants may invoke the implied warranty of habitability under the modern trend, but not under the traditional common law approach. **Answer (C) is incorrect** because under constructive eviction, the landlord's actions (or inaction) are determinative, not the landlord's intent. As long as the consequences are the natural and probable consequences of the landlord's actions (or inaction), the landlord is responsible for the condition. **Answer (D) is incorrect** because the landlord is responsible for conditions which arise on property owned by the landlord, whether or not those premises are the same as the premises on which the tenants reside. **Answer (E) is incorrect** because as long as the landlord has it within his or her power to control the condition (or the parties creating the condition), the landlord is obligated to correct the problem even if the problem is caused by other parties.

- **Additional references**: *See* 2 RICHARD R. POWELL, POWELL ON REAL PROPERTY ch. 16B, §§ 16B.03[1]-[3], 16B.04[2] (Patrick J. Rohan ed. 1999); 5 THOMPSON ON REAL PROPERTY, SECOND THOMAS EDITION §§ 40.22(c)(3)(i)-(ii), 40.23(c)(8) (1994 & Supp. 2006); WILLIAM B. STOEBUCK & DALE A. WHITMAN, THE LAW OF PROPERTY § 6.30-34, 6.38 (3d ed. 2000); Blackett v. Olanoff, 358 N.E.2d 817 (Mass. 1977)

20. **The best answer is (B).** The first issue is who has the legal right to possession on January 1, 2005. The answer to that turns on what type of tenancy Betsy held when she entered into possession on January 1, 2000.

A term of years lease is a lease with a fixed duration which is determinable on the first day of the lease. A term of years lease does not require notice to terminate since the termination date is determinable from the original terms of the lease.

A periodic tenancy is a lease for a fixed period but with no fixed termination date. Since the lease lacks a fixed termination date, the lease continues from fixed period to fixed period until properly terminated. Classic examples of periodic leases are leases for month-to-month or year-to-year. Since the terms of the lease provide for a fixed period which is to repeat, the lease does not terminate until proper notice is given by either the tenant or the landlord. How much notice is required depends on the length of the fixed period. The general common law rule was that the notice had to be at least as long as the duration of the fixed period, but in no event to exceed six months. The notice was also to specify that the lease was to terminate on the last day of the fixed period.

As applied to the facts of the problem, although the lease specified that rent was $12,000 a year, to be paid monthly, the rental payment scheme should not override the express intent of the parties that the lease was to commence January 1, 2000 and terminate December 31, 2004. The duration of the lease can be calculated on the first day of the lease. The lease constitutes a term of years lease with a fixed termination date. Since the termination date is fixed from the outset, there is no need for notice to terminate. The term of years lease terminates automatically on December 31, 2004. Alice was entitled to legal possession on that day.

Whose problem is it that Betsy held over? Under the traditional American approach, the landlord has no duty to deliver **actual** possession on the first day of the lease. As long as the landlord delivers **legal** possession on the first day of the lease, the landlord has fulfilled her duty. Absent an express clause in the lease requiring actual possession, the tenant assumes the risk that someone else may be in possession of the leased premises on the first day of the lease.

The fact that Betsy held over is Cindy's problem, not Alice's. Alice has not breached any duty she owed to Cindy under the American approach. Cindy has no grounds to rescind the lease. Cindy is still liable under the lease with Alice.

Answer (A) is incorrect because it implicitly misstates the American approach to the issue of whether the landlord has the duty to provide actual possession to the tenant on the first day of a lease. Under the American approach, the landlord has no duty to provide actual possession on the first day of the lease, so Cindy has no grounds to rescind the lease. **Answers (C) and (D) are incorrect** because they implicitly incorrectly analyze Alice's lease with Betsy as a periodic lease. Although the rent is set forth on an annual basis to be paid monthly, the express starting and ending date control. The lease is a term of years lease. Since it is a term of years lease, it ended automatically on

5

December 31, 2004 despite the absence of any notice to terminate. The legal right to possession reverted to Alice, who had the right to convey it to Cindy. Alice did not breach the covenant of quiet enjoyment.

- **Additional references**: *See* 2 RICHARD R. POWELL, POWELL ON REAL PROPERTY ch. 16, §§ 16.03[1], 16.03[7][a], ch. 16B, § 16B.02[1][a] (Patrick J. Rohan ed. 1999); 4 THOMPSON ON REAL PROPERTY, SECOND THOMAS EDITION §§ 39.05(a), 39.06(b)(1) (2004 & Supp. 2006); 5 THOMPSON § 40.22(b)(1); RALPH E. BOYER ET. AL., THE LAW OF PROPERTY: AN INTRODUCTORY SURVEY §§ 9.1, 9.2 (4th ed. 1991).

21. **The best answer is** (C). The issues raised by this problem involve privity and tacking for adverse possession purposes.

Tacking permits one adverse possessor to add his or her time of actual possession to that of a previous adverse possessor. Tacking requires privity between the parties. The degree of privity depends on whether the jurisdiction follows the English approach or the American approach. The English approach is more consistent with the objective, statute of limitations approach to adverse possession. The statute of limitations approach punishes the true owner for sleeping on his or her rights. As applied to privity, the English approach holds that tacking is permitted as long as there is no significant gap in possession between the successive adverse possessors. As long as there was no significant gap in possession, if the true owner had walked the property he or she would have noticed the adverse possessor. Here, the facts indicate that following the conveyance between Andy and Betty, she "promptly" moved onto the property. There appears to have been no significant gap in actual possession. Under the English approach, there is sufficient privity to permit Betty to tack her period of actual possession onto Andy's period of actual possession.

The American approach to privity takes much more of a subjective approach, which is more consistent with the earnings approach to adverse possession. The American approach requires that there must be a reasonable relationship between the successive adverse possessors before it permits tacking. Because what constitutes a 'reasonable relationship' is a soft, fact-sensitive standard, courts have offered additional guidance. Some courts have said that there must be a voluntary transfer or a meeting of the minds between the adverse possessors. Another way to think about it is that the subsequent adverse possessor must believe that he or she is receiving the prior adverse possessor's right to possession. Here, Andy voluntary sold his right to possession to Betty. There was a voluntary transfer, a meeting of the minds, Betty thought that she was receiving Andy's right to possession from him. Under the American approach, there is sufficient privity to permit Betty to tack her period of actual possession to Andy's period of actual possession.

Betty can tack her period of actual possession to Andy's regardless of whether the jurisdiction applies the English approach or the American approach.

Answer (A) is incorrect because it fails to acknowledge that Betty can also tack under the American approach. **Answer (B) is incorrect** because it fails to acknowledge that Betty can also tack under the English approach. **Answer (D) is incorrect** because it fails to acknowledge that Betty can tack under both the American and the English approach.

- **Additional references**: *See* 16 RICHARD R. POWELL, POWELL ON REAL PROPERTY ch. 91, §§ 91.10-91.10[2] (Patrick J. Rohan ed. 1999); 10 THOMPSON ON REAL PROPERTY, SECOND THOMAS EDITION § 87.13 (1998 & Supp. 2006).

22. **The best answer is (C).** Adverse possession requires actual entry which gives rise to actual possession which is open and notorious, adverse, exclusive, under a claim of right, and continuous for the statutory period. Here, the statutory period is 10 years. Because Betty was in actual possession of Homeacres for only eight years, her only chance of satisfying the statutory requirements is if she tacks her actual possession onto Andy's actual possession. As the answer to problem 21 above showed, there is sufficient privity between Andy and Betty to permit tacking. Because each element must be satisfied for the whole statutory period, where there is tacking, each adverse possessor's actual possession must satisfy the elements. Each element then must be analyzed in light of the respective parties' actual possession.

Actual entry is required to start the statute of limitations running on the true owner's cause of action for ejectment. It starts the statutory period for adverse possession as long as all of the elements are satisfied. Here, Andy entered the property in 1992. The statutory period is 10 years. Assume all of the elements are satisfied for the whole statutory period, Betty's claim of adverse possession will vest in 2002.

Open and notorious requires possession which would give the true owner constructive notice - if the true owner were to walk the property he or she would see the adverse possessor. Here, both Andy and Betty lived on the property and either farmed it or gardened it. Such activities, particularly living on the property, is sufficiently open and notorious that if Olivia had walked the property she would have noticed. The adverse possession was open and notorious.

Adverse requires the adverse possessor to be there without the true owner's permission, not subservient to the true owner. Andy's possession was clearly without the true owner's permission. Andy broke into the property. He was not there with Olivia's permission. There is no evidence that Betty ever had Olivia's permission either. Andy and Betty's adverse possession was adverse.

Exclusive requires that the adverse possessor regulate access to the property like a true owner would. During Andy's period of actual possession, there is no evidence that anyone other than Andy, and possibly his guests, were on the property. During Betty's period of actual possession, there is no evidence that anyone other than Betty, and possibly her guests, were on the property. Both Andy and Betty regulated access to Homeacres as a true owner would. Andy and Betty's actual possession was exclusive.

Claim of right varies by the jurisdiction. Some jurisdictions take a subjective approach to the element. Under the subjective approach, the jurisdictions look to the adverse possessor's state of mind to see if the adverse possessor has the requisite claim of right. Some jurisdictions take the 'good faith' approach to claim of right element, which requires the adverse possessor believe, in good faith, that he or she owned an interest in the property. Some jurisdictions take a 'bad faith' approach to the claim of right element, which requires that the adverse possessor know that he or she has no interest in the property yet he or she intends to claim it anyway. Here, Andy knew that he had no right to the property - he broke in to take actual possession of the house on Homeacres. Andy would satisfy the bad faith approach, but not the good faith approach. Betty on the other hand, believed in good faith that she was purchasing the property from Andy. There is nothing to indicate that Betty knew that Andy was not the rightful owner. Betty would satisfy the good faith approach, but not the bad faith approach. Because the element has to be satisfied for the whole statutory period, if the jurisdiction takes either the good faith or the bad faith approach, Betty cannot satisfy the claim of right element even with tacking. A majority of jurisdictions, however, take an objective approach to claim of right. Instead of focusing on the adverse possessor's state of mind, the objective approach focuses on the adverse possessor's actions - whether they evidence a claim to the property. Here, Andy and Betty's living on the property and farming/gardening it would constitute sufficient acts to satisfy the claim of right element under the objective approach.

Continuous for the statutory period requires the adverse possessor to occupy the land as continuously as an average owner of similarly situated property would occupy it. Here, both Andy and Betty lived on Homeacres year round, just as an ordinary owner would. And because Betty can tack her period of actual possession on to Andy's period of actual possession (see the answer to problem 21 above), Betty can prove that there was continuous adverse possession of Homeacres for the statutory period: from 1992 (Andy's entry) until 2007 (when Olivia returned to the property).

If the jurisdiction applies the objective approach to claim of right, Betty can prove that she has successfully adversely possessed Homeacres. If, however, the jurisdiction were to apply either of the subjective approaches to claim of right (the good faith or the bad faith approach), Betty could not prove that all of the elements had been satisfied for the statutory period, even with tacking.

Answer (A) is incorrect because to invoke the disability doctrine, the party with the right to possession on the day the adverse possession began must have a qualifying disability (minor, unsound mind, imprisoned). Here, Olivia had no disability on the day Andy entered the property and began adversely possessing the property. Olivia's mother was recovering from a stroke, but a court would be hard-pressed to extend the language in the statute to include disabilities in a family member of the party who had the right to possession. Morever, it is unclear whether a stroke would constitute a qualifying disability. The disability doctrine is not applicable to the fact pattern. **Answer (B) is incorrect** because if the jurisdiction takes the subjective approach to the claim of right element, Andy and Betty had different subjective intents with respect to the property. Andy was claiming the property in bad faith; Betty was claiming the property in good faith. Their possession's cannot be tacked if the jurisdiction takes either subjective approach to claim of right. **Answer (D) is incorrect** because it fails to recognize that Betty cannot tack under the subjective approach because she and Andy had different states of mind with respect to their respective claim of right.

- **Additional references:** *See* 16 RICHARD R. POWELL, POWELL ON
  REAL PROPERTY ch. 91, §§ 91.10-91.13 (Patrick J. Rohan ed. 1999);
  10 THOMPSON ON REAL PROPERTY, SECOND THOMAS EDITION §§
  87.05-87.15, 87.18 (1998 & Supp. 2006); WILLIAM B. STOEBUCK &
  DALE A. WHITMAN, THE LAW OF PROPERTY §§ 11.7 (3d ed. 2000).

23. **The best answer is (D).** This question raises the issue of whether color
of title applies to the claim of adverse possession.

Assuming a party is successful in claiming adverse possession, he or she
gets title, by operation of law, to the land he or she actually possessed
unless he or she is claiming under color of title. Color of title is where a
party is claiming the land in question under a defective written
instrument. Where a party successfully claims adverse possession under
color of title, the adverse possessor gets title not only to the land that he
or she actually possessed but also to the land that he or she
constructively possessed under the terms of the defective written
instrument. Here, Betty is claiming under the deed that she received
from Andy that purported to transfer title to her, but did not because
Andy did not have title to transfer. At first blush it would appear that
Betty is entitled to all three acres of Homeacres because she is claiming
under color of title. But Betty's claim of adverse possession is successful
only because she tacked her time of actual possession to Andy's time of
actual possession. Andy's claim of adverse possession was not based on
any defective written instrument. Inasmuch as Betty's claim of adverse
possession is dependent on her ability to tack to Andy's actual
possession, and inasmuch as Andy cannot invoke color of title, it would
be against public policy to permit Betty to invoke color of title to
increase the amount of land that she can claim. If the courts were
permitting a subsequent adverse possessor with color of title to tack onto
a prior adverse possessor without color of title, adverse possessors would
have an incentive to transfer their claims immediately before vesting to
increase the land they could claim. Color of title should be tacked only
where all of the adverse possessors whose period of actual possession is
being tacked were operating under color of title. Inasmuch as Betty
cannot invoke color of title, she is entitled only to the land that was
actually possessed for the requisite statutory period. Although Andy
actually possessed two of the three acres, Betty only actually possessed
one of those acres. Betty is entitled to only one acre of Homeacres.
Olivia still owns the other two acres.

Answer (A) is incorrect because it fails to recognize that color of title
can be tacked only where all the parties in question were operating under

the same color of title. **Answer (B) is incorrect** because in the absence of color of title, the adverse possessor is entitled to only as much land as has been actually possessed for the statutory period. Neither Andy nor Betty actually possessed all three acres of Homeacres. **Answer (C) is incorrect** because although Andy actually possessed two of the acres by farming acres one and two, he did not actually possess them for the statutory period and Betty actually possessed only one of the acres, acre two. Betty can tack only with respect to the acre that both she and Andy actually possessed. **Answer (E) is incorrect** because it fails to recognize that Betty and Andy did continuously occupy one of the acres, acre two, in addition to their living in the house. Betty can tack the actual possession of the house and of acre two.

- **Additional references**: *See* 16 RICHARD R. POWELL, POWELL ON REAL PROPERTY ch. 91, §§ 91.08[1]-91.08[2] (Patrick J. Rohan ed. 1999); 10 THOMPSON ON REAL PROPERTY, SECOND THOMAS EDITION §§ 87.07, 87.12 (1998 & Supp. 2006); WILLIAM B. STOEBUCK & DALE A. WHITMAN, THE LAW OF PROPERTY §§ 11.7 (3d ed. 2000).

24. **The best answer is (A).** The problem raises a number of potential issues with respect to the rights and obligations of co-tenants, but the first has to do with the creation of co-tenancies.

At common law, as long as the four unities of time, title, interest, and possession where satisfied, the default co-tenancy estate was joint tenancy. The unity of time required the parties to acquire their interests at the same time. The unity of title required the parties to acquire their interest through the same instrument. The unity of interest required the parties to hold equal shares of the same duration. The unity of possession required the parties to each hold the right to possess the whole. If the fifth unity of marriage was also present at the time the parties acquired their interests, the default and presumed co-tenancy estate was tenancy by the entirety. Both joint tenancy and tenancy by the entirety are characterized by a right of survivorship. Under the right of survivorship, upon the death of one co-tenant, his or her share expires and the shares of the surviving co-tenants are re-calculated. Shares in a joint tenancy or tenancy by the entirety are not devisable or inheritable. Co-tenants can opt out of the default estates, but there must be clear and express language in the instrument creating the co-tenancy to opt out of the default co-tenancy if the unities are present.

H and W held the respective parcels as tenants by the entirety. Although the facts are a bit unclear as to from whom they acquired the parcels, there is no evidence that either had an interest in the parcels before they acquired the parcels together. They acquired their interests at the same time, and apparently through the same deed. There is no evidence to contradict the natural assumption that they held equal shares and equal rights to possess the whole of each parcel. The four unities of time, title, interest, and possession were satisfied. In addition, H and W were married when they acquired each parcel. Since the five unities are satisfied, H and W hold each parcel as tenants by the entirety, unless there is clear and express language in the deeds expressing a contrary intent. (At early common law, the parties could not expressly opt out of tenancy by the entirety even with express language to the contrary.) The word "jointly" is ambiguous at best and does not constitute adequate intent to create tenancy in common, assuming that the parties had the power to opt out of the tenancy by the entirety presumption.

Because H and W held the respective parcels as tenants by the entirety, when H died no interest could pass by will or intestacy to C. W alone owns each parcel. C has no rights in either parcel. C has no claim against W.

Answers (B), (C), (D) and (E) are incorrect because each is implicitly based upon the assumption that C has some interest in the parcels. The only way C could have an interest is if H and W held the parcels as tenants in common. Inasmuch as the necessary unities were present to come within the scope of the default rule that the parties intended a tenancy by the entirety, the only way C could have an interest is if the express language of the deeds expressed an intent to create a tenancy in common. The express language does not express such an intent. Since C has no interest in either parcel, C has no claim against W or the parcels.

- **Additional references**: *See* 7 RICHARD R. POWELL, POWELL ON REAL PROPERTY ch. 52, §§ 621[2], 620[1] (Patrick J. Rohan ed. 1999); 4 THOMPSON ON REAL PROPERTY, SECOND THOMAS EDITION §§ 33.06(a), 33.07 (2004 & Supp. 2006); WILLIAM B. STOEBUCK & DALE A. WHITMAN, THE LAW OF PROPERTY § 5.5 (3d ed. 2000).

25. **The best answer is (E).** The problem raises a number of issues concerning the creation of co-tenancies and the relationship between co-tenants.

The first issue is which type of co-tenancy was created under the express terms of the deeds. Under the common law approach, the default and presumed co-tenancy is joint tenancy with right of survivorship as long as the four unities of time, title, interest, and possession were satisfied (tenancy by the entirety if the parties are married.) Under the modern trend, however, the preferred and presumed co-tenancy is tenancy in common. Under the modern trend, even if the four (or even five) unities are satisfied, the co-tenancy will be a tenancy in common unless there is a clear and express intent to opt into joint tenancy or tenancy by the entirety (if tenancy by the entirety is available - in many jurisdictions tenancy by the entirety has been abolished under the modern trend).

Here, there is no clear and express intent to opt into joint tenancy or tenancy by the entirety. At a minimum, most jurisdictions require some express reference to a right of survivorship. The word "jointly" falls well short of the express language necessary to overcome the modern trend presumption in favor of tenancy in common. H and W held each parcel as tenants in common. One of the key attributes of the tenancy in common is that it lacks a right of survivorship. Each tenant's share is devisable and inheritable. When H died, his share passed into probate, and since he died intestate, passed through intestacy. W received 2/3rds of his one half interest, and C received the other 1/3rd. C holds 1/3 of ½, or a 1/6 interest in each parcel as tenant in common with her mother, W, who holds 5/6s.

Inasmuch as W has been residing in the big house and leasing out the little house since H died in 1985, is W entitled to sole ownership of both under adverse possession? Although W's actions with respect to both parcels are probably enough to satisfy the requirements of adverse possession if she were not a co-tenant, the issue is what difference, if any, should it make that she is a co-tenant. Most jurisdictions reason that since each co-tenant is entitled to possess the whole, the co-tenant's exclusive possession of the whole is not adverse. In cases of claims of adverse possession, the courts generally treat the co-tenants as if they owe each other a fiduciary duty. For one co-tenant to successfully start a claim of adverse possession against another, the co-tenant in exclusive possession has to give what amounts to actual notice of the adverse claim. Since W has done nothing during her time in exclusive possession to give C actual notice that W was claiming adverse possession, W will not prevail on her claim. (Even in those jurisdictions where a tenant in exclusive possession for a long time is presumed to be claiming adverse possession, the claim usually does not begin until the tenant has been in exclusive possession for 10 years or so. If the jurisdiction were to apply this approach, W's claim of adverse possession did not start until 1995, so she still falls short.)

Inasmuch as W and C are tenants in common, what rights does C have? First, the fact that W is a surviving spouse is of no significance under basic property law. (Under a state's probate code, a surviving spouse may be entitled to claim a homestead exemption, but the details of what that means and the legal significance of it are beyond the scope of first year property courses and this problem.) Under both the common law and the modern trend, co-tenants have to account for rents received from third parties. W must account to C for the rents from the little house. Is W liable for rent for the time she has been in exclusive possession of the big house? At common law, a co-tenant in exclusive possession was not liable for rent to a co-tenant out of possession absent ouster (physically excluding the other co-tenant). There is no evidence that W ever physically barred C from entering the property. Under the modern trend, however, a co-tenant in exclusive possession is liable for rent to the co-tenants out of possession.

W must account to C for C's share (1/6th) of the 15 years worth of rents W has received, and W is liable to C for C's share (1/6th) of the fair market rental value of the big house for the 15 years she has been in exclusive possession.

Answer (A) is incorrect because it implicitly is based upon the assumption that W held the property with H under a co-tenancy which had a right of survivorship. Under the modern trend, the express language is inadequate to opt into such a co-tenancy, and the default co-tenancy, tenancy in common, does not have a right of survivorship. **Answer (B) is incorrect** because it is extremely difficult for one co-tenant to adversely possess against another co-tenant. The threshold necessary to meet the adverse requirement requires that the co-tenant give actual notice of the adverse claim to the other co-tenants. There is no evidence W ever did so. **Answer (C) is incorrect** because surviving spouses get no special treatment under the laws of co-tenancy unless they held a tenancy by the entirety. H and W did not hold a tenancy by the entirety under the modern trend, so she gets no special rights as a co-tenant merely as a surviving spouse. **Answer (D) is incorrect** because it fails to take into consideration the modern trend on the duty of a co-tenant in exclusive possession to pay rent. Although no such duty existed at common law, there is a duty under the modern trend.

- **Additional references:** *See* 7 RICHARD R. POWELL, POWELL ON REAL PROPERTY ch. 50, ¶¶ 602[2], 601[2], 603[1][b], 603[1][a], 604[1] (Patrick J. Rohan ed. 1999); 4 THOMPSON ON REAL PROPERTY, SECOND THOMAS EDITION §§ 32.03, 32.07(c) (2004 & Supp. 2006); WILLIAM B. STOEBUCK & DALE A. WHITMAN, THE LAW OF PROPERTY §§ 5.2, 5.8 (3d ed. 2000); McKnight v. Basilides, 143 P.2d 307 (Wash. 1943).

PROPERTY
ANSWER KEY AND EXPLANATIONS

EXAM IV

1. **The best answer is (D).** License, easements and profits all grant the benefitting party the non-possessory right to enter real property owned by another and use it in a limited way which would otherwise constitute trespass.

The critical differences between and among a license, a profit and an easement are (1) the revocability of the interest, and (2) the scope of the permission granted. A **license** is a personal relationship between the grantor and grantee. Arguably the distinguishing characteristic of a license is that it is revocable at will by the owner of the burdened ("servient") estate. A license can become irrevocable, however, if the party who holds the license, with the consent or acquiescence of the party who has granted the license, changes his or her position and makes substantial expenditures in reasonable reliance upon the license. Under such circumstances, the grantor is estopped from revoking the license. On the other hand, an **easement** is a more substantive interest. The key characteristic of an easement is that it is irrevocable. Inasmuch as an easement is a more substantial incorporeal interest in real property, it should be created expressly in a written instrument which complies with the Statute of Frauds. A license creates no such interest and thus does not need to be created in writing (though it may be). Lastly, the distinguishing characteristic of a **profit** is that it not only permits the grantee to enter the real property of another, it permits the grantee to remove property (crops, minerals, trees, etc. - typically property which is attached to the real property) from the real property. Like easements, profits create a property interest and should be created in writing. Many commentators and treatises treat profits as simply a subset of easements.

Inasmuch as a license *may* be created in writing, while an easement *must* (as a general rule) be created in writing, where the right to enter and use another's property is created in writing there is often difficulty in determining whether the right is an easement or a license. Formally, the difference turns on the intent of the parties with respect to the revocability of the right. Where there is no clear intent expressed in the writing, the courts look to the totality of the circumstances. If the courts cannot determine the intent of the parties, the courts tend to favor holding the right to be merely a license so as to minimize the burden on the servient estate.

In determining whether Carrie's right to enter and hike is an easement or a license, the starting point is the intent of the parties as expressed in the instrument conveying the right. Here, Aman's note gave Carrie the right to enter the property and hike "for as long as I [Aman] own the land." That language appears to express an intent that the right is not revocable at will, but rather that it endures for as long as Aman owns the land (a life estate determinable). Because the right is not revocable at will by the owner of the servient estate, the right is an easement, not a license. Since Aman conveyed the right in writing in his signed note, there should not be any Statute of Frauds problem with the creation of the property interest. The easement is not a profit since there is no indication that it includes the right to remove any property from the land.

Answer (A) is incorrect because a license is revocable at will by the owner of the servient estate. Here, Aman expressly stated that Carrie's right to enter and hike was to endure for as long as Aman owned the land, indicating that the right was not revocable at will. **Answer (B) is incorrect** because the interest was not a license to begin with, and even if it were construed to be one, there is no evidence that Carrie has made substantial expenditures in reliance on the right or that the grantor stood by and expressly or implicitly consented to or acquiesced in the expenditures in the reliance on the right. Carrie's purchasing new hiking boots, even expensive ones, is not substantial enough to justify estoppel, nor is there any evidence that Aman knew about or acquiesced in the expenditure. **Answer (C) is incorrect** because a profit includes the right to remove property (crops, minerals, trees, etc.) from the real property. The right to hike which Aman conveyed to Carrie does not expressly or implicitly include the right to remove any property. **Answer (E) is incorrect** because each co-tenant has the right to unilaterally convey permission to another party to enter and use the property.

- **Additional references:** *See* 4 RICHARD R. POWELL, POWELL ON REAL PROPERTY ch. 34, §§ 34.01, 34.02, 34.24, 34.25 (Michael Allan Wolf ed., 2000); 7 THOMPSON ON REAL PROPERTY, SECOND THOMAS EDITION §§ 60.02(a), 60.02(b), 60.02(g), 60.03(a), 60.03(a)(7)(iv) (2006); WILLIAM B. STOEBUCK & DALE A. WHITMAN, THE LAW OF PROPERTY § 8.1 (3d ed. 2000); Wangen v. Kecskes, 845 P.2d 721 (Mont. 1993).

2. **The best answer is (A).** Where multiple parties own real property concurrently, each party has an equal right to possess the whole. This is true whether the concurrent estate is a joint tenancy or a tenancy in common (the third possibility is a tenancy by the entirety, but since Aman and Bill are not married, a requirement for tenancy by the entirety, there is no need to consider that option). Here, the facts do not provide enough information to determine which co-tenancy the parties held, but either way, each has the right to possess the whole. (Just because the facts indicate that the parties own the land "jointly," that does not necessarily mean that the parties hold the land in joint tenancy. "Jointly" simply indicates that multiple parties own the land. "Jointly" does not indicate whether the required "unities" have been satisfied, and without knowing whether the jurisdiction follows the common law or modern trend approach, you do not know what the default estate is.)

Co-tenants can convey their right to possession unilaterally to third parties. The third party who receives the right to possession steps into the shoes of the conveying co-tenant. The third party holds the same rights and obligations with respect to the conveyed interest as the co-tenant who conveyed the interest held. As long as the party does not interfere with the rights of the other co-tenants or oust the other co-tenants, the third party is not liable to the co-tenants for using the land. The co-tenants may, however, be able to sue the co-tenant who granted permission to use the land for an accounting for their share of the rents being generated in excess of the granting co-tenant's share.

Aman has the right to unilaterally convey his right to possession to Carrie. Included within the right to possession is the right to permit others to enter and use the property. Bill has no more right to stop Carrie from entering the property and hunting than Bill would have to stop Aman. As long as Carrie is not interfering with Bill's right to possess the land (as long as she is not ousting him), she has no liability to him. In addition, although Bill could sue Aman for an accounting if Aman were profiting from Carrie's use of the land, Carrie is not paying for the right to use the land and thus Aman has no revenues to share with Bill in an accounting. Bill's letter has no affect on Carrie's right to enter and hike on the ranch, and neither Aman nor Carrie is liable to Bill for Carrie's using the land.

Answer (B) is incorrect because each co-tenant may grant third parties the right to use and enjoy the property. The third party has the same rights and obligations as the original co-tenant. The grantee is not liable to a co-tenant unless he or she interferes with the co-tenant's right to possession or ousts the co-tenant, and the granting tenant is liable to his or her co-tenants only for profits generated in excess of his or her share. Carrie is not interfering with Bill's right to use the land, and Aman has not received any money in connection with Carrie using the land. **Answer (C) is incorrect** because each co-tenant has the right to unilaterally convey permission to another party to enter and use the property. **Answer (D) is incorrect** because each co-tenant has the right to possess and use the property concurrently held. Each co-tenant may convey this right to third parties, and the other co-tenant has no right to exclude the third parties who have permission to be on the property.

- **Additional references**: *See* 7 RICHARD R. POWELL, POWELL ON REAL PROPERTY ch. 50, ¶¶ 602[9], 603[1], 603[1][a], 604[1], ch. 51, ¶ 617[4] (Michael Allan Wolf ed., 2000); 4 THOMPSON ON REAL PROPERTY, SECOND THOMAS EDITION §§ 31.07, 31.07(c), 31.07(d), 32.07, 32.07(c), 32.07(d) (2004 & Supp. 2006); WILLIAM B. STOEBUCK & DALE A. WHITMAN, THE LAW OF PROPERTY §§ 5.2, 5.3, 5.8 (3d ed. 2000).

3. **The best answer is (D).** There are a number of different ways one can establish a property interest in a wild animal. One can claim the animal under occupancy if one: (1) manifests an unequivocal intent to appropriate the animal to one's own use, (2) deprives the animal of its natural liberty, and (3) brings the animal under certain control. By shooting and killing the deer, and then selling it, Carrie established her intent to appropriate the animal to her individual use, deprived it of its natural liberty, and brought it under her certain control. Carrie can claim the deer under occupancy.

One can also claim a property interest in a wild animal under rationi soli. Rationi soli provides that the owner of real property has constructive possession of all wild animals on his or her real property to deter trespassing. Bill can claim that as the owner of the ranch where the deer was shot and killed, he had constructive possession of the deer while it was on the ranch. Ordinarily, rationi soli trumps occupancy so as to deter trespass, at least where the party claiming under occupancy is a trespasser. Carrie, however, will claim that she is not a trespasser. She has Aman's permission to be on the ranch.

Under the limited purpose doctrine, however, where one is permitted onto the land of another for a limited purpose, any acts the person performs on the land which exceed the scope of the limited purpose for which he or she was permitted onto the land constitute a trespass. Carrie holds an easement to enter and hike on the ranch, not to hunt wild animals. Although Carrie may try and argue that the scope of the easement to hike should implicitly include the right to hunt, the argument is too much of a stretch. Where an easement is gratuitous, courts are much more likely to construe the easement narrowly.

Moreover, since the right to hunt would constitute a profit (the right to enter and remove something from the real property), the courts would be reluctant to read a profit into language which appears to only convey an easement. The intent of the parties should control. The best evidence of the intent of the parties is the express language in the instrument creating the easement. Since Carrie's easement does not include the right to hunt, when Carrie shot and killed the deer, she was trespassing. Bill's rationi sole claim should prevail over Carrie's occupancy claim.

Although Bill should prevail over Carrie, Bill is merely a co-tenant of the property. The general rule is that co-tenants cannot act as agents for other co-tenants. When Bill sues Carrie, Bill can only assert his interest in the ranch as against Carrie's claim, not Aman's interest in the ranch. Assuming Aman does not assert his half interest, Carrie's occupancy claim will prevail as to half of the deer since no one with a superior claim is asserting a claim to that half of the deer. Bill will prevail as to his one-half interest, and Carrie will prevail as to the other half. The court will not assert Aman's claim for him.

- **Additional references:** *See* RAY A. BROWN, THE LAW OF PERSONAL PROPERTY, 14-18 (Walter B. Raushenbush 3d ed. 1975); 4 RICHARD R. POWELL, POWELL ON REAL PROPERTY ch. 34, §§ 34.12-34.20 (Michael Allan Wolf ed., 2000); 7 POWELL ch. 50, ¶ 606[3]; 7 THOMPSON ON REAL PROPERTY, SECOND THOMAS EDITION §§ 60.04(a), 60.06(a) (2006); WILLIAM B. STOEBUCK & DALE A. WHITMAN, THE LAW OF PROPERTY §§ 5.2, 5.3, 5.8 (3d ed. 2000); RALPH E. BOYER ET. AL., THE LAW OF PROPERTY: AN INTRODUCTORY SURVEY § 1.2 (4th ed. 1991); Gissel v. State, 727 P.2d 1153 (Idaho 1986)

4. **The best answer is (D).** The issue of whether Carrie can assign her easement to Dottie turns in part on whether the easement is an easement appurtenant or an easement in gross. An easement appurtenant is where the benefit of the easement is conveyed to the owner of a parcel of real property. The benefit attaches to the real property, not to the individual who happens to own the parcel currently. If the property is sold, the benefit stays with the real property and is transferred to the new owner.

An easement appurtenant cannot be transferred to someone who does not hold an interest in the real property to which the benefit is appurtenant. In contrast, if the easement is an easement in gross, the benefit of the easement is held by an individual. The benefit stays with the individual wherever the individual may reside. To the extent the conveyance is ambiguous, easements appurtenant are favored over easements in gross.

Here, there is no evidence that Carrie owned any property in the area or that Aman intended to create an easement appurtenant as opposed to an easement in gross. The profit should be considered in gross.

The issue of the transferability of easements in gross troubled the courts because of the unlimited potential for subdivision, thereby overburdening the servient estate. Easements appurtenant, by definition, are limited in the extent to which they can burden the servient estate by the size of the dominant estate. Because of the concern that easements in gross, if transferable, might be subdivided and overburden the servient estate, at common law easements in gross were not transferable. With time, however, the courts came to realize the importance of permitting easements to be transferable. At first, the courts permitted the easement in gross to be transferable if the parties so intended or if commercial in nature. The Restatement (Third) of Property, however, presumes that all easements in gross are transferable unless the easement is personal.

Carrie holds an easement in gross. Under the common law approach, the easement is not transferable. The judicial modern trend permits an easement in gross to be transferable only if the parties intended it to be so or if the easement is commercial in nature. There is no express language in the instrument creating the easement that indicates that Aman intended for it to be transferable, nor is the easement to hike commercial in nature. The Restatement (Third) of Property creates a presumption that all easements in gross are transferable unless the easement is personal. Although The Restatement (Third) approach creates a presumption that Carrie can transfer her easement, the easement arguably is personal in nature. The Restatement considers the totality of the circumstances in determining whether the easement is personal. Here, the relationship between Aman and Carrie (they were engaged), the fact that the easement was gratuitous, the duration of the easement (limited to Aman's life estate), and the nature of the easement (hiking) combine to support the conclusion that the easement would probably be characterized as personal and would not be transferable even under the Restatement (Third) approach.

Answers (A) is incorrect because it fails to recognize that at common law easements in gross were not transferable. **Answer (B) is incorrect** because it implicitly misstates the common law approach (easements in gross were not transferable). **Answer (C) is incorrect** because it implicitly misapplies the modern trend approach. Although easements in gross are transferable under the modern trend approach, *personal* easements in gross are *not* transferable and Carrie's right to hike arguably is personal in nature.

- **Additional references**: *See* 4 RICHARD R. POWELL, POWELL ON REAL PROPERTY ch. 34, §§ 34.02[2][d], 34.16 (Michael Allan Wolf ed., 2000);7 THOMPSON ON REAL PROPERTY, SECOND THOMAS EDITION §§ 60.02(f)(1)-(5), 60.07(c)(1)-(3) (2006); WILLIAM B. STOEBUCK & DALE A. WHITMAN, THE LAW OF PROPERTY §§ 8.2, 8.10 (3d ed. 2000).

5. **The best answer is (A).** A covenant runs with the land, as opposed to being a personal covenant between the original parties, only if the covenant qualifies as either an equitable servitude or a real covenant. *The same covenant can qualify as either an equitable servitude or a real covenant - or both.* If the same covenant can be either (or both), what is the difference? First and foremost, the difference between an equitable servitude and a real covenant is the relief the plaintiff is seeking. If the plaintiff is seeking *equitable relief (an injunction)*, for the covenant to run with the land and be enforceable against the defendant the covenant has to qualify as an *equitable servitude.* If the plaintiff is seeking *damages*, for the covenant to run to the defendant the covenant has to qualify as a *real covenant.* Once it is determined which relief the plaintiff is seeking (or both), then it is simply a question of applying the different requirements for the respective doctrines.

Restatement of Property Approach:
↓
Does the covenant run with the land?
↓
Depends on the relief sought:
↙   ↘

If *equitable relief* (injunction)   If *damages*
↓   ↓
must show covenant qualifies as   must show covenant qualifies as
an *equitable servitude*; must show: a *real covenant*; must show:
   1. notice   1. privity
   2. intent   2. intent
   3. touch & concern   3. touch & concern

<u>Analysis of the covenant as an equitable servitude</u>. To recover equitable relief, the party must show that the covenant qualifies as an equitable servitude. To qualify as an equitable servitude, the general rule (Restatement of Property approach) is that the plaintiff must show: (1) **notice** - that the party against whom the covenant would be enforced had notice of the covenant, (2) **intent** - that the original parties to the covenant intended for the covenant to run with the land (as opposed to merely being a personal agreement between the two original parties to the covenant), and (3) **touch and concern** - that the covenant touches and concerns the land (that it affects the parties' use and enjoyment of the real property in question).

The facts indicate that the deed which created the covenant was recorded, so all subsequent grantees have constructive record notice of the covenant. Professor had notice of the covenant. The deed expressly provided that Owner covenanted for "herself, *her heirs and assigns* to provide spring water to the western half of Blackacres . . . ." (Emphasis added.) The wording also indicates that the original parties to the covenant *intended for the covenant to run* with the land to remote grantees. Lastly, the covenant must touch and concern the land.

An important variable in whether a covenant touches and concerns the land is whether the covenant is affirmative or negative. Affirmative covenants are covenants which require the burdened party to the covenant (typically the owner of the servient estate) to take affirmative action to comply with the covenant (i.e., to trim the trees, to maintain an easement, etc.). Negative covenants are covenants which restrict how the burdened party to the covenant (typically the owner of the servient estate) can use the property (i.e., for residential purposes only; cannot be used for commercial purposes, etc.). The covenant here requires the owner of the burdened estate to provide water to the benefited estate. The covenant is affirmative.

Courts generally are skeptical of affirmative covenants touching and concerning the land because of the risk of unlimited and perpetual liability on the owners of the burdened estate and the need for ongoing judicial supervision of the parties' performance. Where affirmative covenants are limited in duration and scope, and reasonably necessary for the use and enjoyment of the property, however, courts will enforce the affirmative covenant. Since the covenant in question is limited in duration and reasonably necessary for the use and enjoyment of the dominant estate, there is a good probability that a court would find that the covenant touches and concerns the land. The Heavy Metal band would probably be able to obtain equitable relief against the Professor.

Analysis of the covenant as a real covenant. To obtain damages, the covenant must qualify as a real covenant. For a real covenant to run at law, the general rule (Restatement of Property approach) is that the plaintiff must show: (1) **intent** - that the original parties to the covenant must have intended that the covenant run to remote grantees, (2) **touch and concern** - the covenant must touch and concern the land, and (3) **privity** - the requisite privity must exist. The degree of privity depends on whether the burden side of the covenant or the benefit side of the covenant is running to remote grantees. If the plaintiff is not an original party to the covenant, the plaintiff must show that the benefit runs with the land to the plaintiff. If the defendant is not an original party to the covenant, the plaintiff must show that the burden runs with the land to the defendant. Horizontal privity refers to the relationship between the *original parties to the covenant*. Vertical privity refers to the relationship between an original party to the covenant and his or her successive grantees.

As established above, under the facts given the parties intended for the covenant to run with the land, and the covenant arguably touches and concerns the land. The question is whether the requisite privity exists. The question of whether the requisite privity exists depends on which side of the covenant the party must prove runs: the burden side or the benefit side. Under the typical scenario, which side must run depends on who the parties to the litigation are.

Which side of the covenant must the plaintiff show runs? If the *plaintiff* is *not* one of the *original* parties to the covenant, the plaintiff must show the *benefit* runs to the plaintiff. To show the benefit runs to the plaintiff, he or she need not show any horizontal privity between the original parties to the covenant, but he or she must show the requisite vertical privity which is that an estate of any duration passed from one of the original parties to the covenant to the plaintiff. If the *defendant* is *not* one of the *original* parties to the covenant, the plaintiff must show the *burden* runs to the defendant. The plaintiff must show (1) the requisite mutual or successive horizontal privity between the original parties to the covenant and (2) the requisite vertical privity between one of the original parties to the covenant and the plaintiff – the requisite privity being an estate of the exact same duration was passed from the original party to the covenant and the plaintiff. (If neither the plaintiff nor the defendant were parties to the original covenant, the plaintiff must show that both the benefit and the burden run to the respective parties.)

Since neither the Heavy Metal band nor Professor were party to the original agreement, the band must show that both the burden and the benefit of the covenant run with the land in order to recover damages from Professor. For the benefit to run, no horizontal privity is necessary between the original parties to the covenant, and the benefit runs to a successor in interest as long as any interest in the land passes from the original party to the covenant to the plaintiff. Heavy Metal band is leasing from Buyer. A leasehold interest qualifies as an interest in the land such that the benefit will run to Heavy Metal band. On the other side, for Heavy Metal band to recover damages from Professor, the band has to show that the burden runs from Owner to Professor.

For the burden to run, there must have been horizontal privity between the original parties to the covenant, and the burden will not run to a remote grantee unless the remote grantee takes an estate of the exact same duration that the original party held. Horizontal privity can be either successive privity (the original parties to the covenant had a grantor-grantee relationship with respect to a property interest other than the covenant) or mutual privity (the original parties to the covenant hold a property interest in the land other than the covenant).

Inasmuch as the covenant was created in the deed which conveyed the western half of Blackacres, there is horizontal privity (successive privity) between the original parties to the covenant. And inasmuch as Professor purchased Owner's fee simple absolute interest in the property, Professor holds the same estate in duration as the original party to the covenant.

Since there is both horizontal and vertical privity, the burden runs. Since both the benefit and burden run, the real covenant runs at law and Heavy Metal Band could recover damages from Professor.

Answer (B) is incorrect because it fails to recognize that the band may recover damages if it wishes. The covenant meets the requirements for a real covenant to run at law. **Answer (C) is incorrect** because it fails to recognize that the band is entitled to equitable relief if it wishes. The covenant meets the requirements for an equitable servitude to run at equity. **Answer (D) is incorrect** because it fails to recognize that the band may recover either damages or equitable relief. The covenant meets the requirements for it to run as either a real covenant at law or an equitable servitude.

- **Additional references**: *See* 9 RICHARD R. POWELL, POWELL ON REAL PROPERTY ch. 60, §§ 60.04[1]-60.04[2][d] (Michael Allan Wolf ed., 2000); 7 THOMPSON ON REAL PROPERTY, SECOND THOMAS EDITION §§ 62.03-62.13 (2006); ROGER A. CUNNINGHAM ET AL., THE LAW OF PROPERTY: AN INTRODUCTORY SURVEY §§ 8.13-8.19, 8.22-8.29 (3d ed. 2000).

6. **The best answer is (A).** The first step in analyzing whether a grantee may use an existing easement is whether the easement is an easement appurtenant or an easement in gross.

An easement in gross has a servient estate but not a dominant estate. Instead, the benefit is held personally by the holder of the benefit of the easement. The easement in gross stays with the holder of the easement regardless of which parcel of land the easement holder owns, or even if the easement holder holds real property at all. Easements in gross historically were not transferable. The modern trend is to hold that easements in gross are transferable if commercial in nature or if the parties expressly intend for the easement in gross to be transferable.

An easement appurtenant, on the other hand, has both a dominant and a servient estate. The servient estate is the parcel of real property which is burdened by the easement. The dominant estate is the parcel of real property which is benefitted by the easement. The benefit of the easement attaches to the dominant estate and runs with the dominant estate regardless of who owns the dominant estate and regardless of subsequent transfers of the dominant estate. Absent evidence to the contrary, the duration of an easement appurtenant is fee simple absolute, unless terminated under one of the easement termination doctrines.

Where the facts are ambiguous as to whether the parties intended the easement to be appurtenant or in gross, the courts favor an easement appurtenant.

Although at first blush the key to answering this problem appears to be whether the easement is appurtenant or in gross, in fact that distinction makes no difference under these facts. There is no direct evidence which supports whether the easement is appurtenant or in gross, but under either characterization of the easement, E is not entitled to use the easement.

To the extent that the facts are unclear as to whether the easement should be classified as an easement in gross or an easement appurtenant, the courts prefer to classify the easement as an easement appurtenant. Assuming, *arguendo*, that the easement is an easement appurtenant, the easement is terminated under the merger doctrine. A positive easement gives a party the right to enter another's real property and use it in a way which would otherwise constitute a trespass. The key is that it gives one party limited rights to use *another party's* real property. Accordingly, one cannot have an easement in one's own real property. The merger doctrine is based upon that logic. If one holds an easement and thereafter acquires title to the servient estate (the burdened estate), the easement mergers into the fee simple title to the servient estate and is extinguished. Initially, B held an easement in Blackacre, A's property. When A sold Blackacre to C, C took the property subject to B's easement. When B sold Whiteacre to C, if the easement is appurtenant, the easement is attached to Whiteacre and passes with the title to Whiteacre to C. C now holds both the easement and the servient estate. Since C does not need an easement in C's own property to cross it, the easement is extinguished under the merger doctrine.

The only remaining issue under the easement appurtenant option is whether the easement is revived when C severs Blackacre and Whiteacre. The general rule is that once an easement is extinguished under merger, it is not automatically revived when the dominant estate and servient estate are separated again. The easement must be properly recreated again under one of the doctrines for creation of an easement. There is no evidence which indicates that the easement was properly recreated when C sold Blackacre to D and Whiteacre to E.

Assuming, *arguendo*, that the easement was an easement in gross, under the traditional common law B could not transfer it, so E would have no right to use it. Under the modern trend, although easements in gross are transferable if commercial or if the parties intended the easement to be transferable, there is no evidence that the easement was commercial in nature or that the parties intended the easement to be transferable.

Answer (B) is incorrect because E has no right to use the easement whether the easement was classified as an easement appurtenant or an easement in gross. If appurtenant, the easement was terminated under the merger doctrine. If in gross, the easement stayed with the original holder of the easement, B. **Answer (C) is incorrect** because whether an easement is express or implied, in and of itself, does not control a remote grantee's ability to claim the benefit of the easement. **Answer (D) is incorrect** because whether an easement is recorded or not, in and of itself, does not control a remote grantee's ability to claim the benefit of the easement.

- **Additional references**: *See* 4 RICHARD R. POWELL, POWELL ON REAL PROPERTY ch. 34, §§ 34.02[2][d], 34.22 (Michael Allan Wolf ed., 2000); 7 THOMPSON ON REAL PROPERTY, SECOND THOMAS EDITION §§ 60.02(f)(5), 60.08(b)(1) (2006); WILLIAM B. STOEBUCK & DALE A. WHITMAN, THE LAW OF PROPERTY §§ 8.2, 8.12 (3d ed. 2000).

7. **The best answer is (D).** Both a license and an easement grant the benefiting party the non-possessory right to enter real property owned by the grantor and use it in a limited way which would otherwise constitute trespass.

The critical difference between a license and an easement is that the former is a personal relationship between the grantor and grantee which is revocable at will by the owner of the servient (burdened) estate, while the latter is a more substantive relationship which is irrevocable. An easement is a substantial interest in real property which should be created expressly in a written instrument which complies with the Statute of Frauds. A license does not need to be created in writing, though it may be.

Student's right to cross Owner's property appears more substantive than a mere revocable license. Student's right to cross was created by a written instrument, in exchange for consideration, and Owner bound himself, his heirs and assigns. Student holds an easement.

As to Undergraduate's right to use the easement, the issue is whether the easement is appurtenant or in gross. An easement appurtenant has both a dominant and a servient estate. The servient estate is the parcel of real property which is burdened by the easement. The dominant estate is the parcel of real property which is benefited by the easement. The benefit of the easement attaches to the dominant estate and runs with it, regardless of who owns the dominant estate and regardless of subsequent transfers of the dominant estate. An easement in gross, on the other hand, has a servient estate but not a dominant estate. Instead, the benefit is held personally by the holder of the benefit of the easement. The easement in gross stays with the holder of the easement regardless of which parcel of land the easement holder owns, or even if the easement holder holds no real property at all. Where the evidence is ambiguous, the courts tend to favor an easement appurtenant over an easement in gross.

Here, the easement is most likely an easement in gross. Student lives in the dormitories. There is no evidence that Student owns any real property to which the benefit of the easement could attach. The easement held by Student is an easement in gross.

When Student attempted to convey the easement to Undergraduate, that gave rise to the issue of the transferability of the easement in gross. Historically, easements in gross were not transferable. The modern trend is to hold that easements in gross are transferable if commercial in nature or if the parties expressly intended for the easement in gross to be transferable. Under The Restatement (Third) of Property, easements in gross are presumed transferable unless personal in nature. Whether an easement is personal depends upon the circumstances surrounding the creation of the easement.

Under the facts of the case, the easement does not appear to be assignable. There is no evidence that the easement is commercial in nature. It appears to be purely recreational in nature for Student's personal use. Nor is there any evidence in the instrument which created the easement that the parties intended the benefit to be transferable. The fact that Owner and his heirs and assigns covenanted to maintain the road is consistent with the fact that the burden of an easement runs with the land to remote grantees, but it is not determinative as to the issue of whether the benefit is transferable. There is no express evidence that the parties intended it to be transferable.

Under The Restatement (Third) of Property approach, Student can argue that the easement is presumed transferable. Student can support this presumption by pointing out that he paid consideration for the easement and that the instrument expressly provides that the easement is to run with the land. On the other hand, Purchaser will argue that the easement is personal. Purchaser will emphasize that the easement is recreational in nature, not commercial, and that the nature assumption would be that a recreational easement is personal. Moreover, Owner used the words "heirs and assigns" to indicate that the covenant was to run to remote grantees, demonstrating that Owner knew how to express the intent that a property interest which was transferable should pass to subsequent grantees. Owner's failure to use such words when describing the easement arguably indicates that the Owner intended the easement to be personal and not transferable. The issue of whether Student's easement is transferable is much tougher under The Restatement (Third) approach. The most likely result, however, is that easement in gross is not transferable to Undergraduate. Undergraduate has no right to use the easement.

Answers (A) and (B) are incorrect because they underestimate the nature of the property interest created. A license is a personal relationship between the parties which generally is revocable at will by either party, and any act which is inconsistent with the license continuing is construed as an implied revocation. If the interest were merely a license, there would be no need for a written instrument to create it, and there would be no purpose served by expressly providing that the grantor covenanted for the grantor and his heirs and assigns to maintain the road. The fact that grantor expressly covenanted for himself, his heirs and assigns indicates that the parties intended the right to use the road to continue even after the grantor conveyed the servient estate. The better argument is that the right to use the road is an easement, not merely a license. **Answer (C) is incorrect** because it incorrectly concludes that the easement is assignable. The easement is not commercial in nature nor is there any evidence that the parties intended the benefit to be transferable. If the jurisdiction were to apply The Restatement (Third) of Property approach, however, the answer very well could be answer (C).

- **Additional references**: *See* 4 RICHARD R. POWELL, POWELL ON REAL PROPERTY ch. 34, §§ 34.02[d], 34.16 (Michael Allan Wolf ed., 2000); 7 THOMPSON ON REAL PROPERTY, SECOND THOMAS EDITION §§ 60.02(f)(5), 60.03(a)(7)(iv), 60.07(c)(1)-(2) (2006); WILLIAM B. STOEBUCK & DALE A. WHITMAN, THE LAW OF PROPERTY §§ 8.2, 8.10 (3d ed. 2000).

8. **The best answer is (C).** A covenant runs with the land, as opposed to being a personal covenant between the original parties, only if the

covenant qualifies as either an equitable servitude or a real covenant. *The same covenant can qualify as either an equitable servitude or a real covenant - or both.* If the same covenant can be either (or both), what is the difference? First and foremost, the difference between an equitable servitude and a real covenant is the relief the plaintiff is seeking. If the plaintiff is seeking *equitable relief (an injunction)*, for the covenant to run with the land and be enforceable against the defendant the covenant has to qualify as an *equitable servitude*. If the plaintiff is seeking *damages*, for the covenant to run to the defendant the covenant has to qualify as a *real covenant*. Once it is determined which relief the plaintiff is seeking (or both), then it is simply a question of applying the different requirements for the respective doctrines. The common law courts were reluctant to grant damages for a variety of reasons, so the requirements for a real covenant are more difficult to establish than the requirements for an equitable servitude.

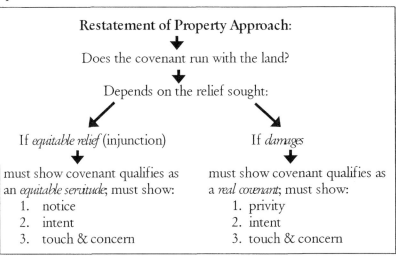

Restatement of Property Approach:

↓

Does the covenant run with the land?

↓

Depends on the relief sought:

↙   ↘

If *equitable relief* (injunction)   If *damages*

↓   ↓

must show covenant qualifies as   must show covenant qualifies as
an *equitable servitude*; must show: a *real covenant*; must show:
   1. notice   1. privity
   2. intent   2. intent
   3. touch & concern   3. touch & concern

<u>Analysis of the covenant as an equitable servitude.</u> To recover equitable relief, the party must show that the covenant qualifies as an equitable servitude. To qualify as an equitable servitude, the general rule (Restatement of Property approach) is that the plaintiff must show: (1) **notice** - that the party against whom the covenant would be enforced had notice of the covenant, (2) **intent** - that the original parties to the covenant intended for the covenant to run with the land (as opposed to merely being a personal agreement between the two original parties to the covenant), and (3) **touch and concern** - that the covenant touches and concerns the land (that it affects the parties' use and enjoyment of the real property in question).

The covenant should qualify as an equitable servitude, and Student should be able to obtain equitable relief against Purchaser. The facts indicate that the deed which created the covenant was recorded, so all subsequent grantees have constructive record notice of the covenant. Purchaser had notice of the covenant. The deed expressly provided that "Owner, his heirs and assigns promise to maintain the road." The wording indicates that the original parties to the covenant intended for the burden of the covenant to run with the land to remote grantees. Lastly, the covenant must touch and concern the land.

The touch and concern requirement is difficult to define. It is the requirement the courts use most often to regulate which covenants should run to remote grantees and which should not. An important variable in whether a covenant touches and concerns the land is whether the covenant is affirmative or negative. Affirmative covenants are covenants which require the burdened party to the covenant (typically the owner of the servient estate) to take affirmative action to comply with the covenant (i.e., to trim the trees, to maintain an easement, etc.). Negative covenants are covenants which restrict how the burdened party to the covenant (typically the owner of the servient estate) can use the property (i.e., for residential purposes only; cannot be used for commercial purposes, etc.). The covenant here requires the owner of the burdened estate to maintain the road. The covenant is affirmative.

Although courts are somewhat reluctant to enforce affirmative covenants on burdened landowners, this judicial reluctance is not nearly as strong where the duration of the burden is limited and the affirmative acts are to be performed on and to the servient estate. Here, because the easement is an easement in gross, its duration is, by definition, limited. In addition, the affirmative acts are to be performed on and to the servient estate. Maintaining the easement will provide an indirect benefit to the servient estate by improving its appearance and by protecting against indirect damage to the servient estate from the easement. Moreover, the benefit of the covenant (the maintenance of the easement) arguably touches and concerns the easement, thereby making Student's property interest in the easement more valuable. Since the covenant in question is limited in duration and reasonably necessary for the use and enjoyment of the easement, there is a good probability that a court would find that the covenant touches and concerns the land. The covenant should qualify as an equitable servitude, and Student should be able to obtain equitable relief against Purchaser.

<u>Analysis of the covenant as a real covenant</u>. To obtain damages, the covenant must qualify as a real covenant. For a real covenant to run at law, the general rule (Restatement of Property approach) is that the plaintiff must show: (1) **intent** - that the original parties to the covenant must have intended that the covenant run to remote grantees, (2) **touch and concern** - the covenant must touch and concern the land, and (3) **privity** - the requisite privity must exist. The degree of privity depends on whether the burden side of the covenant or the benefit side of the covenant is running to remote grantees. If the plaintiff is not an original party to the covenant, the plaintiff must show that the benefit runs with the land to the plaintiff. If the defendant is not an original party to the covenant, the plaintiff must show that the burden runs with the land to the defendant. Horizontal privity refers to the relationship between the *original parties to the covenant*. Vertical privity refers to the relationship between an original party to the covenant and his or her successive grantees.

As established above, under the facts given, the parties intended for the covenant to run with the land, and the covenant arguably touches and concerns the land. The question is whether the requisite privity exists. Whether the requisite privity exists depends on which side of the covenant the plaintiff must show runs – the burden side or the benefit side (or both).

Which side of the covenant must the plaintiff show runs? If the *plaintiff* is *not* one of the *original* parties to the covenant, the plaintiff must show the *benefit* runs to the plaintiff. To show the benefit runs to the plaintiff, he or she need not show any horizontal privity between the original parties to the covenant, but he or she must show the requisite vertical privity which is that an estate of any duration passed from one of the original parties to the covenant to the plaintiff. If the *defendant* is *not* one of the *original* parties to the covenant, the plaintiff must show the *burden* runs to the defendant. The plaintiff must show: (1) the requisite mutual or successive horizontal privity between the original parties to the covenant and (2) the requisite vertical privity between one of the original parties to the covenant and the plaintiff – the requisite privity being an estate of the exact same duration passed from the original party to the covenant and the plaintiff. (If neither the plaintiff nor the defendant were parties to the original covenant, the plaintiff must show that both the benefit and the burden run to the respective parties.)

Because Student was a party to the original agreement, for Student to recover damages from Purchaser, Student need not show that the benefit runs, only that the burden runs from the original grantor, Owner, to Purchaser. For the burden to run, there must have been horizontal privity (between the original parties to the covenant), and there must be vertical privity (between the original party and the grantee being charged with the burden). Horizontal privity can be either successive privity (the original parties to the covenant had a grantor-grantee relationship with respect to a property interest other than the covenant) or mutual privity (the original parties to the covenant share a property interest in the land other than the covenant). Vertical privity requires that the remote grantee being charged with the burden of the covenant must take the exact same estate in duration as the original party to the covenant held.

Under the facts given, horizontal privity is present. The deed which created the covenant also conveyed an easement from Owner to Student. Thus Owner and Student had a grantor-grantee relationship with respect to a property interest other than the covenant, i.e. the easement. There is successive horizontal privity. The easement also created mutual horizontal privity since it created a shared property interest in the servient estate. Owner held a fee simple absolute in the property, and Student held an easement in the real property. Horizontal privity existed between Owner and Student.

For the burden of a covenant to run to remote grantees, in addition to horizontal privity there must be the requisite vertical privity. In particular, the remote grantee must hold the same possessory estate in duration as the original party to the agreement held. Owner transferred his fee simple absolute interest to Purchaser. Purchaser took the same estate in duration. There is the requisite degree of vertical privity between Owner and Purchaser.

The covenant qualifies as a real covenant which runs with the land to the servient estate's remote grantees. There was intent for the covenant to run to Owner's remote grantees, the covenant touches and concerns the land, and the requisite privity was present. (In addition, since the writing creating the easement was recorded, Purchaser cannot claim protection under the recording act in the jurisdiction, regardless of which approach the jurisdiction takes.)

Answer (A) is incorrect because it fails to recognize that Student may recover damages if he wishes. The covenant meets the requirements for a real covenant to run at law. **Answer (B) is incorrect** because it fails to recognize that Student is entitled to equitable relief if he wishes. The covenant meets the requirements for an equitable servitude to run at equity. **Answer (D) is incorrect** because there are no grounds for invalidating the covenant.

- **Additional references:** *See* 9 RICHARD R. POWELL, POWELL ON REAL PROPERTY ch. 60, §§ 60.04[1]-60.04[2][d] (Michael Allan Wolf ed., 2000); 7 THOMPSON ON REAL PROPERTY, SECOND THOMAS EDITION §§ 62.03-62.13 (2006); WILLIAM B. STOEBUCK & DALE A. WHITMAN, THE LAW OF PROPERTY §§ 8.13-8.19, 8.22-8.29 (3d ed. 2000).

9. **The best answer is (C).** A covenant runs with the land, as opposed to being a personal covenant between the original parties, only if the covenant qualifies as either an equitable servitude or a real covenant. *The same covenant can qualify as either an equitable servitude or a real covenant - or both.* If the same covenant can be either (or both), what is the difference? First and foremost, the difference between an equitable servitude and a real covenant is the relief the plaintiff is seeking. If the plaintiff is seeking *equitable relief (an injunction)*, for the covenant to run with the land and be enforceable against the defendant the covenant has to qualify as an *equitable servitude*. If the plaintiff is seeking *damages*, for the covenant to run to the defendant the covenant has to qualify as a *real covenant*. Once it is determined which relief the plaintiff is seeking (or both), then it is simply a question of applying the different requirements for the respective doctrines. The common law courts were reluctant to grant damages for a variety of reasons, so the requirements for a real covenant are more difficult to establish than the requirements for an equitable servitude.

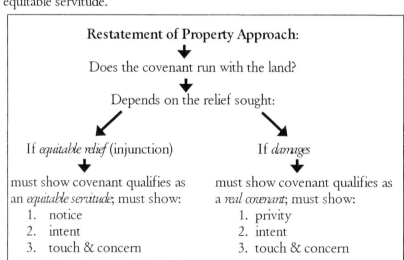

Restatement of Property Approach:

↓

Does the covenant run with the land?

↓

Depends on the relief sought:

↙   ↘

If *equitable relief* (injunction)   If *damages*

↓   ↓

must show covenant qualifies as   must show covenant qualifies as
an *equitable servitude*; must show: a *real covenant*; must show:
1. notice   1. privity
2. intent   2. intent
3. touch & concern   3. touch & concern

Analysis of the covenant as an equitable servitude. To recover equitable relief, the party must show that the covenant qualifies as an equitable servitude. To qualify as an equitable servitude, the general rule (Restatement of Property approach) is that the plaintiff must show: (1) **notice** - that the party against whom the covenant would be enforced had notice of the covenant, (2) **intent** - that the original parties to the covenant intended for the covenant to run with the land (as opposed to merely being a personal agreement between the two original parties to the covenant), and (3) **touch and concern** - that the covenant touches and concerns the land (that it affects the parties' use and enjoyment of the real property in question).

S should be entitled to equitable relief against C. The facts indicate that the deed which created the covenant was recorded, so all subsequent grantees have constructive record notice of the covenant. C had notice of the covenant. The deed expressly provides that "the covenant is to run with the lot conveyed and the adjacent land which O retains, to all subsequent grantees." The wording indicates the original parties to the covenant intended for the covenant to run with the land to remote grantees. The issue is whether the covenant touches and concerns the land. Negative covenants which restrict the purposes to which the burdened estate can be put to use almost invariably touch and concern the land. Such covenants are the prototypical equitable servitude. The covenant here expressly restricts the purposes to which the burdened property can be put to residential uses. The covenant touches and concerns the land. S should be able to obtain equitable relief against C.

Analysis of the covenant as a real covenant. To obtain damages, the covenant must qualify as a real covenant. For a real covenant to run at law, the general rule (Restatement of Property approach) is that the plaintiff must show: (1) **intent** - that the original parties to the covenant must have intended that the covenant run to remote grantees, (2) **touch and concern** - the covenant must touch and concern the land, and (3) **privity** - the requisite privity must exist. The degree of privity depends on whether the burden side of the covenant or the benefit side of the covenant is running to remote grantees. If the plaintiff is not an original party to the covenant, the plaintiff must show that the benefit runs with the land to the plaintiff. If the defendant is not an original party to the covenant, the plaintiff must show that the burden runs with the land to the defendant. Horizontal privity refers to the relationship between the *original parties to the covenant*. Vertical privity refers to the relationship between an original party to the covenant and his or her successive grantees.

As established above, under the facts given the parties intended for the covenant to run with the land, and the covenant touches and concerns the land. The question is whether the requisite privity exists. Whether the requisite privity exists depends on which side of the covenant the plaintiff must show runs – the burden side or the benefit side.

Which side of the covenant must the plaintiff show runs? If the *plaintiff* is *not* one of the *original* parties to the covenant, the plaintiff must show the *benefit* runs to the plaintiff. To show the benefit runs to the plaintiff, he or she need not show any horizontal privity between the original parties to the covenant, but he or she must show the requisite vertical privity which is that an estate of any duration passed from one of the original parties to the covenant to the plaintiff. If the *defendant* is *not* one of the *original* parties to the covenant, the plaintiff must show the *burden* runs to the defendant. The plaintiff must show: (1) the requisite mutual or successive horizontal privity between the original parties to the covenant and (2) the requisite vertical privity between one of the original parties to the covenant and the plaintiff – the requisite privity being an estate of the exact same duration was passed from the original party to the covenant and the plaintiff. (If neither the plaintiff nor the defendant were parties to the original covenant, the plaintiff must show that both the benefit and the burden run to the respective parties.)

Since neither B nor C was party to the original agreement, for B to recover damages from C, B must show that both the burden and the benefit of the covenant run with the land. For the benefit to run, no horizontal privity is necessary between the original parties to the covenant and the benefit runs to a successor in interest as long as any interest in the land passes. B is leasing from O. A leasehold interest qualifies as an interest in the land such that the benefit will run to B.

The issue is whether the burden runs from A to C. For the burden to run, there must have been horizontal privity between the original parties to the covenant, and the remote grantee must take the exact same estate in duration as the original party held. Horizontal privity can be either successive privity (the original parties to the covenant had a grantor-grantee relationship with respect to a property interest other than the covenant) or mutual privity (the original parties to the covenant hold a property interest in the land other than the covenant). Inasmuch as the covenant was created in the deed which conveyed lot 1 to A, there is successive horizontal privity between the original parties to the covenant. The question is whether the requisite vertical privity is present for the burden to run.

Inasmuch as C is only leasing from A, C does not hold the same estate in duration as the original party to the covenant. Since there is not the requisite degree of vertical privity, the burden will not run. Since the burden does not run to C, the real covenant does not run at law, and B cannot recover damages from C.

Answers (A) and (D) are incorrect because although B is entitled to injunctive relief, B is not entitled to damages. For the burden to run for purposes of recovering damages, the defendant must hold the exact same estate as the original party to the covenant. Since C is only leasing from A, C does not hold the exact same estate. The burden does not run, so B is not entitled to damages. **Answers (B) and (D) are incorrect** because B is entitled to injunctive relief against C. There was intent for the covenant to run to remote parties. C had notice since the deed creating the covenant was recorded. The terms of the covenant restricting use of the land to residential purposes touch and concern the land. The covenant is enforceable as an equitable servitude, and B is entitled to injunctive relief.

- **Additional references**: *See* 9 RICHARD R. POWELL, POWELL ON REAL PROPERTY ch. 60, §§ 60.04[1]-60.04[2][d] (Michael Allan Wolf ed., 2000); 7 THOMPSON ON REAL PROPERTY, SECOND THOMAS EDITION §§ 62.03-62.13 (2006); WILLIAM B. STOEBUCK & DALE A. WHITMAN, THE LAW OF PROPERTY §§ 8.13-8.19, 8.22-8.29 (3d ed. 2000).

10. **The best answer is (C).** A covenant runs with the land, as opposed to being a personal covenant between the original parties, only if the covenant qualifies as either an equitable servitude or a real covenant. *The same covenant can qualify as either an equitable servitude or a real covenant - or both.* If the same covenant can be either (or both), what's the difference? First and foremost, the difference between an equitable servitude and a real covenant is the relief the plaintiff is seeking. If the plaintiff is seeking *equitable relief (an injunction)*, for the covenant to run with the land and be enforceable against the defendant the covenant has to qualify as an *equitable servitude*. If the plaintiff is seeking *damages*, for the covenant to run to the defendant the covenant has to qualify as a *real covenant*. Once it is determined which relief the plaintiff is seeking (or both), then it is simply a question of applying the different requirements for the respective doctrines. The common law courts were reluctant to grant damages for a variety of reasons, so the requirements for a real covenant are more difficult to establish than the requirements for an equitable servitude.

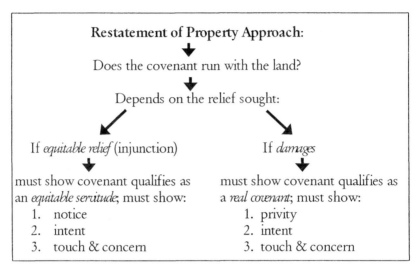

Restatement of Property Approach:

Does the covenant run with the land?

Depends on the relief sought:

If *equitable relief* (injunction)

must show covenant qualifies as an *equitable servitude*; must show:
1. notice
2. intent
3. touch & concern

If *damages*

must show covenant qualifies as a *real covenant*; must show:
1. privity
2. intent
3. touch & concern

<u>Analysis of the covenant as an equitable servitude</u>. To recover equitable relief, the party must show that the covenant qualifies as an equitable servitude. To qualify as an equitable servitude, the general rule (Restatement of Property approach) is that the plaintiff must show: (1) **notice** - that the party against whom the covenant would be enforced had notice of the covenant, (2) **intent** - that the original parties to the covenant intended for the covenant to run with the land (as opposed to merely being a personal agreement between the two original parties to the covenant), and (3) **touch and concern** - that the covenant touches and concerns the land (that it affects the parties' use and enjoyment of the real property in question).

The party against whom the plaintiff is seeking equitable relief must have had notice of the covenant. The facts indicate that the deed which created the covenant was recorded, so all subsequent grantees have constructive record notice of the covenant. Betty is seeking relief against Alice, one of the original parties to the covenant. Alice had notice of the covenant.

The intent that the covenant is to run with the land, as opposed to being merely personal between the original parties to the agreement, is usually express in the instrument ("heirs, successors, and assigns") which created the covenant. Here, there are no such words indicating an intent that the covenant run. Nevertheless, courts will imply an intent that the covenant is to run when the nature, purpose and circumstances of the covenant justify it. Here, the nature of the covenant is not to benefit Olivia personally, but to benefit the land: to prevent the land from being flooded. Although not express, the intent appears to be that the covenant should last in perpetuity. The intent was to protect the land and crops from the regular flooding of the Mississippi, not for some short term arrangement, but in perpetuity. The circumstances surrounding the covenant's creation and the nature and purpose of the covenant support the conclusion that the parties intended for the covenant to run with the land, despite the absence of the traditional terms expressing such an intent in the creating instrument.

The touch and concern requirement is difficult to define. It is the requirement the courts use most often to regulate which covenants should run to remote grantees and which should not. An important variable in whether a covenant touches and concerns the land is whether the covenant is affirmative or negative. Affirmative covenants are covenants which require the burdened party to the covenant (typically the owner of the servient estate) to take affirmative action to comply with the covenant (i.e., to trim the trees, to maintain an easement, etc.). Negative covenants are covenants which restrict how the burdened party to the covenant (typically the owner of the servient estate) can use the property (i.e., for residential purposes only; cannot be used for commercial purposes, etc.). The covenant here requires the owner of the burdened estate to maintain part of the levee. The covenant is affirmative.

Generally courts are skeptical of affirmative covenants touching and concerning the land because of the risk of unlimited and perpetual liability on the owners of the burdened estate and the need for ongoing judicial supervision of the parties' performance. Where, however, affirmative covenants are to be performed on and to the servient estate, and a direct benefit flows back to the servient estate, courts usually enforce the affirmative covenant. Although the covenant in question requires Alice to maintain the levee, the acts are to be performed on and to the servient estate and the acts benefit not only Olivia's estate but also Alice's property. The court should find that the covenant touches and concerns the land. Betty should be able to obtain equitable relief against Alice.

Analysis of the covenant as a real covenant. To obtain damages, the covenant must qualify as a real covenant. For a real covenant to run at law, the general rule (Restatement of Property approach) is that the plaintiff must show: (1) **intent** - that the original parties to the covenant must have intended that the covenant run to remote grantees, (2) **touch and concern** - the covenant must touch and concern the land, and (3)

privity - the requisite privity must exist. The degree of privity depends on whether the burden side of the covenant or the benefit side of the covenant is running to remote grantees. If the plaintiff is not an original party to the covenant, the plaintiff must show that the benefit runs with the land to the plaintiff. If the defendant is not an original party to the covenant, the plaintiff must show that the burden runs with the land to the defendant. Horizontal privity refers to the relationship between the *original parties to the covenant*. Vertical privity refers to the relationship between an original party to the covenant and his or her successive grantees.

As established above, under the facts given the parties intended for the covenant to run with the land, and the covenant arguably touches and concerns the land. The issue is whether the requisite privity exists. Whether the requisite privity exists depends on which side of the covenant the plaintiff must show runs – the burden side or the benefit side (or both).

Which side of the covenant must the plaintiff show runs? If the *plaintiff* is *not* one of the *original* parties to the covenant, the plaintiff must show the *benefit* runs to the plaintiff. To show the benefit runs to the plaintiff, he or she need not show any horizontal privity between the original parties to the covenant, but he or she must show the requisite vertical privity which is that an estate of any duration passed from one of the original parties to the covenant to the plaintiff. If the *defendant* is *not* one of the *original* parties to the covenant, the plaintiff must show the *burden* runs to the defendant. The plaintiff must show: (1) the requisite mutual or successive horizontal privity between the original parties to the covenant and (2) the requisite vertical privity between one of the original parties to the covenant and the plaintiff – the requisite privity being an estate of the exact same duration was passed from the original party to the covenant and the plaintiff. (If neither the plaintiff nor the defendant were parties to the original covenant, the plaintiff must show that both the benefit and the burden run to the respective parties.)

Since Alice was a party to the original agreement, for Betty to recover damages from Alice, Betty must show only that her side of the covenant (since Betty is the plaintiff that would be the benefit side) runs from the original party to the covenant to her. For the benefit to run, no horizontal privity is necessary between the original parties to the covenant, and the benefit runs to a successor in interest as long as any interest in the land passes. Betty purchased fee simple absolute from Alice. Betty's interest qualifies as an interest in the land such that the benefit will run to Betty. Since the benefit runs to Betty, the real covenant runs at law, and Betty can recover damages from Alice.

Answer (A) is incorrect because the courts will imply that the parties intended that the covenant was to run with the land, despite the absence of express language to that effect, from the nature and circumstances surrounding the creation of the covenant. **Answer (B) is incorrect** because even though the covenant is an affirmative covenant, which common law courts were wary of because of the burden imposed in perpetuity upon the servient estate owner, a court would likely hold that the covenant touches and concerns the land because the affirmative act is to be performed upon the servient estate and a direct and real benefit flows to the servient estate. **Answer (D) is incorrect** because the covenant qualifies as a real covenant. The parties intended for the covenant to run to remote grantees, the covenant touches and concerns the land, and the requisite degree of vertical privity is present for the benefit to run to Betty, a remote grantee.

• **Additional references**: *See* 9 RICHARD R. POWELL, POWELL ON REAL PROPERTY ch. 60, §§ 60.04[1]-60.04[2][d] (Michael Allan Wolf ed., 2000); 7 THOMPSON ON REAL PROPERTY, §§ 62.03-62.13 (2006); WILLIAM B. STOEBUCK & DALE A. WHITMAN, THE LAW OF PROPERTY §§ 8.13-8.19, 8.22-8.29 (3d ed. 2000).

11. **The best answer is (C).** A covenant may terminate either naturally pursuant to its express terms or prematurely by being extinguished (terminated prematurely under one of several doctrines). A covenant may be extinguished by merger, release, abandonment (waiver), through prescriptive adverse use, estoppel, the changed conditions doctrine, or if the party is entitled to protection under the jurisdiction's recording act.

Abandonment of a covenant can extinguish the covenant. Abandonment arguably constitutes an implied release (giving up one's rights under the covenant). Abandonment requires a failure to enforce a covenant coupled with an intent to release. (If the failure to enforce lasts long enough in the face of conditions violating the covenant, the circumstances may rise to the level of prescriptive adverse use even in the absence of the intent to release.) Failure to enforce a covenant, in and of itself, however, generally does not constitute abandonment. Most courts require some conduct which demonstrates an intent to release the covenant. In order for community violations to constitute abandonment, the community violations must be so general as to frustrate the original purpose of the covenant.

Here, none of the property owners are in full compliance, and only 18 had taken substantial steps toward compliance. There is substantial and wide spread noncompliance. There has been substantial and general non-enforcement. Under such conditions, the covenant will be deemed abandoned.

Answers (A) and (B) are incorrect because they fail to reflect that the covenant has been extinguished. Although the technical requirements for enforcing the covenant as an equitable servitude or a real covenant may appear to exist, the covenant is not enforceable since it has been waived. **Answer (D) is incorrect** because the doctrine of changed conditions requires that the conditions in and around the neighborhood have changed so much that the objects and purposes of the covenant have been thwarted. There is no evidence that the conditions in and around the neighborhood have changed other than the failure of the residents to comply with the covenant. Enforcing the covenant could still achieve its intended objects and purposes if all residents fully complied. There arguably are no changed conditions which render the objects and purposes thwarted. Answer (C) is a better answer.

- **Additional references**: *See* 9 RICHARD R. POWELL, POWELL ON REAL PROPERTY ch. 60, §§ 60.10[1]-[2] (Michael Allan Wolf ed., 2000); 7 THOMPSON ON REAL PROPERTY, SECOND THOMAS EDITION §§ 62.15-62.16 (2006); WILLIAM B. STOEBUCK & DALE A. WHITMAN, THE LAW OF PROPERTY §§ 8.20-8.30 (3d ed. 2000); B. B. P. Corp. v. Carroll, 760 P.2d 519 (Alaska 1988).

12. **The best answer is (D).** An easement is a non-possessory interest in real estate. Under the Statute of Frauds, transfer of an interest in real property must be in writing and signed by the party to be charged. Inasmuch as the deed between O and X makes no mention of an easement across the eastern lot for the benefit of the western lot, the Statute of Frauds supports X's claim that O has no right to cross the eastern lot to reach the house at the back corner of the western lot.

Nevertheless, in most jurisdictions, courts will imply an easement under appropriate circumstances. A license coupled with estoppel results in an irrevocable license, which is tantamount to an easement for most purposes. A license coupled with estoppel requires the owner of the servient estate to grant permission (either expressly or implicitly) to another to cross the servient estate and to stand by while the holder of the license changes his or her position and expends money in reliance on the license. The license becomes irrevocable to the extent necessary to protect the investment in reasonable reliance upon the permission granted.

Under the facts of the problem, there is no evidence that X ever granted O permission to use the road or that O expended money in reliance on such permission from X. O does not have a viable claim under license coupled with estoppel.

An implied easement by necessity arises when an owner who owns a large parcel of land severs part of the land, and as a result of the transfer, one of the parcels has no access and is landlocked. The courts will imply an easement by necessity across the parcel from which the landlocked parcel was severed. The western lot which O still holds after the conveyance is not legally landlocked since it fronts on PCH. O would have to argue that the test for landlocked should not be legally landlocked, but practically landlocked. Even under this approach, however, there is a serious question of fact as to how landlocked the western parcel is since the only barrier is a steep hill. That is hardly enough "necessity" to support implying an easement by necessity, particularly when O can also claim an implied easement based upon prior existing use.

An implied easement based on prior existing use arises when an owner who owns a large parcel of land severs part of the land, and prior to severance, the owner held a quasi-easement. A quasi-easement exists when an owner uses part of her property to benefit another part of her property (the use cannot be an easement since one cannot hold an easement in his or her own property). Before the courts will imply an easement based on prior existing use, the quasi-easement must have been apparent at the time the parcels were severed, and it must be reasonably necessary that the quasi-easement continue after severance of the parcels. Here, prior to O conveying the eastern lot to X, the road traversing O's property constituted a quasi-easement whereby O used the road which crossed the eastern half of O's property to access the house on the western half. The road was apparent and use of the road to access the house following severance of the eastern parcel is reasonably necessary in light of the practical problems inherent in building a new road up the very steep hill along the front of the western lot along PCH. O has a stronger claim for an implied easement based on prior existing use as opposed to easement by necessity.

Having said that, however, at common law the courts were rather strict in interpreting the degree of necessity which supported implying the easement based upon prior existing use depending on whether the easement was an implied reservation or an implied grant. Whether the implied easement is an implied reservation or an implied grant depends upon whether the grantor retains the dominant estate or the servient estate following severance of the parcels. Where the grantor retains the dominant estate, the effect of implying the easement is to imply a reservation in favor of the grantor. Where the grantor retains the servient estate, the effect of implying the easement is to imply a grant in favor of the grantee. Inasmuch as the grantor is responsible for drafting the deed, the common law courts were much more prone to find an implied easement based upon prior existing use when the implied easement was an implied grant as opposed to an implied reservation.

Under the facts of the case, O, the grantor, is the party claiming the implied easement by prior existing use. O is asking the court to imply a reservation in favor of the grantor, despite O's express deed which failed to provide for such a property interest. Under the modern trend, however, the courts put less weight on whether the implied easement is an implied reservation or an implied grant and look at the totality of the circumstances. The most likely result is that a court will imply an easement based on prior existing use, and this claim has a better chance of prevailing under the modern trend than the common law.

Answer (A) is incorrect because although easements are property interests which should be created in compliance with the Statute of Frauds, the general rule is that courts will imply an easement under appropriate circumstances. **Answer (B) is incorrect** because before courts imply an easement by necessity, the parcel claiming the easement must be landlocked. Here, the western lot is not legally landlocked since it fronts on PCH. **Answer (C) is incorrect** because common law courts were much tougher on claims of implied easement based upon prior existing use when the party claiming the easement is the grantor. **Answer (E) is incorrect** because there is no evidence that O, the grantor had a license or that O expended money in reliance upon a license.

- **Additional references:** *See* 4 RICHARD R. POWELL, POWELL ON REAL PROPERTY ch. 34, §§ 34.03, 34.07-34.08[4] (Patrick J. Rohan ed. 1999); 7 THOMPSON ON REAL PROPERTY, SECOND THOMAS EDITION §§ 60.03(a)(5), 60.03(b)(3)-60.03(b)(5)(iii) (2006); WILLIAM B. STOEBUCK & DALE A. WHITMAN, THE LAW OF PROPERTY §§ 8.1, 8.4, 8.5, 8.8 (3d ed. 2000).

13. **The best answer is (D).** Assuming, arguendo, that the court grants O an easement based upon prior existing use, the issue is how long does such an easement last?

While an implied easement by necessity lasts only as long as necessary, an implied easement by prior existing use is based upon the presumed intent of the parties. Accordingly, if implied, it is implied in fee simple absolute. If the holder of the easement secures alternative access to the property, that does not affect the implied easement. In addition, even if the holder of the easement stops using the easement to access the property, mere non-use does not constitute abandonment.

The implied easement based upon prior existing use, however, is an easement appurtenant. That means that the benefit of the easement attaches to each and every inch of the dominant estate, but to no other property. O still has the right to use the easement across the eastern lot to access the western lot, but O cannot use the easement to access the lot O just purchased to the west of the western lot. If O uses the easement to access land which is not part of the dominant estate, O is exceeding the scope of the easement and is trespassing. X will be entitled to injunctive relief to stop O's trespassing, and if injunctive relief is not capable of controlling the trespassing, the court can order the easement forfeited.

Answer (A) is incorrect because it incorrectly assumes that the easement implied is an easement based upon necessity. The easement is implied based upon prior existing use. **Answer (B) is incorrect** because the facts do not support that O has abandoned the implied easement. The general rule is lack of use does not constitute abandonment. Here, there is not even evidence of lack of use, only of construction of an alternative method of accessing the dominant estate. O has not abandoned the implied easement. **Answer (C) is incorrect** because while an easement attaches to each and every inch of the dominant estate, using the easement to access property not included within the dominant estate exceeds the scope of the easement and constitutes trespass.

The owner of the servient estate is entitled to injunctive relief to insure that the scope of the easement is not exceeded, and if the use cannot be properly regulated, the easement may be terminated.

- **Additional references**: *See* 4 RICHARD R. POWELL, POWELL ON REAL PROPERTY ch. 34, §§ 34.17, 34.19 (Patrick J. Rohan ed. 1999);

7 Thompson on Real Property, Second Thomas Edition §§
60.03(b)(4), 60.08(b)(3), 60.04(a)(1)(ii) (2006); William B.
Stoebuck & Dale A. Whitman, The Law of Property §§ 8.12,
8.9 (3d ed. 2000).

14. **The best answer is (B).** The issue is whether Jesse can successfully
claim a prescriptive easement.

A prescriptive easement is an easement which arises by operation of law
and against the will of the servient estate owner. The doctrine is very
similar to adverse possession. Adverse possession is based on adverse
possession and, if successful, results in the claimant receiving title to the
property actually possessed. Prescriptive easement, on the other hand, is
based on adverse **use** and, if successful, results in the claimant receiving
the right to use the property actually used.

Prescriptive easement requires that there be actual use of another's
property which is adverse, exclusive, open and notorious, under claim of
right, and continuous for the statutory period. Jesse's use appears to
satisfy the requirements. He actually used George's property to get to
the beach each day. Jesse's use was adverse in that George never gave
him permission. Jesse's use was exclusive in that Jesse excluded others
and made sure that he was able to continue his use. Jesse's use was open
and notorious in that all who looked could see it. The use was
sufficiently open to give notice to the true owner, George, that someone
was using his land to get to the beach. Jesse's use was under claim of
right in that he has been acting as if he had the right to use George's
property to get to the beach. Jesse's use has been continuous for longer
than the statutory requirement.

The issue is what effect, if any, did George's comment to Jesse have?
Interruption is an adverse possession doctrine which requires the true
owner to take affirmative steps to oust the adverse possessor if the true
owner's reaction is to have any legal significance. Here, George's
comments fall well short of what is necessary to indicate affirmative
action to stop the adverse nature of Jesse's use.

Under prescriptive easement, however, the courts draw a distinction
based on the whether the jurisdiction follows the lost grant theory or not.
Under the lost grant theory, the fiction is that the owner of the servient
estate granted the user an easement, it is just that the written instrument
has been lost. Under the lost grant approach, any actions or statements
by the owner of the servient estate which are inconsistent with the fiction

that the owner actually granted an express easement is enough to defeat the claim. If the jurisdiction does not apply the lost grant theory, however, the owner must interrupt the adverse use to stop the statute of limitations.

George's statements to Jesse indicate that George never granted Jesse an easement to cross George's property. If the jurisdiction follows the lost grant theory of prescriptive easements, George's statements are enough to defeat Jesse's claim of prescriptive easement.

Answer (A) is incorrect because while interruption will stop a claim of prescriptive easement, interruption requires more aggressive and more substantive action on the part of the property owner. Oral statements alone are not enough to constitute interruption. George has not interrupted Jesse's prescriptive use. **Answer (C) is incorrect** because the lost grant theory is based on the assumption that at some point in the past there actually was an express easement. Any actions or statements by the owner of the servient estate which are inconsistent with an actual grant in the past are adequate to interrupt the adverse use. Under the lost grant approach, George's comments are inconsistent with a past grant of an easement and thus are enough to defeat the claim of prescriptive easement. **Answer (D) is incorrect** because there was no license. George never granted Jesse express permission. Although the permission may be implied if the true owner stands by and watches while the user changes his or her position in reliance on the belief that he or she will be permitted to continue to use the property, there is no basis for claiming implied permission. Although Jesse changed his position in purchasing the lot across the street from George's, Jesse had not started crossing George's property yet. Jesse assumed that George would not mind, but such an assumption coupled with a change in position is not enough to constitute license coupled with estoppel. George had no way of knowing about or objecting to Jesse's assumption.

- **Additional references:** *See* 2 AMERICAN LAW OF PROPERTY § 8.58 (A.J. Casner ed. 1952); 4 RICHARD R. POWELL, POWELL ON REAL PROPERTY ch. 34, § 34.10 (Patrick J. Rohan ed. 1999); 7 THOMPSON ON REAL PROPERTY, § 60.03(b)(6) (2006); WILLIAM B. STOEBUCK & DALE A. WHITMAN, THE LAW OF PROPERTY § 8.7 (3d ed. 2000).

15. **The best answer is (A).** Since there is no express restriction in the deed conveying lot 7 to X or in any of the prior deeds conveying lots 1-6 restricting the lots retained by the grantor, the only basis for creating such a restriction would be the common scheme doctrine.

In most jurisdictions, courts will imply an equitable servitude if a common scheme exists. A common scheme exists if the owner of two or more lots, so situated as to bear the relation, sells one or more with express restrictions which benefit the lots retained by the owner. If the lots "bear the relation," the restriction becomes mutual and is implied back against the lots retained by the owner. The crux is whether the lots "bear the relation," yet there is no clear definition of what the courts mean by that. The doctrine is a very fact sensitive, equitable doctrine designed to protect the reasonable expectations of the other purchasers. Some jurisdictions, however, will not imply an equitable servitude using the common scheme doctrine. These jurisdictions reason that the common scheme doctrine is simply too violative of the Statute of Frauds.

The Statute of Frauds requires that to transfer a property interest, there must be a writing signed by the party to be charged. There is no evidence of a writing creating an equitable servitude restricting lot 7. If the jurisdiction strictly adheres to the Statute of Frauds, A is not entitled to relief. Although the facts appear to support implying an equitable servitude under the common scheme doctrine, inasmuch as the jurisdiction strictly interprets and applies the Statute of Frauds, it is unlikely that the courts will imply an equitable servitude. X is free to use the land as X wishes.

Answer (B) is incorrect because the question states that the jurisdiction strictly interprets and applies the Statute of Frauds. Although most jurisdictions will imply an equitable servitude under the common scheme doctrine, those jurisdictions which strictly interpret and apply the Statute of Frauds do not recognize the common scheme doctrine to create an equitable servitude. **Answer (C) is incorrect** because there is no basis for concluding that the multi-family dwelling would constitute a private nuisance. There is no evidence that the multi-family dwelling will substantially and unreasonably interfere with the use and enjoyment of the surrounding parcels or that building the multi-family dwelling is unreasonable. Nor is there any basis for concluding that the multi-family dwelling would constitute a public nuisance. There is no evidence that the dwelling injures the public health, morals, safety or general welfare. **Answer (D) is incorrect** because it assumes that a covenant restricting the use of the land exists. There is no express restriction, and if the jurisdiction strictly interprets and applies the common scheme, the jurisdiction will not imply an equitable servitude. If a covenant were to exist, A would likely have standing under the common scheme doctrine (which some jurisdictions use to determine which parties have standing to enforce a covenant, but not to create a covenant).

- **Additional references:** *See* 9 RICHARD R. POWELL, POWELL ON REAL PROPERTY ch. 60, §§ 60.02- 60.03 (Patrick J. Rohan ed. 1999); 7 THOMPSON ON REAL PROPERTY, SECOND THOMAS EDITION §§ 62.11, 62.14 (2006); WILLIAM B. STOEBUCK & DALE A. WHITMAN, THE LAW OF PROPERTY § 8.23, 8.32 (3d ed. 2000).

16. **The best answer is (C).** A covenant runs with the land, as opposed to being a personal covenant between the original parties, only if the covenant qualifies as either an equitable servitude or a real covenant. *The same covenant can qualify as either an equitable servitude or a real covenant - or both.* If the same covenant can be either (or both), what is the difference? First and foremost, the difference between an equitable servitude and a real covenant is the relief the plaintiff is seeking. If the plaintiff is seeking *equitable relief (an injunction)*, for the covenant to run with the land and be enforceable against the defendant the covenant has to qualify as an *equitable servitude*. If the plaintiff is seeking *damages*, for the covenant to run to the defendant the covenant has to qualify as a *real covenant*. Once it is determined which relief the plaintiff is seeking (or both), then it is simply a question of applying the different requirements for the respective doctrines.

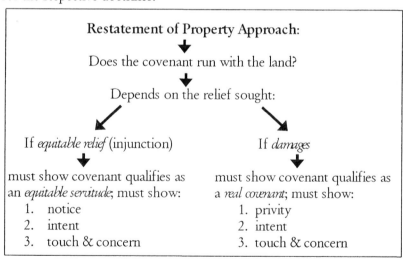

Because Andy sues Betty for damages, the issue is whether the covenant qualifies as a real covenant. For a real covenant to run at law, the general rule (Restatement of Property approach) is that the plaintiff must show: (1) **intent** - that the original parties to the covenant must have intended that the covenant run to remote grantees, (2) **touch and concern** - the covenant must touch and concern the land, and (3) **privity** - the requisite privity must exist. The degree of privity depends on whether the burden side of the covenant or the benefit side of the covenant is running to remote grantees. If the plaintiff is not an original party to the covenant, the plaintiff must show that the benefit runs with the land to the plaintiff. If the defendant is not an original party to the covenant, the plaintiff must show that the burden runs with the land to the defendant. Horizontal privity refers to the relationship between the *original parties to the covenant*. Vertical privity refers to the relationship between an original party to the covenant and his or her successive grantees.

The facts indicate that Treehugger and Sunshine intended for the covenant to run. The parties expressly included in the instrument which created the covenant the provision that the covenant was to run to their respective "heirs and assigns." The requirement that the covenant touch and concern the land is the requirement which the courts use to regulate whether a covenant is the type which should run with the land. Covenants which are merely personal in nature should not bind remote grantees. Covenants which are intrinsically related to the land in question and which properly regulate the use of the land should run with the land and bind remote grantees. Generally, negative covenants are deemed to touch and concern the land since they usually limit the uses to which the servient estate can be put. A covenant restricting the use of the land to residential purposes is a classic negative covenant which will be deemed to touch and concern the land. The issue is whether the requisite privity is present. Whether the requisite privity exists depends on which side of the covenant the plaintiff must show runs – the burden side or the benefit side (or both).

Which side of the covenant must the plaintiff show runs? If the *plaintiff* is *not* one of the *original* parties to the covenant, the plaintiff must show the *benefit* runs to the plaintiff. To show the benefit runs to the plaintiff, he or she need not show any horizontal privity between the original parties to the covenant, but he or she must show the requisite vertical privity which is that an estate of any duration passed from one of the original parties to the covenant to the plaintiff. If the *defendant* is *not* one of the *original* parties to the covenant, the plaintiff must show the *burden* runs to the defendant. The plaintiff must show: (1) the requisite mutual or successive horizontal privity between the original parties to the covenant and (2) the requisite vertical privity between one of the original parties to the covenant and the plaintiff – the requisite privity being an estate of the exact same duration was passed from the original party to the covenant and the plaintiff. (If neither the plaintiff nor the defendant were parties to the original covenant, the plaintiff must show that both the benefit and the burden run to the respective parties.)

Since neither Andy or Betty were party to the original covenant, Andy must show that both the benefit and the burden side of the covenant runs with the land to the present remote grantees.

Andy is claiming the benefit of the covenant (Andy wants to preserve the residential character of the property). Under the original Restatement of Property approach, for the benefit to run, no horizontal privity is necessary between the original parties to the covenant, and the benefit runs to a successor in interest as long as *any interest* in the land passes. Even Andy did not take a possessory interest in Treehugger's property, but a possessory interest is not necessary. All that is necessary is that the successor in interest take *some interest*. Andy's easement constitutes a property interest. The requisite vertical privity is present for the benefit to run to Andy.

For the burden to run to a remote grantee, there must have been horizontal privity between the original parties to the covenant, and the burden will not run to a remote grantee unless the remote grantee takes the exact same estate in duration as the original party held. Horizontal privity can be either successive (the original parties to the covenant had a grantor-grantee relationship with respect to a property interest other than the covenant) or mutual privity (the original parties to the covenant hold a property interest in the land other than the covenant).

Here, the requisite vertical privity exists for the burden to run. Betty bought Sunshine's interest. Assuming Sunshine held a fee simple absolute, Betty holds the exact same estate in duration, fee simple absolute, that Sunshine held. The requisite horizontal privity, however, is missing. Horizontal privity focuses exclusively on the original parties to the covenant. Treehugger and Betty were neighbors. They did not share a mutual property interest in either parcel, so there was no mutual horizontal privity. There was no grantor-grantee relationship between Treehugger and Sunshine with respect to a property interest other than the covenant.

Answer (A) is incorrect because the requisite degree of horizontal privity is lacking. Treehugger and Sunshine did not share a mutual property interest (other than the claimed covenant) in either parcel, nor was there a grantor-grantee relationship between them, at the exact moment they entered into the covenant, with respect to a property interest other then the covenant. **Answers (B) and (D) are incorrect** because the requisite degree of vertical privity is present. For the benefit to run, just some interest has to pass to the remote grantee and Andy took an easement from Treehugger, the original party on the benefit side. For the burden to run, the estate of the exact same duration has to run, and Betty purchased the fee simple absolute that Betty held.

- **Additional references**: *See* 9 RICHARD R. POWELL, POWELL ON REAL PROPERTY ch. 60, §§ 60.04[1]-60.04[2][d] (Michael Allan Wolf ed., 2000); 7 THOMPSON ON REAL PROPERTY, SECOND THOMAS EDITION §§ 62.03-62.13 (2006); WILLIAM B. STOEBUCK & DALE A. WHITMAN, THE LAW OF PROPERTY §§ 8.13-8.19, 8.22-8.29 (3d ed. 2000).

17. **The best answer is (A).** Where a party not an original party to a covenant sues seeking damages, the party must show that the covenant qualifies as a real covenant which runs to remote grantees. Traditionally, for a real covenant to run at law: (1) the original parties to the covenant must have intended that the covenant run to remote grantees, (2) the covenant must touch and concern the land, and (3) the requisite degree of privity must exist.

As established above, see answer to problem 16, the facts indicate that Treehugger and Sunshine intended for the covenant to run with the land. As for the touch and concern requirement, the **Restatement (Third) of Property** discards the requirement in favor of a more flexible approach (emphasizing reasonableness) which gives the courts a variety of grounds upon which to uphold or strike down (either at creation or subsequently) a covenant. This change has its greatest effect with respect to affirmative covenants and negative covenants which arguably have become obsolete. Neither of these situations apply in the current problem, and under the facts given the negative covenant appears reasonable. The issue is whether the requisite privity is present.

The new Restatement (Third) of Property rejects the first Restatement of Property approach with respect to the requisite privity. The Restatement (Third) eliminates the requirement of horizontal privity for a covenant to run. As for the degree of vertical privity, the Restatement (Third) rejects the burden-benefit distinction and instead adopts a negative covenant-affirmative covenant distinction. Negative covenants run with the land regardless of the degree of privity or even if the successive party takes any interest. Affirmative covenants require the traditional degree of privity, but vertical privity is expanded to include adverse possessors.

As noted above, the covenant that Treehugger and Sunshine entered into is negative in nature. Under the new Restatement (Third) of Property approach, the covenant runs regardless of the degree of privity between the original parties and the remote parties. No horizontal privity is necessary, and no vertical privity is necessary. The covenant runs with the land much like an easement appurtenant.

Answers (B), (C) and (D) are incorrect because they all assume that some degree of either horizontal or vertical privity is necessary for the covenant to run. Under the new Restatement (Third) of Property, negative covenants are treated much like appurtenant easements which automatically run with the land as long as the parties intend for the covenant to run with the land and the covenant is reasonable.

- **Additional references**: *See* 9 RICHARD R. POWELL, POWELL ON REAL PROPERTY ch. 60, §§ 60.11[1]-60.11[5] (Michael Allan Wolf ed., 2000); 7 THOMPSON ON REAL PROPERTY, SECOND THOMAS EDITION §§ 62.03-62.08 (2006).

18. **The best answer is (A).** There are several different doctrines which may be invoked to support a claimed right to enter and use another's real property.

The right to enter and use another's real property is either an easement or a license. An easement is a property interest which should be created expressly in a written instrument which complies with the Statute of Frauds. Alice *told* Betty that Betty had permission to cross Malibuacres to access the beach. Alice does not hold an express easement since the right to cross Malibuacres was not granted in a written instrument which complied with the Statute of Frauds. Betty appears to hold merely a license. Licenses are revocable and generally are not transferable (absent intent that they be transferable). Betty had no power to transfer her license to Kristin, and even if she did, Alice clearly revoked the license when she told Kristin she had no right to come on her land.

One can bootstrap him or herself into an easement under the doctrine of license coupled with estoppel. A license is very similar to an easement in that it gives one the right to enter another's property and use it in a manner which would otherwise constitute trespass. A key characteristic of a license, however, is that it is revocable. If, however, the holder of the license can claim license coupled with estoppel, the license becomes tantamount to an easement. License coupled with estoppel requires the owner of the servient estate to grant permission, either expressly or implicitly, to another to use the servient estate. The grantee of such permission then must change his or her position and make substantial investment in reasonable reliance upon the permission granted, and the licensor must know or should know about the licensee's change in position. The party who granted the permission is then estopped from revoking the license for as long as is necessary to recoup the expenditure made in reliance upon the license.

Here, Alice clearly granted Betty permission to walk across Malibuacres to get to the beach. There is no evidence, however, that Betty ever changed her position and made substantial expenditures in reasonable reliance upon the permission granted. Betty cannot successfully claim license coupled with estoppel. As for Kristin, although she might argue that she has changed her position and made substantial expenditure on her assumption that she would be able to continue to walk across Malibuacres to get to the beach, she was never given permission by Alice and Betty cannot transfer the license to her. Nor is there any reason to believe that Alice knew or should have known that Kristin was changing her position in reliance upon the right to continue to walk across Malibuacres to get to the beach. Kristin cannot successfully invoke license coupled with estoppel.

An implied easement based upon prior existing use requires: (1) that there be a single parcel, (2) that the owner of the parcel uses part of the parcel to benefit another part of the parcel, (3) that this quasi-easement must be apparent, (4) that the quasi-dominant part of the parcel must be severed from the quasi-servient part of the parcel, and (5) that following severance, continuance of the use must be reasonably necessary for the reasonable enjoyment of the quasi-dominant part of the parcel. Here, there is no evidence that the two parcels were ever one. Nor is there any basis for claiming a quasi-easement. Betty's crossing of Malibuacres began after the parcels were separate parcels. There is no factual support for an implied easement based upon prior existing use.

A prescriptive easement is an easement which arises by operation of law when a party enters and uses the real property of another, adversely, under a claim of right, exclusively, in an open and notorious manner, and continuously for the statutory period. The problem here is that Betty's use was not adverse (without the true owner's permission). Alice had expressly granted Betty a license, so Betty cannot claim a prescriptive easement, even under the lost grant theory, since her use was with permission. The use is not prescriptive until Kristin starts to use it, and Alice immediately stopped her. There is no chance that a prescriptive use has lasted for the statutory period.

Answer (B) is incorrect because an express easement must be created in a written instrument which complies with the Statute of Frauds. Alice orally told Betty that Betty could cross Malibuacres to get to the beach. Alice created a license, not an easement, and that arguably was all Alice intended to create (not an easement). **Answer (C) is incorrect** because although Betty held a license, she did not change her position and make substantial expenditures in reliance upon her belief that she would have the right to continue to use the license. Although Kristin did change her position and make substantial expenditure in reliance upon her belief that she would have the right to continue to cross Malibuacres, Kristin had no right to rely upon that assumption since she never held the license. Betty cannot transfer the license to her. And Alice was not aware of Kristin's expenditures in reliance upon her assumption, so there is no equitable basis for estopping Alice from being able to stop Kristin from trespassing on Malibuacres. **Answer (D) is incorrect** because there is no evidence that the lots were ever one or that the use could qualify as a quasi-easement prior to any such severance. **Answer (E) is incorrect** because there is no evidence that Betty's crossing Malibuacres was adverse prior to Kristin purchasing Gullsway from Betty. Betty held a license, and thus had permission, thereby preventing her from claiming prescriptive use. Moreover, not enough time has elapsed between when Kristin purchased the land and when Alice stopped her to satisfy the requirement that she adversely used the property for the statutory period.

- **Additional references**: *See* 4 RICHARD R. POWELL, POWELL ON REAL PROPERTY ch. 34, §§ 34.03, 34.25, 34.26, 34.08, 34.10 (Patrick J. Rohan ed. 1999); 7 THOMPSON ON REAL PROPERTY, SECOND THOMAS EDITION §§ 60.03(a)(5), 60.03(b)(3)-(4), 60.03(b)(6) (2006); 8 THOMPSON §§ 64.02(a)-(b); WILLIAM B. STOEBUCK & DALE A. WHITMAN, THE LAW OF PROPERTY §§ 8.1, 8.3, 8.4, 8.7, 8.8 (3d ed. 2000).

19. **The best answer is (B).** The Statute of Frauds requires that to transfer a property interest there must be a writing signed by the party to be charged. When A sues to enjoin B's construction of a gas station, A is asking the court to impose an equitable servitude on lot 30, the lot owned by B. An equitable servitude is a property interest and therefore, under the Statute of Frauds, should be created by written instrument signed by the party to be charged. There is no evidence of a writing creating an equitable servitude restricting lot 30, so if the jurisdiction strictly adheres to the Statute of Frauds, A is not entitled to relief.

In most jurisdictions, however, courts will imply an equitable servitude if a common scheme exists. A common scheme exists if the owner of two or more lots, so situated as to bear the relation, sells one or more with express restrictions which benefit the lots retained by the owner. The restriction then becomes mutual and is implied back against the lots retained by the owner. The crux is whether the lots "bear the relation," yet there is no clear definition of what the courts mean by that. The doctrine is a very fact sensitive, equitable doctrine designed to protect the reasonable expectations of the other purchasers. For there to be a common scheme, usually well over half of the pertinent lots must have the express restriction the plaintiff is asking the court to imply. What constitutes the pertinent lots depends upon the nature and configuration of the claimed common scheme.

Under the facts of the problem, O, the common owner of 50 lots, sold 45 with an express restriction that the lots were to be used for residential purposes only. The issue is why did O sell 5 of the lots without the express restriction: was it intentional or an oversight? Where such a high percentage of the lots are expressly restricted, absent additional evidence which might explain why 5 lots were sold without the express restrictions, the presumption is that it is more likely that the absence of the restrictions is due to an oversight than an intent not to restrict these lots. The court will likely imply an equitable servitude against lot 30 despite the absence of an express restriction.

Even where the court will imply an equitable servitude, however, there is the issue of whether the plaintiff has standing to enforce the equitable servitude. At common law, the benefit of a restriction could not be conveyed to a stranger to the deed. The benefit flowed back to the grantor and the land retained by the grantor. When the grantor sold the 30th lot, the benefit of the implied equitable servitude arguably flowed back only to the grantor and the lots retained by the grantor at that time. A, owner of the 10th lot sold, would have no standing to sue under this traditional approach to the issue of standing.

Most jurisdictions, however, use the common scheme doctrine not only to imply equitable servitudes, but also to determine who has standing to enforce a covenant. If a common scheme exists, it arose upon the sale of the first lot with the express restriction. Under this approach, though lot 30 was not expressly restricted when it was sold, it was implicitly restricted when lot 1 was sold. At that point in time, each and every lot in the common scheme was both burdened and benefited. Each owner of land within the common scheme has standing to enforce the burdens against other lots within the common scheme, regardless of the order of sale of the lots. Even jurisdictions which will not use the common scheme approach to imply an equitable servitude may use it to determine who has standing to enforce express restrictions within a common scheme.

Answer (A) is incorrect because although those jurisdictions which are serious about the Statute of Frauds will not imply an equitable servitude, the majority of jurisdictions will imply an equitable servitude if there is a common scheme. **Answer (C) is incorrect** because most courts which use the common scheme to imply the equitable servitude also use it to determine who has standing to enforce the covenants. Under the common scheme approach, the covenants are deemed to have been created at the moment the first lot so restricted is sold, thereby providing standing to all owners within the common scheme to enforce the covenants of the common scheme against each other. **Answer (D) is incorrect** because there is adequate evidence of a common scheme. Although the common scheme doctrine is extremely fact sensitive, here 90% of the lots were expressly restricted and there is no apparent reason why the 5 lots without the express restrictions were excluded. A court would probably find that a common scheme existed under these facts.

- **Additional references**: *See* 9 RICHARD R. POWELL, POWELL ON REAL PROPERTY ch. 60, §§ 60.02, 60.03, 60.04[3] (Patrick J. Rohan ed. 1999); 7 THOMPSON ON REAL PROPERTY, SECOND THOMAS EDITION §§ 62.03, 62.14 (2006); WILLIAM B. STOEBUCK & DALE A. WHITMAN, THE LAW OF PROPERTY §§ 8.23, 8.32 (3d ed. 2000).

20. **The best answer is (C).** License, easements and profits all grant the benefiting party the non-possessory right to enter real property owned by another and use it in a limited way which would otherwise constitute trespass.

The critical differences between and among a license, a profit and an easement are (1) the revocability of the interest, and (2) the scope of the permission granted. A **license** is a personal relationship between the grantor and grantee. Arguably the distinguishing characteristic of a license is that it is revocable at will by the owner of the burdened ("servient") estate. A license can become irrevocable, however, if the party who holds the license, with the consent or acquiescence of the party who has granted the license, changes his or her position and makes substantial expenditures in reasonable reliance upon the license. Under such circumstances, the grantor is estopped from revoking the license.

On the other hand, an **easement** is a more substantive interest. The key characteristic of an easement is that it is irrevocable. Inasmuch as an easement is a more substantial interest in real property, it should be created expressly in a written instrument which complies with the Statute of Frauds. A license does not need to be created in writing (though it may be). Lastly, the distinguishing characteristic of a **profit** is that it not only permits the grantee to enter the real property of another, it permits the grantee to remove property from the real property (typically property which is attached to the real property, though it need not be attached). Like easements, profits create a property interest and should be created in writing. Many commentators and treatises treat profits as simply a subset of easements.

Inasmuch as a license *may* be created in writing, while an easement *must* (as a general rule) be created in writing, where the right to enter and use another's property is created in writing there is often difficulty in determining whether the right is an easement or a license. Formally, the difference turns on the intent of the parties with respect to the revocability of the right. Where there is no clear intent expressed in the writing, the courts look to the totality of the circumstances. If the courts cannot determine the intent of the parties, the courts appear to favor holding the right to be merely a license so as to minimize the burden on the servient estate.

In determining whether The Rifleman Hunting Club's right to enter, hunt and fish is an easement or a license, the starting point is the intent of the parties as expressed in the instrument conveying the right. Here, the writing expressly provided that the club acquired "the exclusive right to all fishing and shooting privileges to Deliveranceacres, and the perpetual right to enter upon and fully and exclusively enjoy and use the same for its current and future stockholders." The express provision that the club had the "perpetual right" to enter and enjoy the right to hunt and fish expresses an intent that the right is not revocable at will, but rather that it endures in perpetuity (fee simple). Because the right is not revocable at will by the owner of the servient estate, the right is an easement, not a license. Since Charlton conveyed the right in writing and signed it, there should not be any Statute of Frauds problem with the creation of the property interest.

The easement, however, includes not only the right to enter Deliveranceacres, but also the right to hunt and fish. Barring any express limitation that the hunters must employ a "catch and release" approach to the hunting and fishing, the reasonable interpretation of the scope of the property interest conveyed is that the hunters have the right to take whatever they catch off the property. Since the right to hunt and fish inherently includes not only the right to enter but also the right to remove the wildlife from the land, the interest is more appropriately called a profit than an easement (though many treatises treat the profit as a subset of easement law).

Answer (A) is incorrect because a license is revocable at will by the owner of the servient estate. Here, Charlton expressly stated that the hunting club's right to enter and hunt and fish was to endure forever, indicating that the right was not revocable at will. **Answer (B) is incorrect** because an easement includes the right to enter another's real property and use it in a way which would otherwise constitute a trespass, but not the right to remove any property from the real property. A profit includes the right to remove property from the real property. The right to hunt and fish which Charlton conveyed to The Rifleman Hunting Club implicitly includes the right to remove from Deliveranceacres any wildlife captured on the land. **Answer (D) is incorrect** because a leasehold interest is an exclusive right to possession. Here, Charlton conveyed merely a nonpossessory right, the right to enter and use Deliverance for hunting and fishing, not the exclusive right to possession. The interest is not a leasehold interest.

- **Additional references**: *See* 4 RICHARD R. POWELL, POWELL ON REAL PROPERTY ch. 34, §§ 34.01[1], 34.02[2][a], 34.03, 34.24, 34.25 (Michael Allan Wolf ed., 2000); 7 THOMPSON ON REAL PROPERTY, SECOND THOMAS EDITION §§ 60.02(a), 60.02(b), 60.02(g), 60.03(a), 60.03(a)(7)(iv) (2006); WILLIAM B. STOEBUCK & DALE A. WHITMAN, THE LAW OF PROPERTY § 8.1 (3d ed. 2000).

21. **The best answer is (A).** Profits are a subset of the law of easements. A profit/easement is a nonpossessory interest in the servient estate. Where a profit/easement is express, the scope of the profit/easement includes all rights expressly granted and those necessarily incident to the express rights. All remaining rights, however, are retained by the owner of the servient estate, and the owner of the servient estate may make any use of the servient estate which does not unreasonably interfere with the profit/easement.

Here, following the conveyance of the express profit to the Rifleman Hunting Club, Charlton and his subsequent grantees (i.e., PETA, the current owner) retained the power and the right to use Deliverance for any and all purposes which do not unreasonably interfere with the club's exclusive right to hunt and fish. The issue is whether PETA's proposed development unreasonably interferes with the hunting club's exclusive right to hunt and fish. The development would contain an express provision that the owners of the condominiums would not be able to hunt or fish on the property. The new owners would not compete with the members of the Rifleman Hunting Club. There would not be an increase in the numbers of hunters or fishermen. No doubt PETA would maintain that since the new owners would be prohibited from hunting or fishing, there would be no increased burden on the servient estate with respect to these activities.

The problem, however, is not the increase in the numbers of hunters or fisherman, but the effect that the increased development would have upon the presence of wildlife. The issue is whether the mere presence of the proposed development is inherently incompatible with the hunting and fishing rights of the club, such that the presence of the development would actually and unduly interfere with the club's profit. As a result of the proposed development, there arguably would be, at a minimum, twenty-six times the current number of residents, visitors and vehicles on and about the property. Boat traffic would increase greatly. PETA also planned to add a park and playground, along with walking and bridle paths through the undeveloped land. Such development arguably would virtually destroy the forty-acres for hunting and fishing purposes. Such a drastic effect substantially interferes with the hunting and fishing rights of the hunting club. The Rifleman Hunting Club would probably be entitled to injunctive relief to prevent the proposed development.

Answer (B) is incorrect because the right to enter and hunt and fish attaches to every inch of the servient estate. The proposed development would virtually destroy that part of Deliveranceacres, over 10% of the original servient estate, for purposes of hunting. The hunting club actively uses that part of Deliveranceacres in its annual hunting activities. The proposed development would substantially and unreasonably interfere with the right to hunt on that part of the servient estate. **Answer (C) is incorrect** because it assumes that the original profit was nontransferable. Inasmuch as profits are a subset of the law of easement, the issue is first whether the interest was appurtenant or in gross, and second, if in gross, whether it was transferable. At the time the hunting club acquired the interest, there was no evidence that it owned any nearby land to which the rights could attach and become appurtenant. In the absence of such land, the right appears to have been in gross. This conclusion, however, does not end the analysis, since the modern trend is that profits/easements are transferable as long as the parties intended the interest to be transferable. Here, the language of the conveyance expressly indicates that the interest was transferable since it provided that the interest was to be perpetual in nature, for the benefit of current and future stockholders of the hunting club. **Answer (D) is incorrect** because it confuses (and applies) the law with respect to the development of the dominant estate in an easement appurtenant with the situation at hand which involves the development of the servient estate. The rules are not the same, and application of the rule governing the dominant estate to a situation involving a servient estate is inappropriate.

- **Additional references**: *See* 4 RICHARD R. POWELL, POWELL ON REAL PROPERTY ch. 34, § 34.02[1] (Patrick J. Rohan ed. 1999); 7 THOMPSON ON REAL PROPERTY, SECOND THOMAS EDITION §§ 60.04(b)(1)-(2) (2006); WILLIAM B. STOEBUCK & DALE A. WHITMAN, THE LAW OF PROPERTY § 8.9 (3d ed. 2000); Figliuzzi v. Carcajou Shooting Club of Lake Koshkonong, 516 N.W.2d 410 (Wis. 1994).

22. **The best answer is (C).** A profit is generally considered to be a subset of the law of easement. An easement granted for a particular purpose terminates when its purpose ceases to exist or is completed or when the easement is abandoned or rendered impossible of performance. The issue is how does the fact that no animals or fish had been captured, killed or even seen in years on PETA's land relate the different possible ways an easement may be terminated.

Although an easement may be terminated when its purpose is completed, this doctrine is not applicable to the hunting club's right to hunt and fish. An easement for hunting and fishing arguably cannot be "completed." If properly managed, the easement is perpetual in nature. This is especially true under the facts of this problem where the instrument creating the profit expressly sets forth the intent that the holders of the easement would have the "perpetual" right to enter, hunt and fish. This profit/easement, by its very nature, does not have a purpose which may be "completed" within the generally understood use of that word.

Although an easement may be terminated if it is abandoned, this doctrine is not applicable to the hunting club's right to hunt and fish. Abandonment arguably constitutes an implied release. Abandonment requires not only a failure to use the profit/easement, but also an intent to release the right to use the profit/easement. Failure to use an easement, in and of itself, however, generally does not constitute abandonment. Most courts require some conduct which demonstrates an intent to release the easement. Here, the fact that no animals or fish have been captured, killed or even seen in years on PETA's land does not constitute abandonment. First of all, even though no animals or fish have been captured, killed or seen in years, that does not mean that the members of the Rifleman Hunting Club are not hunting and fishing. Many a fisherman has spent countless hours without even a nibble, yet they continue to fish. Many a hunter have spent countless hours without seeing hide or hair of an animal, yet they continue to hunt. The fact that no animals have been captured, killed or even seen in years does not go to the issue of the use of the easement. And even if it did, mere failure to use does not constitute abandonment. There must be the additional element of the intent to release. There is no evidence that the Rifleman Hunting Club intends to release its right to hunt and fish.

An easement for a specific purpose may be terminated when the specific purpose becomes impossible of performance. This is PETA's strongest argument. To the extent that the express easement in question was to come onto the land and hunt and fish, arguably there has to be something to hunt and fish. If there are no wild animals or birds left to hunt, then it is factually impossible for the hunters to hunt. If there are no fish left because the waters are too polluted, then it is factually impossible for the fishermen to fish. Arguably, it has become impossible for the Rifleman Hunting Club to perform the specific purposes of the easement. Under such circumstances, a court may terminate an easement. (The argument against terminating the easement under these facts is that although the current conditions appear to make the specific purposes impossible, the conditions may change. It may be possible to clean up and restock the waters. It may be possible to reintroduce some of the wild animals to the land. Even if these acts are economically not plausible, the courts generally will not terminate the easement merely because the steps necessary to continue use of the easement are economically implausible. It is not for the courts to judge what is efficient behavior. The standard is that the specific purpose must be impossible to perform. While that may be true under the current conditions, it is plausible that the Rifleman Hunting Club may be able to take steps to rectify the situation so as to permit performance under the specific conditions.)

As for the doctrine of changed conditions, it applies primarily to real covenants and equitable servitudes, not easements. One could argue that it is the flip side of the same coin as the impossibility of performance doctrine. Both doctrines arguably deal with the scenario where the specific purpose of a servitude is so frustrated that the servitude appears to have lost its usefulness and basis for existence. Yet the courts appear to apply the changed conditions doctrine only to real covenants and equitable servitudes; and they appear to apply the impossibility of performance doctrine only to easements.

Answer (A) is incorrect because the specific purpose (hunting and fishing) has not been fulfilled as much as it has been frustrated. Hunting and fishing, by nature, are on-going activities which if managed properly, arguably are not capable of being accomplished. **Answer (B) is incorrect** because there is no evidence that the Rifleman Hunting Club has either stopped hunting and fishing or that they intend to relinquish their right to hunt and/or fish. Abandonment turns on the actions and mind set of the holder of the profit/easement, not the current conditions on the servient estate. **Answer (D) is incorrect** because the doctrine of changed conditions appears to apply only to real covenants and equitable servitudes, not easements. (One could argue that the changed conditions and impossibility of performance doctrines are basically one and the same, and that drawing any distinction between the two is exalting form over substance, yet the courts appear to draw just such a distinction.)

- **Additional references:** *See* 4 RICHARD R. POWELL, POWELL ON REAL PROPERTY ch. 34, §§ 34.19, 34.20 (Patrick J. Rohan ed. 1999); 7 THOMPSON ON REAL PROPERTY, SECOND THOMAS EDITION §§ 60.08(a)(3), 60.08(b)(3)(i)-(ii) (2006); WILLIAM B. STOEBUCK & DALE A. WHITMAN, THE LAW OF PROPERTY §§ 8.12, 8.20, 8.30 (3d ed. 2000).

23. **The best answer is (A).** There are several different ways one can establish property rights in a wild animal. In assessing the claims of the different parties, however, one also has to remember that property rights are relative.

Occupancy provides that one acquires a property interest in a wild animal when one (1) demonstrates an intent to appropriate the animal to one's individual use, (2) deprives the animal of its natural liberty, and (3) brings the animal under certain control. Trapper will claim the fox based on occupancy. When Trapper captured the fox, the act of capturing the fox deprived it of its natural liberty, brought it under certain control, and demonstrated Trapper's intent to appropriate the fox to his individual use.

The doctrine of rationi soli provides that the owner of the real property has constructive possession of all wild animals on one's property. Here,

there is an issue as to who may assert rationi soli. PETA owns
Deliverancacres where the fox was captured, so ordinarily, PETA would
be entitled to assert the doctrine. The Rifleman Hunting Club, however,
has the exclusive right to hunt and fish on Deliveranceacres. Although
they do not hold title to Deliveranceacres, their profit gives them the
exclusive right to hunt animals on the land. Since the profit is exclusive,
as between PETA and The Rifleman Hunting Club, the latter has the
superior right to the fox.

Ordinarily, a claim based on rationi soli will trump a claim based on
occupancy. The purpose of the rationi soli is to deter trespass. If the
party claiming occupancy were to prevail, that would encourage parties to
trespass on other's real property while hunting. If rationi soli prevails
over occupancy, parties will be less inclined to trespass on other's
property while hunting. Here, however, The Rifleman Hunting Club is
not claiming the fox. Although they may have the strongest claim to the
fox, the court will resolve the dispute as between the parties before the
court. The issue then becomes the relative rights of PETA and Trapper.

Inasmuch as PETA owns Deliveranceacres, Trapper's hunting on
Deliveranceacres trespassed not only on The Rifleman's exclusive right
to hunt but it also trespassed on PETA's general right to exclusive
possession of Deliveranceacres. Accordingly, normally PETA would
prevail over Trapper. PETA, however, did not wait to assert her rights
through the judicial system. Instead, PETA used self-help in trespassing
onto Trapper's property and taking the fox back. Although self-help was
generally permissible at common law, under the modern trend self-help is
disfavored due to the potential for violence (both to the parties and to
the other members of the community). In light of PETA's self-help in
trespassing on Trapper's property to reclaim the fox, Trapper has a
superior claim to the fox under the facts of the problem.

Answer (B) is incorrect because although PETA ordinarily would have
a superior right to the fox because rationi soli usually trumps occupancy,
here PETA has engaged in self-help to reclaim the fox. Under the
modern trend, the courts disfavor self-help because of its potential for
violence. Under the modern trend, a court would likely rule in favor of
Trapper to discourage parties from using self-help to assert their property
rights. **Answers (C) and (D) are incorrect** because property rights are
relative and courts resolve disputes based upon the arguments made by
the parties before the court. A court will not go out looking for parties
but will resolve the dispute as between the parties before it. Because the
Rifleman Hunting Club never asserted a claim to the fox (though it had

the strongest claim to the fox based on its exclusive right to hunt), it is not entitled to the fox.

- **Additional references:** *See* 2 THOMPSON ON REAL PROPERTY, SECOND THOMAS EDITION § 13.03(c) 2000 & Supp. 2006); RALPH E. BOYER ET AL., THE LAW OF PROPERTY: AN INTRODUCTORY SURVEY §§ 1.1-1.2 (4th ed. 1991); RAY A. BROWN, THE LAW OF PERSONAL PROPERTY, 14-18 (Walter B. Raushenbush 3d ed. 1975).

24. **The best answer is (B).** There are several different doctrines which may be invoked to support a claimed right to enter and use another's real property.

An implied easement by necessity arises if there is a single parcel, severance of part of the parcel, and following the severance, one of the parcels is legally landlocked. Here, there is no evidence of any severance, and there is no evidence that either parcel is legally landlocked since the facts indicate that a roadway runs along the southern boundary of both lots. Olivia will not succeed under an implied easement based upon necessity.

An implied easement based upon prior existing use requires that there be a single parcel, that the owner of the parcel uses part of the parcel to benefit another part of the parcel, that the quasi-easement be apparent, that the quasi-dominant portion of the parcel must be severed from the quasi-servient portion of the parcel, and that following severance continuance of the use must be reasonably necessary for the reasonable enjoyment of the quasi-dominant part of the parcel. Again, there is no evidence of any quasi-easement or of any severance. The evidence appears to indicate that Olivia did not begin to use the strip of land inside lot 2 until after the two lots were severed (assuming they were part of one parcel at some time in the past). Based upon the facts given, Olivia will not succeed under an implied easement based upon prior existing use.

License coupled with estoppel requires the owner of one parcel to grant permission, either expressly or implicitly, to another to use his or her parcel. The grantee of such permission then must change his or her position and make substantial investment in reasonable reliance upon the permission granted. Here, there is no evidence of any express permission for Olivia to use part of lot 2 to build a road. Although permission may be implied where the owner of the servient estate stands by and watches while another uses his or her property and invests substantially in reliance on the presumed ability to continue to use the property, there is no evidence here that Nellie had any idea that Olivia was building the road. To permit absence of knowledge on the part of the servient estate owner to constitute permission would be a dangerous precedent which would encourage neighbors to trespass on vacant land and make substantial investments in reliance on the continued trespass.

Olivia's best argument is either adverse possession or prescriptive easement. The two doctrines are very similar in many respects. One critical difference is that adverse possession grants the claimant full title to the property adversely possessed while prescriptive easement grants the claimant only a right to continue to use the property in question. Olivia's claim appears to rest more on the right to use the strip of land in question than on the right to title to the strip of land. On the other hand, however, since Olivia built a road, there is a permanent improvement on the strip of land in question which arguably constitutes possession, not mere use. Nevertheless, from an equitable approach, a court is more likely to award Olivia the continued right to use the strip in question, which does not deprive Nellie and Betty of all rights to the strip of land, than to award full title. Olivia's best claim is probably prescriptive easement. (In addition, in some jurisdictions, to claim adverse possession the party must pay taxes. There is no evidence that Olivia has paid taxes on the strip of land in question.)

Answer (A) is incorrect because Olivia has not "possessed" the strip of land in question as much as she is merely "using" the strip of land in question. If successful, adverse possession grants title to the land actually possessed, while prescriptive easement grants the right to continue to use the land in question. Olivia has a stronger claim for prescriptive easement than adverse possession. **Answer (C) is incorrect** because there is no evidence that the owner of the servient estate expressly or implicitly granted Olivia permission to use the strip of land in question. **Answer (D) is incorrect** because there is no evidence that the two lots in question were ever one lot, and there is no evidence that lot 1 is legally landlocked. **Answer (E) is incorrect** because there is no evidence that the two lots in question were ever one lot, and there is no evidence that a quasi-easement existed prior to severance of the one lot.

- **Additional references:** *See* 4 RICHARD R. POWELL, POWELL ON REAL PROPERTY ch. 34, §§ 34.07-34.10 (Patrick J. Rohan ed. 1999); 7 THOMPSON ON REAL PROPERTY, SECOND THOMAS EDITION §§ 60.03(b)(3)-60.03(b)(6) (2006); WILLIAM B. STOEBUCK & DALE A. WHITMAN, THE LAW OF PROPERTY §§ 8.4-8.7 (3d ed. 2000).

PROPERTY

EXAM IV ANSWERS

319

25. The best answer is (D). An easement is a nonpossessory interest in the servient estate. Where an easement is express, the scope of the easement includes all rights expressly granted and those necessarily incident to the express rights. All remaining rights, however, are retained by the owner of the servient estate, and the owner of the servient estate may make any use of the servient estate which does not unreasonably interfere with the easement. The owner of the servient estate can transfer to third parties the right to use the servient estate in any way which does not unreasonably interfere with the easement.

Here, following the conveyance of the express easement to the public utility company, the property owners retained the power and right to use the five foot strip of land for any and all purposes which do not unreasonably interfere with the easement. The property owners had the power to transfer this power and right to the cable company. The issue is whether the cable company's laying cable lines within the same five foot strip unreasonably interferes with the utility company's use of the five foot strip. The cable lines have been in place for several years now, and there is no evidence that they are unreasonably interfering with the current water pipes. It is possible that the public utility may need to expand or change its present piping system, and the presence of the cable lines may prove to unreasonably interfere with the utility's first in time, first in right easement. Until such an irreconcilable conflict arises, however, the uses should be construed as compatible to the extent possible under the facts. As holders of concurrent property interests in the servient estate, both parties' right to use the property in question should be construed, to the extent possible, so as to permit the reasonable use and enjoyment of each party. There is currently no evidence that the uses are incompatible, so the cable easement is valid until it actually and unduly interferes with the utility's easement.

Answer (A) is incorrect because it fails to recognize that the servient estate owner retains the right and power to use the property subject to the easement in any way which does not unreasonably interfere with the easement holder's use. First in time, first in right, in and of itself, does not really address the issue posed by the question, because without unreasonable interference, both parties have the right to use the land in question. **Answer (B) is incorrect** because the express terms of the easement fail to indicate that the easement was intended to be exclusive. Exclusive easements are viewed with disfavor because they are tantamount to fee simple. Absent a clear intent that the parties intended the easement holder to have the exclusive right to use the land in question, the general rule is that the servient estate owner retains the right to use the land in any way which does not unreasonably interfere with the express easement. **Answer (C) is incorrect** because there is no evidence that the cable lines are interfering with the water pipes, and until an irreconcilable conflict arises, the rights of the parties should be construed so as to permit reasonable use and enjoyment of the property in question by both parties.

- **Additional references:** *See* 4 RICHARD R. POWELL, POWELL ON REAL PROPERTY ch. 34, § 34.02 (Patrick J. Rohan ed. 1999); 7 THOMPSON ON REAL PROPERTY, SECOND THOMAS EDITION §§ 60.04(b)(1)-(2) (2006); WILLIAM B. STOEBUCK & DALE A. WHITMAN, THE LAW OF PROPERTY § 8.9 (3d ed. 2000); City of Pasadena v. California-Michigan Land & Water Co., 110 P.2d 983 (Cal. 1941).

ANSWER KEY
EXAM V

EXAM V

1. **The best answer is (B).** The Statute of Frauds provides that no interest in land shall be transferable except by an instrument in writing signed by the party to be charged (the party to be bound). To satisfy the Statute of Frauds, most jurisdictions require the written instrument to (1) describe the property so that it can be identified with reasonable certainty, (2) describe the parties so that they can be identified with reasonable certainty, (3) designate the price, (4) express the intent to convey, and (5) be signed by the party to be charged.

    Here the memo describes the parties with reasonable certainty. The seller is clearly identified in the terms of the memo. Although the purchaser is not identified in the body of the memo, when the ambiguous "I" is coupled with the signature at the end of the memo, the identity of the purchaser can be established with reasonable certainty.

    The memo describes the property with reasonable certainty. The legal description is not necessary. Any reference to or description of the property which permits its identification upon reasonable inquiry suffices. Here, assuming that Olivia owns only one house on Elm Street (the more reasonable assumption in the absence of additional facts), there should be no problem identifying the property being conveyed.

    At early common law, the writing need not include the price to be paid. Today, however, either by statute or case law, most jurisdictions require that the writing specify the price or consideration. Because the courts recognize, however, that the parties may not want to disclose the actual purchase price, a reference to price or consideration that indicates the parties have agreed on the price or the method of determining the price is enough. Here, although the memo does not set forth the exact price, its reference to "$100 and other good and valuable consideration" is enough in most jurisdictions to satisfy the price requirement.

    The requirement that the writing express an intent to convey is implicit in the essence of the Statute of Frauds. Here, Paul's promise to buy the property implicitly expresses the intent to sell the property (or at least Paul's intent to convey consideration in exchange for the property).

The final requirement of the Statute of Frauds is that the agreement has to be signed "by the party to be charged." The party to be charged, in essence, means that if the party attempted to back out of the contract, the other party could sue and a court would enforce the contract against the party. Under the facts of this contract, if Paul Paige attempted to back out of the contract, the contract could be enforced against him because he signed the contract. If, however, Olivia Owen tried to back out of the contract, she could since she did not sign the contract. So although there is an enforceable contract, it is enforceable only against Paul Paige and not against Olivia Owen.

Answer (A) is incorrect because it is an overstatement, it is too broad. The statement is correct as applied to Olivia Owen, but not as applied to Paul Paige. A contract to purchase real property may be enforceable against one party to the contract but not the other. **Answer (C) is incorrect** because the Statute of Frauds requires that the writing be "signed by the party to be charged." Since Olivia Owen did not sign the writing, the contract is not enforceable against her. **Answer (D) is incorrect** because it is an overstatement. The contract is enforceable against Paul Paige, but not Olivia Owen.

- **Additional references**: *See* 14 RICHARD R. POWELL, POWELL ON REAL PROPERTY ch. 81, §§ 81.02[1][c]-81.02[1][e] (Michael Allan Wolf ed., 2000); 12 THOMPSON ON REAL PROPERTY, SECOND THOMAS EDITION §§ 99.02-99.04 (1994 & Supp. 2006); WILLIAM B. STOEBUCK & DALE A. WHITMAN, THE LAW OF PROPERTY § 10.1 (3d ed. 2000).

2. **The best answer is (B).** Title to property passes when there is a properly executed written instrument which complies with the Statute of Frauds and there is delivery. Based upon the facts, there is no reason to doubt that the deed was properly executed in compliance with the Statute of Frauds. The issue is whether the deed was properly delivered.

As used in the real estate conveyance context, "delivery" is a term of art which means that the grantor intends to relinquish control over the real property. Because delivery refers to the grantor's state of mind, a variable for which there often is little direct evidence, there are a set of rebuttable presumptions based on the status of the properly executed deed. If the grantor retains possession of the deed, the presumption is no delivery. If the grantor records the deed, the presumption is delivery. If the grantor transfers possession of the deed to the grantee, the presumption is delivery.

Here the grantor, Othello, transferred possession of the deed to the grantee, Duke. The presumption arises that Othello has "delivered" title to Duke. Othello, however, transferred possession of the deed to Duke only to permit Duke's attorney to review the deed, not to relinquish control over the real property. Othello had no present intent to transfer title, only to transfer the deed for review. Based upon the facts, there appears to be sufficient evidence of grantor's intent to overcome the presumption of delivery. Othello retains title to Greenacre despite the fact that Duke possesses the deed.

Othello then dies with a Last Will and Testament which devises his real property to Rod and his personal property to Iago. If there were an enforceable contract between Othello and Duke, Duke could compel delivery even after Othello's death under the doctrine of equitable conversion. Under equitable conversion ("equity regards as done that which ought to be done"), once the parties have entered into an enforceable contract, the purchaser is regarded as the equitable owner of the real property and the seller's interest is merely a personal property right to payment. Under equitable conversion, the seller's death before closing does not prevent the transaction from being consummated. The purchaser can petition for specific performance. Under the facts of the problem, however, Duke was merely a donee, not a purchaser. Without an underlying enforceable contract, there is no basis for applying equitable conversion. Othello is still the owner of Veniceacre, free and clear of any claims by Duke.

Othello holds the real property interest, not merely a personal property interest. Since Othello's interest is still a real property interest, pursuant to the terms of his will, Veniceacre is devised to Rod.

Answer (A) is incorrect because it mistakenly concludes that there was delivery of the deed to Duke. Although Duke physically possesses the deed, Othello did not intend to relinquish control over title to the property by giving the deed to Duke. **Answer (C) is incorrect** because Othello holds the real property interest. There is no enforceable contract between Othello and Duke which would alter Othello's interest. **Answer (D) is incorrect** because Othello died with a valid Last Will and Testament which will dispose of Othello's property.

- **Additional references**: *See* 14 RICHARD R. POWELL, POWELL ON REAL PROPERTY ch. 81A, §§ 81A.04[2][a][i]-[iii], ch. 81, §§ 81.03[1]-81.03[1][a][i] (Michael Allan Wolf ed., 2000); 11 THOMPSON ON REAL PROPERTY, SECOND THOMAS EDITION § 94.06(g) (2002 & Supp. 2006); 11 THOMPSON ch.99, §§ 99.09, 99.14(b); WILLIAM B. STOEBUCK & DALE A. WHITMAN, THE LAW OF PROPERTY §§ 10.13, 10.5, 11.3 (3d ed. 2000).

3. **The best answer is (D).** A contract to purchase real property is, in reality, a contract to purchase **title** to real property. The quality of title the seller has to deliver is subject to the express terms of the contract. Absent an express provision governing the quality of title to be delivered, the quality is marketable title.

Under the facts of the problem, the contract expressly provides for the quality of title to be delivered. The contract modifies the default standard of marketable title. Purchaser agreed to accept marketable title "free and clear of all encumbrances except all restrictions and easements of record." There are basically three types of defects which may render marketable title unmarketable: (1) chain of title defects; (2) recorded encumbrances; and (3) unrecorded encumbrances. Whether one of these defects would render title unmarketable depends upon which type of defect it is and how serious of a defect it is.

The recorded covenant restricting all homes in the subdivision to one-story constitutes a recorded encumbrance. Recorded encumbrances of this nature (easements, covenants, etc.) generally render title unmarketable. Here, however, the express provision in Purchaser's contract to purchase title "free and clear of all encumbrances *except all restrictions and easements of record*" in essence waives all recorded encumbrances. Thus the recorded covenant has been waived and cannot be used as grounds to claim that the title is unmarketable. In addition, absent further evidence concerning how much Purchaser told Owner about Purchaser's plans, Purchaser cannot make out a claim of frustration of purpose or mutual mistake. The most likely outcome is that Owner is entitled to specific performance since Purchase waived all restrictions and easements of record.

Answer (A) is incorrect because it fails to take into account that the contract expressly waived "all restrictions and easements of record." **Answer (B) is incorrect** because there is no present unrecorded encumbrance. **Answer (C) is incorrect** because there is no evidence that the Owner knew of Purchaser's intended plans.

- **Additional references**: *See* 14 RICHARD R. POWELL, POWELL ON REAL PROPERTY ch. 81, §§ 81.03[6]-81.03[6][d][iv], 81.05[7][a], 81.02[3][c] (Michael Allan Wolf ed., 2000); 11 THOMPSON ON REAL PROPERTY, SECOND THOMAS EDITION §§ 91.01(a)(1)-(3) (2002 & Supp. 2006); 12 THOMPSON §§ 99.10(a)(1), 99.14(b)(1); WILLIAM B. STOEBUCK & DALE A. WHITMAN, THE LAW OF PROPERTY §§ 10.5, 10.12, 10.13 (3d ed. 2000).

4. **The best answer is (C).** Construing recording acts requires careful reading of the statutory language.

Race statutes typically include a reference to the fact that any property interest purported to be created is not valid against subsequent transferees until "the time of registration thereof" or "the time of recording thereof . . . ." Race recording acts do not require the party seeking protection to be without notice of the prior property interest or that they be acting in "good faith," only that they be the first party to record. The statute focuses on the requirement that the instrument in question be "registered" or "recorded."

Notice statutes typically provide that any purported property interest is not valid against subsequent transferees unless the subsequent transferees have "notice of the transfer or the interest is recorded." Notice statutes do not require the party seeking protection to record, but the party seeking protection must not have notice - actual, inquiry, or record notice - of the prior property interest. Such statutes may also, or in the alternative, require that the party be acting in "good faith," since there is great overlap between the notice issue and good faith. A party who has notice of a competing prior claim and proceeds anyway is not acting in good faith; and a party acting in good faith has no notice. In addition, the subsequent party must be a purchaser. He or she must give valuable consideration (i.e., he or she cannot be a donee).

Race-notice statutes typically provide that any purported property interest is not valid against subsequent transferees if the subsequent transferees have acquired the property "in good faith and for valuable consideration, *whose conveyance is first duly recorded.*" Race-notice statutes require not only that the party seeking protection qualify as a subsequent bona fide purchaser without notice of the prior property interest (the same as under the typical notice recording act), but also that the party seeking protection be the first to duly record the instrument creating the property interest.

The statute set forth in the problem contains express language evidencing both a notice approach and a race approach. The statute says that any conveyance is void as against any subsequent purchaser who in "good faith" "first duly records" their conveyance. The requirement of "good faith" implicitly includes the requirement that the party be without notice of the competing first in time, first in right property interest. If the subsequent grantee has notice, be it actual, inquiry, or constructive, the party cannot claim to be a purchaser in good faith. The subsequent purchaser in good faith is not protected, however, unless the party also "first duly records." This recording requirement makes the recording act a race-notice recording act.

Answer (A) is incorrect because under the pure race approach, the subsequent grantee's good faith is irrelevant. The only requirement is that the subsequent grantee duly record his conveyance first. Since the statute in question expressly requires good faith, it cannot be purely a race recording act. **Answer (B) is incorrect** because under a pure notice approach, there is no requirement that the subsequent grantee ever record, much less that the grantee seeking protection "first duly record" his or her conveyance. The requirement that the grantee seeking protection under the recording act "first duly record" his or her conveyance indicates that the recording act has a race component to it.

- **Additional references**: *See* 14 RICHARD R. POWELL, POWELL ON REAL PROPERTY ch. 82, §§ 82.02[1], 82.02[c][i]-[iii], 82.03[2][b][1] (Patrick J. Rohan ed. 1999); 11 THOMPSON ON REAL PROPERTY, SECOND THOMAS EDITION § 92.13(a)-(c), 92.15(b)(2)(A) (2002 & Supp. 2006); WILLIAM B. STOEBUCK & DALE A. WHITMAN, THE LAW OF PROPERTY § 11.9 (3d ed. 2000).

5. **The best answer is (D).** Miner will claim the one-half interest in the mineral rights under first in time, first in right. A properly executed and delivered deed is effective to transfer a property interest even if it is not recorded. If the grantee fails to record, however, the grantee's property interest is vulnerable. The first in time property interest can be trumped by another party if the party qualifies for protection under the jurisdiction's recording act. The jurisdiction in question applies a race-notice recording act. Under the race-notice approach, the party claiming protection has to qualify as a subsequent bona fide purchaser without notice of the prior conveyance, and the party must properly record his or her chain of title back to the common grantor before the prior grantee properly records his chain of title.

When Owner sold Greenacre to Gullible, including the mineral rights, Owner did not own all of the mineral rights to convey to Gullible. Owner still owned one-half of the mineral rights, but Owner had already conveyed half to Miner. Gullible can only receive all of the mineral rights if Gullible can qualify for protection under the jurisdiction's race-notice recording act. Gullible purchased Greenacre, so it is assumed Gullible gave valuable consideration. The issue is whether Gullible had notice.

Notice can be either actual, inquiry or record. There is no evidence that Gullible knew of or had actual notice of the prior conveyance from Owner to Miner. There are no facts which would create suspicion in the mind of a reasonable person that there might have been a prior conveyance of part of the mineral rights; and although Gullible has a duty to physically inspect the real property prior to purchasing it, there are no facts which indicate Gullible would have discovered anything which would have put Gullible on duty to inquire further. Lastly, since Miner has not recorded, Gullible is not on record notice of the prior conveyance. Gullible qualifies as a subsequent bona fide purchaser in good faith without notice.

To be entitled to protection under the race-notice recording approach, however, Gullible must also record prior to the first in time claimant. Gullible never recorded, so Gullible does not qualify for protection under the race-notice recording act. Therefore, when Gullible purports to convey all of Greenacre, including all of the mineral rights to Naive, Gullible only owns half of the mineral rights. The other half is owned by Miner under first in time, first in right.

Naive can receive all of the mineral rights only if Naive qualifies for protection under the race-notice recording act. Starting with the notice prong, there is no evidence that Naive knew of or had actual notice of the prior conveyance from Owner to Miner. There are no facts which would create suspicion in the mind of a reasonable person that there might have been a prior conveyance of part of the mineral rights. Although Naive has a duty to physically inspect the real property prior to purchasing it, there are no facts which indicate Naive would have discovered anything which would have put Naive on duty to inquire further. Although the Owner to Gullible deed is not recorded (which arguably should put Naive on inquiry notice), upon investigation Naive would easily discover that Gullibe has a valid deed and there is nothing in the deed or the failure to record it which would put Naive on notice of Miner's interest. Lastly, since Miner has not recorded, Naive is not on record notice of the prior conveyance. Naive qualifies as a subsequent bona fide purchaser in good faith without notice. But to be protected under the race-notice recording approach, Naive also has to record prior to the first in time claimant.

The issue is what does Naive have to record? Naive recorded the deed from Gullible to Naive, but Naive's recording will constitute a "wild deed" in that it is not connected to the chain of title. Subsequent parties checking through the chain of title for the property, searching under the grantor index, will not find the deed from Owner to Gullible since it was not recorded. Because of this hole in the chain, subsequent parties will not find the deed from Gullible to Naive even though it is recorded. Therefore, under the Zimmer rule, to satisfy the "race" prong of the race-notice recording act, the subsequent bona fide purchaser has to properly record his or her whole chain of title back to the common grantor, not just his or her deed. All deeds necessary to connect the subsequent grantee's deed to the chain of title must be properly recorded.

While this might sound unduly burdensome at first, Naive is charged with having performed a search of the chain of title prior to closing and Naive should have noticed that Gullible had not recorded. Naive could have refused to close until Gullible recorded the deed from Owner to Gullible. Since Naive's whole chain of title back to Owner, the common grantor, has not been properly recorded, Naive has not "recorded" first for purposes of qualifying for protection under the race-notice recording act. Miner's first in time, first in right claim to the property is still superior.

Since the holder of the mineral rights interest inherently needs access to the property to utilize the mineral rights, an easement by necessity will be implied. An easement by necessity arises when part of a parcel of real property is severed from the rest, and the act of severing the part results in part of the property being landlocked. When Owner sold half of the mineral rights, that half in essence was severed from the rest of the property and was landlocked in the sense that Miner, the holder of the property interest, had no way of reaching the property interest without committing trespass. An easement by necessity is implied across Greenacre to permit access to the one-half mineral rights property interest.

Answer (A) is incorrect because although Gullible is a subsequent bona fide purchaser without notice, that is not enough to be protected under the race-notice recording approach. The party seeking protection must also record his or her deed (and all connecting deeds back to the common grantor) before the first in time, first in right party records his or her deed (and all connecting deeds back to the common grantor). **Answer (B) is incorrect** because although Naive is a subsequent bona fide purchaser without notice who recorded first, the answer fails to take into account the <u>Zimmer</u> rule. The party seeking protection must record not only his or her deed first, but he or she must record all deeds connecting back to the common grantor to insure that the recording is not a wild deed. Naive's recording is a wild deed without the Owner to Gullible deed being recorded. Naive has not recorded Naive's whole chain of title back to the common grantor, Owner. **Answer (C) is incorrect** because without an easement, the mineral interest is landlocked in that the holder of the interest has no way to access the property interest. The courts will imply an easement by necessity to permit access to the property interest.

- **Additional references**: *See* 4 RICHARD R. POWELL, POWELL ON REAL PROPERTY ch. 34, § 34.07, 14 POWELL ch. 82, §§ 82.02[1][c][iii], 82.03[2][b][1] (Michael Allan Wolf ed., 2000); 11 THOMPSON ON REAL PROPERTY, SECOND THOMAS EDITION §§ 92.13(c), 92.14, 92.15(b)(2)(A) (2002 & Supp. 2006); WILLIAM B. STOEBUCK & DALE A. WHITMAN, THE LAW OF PROPERTY §§ 11.10, 11.11 (3d ed. 2000); Zimmer v. Sundell, 296 N.W. 589 (Wis. 1941).

6. **The best answer is (A).** Where a party has to qualify as a subsequent bona fide purchaser without notice, for purposes of either a notice recording act or race-notice recording act, the requirement of notice applies to the subsequent party at the moment the party changes position in reliance upon the apparent state of the title. The subsequent party changes position, typically, when the party gives valuable consideration in exchange for the deed. Any notice of the first in time, first in right interest which the party subsequently acquires is irrelevant with respect to the requirement that the party be without notice. Notice is tested typically at the time of closing.

Here, as established above in the answer to problem 5, Naive had no notice of Miner's claim when Naive purchased Greenacre from Gullible. Naive arguably paid more on the state of title as it appeared at that time, which was that Gullible held title to all of the surface rights and the mineral rights. If Naive can satisfy the race prong of the race-notice recording act, Naive should be entitled to protection even if Naive learns of Miner's interest before recording, since the key point in time is when

Naive gave valuable consideration on the apparent state of the title. As long as the subsequent grantee's chain of title is properly recorded before the prior grantee records, the subsequent grantee is protected under the race prong even if the party had notice at the time of recording.

When Gullible records the deed from Owner to Gullible, that recording connects Naive's recording to the chain of title and entitles Naive to protection under the race-notice recording act. Although Gullible's recording is late, it is still the first deed recorded under Owner's name as grantor purporting to transfer title to a grantee. A grantee checking the grantor index under Owner would keep searching under Owner's name until the grantee found the deed from Owner to Gullible which is recorded. The grantee would then switch names in the grantor index and begin looking under Gullible's name. The key question is: *When*, in the grantor index, would the grantee start searching under Gullible's name?

A standard scope of the search requires the grantee to search under each grantor's name from the ***date of execution of the deed*** purporting to transfer the property interest to the grantor to the date of recording of the first deed recorded purporting to transfer that property interest to another party. The grantee would start searching under Gullible's name in the grantor index from the date of the deed from Owner to Gullible, not the date the deed was recorded. Starting with the date the deed from Owner to Gullible was executed and delivered, and looking under Gullible's name in the grantor index, a grantee would discover the Gullible to Naive deed. Despite the delay in recording the Owner to Gullible deed, a party performing a standard search of the grantor-grantee indexes would discover Naive's whole chain of title back to Owner, the common grantor. Naive is entitled to protection under the recording act.

Answer (B) is incorrect because notice is relevant only at the time the subsequent grantee changes position in reliance upon the apparent state of the title. As long as the subsequent grantee has no notice at that time, typically at the time of closing, it does not matter whether the subsequent grantee acquires notice prior to recording. Naive had no notice of Miner's interest when Naive purchased Greenacre. Naive's subsequent discovery of Miner's interest is irrelevant if Naive's whole chain of title is recorded prior to Miner's. **Answers (C) and (D) are incorrect** because all of the relevant deeds would be found under a standard search of the grantor-grantee index. The standard scope of search requires a grantee to search under each grantor's name from the date of the deed purporting to transfer title to the party, to the date of the first recorded deed under the party's name purporting to transfer the property interest to another party. When searching under Owner's name in the grantor's index, the first deed recorded purporting to transfer title out to another party is the deed from Owner to Gullible. Although recorded late, there are no other intervening recordings under Owner's name. Switching to Gullible's name in the grantor's index and starting with the date of the deed purporting to transfer title to Gullible (and not the date that deed was recorded), a grantee would find the recorded deed from Gullible to Naive. Naive's whole chain of title back to the common grantor, Owner, is properly recorded under a standard scope of the search before Miner records the Owner to Miner deed.

- **Additional references**: *See* 14 RICHARD R. POWELL, POWELL ON REAL PROPERTY ch. 82, §§ 82.02[1][d], 82.03[2][i], 82.03[2][b][1] (Michael Allan Wolf ed., 2000); 11 THOMPSON ON REAL PROPERTY, SECOND THOMAS EDITION §§ 92.13(c), 92.14, 92.14(b), 92.07(d), 92.15(b)(2)(A) (2002 & Supp. 2006); WILLIAM B. STOEBUCK & DALE A. WHITMAN, THE LAW OF PROPERTY §§ 11.9-11.11 (3d ed. 2000).

7. **The best answer is (B).** Under traditional common law principles, when the seller and purchaser enter into a binding contract to purchase, under the doctrine of equitable conversion the buyer becomes the owner for many purposes.

Equitable conversion is based upon the principle that "equity regards as done that which ought to be done." Under that principle, once there is an enforceable contract, since the parties "ought to" honor their agreement and close on the contract, equity regards it as done. Thus, equitably, title passes to the purchaser the moment the parties enter into a binding contract. Under equitable conversion, the buyer assumes the risk of loss or change with respect to the property during the escrow period between executing the contract and closing. Inasmuch as the contract to purchase is to purchase title to the property, changes to structures on the property or zoning changes which do not affect title per se are not seen as grounds for permitting the buyer to rescind the contract.

Under the doctrine of equitable conversion, the fact that the city rezoned the property in question would not affect the buyer's contractual obligation to purchase the property for the agreed upon price. Under the modern trend, courts are increasingly coming to the rescue of the buyer in such a situation, using a number of different approaches depending upon the nature of the change which occurs to the property during the escrow period. Where the change is a change in zoning which frustrates the buyer's plans for the property, courts are increasingly using the contract doctrines of mutual mistake or frustration of purpose to rescue the buyer. Modern statutory developments also tend to shift the risk of loss to the seller until legal title or possession has been transferred. The typical statutory language, however, expressly covers losses due to natural causes which leaving unclear whether the statutory provisions cover losses caused by zoning changes during the executory/escrow period.

Answer (A) is incorrect because it fails to take into account that the modern trend is much more protective of the buyer and increasingly provides the buyer with grounds for voiding the contract where there are substantial changes affecting the improvements to the property or uses to which the property may be put during the escrow period. **Answer (C) is incorrect** because it has the modern trend and the common law mixed up. The seller is entitled to specific performance under the common law but not under the modern trend. **Answer (D) is incorrect** because it fails to take into account that the common law favored the seller.

- **Additional references:** *See* 14 RICHARD R. POWELL, POWELL ON REAL PROPERTY ch. 81, §§ 81.03[1], 81.03[2], 81.03[b][e][ii][B], 81.02[3][c], 81.03[2][a] (Michael Allan Wolf ed., 2000); 12 THOMPSON ON REAL PROPERTY, SECOND THOMAS EDITION §§ 99.09, 99.09(c) (1994 & Supp. 2006); WILLIAM B. STOEBUCK & DALE A. WHITMAN, THE LAW OF PROPERTY § 10.13 (3d ed. 2000).

8. **The best answer is (E).** A general warranty deed contains the full set of present and future covenants. The present covenants are covenants of seisen (grantor warrants that she owns what she purports to convey), right to convey (grantor warrants that she has the power to convey what she purports to convey), and covenant against encumbrances (grantor warrants that what she purports to convey is free of encumbrances). The future covenants are covenants of general warranty (grantor warrants that she will defend the purchaser against superior title), quiet enjoyment (grantor warrants that purchaser's legal possession will not be disturbed by one asserting a superior title), and further assurances (grantor warrants that she will execute whatever additional documents are necessary to perfect the title conveyed). A general warranty deed makes all of these covenants not only with respect to the grantor's actions, but also with respect to the actions of all prior owners of the property.

Inasmuch as Oscar did not have title to Greeancre to convey to Patty, Oscar breached the present covenants of seisen and right to convey. The problem is that present covenants are breached, if at all, at the moment the deed is conveyed, i.e., at closing. The statute of limitations is typically 10 years. Although Oscar breached the present covenants of seisen and right to convey, the most likely scenario is that the statute of limitations has run. Patty's claims based on the present covenants most likely will be barred.

The future covenants are not breached, however, until the assertion of the superior title. Although this moots the statute of limitations problem which barred Patty's claim on the present covenants, it presents its own set of problems for Patty. To prove a breach of the future covenants, Patty has to show an *assertion* of a superior property interest. Although Patty now realizes that a superior property interest exists, no one is presently asserting that superior property interest. Patty has no present cause of action for breach of the future covenants. (In addition, she appears unable to satisfied the requirements for adverse possession because she never took actual possession)

Lastly, in a contract to purchase, the seller implicitly, if not expressly, represents that he or she has marketable title to convey. Under the merger doctrine, however, the provisions of the contract merge into the deed, and after closing, the buyer's recourse is under the covenants in the deed. Although the modern trend is to construe the merger doctrine narrowly and to construe broadly the exceptions to the doctrine for promises deemed collateral to the deed, the core of the merger doctrine still applies to the quality of title and the quantity of land to be delivered. Since the alleged breach of contract goes directly to the core of the merger doctrine - the quality of title delivered - even under the modern trend Patty is probably barred from suing Oscar for breach of contract.

Answer (A) is incorrect because although Oscar breached the present covenants, the statute of limitations has probably run; there is no breach of the future covenants since no one has asserted a superior property interest; and the merger doctrine bars Patty from suing under the terms of the contract. **Answer (B) is incorrect** because although Oscar breached the present covenants, the statute of limitations has probably run; and there is no breach of the future covenants since no one has asserted a superior property interest. **Answer (C) is incorrect** because although Oscar breached the present covenants, the statute of limitations has probably run. **Answer (D) is incorrect** because the future covenants are not breached until the party holding the superior property interest asserts the interest, and no one has asserted a superior property interest.

- **Additional references**: *See* 14 RICHARD R. POWELL, POWELL ON REAL PROPERTY ch. 81A, §§ 81A.03[b][i], 81A.06[1], 81A.06[2], ch. 81, § 81.03[6][h] (Michael Allan Wolf ed., 2000); 9 THOMPSON 82.10(c)(1)-(6), 82.13(d) (1999 & Supp. 2006); 11 THOMPSON ON REAL PROPERTY, SECOND THOMAS EDITION §§ 94.07(b)(1), 94.07(c)(1); WILLIAM B. STOEBUCK & DALE A. WHITMAN, THE LAW OF PROPERTY § 11.13 (3d ed. 2000).

9. **The best answer is (B).** A promissory note evidences a loan between the parties to the note and establishes personal liability on the part of the borrower. A mortgage is security for the borrower's performance - the borrower's duty to pay off the loan. If the borrower fails to pay off the loan, the mortgage permits the lender to foreclose on the asset. A due on sale clause means that the outstanding debt due under a note, typically secured by a mortgage, becomes immediately payable upon the sale or transfer of the property.

Under the facts, the promissory note and mortgage which Purchaser executed as part of the purchase of Greenacre did not contain a due on sale clause. So when Purchaser sold Greenacre to Buyer, the sale did not affect the note or mortgage. Since Owner has not executed any release, Purchaser remains personally liable on the note and Greenacre remains subject to the mortgage. Thus, under first in time, first in right, Owner's mortgage interest in Greenacre is a superior property interest to Buyer's interest in Greenacre unless Buyer can qualify for protection under the jurisdiction's recording act.

Since Owner recorded the mortgage before Buyer purchased Greenacre, Buyer is not entitled to protection under any of the possible approaches to the recording act. Under the race recording act, the subsequent purchaser is entitled to protection only if he or she properly records his or her deed before the first in time, first in right party. Since Owner recorded the mortgage before Buyer even purchased Greenacre, there is no way Buyer could have recorded before Owner.

Under the notice recording act, the subsequent purchaser is entitled to protection only if the subsequent purchaser qualifies as a bona fide purchaser without notice. Buyer has actual notice since the contract expressly provided that Buyer purchased "subject to the mortgage," and Buyer has constructive notice of Owner's mortgage since Owner's proper recording of the mortgage puts the whole world on notice of the mortgage. Buyer does not qualify for protection under the notice recording act.

Under the race-notice recording act approach, the subsequent purchaser must qualify as a subsequent bona fide purchaser without notice and the subsequent purchaser must properly record his or her deed prior to the first in time grantee. As established above, Buyer cannot qualify as either a subsequent bona fide purchaser without notice or win the race to the recorder's office. Buyer is not entitled to protection under any of the approaches to the recording acts. Accordingly, Buyer takes Greenacre subject to Owner's first in time, first in right mortgage.

When Buyer bought Greenacre, Buyer was purchasing the equity in Greenacre. To protect that equity, Buyer will take over primary responsibility for paying off the debt on Greenacre. Since Buyer bought Greenacre "subject to the mortgage," if Buyer defaults on the payments, Owner can still foreclose on Greenacre. Owner can sell Greenacre, even though Buyer is now the title holder.

Although Greenacre is still subject to the mortgage, Buyer is not personally liable for the note. There is no privity of contract between Buyer and Owner. Buyer did not expressly "assume the mortgage" which would have made Buyer personally liable for the note. Owner still has recourse against Purchaser under the promissory note between Purchaser and Owner, and Owner still has recourse against Greenacre under the mortgage, since Buyer purchased "subject to the mortgage." Because Buyer did not "assume the mortgage," however, Owner has no recourse against Buyer personally.

Answers (A) and (C) are incorrect because there is no basis for holding Buyer personally liable under the note. Buyer was not a party to the note, nor did Buyer expressly assume the note or mortgage. **Answer (D) is incorrect** because the provision that Buyer took "subject to the mortgage" insured that Owner's mortgage interest and rights continued in Greenacre even though Purchaser was selling the land to Buyer, and Buyer had notice of the fact that Buyer was purchasing Greenacre "subject to the mortgage."

• **Additional references**: *See* 4 RICHARD R. POWELL, POWELL ON REAL PROPERTY ch. 37, §§ 37.12[2], 37.30[3]-[5] (Michael Allan Wolf ed., 2000); 12 THOMPSON ON REAL PROPERTY, SECOND THOMAS EDITION §§ 101.05(a)(5) (1994 & Supp. 2006); RALPH E.

BOYER ET. AL., THE LAW OF PROPERTY: AN INTRODUCTORY SURVEY §§ 18.1 (4th ed. 1991).

10. **The best answer is (A).** The Statute of Frauds requires that to transfer an interest in real property, there should be a writing signed by the grantor which contains all of the material provisions. The issue is whether this writing is sufficient to satisfy the Statute of Frauds. There is a writing. It is signed by John Doe, the grantor. Does the writing contain all of the material provisions? What constitute the material provisions?

Although the answer to that question varies a bit from jurisdiction to jurisdiction, depending on the jurisdiction's approach to how strictly the Statute of Frauds should be construed and enforced, the general rule is that for a valid deed, the instrument should identify the parties (grantor and grantee) with reasonable certainty, identify the property interest being conveyed with reasonable certainty, and contain words expressing the intent to convey. Although a reference to consideration is a good idea (in case the grantee needs to claim he or she is a subsequent bona fide **purchaser**), obviously a grantor can convey a property interest by gift, so consideration is not a prerequisite to a valid deed. Likewise, although an attestation clause or acknowledgment is a good idea because most jurisdictions will not record a deed unless it has been witnessed or acknowledged, an attestation clause or acknowledgment is not a prerequisite to a valid deed, at least as between the grantor and grantee.

Applying these simple requirements to the written instrument set forth in the problem, the parties are described adequately so that they can be identified with reasonable certainty. The property is described adequately so that it can be identified with reasonable certainty. The instrument expresses the intent to presently pass a property interest ("hereby grant"). The instrument is signed by the grantor. The writing should satisfy the Statute of Frauds' requirements for a valid deed. The fact that the grantor gave the deed to the grantee in exchange for valuable consideration creates the presumption that the grantor had the present intent to transfer title to the property such that the deed has been properly delivered.

Answer (B) is incorrect because consideration is not required for a valid deed. Where consideration is involved in the conveyance, it is good to acknowledge either the amount or that the conveyance is in exchange for good and valuable consideration in case the party needs to qualify as a subsequent bona fide purchaser under the jurisdiction's recording act;

but reciting consideration in the deed is not required. **Answer (C) is incorrect** because attestation or acknowledgment is not required for a valid deed. Many jurisdictions require that a deed be attested or acknowledged prior to it being recorded, but as between the parties the deed is valid even if not attested or acknowledged. **Answer (D) is incorrect** because a deed need not be recorded to be valid. Although recording protects the grantee against claims of subsequent grantees seeking protection under the jurisdiction's recording act, recording is not a prerequisite to the deed's validity. **Answer (E) is incorrect** because it merely combines the incorrect requirements in answers (B), (C), and (D).

• **Additional references**: *See* 14 RICHARD R. POWELL, POWELL ON REAL PROPERTY ch. 81A, § 81A.02 (Michael Allan Wolf ed., 2000); 9 THOMPSON ON REAL PROPERTY, SECOND THOMAS EDITION § 82.08(a)-(c) (1999 & Supp. 2006); WILLIAM B. STOEBUCK & DALE A. WHITMAN, THE LAW OF PROPERTY § 11.1 (3d ed. 2000).

11. **The best answer is (C).** Inasmuch as O owned Whiteacre, when A purported to convey Whiteacre to B, B took nothing. B can successfully claim an interest in Whiteacre only if B successfully qualifies for protection under the jurisdiction's recording act.

Under a notice recording act, a party is entitled to protection and will trump the first in time, first in right only if the subsequent in time party qualifies as a subsequent bona fide purchaser without notice of the first in time interest. B is not entitled to protection under the jurisdiction's notice recording act. As a grantee, B is charged with whatever information a search of the grantor-grantee index would have disclosed. If B had performed a title search, B would have realized that A had no interest in Whiteacre to convey to B. B is not entitled to protection under the recording act.

Nevertheless, when O subsequently conveys to A, estoppel by deed kicks in. Estoppel by deed provides that if a party who purports to convey a property interest that the party does not rightly own subsequently acquires the property interest in question, the party is estopped from denying his or her prior conveyance of the property interest. By operation of law, the property interest immediately transfers to the prior grantee who took nothing at the time of the prior conveyance. The moment O conveyed Whiteacre to A, by operation of law under estoppel by deed, the deed from A to B is deemed effective. B holds title to the property under first in time, first in right based on the O to A, A to B series of deeds.

When A then purports to convey Whiteacre to C, A has nothing to convey to C. C will take nothing unless C can qualify for protection under the recording act. Under the notice recording act, C will have to be a subsequent bona fide purchaser without notice of any defects in the conveyance. Inasmuch as C purchased Whiteacre, C qualifies as a subsequent purchaser. The issue is whether C qualifies as a bona fide purchaser without notice. There are three different types of notice: actual, inquiry and record. There is no evidence that C had actual notice of B's claim to Whiteacre. Although a grantee has a duty to physically inspect the property prior to purchasing it, there is no evidence that B was in possession or that there were any other facts which would have put C on inquiry notice of B's claim to Whiteacre.

The question is whether C had record notice. As a grantee, C is charged with whatever information a search of the grantor-grantee index would have disclosed. Because the doctrine of estoppel by deed often results in the grantee's deed being recorded prior to the grantor's deed, some jurisdictions require an expanded search of the grantor-grantee index which requires each grantee to search under each grantor's name not from the date of execution of the deed purporting to transfer title to the grantor, but rather from the date of the grantor's birth.

In this case, however, B never recorded. There is no way C could have found the deed from A to B even if C had performed an expanded scope of the search under B's name. Regardless of whether the jurisdiction applies a standard scope of the search or an expanded scope of the search, since B did not record the deed from A to B, there is no way C could have discovered it. C qualifies as a subsequent bona fide purchaser without notice and is entitled to protection under the jurisdiction's notice recording act.

Answers (A) and (B) are incorrect because they are under-inclusive. Each is correct, but not the most complete answer. Since B never recorded the deed from A to B, C qualifies as a subsequent bona fide purchaser without notice regardless of the scope of the required search of the grantor-grantee index. **Answers (D) and (E) are incorrect** because there is no evidence that C had notice of B's interest, primarily because B failed to record.

• **Additional references**: *See* 14 RICHARD R. POWELL, POWELL ON REAL PROPERTY ch. 82, §§ 82.02[c][ii], 82.03[2][b][i], ch. 84, §§ 84.02[1], 84.02[2], 84.02[3][e] (Michael Allan Wolf ed., 2000); 9 THOMPSON ON REAL PROPERTY, SECOND THOMAS EDITION §

82.11 (1999 & Supp. 2006); 11 THOMPSON §§ 92.13(b), 92.07(d), 92.15-92.15(c)(3); WILLIAM B. STOEBUCK & DALE A. WHITMAN, THE LAW OF PROPERTY §§ 11.5, 11.9-11.11 (3d ed. 2000).

12. **The best answer is (A).** Solving this problem involves two steps: (1) properly analyzing which recording act the jurisdiction adopted, and (2) properly analyzing the facts under the recording act.

<u>Recording act construction.</u> Construing recording acts requires careful reading of the statutory language.

Race statutes typically include a reference to the fact that any property interest purported to be created is not valid against subsequent transferees until "the time of registration thereof" or "the time of recording thereof . . . ." Race recording acts do not require the party seeking protection to be without notice of the prior property interest or that they be acting in "good faith," only that they be the first party to record. The statute focuses on the requirement that the instrument in question be "registered" or "recorded."

Notice statutes typically provide that any purported property interest is not valid against subsequent transferees unless the subsequent transferees have "notice of the transfer or the interest is recorded." Notice statutes do not require the party seeking protection to record, but the party seeking protection must not have notice - actual, inquiry, or record notice - of the prior property interest. Such statutes may also, or in the alternative, require that the party be acting in "good faith," since there is great overlap between the notice issue and good faith. A party is not acting in good faith if it has notice of a competing, prior in time claim to the property but proceeds anyway; and a party acting in good faith has no notice. In addition, the subsequent party must be a purchaser or otherwise give valuable consideration.

Race-notice statutes typically provide that any purported property interest is not valid against subsequent transferees if the subsequent transferees have acquired the property "in good faith and for valuable consideration, *whose conveyance is first duly recorded.*" Race-notice statutes require not only that the party seeking protection qualify as a subsequent bona fide purchaser without notice of the prior property interest (the same as under the typical notice recording act), but also that the party seeking protection be the first to duly record the instrument creating the property interest.

Here, the express language of the recording act reads like a typical notice recording act until the last clause. Up until the last clause, the act basically provides that no conveyance is good against a subsequent purchaser without notice. The last clause, however, provides "unless the same be recorded according to law." The last clause throws some ambiguity into the analysis. What is the antecedent reference for the clause "the same?" Is it the first in time conveyance, in which case the statute is a notice recording act, or is it the subsequent conveyance, in which case the statute is a race-notice recording act. The antecedent reference is the initial, first in time, first in right conveyance. All the clause is saying is that a subsequent bona fide purchaser without notice will prevail over a first in time party "unless the same [the first in time deed] be recorded." If the first in time deed is properly recorded, all subsequent grantee will be on constructive notice of the first in time conveyance and will not trump the first in time conveyance.

Analysis of fact pattern under the notice recording act. When O properly conveyed Blackacre to A, A received title to the land under first in time, first in right. Although A held title to the land, A's title was vulnerable because A failed to record the deed from O to A. A subsequent party who took from O could trump A, *if* the party qualified for protection under the recording act.

When O purported to convey Blackacre to B, O did not have actual title to convey to B. B can receive good title to the land only if B qualifies for protection under the recording act. To prevail under a notice recording act, the subsequent grantee has to be a bona fide purchaser ("BFP") without notice of the prior conveyance. Whether the subsequent grantee qualifies as a BFP without notice is tested at time of closing, for that is when the purchaser gives his or her consideration and is entitled to protection, if at all. Notice can be either actual notice, inquiry notice, or constructive notice.

Since B had actual notice of the prior conveyance to A, B cannot qualify as a subsequent BFP without notice. A still holds good title to Blackacre.

When B conveyed to C, B did not have actual title to convey to C. C can receive good title to the land only if C qualifies for protection under the recording act as a subsequent bona fide purchaser without notice.

There is no evidence that C had actual knowledge of the deed from O to A. C is charged with whatever information a proper search of the chain of title would reveal. Because A did not record the deed from O to A until after B recorded the deed from O to B and B purported to convey Blackacre to C, C does not have record notice of A's interest in the property. The grantee is charged with knowledge of whatever a proper search of the grantor-grantee index would reveal at the time of closing. Since A did not record until after C closed on C's purchase from B, C cannot be charged with knowledge of A's recording under any scope of the search, standard or expanded.

C, however, is charged with knowledge of A's interest under inquiry notice. Prior to purchasing real property, a purchaser has a duty to physically inspect the property. During the inspection, if the purchaser discovers any facts suggesting any possible property interests, the purchaser has a duty to inquire as to the extent of the property interest. If a party other than the grantor is in possession of the property, the purchaser has a duty to inquire as to the extent of the possessor's claimed property interest. Under the facts, A was in possession of the property. A's possession put C on inquiry notice of A's potential interest in the property.

Since C was on inquiry notice of A's potential interest in the property, C does not qualify for protection under the notice recording act. A still holds title to the property.

Answers (B) and (C) are incorrect because they address the issue of a grantee having record constructive notice based upon an expanded search of the grantor-grantee index. A did not record the deed from O to A until after B recorded the deed from O to B and after the B to C conveyance. A grantee is charged with whatever knowledge the grantee would have discovered if the grantee performed a proper search of the grantor-grantee index *immediately prior to closing*. Since A did not record until after C closed, under any scope of the search of the grantor-grantee index, C would not have found the deed from O to A. **Answer (D) is incorrect** because a grantee can claim protection under the shelter doctrine only if a prior grantor in the grantee's chain of title was entitled to protection under the notice recording act. B was not entitled to protection under the notice recording act because B had actual knowledge of the prior in time conveyance from O to A. C does not qualify in his or her own right because C is on inquiry notice of A's interest based on A's possession of Blackacre.

- **Additional references**: *See* 14 RICHARD R. POWELL, POWELL ON REAL PROPERTY ch. 82, §§ 82.02[1][c][i]-[iii], 82.03[2][b][i], 82.02[d][iii][A], 82.03[2][b][1] (Michael Allan Wolf ed., 2000); 11

THOMPSON ON REAL PROPERTY, SECOND THOMAS EDITION §§ 92.13(a)-(c), 92.07(d), 92.15(b)(2)(A), 92.15(c)(1) (2002 & Supp. 2006); WILLIAM B. STOEBUCK & DALE A. WHITMAN, THE LAW OF PROPERTY §§ 11.9-11.11 (3d ed. 2000).

13. **The best answer is (D).** Solving this problem involves two steps: (1) properly analyzing which recording act the jurisdiction adopted, and (2) properly analyzing the facts under the recording act.

Recording act construction. Construing recording acts requires careful reading of the statutory language.

Race statutes typically include a reference to the fact that any property interest purported to be created is not valid against subsequent transferees until "the time of registration thereof" or "the time of recording thereof . . . ." Race recording acts do not require the party seeking protection to be without notice of the prior property interest or that they be acting in "good faith," only that they be the first party to record. The statute focuses on the requirement that the instrument in question be "registered" or "recorded."

Notice statutes typically provide that any purported property interest is not valid against subsequent transferees unless the subsequent transferees have "notice of the transfer or the interest is recorded." Notice statutes do not require the party seeking protection to record, but the party seeking protection must not have notice - actual, inquiry, or record notice - of the prior property interest. Such statutes may also, or in the alternative, require that the party be acting in "good faith," since there is great overlap between the notice issue and good faith. A party is not acting in good faith if it has notice of a competing, prior in time claim to the property but proceeds anyway; and a party acting in good faith has no notice. In addition, the subsequent party must be a purchaser or otherwise give valuable consideration.

Race-notice statutes typically provide that any purported property interest is not valid against subsequent transferees if the subsequent transferees have acquired the property "in good faith and for valuable consideration, *whose conveyance is first duly recorded.*" Race-notice statutes require not only that the party seeking protection qualify as a subsequent bona fide purchaser without notice of the prior property interest (the same as under the typical notice recording act), but also that the party seeking protection be the first to duly record the instrument creating the property interest.

Here, the express language of the recording act is completely devoid of any requirement that the subsequent purchaser be "without notice" or that the subsequent grantee be a "bona fide" or "good faith" purchaser. The absence of such requirements indicates that the statute lacks any notice component. By default, the only other option is a race recording act. The express language supports this default conclusion. The language expressly provides that no conveyance is valid until recorded. Implicit is the "race" to the recorder's office.

<u>Analysis of fact pattern under the notice recording act</u>. When O properly conveyed Blackacre to A, A received title to the land under first in time, first in right. Although A held title to the land, A's title was vulnerable because A failed to record the deed from O to A. A subsequent party who took from O could trump A if the party qualified for protection under the recording act.

When O purported to convey Blackacre to B, O did not have actual title to convey to B. B can receive good title to the land only if B qualifies for protection under the recording act. To prevail under a race recording act, the subsequent grantee has to record his or her deed before the deed to the prior conveyance is recorded. Under the pure race approach, whether the subsequent party has notice of the first in time, first in right conveyance is irrelevant. All that matters is who records first. (That statement is somewhat misleading in that the first in time, first in right party holds title unless and until a subsequent grantee qualifies for protection under the recording act. B's only chance to trump A is record first, which creates a race to the courthouse as between A and B. But A's title is good the moment A receives delivery. The race between A and B is only to see if B can trump A. A does not have to record to claim title against O.)

Although B had actual notice of the prior conveyance to A, B still qualifies for protection under the recording act because B recorded first. B holds good title to Blackacre. When B conveyed to C, B had actual title to convey to C. C received good title to the land. The fact that A is on the land is irrelevant. A is a trespasser who lost any claim to the property when B qualified for protection under the recording act. Moreover, C recorded prior to A, though that is not pertinent since A's claim was extinguished when B trumped A.

Answer (A) is incorrect because B qualified for protection under the race recording act, despite the fact that B had notice of A's first in time interest. Notice is irrelevant under the race recording act approach.

Once B won the race by recording first, B trumped A, extinguishing A's claim to the property. **Answers (B) and (C) are incorrect** because they address the issue of a grantee having record constructive notice based upon an expanded search of the grantor-grantee index.   Notice is irrelevant under the race recording act approach. Whoever records first prevails. Since B recorded first, B trumped A and had good title to pass to C.

• **Additional references**: *See* 14 RICHARD R. POWELL, POWELL ON REAL PROPERTY ch. 82, §§ 82.02[1][c][i]-[iii], 82.03[2][b][1] (Michael Allan Wolf ed., 2000); 11 THOMPSON ON REAL PROPERTY, SECOND THOMAS EDITION § 92.13(a)-(c), 92.15(b)(2)(A) (2002 & Supp. 2006); WILLIAM B. STOEBUCK & DALE A. WHITMAN, THE LAW OF PROPERTY § 11.9 (3d ed. 2000).

14. **The best answer is (D).** A contract to purchase real property is, in reality, a contract to purchase **title** to real property. The quality of title the seller has to deliver is subject to the express terms of the contract. Absent an express provision governing the quality of title to be delivered, the quality is marketable title.

Pre-closing, there are basically three types of defects which may render marketable title unmarketable, thereby permitting the buyer to rescind the contract to purchase: (1) chain of title defects; (2) recorded encumbrances; and (3) unrecorded encumbrances. Whether one of these defects would render title unmarketable depends upon which type of defect it is and how serious of a defect it is.

Under the facts of the problem, the first issue is whether the fact that the electrical wiring violates the local housing code constitutes a defect which renders title to the property unmarketable. The housing code violation does not have anything to do with the chain of title (the series of deeds transferring title from one grantor to another) for the property, nor is there any evidence that the problem constitutes a recorded encumbrance (a property interest short of complete title which is recorded against the property).   At best, the electrical wiring problem constitutes an unrecorded encumbrance - a present breach of the housing codes which arguably subjects the purchaser to an unreasonable risk of litigation.

Arguably a buyer should not be forced to accept a lawsuit or potential lawsuit as part of the contract to purchase. If the risk of litigation is serious enough, under the modern trend, some courts may consider a present violation of a housing code sufficient to constitute an unrecorded encumbrance which renders the title unmarketable, thereby permitting the buyer to rescind if the buyer so desires. The majority of courts, however, hold that a present violation of the housing codes does not constitute an unrecorded encumbrance which renders the title unmarketable. The reasoning appears to be that if the present violation rendered title unmarketable, it would be tantamount to making the seller a guarantor of the quality of construction. The courts are reluctant to impose such a burden on the seller.

Post-closing, the question becomes whether the present violation of the housing codes constitutes a breach of one of the covenants in the deed. Under the facts of the problem, Owner gave Buyer a general warranty deed. A general warranty deed contains the full set of present and future covenants. The present covenants are covenants of seisen (grantor warrants that she owns what she purports to convey), right to convey (grantor warrants that she has the power to convey what she purports to convey), and covenant against encumbrances (grantor warrants that what she purports to convey is free of encumbrances). The future covenants are covenants of general warranty (grantor warrants that she will defend the purchaser against superior title), quiet enjoyment (grantor warrants that purchaser's legal possession will not be disturbed by one asserting a superior title), and further assurances (grantor warrants that she will execute whatever additional documents are necessary to perfect the title conveyed). A general warranty deed makes all of these covenants not only with respect to the grantor's actions but also with respect to all prior owners of the property. Inasmuch as the wiring problem existed on the day of closing, the issue is whether the present violation of the housing codes constitutes a breach of the covenant against encumbrances. Consistent with the majority pre-closing approach, post-closing the courts have concluded that a present violation of local housing codes does **not** constitute a breach of the covenant against encumbrances. Again, the reasoning appears to be that if the present violation of the housing code were to constitute a breach, in essence the courts would be making sellers guarantors of the condition of the property. The legal effect would be to impose the implied warranty of quality, currently imposed on builders only, to ordinary sellers. The courts are reluctant to impose such a burden on ordinary sellers.

Answer (A) is incorrect because the courts are reluctant to hold that present violations of local housing codes constitute a breach of the covenant against encumbrances. To hold accordingly would, in essence, make all sellers guarantors of the quality of any and all improvements. **Answer (B) is incorrect** because it misstates the post-closing rule. If anything, courts are more inclined to hold present violations of local housing codes to constitute an unrecorded encumbrance pre-closing than they are to hold that they constitute a breach of the covenant against encumbrances post-closing. Nevertheless, the majority view is that present violations of a housing code are not an unrecorded encumbrance either pre- or post-closing. **Answer (C) is incorrect** because although it states what arguably is the modern trend, the majority rule is still that present violations of a housing code do not constitute an unrecorded encumbrance which makes title unmarketable pre-closing or which breaches the covenant against encumbrances post-closing.

- **Additional references**: *See* 14 RICHARD R. POWELL, POWELL ON REAL PROPERTY ch. 81, §§ 81.03[6], 81.03[6][e][iii] (Michael Allan Wolf ed., 2000); 11 THOMPSON ON REAL PROPERTY, SECOND THOMAS EDITION § 91.09(a)(3) (2002 & Supp. 2006); 9 THOMPSON § 82.10(c)(3); WILLIAM B. STOEBUCK & DALE A. WHITMAN, THE LAW OF PROPERTY §§ 10.12, 11.13 (3d ed. 2000).

15. **The best answer is (B).** Both a special warranty deed and a general warranty deed usually contain all six covenants - the three present and the three future. The present covenants are covenants of seisen (grantor warrants that she owns what she purports to convey), right to convey (grantor warrants that she has the power to convey what she purports to convey), and covenant against encumbrances (grantor warrants that what she purports to convey is free of encumbrances).

The present covenants are breached, if at all, by the mere existence of a superior property interest at the time of closing. A special warranty deed warrants the grantor's actions only, not the actions of any prior grantor. A general warranty deed warrants not only the grantor's actions but also the actions of all prior grantors.

When Slick purported to convey Getawayacre to Bertha, Slick breached the present covenants of seisen and right to convey. Slick did not own Getawayacre or have the power to convey it. These present covenants were breached in 1995 when Slick delivered the deed to Bertha. Bertha's cause of action against Slick began to run at that point in time. By 2000, the statute of limitations had run on Bertha's cause of action for breach of the present covenant against encumbrances. Bertha can no longer sue Slick on the present covenants.

When Bertha purported to convey Getawayacre to Chris, Bertha breached the present covenants of seisen and right to convey. Since

Bertha did not receive title to Getawayacre from Slick and cannot claim title under adverse possession, she did not own Getawayacre or have the power to convey it. These present covenants were breached in 2003 when Bertha delivered the deed to Chris. Chris's cause of action against Bertha began to run at that point in time. The statute of limitations has not run on Chris's cause of action for breach of the present covenants of seisen and right to convey. Chris can sue Bertha. Although Slick caused the problem, not Bertha, Bertha conveyed a general warranty deed to Chris. The general warranty deed warrants not only her actions as owner, but also the actions of all prior owners - including Slick's.

If Chris sues Bertha for breach of the present covenants, Bertha cannot turn around and sue Slick for breach of the present covenants. Slick breached the present covenants when Slick purported to convey title to Bertha in 1995. The statute of limitations has run on Bertha's cause of action against Slick on the present covenants. The statute does not start anew when Bertha purported to convey title to Chris or when Chris sues Bertha.

Nor can Chris sue Slick for breach of the present covenants in Slick's deed to Bertha. Present covenants do not run to remote grantees. The present covenants in Slick's deed were breached, if at all, when Slick delivered the deed to Slick's immediate grantee, Bertha. The cause of action for breach of the present covenants arose at that time. If Bertha had conveyed to Chris before the statute of limitations had expired, could Chris have sued Slick for breach of the present covenants? Under the traditional common law view, causes of action were not assignable. Even if the statute of limitations had not expired, Bertha could not have assigned her cause of action against Slick for breach of the present covenants in Slick's deed to Chris. Moreover, the present covenants in Slick's deed are not re-asserted when Bertha conveys to Chris. Chris cannot sue Slick on the present covenants (under common law because Bertha's cause of action against Slick was not assignable, and the statute of limitations has run).

Answer (A) is incorrect because the present covenants in Slick's deed were breached, if at all, when the deed was delivered to Bertha. At common law, causes of action were not assignable, and under our facts, even if they were, the statute of limitations has run on Bertha's cause of action against Slick for breach of the present covenants. **Answer (C) is incorrect** because present covenants do not run to remote grantees, so Chris cannot sue Slick for breach of the present covenants in Slick's deed. At best Bertha's cause of action may have been assigned to Chris, but at common law, causes of action were not assignable. Moreover, if Chris sues Bertha, Bertha cannot sue Slick for breach of the present covenants because the statute of limitations on Bertha's cause of action has run. **Answer (D) is incorrect** because present covenants do not run to remote grantees. The present covenants in Slick's deed were breached when he delivered his deed to Bertha. The cause of action arose at that time; but at common law, the cause of action was not assignable. So Chris cannot sue Slick for breach of the present covenants in Slick's deed. **Answer (E) is incorrect** because Bertha did breach the present covenants in her deed to Chris, and the statute of limitations has not run on Chris's cause of action against Bertha.

- **Additional references**: *See* 14 RICHARD R. POWELL, POWELL ON REAL PROPERTY ch. 81A, §§ 81A.06[2][a]-[f], 81A.03[1][b][i]-[iii], 81A.06[5][b] (Michael Allan Wolf ed., 2000); 9 THOMPSON ON REAL PROPERTY, SECOND THOMAS EDITION §§ 82.10(c)(1)-(6), 82.10(d) (1999 & Supp. 2006); WILLIAM B. STOEBUCK & DALE A. WHITMAN, THE LAW OF PROPERTY § 11.13 (3d ed. 2000); RALPH E. BOYER ET. AL., THE LAW OF PROPERTY: AN INTRODUCTORY SURVEY § 17.1 (4th ed. 1991); Rockafellor v. Gray, 191 N.W. 107 (Iowa 1922).

16. **The best answer is (B).** Both a special warranty deed and a general warranty deed usually contain all six covenants, the three present and the three future. The future covenants are covenants of general warranty (grantor warrants that she will defend the purchaser against superior title), quiet enjoyment (grantor warrants that purchaser's legal possession will not be disturbed by one asserting a superior title), and further assurances (grantor warrants that she will execute whatever additional documents are necessary to perfect the title conveyed).

The future covenants are breached when a superior property interest is asserted. A special warranty deed warrants the grantor's actions only, not the actions of any prior grantor. A general warranty deed warrants not only the grantor's actions but also the actions of all prior grantors of the property.

When Slick purported to convey Getawayacre to Bertha, Slick did not own Getawayacre. Oscar held title to Getawayacre. The mere existence of a superior title, however, does not constitute a breach of the future covenants. The party holding the superior title must assert the superior property interest. Oscar did not assert his superior property interest while Bertha owned Getawayacre. Bertha's quiet enjoyment was not disturbed during her time of ownership. At this point, she has no cause of action against Slick for breach of the future covenants.

When Bertha purported to convey Greenacre to Chris, Bertha did not own Getawayacre. Oscar held title to Getawayacre. The mere existence of a superior title, however, does not constitute a breach of the future covenants. The party holding the superior title must assert the superior property interest. In 2004, however, when Oscar takes possession of Getawayacre and refuses to relinquish possession, Oscar is adequately asserting his superior property interest. (Some authorities say that the assertion has to rise to the level of an "eviction," but "eviction" has become a term of art and may not require actual eviction. The assertion of the superior property interest must be sufficient to disrupt the grantee's quiet enjoyment of the property. What constitutes a sufficient "assertion" can be a difficult and fact sensitive inquiry under the appropriate facts.)

Chris's quiet enjoyment has been breached. Chris has a cause of action against Bertha for breach of the future covenants of quiet enjoyment and general warranty. Although Slick caused the problem, not Bertha, Bertha conveyed a general warranty deed to Chris. The general warranty deed warrants not only her actions as owner, but also the actions of all prior owners - including Slick's. The statute of limitations begins to run when the superior property interest is asserted. Oscar asserted his superior property interest in 2004. The statute of limitations has not run.

Although future covenants generally run to remote grantees, Chris cannot sue Slick under the facts of this case and the general common law approach. The general common law approach was that future covenants ran to remote grantees as long as there was privity of estate between the parties. Privity of estate exists if (1) there is a deed which conveys some good title between the parties, or (2) there is no deed or the deed does not convey any good title, but the parties pass actual possession from one to another. Here, Slick had no title to convey to Bertha, and Bertha had no title to convey to Chris. The deeds in question passed no title whatsoever. Nor is there privity of estate based on actual possession. Neither Bertha nor Chris ever went into actual possession of the property. Since there is no privity of estate, the future covenants do not run to the remote grantee. The future covenants in Slick's deed do not run to Chris. Chris cannot sue Slick on the future covenants.

If Chris sues Bertha for breach of the future covenants of quiet enjoyment and general warranty, can Bertha sue Slick? Bertha cannot invoke the doctrine of subrogation to step into Chris's shoes because Chris could not sue Slick. Can Bertha sue Slick based on the future covenants in the deed from Slick to Bertha? No, according to the common law courts. Once the grantee conveyed title to a new grantee, if the future covenants did not run to the new grantee, the future covenants, for all practical purposes, expired. Even if Chris were to sue and recover from Bertha, Bertha cannot sue Slick on the future covenants in Slick's deed to Bertha. Since the covenants did not run, they expired when the grantee, Bertha, conveyed the property.

Answer (A) is incorrect because Bertha cannot sue Slick for breach of the future covenants even if Chris recovers from Bertha. Under the general common law approach, since future covenants do not run to a remote grantee, the covenants effectively expired upon the grantee conveying the property. Here, Slick's future covenants in the deed to Bertha effectively expired upon Bertha's conveying the property. The breach did not arise until after Bertha conveyed the property, so Bertha cannot sue Slick on the future covenants in his deed to her. **Answers (C) and (D) are incorrect** because Chris cannot sue Slick. Although the general rule is that future covenants run to remote grantees, at common law that was true only if there was privity of estate between the parties. There is no privity of estate between Slick and Chris because the deeds in question did not convey any title, and none of the parties were in actual possession. **Answer (E) is incorrect** because Chris can sue Bertha for breach of the future covenants.

- **Additional references**: *See* 14 RICHARD R. POWELL, POWELL ON REAL PROPERTY ch. 81A, §§ 81A.06[2][a]-[f], 81A.03[1][b][i]-[iii], 81A.06[5][c]-[d][iii] (Michael Allan Wolf ed., 2000); 9 THOMPSON ON REAL PROPERTY, SECOND THOMAS EDITION §§ 82.10(c)(1)-(6), 82.10(d) (1999 & Supp. 2006); WILLIAM B. STOEBUCK & DALE A. WHITMAN, THE LAW OF PROPERTY § 11.13 (3d ed. 2000); RALPH E. BOYER ET. AL., THE LAW OF PROPERTY: AN INTRODUCTORY SURVEY § 17.1 (4th ed. 1991); Rockefellor v. Gray, 191 N.W. 107 (Iowa 1922); Wead v. Larkin, 54 Ill. 489 (1870).

17. **The best answer is (B).** The basic analysis of this problem is the same as for problem 15, above. The difference between the common law and the modern trend is that although present covenants do not "run" to remote grantees, the cause of action which arises when the present covenant is breached is assignable from the grantee to the remote grantee. If the grantor breaches any of the present covenants when he or she conveys to the grantee, the cause of action which arises upon the

breach is assignable to the grantee's grantee (i.e., a remote grantee relative to the original grantor). The remote grantor can sue the original grantor for breach of the present covenants in the grantor's original deed *if the statute of limitations has not run.* When Slick delivered the deed to Bertha, Slick breached the present covenants of seisen and right to convey. The breach gave rise to a cause of action. When Bertha delivered the deed to Chris, the deed is construed to assign Bertha's cause of action against Slick to Chris. The assignment is implied even in the absence of an express provision in the deed assigning the cause of action. Chris can sue Slick for breach of the present covenants in the deed from Slick to Bertha *if the statute of limitations has not run on the cause of action.* The conveyance from Bertha to Chris does not re-start the statute of limitations. It starts to run, if at all, when Slick delivered his deed to Bertha.

As applied to the facts in question, the statute of limitations has run on Bertha's cause of action against Slick for breach of the present covenants. Since the statute of limitations has run, Bertha has nothing to assign to Chris. The rest of the analysis is the same as under the common law approach. See answer to problem 15 above.

Answer (A) is incorrect because the present covenants in Slick's deed were breached, if at all, when the deed was delivered to Bertha, and the statute of limitations has run on Bertha's cause of action against Slick for breach of the present covenants. **Answer (C) is incorrect** because although under the modern trend present covenants are assignable to remote grantees, here the statute of limitations has run on any claims against Slick for breach of the present covenants in his deed to Bertha. Chris cannot sue Slick for breach of the present covenants in Slick's deed. Moreover, if Chris sues Bertha, Bertha cannot sue Slick for breach of the present covenants because the statute of limitations on Bertha's cause of action has run. **Answer (D) is incorrect** because although under the modern trend present covenants are assignable to remote grantees, the statute of limitations has run on any claim against Slick for breach of the present covenants in Slick's deed. Moreover, since Bertha used a general warranty deed to convey Getawayacre, she has warranted not only her actions but Slick's as well. Therefore, Chris can sue Bertha. **Answer (E) is incorrect** because Bertha did breach the present covenants in her deed to Chris, and the statute of limitations has not run on Chris's cause of action against Bertha.

- **Additional references:** *See* 14 RICHARD R. POWELL, POWELL ON REAL PROPERTY ch. 81A, §§ 81A.06[2][a]-[f], 81A.03[1][b][i]-[iii],

81A.06[5][b] (Michael Allan Wolf ed., 2000); 9 THOMPSON ON REAL PROPERTY, SECOND THOMAS EDITION §§ 82.10(c)(1)-(6), 82.10(d) (1999 & Supp. 2006); WILLIAM B. STOEBUCK & DALE A. WHITMAN, THE LAW OF PROPERTY § 11.13 (3d ed. 2000); RALPH E. BOYER ET. AL., THE LAW OF PROPERTY: AN INTRODUCTORY SURVEY § 17.1 (4th ed. 1991); Rockefellor v. Gray, 191 N.W. 107 (Iowa 1922).

18. **The best answer is (C).** Both a special warranty deed and a general warranty deed usually contain all six covenants, the three present and the three future. The future covenants are the covenants of general warranty (grantor warrants that she will defend the purchaser against superior title), quiet enjoyment (grantor warrants that purchaser's legal possession will not be disturbed by one asserting a superior title), and further assurances (grantor warrants that she will execute whatever additional documents are necessary to perfect the title conveyed).

The future covenants are breached when a superior property interest is asserted. A special warranty deed warrants the grantor's actions only, not the actions of any prior grantor. A general warranty deed warrants not only the grantor's actions but also the actions of all prior grantors of the property.

When Slick purported to convey Getawayacre to Bertha, Slick did not own Getawayacre. Oscar held title to Getawayacre. The mere existence of a superior title, however, does not constitute a breach of the future covenants. The party holding the superior title must assert the superior property interest. Oscar did not assert his superior property interests while Bertha owned Getawayacre. Bertha's quiet enjoyment was not disturbed during her time of ownership. At this point, she has no cause of action against Slick for breach of the future covenants.

When Bertha purported to convey Getawayacre to Chris, Bertha did not own Getawayacre. Oscar held title to Getawayacre. The mere existence of a superior title, however, does not constitute a breach of the future covenants. The party holding the superior title must assert the superior property interest. In 2004, however, when Oscar takes possession of Getawayacre and refuses to relinquish possession, Oscar is asserting his superior property interest. Chris's quiet enjoyment has been breached. Chris has a cause of action against Bertha for breach of the future covenants of quiet enjoyment and general warranty. Although Slick caused the problem, not Bertha, Bertha conveyed a general warranty deed to Chris. The general warranty deed warrants not only her actions as owner, but also the actions of all prior owners - including Slick's. The statute of limitations begins to run when the superior property interest is asserted. Oscar asserted his superior property interest in 2004. The statute of limitations has not run.

As for whether Chris can sue Slick, under the modern trend approach, the future covenants run to remote grantees as long as there is either privity of estate or privity of contract. As establish above, in the answer to problem 16, there is no privity of estate between Slick and Chris. There is, however, privity of contract. Privity of contract exists between parties to the same contract. Slick and Bertha have privity of contract based on the contract and deed between them. Bertha and Chris have privity of contract based on the contract and deed between them. Because of the privity of contract between Slick and Bertha on the one hand, and Bertha and Chris on the other hand, Slick's future covenants to Bertha are deemed to have been passed along from Bertha to Chris when Bertha contracted with Chris. Thus, there is privity of contract between Slick and Chris which supports Slick's future covenants running to Chris. Chris can sue Slick for breach of the future covenants in Slick's deed to Bertha.

If Chris sues Bertha for breach of the future covenants of quiet enjoyment and general warranty, can Bertha sue Slick? Since Chris could have sued either Bertha or Slick, Bertha can invoke the doctrine of subrogation to step into Chris's shoes and sue Slick. (Subrogation permits one to step into the shoes of another and assert any and all claims that party could have asserted.) In addition, Bertha can sue Slick based on the future covenants in the deed from Slick to Bertha. The statute of limitations has not run yet because it does not begin to run until the superior title is asserted.

Answers (A) and (B) are incorrect because Chris can sue Slick for breach of the future covenants set forth in the deed from Slick to Bertha. Under the modern trend, there is privity of contract between the parties which is sufficient to support the running of Slick's future covenants to remote grantees, namely Chris. The statute of limitations has not run because it does not begin to run until Oscar asserts his superior title. **Answer (D) is incorrect** because Chris can sue Bertha. Bertha gave Chris a general warranty deed which warrants not only Bertha's actions but also those of her prior grantors - including the actions of Slick. **Answer (E) is incorrect** because Chris can sue Bertha and/or Slick for breach of the future covenants.

- **Additional references**: *See* 14 RICHARD R. POWELL, POWELL ON REAL PROPERTY ch. 81A, §§ 81A.06[2][a]-[f], 81A.03[1][b][i]-[iii], 81A.06[5][b] (Michael Allan Wolf ed., 2000); 9 THOMPSON ON REAL PROPERTY, SECOND THOMAS EDITION §§ 82.10(c)(1)-(6), 82.10(d) (1999 & Supp. 2006); WILLIAM B. STOEBUCK & DALE A. WHITMAN, THE LAW OF PROPERTY § 11.13 (3d ed. 2000); RALPH E. BOYER ET. AL., THE LAW OF PROPERTY: AN INTRODUCTORY SURVEY § 17.1 (4th ed. 1991); Rockefellor v. Gray, 191 N.W. 107 (Iowa 1922).

19. **The best answer is (C).** Both a general warranty deed and a special warranty deed usually contain all six covenants, the three present and the three future.

   The present covenants are the covenants of seisen (grantor warrants that she owns what she purports to convey), right to convey (grantor warrants that she has the power to convey what she purports to convey), and covenant against encumbrances (grantor warrants that what she purports to convey is free of encumbrances). The present covenants are breached by the mere existence of a superior property interest at the time of closing.

   The future covenants are covenants of general warranty (grantor warrants that she will defend the purchaser against superior title), quiet enjoyment (grantor warrants that purchaser's legal possession will not be disturbed by one asserting a superior title), and further assurances (grantor warrants that she will execute whatever additional documents are necessary to perfect the title conveyed). The future covenants are breached by the assertion of a superior property interest.

   Under the facts of the problem, Chris thought she was purchasing good title to Getawayacre, only to find out later that Bertha did not have good title to convey to Chris. First, Chris will want to sue her immediate grantor, Bertha. Bertha gave Chris a general warranty deed. A general warranty deed contains the same six covenants which cover not only the grantor's actions, but also the actions of all prior grantors. By using a general warranty deed, Bertha warranted not only her own actions, but also the actions of all prior grantors in Bertha's chain of title. Although Bertha arguably did nothing wrong during her time in possession of Getawayacre, the scope of Bertha's general warranty deed makes her liable not only for her actions but also the actions of her prior grantors.

Although Slick is the party responsible for the problem, Bertha has warranted Slick's actions by virtue of Bertha's general warranty deed. Chris can sue Bertha for breach of the present covenants because (1) a superior property interest (Oscar's right to the property) existed at the time of closing, and (2) the statute of limitations has not expired. Chris can also sue Bertha for breach of the future covenants - Oscar is asserting his superior property interest.

A grantor's liability under a warranty deed is limited to the amount of consideration which the grantor received from the sale of the property in question. Inasmuch as Bertha received only $150,000 when she sold the property to Chris, Chris can sue Bertha for only the amount of consideration she received: $150,000.

Under the modern trend, Chris can also sue Slick. (Though Chris can sue Bertha and/or Slick under the modern trend, Chris can only recover once). Under the modern trend, the future covenants run to remote grantees as long as there is privity of estate or privity of contract. Although there is no privity of estate between Slick and Chris, there is privity of contract. At a minimum, Chris can sue Slick for $150,000. (If Chris could show the value of the property was actually $200,000, the courts are split over whether Chris is limited to the consideration he paid his immediate grantor or whether he can sue Slick for up to $200,000 since that is the amount of consideration Slick received.)

If Chris sues Bertha and recovers from her, Bertha will want to sue Slick. Bertha can sue Slick only is Chris recovers damages from her. Bertha cannot sue Slick for breach of the present covenants because even though a superior property interest existed at the time of closing (Oscar's rights to the property), the statute of limitations has expired. Bertha, however, can sue Slick for breach of the future covenants because Oscar is asserting his superior property interest. Although Slick received $200,000 from Bertha, Bertha's liability to Chris is only $150,000, so Bertha's damages arguably are only $150,000 (unless Bertha can show that the reason she could sell Getawayacre for only $150,000 was because of concerns about the quality of title).

Some jurisdictions take a rescissionary approach to damages and permit the buyer to rescind the contract and recover whatever consideration he or she paid. If the jurisdiction applies the rescissionary approach, Bertha will be entitled to rescind the deal and recover the $200,000 she paid to Slick. This approach has the additional equitable benefit of depriving the party at fault of any possible gain from the scenario.

Answer (A) is incorrect because it fails to take into account the modern trend that future covenants run to remote grantees as long as there is privity of contract. There is privity of contract between Slick and Bertha, and between Bertha and Chris, so Slick's future covenants run to Chris. Chris can sue Slick. **Answer (B) is incorrect** because it fails to recognize that Chris can sue Bertha for breach of the present and future covenants. Although Bertha arguably did nothing wrong during her ownership, since she gave a general warranty deed, she warrants not only her own actions as owner, but also the actions of all prior grantors in her chain of title - including Slick. **Answer (D) is incorrect** because it fails to reflect the scope of the rescissionary approach. Under the rescissionary approach, the buyer is permitted to rescind the contract and recover whatever consideration the buyer gave, even if the value of the land has dropped since the buyer purchased the property. **Answer (E) is incorrect** because it fails to recognize that Chris has causes of action against both Bertha and Slick for breach of the covenants.

- **Additional references:** *See* 14 RICHARD R. POWELL, POWELL ON REAL PROPERTY ch. 81A, § 81A.06[4][b], ch. 81, §§ 81.04[3][a], 81.04[3][c] (Michael Allan Wolf ed., 2000); 9 THOMPSON ON REAL PROPERTY, SECOND THOMAS EDITION § 82.10(d) (1999 & Supp. 2006); WILLIAM B. STOEBUCK & DALE A. WHITMAN, THE LAW OF PROPERTY § 11.13 (3d ed. 2000); RALPH E. BOYER ET. AL., THE LAW OF PROPERTY: AN INTRODUCTORY SURVEY § 17.1 (4th ed. 1991); Rockefellor v. Gray, 191 N.W. 107 (Iowa 1922).

20. **The best answer is (C).** Under traditional common law principles, when the seller and purchaser enter into a binding contract to purchase, under the doctrine of equitable conversion, the buyer becomes the owner for most purposes.

   Equitable conversion is based upon the principle that "equity regards as done that which ought to be done." Assuming an enforceable contract, for most purposes title passed the moment the parties entered into a binding contract. Under equitable conversion, the buyer assumes the risk of loss or change with respect to the property during the escrow period between executing the contract and closing. The contract to purchase is to purchase title to the property. Changes to structures on the property or zoning changes which do not affect title per se are not seen as grounds for permitting the buyer to rescind the contract.

   Under the doctrine of equitable conversion, the fact that the earthquake severely damaged the property in question will not affect the buyer's contractual obligation to purchase the property for the agreed upon price. The Owner is still entitled to specific performance.

Where the seller has insured the property, there is the additional issue of who is entitled to the insurance proceeds. Although both the seller and the buyer have insurable interests under equitable conversion, the seller's interest has been reduced to a personal property claim for the contract proceeds. Although a minority of courts have reasoned that the issue of the seller's insurance coverage of the property is completely independent from the issue of equitable conversion, the majority rule is that it would be unconscionable to permit the seller to get specific performance under equitable conversion for the full sale price and to keep the insurance proceeds for the damage the property sustained during the escrow period.

The principle of equitable conversion reasons that once the parties have entered into an enforceable contract of sale, the seller holds merely legal title and the buyer holds equitable title. Likewise, the courts apply the same reasoning to any insurance policy the seller may hold on the property. The seller holds legal title to the policy and insurance proceeds to be paid thereunder, but the buyer holds equitable title. Using the constructive trust doctrine to prevent unjust enrichment, the courts order the seller to convey the insurance proceeds to the buyer. At least where the seller has insured the property, the American approach to the issue of insurance proceeds reduces the harshness of the equitable conversion doctrine as applied to the buyer.

Answers (A) and (B) are incorrect because each fails to take into account the doctrine of equitable estoppel. Under equitable estoppel, once the parties enter into an enforceable contract, the purchaser assumes all risks with respect to changes in the physical condition of the premises or the uses to which the property may be put. **Answer (D) is incorrect** because it fails to take into account the American approach to the issue of the seller's insurance policy. Under the American approach, the insurance policy on the property is, in essence, deemed part of the sale contract and buyer may claim the benefit of the insurance policy.

- **Additional references**: *See* 14 RICHARD R. POWELL, POWELL ON REAL PROPERTY ch. 81, §§ 81.03[1], 81.03[2]-81.03[2][b] (Michael Allan Wolf ed., 2000); 12 THOMPSON ON REAL PROPERTY, SECOND THOMAS EDITION § 99.09(a) (1994 & Supp. 2006); RALPH E. BOYER ET. AL., THE LAW OF PROPERTY: AN INTRODUCTORY SURVEY § 14.4 (4th ed. 1991).

21. **The best answer is (A).** Under the modern trend, more and more courts are recognizing that the true intent of the parties was not to purchase the land *per se*, but to purchase the land with its improvements - in particular, the house. The parties presume that the land will be delivered in the same condition as it was when the parties entered into the contract. Moreover, the modern trend reasons that the seller is in the best position to take precautions against and to insure against changes to the property during the escrow period between the time of contracting and the time of closing.

    Under the modern trend, to the extent the property changes substantially or materially between the time of contracting and the time of closing, it is unfair to impose that change upon the buyer. The buyer is entitled to rescind the contract. In the alternative, if the change in condition of the property is relatively minor, the seller may still be entitled to specific performance, but the buyer is entitled to an abatement in the purchase price.

    Under the facts, the house is seriously damaged by the earthquake which hit during the escrow period. Under the modern trend, Buyer would be entitled to rescind the contract.

    Answer (B) is incorrect because it fails to take into account, under the modern trend, the difference in the degree of damage to the property. Under the modern trend, if the property is damaged during the escrow period, the seller is entitled to specific performance only if the damage is relatively minor. **Answers (C) and (D) are incorrect** because they fail to reflect that, under the modern trend, the buyer is entitled to rescind the contract if the damage is substantial.

    - **Additional references**: *See* 14 RICHARD R. POWELL, POWELL ON REAL PROPERTY ch. 81, §§ 81.03[2], 81.03[2][a] (Michael Allan Wolf ed., 2000); 12 THOMPSON ON REAL PROPERTY, SECOND THOMAS EDITION § 99.09(a) (1994 & Supp. 2006); RALPH E. BOYER ET. AL., THE LAW OF PROPERTY: AN INTRODUCTORY SURVEY § 14.4 (4th ed. 1991).

22. **The best answer is (A).** The first issue is whether Nelson retained any interest in his residence so as to be able to convey it to Jonathan after Nelson executed a will devising all of his property to his four daughters. A will is executory in nature, which means that for most purposes it is not effective until the testator's death. The will disposes of the property which the testator (the person who executed the will) owns at the time of

the testator's death. Testator is free to dispose of his or her property as she wishes until the time of death, and any property disposed of inter vivos (while the testator is alive) is no longer subject to the terms of the will, since the property is no longer the testator's.

In 2000 Nelson properly executed and delivered a quitclaim deed which transferred title to his residence to Jonathan, but which reserved a life estate with the power to revoke. There is no problem with the execution and delivery of the deed. The issue is whether the life estate coupled with the power to revoke the remainder made the deed so testamentary in nature that the instrument must be executed with wills act formalities (the technical execution requirements for a valid will). A typical deed does not comply with the requirements for a valid will. If the deed should have been executed with wills act formalities, the deed will fail to pass any interest to Jonathan.

At common law, the courts reasoned that since the deed was revocable, the deed passed no interest to Jonathan inter vivos, but only upon Nelson's death if not revoked. Under that characterization, the common law courts generally held that such deeds were testamentary in nature and failed to pass any interest to the remainderman, since the deed was not executed with wills act formalities.

Answer (B) is incorrect because a quitclaim deed is effective to transfer a property interest, and a will devises only property which is still the testator's property at the time of death. If the testator holds only a life estate interest in the property, the testator's interest expires upon the testator's death and there is no interest in the property for the will to transfer. **Answer (C) is incorrect** because although plausible, the common law courts were very protective of the wills act formalities and generally held that anything which appeared to transfer a property interest at time of death had to comply with wills act formalities (which a typical deed did not satisfy). **Answer (D) is incorrect** because the courts require strict compliance with the wills act formalities, and any transfer which appeared to transfer a property interest at time of death had to comply strictly with wills act formalities (which a typical deed did not satisfy).

- **Additional references:** *See* 14 RICHARD R. POWELL, POWELL ON REAL PROPERTY ch. 81A, § 81A.04[2][a][iii] (Michael Allan Wolf ed., 2000); 9 THOMPSON ON REAL PROPERTY, SECOND EDITION § 83.03(c) (1999 & Supp. 2006); RALPH E. BOYER ET. AL., THE LAW OF PROPERTY: AN INTRODUCTORY SURVEY § 6.1 (4th ed. 1991).

23. The best answer is (C). The first issue is whether Nelson retained any interest in his residence, so as to be able to convey it to Jonathan after Nelson executed a will devising all of his property to his four daughters.

A will is executory in nature, which means that for most purposes it is not effective until the testator's death. The will disposes of the property which the testator (the person who executed the will) owns at the time of the testator's death. Testator is free to dispose of his or her property as she wishes until time of death, and any property disposed of inter vivos (while the testator is alive) is no longer subject to the terms of the will since the property is no longer the testator's.

In 2000, Nelson properly executed and delivered a quitclaim deed which transferred title to his residence to Jonathan, but which reserved a life estate with the power to revoke. There is no problem with the execution and delivery of the deed. The issue is whether the life estate coupled with the power to revoke the remainder made the deed so testamentary in nature that the instrument must be executed with wills act formalities (the technical requirements for a valid will). A typical deed does not comply with the requirements for a valid will. If the deed should have been executed with wills act formalities, the deed will fail to pass any interest to Jonathan.

The modern trend focuses more on the intent of the grantor, whether there was any risk of fraud, and whether the act of executing the deed fulfills the functions underlying the wills act formalities. The modern trend has been to hold that a deed which purports to transfer title subject to a retained life estate and power to revoke is valid to pass a property interest to the party holding the future interest. Although Nelson retained a life estate, Jonathan took a remainder in fee simple the moment the deed was delivered. That Nelson retained the power to revoke Jonathan's interest may have made the remainder subject to divestment, but under the modern trend analysis, Jonathan still took an adequate property interest so that the transfer is valid even though it does not comply with the wills act formalities.

Answer (A) is incorrect because under the modern trend, revocable deeds are effective to transfer a property interest, even though the deed fails to comply with wills act formalities. **Answer (B) is incorrect** because a quitclaim deed is effective to transfer a property interest, and a will only devises property which is still the testator's property at time of death. If the testator holds only a life estate interest in the property, the testator's interest expires upon testator's death and there is no interest in the property for the will to transfer. **Answer (D) is incorrect** because the courts still require strict compliance with the wills act formalities generally, although the modern trend is for the courts to show greater leniency towards the formalities with some jurisdictions going so far as to adopt substantial compliance as the required standard of compliance.

- **Additional references**: *See* 15 RICHARD R. POWELL, POWELL ON REAL PROPERTY ch. 85, § 85.07, 14 POWELL ON REAL PROPERTY ch. 81A, § 81A.04[2][a][iii] (Michael Allan Wolf ed., 2000); 9 THOMPSON ON REAL PROPERTY, SECOND THOMAS EDITION § 83.03(c) (1999 & Supp. 2006); RALPH E. BOYER ET. AL., THE LAW OF PROPERTY: AN INTRODUCTORY SURVEY § 6.1 (4th ed. 1991).

24. **The best answer is (B).** The problem presents a classic example of what is known as circular priorities. A's claim is first in time, first in right, but A failed to record A's mortgage. B's claim is second in time and thus, in order of priority, stands in line behind A's mortgage. The only way B could jump ahead of A's claim is if B could qualify for protection under the jurisdiction's recording act.

To qualify for protection under a notice recording act, the claimant must qualify as a subsequent bona fide purchaser without notice of the prior conveyance. B cannot trump A because B knows of A's mortgage. When C comes along and receives a mortgage from Bluto, C is third in line unless C qualifies for protection under the recording act. C lent money to Bluto, so C qualifies as a subsequent purchaser with respect to C's property interest - the mortgage. The question is whether C had notice of the prior conveyances. There is no evidence that C had actual or inquiry notice of the prior mortgages. Did C have constructive notice? B recorded B's mortgage, so C is on constructive notice of B's interest, but A never recorded A's mortgage. C takes subject to B's claim (i.e., behind B's claim) but before A's claim, since C is entitled to protection against A's claim under the recording act. So A takes before B, who takes before C, who takes before A. A classic example of circular priorities. Although there are several competing theories as to how to resolve the problem, the prevailing "expectations" theory says give each party what he or she expects, starting with the last party to receive an interest. C was last, so ask, from C's perspective: What did C think the situation was? C thought C stood in line behind B. So credit what B is entitled to against the sale proceeds and then see how much is left to satisfy C's claim. The foreclosure sale brought in $70,000. B's mortgage is for $40,000. Giving B what C expected would happen, there would only be $30,000 left over for C. C takes $30,000.

Repeat the analysis for B, using the *full* amount of the sale proceeds. B thought B stood in line behind A. So credit what A is entitled to against the sale proceeds, and then see how much is left to satisfy B's claim. The foreclosure sale brought in $70,000. A's mortgage is for $40,000. Giving A what B expected would happen, there would only be $30,000 left over for B. B takes $30,000. Lastly, there is A. Since A was the root of the problem, because A failed to record, give A whatever money is left over. C took $30,000, and B took $30,000 for a total of $60,000. The foreclosure sale proceeds were only $70,000. There is only $10,000 left over for A.

Answer (A) is incorrect because it fails to take into account the circular priorities. Answer (A) simply reflects the order of takers if A came first, B second, and C last. But C is entitled to protection against A's claim. C is entitled to take before A. **Answer (C) is incorrect** because it simply reduces each claimant's claim by $10,000. But that fails to take into account the expectations of each party and the relative fault of each party. **Answer (D) is incorrect** because it simply is another attempt at an equitable solution to the matter. But is also fails to take into account the expectations of each party and the relative fault of each party. **Answer (E) is incorrect** because from a law and economics perspective, the market sets the value of the property, not what some people think should be the value (moreover, it is in there just to see if you are still awake!).

- **Additional references:** *See* 14 RICHARD R. POWELL, POWELL ON REAL PROPERTY ch. 82, §§ 82.02[c][ii], 82.02[d][i]-[iii], 82.03[2][b][i] (Michael Allan Wolf ed., 2000); 11 THOMPSON ON REAL PROPERTY, SECOND THOMAS EDITION §§ 92.13(b), 92.14, 92.15(b)(2)(A), 92.07(d) (2002 & Supp. 2006); WILLIAM B. STOEBUCK & DALE A. WHITMAN, THE LAW OF PROPERTY §§ 11.9-11.11 (3d ed. 2000).

25. **The best answer is (B).** A fraudulent deed is a deed which the true owner actually signs, but under an intentional misrepresentation by a third party. A forged deed is a deed which the true owner does not sign. Someone other than the true owner signs the true owner's name on the deed without the owner's authority.

A forged deed is void. It can never pass good title, even if conveyed to one who qualifies for protection under the jurisdiction's recording act. A fraudulent deed is either void or voidable, depending on the grantor's culpability. If the deed is void, then the deed can never pass good title, even if conveyed to one who qualifies for protection under the jurisdiction's recording act. If the deed is voidable, as between the grantor and grantee, the grantor still has a superior claim to the property and can void the deed. If, however, the grantee conveys it to a party who qualifies for protection under the jurisdiction's recording act, the subsequent bona fide purchaser will be protected against the claim of the true owner.

Under the facts of the problem, Ron, the true owner, never signed the deed. Darth forged Ron's signature. The deed is void. The deed cannot pass good title, even to one who otherwise qualifies for protection under the jurisdiction's recording act.

Answer (A) is incorrect because a fraudulent deed is a deed which the grantor actually signs, but under fraudulent conditions. Ron never signed the deed purporting to transfer title from Ron to Darth. The deed is a forged deed, not a fraudulent deed. **Answers (C) and (D) are incorrect** because a forged deed is void and can never pass good title, even to subsequent grantees in the chain of title who qualify for protection under the recording act.

*   **Additional references**: *See* 14 RICHARD R. POWELL, POWELL ON REAL PROPERTY ch. 81A, § 81A.04[1][e], ch. 82, § 82.02[1] (Patrick J. Rohan ed. 1999); 11 THOMPSON ON REAL PROPERTY, SECOND THOMAS EDITION §§ 94.07(m) (2002 & Supp. 2006); RALPH E. BOYER ET. AL., THE LAW OF PROPERTY: AN INTRODUCTORY SURVEY § 17.3[B] (4th ed. 1991).

ANSWER KEY
EXAM VI

PROPERTY
ANSWER KEY AND EXPLANATIONS

EXAM VI

1. **The best answer is (C).** The Statute of Frauds requires that to transfer an interest in land, there must be a writing signed by the party to be charged which contains the material provisions. Inasmuch as the agreement between O and B was oral, strict application of the Statute of Frauds would mean that B has no cause of action.

   Because of the harshness and inequity which the Statute of Frauds may cause in some situations, most jurisdictions recognize an exception to the Statute of Frauds: part performance. Under part performance, the parties' conduct may so evidence the agreement that the court may enforce the agreement even in the absence of a writing which satisfies the Statute of Frauds. Under part performance, the courts focus on three factors: (1) whether the buyer has taken possession of the property, (2) whether there has been payment of all or part of the purchase price, and (3) whether the buyer has made any valuable improvements. Although the exact relationship of the three factors is unclear, many authorities argue that if the plaintiff can show the buyer has taken possession and that the buyer can satisfy one of the other two factors, the plaintiff should prevail. Obviously, if the plaintiff can show all three factors, the plaintiff has an even stronger claim.

   Historically, partial performance was the only exception to the rule that an agreement to sell real property had to be in writing. The exception had two theoretical justifications: an evidentiary basis and an estoppel basis. The modern trend (as set forth in the Uniform Land Transaction Act), however, arguably recognizes estoppel as a distinct exception to the Statute of Frauds, not just as a theoretical justification for the part performance exception.

   In contrast to the traditional, three factor approach to part performance, estoppel takes a more holistic approach to the facts. Courts may apply estoppel to prevent unjust enrichment by the party invoking the Statute of Frauds or to prevent unconscionable injury to the party who has relied on the alleged contract in good faith and has changed his or her position in reliance on the oral agreement. What constitutes "unjust enrichment" or "unconscionable injury" is very fact sensitive and it is difficult to predict how a court will rule on such claims.

Since B can show all three factors which the courts look to for part performance, B has a stronger claim under part performance than estoppel. B has taken possession of Farmland. B has made partial payment, a down payment, towards the purchase price. B has made substantial improvements to the land by investing in the land by planting a crop. While B could assert a claim under the very fact sensitive and amorphous doctrine of estoppel, B has a stronger claim under part performance because B can clearly establish all three factors which the courts look for under the doctrine of part performance.

Answer (A) is incorrect because the agreement between A and O is oral, and the Statute of Frauds requires that all agreements to convey real property must be in writing. **Answer (B) is incorrect**, arguably, because part performance is a slightly clearer doctrine than estoppel, and B can clearly satisfy all three of the factors the courts look at in determining whether to apply part performance. B has a stronger claim under part performance than B would have under the more amorphous estoppel. **Answer (D) is incorrect** because equitable conversion applies once there is an enforceable contract. Since the issue here is *whether* there is an enforceable contract between O and B, equitable conversion is of no help.

- **Additional references:** *See* 14 RICHARD J. POWELL, POWELL ON REAL PROPERTY ch. 81, §§ 81.02[1]-81.02[2][e] (Patrick J. Rohan ed. 1999); WILLIAM B. STOEBUCK & DALE A. WHITMAN, THE LAW OF PROPERTY §§ 10.1-10.2 (3d ed. 2000). RALPH E. BOYER ET. AL., THE LAW OF PROPERTY: AN INTRODUCTORY SURVEY §§ 14.2-14.4 (4th ed. 1991).

2. **The best answer is (C).** A contract to purchase real property is not really a contract to purchase property; it is a contract to purchase title to real property. One of the keys to analyzing the contract then is to determine the quality of title called for in the contract. Where the contract is silent, the default rule is that the seller must deliver marketable title. Marketable title is title which is free from reasonable doubt and risk of litigation, and which a reasonable buyer would be willing to accept in exchange for valuable consideration.

Basically, there are three types of defects which may render title unmarketable: chain of title defects, recorded encumbrances, and unrecorded encumbrances. Whether one of these types of encumbrances actually renders title unmarketable depends upon which type of defect it is, and how substantial the defect is. Here, inasmuch as the seller is operating a business in violation of the local zoning ordinance, the present violation of the zoning law arguably constitutes an unrecorded encumbrance. The issue is whether the violation is substantial enough to render the title unmarketable. While additional facts may be necessary to resolve that question, the issue is moot since the contract here does not call for marketable title but only insurable title.

Where the contract calls for insurable title, the issue of whether the title is acceptable or not is not for the buyer or even the court to determine, but for a title insurance company to decide. As long as the seller can find a reputable title insurance company to insure the property with the claimed defect, the buyer has no grounds to object. The buyer contracted for insurable title, and that is what the buyer would get. If O can find a title insurance company which will assume the risk of subsequent litigation over the use of the property for business purposes, the buyer has no grounds to object.

Answer (A) is incorrect because the purchaser contracted for only "insurable title" which means that purchaser has agreed to accept the property, even if the property is subject to some encumbrances, as long as a title insurance company will insure the property. Under "insurable title" the ultimate decision of whether the risk of litigation is too great is for the insurance company to decide, not the purchaser. **Answer (B) is incorrect** because the purchaser contracted for "insurable title," not "marketable title." Under marketable title, a present violation of a zoning ordinance generally makes title unmarketable since it subjects the purchaser to an unreasonable risk of litigation. Under insurable title, however, what constitutes an unreasonable risk of litigation is for the insurance company to decide, not the purchaser or the court. **Answer (D) is incorrect** because although the risk of litigation may be great, if the insurance company is willing to assume that risk and insure the title, the purchaser has no grounds to rescind the contract since the seller is providing the quality of title called for in the contract - insurable title.

- **Additional references**: *See* 12 THOMPSON ON REAL PROPERTY, SECOND EDITION § 99.10(a)(2) (1994 & Supp. 2006); WILLIAM B. STOEBUCK & DALE A. WHITMAN, THE LAW OF PROPERTY § 10.12 (3d ed. 2000); RALPH E. BOYER ET. AL., THE LAW OF PROPERTY: AN INTRODUCTORY SURVEY § 14.6 (4th ed. 1991); 14 RICHARD J. POWELL, POWELL ON REAL PROPERTY ch. 81, § 81.03[6][a].

3. **The best answer is (C).** A's mortgage interest in Blackacre constitutes a property interest as real as if it were an easement. Inasmuch as A received the mortgage from O, the true owner of the property, there is no problem with the creation of the property interest. A will claim the mortgage interest in Blackacre based on first in time, first in right.

When O conveys Blackacre to B with no mention of the mortgage, O is conveying more than O has. O no longer owns Blackacre free and clear of any other property interests. O owns Blackacre subject to A's mortgage. The only way B can receive Blackacre free and clear of A's mortgage interest is if B can qualify for protection under the jurisdiction's recording act.

The jurisdiction applies the notice recording act. To qualify for protection under a notice recording act, the party claiming protection from a prior in time property interest must be a subsequent bona fide purchaser without notice of the competing property claim. Inasmuch as O sold Blackacre to B, B qualifies as a subsequent purchaser (subsequent to A's competing property claim). The question is whether B had notice of the competing property claim.

There are three types of notice: actual, inquiry and constructive. There are no facts which indicate that B had either actual or inquiry notice, and the call of the question expressly says to assume that none of the parties had actual notice of any of the prior transactions. There is no evidence which would create suspicions in a reasonable person that there may be a mortgage interest in the property. Thus, there is no evidence of inquiry notice. Did B have constructive notice? Constructive notice typically is based upon record notice if the deed from the prior transaction has been properly recorded. Notice is assessed at the time the subsequent grantee gives consideration for his or her property interest. Since A did not record the mortgage, B has no record notice of the mortgage. A search of the grantor-grantee index would not have revealed the mortgage.

At the time B purchased Blackacre (at closing when B gave consideration for the deed to Blackacre), B qualified as a subsequent bona fide purchaser without notice and is entitled to protection from A's mortgage interest in Blackacre. The fact that B did not record is irrelevant under a notice recording act. B is entitled to protection from A's mortgage, enabling B to receive title to Blackacre free and clear of A's claimed mortgage interest. B has good title to Blackacre to convey to C.

Inasmuch as B held good title to Blackacre, when B conveyed to C, C received whatever title B held. C holds Blackacre free and clear of any competing property interests. The subsequent recordings by C, A, and B record, do not affect the analysis under a notice recording act. Whether the party claiming protection is entitled to protection depends solely on the party's status at the moment of closing. Recording is not required to qualify for protection under the notice approach.

Answer (A) is incorrect because it fails to take into account that B conveyed Blackacre to C by quitclaim deed. A quitclaim deed conveys whatever interest the grantor holds, if any, to the grantee. Because B held Blackacre free and clear of A's mortgage, C received Blackacre free and clear of A's mortgage. **Answer (B) is incorrect** because it fails to take into account that B conveyed Blackacre to C, as just analyzed, and that B took Blackacre free and clear of A's mortgage. B qualified for protection under the notice recording act, because there is no evidence that B knew or should have known of A's mortgage. **Answer (D) is incorrect** because C took whatever title B held, and B held Blackacre free and clear of A's mortgage.

• **Additional references**: *See* 14 RICHARD J. POWELL, POWELL ON REAL PROPERTY ch. 82, §§ 82.01-82.02 (Patrick J. Rohan ed. 1999); 11 THOMPSON ON REAL PROPERTY, SECOND EDITION §§ 92.13-92.15(c)(3) (2002 & Supp. 2006); WILLIAM B. STOEBUCK & DALE A. WHITMAN, THE LAW OF PROPERTY §§ 11.9-11.11 (3d ed. 2000).

4. **The best answer is (D).** As established above (see answer to problem 3), there is no problem with the creation of A's mortgage interest in Blackacre. Since O holds good title to Blackacre, A's mortgage is valid under the first in time, first in right principle. When O purports to convey Blackacre free and clear of any competing mortgage interest, O is incapable of conveying such a title to Blackacre. The only way B can receive title to Blackacre free and clear of A's mortgage interest is if B qualifies for protection under the jurisdiction's recording act.

    Under the race-notice recording act, B has to qualify as a subsequent bona fide purchaser without notice, and B has to properly record his or her deed before the deed which created the competing property interest is recorded. As established above (see answer to problem 3), B qualifies as a subsequent bona fide purchaser without notice. Under the race-notice approach, however, that is not enough. The party seeking protection must also win the race to the recorder's office and record his or her deed properly.

B did not record immediately. At that point in time, B is not entitled to protection. When B purports to convey title to Blackacre to C free and clear of any mortgage interest, B does not have such title to convey. A's mortgage interest in Blackacre is still valid under first in time, first in right. The only way C can receive Blackacre free and clear of A's mortgage interest is if C qualifies for protection under the recording act.

Under the race-notice approach, C has to qualify as a subsequent bona fide purchaser without notice, and C must also win the race to the recorder's office and properly record his or her deed. Inasmuch as C gave valuable consideration in exchange for Blackacre, C qualifies as a subsequent purchaser. Did C have notice of the competing property interest - A's mortgage? There are three types of notice: actual, inquiry and constructive. The call of the question expressly says to assume that none of the parties had actual notice of any of the prior transactions.

Does the fact that B gave C a quitclaim deed give rise to inquiry notice? The defining characteristic of the quitclaim deed which distinguishes it from the special warranty deed and the general warranty deed is that the quitclaim contains no warranties as to the quality of title which the grantor is purporting to convey. Should the fact that the grantor refuses to warrant the quality of title being conveyed be enough to give rise to at least inquiry notice of a possible defect with the title? No. The general rule is that a quitclaim deed is not enough to give rise to inquiry notice.

Does C have constructive notice? Constructive notice typically is based upon record notice - if notice of the prior transaction has been properly recorded. Notice is assessed at the time the subsequent grantee gives consideration for his or her property interest. At the time C purchased Blackacre (at closing when C gave consideration for the deed to Blackacre), A had not recorded the mortgage. There is no way C could have found A's mortgage if C had searched the grantor-grantee index. C qualified as a subsequent bona fide purchaser without notice.

Did C win the race and properly record his or her deed first? At first blush, it would appear so. C records first, then A records, and then B records. The key, though, is understanding what is meant by the requirement that the party claiming protection must "properly record" his or her deed first.

Under the *Zimmer* rule, properly recording the deed means that all the deeds connecting the party who is claiming protection back to the chain of title for the property (back to the common grantor) must be properly recorded. When C recorded his or her deed, at that point in time the deed constituted a wild deed. There is no way any subsequent grantee searching the grantor-grantee index could have found the deed C recorded as it related to Blackacre.

Although C recorded the B to C deed first, C's whole chain of title back to the common grantor, O, is not properly recorded. B's failure to record creates a hole in the chain of title. Once A recorded, A closed the opportunity C had to trump A's interest. C's whole chain of title cannot be properly recorded before the first in time, first in right's chain of title. C does not qualify for protection under the race-notice recording act. C takes subject to A's competing property interest. C holds Blackacre subject to A's mortgage.

Answer (A) is incorrect because it fails to take into account that B failed to record the O to B deed before A recorded the mortgage. For B to hold Blackacre free and clear of A's first in time, first in right mortgage, under the race-notice recording act approach, B not only had to qualify as a subsequent bona fide purchaser without notice, but B also had to record B's deed before A recorded the mortgage. B failed to record before A. B was not entitled to protection. **Answer (B) is incorrect** because it fails to take into account that B conveyed whatever interest B had to C. **Answer (C) is incorrect** because it fails to take into account the *Zimmer* rule. Although C recorded the B to C deed before A recorded the mortgage, C's whole chain of title back to the chain of title for the property (back to the common grantor) was not properly recorded before A recorded. C did not win the recording race and was not entitled to protection.

- **Additional references**: *See* 14 RICHARD J. POWELL, POWELL ON REAL PROPERTY ch. 82, §§ 82.01-82.02 (Patrick J. Rohan ed. 1999); 11 THOMPSON ON REAL PROPERTY, SECOND THOMAS EDITION §§ 92.13-92.15(c)(3) (2002 & Supp. 2006); WILLIAM B. STOEBUCK & DALE A. WHITMAN, THE LAW OF PROPERTY §§ 11.9-11.11 (3d ed. 2000); Zimmer v. Sundell, 237 Wis. 270, 296 N.W. 589 (1941).

5. **The best answer is (C).** Title to property passes when there is (1) a properly executed written instrument which complies with the Statute of Frauds, (2) delivery, and (3) acceptance. Acceptance is presumed in the absence of facts indicating otherwise. As for the Statute of Frauds, there is no reason to doubt that the deed was properly executed in compliance with the Statute. The issue is whether there was delivery.

As used in the real estate conveyance context, delivery is a term of art which means that the grantor presently intends to relinquish control over the real property. Because delivery refers to the grantor's state of mind, a variable for which there often is little direct evidence, there are a set of rebuttable presumptions based on the status of the properly executed deed. If the grantor retains possession of the deed, the presumption is no delivery. If the grantor records the deed, the presumption is delivery. If the grantor transfers possession of the deed to the grantee, the presumption is delivery. Here, inasmuch as O physically delivered possession of the deed to S, the presumption arises that there was a valid delivery.

The presumption, however, is a rebuttable one. The facts indicate that O did not intend to presently relinquish control over the property. O remained in possession of Blackacre and did not want title to pass to S unless she died of cancer. O should be able to overcome the presumption of delivery. To prevent unjust enrichment, the court should impose a constructive trust on S and order S to convey the title back to O.

Under a traditional, strict approach to the Statute of Frauds, a court might bar the extrinsic evidence of the mother's oral statements to the son. Under the modern trend approach, however, the court would probably admit the extrinsic evidence to prevent unjust enrichment by the son.

Answers (A) and (B) are incorrect because they fail to take into account the presumption that there was a valid delivery since S is in actual possession of the deed purporting to transfer title to S. **Answer (D) is incorrect** because it fails to take into account the factual evidence that O never intended to relinquish control over title to the property.

- **Additional references:** *See* 9 THOMPSON ON REAL PROPERTY, SECOND THOMAS EDITION §§ 83.03-83.04 (1999 & Supp. 2006); 14 RICHARD J. POWELL, POWELL ON REAL PROPERTY ch. 81A, § 81A.04[2][a][i]-[iv] (Patrick J. Rohan ed. 1999); WILLIAM B. STOEBUCK & DALE A. WHITMAN, THE LAW OF PROPERTY § 11.3 (3d ed. 2000).

6. **The best answer is (D).** A valid escrow arrangement requires that the grantor convey the properly executed deed to an independent third party who is to deliver the deed to the grantee only upon the occurrence of a condition which is beyond the control of the grantor. A valid delivery

requires the grantor to relinquish control over the deed. If the grantor retains control over "escrow" or delivery of the deed to the grantee, there is not a valid escrow arrangement. The holder of the deed is no more than an agent of the grantor. For most purposes, the deed may as well still be in the grantor's possession.

Under the facts of the problem, although O (the grantor) physically turned the deed over to her attorney, the attorney does not qualify as an independent escrow agent because the grantor retained the power to recall the deed. The attorney is to deliver the deed to her son, S, one year from the date of delivery to the attorney only if O, the grantor, did not change her mind and ask for it back. The instructions to the attorney indicate that the grantor has not relinquished control over whether the deed is delivered to the grantee. O, the grantor, has retained control over the issue of delivery. Therefore, the attorney is merely O's agent, and for purposes of a creditor's ability to reach the property, the property is still held by the grantor, O.

Answer (A) is incorrect because although O's attorney physically possessed the deed, O retained control over the attorney. The attorney does not qualify as an independent escrow agent. The attorney was simply an agent for O. Because O's attorney is merely O's agent, O is deemed to still be in possession of the deed and the property, and O's creditors may reach the asset. **Answer (B) is incorrect** because although oral conditions generally are enforceable against an independent escrow agent, here O's attorney does not qualify as an independent escrow agent. The key oral condition is that delivery to O's son is to occur *only if O does not ask for the deed back*. The latter oral condition evidences that O still has control of the deed. **Answer (C) is incorrect** because it fails to reflect that creditors of a grantor cannot reach the property while it is in the hands of an independent escrow agent if the agent is truly an independent escrow agent. The problem here is that O's attorney does not qualify as an independent escrow agent since O has control over the condition controlling when, if ever, the second delivery will take place.

- **Additional references**: *See* 14 RICHARD J. POWELL, POWELL ON REAL PROPERTY ch. 81A, § 81A.04[2][a][v][B] (Patrick J. Rohan ed. 1999); 9 THOMPSON ON REAL PROPERTY, SECOND THOMAS EDITION §§ 83.03-83.05, 83.05(b) (1999 & Supp. 2006); WILLIAM B. STOEBUCK & DALE A. WHITMAN, THE LAW OF PROPERTY §§ 11.4 (3d ed. 2000)

7. **The best answer is (C).** The seller's duty to disclose varies depending on whether the jurisdiction applies the traditional common law approach or the modern trend. At common law, the prevailing doctrine was caveat emptor: buyer beware. A buyer should perform a reasonable inspection and investigation of the property to assess its fitness and value. The seller has no duty to disclose information to the buyer unless (1) there is a confidential relationship between the parties; (2) the seller engages in active concealment; or (3) there is partial disclosure. At common law, the seller is not liable under a duty to disclose for mere failure to disclose (nonfeasance), only for misrepresentations (misfeasance).

There is no evidence to suggest that any of the exceptions to the traditional common law rule apply. The parties are not in a confidential relationship. There is no evidence that O has actively concealed, or only partially disclosed, the house's prior history. Under the traditional common law approach, O has no liability to P for breach of the duty to disclose.

The modern trend approach, on the other hand, imposes a broader duty to disclose on the seller. If the seller knows of facts affecting the desirability or value of the property which are known or ascertainable only to the seller, and the seller knows that such facts are not known to the buyer or discoverable by the buyer during a reasonable inspection, the seller is under a duty to disclose the facts to the buyer.

Under the modern trend approach to the duty to disclose, O has a duty to disclose the house's history. O, the seller, knows that a bloody murder occurred in the house. O knows or should know that such a fact affects the value and desirability of the property. O knows or should know that P does not know about the house's history and that such information is not readily discoverable during an inspection of the property. P's best chance of prevailing is if P sues O in a jurisdiction which applies the modern trend approach. (A number of states which have adopted the modern trend approach have enacted statutes which specifically exempt from the duty to disclose that a serious crime, such as murder, has occurred on the property.)

Answer (A) is incorrect because the implied warranty of habitability generally applies to the quality of the construction as opposed to the reputation of the property. Physically, the structure is habitable. Although P could make an argument under the implied warranty of habitability, it would be quite a stretch. **Answers (B) and (D) are incorrect** because the traditional common law approach was caveat emptor - buyer beware. The seller is not liable under a duty to disclose for mere failure to disclose (nonfeasance), only for misrepresentations (misfeasance). O made no misrepresentations about the condition of the house. O would not be liable for failure to disclose under the common law approach.

- **Additional references**: *See* 14 RICHARD J. POWELL, POWELL ON REAL PROPERTY ch. 84A, §§ 84A.02[1], 84A.03[4][b] (Patrick J. Rohan ed. 1999); WILLIAM B. STOEBUCK & DALE A. WHITMAN, THE LAW OF PROPERTY § 11.16 (3d ed. 2000); RALPH E. BOYER ET. AL., THE LAW OF PROPERTY: AN INTRODUCTORY SURVEY § 14.9 (4th ed. 1991).

8. **The best answer is (B).** There is no problem with O granting X an easement to cross Blackacre. Since O holds good title to Blackacre, X's easement is valid under the first in time, first in right principle. When O purports to convey Blackacre free and clear of any competing property interest, O is incapable of conveying such a title to Blackacre. The only way A can receive title to Blackacre free and clear of X's easement is if A qualifies for protection under the jurisdiction's recording act.

Under a notice recording act, A has to qualify as a subsequent bona fide purchaser without notice. Inasmuch as A gave O valuable consideration for Blackacre, A qualifies as a subsequent purchaser. The question is whether A had notice of the competing property claim. There are three possible types of notice: actual, inquiry and constructive. There are no facts which indicate that A had actual notice. Although a purchaser of real property has a duty to inspect the property prior to closing and is on notice of any and all competing property interests which would be disclosed by a reasonable inspection, there is no evidence of a path or any other evidence of X's easement which would have put A on inquiry notice (and the call of the question expressly stated to assume that A had no inquiry notice).

Does A have constructive notice? Constructive notice typically is based upon record notice if the deed from the prior transaction has been properly recorded. Notice is assessed at the time the subsequent grantee gives consideration for his or her property interest. At the time A purchased Blackacre (at closing, when A gave consideration for the deed to Blackacre), X had not recorded the easement. A qualified as a subsequent bona fide purchaser without notice. Under a notice recording act approach, A qualifies for protection. A takes Blackacre free and clear of X's claimed easement.

When A conveys to B, under the shelter doctrine, since A is entitled to protection under the notice recording act, all subsequent grantees claiming title from A are also protected (they are sheltered by the protection A receives.) Under the notice approach, B takes Blackacre free and clear of X's claimed easement.

Under the race-notice recording act, the subsequent grantee claiming protection from a prior in time, properly created property interest has to (1) qualify as a subsequent bona fide purchaser without notice, and (2) properly record his or her deed before the deed which created the competing property interest is recorded.

Starting with the notice prong first, as established above, A qualifies as a subsequent bona fide purchaser without notice. Under the race-notice approach, however, that is not enough. The party seeking protection must also win the race to the recorder's office and properly record his or her deed. A did not record immediately. At that point in time, A is not entitled to protection. So when A purports to convey title to Blackacre to B free and clear of any easements, A does not have such title to convey to B. X's easement in Blackacre is still valid under first in time, first in right.

The only way B can receive Blackacre free and clear of X's easement is if B qualifies for protection under the recording act. Under the race-notice approach, B has to qualify as a subsequent bona fide purchaser without notice, and B must also win the race to the recorder's office and record his or her deed properly. Inasmuch as B gave valuable consideration in exchange for Blackacre, B qualifies as a subsequent purchaser. Did B have notice of the competing property interest - X's easement? There are three possible types of notice: actual, inquiry and constructive. There is no evidence that B had actual notice of the prior transactions. Although a purchaser of real property has a duty to inspect the property prior to closing and is on notice of any competing property interests which would be disclosed by a reasonable inspection, there are no facts which would have put B on inquiry notice (and the call of the question expressly says to assume that neither party had inquiry notice of X's easement).

Does the fact that A gave B a quitclaim deed give rise to inquiry notice? The defining characteristic of the quitclaim deed which distinguishes it from the special warranty deed and the general warranty deed is that the quitclaim deed contains no warranties as to the quality of title which the grantor is purporting to convey. Should the fact that the grantor refuses to warrant the quality of title being conveyed be enough to give rise to at least inquiry notice as to a possible defect in title? No. The general rule is that a quitclaim deed is not enough to give rise to inquiry notice.

Does B have constructive notice? Constructive notice typically is based upon record notice - if notice of the prior transaction has been properly recorded. Notice is assessed at the time the subsequent grantee gives consideration for his or her property interest. At the time B purchased Blackacre (at closing, when B gave consideration for the deed to Blackacre), X had not yet recorded the easement. B qualified as a subsequent bona fide purchaser without notice.

Did B win the race and properly record his or her deed first? Under the *Zimmer* rule, properly recording the deed means not just that the grantee in question records his or her deed first, but all the deeds connecting the grantee to the chain of title for the property must be properly recorded first. For B to win the recording race, not only must B record the deed from A to B, but A must record the deed from O to A prior to X recording the deed from O to X which created the easement. X recorded prior to both B and A. Once X recorded, X closed any opportunity B had to trump X's easement. B's whole chain of title was not properly recorded before X's chain of title. B does not qualify for protection under the race-notice recording act. B would take subject to X's competing property interest. B holds Blackacre subject to X's easement.

Answer (A) is incorrect because although B prevails under a notice recording act approach, B is not entitled to protection under the race-notice recording act approach. Under the *Zimmer* rule, B's whole chain of title back to the chain of title for the property (back to the common grantor) must be properly recorded before the first in time property interest is properly recorded. X recorded prior to B or A, preventing B from qualifying for protection under the race-notice approach. **Answer (C) is incorrect** because it confuses the outcome under the two different recording acts. B qualifies for protection under the notice approach and not under the race-notice approach. **Answer (D) is incorrect** because it fails to recognize that B qualifies for protection under the notice recording act.

- **Additional references:** *See* 14 RICHARD J. POWELL, POWELL ON REAL PROPERTY ch. 82, §§ 82.01-82.02 (Patrick J. Rohan ed. 1999); 11 THOMPSON ON REAL PROPERTY, SECOND THOMAS EDITION §§ 92.13-92.15(c)(3) (2002 & Supp. 2006); WILLIAM B. STOEBUCK &

DALE A. WHITMAN, THE LAW OF PROPERTY §§ 11.9-11.11 (3d ed. 2000); Zimmer v. Sundell, 237 Wis. 270, 296 N.W. 589 (1941).

9.   **The best answer is (E) (though a strong argument can be made for A).** Pursuant to common law, first in time, first in right principles, once a party conveys his or her real property interest, a subsequent grantee cannot acquire the same property interest from the original grantor. The original grantor no longer has the property interest, so he or she has nothing to convey. Under a recording act analysis, however, a subsequent grantee from the original grantor may still be entitled to acquire the conveyed property interest, if the subsequent grantee qualifies for protection under the recording act. Although the exact requirements of the recording acts vary from jurisdiction to jurisdiction depending on whether the recording act adopts the race, notice, or race-notice approach, virtually all of the recording acts require the subsequent grantee to be a purchaser. Although a broad approach is taken to who qualifies as a purchaser, the subsequent grantee must give valuable consideration to qualify as a purchaser.

O conveyed Legaland to A. Inasmuch as O had rightful title to Legaland, A takes under first in time, first in right. As a grantee receiving title from a grantor who holds rightful title, A does not need to give consideration. A is claiming based on first in time, first in right. When O purports to convey Legaland to B as a wedding gift, O has nothing left to give to B. B will receive title to Legaland only if B qualifies for protection under the jurisdiction's recording act.

Both the notice and race-notice recording acts require, among other things, that the party claiming protection be a subsequent bona fide **purchaser**. There is no evidence that B agreed to get married in exchange for receiving Legaland. Since B is a donee and did not give any valuable consideration, B cannot qualify for protection under either a notice or race-notice approach. B's only hope is under a race approach

Although being a purchaser is not an intrinsic element under the race approach, some race statutes add this requirement as an equitable matter. The problem is there are very few pure race recording acts, and some of them do not expressly mention whether the subsequent grantee must be a purchaser. Several of the leading treatises simply assert that the subsequent grantee under the race approach must be a purchaser, while the Stoebuck & Whitman hornbook implies that there simply are not enough race statutes to conclude definitively whether the general rule is that the subsequent grantee must be a purchaser under the race approach. Inasmuch as the majority of the leading treatises say that the subsequent grantee under the race approach must be a purchaser, under that interpretation of the race approach, B does not qualify for protection since B is a donee.

Answers (A) is incorrect under the majority view that a subsequent grantee under a race approach has to be a grantee (though the leading treatises are in conflict on this issue and there is plenty of room for argument). **Answers (B), (C) and (D) are incorrect** because they fail to recognize that the party seeking protection under the notice and race-notice recording acts must be a purchaser - the party seeking protection must give valuable consideration. Here, B is merely a donee. B gave no consideration. B is not entitled to protection.

- **Additional references**: *See* 14 RICHARD J. POWELL, POWELL ON REAL PROPERTY ch. 82, §§ 82.01[2][a], 82.02[1][c][1], 82.03[2][b][1] (Patrick J. Rohan ed. 1999); 11 THOMPSON ON REAL PROPERTY, SECOND THOMAS EDITION §§ 92.13(a), 92.14(b), 92.14(b)(1), 92.15(b)(2)(A) (2002 & Supp. 2006); WILLIAM B. STOEBUCK & DALE A. WHITMAN, THE LAW OF PROPERTY §§ 11.9-11.10 (3d ed. 2000).

10. **The best answer is (A).** A mortgagee executing a power of sale must comply not only with the applicable statutory regulations but also with the general duty to protect the interests of the mortgagor through the exercise of good faith and due diligence. Good faith is a subjective requirement which looks at the intentions of the mortgagee in carrying out the foreclosure sale. Good faith is breached by evidence that the mortgagee acted in bad faith - an intentional disregard of duty or a purpose to injure. Due diligence is an objective requirement which looks at the reasonableness of the mortgagor's actions. The mortgagee must make every reasonable effort to obtain a fair and reasonable price under the circumstances. Good faith and due diligence are distinct requirements. Breach of the former arguably is more heinous than breach of the latter. Bad faith requires a culpable state of mind, while breach of due diligence requires simple negligence.

The fact that breach of the duty of good faith is more heinous than breach of the duty of due diligence is supported by the difference in the damages. The measure of damages is greater for a breach of the duty of good faith than it is for a breach of the duty of due diligence. Fair market value is the value the property would support if sold under normal market conditions (a non-foreclosure sale). Fair price is the value the property would support if sold under normal foreclosure conditions. Under normal conditions, fair market value is assumed to be greater than fair price, which in turn is assumed to be greater than the actual price where the mortgagee does exercise good faith and due diligence. Where the mortgagee breaches its duty of good faith, the mortgagor is entitled to the difference between fair market price and the actual sale price. Where the mortgagee breaches its duty of due diligence, the mortgagor is entitled to the difference between fair price and the actual sale price.

Applied to the facts of the problem, there is no evidence that the mortgagee acted in bad faith, only that it failed to exercise due diligence in advertising the sale. The mortgagee is entitled to damages measured by the difference between the actual sale price and the fair price.

Answer (B) is incorrect because it misstates the measure of damages for breach of the duty to exercise due diligence. The measure of damages is the difference between the sale price and a fair price under foreclosure conditions, not the difference between the sale price and a fair market price which would not take into consideration foreclosure conditions. **Answers (C) and (D) are incorrect** because there is no evidence to support the conclusion that the mortgagee acted in bad faith. The mortgagee was merely negligent in failing to exercise due diligence in advertising the sale. **Answer (E) is incorrect** because the measure of damages for breach of due diligence is not simply whether the foreclosure price exceeds the outstanding balance on the mortgage, but whether the sale price exceeds a fair price under foreclosure conditions.

- **Additional references:** *See* GRANT S. NELSON & DALE A. WHITMAN, REAL ESTATE FINANCE LAW § 7.22 (3d ed. 1994); Murphy v. Financial Development Corporation, 126 N.H. 536, 495 A.2d 1245 (1985).

11. **The best answer is (C).** There is no problem with O granting Greenacre to A. Since O holds good title to Blackacre, A's ownership of Greenacre is valid under first in time, first in right. A need not record the deed for the transfer to be valid. A holds good title, although it is a vulnerable title since A has not recorded the deed. Since A has not recorded the deed, a subsequent grantee from O may qualify for protection under the jurisdiction's recording act and trump A's title.
When O purports to convey Greenacre to B, O does not have title to convey. The only way B can receive title to Greenacre is if B qualifies for protection under the jurisdiction's recording act. Under a notice recording act, B must qualify as a subsequent bona fide purchaser

without notice. Inasmuch as B gave O valuable consideration for Blackacre, B qualifies as a subsequent purchaser. The question is whether B had notice of the competing property claim. There are three possible types of notice: actual, inquiry and constructive. There are no facts which indicate that B had either actual or inquiry notice. Although a purchaser of real property has a duty to inspect the property prior to closing and is on notice of any and all competing property interests which would be disclosed by a reasonable inspection, there is no evidence that A took possession of the property or otherwise put B on inquiry notice.

Does B have constructive notice? Constructive notice typically is based upon record notice - if the deed from the prior transaction has been properly recorded. Notice is assessed at the time the subsequent grantee gives consideration for his or her property interest. At the time B purchased Greenacre (at closing when B gave consideration for the deed to Greenacre), A had not recorded the O to A deed. B qualified as a subsequent bona fide purchaser without notice. Under a notice recording act approach, B qualifies for protection. B need not record to qualify for protection under the notice recording act, so the issue of the patent defect in the deed from O to B is irrelevant to B's status.

Inasmuch as B qualifies for protection under the recording act, B holds title and has good title to transfer to C under first in time, first in right. Under the notice approach, C takes Greenacre free and clear of A's claim to the property.

Answer (A) is incorrect because B is entitled to protection under the notice recording act. B is a subsequent bona fide purchaser without notice of A's first in time, first in right interest. **Answer (B) is incorrect** because B conveyed B's interest to C even though the deed between O and B has a defect in the acknowledgment. A defect in the acknowledgment may be relevant to whether the deed gives notice if recorded, but it does not affect the validity of the deed as between the parties to the deed. **Answer (D) is incorrect** because although O started with good title, O properly conveyed all of O's interest to A, even though the deed was not recorded. Failure to record the deed will affect how much notice the deed gives, but it does not affect the validity of the deed as between the parties to the deed.

- **Additional references**: *See* 14 RICHARD J. POWELL, POWELL ON REAL PROPERTY ch. 82, §§ 82.01-82.02 (Patrick J. Rohan ed. 1999); 11 THOMPSON ON REAL PROPERTY, SECOND THOMAS EDITION §§

92.13-92.15(c)(3) (2002 & Supp. 2006); WILLIAM B. STOEBUCK & DALE A. WHITMAN, THE LAW OF PROPERTY §§ 11.9-11.11 (3d ed. 2000).

12. **The best answer is (A).** As established above (see the answer to problem 11 above), there is no problem with O granting Greenacre to A. A's ownership of Greenacre is valid under first in time, first in right. A need not record the deed for the transfer to be valid. When O purports to convey Greenacre to B, O does not have title to convey. The only way B can receive title to Greenacre is if B qualifies for protection under the jurisdiction's recording act.

Under a race-notice recording act, B has to qualify as a subsequent bona fide purchaser without notice, and B must properly record B's chain of title back to the chain of title for the property (back to the common grantor, O) before A properly records A's chain of title. As established above, (see the answer to problem 11), B satisfies the notice prong of the race-notice recording act. The issue is whether B's recording satisfies the race prong. Although B recorded the deed from O to B before A recorded the deed from O to A, the issue is what effect, if any, does the patent defect in the deed from O to B have on its recording?

The general rule is that a deed with a patent defect, a defect apparent on the face of the instrument, is treated legally as if it were not recorded; and it provides no constructive notice. Although that general rule applies more to the 'notice' effect of a recorded deed with a patent defect, courts have reasoned that for purposes of consistency, the effect of the patent defect on the 'recording' prong is to treat the deed as if it were never recorded. Therefore, although the deed from O to B was actually recorded, legally it is treated as if it were not recorded. B is not entitled to protection under the race-notice recording act. A still holds good title to Greenacre.

Therefore, when B purports to convey title to C, B has no title to convey to C. C will receive title to Greenacre only if C qualifies for protection under the jurisdiction's race-notice recording act. C must qualify as a subsequent bona fide purchaser without notice of the conveyance from O to A, and C must properly record C's whole chain of title before A. Inasmuch as C gave B valuable consideration for Greenacre, C qualifies as a subsequent purchaser. The question is whether C had notice of the competing property claim. There are three possible types of notice: actual, inquiry and constructive. There are no facts which indicate that C had either actual or inquiry notice. Although a purchaser of real property has a duty to inspect the property prior to closing and is on notice of any and all competing property interests which would be disclosed by a reasonable inspection, there is no evidence of any facts which would have put C on inquiry notice. There is no evidence that A took possession of Greenacre.

Does C have constructive notice? Typically constructive notice is based upon record notice if the deed from the prior transaction has been properly recorded. Notice is assessed at the time the subsequent grantee gives consideration for his or her property interest. At the time C purchased Greenacre (at closing when C gave consideration for the deed to Greenacre), A had not recorded the deed from O to A. C qualifies as a subsequent bona fide purchaser without notice.

The issue is whether C has properly recorded C's chain of title. Although C records the deed from B to C before A records the deed from O to A, the issue is whether C's whole chain of title was properly recorded. Under the *Zimmer* rule, C's whole chain of title back to the common grantor, O, must be properly recorded. Inasmuch as the O to B deed has a patent defect, the deed is legally treated as if it were not recorded. C's recording legally is a wild deed. It is not properly connected to the chain of title of Greenacre. The hole in the chain of title means that A recorded before C's whole chain of title was properly recorded. C is not entitled to protection.

While this result may appear inequitable, the counter-argument is that C performed a title search and should have noticed the patent defect in the deed from O to B. This defect made the title B was purporting to transfer to C unmarketable, and C should have refused to close until B corrected the problem.

Answer (B) is incorrect because B did not satisfy the 'race' prong of the race-notice recording act approach. Although B appears to have recorded before A, legally B is treated as having not recorded because a deed with a patent defect in the acknowledgment is treated as not having been recorded for notice and recording purposes. A properly recorded before B properly recorded. **Answer (C) is incorrect** because under the *Zimmer* rule, the party seeking protection under the recording act must properly record his or her whole chain of title back to chain of title for the property before the first in time party. Here, although C properly recorded before A, C's whole chain of title is not properly recorded because of the patent defect in the acknowledgment of B's deed. A properly recorded before C properly recorded C's whole chain of title.

Answer (D) is incorrect because although O started with good title, O properly conveyed all of O's interest to A, even though the deed was not recorded. Failure to record the deed will affect how much notice the deed gives, but it does not affect the validity of the deed as between the parties to the deed.

- **Additional references**: *See* 14 RICHARD J. POWELL, POWELL ON REAL PROPERTY ch. 82, §§ 82.01-82.02 (Patrick J. Rohan ed. 1999); 11 THOMPSON ON REAL PROPERTY, SECOND THOMAS EDITION §§ 92.13-92.15(c)(3) (2002 & Supp. 2006); WILLIAM B. STOEBUCK & DALE A. WHITMAN, THE LAW OF PROPERTY §§ 11.9-11.11 (3d ed. 2000); Zimmer v. Sundell, 237 Wis. 270, 296 N.W. 589 (1941).

13. **The best answer is (B).** The sales contract provided that S, the seller, was to provide marketable title. Marketable title is title which is free from reasonable doubt and risk of litigation, and which a reasonable buyer would be willing to accept in exchange for valuable consideration. Basically, there are three types of defects which may render title unmarketable: chain of title defects, recorded encumbrances, and unrecorded encumbrances. Whether one of these types of encumbrances renders title unmarketable depends upon which type of defect it is, and how substantial the defect is.

Here, the contract for sale expressly waived 7 recorded encumbrances. The contract did not, however, waive the recorded easement for the public utility's above ground electrical poles and lines. The general rule at common law was that easements constituted title defects which rendered title per se unmarketable. At common law, the encumbrance was deemed substantial enough to render title unmarketable, and P would prevail. Under the modern trend, however, courts have held that easements for public utilities, which are open and obvious and which provide basic services to the property, do not render title unmarketable.

Answer (A) is incorrect because as a general rule, easements which are not expressly excepted from the deed constitute a breach of the covenant against encumbrances which render title unmarketable. **Answer (C) is incorrect** because although the common law approach was to treat all easements as *per se* violations of the covenant against encumbrances, the modern trend holds that open and notorious public easements for utilities do not constitute encumbrances that breach the covenant against encumbrances. **Answer (D) is incorrect** because the modern trend holds that open and notorious public easements for utilities do not breach the covenant against encumbrances. Arguing that the public easement constitutes a breach of the covenant of quiet enjoyment is simply an attempt to end run the modern trend which, if recognized, would emasculate the modern trend.

- **Additional references**: *See* 14 RICHARD J. POWELL, POWELL ON REAL PROPERTY ch. 81, §§ 81.03[6][a], 81.03[6][d][iii] (Patrick J. Rohan ed. 1999); 11 THOMPSON ON REAL PROPERTY, SECOND THOMAS EDITION § 91.09(a)(3) (2002 & Supp. 2006); WILLIAM B. STOEBUCK & DALE A. WHITMAN, THE LAW OF PROPERTY § 10.12 (3d ed. 2000).

14. **The best answer is (A).** Traditional common law reasoned that the real estate broker's contractual obligation was to produce a ready, willing, and able buyer. Once the buyer enters into an enforceable contract, the real estate broker has performed his or her job and is entitled to his or her commission, regardless of whether the contract closes. B produced X, a ready, willing, and able buyer, who signed an enforceable contract to purchase. Under the traditional common law approach, B is entitled to B's commission.

As for whether X can legally repudiate the contract, where the contract is silent as to the quality of title the seller is required to deliver, the seller must deliver marketable title. Zoning laws in effect at the time the parties enter into the contract are not considered unrecorded encumbrances which make title unmarketable. At common law, buyers were presumed to know the zoning laws governing the property. The fact that the zoning laws governing the property prohibit X's contemplated use does not render the title unmarketable.

Moreover, the traditional common law approach took a property approach to the transaction. Courts were not inclined to apply the contractual doctrine of mutual mistake. The most likely result is that B is entitled to B's commission, and O is entitled to specific performance.

Answers (B) and (C) are incorrect because the seller, O, is entitled to specific performance. The zoning laws which apply to a property are a matter of public notice and are not considered unrecorded encumbrances. The fact that current zoning regulations prohibit the purchaser's intended use is not grounds to rescind the contract. Moreover, common law courts were not inclined to apply contract doctrines such as mutual mistake. **Answers (C) and (D) are incorrect** because under the traditional common law approach, a real estate broker had completed his or her contractual obligations once the broker produced a ready, willing, and able purchaser who entered into an enforceable contract. B has produced a ready, willing, and able purchaser who entered into an enforceable contract, so B is entitled to B's commission.

- **Additional references**: *See* 14 RICHARD J. POWELL, POWELL ON REAL PROPERTY ch. 81, §§ 81.03[6][e][ii][A], 81.02[3][c], 15 POWELL ON REAL PROPERTY ch. 84C, § 84C.05[1] (Patrick J. Rohan ed. 1999); 11 THOMPSON ON REAL PROPERTY, SECOND THOMAS EDITION §§ 92.12(k), 95.07(d)(1) (2002 & Supp. 2006); WILLIAM B. STOEBUCK & DALE A. WHITMAN, THE LAW OF PROPERTY § 10.12 (3d ed. 2000); RALPH E. BOYER ET. AL., THE LAW OF PROPERTY: AN INTRODUCTORY SURVEY § 14.1 (4th ed. 1991); Annot., 39 A.L.R.3d 362 (1971).

15. **The best answer is (C).** The modern trend looks more to the presumed intent of the parties. A seller presumes that he or she will pay real estate commissions upon sale of the property, not upon production of a ready, willing and able purchaser. Accordingly, under the modern trend, a seller is liable for real estate commissions only if (1) the agent produces a ready, willing, and able purchaser, and (2) *the parties close on the contract* (unless the failure to close on the contract is the seller's fault, in which case the seller is liable for real estate commissions even though the parties did not close).

Here, although B produced X, a ready, willing, and able buyer, the parties failed to close on the contract because the local zoning laws prohibited X's intended use. The reason the parties failed to close on the contract was beyond the control of, and not the fault of, the seller. Under the modern trend approach, B is not entitled to B's commission.

As for whether X can legally repudiate the contract, under the modern trend, zoning laws are not considered an unrecorded encumbrance which make title unmarketable. The fact that the zoning laws prohibit X's contemplated use does not render the title unmarketable.

The modern trend approach, however, takes more of a contractual approach to the real estate transaction. More and more, courts are inclined to apply the contractual doctrine of mutual mistake. Under mutual mistake, if both the buyer and the seller are operating under a mutual mistake, there is no meeting of the minds and no enforceable contract. Here, both O and X presumed that X's intended use was permitted under the local zoning laws. Inasmuch as that assumption proved false, there was no meeting of the minds. Under mutual mistake, X is permitted to rescind the contract.

Answers (A) and (B) are incorrect because under the modern trend a real estate broker is not entitled to his or her commission unless the contract closes or the failure to close is the seller's fault. **Answers (A) and (D) are incorrect** because increasingly under the modern trend courts are willing to apply contract doctrines such as mutual mistake to permit buyers to rescind contracts where local zoning ordinances in existence at the time of the contract prevent the purchaser from using the property as intended, especially where the seller knew about the purchaser's plans.

- **Additional references**: *See* 14 RICHARD J. POWELL, POWELL ON REAL PROPERTY ch. 81, §§ 81.03[6][e][ii][A], 81.02[3][c], 15 POWELL ch. 84C, § 84C.05[1] (Patrick J. Rohan ed. 1999); 11 THOMPSON ON REAL PROPERTY, SECOND THOMAS EDITION § 95.07(d)(2) (2002 & Supp. 2006); WILLIAM B. STOEBUCK & DALE A. WHITMAN, THE LAW OF PROPERTY § 10.12 (3d ed. 2000); RALPH E. BOYER ET. AL., THE LAW OF PROPERTY: AN INTRODUCTORY SURVEY § 14.1 (4th ed. 1991); Annot., 39 A.L.R.3d 362 (1971).

16. **The best answer is (A).** The first issue is whether the deed constitutes a valid deed.

Under the Statute of Frauds, to transfer an interest in real property, there must be a writing signed by the party to be charged which contains the necessary material provisions. There is a deed which is properly executed by O, the party to be charged. The question is whether it contains the necessary material provisions. The deed must describe the parties with reasonable certainty, the property with reasonable certainty, and express the intent to convey the property interest in question. Assuming O has only one niece named Carolyn, the court will admit extrinsic evidence to ascertain who O's favorite niece is. Since O signed the deed, the parties can be identified with reasonable certainty. Although there is no detailed description of the property being transferred, a Mother Hubbard clause permits a grantor to convey all the property he or she owns within a specified jurisdiction, without an exact description of the property interests, as long as the grantor expresses the intent to do so. The clause in O's deed arguably constitutes a Mother Hubbard clause which transfers all of O's property holdings in California to Carolyn. Under the modern trend, the deed is a valid deed which contains all of the necessary material provisions.

The second issue is whether the deed was properly delivered. When O gives the deed to Edward, O is attempting to create an escrow arrangement. When a grantor gives the deed to a third party to deliver to the grantee upon the occurrence of a specific condition, the escrow arrangement is valid only if the condition controlling the escrow's delivery to the grantee is beyond the control of the grantor. Technically speaking, one could argue that O has not relinquished complete control over the deed when O delivered it to Edward because O has control over whether Carolyn survives O or not. O could commit suicide, insuring that Carolyn survives O. Nevertheless, under the modern trend, the courts have concluded that where the escrow's delivery to the grantee is conditioned on the grantee surviving the grantor, the grantor has effectively relinquished control over the deed.

There is also the issue of whether the delivery is so testamentary in nature that it should have to meet the wills act formalities which are necessary for a valid will. Edward is to deliver the deed to Carolyn only after O's death, so the transfer appears to occur at the time of O's death which arguably makes it testamentary. Although some courts have trouble with the apparent testamentary nature of the transfer, under the modern trend the courts use the relation back doctrine to find that the second delivery dates back to the date of the first delivery from the grantor to the escrow agent. The delivery to the grantee is no longer testamentary in nature but rather inter vivos. The delivery from Edward to Carolyn will relate back and be dated as of the date of the delivery from O to Edward.

Lastly, although oral conditions to a deed are generally ineffective and unenforceable, oral conditions to an escrow agent are effective and enforceable. The oral condition telling Edward when to deliver the deed to Carolyn concerns the personal relationship between the grantor and the escrow agent and not the deed per se. Oral conditions to escrow agents are valid. Carolyn takes the property.

Answer (B) is incorrect because the description of the beneficiary and the property is adequate. The description of the property is adequate because a Mother Hubbard clause permits a grantor to convey all the property he or she owns within a specified jurisdiction, without an exact description of the property interests, as long as the grantor expresses the intent to do so. Assuming O has only one niece named Carolyn, the court will admit extrinsic evidence to ascertain who Carolyn is, and since O signed the deed, the parties can be identified with reasonable certainty. **Answer (C) is incorrect** because the oral condition goes to the relationship between the grantor and the escrow agent, not to the deed *per se.* Oral conditions governing when the escrow agent is to deliver the deed are valid. **Answer (D) is incorrect** because under the relation back doctrine, as long as there is an independent escrow agent, the delivery from the escrow agent to the grantee will relate back to the date the grantor delivered the deed to the escrow agent. Under the relation back doctrine, the second delivery is not testamentary but inter vivos.

- **Additional references**: *See* 9 THOMPSON ON REAL PROPERTY, SECOND THOMAS EDITION §§ 82.08(a)(1), 82.08(c), 83.05(b) (1999 & Supp. 2006); WILLIAM B. STOEBUCK & DALE A. WHITMAN, THE LAW OF PROPERTY §§ 11.1, 11.2, 11.4 (3d ed. 2000); RALPH E. BOYER ET. AL., THE LAW OF PROPERTY: AN INTRODUCTORY SURVEY § 16.4 (4th ed. 1991).

17. **The best answer is (D).** The issue is whether the writing constitutes an enforceable contract. Under the Statute of Frauds, to transfer an interest in real property, there must be a writing signed by the party to be charged which contains the necessary material provisions. There is a writing which is properly executed by O and A. The question is whether it contains the necessary material provisions.

The contract must (1) describe the parties with reasonable certainty, (2) describe the property with reasonable certainty, and (3) express the intent to convey the property interest in question. Although there is some disagreement among the jurisdictions as to whether the price is required if it has been agreed upon, or at least a method of determining price, the writing here includes a method of determining the price, so that should not be a problem. The writing adequately describes the parties to the contract, O and A, and the writing expresses the intent to convey a property interest.

The question is whether the writing describes the property interest to be conveyed with reasonable certainty. O is selling part of Blackacre, a 500 acre farm O owns. The problem is A is not purchasing all of it, only the farmhouse and enough land for a garden. The contract fails to indicate how much land is necessary for the garden or a method of determining either the amount of land or which part of the land surrounding the farmhouse is to be conveyed. Inasmuch as one cannot determine the actual property to be conveyed, the contract fails to meet the requirements of the Statute of Frauds.

Answer (A) is incorrect because the contract fails to meet the requirements of the Statute of Frauds. The terms of the contract fail to provide an adequate description of the property being conveyed so as to permit its identification with reasonable certainty. **Answer (B) is incorrect** because the contract adequately describes the parties to the contract so as to permit their identification with reasonable certainty, as required by the Statute of Frauds. **Answer (C) is incorrect** because the Statute of Frauds does not require the contract to set forth the purchase price, only a method of determining the price. Here, the contract sets forth a method of determining the price, a method which both parties have accepted. Accordingly, the material terms concerning the price are adequately set forth in the contract.

- **Additional references:** *See* 14 RICHARD J. POWELL, POWELL ON REAL PROPERTY ch. 81A, § 81A.05[1][c][i] (Patrick J. Rohan ed. 1999); 9 THOMPSON ON REAL PROPERTY, SECOND THOMAS EDITION § 82.08(c) (1999 & Supp. 2006); RALPH E. BOYER ET. AL., THE LAW OF PROPERTY: AN INTRODUCTORY SURVEY § 16.2 (4th ed. 1991).

18. **The best answer is (B).** Under estoppel by deed, if a party purports to transfer a property interest which the party does not own, and then subsequently the party comes into ownership of that property interest, the party is estopped from denying the prior conveyance. By operation of law, the grantee of the prior conveyance holds title to the property interest.

When A purported to convey Greenacre to B, A did not own it. B took nothing. O, the rightful owner of Greenacre, still owns it. (B cannot claim protection under the jurisdiction's recording act because a grantee of real property is charged with whatever information a search of the chain of title would have revealed. If B had performed a title search on Greenacre, B would have realized that O, not A, was the rightful owner of Greenacre.) Thereafter, A purports to convey Greenacre to C. Again, A owned nothing, so A had nothing to give C, and C cannot claim protection under the jurisdiction's recording act for the same reasons B could not. Thereafter, A acquires title to Greenacre from O. Applying estoppel by deed, the moment A acquires title, by operation of law title will transfer to any prior grantee to whom A purported to transfer Greenacre.

The problem is that A purported to transfer Greenacre two different times prior to acquiring title to it: first to B, and then to C. As between B and C, who has a better claim to it? B can claim it under first in time, first in right. C, then, must qualify for protection under the jurisdiction's recording act.

Under the notice recording act, the party claiming protection must qualify as a subsequent bona fide purchaser without notice. C bought from A subsequent to the A to B conveyance, so C qualifies as a subsequent purchaser. Did C have notice of the prior conveyance from A to B? Although B's recording constituted a wild recording at the time it was recorded, since A had no interest in Greenacre, the courts still reason that at a minimum C should have searched the record system of the name of C's grantor, A. If C had searched the record system under A's name as grantor, C would have found the deed B recorded showing that A had already conveyed Greenacre to B. Under this reasoning, C is on constructive notice of the prior conveyance from A to B, and C is not entitled to protection under the jurisdiction's recording act. B owns Greenacre.

Answer (A) is incorrect because it fails to take into account estoppel by deed. Under estoppel by deed, if a party purports to transfer a property interest which the party does not own, and then subsequently the party comes into ownership of that property interest, the party is estopped from denying the prior conveyance. By operation of law the grantee of the prior conveyance holds title to the property interest. A purported to transfer Greenacre to B before A owned Greenacre, so when A subsequently acquired Greenacre, A would be estopped from denying A's prior transfer of Greenacre to B. B is deemed to own Greenacre by operation of law. **Answer (C) is incorrect** because C does not qualify for protection under the jurisdiction's recording act. Since A had previously conveyed Greenacre to B, A had no interest left to convey to C. Nor can C qualify for protection under the notice recording act, since if C had checked the grantor index under C's grantor, A, C would have found B's recording. C is not a subsequent bona fide purchaser without notice. **Answer (D) is incorrect** because O validly transferred O's interest in Greenacre to A.

• **Additional references:** *See* 14 RICHARD J. POWELL, POWELL ON REAL PROPERTY ch. 84, §§ 84.02[2][a], 84.02[3][e], ch. 82, § 82.02[c][ii], 82.03[2][b][1] (Patrick J. Rohan ed. 1999); 9 THOMPSON ON REAL PROPERTY, SECOND THOMAS EDITION § 82.11, 11 THOMPSON §§ 92.13(b), 92.15(b)(2)(A) (1999 & Supp. 2006); WILLIAM B. STOEBUCK & DALE A. WHITMAN, THE LAW OF PROPERTY § 11.5 (3d ed. 2000).

19. **The best answer is (C).** Much of the land description in the United States is based upon the original government land surveys conducted for the General Land Office beginning in 1785. The land was surveyed into rectangles using meridians and base lines. The rectangles were then subdivided into smaller areas by using range lines and township lines running parallel to the meridian and base lines. The range lines run north and south, the township lines run east and west. The resulting squares are approximately 6 miles by 6 miles. The resulting squares are commonly known as townships.

Each township can be described by reading its location on the township grid, reading from the intersection of the nearest meridian and base lines. When moving north and south from the base line, the term "township" is used to describe the location on the grid. When moving east and west from the meridian line, the term "range" is used to describe the location on the grid. The township location is given first. Accordingly, for the township marked above, the square is 2 squares to the north of the base line, so Township 2 North; and the square is 2 squares to the east of the meridian line, so Range 2 East. The full description would be Township 2 North, Range 2 East. (Each township, in turn, is typically broken down further into 36 sections.)

Answer (A) is incorrect because it confuses the terms Range and Township. Township indicates the north-south enumeration, Range the east-west. In addition, the square is 2 spots north of the base line, not south. **Answer (B) is incorrect** because it confuses which direction is north vs. south, and which direction is east vs. west. **Answer (D) is incorrect** because it confuses the terms Range and Township. Township indicates the north-south enumeration, Range the east-west enumeration.

- **Additional references:** *See* 14 RICHARD J. POWELL, POWELL ON REAL PROPERTY ch. 81A, § 81A.05[2][c][ii] (Patrick J. Rohan ed. 1999); WILLIAM B. STOEBUCK & DALE A. WHITMAN, THE LAW OF PROPERTY § 11.2 (3d ed. 2000).

20. **The best answer is (E).** Marketable title is title which is free from reasonable doubt and risk of litigation - title which a reasonable buyer would be willing to accept in exchange for valuable consideration. Basically, there are three types of defects which may render title unmarketable: chain of title defects, recorded encumbrances, and unrecorded encumbrances. Whether one of these types of encumbrances actually renders title unmarketable depends upon which type of defect it is, and how substantial the defect is.

Here, inasmuch as S is claiming ownership to part of the property to be conveyed based on adverse possession, it would appear as if the title were subject to some doubt and that there was risk of litigation. But the mere fact that there may be some doubt as to part of the title, and some risk of litigation, is not enough to make title unmarketable. The doubt must be reasonable, and the risk of litigation must be meaningful. For S to prevail, at a minimum the court must determine that it is likely that S has established title by adverse possession to the portion of the property in question. That, however, is not enough. A purchaser does not want to purchase a lawsuit. The court must also conclude that the risk that the true owner would actually sue to reclaim the portion of the property in question is unlikely.

Answer (A) is incorrect because the common law courts reasoned that each parcel of land is unique and damages are too difficult to ascertain. The preferred remedy is specific performance. **Answer (B) is incorrect** because the mere fact that the seller does not have good record title to all of the property the seller is purporting to convey does not necessarily make title unmarketable. The seller can still deliver marketable title if the seller can convince the court that there is little chance that the original owner will ever sue to reclaim the property in question, and that if the seller were to sue, there is little chance that the original owner would prevail. **Answers (C) and (D) are incorrect** because they are incomplete. The fact that the adverse possessor is likely to prevail is not enough. A buyer of real property does not want to buy a law suit, even if the purchaser were likely to prevail. In addition to showing that the seller is likely to prevail if there were a suit, the seller must also show that it is unlikely that there will be litigation.

- **Additional references**: *See* 14 RICHARD R. POWELL, POWELL ON REAL PROPERTY ch. 81, §§ 81.03[6][a], 81.03[6][d][ii] (Michael Allan Wolf ed., 2000); WILLIAM B. STOEBUCK & DALE A. WHITMAN, THE LAW OF PROPERTY § 10.12 (3d ed. 2000); 11 THOMPSON ON REAL PROPERTY, SECOND THOMAS § 91.09(a)(4) (2002 & Supp. 2006).

21. **The best answer is (C).** A home buyer's ability to recover from the builder for poor workmanship in the construction of a home was greatly hampered at common law. To recover in tort under negligence, a plaintiff had to prove personal injury, not just economic loss. Economic loss is recoverable in contract, but to recover in contract under an implied warranty, a plaintiff had to prove privity of contract - that he purchased from the builder. At common law, all but the first buyer of the home were stuck between a rock and a hard place.

The modern trend, however, has come to the rescue of the buyer of a defectively constructed home. The modern trend has created an implied warranty of quality which runs to remote purchasers of the home, not just to the original purchaser. The courts have been somewhat vague about whether the doctrine is based in torts, contracts, or some hybrid of the two, but the result is the same. Original or subsequent purchasers of defectively constructed homes may sue the builder, as long as the statute of limitations has not run (ten years is the norm).

The implied warranty of quality relates to the quality of the improvements on the property, not the state of the title (covered by the implied warranty of marketable title). The merger doctrine does not apply because the warranty is collateral to the contract to purchase. The warranty is collateral because it covers the improvements to the property, not the quantity of land or quality of title.

Answer (A) is incorrect because it invokes the wrong warranty. The implied warranty of marketable title applies pre-closing. Marketable title goes to the quality of the title the seller has to deliver to the buyer at closing, not to the quality of the improvements on the land. **Answer (B) is incorrect** because it reflects the common law requirement that to invoke an implied warranty, the plaintiff had to be in privity of contract with the builder. The privity requirement greatly limited the protection provided by the implied warranty of quality, because only the original purchaser could invoke the warranty. The modern trend rejects the privity requirement to provide greater protection to buyers. **Answer (D) is incorrect** because the merger doctrine applies primarily to claims involving the quantity of land or the quality of title which the seller was supposed to deliver under the terms of the contract. These matters go to the heart of the deed, and under the merger doctrine, the contractual obligations are deemed to have merged into the deed which was delivered. The implied warranty of quality applies to improvements on the property, a matter collateral to the deed.

- **Additional references**: *See* 12 THOMPSON ON REAL PROPERTY, SECOND THOMAS EDITION §§ 99.06(a)(2)(A), 99.06(a)(2)(B) (1994 & Supp. 2006); WILLIAM B. STOEBUCK & DALE A. WHITMAN, THE LAW OF PROPERTY § 11.16 (3d ed. 2000); 14 RICHARD J. POWELL, POWELL ON REAL PROPERTY ch. 84A, §§ 84A.03[1], 84A.02[A] (Patrick J. Rohan ed. 1999).

22. **The best answer is (C).** Under estoppel by deed, if a party purports to transfer a property interest which the party does not own, and then

subsequently the party comes into ownership of that property interest, the party is estopped from denying the prior conveyance. By operation of law the grantee of the prior conveyance holds title to the property interest. When A purported to convey Blackacre to B, A did not own it. B took nothing. O, the rightful owner of Blackacre, still owns it. (B cannot claim protection under the jurisdiction's recording act because a grantee of real property is charged with whatever information a search of the chain of title would have revealed. If B had performed a title search on Blackacre, B would have realized that O, not A, was the rightful owner of Blackacre.)

Thereafter, A acquires title to Blackacre from O. Applying estoppel by deed, the moment A acquires title, by operation of law, title will transfer to any prior grantee to whom A purported to transfer Blackacre. B, not A, holds title to Blackacre. Thereafter, A purports to convey Blackacre to C. Because of estoppel by deed, however, A owned no interest in Blackacre to convey to C. C receives no interest in Blackacre unless C can qualify for protection under the jurisdiction's recording act.

Under the notice recording act, the party claiming protection must qualify as a subsequent bona fide purchaser without notice. C bought from A subsequent to B purchasing from A, so C qualifies as a subsequent purchaser. Did C have notice of the prior conveyance from A to B? Although B recorded the deed from A to B, the recording constituted a wild deed at the time it was recorded. Under the standard scope of the search of the chain of title, as C searches through the grantor index, C is obligated to search under each grantor's name from the date of the deed purporting to transfer the property to the grantor to the date of the first deed recorded which purports to transfer that property interest to another party.

When performing a standard scope of the search of the grantor-grantee index under the facts of this problem, C would never find B's recording. C would search under O's name until C found the recorded deed from O to A. At that point, C would switch to A's name and search forward from the date of the deed purporting to transfer title to A to the present, searching under A's name. C would not find the deed from A to B because it was recorded prior to the deed from O to A. Assuming C did not have actual notice or inquiry notice of the conveyance from O to A, C would not have constructive notice since there is no way C would find the deed from A to B under a standard scope of the recording system. C has no notice of the prior conveyance from A to B, and C is entitled to protection under the jurisdiction's recording act. C owns Blackacre.

(Notice that estoppel by deed may not be that effective in protecting the intended grantee if the jurisdiction requires only a standard search of the grantor index. For that reason, many jurisdictions which recognize the doctrine of estoppel by deed require a grantee to perform an expanded scope of the search of the grantor index, searching under each grantor's name not from the date of the deed purporting to transfer title to that grantor, but searching under each grantor's name from the date of the grantor's birth.)

Answer (A) is incorrect because it fails to take into account estoppel by deed. A purported to transfer Blackacre to B before A owned Blackacre, so when A subsequently acquired Blackacre, A would be estopped from denying A's prior transfer of Blackacre to B. B is deemed to own Blackacre by operation of law. **Answer (B) is incorrect** because C qualifies for protection under the notice recording act. Although B recorded the A to B deed, since A did not own Blackacre at the time, B's recording is a wild deed since there is no way to connect the recorded deed to the chain of title for Blackacre. When A subsequently acquires title and records the O to A deed, under a standard scope of the grantor-grantee index, a subsequent grantee will never find the deed B recorded. When C takes from A, C has no notice of B's recorded deed and qualifies for protection under the recording act. **Answer (D) is incorrect** because O validly transferred O's interest in Blackacre to A.

- **Additional references:** *See* 14 RICHARD J. POWELL, POWELL ON REAL PROPERTY ch. 84, §§ 84.02[2][a], 84.02[3][e], ch. 82, § 82.02[c][ii], 82.03[2][b][1] (Patrick J. Rohan ed. 1999); 9 THOMPSON ON REAL PROPERTY, SECOND THOMAS EDITION § 82.11, 11 THOMPSON §§ 92.13(b), 92.15(b)(2)(A) (1999 & Supp. 2006); WILLIAM B. STOEBUCK & DALE A. WHITMAN, THE LAW OF PROPERTY § 11.5 (3d ed. 2000).

23. **The best answer is (B).** Under estoppel by deed, if a party purports to transfer a property interest which he or she does not own, and then subsequently the party acquires ownership of the property, the party is estopped from denying the prior conveyance. By operation of law the grantee of the prior conveyance holds title to the property interest.

When A purported to convey Blackacre to B, A did not own it. B took nothing. O, the rightful owner of Blackacre, still owns it. (B cannot claim protection under the jurisdiction's recording act, because a grantee of real property is charged with whatever information a search of the chain of title would have revealed. If B had performed a title search on

Blackacre, B would have realized that O, not A, was the rightful owner of Blackacre.) Thereafter, A acquires title to Blackacre from O.

Applying estoppel by deed, the moment A acquires title, by operation of law, title will transfer to any prior grantee to whom A purported to transfer Blackacre. B, not A, holds title to Blackacre. Thereafter, A purports to convey Blackacre to C. Because of estoppel by deed, however, A owned no interest in Blackacre to convey to C. C receives no interest in Blackacre unless C can qualify for protection under the jurisdiction's recording act.

Under the notice recording act, the party claiming protection must qualify as a subsequent bona fide purchaser without notice. C bought from A subsequent to B purchasing from A, so C qualifies as a subsequent purchaser. Did C have notice of the prior conveyance from A to B? Under the expanded scope of the search of the chain of title, each grantee must search under each grantor's name not from the date of the deed purporting to transfer title to that grantor, but rather the grantee must search under each grantor's name from the date of the grantor's birth. As C was searching through the grantor index under A's name, C was responsible to search under A's name prior in time to the date of the deed purporting to transfer title from O to A. C would have to search under A's name, in theory, all the way back to the date of A's birth to see if A might have purported to have transferred the property prior to owning it. When performing such an expanded search under the facts of this problem, C would have found the deed from A to B which B recorded that purported to transfer Blackacre to B before A owned it. C would then be on inquiry notice at a minimum and would not qualify as a subsequent bona fide purchaser without notice.

Under an expanded scope of the recording system, C has notice of the prior conveyance from A to B, and thus C is not entitled to protection under the jurisdiction's recording act. B owns Blackacre.

Answer (A) is incorrect because it fails to take into account estoppel by deed. Under estoppel by deed, if a party purports to transfer a property interest which the party does not own, and then subsequently the party comes into ownership of that property interest, the party is estopped from denying the prior conveyance. By operation of law the grantee of the prior conveyance holds title to the property interest. A purported to transfer Blackacre to B before A owned Blackacre, so when A subsequently acquired Blackacre, A would be estopped from denying A's prior transfer of Blackacre to B. B is deemed to own Blackacre by operation of law. **Answer (C) is incorrect** because it fails to take into account the expanded scope of the search under each grantor's name before the date of the deed purporting to transfer title to the grantor. Under the expanded scope of the search, each grantee must search under each grantor's name from the date of the grantor's birth. Searching the grantor index under A's name even before the date of the deed purporting to transfer title to A, C would have found the deed from A to B which purports to transfer title to Blackacre from A to B. C would have notice of B's first in time, first in right interest in Blackacre and would not qualify for protection under the recording act. **Answer (D) is incorrect** because O validly transferred O's interest in Blackacre to A.

- **Additional references**: *See* 14 RICHARD J. POWELL, POWELL ON REAL PROPERTY ch. 84, §§ 84.02[2][a], 84.02[3][e], ch. 82, § 82.02[c][ii], 82.03[2][b][1] (Patrick J. Rohan ed. 1999); 9 THOMPSON ON REAL PROPERTY, § 82.11, 11 THOMPSON §§ 92.13(b), 92.15(b)(2)(A) (1999 & Supp. 2006); WILLIAM B. STOEBUCK & DALE A. WHITMAN, THE LAW OF PROPERTY § 11.5 (3d ed. 2000).

24. **The best answer is (D).** Under traditional common law principles, when the seller and buyer enter into a binding contract to purchase real property, under the doctrine of equitable conversion the buyer becomes the owner for most purposes.

Equitable conversion is based upon the principle that "equity regards as done that which ought to be done." Under that principle, assuming an enforceable contract, for many purposes title passes the moment the parties enter into a binding contract. Under equitable conversion, the buyer assumes the risk of loss or change with respect to the property during the escrow period between executing the contract and closing. Inasmuch as the contract to purchase is to purchase *title* to the property, changes to structures on the property or zoning changes which did not affect title *per se* were not seen as grounds for permitting the buyer to rescind the contract.

The modern trend takes stock of the fact that where the real property has been improved, the primary purpose of most contracts to purchase is to acquire the improvement as is, not just the underlying land. Accordingly, if the improvement constitutes an important part of the contract, and the improvement is substantially damaged during the escrow period, the buyer can rescind the contract. If, however, the damage is not substantial, either party can enforce the contract, but the purchase price may be abated to reflect the damage to the improvement.

Under the facts of the problem, the damage to the house appears to be substantial. The owner is not entitled to specific performance since delivery of the house in substantially the same condition as it was on the date the parties entered into an enforceable contract is an implied condition precedent under the modern trend.

Answer (A) is incorrect because it reflects the answer under the traditional common law, equitable conversion approach to the problem. Under equitable conversion, the buyer is treated as owner of the property once the parties enter into an enforceable contract. The buyer assumes the risk of loss during the escrow period. The modern trend, however, rejects placing the risk of loss on the purchaser during the escrow period. **Answer (B) is incorrect** because it misstates the modern trend rule. The seller is entitled to specific performance and abatement only if the damage is not substantial. Here, the damage is substantial, and the house appears to be an important part of the contract. The buyer can rescind the contract. **Answer (C) is incorrect** because although it implicitly states the modern trend rule, it misapplies it. The issue is whether the house was substantially damaged. The house sustained $300,000 worth of damage, almost 1/3 of its value. The damage arguably was substantial.

- **Additional references**: *See* 14 RICHARD J. POWELL, POWELL ON REAL PROPERTY ch. 81, § 81.03[2] (Patrick J. Rohan ed. 1999); 12 THOMPSON ON REAL PROPERTY, SECOND THOMAS EDITION § 99.09(a) (1994 & Supp. 2006); WILLIAM B. STOEBUCK & DALE A. WHITMAN, THE LAW OF PROPERTY § 11.13 (3d ed. 2000).

25. **The best answer is (D).** Marketable title acts are designed to limit the scope of the search of the chain of title that a grantee must perform by providing that if a property interest is not re-recorded within the statutory period, the property interest is extinguished.

The key to applying and analyzing a marketable title act is to understand the significance of the "root of title." Under a marketable title act, start with the latest point in time in the facts. From that date, go back in time the number of years expressly required in the statute. From that date, keep going back in time until you find the first recorded transfer of fee simple for that property. That is the current root of title for the property. The general rule is that property interests which are inconsistent with the chain of title from the root of title to the present (i.e. which are not recited in the root of title or re-recorded) are extinguished.

Under the facts given, the latest point in time in the facts is 2004. From 2004, go back in time the number of years expressly required by the statute: 30 years. Subtracting 30 years from 2004 yields 1974. Keep going back in time until the first recorded conveyance of Blueacre prior to 1974 is found - that will be the "root of title." The first recorded conveyance of Blueacre found prior to 1974 is the 1970 recorded deed which conveyed Blueacre from A to B. There is no mention of X's leasehold in the deed or in any other recording thereafter during the statutory period. Inasmuch as C holds an unbroken chain of title from the 1970 root of title for over 30 years, the statutory period, X's leasehold interest is extinguished.

The fact that B and C had actual knowledge of X's leasehold interest is irrelevant under the marketable title act. The property interest must be re-recorded within the statutory period of the interest or it is extinguished.

Answers (A) and (B) are incorrect because actual knowledge of the property interest in question is irrelevant under the marketable title act. The question is simply whether the property interest is recorded within the root of title or statutory period thereafter. **Answer (C) is incorrect** because the root of title is the 1970 deed from A to B which does not mention the lease, not the 1960 deed from O to A which mentions the lease. If the property interest is mentioned in the root of title, the interest is not extinguished. Here, however, it is not becasue the root of title is the 1970 deed. **Answer (E) is incorrect** because it refers to the wrong root of title. Start with the latest point in time in the fact pattern, here 2004, and go back the statutory period, here 30 years. That takes you to 1974. Do not go forward in time from that point in time, but rather continue to go back in time until you find the first recorded fee simple deed. That would be the deed from A to B which was recorded in 1970.

- **Additional references:** *See* 14 RICHARD J. POWELL, POWELL ON REAL PROPERTY ch. 82, §§ 82.04[1], 82.04[3][a][i] (Patrick J. Rohan ed. 1999); 11 THOMPSON ON REAL PROPERTY, SECOND THOMAS EDITION § 91.09(b)(1) (2002 & Supp. 2006); WILLIAM B. STOEBUCK & DALE A. WHITMAN, THE LAW OF PROPERTY § 11.12 (3d ed. 2000).

ANSWER KEY
EXAM VII

PROPERTY
ANSWER KEY AND EXPLANATIONS

EXAM VII

1. **The best answer is (B).** Analyzing recording act statutes requires a careful reading of the statutory language.

    Race statutes typically include a reference to the fact that any property interest purported to be created is not valid against subsequent transferees until "the time of registration thereof" or "the time of recording thereof." Race recording acts do not require the party seeking protection to be without notice of the prior property interest, only that the party be the first to record. The statute focuses on the requirement that the instrument in question be "registered" or "recorded."

    Notice statutes typically provide that any purported property interest is not valid against subsequent transferees unless the subsequent transferees have "notice of the transfer or the interest is recorded." Notice statutes do not require the party seeking protection to record, but the party seeking protection must not have notice - actual, inquiry, or record notice - of the prior property interest. In addition, the subsequent party must be a purchaser or otherwise give valuable consideration.

    Race-notice statutes typically provide that any purported property interest is not valid against subsequent transferees if the subsequent transferees have acquired the property "in good faith and for a valuable consideration, *whose conveyance is first duly recorded*." Race-notice statutes require not only that the party seeking protection qualify as a subsequent bona fide purchaser without notice of the prior property interest, but also that the party seeking protection be the first to duly record the instrument creating the property interest.

    Looking at the statute here, the statutory language basically provides that a conveyance is not good against "subsequent purchasers for valuable consideration and without notice, unless the same [the first in time, first in right conveyance] be recorded according to the law." The conveyance is good unless the subsequent party qualifies as a subsequent bona fide purchaser without notice. That is the essence of a notice recording act. The statute is a notice recording statute.

Answers (A) and (C) are incorrect because the statute does not have a race component and therefore is neither a pure race or race-notice recording act. The statute does not include any reference to the subsequent party's conveyance being duly recorded first. The statute does not require the subsequent grantee to record to be entitled to protection. The conveyance is good unless the subsequent grantee qualifies as a subsequent bona fide purchaser without notice. That is the essence of a notice recording statute.

- **Additional references**: *See* 14 RICHARD R. POWELL, POWELL ON REAL PROPERTY ch. 82, §§ 82.02[1][c][i]-[iii], 82.03[2][b][1] (Patrick J. Rohan ed. 1999); 11 THOMPSON ON REAL PROPERTY, SECOND THOMAS EDITION § 92.13(a)-(c), 92.15(b)(2)(A) (2002 & Supp. 2006); WILLIAM B. STOEBUCK & DALE A. WHITMAN, THE LAW OF PROPERTY § 11.9 (3d ed. 2000).

2. **The best answer is (D).** At the start of the facts, Olivia is the rightful owner of Greenacre. Thus, Andy has no interest in Greenacre to transfer to Barb when he executes and delivers the special warranty deed to Barb. (The fact that the deed has a defective acknowledgment does not affect whether the deed is valid, but is does affect whether the deed gives constructive notice. See answer to problem 3 for further discussion of this point.) Nor can Barb claim protection under the jurisdiction's recording act.

To qualify for protection under a notice recording act, the party claiming protection must qualify as a subsequent bona fide purchaser without notice of the prior competing interest. A grantee of real property is charged with knowledge of whatever a search of the recording system would have revealed. If Barb had searched the recording system, she would have discovered that O was the rightful owner of Greenacre and that Andy had no interest to convey to Barb. Thus, Barb is charged with constructive notice of the fact that Olivia, not Andy, is the rightful owner.

When Olivia subsequently conveys Greenacre to Andy, however, Barb can now successfully claim title to Greenacre under estoppel by deed. Estoppel by deed provides that where a party purports to convey title to a property interest which the party does not own, if the party subsequently acquires title to the property, the party is estopped from denying the prior deed which the party executed and delivered. The effect is to transfer title, by operation of law, to the party to whom the prior ineffective deed was transferred. Since Olivia had good title to transfer to Andy, the moment delivery is effective, by operation of law, title transfers to Barb by virtue of the prior deed from Andy to Barb. Barb holds good title to Greenacre.

Thus, when Andy purports to convey to Carl, Andy has no interest in Greenacre to convey to Carl. Carl can acquire a property interest in Greenacre only if Carl qualifies for protection under the jurisdiction's recording act. Under a notice recording act, the party seeking protection must qualify as a subsequent bona fide purchaser without notice. Andy's purported conveyance of Greenacre to Carl was subsequent to Barb acquiring her interest in Greenacre, and Carl paid valuable consideration, $40,000, for the deed. Carl qualifies as a subsequent purchaser. Did Carl purchase without notice of Barb's claim to the property? The facts state that Carl knew of the prior deed from Andy to Barb. Carl has actual notice of Barb's claim to the property and therefore cannot qualify as a subsequent bona fide purchaser without notice. Barb still holds good title to Greenacre under first in time, first in right.

Carl has no interest in the property to convey to Deb. Deb can acquire a property interest in Greenacre only if Deb qualifies for protection under the recording act as a subsequent bona fide purchaser without notice. Carl's purported conveyance of Greenacre to Deb was subsequent to Barb acquiring her interest in Greenacre, and Deb paid valuable consideration, $75,000, for the deed. Deb qualifies as a subsequent purchaser. Did Deb purchase without notice of Barb's claim to the property? There are three types of notice: actual, inquiry, and constructive. There is no evidence that Deb had actual notice of Barb's claim to the property. Although a grantee of real property has a duty to inspect the property prior to purchasing and to ascertain the scope and nature of any claimed property interests by any parties in possession, there is no evidence that Barb ever took possession. (The facts imply that Barb had not taken possession since the facts state that Barb came forward after the Carl to Deb deed was recorded.)

The only question is whether Deb had constructive notice. A grantee is charged with notice of whatever a proper search of the chain of title would have revealed, whether the party actually searched the chain of title or not. If Deb had performed a standard scope of the search of the chain of title, when she was coming forward in the grantor-grantee index, she would have continued searching under Olivia's name until she found the Olivia to Andy recording. At that point, she would have shifted to Andy's name and searched under Andy's name from the date of the Olivia to Andy deed forward. She would not have found the Andy to

Barb deed because it is a wild deed. It was recorded prior to the Olivia to Andy deed. Thus, under a standard scope of the search, which requires the grantee to search from the date of execution of the deed purporting to transfer title to the grantee to the date of the first recorded deed which purports to transfer title out to another grantee, Deb would not have found the recording of the Andy to Barb deed. Searching under Andy's name, she would have found the Andy to Carl deed. Switching to Carl's name, and performing the standard scope of the search under Carl's name, Deb would not find a deed recorded under Carl's name which purports to convey title out to another party. Deb would think, in good faith, that Carl has good title to convey to her. Deb qualifies as a subsequent bona fide purchaser without notice and is entitled to protection under the notice recording act. Deb holds title to Greenacre.

Answer (A) is incorrect because under estoppel by deed, once Andy received good title to Greenacre, he is estopped from denying his earlier purported conveyance of Greenacre to Barb. By operation of law, title is transferred from Andy to Barb. The patent defect in the acknowledgment does not affect the validity of the deed, only whether the recorded deed gives constructive notice. **Answer (B) is incorrect** because although Barb recorded the Andy to Barb deed, the recording is a wild deed since Andy had no connection to the chain of title for Greenacre at that point in time. Barb's title is vulnerable. Although Carl did not qualify for protection under the notice recording act because he had actual knowledge of Barb's interest, and thus had no interest to pass to Deb, Deb did not have notice of Barb's interest and qualifies for protection under the recording act because she would not find Barb's deed under a standard search of the grantor-grantee index. **Answer (C) is incorrect** because when Carl received the deed from Andy, Carl had actual knowledge of the prior deed from Andy to Barb. Under estoppel by deed, Andy had no interest to give Carl, and Carl does not qualify for protection under the notice recording act, since he had actual notice of Barb's interest. **Answer (E) is incorrect** because Olivia properly executed and delivered a deed transferring title to Greenacre to Andy.

- **Additional references:** *See* 14 RICHARD R. POWELL, POWELL ON REAL PROPERTY ch. 84, §§ 84.02[2][a], 84.02[3][e], ch. 82, §§ 82.02[1][c][ii], 82.03[2][b][1] (Patrick J. Rohan ed. 1999); 9 THOMPSON ON REAL PROPERTY, SECOND THOMAS EDITION § 82.11, 11 THOMPSON §§ 92.13(b), 92.15(b)(2)(A) (1999 & Supp. 2006); WILLIAM B. STOEBUCK & DALE A. WHITMAN, THE LAW OF PROPERTY §§ 11.5, 11.9-11.11 (3d ed. 2000).

3. **The best answer is (C).** The initial analysis of the problem is the same as in problem 2 until the Carl to Deb conveyance. When Andy conveyed to Barb, he had no interest in Greenacre to convey. Barb took nothing. Barb cannot qualify for protection under the notice recording act because she is charged with the knowledge that Olivia, not Andy, owns Greenacre. When Olivia conveyed to Andy, under estoppel by deed, title transferred by operation of law to Barb. When Andy conveyed to Carl, Andy had no interest to convey to Carl. Carl cannot qualify for protection under the recording act because he knows of the prior conveyance to Barb. When Carl conveys to Deb, Carl has no interest in Greenacre to convey.

Deb takes nothing unless she qualifies for protection under the notice recording act, that is, unless she qualifies as a subsequent bona fide purchaser without notice of the competing claim. Deb is a subsequent purchaser. The question is whether she is without notice of Barb's interest in the property. There is no evidence that Deb has actual or inquiry notice of Barb's interest. The question is whether she has constructive notice if the jurisdiction requires an expanded scope of the search of the grantor-grantee index.

Under the expanded scope of the search, the grantee must search the grantor index under each grantor's name starting not with the date of execution of the deed purporting to transfer title to the grantor, but *before* the date of the deed purporting to transfer title to the grantor. Under that scope, when Deb searches under Olivia's name, she will not find anything except the Olivia to Andy deed which was recorded. When she switches to Andy's name and searches the grantor index prior to the date of execution of the Olivia to Andy deed, Deb will find the Andy to Barb deed which was recorded.

The problem is the deed has a patent defect in the acknowledgment. The general rule is that a recorded deed which has a patent defect in the acknowledgment does not give constructive notice, but if a party actually performs a search of the grantor index and finds the deed, the party has actual notice of the deed. If Deb actually performed a title search, she had notice of Barb's interest in Greenacre and does not qualify for protection under the notice recording act. If, however, Deb did not actually perform a title search, she is not charged with constructive notice of the defectively acknowledged deed. Deb would not be charged with the second recording of the Andy to Barb deed because Deb is required to search under each grantor's name only until she finds the first deed recorded which purports to transfer title out from the grantor to another grantor. When Carl recorded the Andy to Carl deed, that marked the end of the scope of the search Deb had to perform in the grantor index under Andy.

Deb qualifies for protection as a subsequent bona fide purchaser without notice if she did not actually search the grantor-grantee index. If, however, she actually searched the grantor-grantee index and found the Andy to Barb deed, she does not qualify for protection under the recording act.

Answer (A) is incorrect because although Andy had no interest to convey at the time he delivered the deed to Barb, under estoppel by deed, when Andy subsequently acquired title to Greenacre he is estopped from denying his earlier deed and title passes, by operation of law, to Barb. A deed is valid even if not notarized, so the defect in the acknowledgment does not affect the validity of the deed as between the parties to the deed. **Answer (B) is incorrect** because it is an overstatement. Deb qualifies for protection only if she does not actually search the grantor-grantee index. If she performs the expanded search, she would find the Andy to Barb deed. If she does not perform the search, however, she is not charged with knowledge of the Andy to Barb deed because the general rule is that a recorded deed with a patent defect in the acknowledgment gives no constructive notice of its recording. **Answer (D) is incorrect** because Deb qualifies for protection under the notice recording act if she does not actually search the grantor-grantee index. The patent defect in the acknowledgment means that the Andy to Barb deed does not give constructive notice even though recorded.

- **Additional references**: *See* 14 RICHARD R. POWELL, POWELL ON REAL PROPERTY ch. 84, §§ 84.02[2][a], 84.02[3][e], ch. 82, §§ 82.02[1][c][ii], 82.03[2][b][1] (Patrick J. Rohan ed. 1999); 9 THOMPSON ON REAL PROPERTY, SECOND THOMAS EDITION § 82.11, 11 THOMPSON § 92.13(b), 92.15(b)(2)(A) (1999 & Supp. 2006); WILLIAM B. STOEBUCK & DALE A. WHITMAN, THE LAW OF PROPERTY §§ 11.5, 11.9-11.11 (3d ed. 2000).

4. **The best answer is (E).** The initial analysis of the problem is the same as in problem 2 until the Carl to Deb conveyance. When Andy conveyed to Barb, he had no interest in Greenacre to convey. Barb took nothing. Barb cannot qualify for protection under the notice recording act because she is charged with the knowledge that Olivia, not Andy, owns Greenacre. When Olivia conveyed to Andy, under estoppel by deed, title transferred, by operation of law, to Barb. When Andy conveyed to Carl,

Andy had no interest to convey to Carl. Carl cannot qualify for protection under the recording act because he knows of the prior conveyance to Barb. When Carl conveys to Deb, Carl has no interest in Greenacre to convey.

Deb takes nothing unless she qualifies for protection under the notice recording act, that is, unless she qualifies as a subsequent bona fide purchaser without notice of the competing claim. Deb is a subsequent purchaser. The question is whether she is without notice of Barb's interest in the property. There is no evidence that Deb has actual or inquiry notice of Barb's interest. The question is whether she has constructive notice if the jurisdiction requires an expanded scope of the search of the grantor-grantee index.

Under the expanded scope of the search, the grantee must search the grantor index under each grantor's name from the date of execution of the deed purporting to transfer title to the grantor up until the date of the proposed transaction to the grantee in question. The grantee cannot stop at the first deed recorded purporting to transfer title out to another party, but must continue searching after that date. When Deb is coming forward in the grantor index searching under Olivia's name, the only recording Deb will find is the Olivia to Andy deed which Andy recorded. Deb would then switch over to Andy's name in the grantor index. Starting with the date of the deed from Olivia to Andy, Deb would search from that date forward until the current date. Deb would not find the original Andy to Barb deed because it was recorded before the point in time in which she is charged with beginning her search. Nor would she find the re-recorded Andy to Barb deed, because the recorder mis-recorded it under the notary's name, Noel. Deb would only find the Andy to Carl deed, and then searching under Carl's name, Deb would not find any recordings. Deb would appear to qualify as a subsequent bona fide purchaser without notice entitled to protection.

Nevertheless, the general rule is that if a grantee takes a properly executed and acknowledged deed to the recorder's office for recording, and the recorder mistakenly records it under the wrong name, the deed is deemed to give constructive notice even though the recording constitutes a wild deed which subsequent grantees cannot find. The reasoning is that the grantee did all he or she was supposed to do, and it is unfair to punish the grantee for the recorder's mistake. (The general rule is subject to criticism. As between the grantee and subsequent grantee, the original grantee is in the best position to discover the mis-recording and correct it. The burden should be on that grantee to check and see if the deed was properly recorded. Placing the burden on that grantee is accomplished by ruling that the mis-recorded deed does not give constructive notice.) Under the general rule, Deb does not qualify for protection, because she has constructive notice of the re-recorded Andy to Barb deed even though from Deb's perspective, the deed constitutes a wild deed.

Answer (A) is incorrect because although Andy had no interest to convey at the time he delivered the deed to Barb, under estoppel by deed, when Andy subsequently acquired title to Greenacre, he is estopped from denying his earlier deed and title passes by operation of law to Barb. A deed is valid even if not notarized, so the defect in the acknowledgment does not affect the validity of the deed as between the parties to the deed. **Answers (B), (C) and (D) are incorrect** because the general rule is that a properly executed deed which is delivered to the recorder's office for recording gives constructive notice even if mis-recorded. Even though the recorder mis-recorded the re-recorded Andy to Barb deed, the deed is deemed by operation of law to have been properly recorded since Barb is not responsible for the mis-recording, the recorder is. Since the deed is deemed properly recorded, Deb is deemed to have constructive notice of it, even though there is no way Deb could have discovered the deed under a proper search of the grantor-grantee index. Since Deb is deemed to have constructive notice of the re-recorded Andy to Barb deed, there is no way Deb can qualify for protection under the notice recording act.

- **Additional references**: *See* 14 RICHARD R. POWELL, POWELL ON REAL PROPERTY ch. 84, §§ 84.02[2][a], 84.02[3][e], ch. 82, §§ 82.02[1][c][ii], 82.03[2][b][1] (Patrick J. Rohan ed. 1999); 9 THOMPSON ON REAL PROPERTY, SECOND THOMAS EDITION § 82.11, 11 THOMPSON § 92.13(b), 92.15(b)(2)(A) (1999 & Supp. 2006); WILLIAM B. STOEBUCK & DALE A. WHITMAN, THE LAW OF PROPERTY §§ 11.5, 11.9-11.11 (3d ed. 2000).

5. **The best answer is (D).** Deb would like to sue her grantor, Carl. In theory, a grantee can sue a grantor under either breach of contract or breach of the covenants in the deed. Under the merger doctrine, however, terms of the contract concerning quantity of land being conveyed and quality of title being conveyed merge into the deed. Although contractual provisions collateral to the quantity of land and quality of title arguably do not merge into the deed, particularly under the modern trend, Deb is suing for failure to deliver good title to Greenacre, so merger most likely will apply to bar her from suing on the contract

even under the modern trend. (Merger does not apply to claims of fraud or mistake, but those claims are beyond the scope of the question.)

As for suing on the covenants in the deed, the key is which type of deed did the grantor deliver. A quitclaim deed contains no covenants. A special warranty deed contains the usual six covenants, three present (seisen, right to convey, and against encumbrances) and three future (general warranty, quiet enjoyment, and further assurances), but only with respect to the grantor's actions. A general warranty deed contains the usual six covenants, but unlike the special warranty deed, the general warranty deed covenants not only the grantor's actions but also all prior grantor's actions. Unfortunately, Deb cannot sue Carl since Carl gave her a quitclaim deed which contains no covenants.

Moving further up the chain of grantors, can Deb sue Andy? Andy conveyed Greenacre to Carl by special warranty deed. A special warranty deed means that Andy warrants his actions only. Andy, however, is at fault for the situation because he conveyed Greenacre to Barb prior to owning it. Under estoppel by deed, when Olivia conveyed to Andy, title passed by operation of law to Barb, and Andy had no title to convey to Carl. Andy breached the covenants of seisen and right to convey when he purported to convey to Carl. The present covenants are breached, if ever, at the time the grantor delivers title to the grantee. The mere existence of a superior property interest breaches the present covenants. The future covenants, on the other hand, are breached by the assertion of a superior property interest. When Barb comes forward and asserts her superior right to Greenacre, the future covenants are breached.

The issue is whether the present and future covenants run to a remote grantee. At common law, present covenants did not run to remote grantees because causes of action were not assignable. Under the modern trend, causes of action are assignable, so the cause of action for breach of the present covenants which arose when the grantor delivered the deed to the immediate grantee is deemed assigned to the remote grantee when the immediate grantee conveys to the remote grantee. The issue is whether the statute of limitations has run on the cause of action. Deb could sue Andy for breach of the present covenants of seisen and right to convey as long as the statute of limitations has not run.

Future covenants run to a remote grantee as long as some title passes from covenantor to remote grantee or actual possession passes from covenantor to remote grantee. Andy had no title to pass to Carl, who in turn had no title to pass to Deb. Future covenants cannot run to Deb since no title passed. Was actual possession passed from Andy to Carl to

Deb? No. None of the parties took actual possession. Although future covenants often run to remote grantees, under the facts of this problem, the future covenants do not run to Deb.

Moving further up in the chain of grantors, can Deb sue Olivia? Olivia conveyed Greenacre to Andy by general warranty deed. Olivia was warranting not only her actions but the actions of all prior grantors. The problems with the title to Greenacre which Deb purported to receive arose after Olivia conveyed Greenacre. The temporal scope of Olivia's actions covers only the time Olivia owned Greenacre and the grantors prior to her ownership, not subsequent grantors and their actions. Deb has no recourse against Olivia.

Answers (A) and (B) are incorrect because Deb cannot sue Carl. Carl used a quitclaim deed when transferring to Deb. A quitclaim deed makes no warranties as to the state of the title. **Answers (C) and (E) are incorrect** because future covenants do not run to remote grantees unless there is privity of estate. Privity of estate exists if the deed passes good title to some of the land in question or if the parties pass actual possession of the property in question. Here, the deeds did not pass good title to any of the land in question, nor were the parties in actual possession of the land. There is no privity of estate to support the running of the future covenants to remote grantees. **Answer (C) is also incorrect** because Deb is not in privity of contract with Andy and therefore cannot sue Andy on the terms of the contract.

- **Additional references:** *See* 14 RICHARD R. POWELL, POWELL ON REAL PROPERTY ch. 81, § 81.03[6][h], ch. 81A, §§ 81A.03[1][b][i]-[iii], 81A.03[1][c], 81A.06[2][a]-[f], 81A.06[5][a]-[d] (Patrick J. Rohan ed.1999); 9 THOMPSON ON REAL PROPERTY, SECOND THOMAS EDITION §§ 82.10(c)(1)-(6), 82.10(d), 82.13(d) (1999 & Supp. 2006), 11 THOMPSON §§ 94.07(b)(1)-(b)(3), 94.07(c)(1), 94.07(e) (2002 & Supp. 2006); WILLIAM B. STOEBUCK & DALE A. WHITMAN, THE LAW OF PROPERTY §§ 10.12, 11.13 (3d ed. 2000).

6. **The best answer is (C).** Barb would like to sue her grantor, Andy. In theory, a grantee can sue a grantor under either breach of contract or breach of the covenants in the deed. Under the merger doctrine, however, terms of the contract concerning quantity of land being conveyed and quality of title being conveyed merge into the deed. Although contractual provisions collateral to quantity of land and quality of title arguably do not merge into the deed, particularly under the modern trend, Deb is suing for failure to deliver good title to Greenacre,

so merger most likely will apply to bar her from suing on the contract even under the modern trend. (Merger does not apply to claims of fraud or mistake, but those claims are beyond the scope of the question.)

As for suing on the covenants in the deed, the key is which type of deed the grantor delivered. A quitclaim deed contains no covenants. A special warranty deed contains the usual six covenants, three present (seisen, right to convey, and against encumbrances) and three future (general warranty, quiet enjoyment, and further assurances), but only with respect to the grantor's actions. A general warranty deed contains the usual six covenants, but a general warranty deed covenants not only the grantor's actions but also the actions of all prior grantors.

Can Barb sue Andy? Andy conveyed Greenacre to Barb by special warranty deed. Andy was warranting only his actions when he used the special warranty deed. Andy, however, is at fault for the situation since he conveyed Greenacre to Barb prior to owning Greenacre. Andy breached the covenants of seisen and right to convey when he purported to convey to Barb. The present covenants are breached, if ever, at the time the grantor delivers title to the grantee. The mere existence of a superior property interest breaches the present covenants. The future covenants, on the other hand, are breached by the assertion of a superior property interest. When Deb comes forward and asserts her superior right to Greenacre, the future covenants are breached.

The issue is whether the defects in the deed from Andy to Barb were cured when title passed from Andy to Barb under estoppel by deed. Applying estoppel by deed, there no longer appears to be a problem. Barb can claim title. But because Barb recorded her initial deed from Andy before he had title, Barb's title is vulnerable. Her recording constituted a wild recording unconnected to the chain of title for Greenacre. To permit estoppel by deed to cure Andy's deed to Barb while leaving Barb vulnerable would be contrary to the purposes behind the warranties in the deed. In addition, Andy's actions in purporting to convey title to Carl, who in turn purports to convey title to Deb, create the superior title in Deb. Andy breached the present and future covenants when he conveyed to Barb, and estoppel by deed should not cure the breaches.

Answer (A) is incorrect because Barb cannot sue Carl. The covenants in a deed run to subsequent grantees. Barb is not a subsequent grantee from Carl. Moreover, Carl used a quitclaim deed when transferring to Deb. A quitclaim deed makes no warranties as to the state of the title.

Answer (B) is incorrect because Barb cannot sue Andy under the contract. Under the merger doctrine, the promises in the contract merge into the deed. Although the modern trend has been to narrow the scope of the merger doctrine and to exclude promises collateral to the deed, the problem here goes to the quality of title, the essence of the deed. Unless the court were willing to abolish the merger doctrine altogether, it would appear to bar Deb's claim under the terms of the contract promising title. **Answer (D) is incorrect** because it is incomplete. Barb can sue not only on the present covenants but also on the future covenants since Deb is asserting a superior title. **Answer (E) is incorrect** because it is incomplete. Barb can sue not only on the future covenants but also on the present covenants. Andy breached the present covenants of seisen and right to convey when he delivered the deed to Barb since he held no interest in Greenacre at that time.

- **Additional references:** *See* 14 RICHARD R. POWELL, POWELL ON REAL PROPERTY ch. 81, § 81.03[6][h], ch. 81A, §§ 81A.03[1][b][i]-[iii], 81A.03[1][c], 81A.06[2][a]-[f], 81A.06[5][a]-[d], ch. 84, §§ 84.02[2][a], 84.02[3][e] (Patrick J. Rohan ed.1999); 9 THOMPSON ON REAL PROPERTY, SECOND THOMAS EDITION §§ 82.10(c)(1)-(6), 82.10(d), 82.11, 82.13(d) (1999 & Supp. 2006), 11 THOMPSON §§ 94.07(b)(1)-(b)(3), 94.07(c)(1), 94.07(e) (2002 & Supp. 2006); WILLIAM B. STOEBUCK & DALE A. WHITMAN, THE LAW OF PROPERTY §§ 10.12, 11.5, 11.13 (3d ed. 2000).

7. **The best answer is (A).** The Statute of Frauds requires that to transfer a property interest there has to be a written instrument signed by the party to be charged. The quitclaim deed which Fred executed satisfies the writing requirement. The property interest does not transfer, however, until the writing is properly delivered.

For purposes of transferring a property interest, "delivery" is a term of art which refers to the grantor's state of mind. Has the grantor relinquished control over the property? Since there rarely is direct evidence of the grantor's intent, certain presumptions arise out of the physical treatment of the deed. If the grantor retains the properly executed deed, the presumption is no delivery. If the grantor records the properly executed deed, the presumption is delivery. If the grantor transfers the deed to the grantee, the presumption is delivery.

Here, Fred handed the deed to Doris. The presumption is that Fred has properly transferred title to Blackacre to Doris. Although Doris hands the deed back to Fred, there is no transfer of title back to Fred. The

Statute of Frauds requires that to transfer a property interest there has to be a written instrument signed by the party to be charged. Doris has not signed any written instrument which purports to transfer title. The fact that she hands the deed which her father executed back to her father does not transfer any property interest back to her father. Doris holds title to Blackacre, which she can assert against Fred, even though Fred holds the deed to the property.

Answer (B) is incorrect because it assumes that a properly executed deed must be recorded to be effective. A properly executed deed need only be delivered to be effective. **Answer (C) is incorrect** because it improperly analyzes the delivery requirement. Whether or not a deed has been delivered is a question of fact concerning the grantor's state of mind: has the grantor relinquished control over title to the property? When Fred handed the properly executed deed to Doris, Fred manifested his intent to relinquish control over title to the property. **Answer (D) is incorrect** because Doris has not satisfied the Statute of Frauds. She has not signed a written instrument which purports to transfer her interest in Blackacre. In addition, there has been no delivery because Doris' state of mind when she asked her father to keep the deed was not to relinquish control over title to the property, but merely to safeguard the deed.

- **Additional references**: *See* 14 RICHARD R. POWELL, POWELL ON REAL PROPERTY ch. 81A, §§ 81A.04[2][a][i]-[iii], 81A.02[2] (Michael Allan Wolf ed., 2000); 9 THOMPSON ON REAL PROPERTY, SECOND THOMAS EDITION §§ 82.03(b)(3), 83.04 (1999 & Supp. 2006); WILLIAM B. STOEBUCK & DALE A. WHITMAN, THE LAW OF PROPERTY § 11.3 (3d ed. 2000).

8. **The best answer is (A).** Under the traditional common law approach, the default concurrent tenancy was joint tenancy as long as the four unities of time, title, interest and possession were satisfied. Each of the joint tenants had to acquire their interest at the same time, each had to acquire their interest through the same instrument, each had to have an equal share of the same duration in the property, and each had to have equal right to possess the whole. At common law, a party who already owned the property could not convey it to him or herself and another as joint tenants without using a straw party. If the party who already owned the property did not use a straw party but rather executed a deed which purported to create a joint tenancy, the unities of time and title would not be satisfied. The common law rule required the 4 unities for a joint tenancy, regardless of the intent of the transferor.

Despite Olivia's clear intent to create a joint tenancy, the transfer from Olivia to Olivia and Doris lacks the 4 unities necessary to create a joint tenancy at common law. Her interest in the parcel predated the deed to Olivia and Doris. Because Olivia did not use a straw party, her transfer from herself to herself and Doris lacks the unities of time and title. Olivia and Doris hold the property as tenants in common, not as joint tenants.

A tenant in common can unilaterally transfer his or her interest to a third party, who then becomes a tenant in common also. The issue is whether the deed which Doris properly executed transferred any property interest to Kile and his children.

Execution of a deed does not transfer the property interest. The property interest is not transferred until the deed is properly delivered. Delivery relates to the grantor's state of mind. Delivery occurs when the grantor intends to relinquish control over the property interest being transferred. Since there is rarely direct evidence of the grantor's state of mind, a presumption of delivery arises if the deed is handed to the grantee or if the deed is recorded. There is a presumption of no delivery when the grantor retains possession of the deed.

As between Olivia and Doris, Olivia recorded the deed, which gives rise to a presumption of delivery, a presumption supported by Doris' actions in securing the necessary permits and beginning construction on the property. Doris then executed a deed which purports to convey her interest to Kile and his children. While there is some issue over which estates were created by the express language of Doris' deed, first there is the issue of whether Doris has delivered the deed. Doris retained possession of the deed, putting it in her safe deposit box for safe keeping. Doris' treatment of the deed gives rise to a presumption that it has not been delivered yet. This presumption arguably is supported by the fact that Doris continued to treat the property as if it were her own, obtaining construction permits and building on the property. The deed from Doris to Kile and his children has not been delivered yet. Olivia and Doris still own the property as tenants in common.

Answer (B) is incorrect because although the default tenancy at common law was joint tenancy, common law was very strict in requiring that the four unities of time, title, interest and possession be met to create a joint tenancy. Despite the clear language of the deed, since Olivia owned the property prior to the conveyance and did not use a straw party, Olivia did not satisfy the unities of time and title. **Answers**

(C), (D) and (E) are incorrect because they presume that the deed Doris executed conveyed a property interest to Kile and his children. A deed is not effective until delivered. Delivery occurs when the grantor intends to transfer the property interest. Here, Doris neither recorded nor transferred the deed to Kile. The presumption is against delivery, a presumption supported by Doris' conduct asserting continued control over the property.

- **Additional references**: *See* 7 RICHARD R. POWELL, POWELL ON REAL PROPERTY ch. 51, ¶ 616[3] (Patrick J. Rohan ed. 1999); 4 THOMPSON ON REAL PROPERTY, SECOND THOMAS EDITION § 31.06(b)-(c) (2004 & Supp. 2006); WILLIAM B. STOEBUCK & DALE A. WHITMAN, THE LAW OF PROPERTY § 5.3 (3d ed. 2000).

9. **The best answer is (B).** A term of years lease is a lease with a fixed term, meaning the last day of the term can be calculated on the first day of the lease. A periodic lease is a lease which has a fixed term which is presumed to repeat term after term until proper notice to terminate is given. A tenancy at will is when a tenant enters with the landlord's permission but there is no fixed term at all. The tenancy continues as long as either party wishes it to continue. A holdover tenancy is where a tenant remains in actual possession of the property after the tenant's legal right to possession has ended.

At first blush, Ali's lease appears to be a term of years lease because the parties expressly refer to the lease as a "term of years" lease in the lease. The parties' characterization, however, is not controlling if the lease fails to meet the requirements for the leasehold. Although the parties call the lease a term of years, the end date cannot be determined on the first day of the lease, so there is no fixed term. The lease provides that it is to run from January 1 until December 31 of each year, but there is no fixed year when it will end. Instead, the lease is a periodic lease. The issue is of which fixed period: month-to-month or year-to-year. The rent is stated annually to be paid monthly. The lease is ambiguous. In resolving ambiguities in the term of a periodic lease, courts often look to the nature of the use of the property as circumstantial evidence of the likely intent of the parties. Generally courts construe ambiguous residential periodic leases to be month-to-month. The prior clause in the lease, however, expressly indicates that the parties intended the lease to run from the first day of each year until the last day of each year. This express intent should control to resolve the ambiguity in favor of a periodic tenancy from year-to-year.

Answer (A) is incorrect because a term of years lease requires that the last day of the lease can be calculated on the first day. Here, since the lease fails to indicate the year in which the lease is to terminate, the last day cannot be calculated. The lease is not a term of years lease regardless of the fact that the parties expressly called it a term of years lease: substance over form. Answer (C) is incorrect because although courts generally construe ambiguous residential periodic leases to be month-to-month, on the assumption that that is probably what the parties intended, here the parties expressly provided that the period was to run from the first of each year to the last of each year. Express intent should control over presumed intent. Answer (D) is incorrect because both the terms of the instrument and the payment of rent demonstrate a periodic nature to the lease. Even if the lease lacked an express periodic term, most courts will boot strap a tenancy at will into a periodic lease based upon the periodic payment of rents. Answer (E) is incorrect because a holdover tenancy arises when a tenant wrongfully remains in possession after termination of the lease. Since the lease is a periodic tenancy, termination would require proper notice. There is no evidence that any notice at all has been given. (Complaining about the smoke does not constitute notice to terminate.) Since the lease has not been properly terminated, Ali cannot be a holdover tenant.

- **Additional references**: *See* 2 RICHARD R. POWELL, POWELL ON REAL PROPERTY ch. 16, §§ 16.03[4], 16.04[1]-[3] (Patrick J. Rohan ed. 1999); WILLIAM B. STOEBUCK & DALE A. WHITMAN, THE LAW OF PROPERTY §§ 6.14, 6.16 (3d ed. 2000); 4 THOMPSON ON REAL PROPERTY, § 39.05(a)-(b)(3) (2004 & Supp. 2006).

10. **The best answer is (C).** At common law, a tenant's principal recourse against a landlord was to claim constructive eviction under the covenant of quiet enjoyment. If the landlord breached a duty the landlord owed to the tenant, and the conditions which arose as a result of the breach were so egregious as to seriously interfere with the beneficial enjoyment of the property or render the property substantially unsuitable for the purposes for which they were leased, the tenant could claim constructive eviction. Under constructive eviction, the tenant had to give the landlord notice of the problem, give the landlord reasonable time to remedy the situation, and then, if the problem were not fixed, vacate in a timely manner.

The tenant could claim breach of the covenant of quiet enjoyment, however, only if the landlord was responsible for the condition - i.e., if the condition arose as a result of the landlord's breach of a duty owed to the tenant. The duty could either be an express duty set forth in the lease, or one of the implied duties at common law: duty to disclose latent defects about which the landlord knew or should have known; duty to maintain common areas; duty to make any promised repairs or repairs the landlord voluntarily undertakes; duty not to fraudulently misrepresent the condition of the property; duty to maintain furnished dwellings leased for short terms; and duty to abate immoral conduct or nuisances which arise on property owned by the landlord.

The facts fail to indicate whether there are any express duties under the terms of the lease, so Ali's only option is to invoke one or more of the implied duties. With respect to the view being blocked, the only possible argument Ali can make is that the building constitutes a nuisance. Not very likely. With respect to the noise, Ali would have to argue that the noise constitutes a nuisance. Depending on how loud the noise is and how constant the noise is, Ali might have a chance. With respect to the smoke, Ali can invoke the duty to abate nuisances and the duty to maintain common areas. Whether the smoke rises to the level of a nuisance is questionable but arguable.

The stronger argument appears to be that the landlord has failed to maintain the common areas. Under a traditional common law approach, however, most jurisdictions require not only that the tenant give notice to the landlord, but if the landlord fails to cure the problem, that the tenant move out. Ali has not moved out. Even if the jurisdiction does not require the tenant to vacate, proving that the smoke and/or noise seriously interfere with the beneficial uses of the property, and that blocking the view renders the apartment substantially unsuitable for the purposes for which it was rented, is an uphill battle.

The illegal lease doctrine applies to violations of a local housing code which exist on the first day of a lease which the landlord knew or should have known existed, and which render the premises unsafe. None of the conditions existed on the first day of the lease, and it is questionable whether any of the conditions violate local housing codes. The illegal lease doctrine is not a viable option for Ali.

Under frustration of purpose, the tenant is relieved of the tenant's duty to pay rent if the purpose of the lease is illegal or if conditions arise which render it impossible for the tenant to use the premises for the purposes leased. The traditional scenario is where there is a change in the law which renders the intended use illegal, or where there is an unforeseen and drastic change in the condition of the premises which renders the intended use impossible.

Ali would have a difficult time meeting the traditional standard. Ali's intended use is not illegal, nor is it likely that she can establish that it is impossible to accomplish the use. Although the blocked view frustrates Ali, it does not render use of the apartment impossible for living purposes. Moreover, although the noise and smoke are bothersome and arguably even damaging, it arguably would be quite a stretch for a court to conclude that either of these conditions render it impossible to use the apartment. Ali has an argument under frustration of purpose, but it arguably is not her strongest argument because of the high threshold courts have traditionally applied to find the intended use frustrated.

The implied warranty of habitability arguably gives a tenant the greatest protection. The tenant's duty to pay rent is contingent upon the landlord's duty to deliver and maintain habitable premises. What constitutes "habitable" varies from jurisdiction to jurisdiction, but the general consensus appears to be what a reasonable person would consider acceptable. Conditions which do not amount to a nuisance or even a breach of local housing codes can render the premises "uninhabitable." Although Ali arguably has no argument that the loss of the view renders the premises uninhabitable, she has a strong argument that the presence of the smoke in her apartment and the noise from the construction may render the apartment uninhabitable. Moreover, Ali is not required to move out to assert her rights under the implied warranty of habitability. Ali's best chance of prevailing is under the implied warranty of habitability.

Answer (A) is incorrect because to show a breach of the covenant of quiet enjoyment, the tenant must prove that the condition is so severe as to constitute a constructive eviction, that the condition was caused by the landlord breaching a duty he or she owed the tenant, and in most jurisdictions, the tenant had to vacate the premises. Although Ali has an argument that the smell of smoke in the common areas breaches the landlord's duty to maintain the common areas, there is serious doubt as to whether the problem rises to the level of a constructive eviction, and even if so, there is no evidence that Ali has vacated. Although Ali has a claim under the covenant of quiet enjoyment, it is probably not her best chance. **Answer (B) is incorrect** because the illegal lease doctrine applies to violations of a local housing code which exist on the first day of a lease which the landlord knew or should have known existed and which render the premises unsafe. None of the conditions existed on the first day of the lease, and it is questionable whether any of the conditions violate local housing codes. **Answer (D) is incorrect** because frustration of purpose requires that the change in conditions render the premises impossible to use for their intended purpose. Despite the annoyances and problems, the apartment is still substantially suitable for living in, its intended purpose.

- **Additional references**: *See* 2 RICHARD R. POWELL, POWELL ON REAL PROPERTY ch. 16B, §§ 16B.03[1][a]-[b]16B.04[2][a]-[b] (Patrick J. Rohan ed. 1999); 5 THOMPSON ON REAL PROPERTY, SECOND THOMAS EDITION §§ 40.22(c)-40.22(c)(7), 40.23(c)(6), 40.23(c)(8)-(c)(8)(vi)(E) (1994 & Supp. 2006); WILLIAM B. STOEBUCK & DALE A. WHITMAN, THE LAW OF PROPERTY §§ 6.27, 6.30-6.33, 6.38 (3d ed. 2000).

11. **The best answer is (D).** This is a tough question, arguably better suited for an essay question than multiple choice.

At common law, the law of finders turned on whether the property was lost or mislaid, and whether the property was found in a public or private location. Lost property found in a public area went to the finder - to reward the finder for coming forward with the find. Lost property found on private property went to the owner of the private property to deter trespass and to protect landowner's expectations. Mislaid property went to the owner of the property where it was found, be it private or public, on the assumption that the owner of mislaid property was more likely to retrace his or her steps in searching for the property.

Many have criticized the common law distinction between lost and mislaid property. The critics argue that owners of *lost* property are just as likely as the owners of *mislaid* property to retrace their steps in an effort to locate lost property. Moreover, if finders of property know the rule that property characterized as mislaid gives the finder no rights to the property, finders would be more reluctant to come forward with the found property, thereby destroying any chance of getting the property back to its true owner.

In addition, many have criticized the lost-mislaid distinction as arbitrary. Lost property is property which the true owner unintentionally relinquishes possession of - usually not realizing it. Mislaid property is property which the true owner intentionally relinquishes possession of, but with the intent to return and pick it up later. The distinction between lost and mislaid property then turns on the intent of the true owner. Yet, the problem is no one knows who the true owner is. How is one to determine the true owner's intent at the time the true owner relinquished possession? The courts assume the true owner's intent from the circumstances surrounding the property when it is found. That, however, assumes that the property has not been moved or changed in any way since it left the true owner's possession.

As applied to the facts of the problem, it is unclear whether the property is lost or mislaid. The true owner may have intentionally placed the money on the chair while removing something else from the safe deposit box and then forgot to pick the money up and put it back in the box; or the money may have fallen out of the true owner's pocket onto the chair.

Assuming the money were characterized as lost, was it found in a public or private location? The Bank generally is open to the public, but access to the safe deposit area is restricted and heavily guarded, arguably making it private. But is it private to protect the Bank's expectations or to protect the safety and privacy of the public who use the area? Arguably the latter, so the Bank's expectations with respect to property found in that area arguably is no different from property found in any other area of the Bank. Moreover, Doris was not trespassing when she found the money, although the Bank could argue that Doris was permitted into that area for a limited purpose - to open and remove items from her safe deposit box only, not other property.

Strong arguments can be made for each party. Under such circumstances, however, a stronger argument can be made that the benefit of the doubt should go to the finder, because if finders are not rewarded for coming forward with their find, there is little chance of the property ever getting back to the true owner. The relevant public policy considerations support awarding the money to Doris.

Answer (A) is incorrect because it is an overstatement. Although the general rule is that the finder has superior title over all but the true owner, that is not always true. A prior finder will prevail over a subsequent finder, and if the property is found in on private property, usually the owner of the property where the item is found will prevail. The statement that a finder has superior title over all but the true owner does not help resolve who has a superior title under these facts. **Answer (B) is incorrect** because it presumes that the money was mislaid. Arguments can be advanced on both sides factually, and legally the distinction between lost and mislaid property can be attacked. To the extent that the proper characterization is ambiguous, arguably doubts should be resolved in favor of the finder. **Answer (C) is incorrect** because the expectations of the landowner are protected only if the property is found on private property. Here, it is unclear whether the location of the find should be characterized as private or public. Although the area where the money was found was a guarded and secure area, the purpose for the security appears to have been more to protect the customers who used that area and their privacy than to promote the private property rights of the Bank. In addition, to the extent that the proper characterization of the locale where the property was found is unclear, arguably, doubts should be resolved in favor of the finder.

- **Additional references**: *See* 2 THOMPSON ON REAL PROPERTY, SECOND THOMAS EDITION §§ 13.04(e)-(e)(2) (2000 & Supp. 2006); RALPH E. BOYER ET. AL., THE LAW OF PROPERTY: AN INTRODUCTORY SURVEY § 1.3 (4th ed. 1991); RAY A. BROWN, THE LAW OF PERSONAL PROPERTY 24-29 (Walter B. Raushenbush 3d ed. 1975).

12. **The best answer is (D).** Although Alice holds no interest in lot 1 in 1999, under the principle of relativity of title, the party in possession has rightful claim to the property until the true owner comes along and asserts his or her superior rights. Alice thinks she is the true owner and is acting as a true owner would in conveying property interests in the land to other parties. Similarly, Bob's interest in the property is rightful against all but Alice, since he takes subservient to her, and the true owner.

The issue is the extent of Bob's interest. A license, an easement, and a profit are all similar in that the holder of each has the right to enter another's land and use it in a way which would otherwise constitute trespass. Each involves a right to use the servient estate, but not to possess it. Each, however, has an additional key attribute. A license is not considered an interest in land and is revocable. An easement is considered an interest in land and is irrevocable. A profit is coupled with an interest in the land, one which typically permits the holder of the interest to remove something attached to the servient (burdened) estate.

Here, Bob has the right "to cut trees in an environmentally friendly manner and haul them away." Since the right to use is coupled with the right to remove something attached to the land, Bob's interest is most accurately described as a profit.

Answer (A) is incorrect because it overlooks the principle of relativity of title. Although Alice is not the true owner, since she is in possession of the property, she has superior rights to all but the true owner. Unless and until the true owner asserts his or her rights, Alice is regarded as and treated as the true owner. She has the right to convey property interests which are consistent with the extent of her interest. **Answers (B) and (C) are incorrect** because they fail to reflect the full extent of Bob's interest. Bob not only has the right to enter the servient estate, which looks like either a license or an easement (more likely an easement since in light of the consideration the right to enter is irrevocable by Alice at least for the extent of the agreement), Bob also has the right to remove property from the premises. Neither a license nor an easement includes the right to remove property from the premises.

- **Additional references**: *See* 8 THOMPSON ON REAL PROPERTY, SECOND THOMAS EDITION §§ 65.04(a), 65.05 (2005 & Supp. 2006); WILLIAM B. STOEBUCK & DALE A. WHITMAN, THE LAW OF PROPERTY §§ 1.3, 8.1 (3d ed. 2000).

13. **The best answer is (D).** This is a tough question, arguably better suited for an essay question than multiple choice. Strong arguments can be made for each party. On balance, however, Alice has the stronger claim.

Alice will claim lot 2 based on adverse possession. To prove adverse possession, there must be actual entry which gives rise to possession which is open and notorious, adverse, under claim of right, exclusive, and continuous for the statutory period.

Actual entry is necessary to start the statute of limitations on the true owner's cause of action for ejectment. Alice entered in 1998.

Exclusive possession is necessary to indicate that the adverse possessor is acting like a true owner in excluding others. Her possession was exclusive in that neither the true owner, Ollie, nor anyone else was on lot 2 during her period of possession. In addition, in granting Bob the profit to lot 1, she showed that she regulated possession of the other lots which she claimed, thereby acting as a true owner would.

The adverse element requires that the adverse possessor not be on the property subservient to the true owner. Alice's possession is adverse in that it is without the consent of the true owner, Ollie.

Claim of right focuses on the state of mind of the adverse possessor. Most jurisdictions follow the objective approach, which regards the state of mind of the adverse possessor as irrelevant as long as the other elements are satisfied. The objective approach emphasizes the adverse possessor's actions as opposed to his or her state of mind. The objective approach is consistent with the statute of limitations approach to adverse possession which focuses on the inaction of the true owner and punishes him or her for sleeping on his or her rights. Claim of right is not really an element under the objective approach. Some jurisdictions take the subjective approach to claim of right, inquiring into the state of mind of the adverse possessor. Under the 'good faith' approach, the adverse possessor must have thought that he or she owned the property in question. A handful of jurisdictions require the 'aggressive trespasser' state of mind - the adverse possessor must know it is not his or her property and yet intend to claim it anyway. Based on the deed from Zack which purported to convey lots 1-3 to Alice, Alice was a good faith trespasser, but Alice would not satisfy the claim of right requirement if the jurisdiction follows the aggressive trespasser approach.

The adverse possession must be open and notorious so as to give the true owner notice of the adverse possessor. The possession need be only as open and notorious as an ordinary owner would use similar property. Here, since the property is undeveloped mountain property, Alice's camping and hiking on the property may be sufficient, especially since Alice left an improvement on the property, the hut. Although the hut is not a house, it arguably is sufficient in light of the nature of the property. If Ollie had walked the property, Ollie would have seen the hut and had notice that someone was living on the property. Moreover, Alice harvested the wild berries which grew on the lots. Although the open and notorious element is debatable, Alice appears to have satisfied her burden.

The element most in doubt, however, is the requirement that the adverse possession be continuous. First, Alice is not there every day, but only on weekends and holidays. The adverse possession need only be as continuous as an owner of similar property would be on his or her property. The property is heavily wooded, mountainous land near Yosemite. That area is very popular for hiking and camping. There is no evidence that any neighbors live year round on the property. Alice's sporadic use is probably continuous enough to demonstrate her exercise of dominion over the land.

The more difficult question is whether Alice's prolonged absence due to her injury constitutes an interruption which requires the statute of limitations to start over. Although at first blush that would appear to be the case, the situation can be analogized to where an adverse possessor is ousted from the property by one who does not have a superior title. Although the adverse possessor is not in actual possession, as long as the adverse possessor's absence was involuntary and the adverse possessor never relinquished her claim to the property, the adverse possessor is still acting like a true owner even though not in possession. To the extent that may appear unfair to the true owner, the statute of limitations can be tolled while Alice is comatose. Even assuming she does not receive credit for the time she was in the coma, she adversely possessed lot 2 continuously from 1998 to 2004 - 4 years, and from January 2006 to May 2007 - another year and 5 months. Alice has possessed the land continuously for over 5 years. She arguably has the strongest claim to lot 2.

An adverse possession who meets the requirements of the doctrine receives title to the land which the adverse possessor actually possessed. If, however, the adverse possessor possessed the land under color of title, the adverse possessor receives title not only to the land actually possessed, but also to the land constructively possessed under color of title. Color of title is where a defective instrument purports to convey title to a grantee, and the grantee enters and actually occupies part of the land described in the defective instrument. If the adverse possessor's occupation under color of title satisfies the requirements for adverse possession, he or she gets title not only to the land actually possessed, but also the land constructively possessed - subject to certain restrictions set forth in the answer to question 14, below.

Here, Alice entered lot 2 under color of title - the defective deed from Zack. Alice has satisfied the adverse possession requirements as to the portion of lot 2 where she maintained her hut. Having satisfied the requirements as to part of lot 2, under color of title, Alice receives title to all of lot 2.

Answer (A) is incorrect because the adverse possessor's possession need only be as open and notorious as other owners in the area use their property as long as it is sufficient to put the true owner on constructive notice that the land is being possessed. Here, since the property was heavily wooded, Alice's camping and hiking on the property may be sufficient, especially since Alice left an improvement on the property, the hut. If Ollie had walked the property, he would have had sufficient opportunity to discover her. In addition, Alice gets credit for Bob's actions, which also arguably constitute constructive notice. **Answer (B) is incorrect** because the adverse possessor's possession need only be as continuous as an ordinary owner holding similar property would use the land. There is no evidence that any of the surrounding owners used their property any more, or even as much as, Alice used the property in question. Her weekend and vacation use of the property should be adequate. **Answer (C) is incorrect** because her absence from the property was not voluntary, and her improvements and Bob's use of the property continued while she was in the coma. The purpose of the continuous requirement is to make sure the true owner would have an opportunity to detect the adverse possessor if the true owner were to check on the property during the statutory period. If Ollie had checked on the land, Ollie would have discovered the adverse possession. Alice should not be required to start the statute of limitations all over again when she comes out of her coma and begins using the property again, since her absence was involuntary and she never relinquished her claim to the property.

- **Additional references**: *See* 16 RICHARD R. POWELL, POWELL ON REAL PROPERTY ch. 91, §§ 91.02-91.08 (Patrick J. Rohan ed. 1999); 10 THOMPSON ON REAL PROPERTY, SECOND THOMAS EDITION §§ 87.05-87.13 (1998 & Supp. 2006); WILLIAM B. STOEBUCK & DALE A. WHITMAN, THE LAW OF PROPERTY § 11.7 (3d ed. 2000).

14. **The best answer is (A).** An adverse possessor who satisfies the requirements for adverse possession receives a new title to the property by operation of law which relates back to the date the adverse possessor entered the property. The title covers only the property the adverse possessor actually possessed, unless the adverse possessor claims the property under color of title. Color of title is when the adverse possessor enters the property in reliance upon a written instrument which purports to convey title to the adverse possessor but is defective for some reason. Under color of title, the adverse possessor receives not only the property which he or she actually possessed, but also the property constructively possessed by virtue of the terms of the written instrument. If, however, the written instrument purports to convey more than one deed, constructive possession applies only to those lots which are contiguous and which are owned by the same party.

Here, Alice entered lot 2 under color of title - the deed from Zack which purported to convey title to lots 1-3 to Alice. The deed was defective because Zack did not own any of the property. Under color of title, Alice can claim not only the section of lot 2 which she actually possessed, but all the rest of lots 1, 2 and 3 based on the constructive possession under the terms of the deed. All three lots are contiguous, and when Alice entered, they were owned by the same party, Ollie. At first blush it would appear Alice is entitled to all 3 lots under color of title. In 2000, however, Ollie conveyed lot 3 to Cindy.

Normally, the adverse possessor adversely possesses against the state of title as it exists on the day the adverse possession starts, and subsequent transfer by the owner does not affect the running of the statute of limitations. The problem with applying that rule to this scenario, however, is that there is no evidence Alice ever entered lot 3. And when Ollie conveyed title to lot 3 to Cindy, Cindy went into actual possession of lot 3. There is no way Cindy could have known of Alice's claim to lot 3. Cindy had no grounds to sue Alice for ejectment. Moreover, one of the basic principles underlying the doctrine of adverse possession is that actual possession (by the adverse possessor) trumps constructive possession (by the absent true owner). Consistent with that principle, Cindy's actual possession trumps Alice's constructive possession. Accordingly, Alice's claim to lot 3 based on constructive possession under color of title fails.

Answer (B) is incorrect because Cindy does not need protection under the recording act. Cindy purported to take her title from Ollie, who was the rightful owner. Cindy is claiming under first in time, first in right. Cindy will prevail unless Alice can rightfully claim title under adverse possession. Even under adverse possession, however, Alice's claim to lot 3 is based on constructive possession. Cindy's actual possession trumps Alice's claim to lot 3 based on constructive possession. Cindy does not need recourse to the recording acts. **Answer (C) is incorrect** because Alice's claim to lot 3 is based on color of title. Color of title gives the adverse possessor not only the land which the party has actually possessed, but also the land which the party has constructively possessed pursuant to the terms of the written instrument. Here, however, Cindy's actual possession of lot 3 based upon her deed from the rightful owner, Ollie, trumps Alice's constructive possession claim. **Answer (D) is incorrect** because Ollie was the first in time, first in right owner of the property. Cindy's claim to title is based upon Ollie's claim to title. Cindy is claiming the land based on first in time, first in right. The fact that Cindy entered lot 3 after Alice entered lot 2 is not controlling on the issue of first in time, first in right.

- **Additional references:** *See* 16 RICHARD R. POWELL, POWELL ON REAL PROPERTY ch. 91, §§ 91.07-91.08[2] (Patrick J. Rohan ed. 1999); 10 THOMPSON ON REAL PROPERTY, SECOND THOMAS EDITION §§ 87.04, 87.07 (1998 & Supp. 2006); WILLIAM B. STOEBUCK & DALE A. WHITMAN, THE LAW OF PROPERTY § 11.7 (3d ed. 2000).

15. **The best answer is (C).** If Alice successfully claims adverse possession (see answer to question 13), since she is claiming under color of title (see answer to question 14), she is entitled not only to the property which she actually possessed, but also the property which she constructively possessed by virtue of the deed she received from Zack.

Alice can claim lot 1 under color of title. Although Bob occasionally entered lot 1, thereby raising questions as to whether Alice's possession of lot 1 was exclusive, Bob entered lot 1 subservient to Alice. He purchased the profit from her and from 1999 to 2002 entered lot 1 subservient to Alice's superior right to lot 1. Not only does Bob's possession from 1999 to 2002 not create problems for Alice's claim to lot 1, Bob's possession only strengthens Alice's claim since she receives credit for Bob's actions. By regulating the access to and use of lot 1, and by putting it to productive use, Alice is acting as a true owner would act. In 2002, however, Bob moves onto lot 1. His possession of lot 1 is inconsistent with the scope of the profit Alice granted Bob. At this point, Bob is trespassing and no longer is acting subservient to Alice. Bob's claim for adverse possession arguably starts at that point.

In response, however, Alice can invoke the disability statute. Although it might appear strange at first blush for an adverse possessor to be invoking the disability statute, notice the statute protects the party who has a cause of action to recover possession. As between Alice and Bob, Alice has superior rights to the property under first in time, first in right, and therefore has a right to eject Bob even if she were not the true owner. Moreover, if an adverse possessor's claim is successful, under the relation back doctrine, the title which the party receives by operation of law dates back to the date when the adverse possession began. Since Alice was successful in claiming adverse possession, Alice's title dates back to 1998, the date Alice entered lot 2. Under the relation back doctrine, when Bob starts adversely possessing lot 1 in 2002, Alice arguably is the true owner.

Under the disability doctrine, if the true owner has a qualifying disability on the day the adverse possession begins, the statute of limitations is tolled until the disability is removed, and then the true owner has two more years within which to bring the cause of action for ejectment. Qualifying disabilities under the statute include imprisonment, being a minor, and unsound mind. The question is whether Alice's coma qualifies as "unsound mind." Assuming that the court construes unsound mind to protect the true owner's interests and consistent with the equities of the case, Alice's coma should qualify. Alice came out of the coma in January of 2006. She has until January of 2008 to bring her cause of action for ejectment. Alice arguably has the strongest claim to lot 1.

As for Bob's improvements, the general rule is still the common law rule. Under the common law rule, improvements made by a trespasser belong to the landowner regardless of whether the improvements were made in good faith or bad faith. (Under the modern trend, an innocent improver is entitled to either remove the improvement or receive compensation for the improvements, but a bad faith improver does so at his or her own risk). Here, Bob knew that he did not have permission to claim title to lot 1. Bob was an aggressive trespasser. Accordingly, under either the common law or the modern trend, he improved the property at his own risk and is not entitled to either remove the improvements or receive compensation for them.

Answer (A) is incorrect because Alice can claim lot 1 under color of title. Assuming that Alice's claim of adverse possession as to the property which she actually possessed is successful, she can successfully claim all of lot 1 under color of title based on the defective deed which she received from Zack. **Answer (B) is incorrect** because it implicitly misstates the rule regarding an adverse possessor's rights to remove improvements when the adverse possessor's claim is unsuccessful. To the extent that Bob's claim of adverse possession to lot 1 is unsuccessful, Bob has no right to remove his improvements. (Although under the modern trend, a good faith adverse possessor is entitled to remove the improvements or is entitled to compensation, Bob knew that he had no right to move onto the property and make improvements. A bad faith improver is not entitled to remove the improvements or to compensation.) **Answer (D) is incorrect** because it fails to properly analyze the issue of permission. There are varying degrees of permission, and when one who enters with permission exceeds the scope of the permission, the party is acting as a trespasser or adverse possessor if he or she remains in possession. Although Bob entered with permission pursuant to the profit, when he moved onto the property he knowingly exceeded the scope of his permission and became an adverse possessor. **Answer (E) is incorrect** because Alice can invoke the disability doctrine as against Bob, even though she is not the rightful owner, because the statute protects one with a cause of action for ejectment. Under relativity of property rights, as the first in time, first in right adverse possessor, Alice has a cause of action against Bob to regain possession. Assuming Alice's coma constitutes a qualifying disability, she has 2 years after the removal of her disability, or until May 2008, to bring her cause of action.

- **Additional references:** *See* 16 RICHARD R. POWELL, POWELL ON REAL PROPERTY ch. 91, § 91.10[3], 9 POWELL ch. 64A, ¶ 707.3[1][c][iii] (Patrick J. Rohan ed. 1999); 10 THOMPSON ON REAL PROPERTY, SECOND THOMAS EDITION §§ 87.12, 87.18 (1998 & Supp. 2006); RALPH E. BOYER ET. AL., THE LAW OF PROPERTY: AN INTRODUCTORY SURVEY §§ 4.8, 4.9 (4th ed. 1991).

16. **The best answer is (A).** A general warranty deed contains the usual six covenants (the present covenants of seisen, right to convey, and covenant against encumbrances, and the future covenants of general warranty, quiet enjoyment, and further assurances). The grantor covenants not only his or her actions, but also the actions of all prior grantors in the property's chain of title. A special warranty deed contains the same six covenants, but the grantor warrants only his or her actions, not the actions of any prior grantors.

Inasmuch as Zack did not have title to the property when he purported to sell it to Alice, the temporal scope of both a special and a general warranty deed would cover Zack's wrongful conduct. Do Zack's actions constitute a breach of the present covenants, the future covenants or both? The present covenants are breached by the mere existence of a superior property interest at the time of conveyance. The future covenants are breached by the *assertion* of a superior property interest. Here, when Zack purported to convey the property to Alice, Ollie held a superior claim to the property. The present covenants were breached at the time of conveyance. Assuming that Alice learned of this in 1999 and Ollie had not yet asserted his superior title, there is no breach of the future covenants. Ollie has not yet asserted his superior title.

Answers (B), (C) and (D) are incorrect because there is no breach of the future covenants until the superior title is asserted. In 1999, no one with a superior title to Alice's is asserting title. Alice cannot sue for breach of the future covenants. **Answers (B) and (C) are incorrect** also because Alice can sue for breach of the present covenants whether the covenant is a general warranty or a special warranty deed. Both types of deeds contain the present covenants of siesen and right to convey which are breached when one purports to convey title to which the party has no rights. **Answer (E) is incorrect** because the existence of a superior property interest constitutes such a cloud on the title which the grantor has purported to convey, the grantee is entitled to recover all or a portion of the consideration paid for the property. With respect to present covenants, damages are presumed even in the absence the superior title being asserted - though most courts award nominal damages only.

- **Additional references**: *See* 14 RICHARD R. POWELL, POWELL ON REAL PROPERTY ch. 81A, § 81A.03[1][b][1]-[iii], 81A.06[4][a] (Patrick J. Rohan ed. 1999); 11 THOMPSON ON REAL PROPERTY, SECOND THOMAS EDITION §§ 94.07(b)(1)-(b)(2)(1), 94.07(c)(2) (2002 & Supp. 2006); WILLIAM B. STOEBUCK & DALE A. WHITMAN, THE LAW OF PROPERTY § 11.13 (3d ed. 2000).

17. **The best answer is (B).** To convey a property interest, there must be a writing which complies with the statute of frauds and there must be delivery. The deed which O executed appears to comply with the statute of frauds (there are no facts which give rise to a reason to doubt that it complies with the statute of frauds). Delivery occurs when the grantor intends to relinquish control over the property in question. A deed need not be recorded to be effective. If the grantor gives the deed to the grantee, there is a presumption that there is delivery.

Here, O gave the deed to A, and there is no reason to doubt that O intended to relinquish control of lot 1 when O gave the deed to A. Delivery has occurred. A owns lot 1. The deed which conveyed lot 1 to A expressly retained an easement to cross lot 1 for O, the grantor. Although a property interest generally cannot be created in a stranger to the deed, a grantor can reserve a newly created property interest in him or herself. When O conveyed lot 1 to A, O expressly reserved an easement to cross lot 1. There should be no problem with the creation of the easement.

The problem is that the deed creating the easement is not recorded. When A purports to convey lot 1 to B free and clear of any easements, A does not have that ability. O holds an easement under first in time, first in right under the express terms of the O to A deed. B can receive lot 1 free and clear of O's superior property interest only if B qualifies for protection under the jurisdiction's recording act. Under a notice recording act, B must qualify as a subsequent bona fide purchaser without notice of the prior property interest. The A to B conveyance is subsequent to the O to A conveyance, and B gave valuable consideration, so B qualifies as a subsequent purchaser. The question is whether B is without notice of the easement.

There are three possible types of notice. Notice can be either actual notice, inquiry notice, or constructive notice. There is no evidence that B had actual notice of O's easement. A properly recorded deed puts the whole world on constructive notice of the property interests set forth in the deed. Since the O to A deed was not recorded, B is not on constructive notice of O's easement. Inquiry notice is notice which arises from facts which put a reasonable person on notice that he or she should inquire further into the state of the affairs. As part of record notice, a subsequent grantee is charged with whatever would be found if the grantee conducted a proper search of the grantee-grantor index. If B had searched the grantee-grantor index, B would not have found the O to A deed.

While that means that B would not have constructive notice of O's easement, it also means that B would be on constructive notice that O is the record owner of lot 1, not A. B would be on inquiry notice to inquire as to the basis of A's claim to the property. A reasonably diligent inquiry would have lead B to ask A the basis of A's claim, which no doubt should have resulted in A showing B the unrecorded deed from O to A. At that point, at a minimum B would have inquiry notice as to the contents of the deed from O to A, and more likely B would have actual notice of O's easement which is set forth in the deed from O to A. So although B does not have record notice of O's easement, at a minimum B should have inquiry notice of O's easement.

Answers (A), (C) and (D) are incorrect because they implicitly conclude that O's express easement has been extinguished. A deed is valid even though not recorded, so the easement O reserved is valid even though the deed from O to A is not recorded. The issue is whether the failure to record means that B is entitled to protection under the recording act as a subsequent bona fide purchaser without notice. A's failure to record creates a hole in A's chain of title which puts B on constructive notice that O is the record owner of lot 1. The discrepancy between O's record title and A's claimed title at a minimum puts O on inquiry notice to determine the extent of the parties' interests. If B fails to investigate, B would be charged with notice of O's easement; and a diligent investigation would reveal the O to A deed with the express easement. A's failure to record the deed creates inquiry notice under these facts. **Answer (C) is also incorrect** because to have an implied easement by necessity, one parcel of land must be landlocked following its severance from another parcel of land. When O sold lot 3, lots 2 and 4 were not landlocked because O retained the right to cross lot 1 to access lots 2 and 4. (At common law, access via a navigable waterway also constituted access sufficient to defeat a claim of easement by necessity.) **Answer (D) is also incorrect** because to have an implied easement based upon prior existing use, continuance of the use must be necessary following severance of the land. Here, O will have an extremely difficult time attacking O's own deed claiming an implied reservation across lot 3 in light of O's express right to cross lot 1. Arguably, O has no need to continue to cross lot 3, O can cross lot 1.

- **Additional references:** *See* 4 RICHARD R. POWELL, POWELL ON REAL PROPERTY ch. 34, §§ 34.07-34.08[3], 14 POWELL §§ 82.02[1][d][ii]-[iii](Patrick J. Rohan ed. 1999); 7 THOMPSON ON REAL PROPERTY, SECOND THOMAS EDITION §§ 60.03(b)(4)-(b)(5)(iii), 11 THOMPSON §§ 92.15(b)-92.15(c)(2) (2006); WILLIAM B. STOEBUCK & DALE A. WHITMAN, THE LAW OF PROPERTY §§ 11.10, 8.4-8.5 (3d ed. 2000).

18. **The best answer is (B).** Where a contract is silent as to the quality of title to be delivered by the seller, the default quality of title is marketable title. Marketable title is title which is free from unreasonable doubt and free from unreasonable risk of litigation. The quality of title which is required under a contract, however, is up to the parties to the contract.

Here, the contract expressly called for marketable title subject to "all restrictions and easements of record applying to the property." Although O's recorded restriction on what may be built on lot 3 ordinarily would constitute a recorded encumbrance which would render title unmarketable, the contract has expressly waived D's right to object to the title on the basis of any and all restrictions and easements of record. C is able to deliver the quality of title called for in the contact, so D has no grounds to object.

Answer (A) is incorrect because the height restriction qualifies as an equitable servitude which will run with the land to remote grantees. An equitable servitude runs with the land if the original parties to the covenant intended for the covenant to run to remote grantees, if the covenant touches and concerns the land, and if the remote grantee had notice of the covenant. The intent that the covenant run to remote grantees is evidenced by the express language in the deed which provides that the height restriction "is to run with the land conveyed, ..." The covenant is a negative servitude which restricts how the burdened estate may be used. Typically negative servitudes are held to touch and concern the land, since they restrict how the land may be used. D, the remote grantee, has notice of the covenant because the deed creating the equitable servitude was properly recorded, thereby putting the whole world on notice of the covenant. The covenant qualifies as an equitable servitude and runs to and binds D, the remote grantee.

Answer (C) is incorrect because frustration of purpose requires either that the seller knew that the buyer had only one intended purpose or that both parties assumed that there would be no problem with the intended use. There is no evidence that C knew that D had only one intended purpose or that both parties assumed that there would be no problem with D's intended use. D is still free to use the premises for any use which does not exceed the height restriction. The land is still capable of being put to many economic uses. D is not entitled to prevail under frustration of purpose under these facts.

Answer (D) is incorrect because it fails to take into account that the contract did not call for marketable title, but rather marketable title subject "to all restrictions and easements of record applying to the property." Although the recorded encumbrance normally would have made the title unmarketable and permitted the buyer to rescind the contract, since D waived all recorded restrictions and easements as grounds for rescinding the contract, D has no basis to complain.

- **Additional references**: *See* 14 RICHARD R. POWELL, POWELL ON REAL PROPERTY ch. 81, §§ 81.03[6], 81.03[6][a], 81.05[7][a] (Patrick J. Rohan ed. 1999); 11 THOMPSON ON REAL PROPERTY, SECOND THOMAS EDITION §§ 91.09(a)(6), 91.09(a)(3) (2002 & Supp. 2006); WILLIAM B. STOEBUCK & DALE A. WHITMAN, THE LAW OF PROPERTY § 10.12 (3d ed. 2000).

19. **The best answer is (D).** At common law, a property interest could not be conveyed to a stranger to the deed. The benefit of a restrictive covenant could only be retained by the grantor and/or the lands retained by the grantor. Under this general rule, the grantor and any subsequent grantees from the grantor would be the only parties with standing to enforce the restrictive covenant.

A number of jurisdictions, however, use the common scheme approach to determine who has standing to enforce an express restrictive covenant. A common scheme exists if the owner of two or more lots, so situated as to bear the relation, sells one or more with express restrictions which benefit the lots retained by the owner, the restriction becomes mutual and is implied back against the lots retained by the owner. The doctrine is a very fact sensitive equitable doctrine designed to protect the reasonable expectations of the other purchasers. Generally, well over half the pertinent lots must have the express restriction the plaintiff is asking the court to imply, and the common scheme starts with the first lot sold with the restriction.

Here, O owns 4 lots. Only lot 3 is restricted. The remaining lots do not appear to be so situated as to bear the relation to justify implying the restriction back against the lots retained by the grantor. And even if a court were so inclined, lot 1 was sold before lot 3 with the express restriction. Inasmuch as lot 1 would not be mutually restricted, the owner of lot 1 would not have the benefit of the restriction either.

The only chance B has to enforce the restrictive covenant against D is if the jurisdiction applies the third party beneficiary approach to determine who has standing to enforce the covenant. Consistent with the modern trend contractual approach to property rights, the third party beneficiary approach reasons that the grantor may extend the benefit of the covenant to any surrounding property owners the grantor wishes to benefit by the restriction. This approach repudiates the old common law rule that a property interest could not be conveyed to a stranger to the deed. Under the third party beneficiary approach, if the grantor intends for other property owners to benefit from the restriction, such property owners have standing to enforce the restrictive covenant.

Inasmuch as the purpose of the restriction was to "maintain to the extent reasonably possible the beautiful views of the ocean and mountains that run along the shoreline" it would appear that B, as a neighbor to D whose view would be obstructed by the apartment complex, has standing to enforce the restrictive covenant under the third party beneficiary approach.

Answer (A) is incorrect because it fails to take into account the modern trend, third party beneficiary approach to determining who has standing to enforce an equitable servitude. Under the third party beneficiary approach, if the grantor intends for the benefit of the covenant to flow not only to the grantor and grantor's retained lands, but also to surrounding lands, the owners of those surrounding lands also have standing to enforce the covenant. B arguably has standing to enforce the covenant under a third party beneficiary approach. **Answer (B) is incorrect** because under the common law approach to who has standing to enforce an equitable servitude, only the grantor or the lots retained by the grantor have standing to enforce an express restriction. Since B owns lot 1, which was sold before the express restriction was created, B would have no standing under the common law approach. **Answer (C) is incorrect** because the facts do not support the existence of a common scheme. There are only four lots, and one has the express restriction in question. Moreover, even if there were a common scheme, it is generally held to start with the sale of the first lot burdened with the express restriction in question. B owns lot 1, which was sold before lot 3, the lot expressly restricted. Even assuming a common scheme were to exist, lot 1 is not part of the common scheme since it was sold prior to the first lot with the express restriction. **Answer (E) is incorrect** because B lacks standing under the common law approach and the common scheme approach. B has standing only in those jurisdictions which recognize the modern trend, third party beneficiary approach.

- **Additional references**: *See* 9 RICHARD R. POWELL, POWELL ON REAL PROPERTY ch. 60, §§ 60.04[2][c], 60.03 (Patrick J. Rohan ed. 1999); 7 THOMPSON ON REAL PROPERTY, SECOND THOMAS EDITION §§ 62.07, 62.14 (2006); WILLIAM B. STOEBUCK & DALE A. WHITMAN, THE LAW OF PROPERTY §§ 8.17, 8.32 (3d ed. 2000).

20. **The best answer is (A).** Title insurance generally insures the party purchasing the policy against defects in the public records. Accordingly, a standard title insurance policy covers chain of title defects and recorded encumbrances (unless expressly excepted out), but not unrecorded encumbrances (such as easements not shown by public records). Under the facts, the first issue is whether there is any type of chain of title defect or recorded encumbrance concerning Greenacres which could be the basis of a title insurance claim.

An easement by necessity arises when an owner severs part of his or her property and conveys it to a third party, and as a result of the severance, one of the parcels of land is landlocked. There is a strong presumption that the parties did not intend for the parcel to be landlocked, and there is a strong public policy interest against permitting land to be landlocked. Accordingly, in most jurisdictions, an easement by necessity will be implied across the parcel from which the landlocked parcel was severed.

When Owner conveyed the eastern half of Greenacres to Purchaser, the half retained by Owner (the western half) became landlocked. To prevent the parcel of land from becoming landlocked, an easement by necessity is implied across the parcel from which it was severed - the eastern half. That defect in the title, however, is not discernable from a search of the records at the recorder's office. Such a defect could only be ascertainable following a physical inspection of the properties. An implied easement by necessity constitutes an unrecorded encumbrance which is not covered by title insurance.

The duty to search and disclose places a burden on the title insurance company to perform a reasonable search of the public records and to disclose to the insured any reasonably discoverable information which the search uncovers which might affect the insured's decision to close on the contract to purchase the property. The insurance company has the duty to disclose the defect even if the insurance company thinks the defect is so minor that the insurance company is willing to insure against it and even if the defect is one which should be discoverable upon a reasonable inspection of the property.

As applied to the facts of the problem, because the defect (the implied easement by necessity) arises by operation of law and is not discoverable during a search of the documents at the recorder's office, the search and disclose duty does not affect the insurance company's liability. The title insurance company is not liable either in contract or in tort for a defect which cannot be discovered from a search of the chain of title in the recorder's office.

Answer (B) is incorrect because tort duty to search and disclose places a burden on the title insurance company to perform a reasonable search of the public records and to disclose to the insured any reasonably discoverable information which the search uncovers which might affect the insured's decision to close on the contract to purchase the property. Here, the easement arose by operation of law and would not be discoverable upon a reasonable inspection of the public records. Since the easement is not discoverable, the title insurance company has no duty to disclose it. **Answer (C) is incorrect** because title insurance generally insures the party purchasing the policy against chain of title defects and recorded encumbrances (unless expressly excepted out), but not unrecorded encumbrances (such as easements not shown by public records). Since the easement here arose by operation of law, it constitutes an unrecorded encumbrance which is not covered by the standard title insurance policy. **Answer (D) is incorrect** because it merely combines answers (B) and (C), both of which are incorrect. Together the two are still incorrect.

- **Additional references:** *See* 16 RICHARD R. POWELL, POWELL ON REAL PROPERTY ch. 92, §§ 92.04[1], 92.11, 92.12 (Michael Allan Wolf ed., 2000); 11 THOMPSON ON REAL PROPERTY, SECOND THOMAS EDITION §§ 93.05(b)(1)-(5), 93.06(d) (2002 & Supp. 2006); WILLIAM B. STOEBUCK & DALE A. WHITMAN, THE LAW OF PROPERTY § 11.14 (3d ed. 2000).

21. **The best answer is (E).** Fran's claim is that she is not subject to the claimed easement across her half of Greenacres because she is entitled to protection under the jurisdiction's recording act.

Recording acts apply only to property interests which are created by written instruments, not property interests which arise by operation of law. Since the easement in question is an implied easement by necessity, it was not created in the deed which sold the eastern half of Greenacres to Purchaser. The easement arose by operation of law. Thus, the issue of whether Fran has notice of the easement is moot since the recording act does not apply to the implied easement.

Answers (A), (B), (C), and (D) are incorrect because each implicitly assumes, incorrectly, that the recording acts apply to the facts. Recording acts apply to property interests which arise by written instrument. Recording acts do not apply to property interests which arise by operation of law. The recording acts do not apply to the implied easement by necessity because it arises by operation of law.

- **Additional references:** *See* 14 RICHARD R. POWELL, POWELL ON REAL PROPERTY ch. 82, § 82.02[3][ii] (Michael Allan Wolf ed., 2000); 11 THOMPSON ON REAL PROPERTY, SECOND THOMAS EDITION §§ 92.12, 92.12(e) (1994 & Supp. 2006); WILLIAM B. STOEBUCK & DALE A. WHITMAN, THE LAW OF PROPERTY § 11.9 (3d ed. 2000).

22. **The best answer is (D).** Even assuming that Fran takes the eastern half of the property subject to the easement, there is still the issue of the scope of the easement.

An easement appurtenant, which an easement by necessity by definition must be, attaches to every square inch of the dominant estate. The general rule is absent an express provision dealing with the scope of an easement, the scope of use of an easement includes increase in the use necessary to accommodate normal development of the dominant estate. This default rule may be modified if the parties' intent indicates as much.

The issue of the parties' intent as to the scope of the easement becomes more complicated when the easement is implied by operation of law. In such cases, the courts have some difficulty defining the scope of the easement. Many courts define the scope of the easement in relation to the circumstances surrounding the creation of the easement. While that approach works for some issues, it arguably does not work for the issue of future increased use of the dominant estate because it would have the effect of preventing virtually all increased use of the dominant estate. Inasmuch as there is no express provision dealing with the issue of the scope of the easement, the general rule arguably should apply: the scope of use of an easement includes increase in the use necessary to accommodate normal development of the dominant estate. Although increased use which unreasonably damages the servient estate or unreasonably interferes with its enjoyment can be enjoined, such increased use must be grossly excessive relative to the property.

Here Grantee is proposing to subdivide his half into 50, one acre lots for single family homes. Such density hardly seems excessive or unreasonable. Arguably, Fran is not entitled to any relief under the facts.

Answer (A) is incorrect because there is no evidence that Grantee is exceeding the permissible scope of the easement. If Grantee were using the easement to reach land which was not originally part of the dominant estate, and Grantee's use of the easement to reach such land could not be adequately enjoined, the court may enjoin the party's use of the easement altogether. There are, however, no facts to support such use of the easement by Grantee. **Answer (B) is incorrect** because it fails to recognize that an easement appurtenant attaches to every inch of the dominant estate and runs with the dominant estate, not the owner of the dominant estate. The owner of the dominant estate may break up the dominant estate and the easement still attaches to every inch of the dominant estate. The benefit of the easement appurtenant runs with the subdivided lots to the new owners. **Answer (C) is incorrect** because there is no evidence that Grantee is exceeding the permissible scope of the easement. If Grantee were, the traditional and general rule is that the plaintiff is entitled to injunctive relief - although a few modern trend opinions have granted the plaintiff damages instead of injunctive relief where the court reasoned that the equities of the case did not warrant enjoining plaintiff's use.

- **Additional references**: *See* 4 RICHARD R. POWELL, POWELL ON REAL PROPERTY ch. 34, § 34.13 (Michael Allan Wolf ed., 2000); 7 THOMPSON ON REAL PROPERTY, SECOND THOMAS EDITION §§ 60.04(a)(1)(i), 60.04(a)(1)(ii) (2006); WILLIAM B. STOEBUCK & DALE A. WHITMAN, THE LAW OF PROPERTY § 8.9 (3d ed. 2000).

23. **The best answer is (B).** <u>Analysis under the race recording act</u>. When O conveys Malibuacres to A, A receives title to the land under first in time, first in right. Because A fails to record the O to A deed, although A holds title to the land, A's title is vulnerable in that a subsequent party

who takes from O could trump A if the party qualified for protection under the recording act. When O conveys Malibuacres to B, O does not have actual title to convey to B. B can receive good title to the land only if B qualifies for protection under the recording act.

To prevail under a race recording act, the subsequent purchaser has to record before the party who actually received title to the land under first in time, first in right. Under the race approach, it doesn't matter if the subsequent party has notice of the prior conveyance to the first in time party. The fact that B learned of O's prior conveyance to A is irrelevant under the race recording act. The issue is simply who properly records first. B recorded the O to B deed prior to A recording the O to A deed. B has satisfied the requirements of the race recording act and will prevail over A.

Analysis under the notice recording act. When O conveys Malibuacres to A, A receives title to the land under first in time, first in right. Because A fails to record the O to A deed, although A holds title to the land, A's title is vulnerable in that a subsequent party who takes from O could trump A if the party qualified for protection under the recording act. When O conveys Malibuacres to B, O does not have actual title to convey to B. B can receive good title to the land only if B qualifies for protection under the recording act. To prevail under a notice recording act, the subsequent grantee has to be a bona fide purchaser ("BFP") who has no notice of the prior conveyance. Whether the subsequent grantee qualifies as a BFP without notice is tested at the time of closing, for that is when the purchaser gives his or her consideration and is entitled to protection, if at all. Notice can be either actual notice, inquiry notice, or constructive notice.

In analyzing whether B qualifies as a subsequent bona fide purchaser without notice (a BFP), B clearly is the subsequent purchaser. The O to B transfer occurred after the O to A transfer. The issue is whether B is a bona fide ("good faith") purchaser: whether B purchased in good faith and without notice of the prior conveyance from O to A? There is no evidence that B had actual notice of the prior conveyance to A. Although B has a duty to inspect the property prior to purchasing and to inquire as to the extent of the property interest claimed by any parties in possession or to inquire as to any possible property interests disclosed during the inspection, there is no evidence that A was in possession of the property so as to put B on inquiry notice. In addition, because A failed to record the deed from O to A, B was not on record constructive notice. Inasmuch as B is a BFP and did not have notice at the time of closing with O, B is entitled to protection under the notice recording act. The fact that B learned of O's prior conveyance of Malibuacres to A **after** B closed with O is irrelevant. B has satisfied the requirements of the notice recording act and will prevail over A.

Analysis under the race-notice recording act. To prevail under a race-notice recording act, the subsequent grantee has to be a subsequent bona fide purchaser ("BFP") who has no notice of the prior conveyance, and the subsequent grantee has to record prior to the first in time grantee. As established above, B qualifies as a BFP without notice. B also recorded the O to B deed prior to A recording the O to A deed. B meets both prongs of the race-notice recording act and is entitled to protection. B prevails over A under the race-notice approach.

Answers (A), (C) and (D) are incorrect because B prevails over A under all three recording acts. Under the **race approach**, if the subsequent purchaser records prior to the first in time party, the subsequent grantee is entitled to protection. Here, B recorded before A, and B's knowledge of the prior O to A conveyance is irrelevant under the race approach. Under the **notice approach**, if the subsequent purchaser has no notice of the prior conveyance at the time the subsequent grantee gives consideration, the subsequent grantee is entitled to protection. B gave valuable consideration, and at the time B did so, B did not know of A's interest. B's subsequent knowledge is irrelevant. Whether the subsequent grantee knew or should of known is tested at the time consideration is conveyed, not at the time of recording. Under the **race-notice approach**, the subsequent grantee has to qualify as a subsequent purchaser without notice who records before the first in time party. As established above, B had no notice at the time B gave consideration for the property, and B recorded before A.

- **Additional references**: *See* 14 RICHARD R. POWELL, POWELL ON REAL PROPERTY ch. 82, §§ 82.02[1][c][i]-[iii], 82.03[2][b][1] (Michael Allan Wolf ed., 2000); 11 THOMPSON ON REAL PROPERTY, SECOND THOMAS EDITION §§ 92.13(a)-(c), 92.15(b)(2)(A) (2002 & Supp. 2006); WILLIAM B. STOEBUCK & DALE A. WHITMAN, THE LAW OF PROPERTY §§ 11.9-11.11 (3d ed. 2000).

24. **The best answer is (B).** Analysis under the race recording act. When O conveyed Malibuacres to A, A received title to the land under first in time, first in right. Because A failed to record, although A held title to the land, A's title was vulnerable in that a subsequent party who took from O could trump A if the party qualified for protection under the

recording act. When O conveyed to B, O did not have actual title to convey to B. B can receive good title to the land only if B qualifies for protection under the recording act.

To prevail under a race recording act, the subsequent purchaser has to record his or her deed before the party who actually received title to the land under first in time, first in right. A recorded the O to A deed prior to B's recording the O to B deed. B cannot satisfy the requirements of the race recording act. A prevails over B in a race recording jurisdiction.

Analysis under the notice recording act. When O conveyed Malibuacres to A, A received title to the land under first in time, first in right. Because A failed to record, although A held title to the land, A's title was vulnerable in that a subsequent party who took from O could trump A if the party qualified for protection under the recording act. When O conveyed Malibuacres to B, O did not have actual title to convey to B. B can receive good title to the land only if B qualifies for protection under the recording act.

To prevail under a notice recording act, the subsequent grantee has to be a bona fide purchaser ("BFP") who has no notice of the prior conveyance. Whether the subsequent grantee qualifies as a BFP without notice is tested at time of closing, for that is when the purchaser gives his or her consideration and is entitled to protection, if at all. Notice can be either actual notice, inquiry notice, or constructive notice.

B did not have notice of A's interest in Malibuacres. There is no evidence that B had actual notice of the prior conveyance to A. Although B has a duty to inspect the property prior to purchasing and to inquire as to the extent of the property interest claimed by any parties in possession or to inquire as to any possible property interests disclosed during the inspection, there is no evidence that A was in possession of the property so as to put B on inquiry notice. Since A failed to record the O to A deed, B was not on record constructive notice.

Inasmuch as B is a BFP and did not have notice at the time of closing with O, B is entitled to protection under the notice recording act. The fact that A recorded the O to A deed **after** B closed with O is irrelevant under the notice recording act approach. B has satisfied the requirements of the notice recording act and will prevail over A.

Analysis under the race-notice recording act. To prevail under a race-notice recording act, the subsequent grantee has to be a bona fide purchaser ("BFP") who has no notice of the prior conveyance, and the subsequent grantee has to record prior to the first in time grantee. As established above, B qualifies as a BFP without notice. B can satisfy the notice prong of the race-notice recording act. As established above, however, A recorded prior to B. Since B cannot meet both prongs of the race-notice recording act, B is not entitled to protection. A prevails over B under the race-notice approach.

Answer (A) is incorrect because A prevails under the race and race-notice approaches. Under the **race approach**, if the subsequent purchaser records prior to the first in time party, the subsequent grantee is entitled to protection. Here, A recorded before B, so B is not entitled to protection under the race approach. Under the **race-notice approach**, the subsequent grantee has to qualify as a subsequent purchaser without notice who records before the first in time party. Although meets the notice requirements of the notice prong (B had no notice of A's interest at the time B gave valuable consideration), B fails to meet the requirements under the race prong. A recorded before B. B is not entitled to protection under the race-notice approach. **Answer (C) is incorrect** because under the race approach, as established above, A prevails. Moreover, under the **notice approach**, B prevails. Under the **notice approach**, if the subsequent purchaser has no notice of the prior conveyance at the time the subsequent grantee gives consideration, the subsequent grantee is entitled to protection. B gave valuable consideration, and at the time B did so, B did not know of A's interest. Whether the subsequent grantee knew or should of known is tested at the time consideration is conveyed, not at the time of recording. B is entitled to protection under the notice approach. **Answer (D) is incorrect** because under the notice approach, as established above, B prevails.

- **Additional references**: *See* 14 RICHARD R. POWELL, POWELL ON REAL PROPERTY ch. 82, §§ 82.02[1][c][i]-[iii], 82.03[2][b][1] (Michael Allan Wolf ed., 2000); 11 THOMPSON ON REAL PROPERTY, SECOND THOMAS EDITION §§ 92.13(a)-(c), 92.15(b)(2)(A) (2002 & Supp. 2006); WILLIAM B. STOEBUCK & DALE A. WHITMAN, THE LAW OF PROPERTY §§ 11.9-11.11 (3d ed. 2000).

25. **The best answer is (B).** When O conveyed Malibuacres to A, A received title to the land under first in time, first in right. Because A failed to record the O to A deed, although A held title to the land, A's title was vulnerable in that a subsequent party who took from O could trump A if the party qualified for protection under the recording act.

When O conveyed to B, O did not have actual title to convey to B. B can receive good title to the land only if B qualifies for protection under the recording act.

To prevail under a notice recording act, the subsequent grantee has to be a bona fide purchaser ("BFP") who has no notice of the prior conveyance. Whether the subsequent grantee qualifies as a BFP without notice is tested at time of closing, for that is when the purchaser gives his or her consideration and is entitled to protection, if at all. Notice can be either actual notice, inquiry notice, or constructive notice.

B did not have notice of A's prior in time interest in Malibuacres. There is no evidence that B had actual notice of the prior conveyance to A. Although B has a duty to inspect the property prior to purchasing and to inquire as to the extent of the property interest claimed by any parties in possession or to inquire as to any possible property interests disclosed during the inspection, there is no evidence that A was in possession of the property so as to put B on inquiry notice. Since A failed to record the O to A deed, B was not on record constructive notice. Inasmuch as B is a BFP and did not have notice at the time of closing with O, B is entitled to protection under the notice recording act.

The fact that A recorded the O to A deed *after* B closed with O is irrelevant. The requirements of the notice recording act are tested at time of closing. B has satisfied the requirements of the notice recording act and will prevail over A.

When B goes to convey Malibuacres to C, however, C will be on constructive notice of the O to A conveyance since A recorded the O to A deed. If C performs a standard search of the chain of title for Malibuacres, as C is charged with having performed, C would discover the O to A recording. Can A claim superior right to the property over C? No.

To protect B's investment and insure that B can recoup his or her investment, the shelter doctrine provides that once a party claiming protection under the recording act is protected against a first in time, first in right claimant, anyone other than the common grantor who takes from a party protected under the notice recording act is likewise protected even if that party does not qualify for protection in his or her own right under the recording act. The remote grantees are sheltered by the protection which was granted to B, the first party who prevailed under the recording act. The first in time, first in right claimant gets only one shot at perfecting his or her title. If he or she loses, the party cannot come back later and claim first in time, first in right against a subsequent grantee from the protected party (unless the subsequent grantee is the common grantor - in this case O).

Once B trumped A under the recording act analysis, as long as B conveys the property to anyone other than O, the common grantor, the subsequent grantee will be protected against A's claim even though the subsequent grantee has notice of A's claim. To permit A to come back and claim first in time, first in right against subsequent takers from B would effectively bar B from conveying the property. It would effectively make B's triumph over A a hollow victory.

Answer (A) is incorrect because C does *not* qualify as a subsequent bona fide purchaser (SBP) without notice of the prior in time conveyance. C is charged with the knowledge which C would have obtained if C had performed a proper search of the grantor-grantee index prior to closing with B. If C had performed the search, C would have found the O to A deed, thereby putting C on notice of O's conveyance of Malibuacres to A. **Answer (C) is incorrect** because under the notice recording act approach, the party claiming protection does not have to record. Whether the party is entitled to protection is tested at the moment the party gives consideration (typically at closing). The fact that A thereafter recorded before B is not relevant under the notice recording approach. **Answer (D) is incorrect** because if fails to consider the shelter doctrine.

- **Additional references**: *See* 14 RICHARD R. POWELL, POWELL ON REAL PROPERTY ch. 82, §§ 82.02[1][c][ii], 82.03[2][b][1] (Michael Allan Wolf ed., 2000); 11 THOMPSON ON REAL PROPERTY, SECOND THOMAS EDITION § 92.13(b), 92.15(b)(2)(A) (2002 & Supp. 2006); WILLIAM B. STOEBUCK & DALE A. WHITMAN, THE LAW OF PROPERTY §§ 11.9-11.11 (3d ed. 2000).

ANSWER KEY
EXAM VIII

EXAM VIII

1. **The correct answer is (C).** One way to challenge an exclusionary zoning ordinance which has racial implications is to challenge it under the Equal Protection Clause of the 14th Amendment to the United States Constitution. The key is the standard of review the courts will apply in reviewing the ordinance. If the court applies the traditional, rational basis level of scrutiny, the ordinance will invariably be upheld. To get the courts to apply a heightened, strict scrutiny standard of review, the plaintiffs must persuade the courts that the exclusionary zoning involves suspect classifications or infringes upon a fundamental right. As for the former, the most common argument is that exclusionary ordinances are racially discriminatory. The issue here, however, is whether a showing of disparate impact is enough, or must the plaintiffs show a racially discriminatory purpose behind the ordinance.

The Supreme Court has ruled that for purposes of an Equal Protection challenge to an exclusionary zoning ordinance, proof that the ordinance has a racially discriminatory effect is not enough. The plaintiffs must prove a racially discriminatory motive. The Court, however, recognized that direct evidence of discriminatory intent is rare. It ruled that even when an ordinance appears neutral on its face, evidence of a discriminatory intent may be derived from a historical pattern of zoning in the community, from a history behind the challenged ordinance, and from any departures from established policies or procedures.

There is evidence that Valleytown's refusal to rezone the proposed project site has a racially discriminatory effect. That, however, is not enough to subject the exclusionary zoning and the decision not to rezone to a heightened scrutiny standard. There must be evidence of a racially discriminatory intent on the part of Valleytown in refusing to rezone the site of the proposed project. There is no direct evidence of discriminatory intent, nor is there any indirect evidence. The decision not to rezone simply upholds the existing zoning scheme. It does not constitute a significant departure from the established zoning policy, nor is there any evidence of any departures in procedure when considering the request. Although the decision not to rezone has a racially discriminatory effect, the decision is explainable arguably on non-racial grounds: maintaining property values in the surrounding area. ACME Housing cannot show that Valleytown's exclusionary zoning and refusal to rezone are based on a racially discriminatory intent on the part of local officials. ACME Housing can show only that there is a racially discriminatory effect, which is not sufficient.

Moreover, if the plaintiffs were to allege that the exclusionary zoning and the decision not to rezone do not substantially advance a legitimate state interest, the Supreme Court has indicated that where a zoning regulation does not exact a benefit from a landowner and does not amount to a categorical taking (that the governmental action "invades" or "occupies" the landowners' property, or that the governmental action denies the landowners all economically beneficial use of the land), heightened judicial review is inappropriate. Here, there was no exaction, and there is no categorical taking. Accordingly, the deferential, fact sensitive balancing approach is the applicable standard of review. The city has asserted a legitimate state interest - protecting property values - and the exclusionary zoning and decision not to rezone conceivably advance that goal. The burden of proof is on the party challenging the regulation, and ACME Housing cannot carry its burden of proof under the facts.

Answer (A) is incorrect because a racially discriminatory effect, no matter how substantial, is not enough by itself. **Answer (B) is incorrect** because there is no evidence, direct or indirect, that Valleytown's exclusionary zoning and refusal to rezone were based upon a racially discriminatory purpose. The city has a legitimate interest in protecting property values, and there is no reason to believe that that goal is a mere pretext under the facts. **Answer (D) is incorrect** because absent evidence of a categorical taking or an exaction, the courts apply the deferential, fact sensitive balancing approach to the issue of whether the governmental action substantially advances a legitimate state interest. Protecting property values is a legitimate state interest. As long as it is conceivable that the exclusionary zoning and refusal to rezone may advance that goal, the city's actions pass the deferential approach.

- **Additional references:** *See* 12 RICHARD R. POWELL, POWELL ON REAL PROPERTY ch. 79C, § 79C.07[4][b] (Michael Allan Wolf ed., 2000); 8 THOMPSON ON REAL PROPERTY, SECOND THOMAS EDITION §§ 66.05, 74.02(c)(3)(i) (2005 & Supp. 2006); WILLIAM B. STOEBUCK & DALE A. WHITMAN, THE LAW OF PROPERTY § 9.26 (3rd ed. 2000); Arlington Heights v. Metropolitan Housing Development Corp., 429 U.S. 252 (1977).

2. **The best answer is (E).** Property owners have the right to use their property as they see fit, but neighboring land owners and the public have the right to be free from unreasonable uses that substantially interfere with their quiet enjoyment of their surrounding lands. The law of nuisance attempts to balance the rights of property owners to use their land as they see fit and the duty of property owners to use their land so as not to unreasonably interfere with the public and their neighbors' right to use their land as they see fit.

The law of nuisance can be divided between public nuisances and private nuisances. Public nuisances are unreasonable activities which injure the community generally and which are contrary to a public good (the public's health, morals, safety or general welfare), regardless of the activity's effect upon another's ability to use his or her land. On the other hand, private nuisances are those activities which constitute an unreasonable use of one's land which substantially interfere with another individual's use of his or her land.

The law of nuisance becomes even murkier when one considers that private nuisances can be divided between nuisances *per se* and nuisances in fact. Nuisances *per se* are those activities which are so unreasonable that they are unreasonable under any circumstances. The problem is that most activities which rise to the level of a nuisance *per se* are also public nuisances.   Common examples of nuisances *per se* are uses which are illegal, uses which a landowner engages in out of malice towards a neighboring landowner, and uses which are patently contrary to public norms. Activities which fall within these categories usually constitute a public nuisance.   The significance of this overlap between public nuisances and private nuisances *per se* is that, as a general rule, only the government may enjoin a public nuisance. Individual citizens may not enjoin a public nuisance unless they can show extraordinary interference with the use of their land.

As applied to the facts of the problem, however, the subtleties of the difference between a public nuisance and a private nuisance *per se* are irrelevant because keeping a dog kennel is neither. Dog kennels are not intrinsically unreasonable activities which injure the common good, nor are they activities which are unreasonable under any circumstances. Properly built and maintained, dog kennels provide a useful service and promote the public good by taking care of dogs - man's best friend. The issue is whether *this* dog kennel constitutes a nuisance in fact.

The doctrine of nuisance in fact is particularly unwieldy. As its name implies, the essence of the doctrine is simply that *under these particular facts*, the use complained of constitutes a nuisance. The same use may not be a nuisance under certain circumstances, yet not be a nuisance under other circumstances. So when is a use a nuisance? Whenever a court decides that the use unreasonably and substantially interferes with a surrounding landowner's ability to use his or her property. Although the law of nuisance, especially what constitutes "unreasonable use", is extremely fact sensitive, the courts and commentators have tried to put some guidelines on the doctrine. In assessing the reasonableness of the defendant's activity, the Restatement (Second) of Torts recommends that the courts consider: (1) the social value of the defendant's conduct, (2) the suitability of the defendant's conduct to the locality, and (3) the defendant's ability to avoid the interference. In assessing whether the harm to the plaintiff is "substantial," the Restatement (Second) of Torts recommends that the court consider: (1) the duration and degree of the harm, (2) the character of the harm, (3) the social value of the plaintiff's enjoyment, (4) the suitability of the plaintiff's use to the locality, and (5) the burden to the plaintiff to avoid the harm. Moreover, the courts have ruled that the magnitude of the harm should be assessed from the objective perspective of a reasonable person, not one hyper-sensitive to the defendant's use. The key elements of the law of nuisance are obviously very soft, nebulous elements: unreasonable interference, substantial interference, contrary to public good. Because of the nature of the doctrine, its application is extremely fact sensitive.

In assessing the relevant factors, the courts have often found that dog kennels in residential or even semi-residential neighborhoods constitute a nuisance in fact. Despite the social utility of dog kennels, the constant yapping of the animals can make it virtually impossible for neighbors to sleep or even to engage in ordinary outdoor activities without substantial disturbance from the dogs. Kennels with as few as 16 dogs more than 150 yards from the nearest house have been found to constitute a nuisance in fact, even where several neighbors testified that the dogs were no problem. Under these facts, the likely result is that the kennel will constitute a nuisance in fact. Roger and Anita will be enjoined from operating the kennel unless they can successfully abate the noise, odor and other problems.

Answer (A) is incorrect because, although who was there first is a factor to consider, it is not a determining factor. The court has to balance the competing interests and uses of the respective parties. Being there first does not automatically permit one to unreasonably and substantially interfere with surrounding landowners' use of their property. **Answer (B) is incorrect** because the facts do not support the factual conclusion it sets forth. Although the magnitude of the harm should be assessed from the objective perspective of a reasonable person, even using that standard, the noise, odor, and related problems generated by over 100 dogs arguably would be unreasonable and substantial absent extraordinary conditions not evidenced in the fact pattern. **Answer (C) is incorrect** because the mere fact that a use is permitted by local zoning laws does not insulate it from a claim that it constitutes a nuisance in fact. **Answer (D) is incorrect** because a nuisance *per se* is one which constitutes a nuisance under any circumstance. It is easy to envision a scenario where a dog kennel does not constitute a nuisance because of its location. As originally built, there is no evidence that Roger and Anita's dog kennel interfered with the use of the surrounding property. It was not until circumstances in the area changed that it became an issue.

- **Additional references:** *See* 9 RICHARD J. POWELL, POWELL ON REAL PROPERTY ch. 64, §§ 64.01[1], 64.02[2]-64.04[2], 64.05[2], 64.05[6] (Patrick J. Rohan ed. 1999); 11 THOMPSON ON REAL PROPERTY, SECOND THOMAS EDITION §§ 67.02(a), 67.03(a)-(b)(3) (2002 & Supp. 2006); WILLIAM B. STOEBUCK & DALE A. WHITMAN, THE LAW OF PROPERTY § 7.2 (3rd ed. 2000); Tichenor v. Vore, 953 S.W.2d 171 (Mo. App. 1997).

3. **The best answer is (A).** A tenant's ability to terminate a lease prematurely is greatly limited, especially where the leasehold is a term of years. The essence of a term of years is that the lease's beginning and ending dates are fixed at the start of the lease. Although a term of years determinable lease is permitted where the parties expressly provide that the lease may terminate prematurely upon a specific condition occurring, there is no evidence in the facts that the lease was a term of years determinable. Absent the lease expressly authorizing a tenant to prematurely terminate a term of years lease, a tenant's ability to terminate the lease is very limited.

At common law, a lease was viewed primarily as a property conveyance. The tenant was given the exclusive right to possession for the term set forth in the lease. The landlord owed the tenant minimal duties, and in the event the landlord breached a duty he or she owed to the tenant, a cause of action for damages arose against the landlord. A breach generally did not give the tenant the right to terminate the lease. The primary exception to this approach was the covenant of quiet enjoyment. Under the covenant of quiet enjoyment, if the landlord breached a duty which he or she owed the tenant, and as a result of the breach conditions arose which substantially interfered with the tenant's ability to use and enjoy the property, the tenant could claim constructive eviction and vacate the property. When the landlord would sue for rent, the tenant could use the constructive eviction and breach of the implied covenant of quiet enjoyment as a defense. If the tenant were successful, the effect of the doctrine would be that the lease was terminated, and the tenant would have no further liability under the terms of the lease.

Here, however, there is no basis for Roger and Anita to claim breach of the covenant of quiet enjoyment. There is no evidence that the landlord, Mickey, has breached a duty to Roger and Anita which is causing the condition which necessitates their leaving the property. Roger and Anita created the condition. Moreover, Roger and Anita are not being constructively evicted from the land. The land is still useable, just not for the particular purpose that they hoped to use it for - a kennel. There is no basis for claiming breach of the covenant of quiet enjoyment against Mickey, the landlord.

While common law took a traditional, property approach to leases, the modern trend takes much more of a contracts approach. Under the contracts approach, there are a couple of doctrines a tenant may invoke in an attempt to prematurely terminate a term of years lease. The first is frustration of purpose. Under frustration of purpose, if the tenant's use of the property is still legal, but in light of changed circumstances the cost of tenant's use has become prohibitively expensive, the tenant may terminate the lease and avoid any further liability under it. The doctrine has several elements: (1) the tenant's intended use must be the use which is now frustrated, (2) the degree of frustration must be complete or near complete, and (3) the event which caused the frustration must not have been reasonably foreseeable by the parties at the time they entered into the lease. In addition, the courts limit the doctrine to situations where: (1) the lease expressly limits the tenant's ability to use the property to the frustrated use, or (2) the landlord knew of the tenant's intended use.

At first blush it would appear as if Roger and Anita could successfully invoke the contract doctrine of frustration of purpose. First, Roger and Anita leased Pongoacres for the purpose of building and maintaining a kennel for the dogs. That purpose has become frustrated in light of the court's finding that the kennel constitutes a nuisance in fact. Second, under the court's finding, Roger and Anita are completely frustrated in their intent to use the property as a kennel for the dogs. As for the final element, that the intervening event was not foreseeable by the parties, arguments can be made on both sides of this element. The arguments, however, are moot in light of the fact that courts limit the frustration of purpose doctrine to situations where (1) the lease expressly limits the tenant's ability to use the property to the frustrated use, or (2) the landlord knew of the tenant's intended use. There is nothing to indicate that the lease expressly limits the use to which Roger and Anita may put the land. Moreover, there is no evidence that Mickey knew of their intended purpose. Under the circumstances, it is unlikely that a court would apply the frustration of purpose doctrine.

The other contract doctrine which courts are applying to leases with increasing frequency under the modern trend approach is supervening illegality. The doctrine of supervening illegality provides that where the lease restricts the tenant's use of the property to one use, and that use becomes illegal after execution of the lease, effectively depriving the tenant of all use of the land, the tenant is relieved of his or her obligations under the terms of the lease. Roger and Anita, however, will not be able to invoke the doctrine successfully. Although the court's nuisance in fact ruling arguably makes what was their legal use illegal, effectively depriving them of *that* use of the land, the lease does not expressly limit their use to a kennel. Roger and Anita are free to use the land for other, legal purposes. Under the circumstances, the doctrine of supervening illegality does not help Roger and Anita.

Under either the property based, common law approach or the contract based, modern trend approach, Roger and Anita are not entitled to terminate the lease prematurely just because their kennel has been found to constitute a nuisance in fact.

Answer (B) is incorrect because it implicitly misapplies the modern trend approach. Although the contracts based, modern trend approach to leases is more willing to permit a tenant to terminate a lease prematurely under frustration of purpose or supervening illegality, both doctrines require either that the lease expressly limits the permissible use to the frustrated/illegal use or that the landlord knew of the tenant's specific purpose. Here, there is no evidence that Mickey knew that Roger and Anita intended to use the land as a kennel, and there is no evidence that the lease expressly limited the use of Pongoacres to a kennel. **Answer (C) is incorrect** because it confuses the common law and modern trend approaches. The tenant has a better chance under the contracts based, modern trend approach than he or she has under the property based, common law approach. Nevertheless, even under the contracts based, modern trend approach the most likely result is that the tenant will not be able to terminate the contract prematurely. **Answer (D) is incorrect** because it implicitly misstates both the common law and modern trend approaches to the issue. Under the common law, Roger and Anita would not be able to prove the Mickey, the landlord, breached the covenant of quiet enjoyment; and under the modern trend Roger and Anita would not be able to show frustration of purpose or supervening illegality since they can still use the land for other purposes (and Mickey did not know of their particular intended use).

> • **Additional references**: *See* 2 RICHARD J. POWELL, POWELL ON REAL PROPERTY ch. 16B, §§ 16B.07[2][a]-[b], 16B.04[1]-[2] (Patrick J. Rohan ed. 1999); 5 THOMPSON ON REAL PROPERTY, SECOND THOMAS EDITION §§ 40.16(b), 40.17, 40.23(c)(8)-(c)(9) (1994 & Supp. 2006); WILLIAM B. STOEBUCK & DALE A. WHITMAN, THE LAW OF PROPERTY §§ 6.28, 6.33, 6.87 (3rd ed. 2000).

4. **The best answer is (E).** In a typical loan transaction, the borrower executes both a promissory note and a mortgage. The promissory note creates personal liability between the lender and the borrower. The mortgage gives the lender (the mortgagee) a security interest in the property in question which permits the lender to foreclose on the borrower's (mortgagor's) property interest if necessary to satisfy the debt evidenced by the promissory note. Absent express restrictions in the loan documents, the mortgagor can transfer the mortgaged property. The issue is what right, if any, does the mortgagee have following such a transfer by the mortgagor.

When the mortgagor transfers the mortgaged property, the transferee can take the property either "subject to the mortgage" or the transferee can "assume the mortgage." If the transferee "assumes the mortgage," the transferee is agreeing to be personally liable for the outstanding debt underlying the mortgage and can be sued by the mortgagee. If the transferee merely takes the mortgaged property "subject to the mortgage," the transferee is acknowledging that the mortgage is being passed with the property to the transferee, but the transferee is not personally liable for the underlying debt. When a party who is personally liable for the underlying debt transfers the mortgaged property, the party remains personally liable for the underlying debt unless expressly released by the mortgagee.

Under the facts of the problem, Gerri is liable for the debt under the express terms of the promissory note. Although she transferred the mortgaged property, Greenacres, she was not expressly released from the debt. Gerri is still personally liable for the debt to Stagecoach Lenders. So too are any and all subsequent grantees of Greenacres who "assumed the mortgage" when they took the property. Both Carolyn and Paul expressly assumed the mortgage and there is no evidence that either were subsequently expressly released from their liability. Gerri, Carolyn and Paul are all personally liable under the express terms of their respective conveyances.

(Because Paul assumed the mortgage from someone who was not personally liable, some jurisdictions hold that Paul cannot be personally liable on the grounds that the break in personal liability breaks the privity necessary to establish personal liability with the mortgagee. The more likely scenario, however, is to hold Paul liable under a third party beneficiary approach despite the break in privity.)

Answers (A), (B) and (C) are incorrect because each is incomplete. Each answer fails to recognize all the parties that are personally liable under the note either because they were party to the promissory note or they expressly "assumed the mortgage" when they purchased Greenacres. Gerri is personally liable as a party to the note. Both Carolyn and Paul expressly assumed the mortgage. There is no evidence that any of the three were subsequently expressly released from their liability. **Answer (C) is also incorrect, along with answer (D),** because they incorrectly include Kristin as personally liable. When Kristin purchased Greenacres, she agreed to take the property "subject to the mortgage." Taking "subject to the mortgage" recognizes that the property is subject to a pre-existing security interest which has not been completely paid off, but the grantee is not personally assuming, and thus is not personally liable for, the mortgage. Kristin is not personally liable since she did not agree to "assume the mortgage."

- **Additional references:** *See* 4 RICHARD J. POWELL, POWELL ON REAL PROPERTY ch. 37, §§ 37.30[3]-[4] (Patrick J. Rohan ed. 1999); 12 THOMPSON ON REAL PROPERTY, SECOND THOMAS EDITION §§ 101.05(a)(1), 101.05(a)(4)-(a)(5) (1994 & Supp. 2006); RALPH E. BOYER ET. AL., THE LAW OF PROPERTY: AN INTRODUCTORY SURVEY § 18.1 (4th ed. 1991).

5. **The best answer is (C).** Under the power of eminent domain, the government has the power to take property involuntarily from private property owners. Proper exercise of the power of eminent domain requires that the property shall be "taken for public use" and that the aggrieved citizen receive "just compensation." On the other hand, under

the government's police powers, as a general rule the government has the right to regulate the use of private property without compensating the property owner. Where the regulation is excessive, however, it may constitute a taking requiring compensation. Thus, there are basically two possible types of takings: physical (or trespassory) and regulatory (or non-trespassory). An action for inverse condemnation is where a property owners claims that the government has taken property without formally exercising its power of eminent domain and without compensating the property owner as required under the power of eminent domain.

Here, Jessie pleads in the alternative. First, she claims implicitly that the government has no right to take any part of her property because the portion of her property is not being taken for public use as required by the Constitution. The courts have broadly construed what constitutes public use. The Supreme Court has ruled that a taking satisfies the public use requirement as long as it advances a conceivable public purpose, whether that purpose is achieved or not. Here, the purpose of the pathway is to facilitate public access from the Japanese Gardens to the public library, easing traffic congestion. The purpose of the pathway is clearly public, regardless of whether traffic congestion actually is reduced or whether the pathway actually facilitates access between the Gardens and the library.

As for Jessie's inverse condemnation claim, a permanent physical occupation authorized by the government is a classic example of a taking. A taking occurs where real estate is physically invaded by water, earth, sand, artificial structures, and/or people, so as to destroy or impair its use. Where the government physically invades private property without taking title, it has taken part of the property "per se" and must pay for it, no matter how trivial the invasion. The government has taken the landowner's right to exclude and has physically invaded the property.

There is no doubt that the government has "taken" some of Jessie's property. The government concedes that about one yard of its pathway crosses onto Jessie's property. As to that one yard, Jessie has lost her right to exclude. The government has physically invaded her property. Whether the degree of invasion constitutes an easement or a taking of full title, and the fact that the intrusion was over a portion of Jessie's property that Jessie did not occupy, go to the issue of damages/compensation, not the issue of whether there was a taking. No matter how trivial the taking may appear, if there is a permanent, physical taking, the landowner is entitled to compensation.

Answer (A) is incorrect because as long as it is conceivable that the purpose is public, the taking is authorized under the power of eminent domain even if the purpose is not achieved. Here, the purpose of facilitating public access between the Japanese Gardens and the library, and reducing traffic congestion, are public purposes regardless of the number of people who take advantage of the pathway (as long as the pathway is open to the public as opposed to a select few, in which case it would more problematic). **Answer (B) is incorrect** because the power of eminent domain permits the government to take property from private property owners regardless of their wishes or investment backed expectations. A property owner's reasonable, investment backed expectations are relevant where it is unclear whether there is a taking. Here, the taking is a permanent, physical occupation of Jessie's property - a classic example of a taking which the government is entitled to do as long as it is for the public's use and the government compensates the property owner. **Answer (D) is incorrect** because the amount of invasion is of no importance where the invasion is a permanent physical occupation authorized by the government. The pathway permanently crossing Jessie's land is a taking.

- **Additional references:** *See* 12 RICHARD R. POWELL, POWELL ON REAL PROPERTY ch. 79B, §§ 79B.01[1]-[2], 79B.03, 11 POWELL ch. 79, § 79.03[2] (Michael Allan Wolf ed., 2000); 9 THOMPSON ON REAL PROPERTY, §§ 80.03(a)-(e), 80.05(b)(2), 81.03-81.04(b) (1999 & Supp. 2006); RALPH E. BOYER ET. AL., THE LAW OF PROPERTY: AN INTRODUCTORY SURVEY § 12.2 (4th ed. 1991).

6. **The best answer is (D).** Under the power of eminent domain, the government has the power to take property involuntarily from private property owners. Proper exercise of the power of eminent domain requires that the property be "taken for public use" and that the aggrieved citizen receive "just compensation." On the other hand, under the government's police powers, as a general rule the government has the right to regulate the use of private property without compensating the property owner. Where the regulation is excessive, however, it may constitute a taking requiring compensation. Thus, there are basically two possible types of takings: physical (or trespassory) and regulatory (or non-trespassory).

An action for inverse condemnation is where a property owners claims that the government has taken property without formally exercising its power of eminent domain and without compensating the property owner as required under the power of eminent domain.

Here, Jessie pleads that the public's use of the pathway rises to the level of a taking. The problem is that Jessie can show neither that the government's actions amount to a physical (trespassory) taking or that they amount to a regulatory (non-trespassory) taking. The evidence clearly states no part of the pathway crosses onto or encroaches upon Jessie's property. There is no physical invasion or occupation of any portion of Jessie's property. Nor is the government regulating the use of Jessie's property. The government is merely using the adjacent land. The negative consequences generated by the public using the pathway do not constitute a taking. While it may appear unfair that Jessie's profits have dropped so significantly as a result of the public footpath, the fact of the matter is that there has not been a taking in this instance - either physical or regulatory. The government has merely constructed a footpath on what is already public property. The government has not, therefore, taken Jessie's property and does not owe her compensation for her loss.

Answers (A) and (B) are incorrect because they implicitly rely upon doctrines which do not apply to the facts. Where the government is accused of a regulatory taking, its regulation of the property may be excessive if: (1) the government regulation compels the landowner to permit a permanent physical "occupation" or "invasion" of the land, or (2) the regulation denies the landowner all economically beneficial or productive use of the land. Here there is no regulation of Jessie's land. The government's use of the adjoining property does not constitute either a physical invasion of Jessie's land or a regulatory taking which denies Jessie of all economically beneficial use of the land. **Answer (C) is incorrect** because it similarly assumes that the cause of the problem is the government's regulation of the affected property. The facts do not involve either a physical or a regulatory taking.

- **Additional references**: *See* 12 RICHARD R. POWELL, POWELL ON REAL PROPERTY ch. 79B, §§ 79B.01[1]-[2], 79B.03, 11 POWELL ch. 79, § 79.03[2] (Michael Allan Wolf ed., 2000); 9 THOMPSON ON REAL PROPERTY, SECOND THOMAS EDITION §§ 80.03(a)-(e), 80.05(b)(2), 81.03-81.04(b) (1999 & Supp. 2006); RALPH E. BOYER ET. AL., THE LAW OF PROPERTY: AN INTRODUCTORY SURVEY § 12.2 (4th ed. 1991).

7. **The best answer is (B)**. Zoning laws are intended to segregate incompatible property uses. Incompatible property uses are those which local planning officials and city councils deem incompatible and which are incorporated into the jurisdiction's zoning ordinance. The

assumption underlying zoning laws is that certain types of property uses give off what an economist would call an externality - a by-product which is not fully internalized by the use. Factories typically emit noise and air pollution which is incompatible with residential uses. The noise and air pollution constitute negative externalities relative to typical residential uses. The premise of zoning law is that by segregating different incompatible uses, the overall use of the land is maximized and negative externalities are minimized. Zoning laws also seek to protect public benefits and/or to maximize the value of property in a given area. The best way to achieve these goals is to separate incompatible uses.

Zoning laws typically begin by segregating uses into at least three basic groups: residential, commercial, and industrial. Residential use is typically considered the "highest" use. These larger groupings are then typically broken down into more specific categories relating to the type and/or density of use within the grouping. For example, within residential use, single-family housing is typically considered the highest use, then two-family homes, then apartments, etc. After residential use comes commercial use, and then industrial use. Within the commercial bracket, there may be further breakdowns, such as convenience shops, shopping centers and overall commercial districts. Industrial use is "lower" than commerce use, and industrial use also has its further subdivisions. The governmental entity in charge of zoning typically breaks the land within its jurisdiction up into various districts and zones based upon what its planners, after carefully studying the situation, determine to be the optimal use for that district (taking all relevant factors and the overall zoning scheme into consideration).

Once an area is zoned into different districts, the zoning can be of two types: exclusionary or cumulative. Exclusionary zoning, as its name implies, is zoning which permits only the type of use for which the district is zoned. All other uses are excluded, even if the other use is a "higher" or lighter use. On the other hand, cumulative zoning permits not only the specifically zoned use, but any and all "higher" uses. Under cumulative zoning, uses which are "higher" are permitted, but not "lower" uses. For example, under exclusionary zoning, if a district is zoned commercial, only commercial uses are permitted in that district. Residential uses are excluded, even though they are a "higher" use. On the other hand, under cumulative zoning, if a district is zoned commercial, commercial and/or residential uses are permitted. Residential uses are permitted because residential use is a "higher" use. "Lower" uses are still not permitted though. Industrial uses would not be permitted in the commercial, cumulative district. Just as cumulative zoning is permitted between groupings, cumulative zoning is permitted within sub-categories to groupings.

Here, the district is zoned for apartments, and the zoning is cumulative. That means that other residential uses which are "higher" are permitted, but not any "lower" uses (commercial or industrial). Therefore C's apartment building is allowed to be there. Under the cumulative uses rule, A and B would also be allowed to be in that district, because both types of housing are "higher" residential uses than the apartment. D and E's uses, however, are both commercial uses. Commercial uses are "lower" uses than the apartment residential zoning. D and E's uses are not permitted in the apartment zoning district even under the cumulative approach.

Answer (A) is incorrect because it excludes C, who is actually the only person who is definitely allowed to be in the district regardless of whether cumulative uses are permitted. **Answer (C) is incorrect** because it is not complete. It does not take into consideration the call of the question, which specifically addressed cumulative uses, and would therefore include A and B. **Answer (D) is incorrect** because it excludes A and B and also because it permits D to remain in the district. D is not legally entitled to be in an apartment district, because his commercial convenience shop is a "lower" use than the housing scheme. **Answer (E) is incorrect** because it similarly allows E to be in the district even though he owns a car lot, a commercial use which is also a "lower" use than the housing scheme.

- **Additional references:** *See* 12 RICHARD R. POWELL, POWELL ON REAL PROPERTY ch. 79C, § 79C.04[1][a] (Michael Allan Wolf ed., 2000); WILLIAM B. STOEBUCK & DALE A. WHITMAN, THE LAW OF PROPERTY § 9.10 (3rd ed. 2000); RALPH E. BOYER ET. AL., THE LAW OF PROPERTY: AN INTRODUCTORY SURVEY p.452 (4th ed. 1991).

8. **The best answer is (B).** When a mortgagee forecloses, the foreclosure wipes out all junior property interests. A junior property interest is any property interest which is created after the time the mortgage was created (unless the later in time property interest qualifies for protection under the jurisdiction's recording act, in which case it is treated as if it were a senior property interest). Senior property interests are those which were created before the mortgage was created. Senior property interests, if properly recorded, are not affected by foreclosure and the purchasing party takes subject to the senior property interests.

Alice's mortgage with Bank of Finance is the first in time property interest. Because Bank properly recorded the mortgage, no junior property interests can qualify for protection under the jurisdiction's recording act. When Bank of Finance forecloses on the mortgage, it will wipe out all the junior property interests. Betsy's lease is a junior property interest because it was created subsequent in time to the properly recorded mortgage. Even though Betsy recorded her lease, she was on notice that the title was subject to the first in time mortgage to Bank of Finance and that if Bank foreclosed, her interest would be wiped out. Betty was properly joined in the foreclosure action, so her leasehold interest is wiped out.

Although the foreclosure wipes out Betsy's lease, she has a claim against Alice for breach of the covenant of quiet enjoyment. The covenant of quiet enjoyment is implied in virtually every lease. It provides that the landlord warrants that the tenant's possession and quiet enjoyment of the leased premises shall not be disrupted by the landlord or anyone claiming title through or paramount to the landlord's. Generally a landlord is not responsible for the acts of a third party which disrupt the tenant's quiet enjoyment of the premises. If, however, the third party is asserting a superior right to possession to the premises, the landlord is liable for breach of the covenant of quiet enjoyment.

When Alice defaulted on her loan with Bank of Finance, under the terms of the mortgage Bank had a right to foreclose on the property, wiping out all junior property interests. Once the Bank forecloses, it holds a paramount claim to title and possession. Betsy's quiet enjoyment was breached when the Bank asserted its superior right. Because the third party which disrupted Betsy's quiet enjoyment has a superior right to title and possession, Alice is liable for the eviction. Alice is liable for breaching the covenant of quiet enjoyment.

Answer (A) is incorrect because although landlords generally are not responsible for the acts of third parties which disrupt a tenant's quiet enjoyment, landlords are responsible for the acts of third parties who hold a superior right to title and/or possession. When the Bank foreclosed on the property, the Bank held a superior right to title and acquired a superior right to possession. Alice is liable for breach of the covenant of quiet enjoyment. **Answers (C) and (D) are incorrect** because when a properly recorded, first in time, first in right mortgagee forecloses, the foreclosure wipes out all junior in time property interests, regardless of whether the junior interest is recorded or whether the foreclosing party has notice of the junior property interests. Because

Bank properly recorded its mortgage, a subsequent in time grantee could not qualify for protection under any approach to the recording acts. The Bank's foreclosure wiped out Betty's lease.

- **Additional references:** *See* 4 RICHARD J. POWELL, POWELL ON REAL PROPERTY ch. 37, §§ 37.37[6]-[7], 14 POWELL, ch. 82, §§ 82.02[1][c][i]-[iii], 82.02[1][d][ii], 82.03[2][a]-[b][ii], 2 POWELL, ch. 16B, § 16B.03[1] (Patrick J. Rohan ed. 1999); 12 THOMPSON ON REAL PROPERTY, SECOND THOMAS EDITION §§ 101.04(b)(1)-(3), 11 THOMPSON §§92.13(a)-(c), 92.15(b), 5 THOMPSON §§ 40.22(c)(1), 40.22(c)(4) (1994 & Supp. 2006); GRANT S. NELSON & DALE A. WHITMAN, REAL ESTATE FINANCE LAW §§ 7.11-7.14 (3d ed. 1994); WILLIAM B. STOEBUCK & DALE A. WHITMAN, THE LAW OF PROPERTY §§ 11.9-11.11, 6.30-6.31 (3rd ed. 2000).

9. **The best answer is (C).** Property owners have the right to use their property as they see fit, but neighboring land owners and the public have the right to be free from unreasonable uses that substantially interfere with their quiet enjoyment of their surrounding lands. The law of nuisance attempts to balance the rights of property owners to use their land as they see fit and the duty of property owners to use their land so as not to interfere unreasonably with the public and their neighbors' right to use their land as they see fit.

The law of nuisance can be divided between public and private nuisances. Public nuisances are unreasonable activities which injure the community generally and which are contrary to a public good (the public health, morals, safety or general welfare), regardless of the activity's effect upon another's ability to use his or her land. Private nuisances are those activities which constitute an unreasonable use of one's land which substantially interfere with another individual's use of his or her land.

The law of nuisance becomes even murkier when one considers that private nuisances can be divided between nuisances *per se*, and nuisances in fact. Nuisances *per se* are those activities which are so unreasonable that they are unreasonable under any circumstances. The problem is that most activities which rise to the level of a nuisance *per se* are also public nuisances. Common examples of nuisances *per se* are uses which are illegal, uses which a landowner engages in out of malice towards a neighboring landowner, and uses which are patently contrary to public norms. Activities which fall within these categories usually constitute a public nuisance. The significance of this overlap between public nuisances and private nuisances *per se* is that, as a general rule, only the government may enjoin a public nuisance. Individual citizens may not enjoin a public nuisance unless they can show extraordinary interference with the use of their land.

The local residents claim is that the proposed halfway house constitutes an unreasonable use which substantially interferes with the local residents' use of their property is based upon (1) their fears for their safety, and (2) concern over depreciation in property values. Depreciation in property values, though a factor, is never enough, in and of itself, to constitute a nuisance. The key then is the neighbors' fear of harm. Though fear of harm is a legitimate concern, their fears are based upon pure conjecture and suppositions. The halfway house has not opened yet. The local residents have no factual support for their assumption that the presence of a halfway house will increase criminal activity in the area. Fears and apprehensions based upon speculation rarely justify injunctive relief. Where plaintiffs are seeking *anticipatory* injunctive relief, based upon the mere *threat* of harm as opposed to actual harm, court usually demand proof of a high probability that harm would result without an injunction. The local residents have failed to meet that standard. That is particularly true here, where the proposed use has an offsetting high social benefit.

There is no reason to presume that a properly operated halfway house will increase the crime rate in the surrounding neighborhood. The local residents have failed to present evidence to support their claim of harm. To enjoin a proposed use based on the fear and speculation that a lawful operation will be operated negligently so as to produce harm would be tantamount to deeming the use in question an inherently dangerous activity which constitutes a nuisance per se. Such speculation is unwarranted. Ron and Mary's proposed halfway house is legal and permitted under the local zoning ordinance.

Although at least one court has enjoined the operation of a halfway house under similar facts, most courts have ruled that a proposed halfway house does not constitute a nuisance because there is insufficient evidence that a halfway house in a residential neighborhood will inevitably lead to increased crime. The resident's fear is too speculative, and the social value of preparing parolees for everyday living after release from prison is high.

Answer (A) is incorrect because while depreciation in value is one of the factors to consider when looking at the character of harm, it is not by itself enough to constitute a nuisance. The factor must be coupled with substantial injury to the residents. **Answer (B) is incorrect** because it assumes too much. Fear of harm, while an important consideration, is not *the* controlling factor; it is merely *a* factor. **Answer (D) is incorrect** because the fact that one's use of her land is consistent with a local zoning ordinance is not controlling in an action for private nuisance. Zoning ordinances are not an absolute defense to a private nuisance suit. The legal use may still be unreasonable under the circumstances and constitute a nuisance.

- **Additional references**: *See* 9 RICHARD R. POWELL, POWELL ON REAL PROPERTY ch. 64, §§ 64.02[1]-[4], 64.04[3], (Michael Allan Wolf ed., 2000); 8 THOMPSON ON REAL PROPERTY, SECOND THOMAS EDITION §§ 67.03(b), 67.03(a)(2) (2005 & Supp. 2006); WILLIAM B. STOEBUCK & DALE A. WHITMAN, THE LAW OF PROPERTY § 7.2 (3rd ed. 2000); Nicholson v. Connecticut Half-Way House, Inc., 153 Conn. 507, 218 A2d 383 (1966).

10. **The best answer is (D).** This is a classic example of the problem of the migrating couple. Property is characterized by the law of the state where it is acquired at the time it is acquired. The spousal protection scheme at time of death is determined by the law of the state where the couple is domiciled at time of death.

Here, H and W live in a community property state at the time W acquires the $600,000 which she holds in her name alone. Under community property principles, earnings of either spouse acquired during the marriage are owned jointly by the community the moment the earning is acquired, regardless of how the earnings are held - i.e., in whose name the earnings are held. (Thereafter the couple may expressly change the legal characterization of the property, a process known as transmutation, but there is no evidence to indicate that occurred here.) Although W holds the initial $600,000 in her name alone, the couple owns the $600,000 jointly as community property.

Thereafter the couple moves to Missouri, a separate property jurisdiction. Once property has been legally characterized, the characterization of the property does not change just because the couple moves to another jurisdiction. The $600,000 W acquired in California, a community property state, remains community property even though the couple has moved to Missouri, a separate property jurisdiction. After moving to Missouri, W acquires another $300,000 in earnings. Since Missouri is a separate property jurisdiction, these earnings are W's separate property. W owns all of the $300,000 as her separate property.

Immediately prior to death, W owns $300,000 in separate property, and H and W own $600,000 as community property. Upon the death of a spouse, any and all community property is split 50-50. Both community property and separate property are probate property. Thus, when W dies, her half of the community property and all of her separate property will pass into her probate estate. W's probate estate consists of her half of the community property ($600,000 divided by 2 = $300,000) plus her $300,000 in separate property. There is $600,000 in her probate estate. H holds the other half of the community property, $300,000, as his property.

The marital domicile for W and H at the time of W's death is Missouri, a separate property jurisdiction. The spousal protection scheme in separate property jurisdictions at time of death is the elective share approach. Under the hypothetical Missouri statute, H is entitled to an elective share of 1/3 of W's probate estate. Assuming H asserts his elective share, H is entitled to 1/3 of W's probate estate. Since W's probate estate is $600,000, 1/3 is $200,000. Combining H's half of the community property ($300,000) with H's elective share ($200,000), H ends up with $500,000.

Answer (A) is incorrect because it takes into account H's elective share but fails to include H's half of the community property. **Answer (B) is incorrect** because it takes into account H's half of the community property but fails to include H's elective share. One may also have reached answer (B) incorrectly if one put all of the community property into W's estate and applied the elective share fraction against the full $900,000. The community property is split upon death, with only the decedent's half going into his or her probate estate. The other half is owned outright by the surviving spouse. **Answer (C) is incorrect**, because that is the amount that W's estate ends up with, not H. **Answer (D) is incorrect**, because that is the amount that goes into W's probate estate, not the amount which H can claim. The $600,000 fails to take into account the elective share or the half of community property that the surviving spouse gets independent of the probate estate.

- **Additional references**: *See* 7 RICHARD J. POWELL, POWELL ON REAL PROPERTY ch. 53, §§ 53.03[1], 53.06[4]-[6] (Michael Allan Wolf ed., 2000); 4 THOMPSON ON REAL PROPERTY, SECOND THOMAS EDITION §§ 37.06(a), 37.08(a), 37.16(c) (2004 & Supp. 2006); WILLIAM B. STOEBUCK & DALE A. WHITMAN, THE LAW OF PROPERTY § 5.14-5.15 (3rd ed. 2000).

11. **The best answer is (D).**   The issue is what right, if any, does Owner have to continue to use the road branching off of PCH to access her house after she sells the land along PCH to Developer.   The non-possessory right to enter real property owned by another and use it in a limited way which would otherwise constitute a trespass can be either a license, an easements or a profit. A profit not only permits the grantee to enter the real property of another, it permits the grantee to remove property (crops, minerals, trees, etc. - typically property which is attached to the real property) from the real property. There is no evidence that Owner sought or was granted the right to remove property from the real property Owner conveyed to Developer. Owner's right to continue to use the road is either a license or an easement.

A license is a personal relationship between the grantor and grantee. Arguably the distinguishing characteristic of a license is that it is revocable at will by the owner of the burdened ("servient") estate. A license can become irrevocable, however, if the party who holds the license, with the consent or acquiescence of the party who has granted the license, changes his or her position and makes substantial expenditures in reasonable reliance upon the license. Under such circumstances, the grantor is estopped from revoking the license.

On the other hand, an easement is a more substantive property interest. The key characteristic of an easement is that it is irrevocable. The Statute of Frauds requires that an easement should be created expressly in a written instrument signed by the party to be charged. A license does not create as substantive an interest and thus does not need to be created in writing (though it may be).

Inasmuch as a license and an easement are so similar, it is often difficult to tell which one was created. In analyzing conveyances which are ambiguous, the courts focus on the intent of the parties. Inasmuch as the principal distinguishing characteristic between the two is the revocability of the right, it should control where there is clear intent on that characteristic. Here, Developer expressly told Owner that Owner could "continue to use the road *forever* to access her house." (Emphasis added.) The use of the word "forever" arguably indicates that the parties intended for the use to be non-revocable. This conclusion is also supported by the hardship which would be created if a mere license were created, and Developer were permitted to revoke it or it terminated upon Developer's subsequent conveyance of the servient estate. Owner would have no ready access to her house, and construction of a new road to the house would be extremely difficult, if not practically impossible, due to the terrain going over the Santa Monica Mountains. All things being equal, it appears as though the parties intended that Owner's right to continue to use the road branching off PCH was to be an easement.

The problem, however, with concluding that Owner has an easement is that because an easement is a property interest, an easement should be created expressly in a writing which complies with the Statute of Frauds. The deed transferring Owner's property along PCH from Owner to Developer makes no reference to an easement. There is no express easement. By default that would appear to leave the license as the sole option. But classifying the right as a mere license would appear to do injustice to the intent of the parties. The key to resolving this apparent dilemma (between calling Owner's right a license, which conflicts with the clear intent of the parties, and calling Owner's right an easement, which conflicts with the Statute of Frauds) is to remember that most jurisdictions permit an easement to be implied under appropriate circumstances; and implied easements are not subject to the Statute of Frauds.

An implied easement by necessity arises when an owner of a large parcel of land transfers part of the land, and as a result of the transfer, one of the parcels of land has no access and is landlocked. The courts will imply an easement by necessity across the parcel from which the landlocked parcel was severed. Although the property which Owner still holds after the conveyance to Developer is not legally landlocked, for all practical purposes Owner's house is landlocked. Access to the house across the Santa Monica Mountains is impracticable. Owner can argue that she should be granted an implied easement by necessity across the land conveyed to Developer to reach her house because otherwise her house is, for all practical purposes, landlocked. Inasmuch as Owner has plenty of legal access to the property on which the house sits, however, the argument that the house is landlocked is a stretch.

Another claim Owner can make is that she should be granted an implied easement based upon prior existing use. An implied easement based upon prior existing use arises when an owner who owns a large parcel of land transfers part of the land. If prior to the transfer, (1) the owner held a quasi-easement (whereby the owner used part of her property to benefit another part of her property), (2) the quasi-easement was apparent, and (3) it is reasonably necessary for the quasi-easement to continue after transfer of the parcel, the courts will imply an easement based upon prior existing use. Here, the road traversing Owner's property constituted a quasi-easement (Owner used the parcel along the ocean to access the house). The road was apparent and use of the road to access the house following severance of the parcel along the ocean is reasonably necessary in light of the practical problems inherent in building a new road through the Santa Monica Mountains.

Owner has a stronger claim for an implied easement based on prior existing use as opposed to easement by necessity. Developer assured Owner that Owner could continue to use the road forever after the land along the ocean was severed from the larger parcel and conveyed to Developer. It appears as the parties intended that an express easement be created, but for some reason the express easement was not set forth in the deed. The implied easement based upon prior existing use presumes that the parties intended to put the easement in the deed but simply forgot. That appears to be what happened between Owner and Developer.

Under the modern trend, the courts tend to focus more on the intent of the parties and less on the Statute of Frauds. Under the modern trend approach, a court is more likely to imply an easement based on prior existing use than to apply the Statute of Frauds strictly and hold that Owner has a mere license.

Answer (A) is incorrect because a profit permits the holder of the profit to enter another's real property and remove part of the property. There is no evidence that Owner is removing any part of the real property or anything attached to it, or that the parties intended for Owner to have that right. **Answer (B) is incorrect** because there is no reference to the easement or the road in the deed from Owner to Developer. **Answer (C) is incorrect** because although Owner can make an argument for an implied easement by necessity, technically the land and the house are not legally landlocked. Owner has a stronger argument under the implied easement based upon prior existing use. **Answer (E) is incorrect** because a license is revocable. Although the initial agreement was oral, which arguably supports the claim that the interest is merely a license, Owner has a stronger argument that the parties intended to create an easement but simply forgot to put the easement in the deed. Hence the interest should be an implied easement based upon prior existing use. If, however, the court were a stickler on the Statute of Frauds and construed the deed against the drafter (more the traditional common law approach), there is a good chance the court may conclude that the interest is merely a license.

- **Additional references**: *See* 4 RICHARD R. POWELL, POWELL ON REAL PROPERTY ch. 34, §§ 34.02[1]-[2][b], 34.03, 34.07, 34.08[1]-[3], 34.23, 34.24 (Michael Allan Wolf ed., 2000); 7 THOMPSON ON REAL PROPERTY, SECOND THOMAS EDITION §§ 60.02(a)-(b), 60.02(g), 60.03(a)(5), 60.03(b)(3)-(b)(5)(iii) (2006); WILLIAM B. STOEBUCK & DALE A. WHITMAN, THE LAW OF PROPERTY §§ 8.1, 8.3-8.5 (3rd ed. 2000).

12. **The best answer is (D).** Assuming the easement is an implied easement by prior existing use, the issue is whether the Santa Monica Conservancy takes subject to the easement. Owner will claim the easement under first in time, first in right. The Santa Monica Conservancy will have to seek protection under the jurisdiction's notice recording act.

To prevail under a notice recording act, the subsequent grantee has to be a bona fide purchaser ("BFP") who has no notice of the prior conveyance. Whether the subsequent grantee qualifies as a BFP without notice is tested at the time of closing, for that is when the purchaser gives his or her consideration and is entitled to protection, if at all. Notice can be either actual notice, inquiry notice, or constructive notice. There is no evidence that the Santa Monica Conservancy had actual notice of the easement. The Santa Monica Conservancy is charged with whatever information a proper search of the chain of title would reveal. Since the easement is an implied easement by prior existing use, and not an express easement, the easement was never recorded. The Santa Monica Conservancy does not have record notice of the implied easement.

Prior to purchasing real property, a purchaser has a duty to physically inspect the property. During the inspection, if the purchaser discovers facts suggesting any possible conflicting property interests, the purchaser has a duty to inquire as to the extent of the property interest. When the Santa Monica Conservancy inspected the property prior to purchase, it should have noticed the road running across the property from Pacific Coast Highway to the house and should have inquired as to the extent of the claimed property interests in the road. Inasmuch as the Santa Monica Conservancy was on inquiry notice of the easement, it does not qualify as a subsequent bona fide purchaser without notice. Once a party has inquiry notice of a possible first in time property interest, the party has a duty to perform a diligent search to ascertain the status of the possible superior property interest. The party is charged with whatever knowledge a diligent inquiry would have performed. Here, if the Conservancy had inquired as to Owner's interest in the road, the

Conservancy would have learned of Owner's claimed interest in the road. The Conservancy is not entitled to protection under the recording act.

In addition, recording acts apply only to property interests which arise expressly in a written instrument. One of the purposes of a recording act is to create an incentive for the grantee to record the instrument. Property interests which arise by operation of law are not created by written instruments. The holder of the interest does not have a written instrument to record. Accordingly, even if the Santa Monica Conservancy were to qualify as a subsequent bona fide purchaser without notice of the claimed easement, they would not be entitled to protection because the recording act does not apply to the implied easement since it arises by operation of law.

Answer (A) is incorrect because the Conservancy is on notice of Owner's right to use the road. Prior to purchasing real property, the buyer has a duty to walk the property and is on inquiry notice of any property interest which may be discovered from the inspection of the property. If the Conservancy had walked the property, it would have noticed the road leading to Owner's house, and at a minimum, would have a duty to inquire as to the extent of Owner's interest in the road, if any. **Answer (B) is incorrect** because Owner's right to use the road is not a license (see answer 9 above), and even if it were, Owner has not expended any money in reliance on Developer's permission to use the road (though one could argue that Owner's decision to sell the land to Developer was a change in position in reliance upon the permission to use the road which should be an adequate basis for estoppel). **Answer (C) is incorrect** because the easement was never set forth in a deed, so the issue of whether an easement may be reserved in a stranger to a deed never arises. (Under common law, easements could not be reserved in favor of a stranger to the deed. Under the modern trend, easements may be created in favor of a stranger to the deed.) Moreover, if the easement had been properly reserved in the deed from Owner to Developer, the easement would have been properly reserved in the grantor, not a stranger to the deed.

- **Additional references:** *See* 14 RICHARD R. POWELL, POWELL ON REAL PROPERTY ch. 82, §§ 82.01[2][b], 82.02[1][c][ii], 82.02[1][d][iii], 82.02[1][d][iii][a], 82.03[a] (Michael Allan Wolf ed., 2000); 11 THOMPSON ON REAL PROPERTY, SECOND THOMAS EDITION §§ 92.12(c), 92.12(e), 92.13(b), 92.15(c)(1) (2002 & Supp. 2006); WILLIAM B. STOEBUCK & DALE A. WHITMAN, THE LAW OF PROPERTY §§ 11.9-11.10 (3rd ed. 2000).

13. **The best answer is (A).** Regulatory takings jurisprudence is one of the most difficult areas of the law. The starting point is the Fifth Amendment Takings Clause, which prohibits the government from taking "private property . . . for public use, without just compensation." There are basically two types of governmental takings: trespassory, physical invasions and non-trespassory, regulatory takings. The former are easier to identify and analyze. The latter defy simple analysis. At one end of the spectrum, the government's police powers permit it to regulate land use. At the other end of the spectrum, excessive governmental regulation amounts to a taking. The challenge is to identify when the regulation has crossed that point on the spectrum where it ceases to be regulation and becomes a taking. The Supreme Court has repeatedly stated that whether a particular regulation amounts to a taking is a fact sensitive inquiry which depends upon the circumstances of each case.

Although the Supreme Court has repeatedly stated that whether a particular regulation amounts to a taking depends upon the particular circumstances of each case, a careful reading of the cases reveals at least four basic scenarios in which a taking claim may arise. The significance of the four different scenarios is that the Court has applied four different approaches to the takings analysis depending on the scenario. The first scenario involves a typical zoning ordinance of broad application. Under this scenario, the courts apply an ad hoc, fact sensitive balancing approach. Inasmuch as the government's police powers permit governments to regulate land use, the approach is very deferential to the governmental regulation. The central question is whether the governmental regulation substantially advances a legitimate state interest. What constitutes a legitimate state interest is construed broadly under the government's police powers. The regulation is deemed to substantially advance the interest as long as it plausibly could advance the interest. The state need not prove that the goal is actually advanced. The courts balance the public and private interests at stake, with deference being given to the claimed governmental interests and means. The courts also take into consideration (1) the economic impact of the regulation on the landowner, (2) the extent to which the regulation has interfered with the landowner's distinct investment-backed expectations, and (3) the character of the governmental action (the nature of the claimed taking and the nature of the public interest). If the ordinance appears to unfairly burden an individual property owner, the court may declare the regulation a taking.

The second and third takings scenarios involve what are considered "categorical" takings. The Supreme Court has identified two forms of "categorical" takings where the above described deferential, ad hoc balancing approach is inappropriate. The first is where the governmental regulation compels the landowner to permit a permanent physical "occupation" or "invasion" of the land. In such a case, the nature of the governmental action, a permanent physical "occupation" or "invasion" of the land dictates that the regulation be treated as a trespassory taking. Just compensation is due. The other scenario where the deferential balancing approach is inappropriate is where the regulation denies the landowner all economically beneficial or productive use of the land. In such a case, to the extent the landowner is denied all economically beneficial or productive use of the land, it is as if the landowner no longer owns the land. The regulation is deemed a categorical taking and just compensation is due.

The fourth takings scenario where the Supreme Court has set forth a distinct analysis is the exaction scenario. The exaction scenario arises where the landowner seeks to put his or her land to a legally permitted use, but the government conditions the landowner's ability to engage in that use upon the landowner dedicating some form of property interest to the public. The Supreme Court has ruled that where the governmental action amounts to an exaction, the governmental action is subject to heightened judicial scrutiny. The government must show that an essential nexus exists between the exaction and a legitimate state interest. An essential nexus exists if (1) the record supports a reasonable relationship between the identified public problem and the landowner's proposed use, and (2) the record establishes rough proportionality between the required exaction and the adverse impact of the landowner's proposed use. There is some disagreement over the exact degree of nexus and relationship which must be established, but this approach sets forth the basics of the exaction analytical approach.

In summary, the default judicial approach to takings claims is an ad hoc, deferential balancing approach unless the landowner can come within either the categorical takings scenarios or the exaction scenario.

Turning to the Town's decision to rezone the golf course from residential use to solely recreational use, the first issue is which analytical approach should be applied to the takings claim. Does the rezoning amount to a categorical takings, does it constitute an exaction, or should be it be subjected to the default, deferential balancing analysis? The rezoning does not really "occupy" or "invade" the landowners' property.

Nor does the rezoning deny Tiger all economically beneficial or productive use of the land." Tiger is still free to operate the land as a golf course, no doubt making good money from its operation. He is free to change the use to another recreational use if he wishes. The rezoning does not constitute a categorical taking. Nor does the rezoning involve any exaction. The Town is not requiring Tiger to dedicate any land to public use. The rezoning merely regulates Tiger's use.

Under the balancing approach, the issue is whether the governmental regulation substantially advances a legitimate state interest. The rezoning resembles a classic application of the government's police powers and should be analyzed as such. Does the rezoning substantially advance a legitimate state interest? Legitimate state goals include protecting open space, preserving and promoting recreational opportunities, and controlling flooding risks. Under the traditional, non-heightened standard of judicial review, the regulatory actions of the Town substantially advance a legitimate state interest if the action bears a reasonable relationship to that objective. Rezoning the golf course clearly bears a reasonable relationship to the stated legitimate state interests.

Nor does the rezoning appear to unfairly burden Tiger. Although the ordinance may diminish the value of the property, that is not enough to constitute a taking. Loss of value as a result of governmental regulation which advances a legitimate state interest is not enough to constitute a taking. The courts have denied takings claims where the governmental regulation has caused over an 80% reduction in value to the affected parcel of land. Although extraordinary reduction in value may give rise to a valid takings claim, that does not appear to be the situation here. Although the problem does not set forth the magnitude of the loss of value following the rezoning, it appears highly unlikely that the loss in value is anywhere near that great. The land can still be put to very productive and valuable use as a golf course. The rezoning does not constitute a taking entitling Tiger to just compensation under the Fifth Amendment.

Answer (B) is incorrect because the rezoning clearly does not deny Tiger all economically beneficial or productive use of the land. The rezoning may have decreased the property's value, but Tiger is still permitted to use the property as a golf course or to use the property for any other recreational use. There are still plenty of economically beneficial uses and/or productive uses of the land permitted under the rezoning. **Answer (C) is incorrect** because the rezoning does not "occupy" or "invade" the golf course in any sense of the word. The rezoning merely regulates what Tiger may do with his property, but it does not in any sense permit the government to invade or occupy the land. **Answer (D) is incorrect** because it implicitly applies the heightened judicial scrutiny approach. The "close nexus" heightened judicial scrutiny, however, is limited to cases where the governmental regulation constitutes an exaction and is not applicable to general zoning ordinances.

- **Additional references:** *See* 12 RICHARD J. POWELL, POWELL ON REAL PROPERTY ch. 79B, §§ 79B.05[1]-[2] (Michael Allan Wolf ed., 2000); 8 THOMPSON ON REAL PROPERTY, SECOND THOMAS EDITION § 74.08, 9 THOMPSON §§ 81.04(a)-(i) (2005 & Supp. 2006); WILLIAM B. STOEBUCK & DALE A. WHITMAN, THE LAW OF PROPERTY § 9.4 (3rd ed. 2000); Bonnie Briar Syndicate, Inc. v. Town of Mamaroneck, 94 N.Y.2d 96, 721 N.E.2d 971 (1999).

14. **The correct answer is (A).** Zoning laws are intended to segregate incompatible property uses. Incompatible property uses are those which local planning officials and city councils deem incompatible and whch are incorporated into the jurisdiction's zoning ordinance. The assumption underlying zoning laws is that certain types of property uses give off what an economist would call an externality - a by-product which is not fully internalized by the use. Factories typically emit noise and air pollution which is incompatible with residential uses. The noise and air pollution constitute negative externalities relative to typical residential uses. The premise of zoning law is that by segregating different incompatible uses, the overall use of the land is maximized and negative externalities are minimized. Zoning laws also seek to protect public benefits and/or to maximize the value of property in a given area. The best way to achieve these goals is by separating conflicting uses.

Once an area is zoned into different districts, the zoning can be of two types: exclusionary or cumulative. Exclusionary zoning, as its name implies, is zoning which permits only the type of use for which the district is zoned. All other uses are excluded, even if the other use is a "higher" or lighter use. On the other hand, cumulative zoning permits not only the specifically zoned use, but any and all "higher" uses. Under cumulative zoning, uses which are "higher" are permitted, but not "lower" uses. Here, the facts specifically state that the block is zoned "exclusively and solely" single family residential. The facts imply that the zoning is exclusionary, which intrinsically would prohibit any type of use but single family residential. The YMCA's recreational complex would not be permitted. Moreover, even if the zoning were cumulative, only "higher" uses would be permitted. It is unlikely that the YMCA recreational complex would be considered a "higher" use. Under either approach, the complex is incompatible with the current zoning.

Although stability in zoning is important, so too is some degree of flexibility. Stability is important because property owners invest money in the land on the reasonable expectation that the zoning for the area and the surrounding uses will not change. On the other hand, some flexibility is important because whenever broadly worded regulations are imposed upon a large area of land it is impossible to take into consideration individual circumstances and consequences. Accordingly, the general rule is that one who purchases in reliance upon existing zoning ordinances acquires no vested property rights that the ordinances will remain as is in perpetuity. While the surrounding property owners' reliance may be taken into consideration in analyzing whether the appropriate zoning body has adequate grounds for varying from the existing zoning ordinance, changes are permitted under the appropriate circumstances. There are a number of different methods of providing for flexibility within a zoning scheme as applied to a single lot.

One method of providing for flexibility within a zoning scheme is the special exception/special-use permit approach. This method must be built into the existing zoning scheme by being set forth expressly in the existing zoning ordinance. If the zoning ordinance permits special exceptions, the ordinance typically will set forth two lists of permitted uses. The first list will set forth those uses which are permitted without any special permission from the local zoning bodies. The second list will set forth those uses which are permitted, but only with special permission from the local zoning bodies. The special exception/special use permit approach recognizes that certain uses are not only not incompatible, but may actually be desirable, but only under appropriate conditions within the district. A classic example of a desirable use but only under appropriate conditions would be a church or other place of worship (putting aside separation of church and state issues).

Under the facts of the problem, the issue would be whether the zoning ordinance has a provision providing for any special use permits, and if so, if the YMCA's planned recreational complex came within the scope of the special exceptions. The facts are not clear, but based upon the few facts mentioned, it does not appear as if the ordinance permits any special exceptions. The facts state that the district was zoned "*exclusively* and *solely* for single family residential use *and no other*." The zoning ordinance does not appear to permit special use exceptions to the general residential, single family scheme.

A second method of providing for flexibility within a zoning ordinance are variances. A variance is simply a waiver from the zoning ordinance as applied to the property in question. The property owner petitions the appropriate zoning body for a variance. Because a variance is an exception to the general principle that similarly situated parties should be treated equally, in essence the applicant needs to establish that he or she is not similarly situated and that application of the zoning ordinance to him or her would result in "hardship." The debate is over the degree of hardship required to justify a variance in the use of the property. The prevailing approach is that the hardship must be extreme, and that variances in use should be granted sparingly.

As applied to the YMCA's plans, there does not appear to be any evidence of extreme hardship if the zoning ordinance is applied to lot 10. In fact, it is difficult to say that there is any hardship at all. Although locating the YMCA's recreational complex on lot 10 may be a convenience, and may even be in the best interest of the public, it is not necessary to relieve a hardship. The YMCA appears to have little chance of prevailing under the variance approach.

A third approach to building some flexibility into a zoning scheme is to permit amendments to a zoning ordinance. Although an argument can be made that any such amendment should be made on a district wide basis, that is not required. The general rule is that zoning amendments can be adopted on a lot-specific basis as long as the amendment meets the requirements for a valid ordinance: that the act promote the health, safety, morals or general welfare of the public and that the act is consistent with the municipality's comprehensive plan.

The YMCA's best chance is to petition to have the property rezoned. There is no evidence the zoning ordinance permits special exceptions. There is no evidence of undue hardship if the ordinance is enforced as written on lot 10. The YMCA needs to try to have the property rezoned. **Answer (B) is incorrect** because there is no evidence that the zoning ordinance governing lot 10 permits special exceptions. On the contrary, the only available evidence implies that the ordinance does not permit special exceptions. (If the ordinance did, and the YMCA's recreational plans fell within the scope of a listed special exception, that would probably be the YMCA's best chance of succeeding.) **Answer (C) is incorrect** because there is no evidence of undue hardship if the ordinance is enforced as written on lot 10. **Answer (D) is incorrect** because zoning ordinances are authorized under the government's general police powers, and absent special circumstances, they are accorded a strong presumption of validity. The residential, single family zoning district is a classic zoning ordinance which will withstand the rational basis judicial scrutiny absent special circumstances not presented by the facts.

• **Additional references**: *See* 12 RICHARD R. POWELL, POWELL ON REAL PROPERTY ch. 79C, §§ 79C.15[4][a], 79C.16[1]-[2][c], (Michael Allan Wolf ed., 2000); WILLIAM B. STOEBUCK & DALE A. WHITMAN, THE LAW OF PROPERTY §§ 9.2, 9.11, 9.21, 9.22, 9.28-9.29 (3rd ed. 2000); 8 THOMPSON ON REAL PROPERTY, SECOND THOMAS EDITION § 74.02(d) (2005 & Supp. 2006).

15. **The best answer is (D) (though a strong argument can be made for answer (B)).** Although zoning amendments are permitted, zoning amendments which rezone a single lot or a small amount of land are closely scrutinized because the assumption is that similarly situated parcels are no longer being treated similarly. There is an assumption that the initial zoning ordinance properly treated the property and surrounding properties. To the extent surrounding properties are not being rezoned and/or the surrounding property owners have invested in their properties in reliance on the original zoning, "spot rezoning" is highly suspect.

First the plaintiffs must show that they have standing to challenge the rezoning. Plaintiffs challenging a rezoning ordinance must show that they are directly affected or aggrieved by the rezoning. Neighboring property owners are almost always found to have standing because usually they will be directly affected by the rezoning. Here, the plaintiffs live on Oak Park Avenue, and one is the immediate neighbor. Under the facts, there appears little doubt that the plaintiffs have standing.

Although original zoning ordinances are generally accorded great deference as a valid exercise of the government's police powers, "spot rezoning" generally is viewed with great suspicion. Courts require that a zoning scheme be reasonably uniform, rather than arbitrary and discriminatory. This means that similar parcels have to be treated in the same way, and the government has to have a valid reason for zoning two similar parcels differently. When like parcels are found to have been treated differently, it is often referred to as "spot zoning," and that portion of the ordinance will be invalid.

"Spot zoning" generally arises in the context of an amendment to an existing plan. There are three factors which are usually present when an amendment is struck down as spot zoning: (1) the use permitted by the re-zoning is generally very different from the prevailing uses in the surrounding area; (2) the area rezoned is generally small - usually one parcel, rarely more than a few; and (3) the rezoning is for the benefit of the sole or few owners whose property has been rezoned, rather than for the benefit of the community.

Spot zoning smacks of unequal treatment, of discrimination in favor of one group of property owners and against another. Rezoning which expands the boundaries of an existing zoning scheme is more likely to be upheld than rezoning which carves out an exception from an existing scheme and from the surrounding parcels. Rezoning which is not in accordance with the municipality's comprehensive plan is more at risk. Rezoning which cannot be justified as the grounds of "change of conditions" or "mistake in the original zoning scheme" are often struck down. If a rezoning generates benefits for the community, that is a relevant, but not controlling, factor. Courts will often examine all of the circumstances, including the harm imposed on neighboring properties.

As applied to the facts of the problem, the rezoning of lot 10 is a classic example of spot zoning. A small, single parcel of land is being singled out for preferential treatment. Although the community at large would receive some benefit, there is no great need for the rezoning. There are other locations better suited for the YMCA's recreational project where the use would be in compliance with the local zoning. The benefits to be derived from locating the project at this site arguably are minimal. Moreover, the rezoning does not appear to be in accordance with Pleasantville's comprehensive plan, and the rezoning cannot be justified on the grounds of "change of conditions" or "mistake in the original zoning scheme." The most likely result is the rezoning will be struck down as improper and illegal spot zoning.

Answer (A) is incorrect because the plaintiffs do have standing to challenge the rezoning. As neighbors in the immediate vicinity of the rezoned lot, the plaintiffs will be directly affected by any change in use permitted on lot 10. As aggrieved parties, the neighbors have standing to sue. **Answer (B) is incorrect** because the courts have the judicial authority to review rezoning ordinances, even those which the local zoning entity deems to be in the best interests of the community. The rezoning must comply with the city's comprehensive plan to be in the best interests of the community, and the rezone must appear fair and reasonable under the circumstances. **Answer (C) is incorrect** because although zoning in general is usually upheld as a valid exercise of the government's police powers, spot zoning is highly suspect and usually struck down as arbitrary and illegal.

- **Additional references:** *See* 12 RICHARD R. POWELL, POWELL ON REAL PROPERTY ch. 79C, §§ 79C.15[4], 79C.19[2], 79C.03[3]-[3][b][iii], (Michael Allan Wolf ed., 2000); WILLIAM B. STOEBUCK & DALE A. WHITMAN, THE LAW OF PROPERTY §§ 9.2, 9.22 (3rd ed. 2000); RALPH E. BOYER ET. AL., THE LAW OF PROPERTY: AN INTRODUCTORY SURVEY § 12.1 (4th ed. 1991).

16. **The best answer is (D).** Zoning is justified under the government's police powers. Zoning regulations are upheld as long as they promote the public welfare. The issue is whether purely aesthetic considerations fall within the scope of the public welfare.

Historically, the courts' answer to that question was "no." The courts reasoned that aesthetic considerations were simply not sufficiently related to the public's health, safety, morals or general welfare. In addition, the courts were concerned that aesthetics are so intrinsically subjective that ordinances prohibiting certain uses or activities on purely aesthetic grounds would be open to claims that the government was acting arbitrarily and/or irrationally.

More recently, however, there is growing support for the proposition that aesthetic considerations come within the scope of the public welfare. Support for aesthetic zoning stems from a Supreme Court opinion where the Court broadly construed the term "public welfare" to include "spiritual as well as physical [considerations], aesthetic as well as monetary [considerations], ..." Based on the Court's statement, zoning for aesthetic purposes is becoming increasingly common. Aesthetic zoning ordinances, however, arguably never consider only aesthetic considerations. Invariably, such ordinances also consider more traditional factors which would fall within a more traditional understanding of the public welfare. Accordingly, the commentators continue to debate whether a pure aesthetic zoning ordinance would be constitutional.

Moreover, even the courts which have upheld contemporary aesthetic zoning ordinances have required them to be "reasonable." While there is room for debate as to what constitutes "reasonable," the courts appear to require that the (1) the prohibited use offends the average, reasonable person, and (2) the prohibited use would decrease property values. To the extent the latter is a requirement, aesthetic zoning looks more and more like traditional zoning which was intended to protect property rights and values.

There is no doubt that the under the traditional approach, the Stewartsville zoning ordinance would be an illegal attempt to regulate aesthetics. Under the modern trend, aesthetic zoning arguably is permitted, but only if reasonable. Under the modern trend, the issue is whether the Stewartsville ordinance is reasonable. The color of Howie's door (while definitely ugly), arguably would not offend the average reasonable person. Martha arguably is being hyper-sensitive. Furthermore, the color of Howie's door is not a significant enough factor to depress the value of nearby properties. Aesthetic zoning ordinances, to the extent they are permitted under the modern trend, should be for more severe cases than the facts given here. A red door is simply a personal choice and is not likely to get much of a reaction from the average, reasonable person.

Answer (A) is incorrect because it implicitly misstates the traditional common law approach and misapplies the modern trend approach. Under the traditional, common law approach, the ordinance would be an invalid attempt at aesthetic zoning. The modern trend permits aesthetic zoning if it is reasonable. As applied to Howie's door, the Stewartsville zoning ordinance arguably is not reasonable. The color of Howie's door arguably is not offensive to the average, reasonable person, and it is not likely to appreciably lessen the property values of nearby homes. **Answer (B) is incorrect** because it confuses the common law and modern trend approaches. The city has no chance under the common law approach - the ordinance would be an invalid attempt at aesthetic zoning. The city's only chance is under the modern trend, which permits aesthetic zoning if it is reasonable. But even there, the Stewartsville zoning ordinance arguably is not reasonable as applied to Howie's door. The color of Howie's door arguably is not offensive to the average, reasonable person, and it is not likely to appreciably lessen the property values of nearby homes. **Answer (C) is incorrect** because although it properly states the law with respect to aesthetic zoning, it fails to take into consideration that under the modern trend the aesthetic zoning ordinance has to be reasonable. As applied to Howie's door, the Stewartsville zoning ordinance is not reasonable. The color of Howie's door arguably is not offensive to the average, reasonable person, and it is not likely to appreciably lessen the property values of nearby homes.

- **Additional references:** *See* WILLIAM B. STOEBUCK & DALE A. WHITMAN, THE LAW OF PROPERTY § 9.20 (3rd ed. 2000); 12 RICHARD R. POWELL, POWELL ON REAL PROPERTY ch. 79C, § 79C.03[2][c][vi] (Michael Allan Wolf ed., 2000); RALPH E. BOYER ET. AL., THE LAW OF PROPERTY: AN INTRODUCTORY SURVEY § 12.1 (4th ed. 1991); Berman v. Parker, 348 U.S. 26 (1954).

17. **The best answer is (C).** When there is only one mortgage on a property and the mortgagee (lender) forecloses, any surplus proceeds after paying off the mortgage constitute the mortgagor's (borrower's) equity and go to the mortgagor. Where there are multiple mortgages or lien holders, however, the distribution scheme may change. If a mortgagee or lien holder forecloses, the effect of the foreclosure is to wipe out the junior mortgages and lien holders. A junior property interest is any property interest which is created after the time the mortgage was created. Because the foreclosure wipes out the junior mortgages and lien holders, any surplus is generally distributed to the junior mortgages and lien holders in order of their priority. Priority is determined under the traditional principle of first in time, first in right (as modified by the jurisdiction's recording act - if applicable to the facts).

(If the later in time property interest qualifies for protection under the recording act, it is treated as if it were a senior property interest. Senior property interests are those which were created before the mortgage or lien was created. Senior property interests, if properly recorded, are not affected by foreclosure and the purchasing party takes subject to the senior property interests.)

Because National Trust & Loan is the foreclosing mortgagee, it is treated as the senior mortgagee for purposes of distribution of the foreclosure proceeds. National Trust & Loan is paid off first, with any surplus proceeds being distributed to the mortgagees and lien holders junior to it in order of their priority. In this case, the surplus would be distributed to 1st Federal Bank and Trust.

Answers (A) and (B) are incorrect because a junior lien holder's foreclosure does not affect a properly recorded senior lien holder's interest. The property is sold at foreclosure subject to the existing senior liens. Since National Trust & Loan is the foreclosing mortgagee, the foreclosure does not affect 1st State Bank's interest in the property. The foreclosure is subject to 1st State Bank's mortgage, which continues to run against the property. Since 1st State Bank's interest and mortgage is not affect by the foreclosure, 1st State Bank has no rights to any of the foreclosure proceeds. **Answer (D) is incorrect** because it fails to recognize that more than one creditor may have an interest in an asset. Jake executed mortgages on the property to several lenders. Each lender stands in line in order of first in time, first in right (assuming each lender's interest is properly recorded), with the borrower standing in line last. When a middle of the line lender forecloses on the property, since the effect of the foreclosure is to wipe out the junior lien holders, each junior lien holder stands in line after the foreclosing lien holder but before the borrower. As a junior lien holder in line after National Trust & Loan, 1st Federal Bank and Trust takes any excess proceeds up to the amount it is owed before Jake receives any of the foreclosure proceeds. **Answer (E) is incorrect** because it fails to recognize the principle of first in time, first in right. As long as the lien holders have properly recorded their interests, they are satisfied in order of priority, not pro rata.

- **Additional references**: *See* 4 RICHARD J. POWELL, POWELL ON REAL PROPERTY ch. 37, § 37.41 (Patrick J. Rohan ed. 1999); 12 THOMPSON ON REAL PROPERTY, SECOND EDITION §§ 101.06(a), 101.04(a)-(b)(1) (1994 & Supp. 2006); GRANT S. NELSON & DALE A. WHITMAN, REAL ESTATE FINANCE LAW § 7.31 (3d ed. 1994).

18. **The best answer is (B).** The general effect of a foreclosure is to wipe out the foreclosing claim and all junior claims, but a foreclosure generally does not affect any senior mortgages or liens. A junior property interest is any property interest which is created after the time the mortgage was created. Senior property interests are those which were created and properly recorded before the mortgage was created. Foreclosure by the senior mortgagee has the effect of cleaning the title of the mortgages. Foreclosure by a junior mortgage or lien holder, however, will not affect the more senior mortgages and lien holders (assuming they were properly recorded).

National Trust & Loan is a junior mortgage (junior in time, i.e., subsequent in time) to 1st State Bank's mortgage. National Trust & Loan's foreclosure wipes out its mortgage and any and all junior mortgages and lien holders (1st Federal Bank and Trust). In essence, the purchaser at National Trust & Loan's foreclosure sale is purchasing the equity which exists above and beyond the mortgage held by 1st State Bank, since the purchaser takes subject to that mortgage.

Answer (A) is incorrect because the effect of the mortgage foreclosure is to wipe out the foreclosing mortgage and any and all junior lien holders. Since National Trust & Loan is the foreclosing mortgagee, National Trust & Loan's mortgage is wiped out, along with the junior mortgage, 1st Federal Bank and Trust. **Answer (C) is incorrect** because the mortgage foreclosure completely wipes out the foreclosing mortgage and any and all junior lien holders, even if the funds generated by the foreclosure sale are not great enough to satisfy the outstanding liens. 1st Federal Bank & Trust's mortgage is completely wiped out, even if the funds from the sale are not enough to cover the mortgage. **Answer (D) is incorrect** because it implicitly fails to recognize the principle of first in time, first in right. As long as the lien holders have properly recorded their interests, they are satisfied in order of priority, not pro rata. The foreclosing mortgage and any and all junior lien holders are completely wiped out. Any mortgages and lien holders senior (recorded prior in time as a general rule) to the foreclosing mortgage remain intact. **Answer (E) is incorrect** because the foreclosure wipes out only the foreclosing mortgage and any and all junior lien holders. Any mortgages and lien holders senior (recorded prior in time as a general rule) to the foreclosing mortgage remain intact.

- **Additional references**: *See* 4 RICHARD J. POWELL, POWELL ON REAL PROPERTY ch. 37, §§ 37.37[6]-[10] (Patrick J. Rohan ed. 1999); 12 THOMPSON ON REAL PROPERTY, SECOND THOMAS EDITION §101.04(b)(1) (1994 & Supp. 2006); GRANT S. NELSON & DALE A. WHITMAN, REAL ESTATE FINANCE LAW § 7.31 (3d ed. 1994).

19. **The best answer is (A)**. The Fifth Amendment to the Constitution provides, "…nor shall private property be taken for public use, without just compensation." The Takings Clause expressly requires that the taking has to be for "public use." In construing what constitutes "public use" for purposes of the Fifth Amendment, the Supreme Court has taken an extremely liberal approach, establishing an extremely low threshold.

Public use does not mean that the public generally, or even a large segment of the public, has to be able to use the property. Public use does not mean that the public generally, or even a large segment of the public, has to benefit directly from the property. Public use does not mean that the public, the government, or some agency of the government has to hold title to the property. All that is necessary is that the taking promotes a "conceivable public purpose." As long as the taking arguably promotes a conceivable public benefit, even if the direct benefit is enjoyed by relatively few, and even title to the property is transferred to private parties, the taking is for a public use.

The crucial question is whether the proposed taking is for the primary benefit of the public or the private user. Here, the controlling purpose of the project is to increase employment and to boost the economy. The Supreme Court has ruled that that a city's exercise of eminent domain power in furtherance of an economic development plan does satisfy the constitutional "public use" requirement. Here, the benefits that the public will enjoy as a result of the plant are sufficient to satisfy the spirit of the law, even though a private party will also ultimately benefit (the reason being that the private benefit is merely incidental to the public benefit). Capitalism may take the property and transfer it to "Toys for You" for use as an assembly plant.

Answer (B) is incorrect because the Takings Clause explicitly states that the government can only take property for "public use" - a reasonable use which is not a public use would not qualify. Moreover, just compensation is a distinct requirement that must be analyzed separately in determining whether the government acted pursuant to its authority. If the purpose for the taking is not a public use, the taking will be declared unconstitutional even if there was just compensation. **Answers (C) and (D) are incorrect** because they reach the wrong conclusion. Even though a private party will also benefit, the underlying purpose of this project is to promote employment and boost the economy, two public benefits. Generally speaking, the government cannot condemn one's property merely to convey it to another private person. If the primary purpose of the transfer from one private party to another is a public benefit though, this use of the power of eminent domain is permitted.

- **Additional references:** *See* 12 RICHARD R. POWELL, POWELL ON REAL PROPERTY ch. 79B, § 79B.01[1] (Michael Allan Wolf ed., 2000); 9 THOMPSON ON REAL PROPERTY, SECOND THOMAS EDITION § 80.03(c) (1999 & Supp. 2006); RALPH E. BOYER ET. AL., THE LAW OF PROPERTY: AN INTRODUCTORY SURVEY § 12.3 (4th ed. 1991); Authority v. Midkiff, 467 U.S. 229 (1984); Kelo v. City of New London, Conn., 545 U.S. 469 (2005).

20. **The best answer is (A).** Although the bank account paperwork indicates that it is a joint tenancy bank account, historically courts have put little weight on the paperwork because banks have not offered customers other options consistent with the depositor's true intent. If the depositor's true intent is something other than a true joint tenancy, the courts will ignore the paperwork and treat the multiple party bank account according to the depositor's true intent.

In assessing the depositor's true intent, there were basically three possibilities. First, the depositor may have intended a true joint tenancy, which immediately grants an equal interest to the other parties on the account and creates a right of survivorship. Second, the depositor may have been trying to create a payment on death account, which transfers no interest to the other parties on the account inter vivos (during the life of the parties), but which transfers the funds upon the death of the depositor (right of survivorship). Lastly, the depositor may have wanted an agency or convenience account. The depositor may have put the other party or parties on the account merely to help the depositor, to act as an agent for the depositor. The agency account transfers no equitable interest to the other parties either during the depositor's life or after the depositor's death.

Historically, banks were reluctant to recognize payment on death accounts or convenience accounts because of the liability risks they posed for the banks. Accordingly, banks would force the depositor to use the joint tenancy bank account even if that was not the depositor's true intent. The common law courts reasoned that the depositor's true intent should control the ultimate disposition of the funds, not the bank's paperwork which was forced upon the depositor.

Here, although O put the funds into a joint bank account, the bank's characterization of the account is not controlling. The question is "Why did O put A on the account?" It appears as if O put A on the account so that A could act as O's agent and pay O's bills while O was away in Europe. O did not intend to transfer any interest to A inter vivos, nor did O intend for A to get the money in the event O were to die while in Europe. Inasmuch as the multiple party bank account was intended to be an agency account, A has no interest in the account. All of the funds in the account will pass into O's probate estate where H, O's heir, will take the funds because O died intestate.

Answer (B) is incorrect because it fails to take into account that the bank's characterization of the account is not controlling. The courts will consider evidence as to O's true intent in putting A on the account. O's true intent will control how the account is characterized and the property rights which follow. **Answer (C) is incorrect** because under the intestate distribution scheme, an heir is entitled to inherit property regardless of the relationship the heir had with the decedent as long as the decedent has not executed a valid will which disposes of the property or properly disposed of the property through non-probate means. **Answer (D) is incorrect** because there is no affirmative evidence to support the position that O wanted A to have the money when O died. The fact that O did not know H and was good friends with A is not enough to constitute an intent that the account be construed as a payment on death account. (And even if it were, at common law payment on death accounts were invalid so the money would still pass into O's probate estate where H would take it as O's heir.) **Answer (E) is invalid** because as a convenience or agency account, the agent takes no interest in the property while the depositor is alive or after his or her death. A took no interest in the joint account, and upon O's death, the funds passed into O's probate estate where H took the money under the laws of intestacy.

- **Additional references**: *See* 2 THOMPSON ON REAL PROPERTY, SECOND THOMAS EDITION §§ 13.10(a)-(c) (2000 & Supp. 2006); RALPH E. BOYER ET AL., THE LAW OF PROPERTY: AN INTRODUCTORY SURVEY §§ 3.6-3.7 (4th ed. 1991); 15 RICHARD J. POWELL, POWELL ON REAL PROPERTY ch. 85, § 85.21[1][a] (Michael Allan Wolf ed., 2000).

21. **The best answer is (A).** As established above (see answer to question 19), under the common law approach, the bank's characterization of the account is not controlling. The courts will take evidence as to the depositor's true intent and that will control the characterization of the account and the legal rights to the money in the account.

The problem with the common law approach is that it leads to excessive litigation. In an attempt to reduce litigation concerning the proper characterization of multiple party bank accounts, the modern trend (as set forth in the Uniform Probate Code) creates rebuttable presumptions as to the parties' rights to the funds and heightens the evidentiary standard necessary to overcome the presumptions. The modern trend presumes that during the life of the parties, the funds are owned in proportion to the parties' contributions, absent clear and convincing evidence of a contrary intent. The modern trend presumes that after the death of one of the parties, the funds remaining in the account are owned by the other parties named on the account, absent clear and convincing evidence of a contrary intent.

Applying the modern trend, absent clear and convincing evidence of a contrary intent, it is presumed that O owned all the funds during O's lifetime, and upon O's death, A owns the funds. O put A's name on the account, however, only as a convenience to O to pay O's bills while O was away in Europe. O never contemplated that O might die during the trip. O did not intend to transfer any interest to A inter vivos, nor did O intend for A to get the money in the event O were to die while in Europe. The only reason O put A on the account was to facilitate paying O's bills. There appears to be clear and convincing evidence that O intended only a convenience account. Thus, A takes no interest in the funds either inter vivos or after O's death. The funds pass through O's probate estate to O's only heir, H.

Answer (B) is incorrect because although the modern trend presumes that following the death of one of the parties on the account, the money is owned by the other parties, that is true only if there is not clear and convincing evidence of a contrary intent. Here, there is clear and convincing evidence that O intended an agency account which grants A no interest upon O's death. **Answer (C) is incorrect** because there is clear and convincing evidence that O intended an agency account. Therefore, upon O's death, A has no interest in the money and it goes into O's probate estate. Under the intestate distribution scheme, an heir is entitled to inherit property regardless of the relationship the heir had with the decedent if the decedent has not properly disposed of the property through non-probate means or executed a valid will. **Answer (D) is incorrect** because there is no affirmative evidence to support that O wanted a payment on death account in favor of A. The fact that O did not know H and was good friends with A is not enough to constitute an intent that the account be construed as a payment on death account. Although that is the presumption under the modern trend, there is clear and convincing evidence that O intended the account to be merely an agency account. The clear and convincing evidence overcomes the modern trend presumption. **Answer (E) is invalid** because as a convenience or agency account, the agent takes no interest in the property. A took no interest, and upon O's death, the funds passed into O's probate estate where H took under the laws of intestacy.

- **Additional references:** *See* UNIFORM PROBATE CODE § 6-103(a); 2 THOMPSON ON REAL PROPERTY, SECOND THOMAS EDITION §§ 13.10(a)-(c) (2000 & Supp. 2006); RALPH E. BOYER ET AL., THE LAW OF PROPERTY: AN INTRODUCTORY SURVEY §§ 3.6-3.7 (4th ed. 1991); 15 RICHARD J. POWELL, POWELL ON REAL PROPERTY ch. 85, § 85.21[1][a] (Michael Allan Wolf ed., 2000); In re Estate of Thompson, 66 Ohio St. 2d 433, 423 N.E.2d 90 (1981).

22. **The best answer is (B).** A Mother Hubbard clause is a clause which conveys all of the grantor's property within a specified area. It is most often used when there is not enough time to determine all of the

grantor's real property holdings and/or to get an accurate description of the properties. A common scenario when such a clause is used in a deed is a death bed scenario where the grantor is about to die. Assuming the grantor has capacity and the rest of the requirements for a valid deed are met, the clause is effective to transfer title to the properties within the specified area to the grantee.

The common law courts reasoned that the clause meets the Statute of Frauds requirement that the deed adequately describe the property to be conveyed because, with recourse to outside sources (the recording index and grantor's papers), the property being conveyed could be determined with reasonable certainty. Courts are becoming increasingly lax on the Statute of Frauds description requirement as long as the grantor's intent is clear and the property interest(s) being conveyed can be determined with reasonable certainty by resorting to extrinsic evidence.

If a deed containing such a clause is recorded, however, the general rule is that the Mother Hubbard clause does not give constructive notice of the transfer of the properties in question without a more accurate description of the properties in question. The grantee under a Mother Hubbard clause should follow-up on the clause and attach a more accurate description of the properties affected by the Mother Hubbard clause. Only if the Mother Hubbard clause has just such an addendum does its recording give constructive notice as to the properties described more accurately in the addendum.

Answers (A), (C) and (D) are incorrect because they refer to the wrong nursery rhymes. (How the clause came to be called a "Mother Hubbard" clause is a good question.) **Answer (D) is incorrect** because, with recourse to outside sources (the recording index and grantor's papers), the property being conveyed can be determined with reasonable certainty.

- **Additional references**: *See* 9 THOMPSON ON REAL PROPERTY, SECOND THOMAS EDITION § 82.08(c) (1999 & Supp. 2006); WILLIAM B. STOEBUCK & DALE A. WHITMAN, THE LAW OF PROPERTY § 11.2 (3rd ed. 2000); 14 RICHARD J. POWELL, POWELL ON REAL PROPERTY ch. 81A, §§ 81A.05[1][a]-[c][ii] (Michael Allan Wolf ed., 2000).

23. **The best answer is (D) (though a strong argument can be made for answer (C)).** Regulatory takings jurisprudence is one of the most difficult areas of the law. The starting point is the Fifth Amendment

Takings Clause, which prohibits the government from taking "private property . . . for public use, without just compensation." There are basically two types of governmental takings: trespassory, physical invasions and non-trespassory, regulatory takings. The former are easier to identify and analyze. The latter defy simple analysis. At one end of the spectrum, the government's police powers permit it to regulate land use. At the other end of the spectrum, excessive governmental regulation amounts to a taking. The challenge is to identify when the regulation has crossed that point on the spectrum where it ceases to be regulation and becomes a taking. The Supreme Court has repeatedly stated that whether a particular regulation amounts to a taking is a fact sensitive inquiry which depends upon the circumstances of each case.

Although the Supreme Court has repeatedly stated that whether a particular regulation amounts to a taking depends upon the particular circumstances of each case, a careful reading of the cases reveals at least four basic scenarios in which a taking claim may arise. The significance of the four different scenarios is that the Court has applied four different approaches to the takings analysis depending on the scenario. The first scenario involves a typical zoning ordinance of broad application. Under this scenario, the courts apply an ad hoc, fact sensitive balancing approach. Inasmuch as the government's police powers permit governments to regulate land use, the approach is very deferential to the governmental regulation. The central question is whether the governmental regulation substantially advances a legitimate state interest. What constitutes a legitimate state interest is construed broadly under the government's police powers. The regulation is deemed to substantially advance the interest as long as it plausibly could advance the interest. The state need not prove that the goal is actually advanced. The courts balance the public and private interests at stake, with deference being given to the claimed governmental interests and means. The courts also take into consideration (1) the economic impact of the regulation on the landowner, (2) the extent to which the regulation has interfered with the landowner's distinct investment-backed expectations, and (3) the character of the governmental action (the nature of the claimed taking and the nature of the public interest). If the ordinance appears to unfairly burden an individual property owner, the court may declare the regulation a taking.

The second and third takings scenarios involve what are considered "categorical" takings. The Supreme Court has identified two forms of "categorical" takings where the above described deferential, ad hoc balancing approach is inappropriate. The first is where the government regulation compels the landowner to permit a permanent physical "occupation" or "invasion" of the land. In such a case, the nature of the governmental action, a permanent physical "occupation" or "invasion" of the land dictates that the regulation be treated as a trespassory taking. Just compensation is due. The other scenario where the deferential balancing approach is inappropriate is where the regulation denies the landowner all economically beneficial or productive use of the land. In such a case, to the extent the landowner is denied all economically beneficial or productive use of the land, it is as if the landowner no longer owns the land. The regulation is deemed a categorical taking and just compensation is due.

The fourth takings scenario where the Supreme Court has set forth a distinct analysis is the exaction scenario. The exaction scenario arises where the landowner seeks to put his or her land to a legally permitted use, but the government conditions the landowner's ability to engage in that use upon the landowner dedicating some form of property interest to the public. The Supreme Court has ruled that where the governmental action amounts to an exaction, the governmental action is subject to heightened judicial scrutiny. The government must show that an essential nexus exists between the exaction and a legitimate state interest. An essential nexus exists if (1) the record supports a reasonable relationship between the identified public problem and the landowner's proposed use, and (2) the record establishes rough proportionality between the required exaction and the adverse impact of the landowner's proposed use. There is some disagreement over the exact degree of nexus and relationship which must be established, but this approach sets forth the basics of the exaction analytical approach.

Summarizing the judicial approach to takings claims, the default approach is the ad hoc, deferential balancing approach unless the landowner can come within either the categorical takings scenarios or the exaction scenario.

As applied to the TRPA temporary moratorium on development, the first issue is which analytical approach should be applied to the takings claim. Does the temporary moratorium amount to a categorical takings, does it constitute an exaction, or should be it be subjected to the default, deferential balancing analysis? The temporary development moratorium does not in any way "occupy" or "invade" the landowners' property. The temporary development moratorium does not constitute an exaction because it does not permit any development. The stronger argument is that the temporary development moratorium "denied the landowners all economically beneficial or productive use of the land." The counter-argument is that the moratorium was merely temporary to give the government an opportunity to study the problem and develop a reasonable response before the problem had developed beyond the point of control. The issue is whether the ordinance can constitute a taking for the time-period that it was in effect.

To argue that the temporary moratorium constitutes a temporary taking is to argue for a temporal, severance approach. Under this approach, property interests are placed on a time line, and segments of that time line constitute independent property interests. Any regulation which denies a property owner of all economically beneficial or productive use of the land for even a segment of the time line constitutes a categorical taking. Most modern cases, including a number of Supreme Court cases, have rejected the conceptual severance approach, except in cases of physical invasion or occupation. Since there is no physical invasion or occupation involved in the TRPA temporary development moratorium, it is unlikely the court would adopt the conceptual severance perspective. Accordingly, since the regulation was only temporary (though for a good number of years), the regulation did not deny the landowners all economically beneficial or productive use of the land.

(The Supreme Court's holding in First English Evangelical Lutheran Church v. County of Los Angeles, 482 U.S. 304 (1987) arguably is not applicable. First English involved an ordinance which banned development of property located in a flood plain. The ordinance was subsequently struck down as unconstitutional, and the issue was whether the landowners were entitled to compensation during the period that the ordinance was in effect. The Supreme Court expressly stated that it was not addressing whether the ordinance constituted a taking, but rather it was addressing only a very narrow issue: assuming a governmental regulation is deemed a taking, if the government subsequently abandons the regulation, is the landowner entitled to compensation for the time period the regulation was in effect? Although the Supreme Court ruled in the affirmative, which appears to support a conceptual severance approach, the Court's opinion expressly limited its holding to situations where the ordinance has been deemed a taking. The opinion arguably is distinguishable, and most courts had continued to hold that temporary development moratoriums do not constitute a taking.)

Under the deferential, fact sensitive balancing approach, the courts have repeatedly held that a temporary development moratorium does not constitute a taking. The temporary development moratorium is an important governmental land-use tool with a long and established tradition. It permits the appropriate planning agency to study the problem without the problem being exacerbated. It insures that land-use plans being developed are not obsolete by the time they are adopted because of development which occurred during the development of the plans. As applied to the temporary development moratorium adopted by the TRPA, it was adopted only as a last resort when prior attempts at regulating the problem proved ineffective. The moratorium's goal of permitting time to develop land use plans which would save the environmentally sensitive Lake Tahoe is clearly an appropriate governmental goal. The temporary nature of the regulations and the conditions which dictated it show that the ordinance was narrowly tailored to secure the permissible governmental goal.

The temporary development moratorium does not constitute a taking entitling the landowners to just compensation under the Fifth Amendment.

Answer (A) is incorrect because a temporary development moratorium does not "occupy" or "invade" the landowners' property in any sense of the word. A development moratorium merely regulates what the landowners may do with their property, but it does not permit the government to invade or occupy the land. **Answer (B) is incorrect** because a *temporary* building moratorium does not deny a landowner all economically beneficial or productive use of the land. The temporary moratorium may have diminished the property's value, but as long as the moratorium is intended to be, and is understood as, temporary, it will not deny the landowner *all* economically beneficial or productive use of the land. **Answer (C) is incorrect** because the courts have rejected applying a conceptual, severance approach to the issue of whether a governmental regulation constitutes a taking (though the Supreme Court has applied a conceptual, severance approach to calculating compensation once a taking has been established).

- **Additional references**: *See* 12 RICHARD J. POWELL, POWELL ON REAL PROPERTY ch. 79C, §§ 79C.08[4][c] (Michael Allan Wolf ed., 2000); WILLIAM B. STOEBUCK & DALE A. WHITMAN, THE LAW OF PROPERTY § 9.4 (3rd ed. 2000); Tahoe-Sierra Preservation Council, Inc. v. Tahoe Regional Planning Agency, 2000 U.S. App. LEXIS 13941; 50 ERC (BNA) 1751; 2000 Cal.Daily Op. Service 4765; 2000 Daily Journal DAR 6356 (9th Cir. 2000).

24. The best answer is (B). Regulatory takings jurisprudence is one of the most difficult areas of the law. The starting point is the Fifth Amendment Takings Clause, which prohibits the government from taking "private property . . . for public use, without just compensation." There are basically two types of governmental takings: trespassory, physical invasions and non-trespassory, regulatory takings. The former are easier to identify and analyze. The latter defy simple analysis. At one end of the spectrum, the government's police powers permit it to regulate land use. At the other end of the spectrum, excessive governmental regulation amounts to a taking. The challenge is to identify when the regulation has crossed that point on the spectrum where it ceases to be regulation and becomes a taking. The Supreme Court has repeatedly stated that whether a particular regulation amounts to a taking is a fact sensitive inquiry which depends upon the circumstances of each case.

Although the Supreme Court has repeatedly stated that whether a particular regulation amounts to a taking depends upon the particular circumstances of each case, a careful reading of the cases reveals at least four basic scenarios in which a takings claim may arise. The significance of the four different scenarios is that the Court has applied four different approaches to the takings analysis depending on the scenario. The first scenario involves a typical zoning ordinance of broad application. Under this scenario, the courts apply an ad hoc, fact sensitive balancing approach. Inasmuch as the government's police powers permit governments to regulate land use, the approach is very deferential to the governmental regulation. The central question is whether the governmental regulation substantially advances a legitimate state interest. What constitutes a legitimate state interest is construed broadly under the government's police powers. The regulation is deemed to substantially advance the interest as long as it plausibly could advance the interest. The state need not prove that the goal is actually advanced. The courts balance the public and private interests at stake, with deference being given to the claimed governmental interests and means. The courts also take into consideration (1) the economic impact of the regulation on the landowner, (2) the extent to which the regulation has interfered with the landowner's distinct investment-backed expectations, and (3) the character of the governmental action (the nature of the claimed taking and the nature of the public interest). If the ordinance appears to unfairly burden an individual property owner, the court may declare the regulation a taking.

The second and third takings scenarios involve what are considered "categorical" takings. The Supreme Court has identified two forms of "categorical" takings where the above described deferential, ad hoc balancing approach is inappropriate. The first is where the government regulation compels the landowner to permit a permanent physical "occupation" or "invasion" of the land. In such a case, the nature of the governmental action, a permanent physical "occupation" or "invasion" of the land dictates that the regulation be treated as a trespassory taking. Just compensation is due. The other scenario where the deferential balancing approach is inappropriate is where the regulation denies the landowner all economically beneficial or productive use of the land. In such a case, to the extent the landowner is denied all economically beneficial or productive use of the land, it is as if the landowner no longer owns the land. The regulation is deemed a categorical taking and just compensation is due.

The fourth takings scenario where the Supreme Court has set forth a distinct analysis is the exaction scenario. The exaction scenario arises where the landowner seeks to put his or her land to a legally permitted use, but the government conditions the landowner's ability to engage in that use upon the landowner dedicating some form of property interest to the public. The Supreme Court has ruled that where the governmental action amounts to an exaction, the governmental action is subject to heightened judicial scrutiny. The government must show that an essential nexus exists between the exaction and a legitimate state interest. An essential nexus exists if (1) the record supports a reasonable relationship between the identified public problem and the landowner's proposed use, and (2) the record establishes rough proportionality between the required exaction and the adverse impact of the landowner's proposed use. There is some disagreement over the exact degree of nexus and relationship which must be established, but this approach sets forth the basics of the exaction analytical approach.

In summary, the default judicial approach to takings claims is an ad hoc, deferential balancing approach unless the landowner can come within either the categorical takings scenarios or the exaction scenario.

As applied to the Town's development requirements for Developer, the first issue is which analytical approach should be applied to the takings claim. Do the development requirements amount to a categorical takings, do they constitute an exaction, or should they be subjected to the default, deferential balancing analysis? Both requirements arguably constitute exactions. Developer's proposed legal land use is conditioned upon Developer dedicating land to public use. One exaction is the dedication of a second roadway for emergency access. A second exaction is the requirement that Developer retain 30 percent of the subdivision as open space. Inasmuch as both requirements constitute exactions, both are subject to the heightened judicial scrutiny.

The Town must show that an essential nexus exists between each exaction and a legitimate state interest. An essential nexus exists if (1) the record supports a reasonable relationship between the identified public problem and the landowner's proposed use, and (2) the record establishes rough proportionality between the required exaction and the adverse impact of the landowner's proposed use. As applied to the requirement of a second access road, a legitimate state interest clearly exists. Public safety is a well recognized legitimate state interest. An essential nexus exists between the public concern and Developer's proposed subdivision because the record supports the fire hazards and emergency access risks inherent in Dead End Road. And the record establishes rough proportionality between the required second access road and the adverse impact of Developer's proposed subdivision. The Fire Department presented evidence as to how the subdivision would increase the problems by extending the road into a hazardous fire area. Limiting access to Dead End Road alone would exacerbate the fire and emergency access concerns. A secondary access road is a reasonable means of alleviating the legitimate public safety concerns and is proportionally related to the increased risks posed by the new development. The requirement that Developer provide a second access road is not a taking.

The requirement that Developer retain 30 percent of the subdivision as open space is a taking. Preserving open space and wildlife areas are legitimate state interests. Moreover, the record supports a reasonable relationship between the identified state interests and Developer's proposed subdivision. Clearly developing the 13.5 acres into 51 developed lots would reduce open space and wildlife areas. The record, however, is completely devoid of any evidence that the 30 percent exaction is roughly proportional to the adverse impact of the proposed subdivision. There are no studies or reports which support why 30 percent is the appropriate figure. Under the heightened scrutiny approach, the burden is on the government to establish the necessary nexus between the exaction and the legitimate state interest, and as to the open space exaction, the Town is unable to meet its burden here.

The requirement that Developer provide a second access road does not constitute a taking entitling Developer to just compensation under the

Fifth Amendment, but the requirement that 30 percent of the site be reserved for open space does constitute a taking entitling Developer to just compensation under the Fifth Amendment.

Answer (A) is incorrect because it fails to recognize that the 30 percent open space requirement fails to meet the heightened judicial scrutiny. Although the exaction is reasonably related to a legitimate state interest, there is no evidence that the exaction is roughly proportional to the adverse impact the subdivision will cause to the community. The government bears the burden of proving the essential nexus between the exaction and the legitimate state interest, and here the Town cannot carry its burden of proof. **Answer (C) is incorrect** because it gets the two exactions backwards. There is an essential nexus between the requirement that Developer provide a second access road and the public safety concerns, and that nexus is supported by the record. The record does not support the conclusion that the 30 percent open space requirement is roughly proportional to the adverse impact the subdivision will cause to the community. The government bears the burden of proving the essential nexus between the exaction and the legitimate state interest, and here the Town cannot carry its burden of proof as to the open space set aside. **Answer (D) is incorrect** because there is an essential nexus between the requirement that Developer provide a second access road and the public safety concerns, and that nexus is supported by the record. Requiring Developer to provide a second access road does not constitute a taking under the record.

- **Additional references:** *See* 11 RICHARD J. POWELL, POWELL ON REAL PROPERTY ch. 79, §§ 79.03[1]-[3], 12 POWELL ch. 79B, §§ 79B.07[1] (Michael Allan Wolf ed., 2000); 8 THOMPSON ON REAL PROPERTY, SECOND THOMAS EDITION §§ 85.12(a)-(e) (2005 & Supp. 2006); WILLIAM B. STOEBUCK & DALE A. WHITMAN, THE LAW OF PROPERTY §§ 9.4, 9.32 (3rd ed. 2000); Isla Verde International Holdings, Inc. v. City of Camas, 99 Wash. App. 127, 990 P.2d 420 (1999).

25. **The best answer is (B).** Property owners have the right to use their property as they see fit, but neighboring land owners and the public have the right to be free from unreasonable uses that substantially interfere with their quiet enjoyment of their lands. The law of nuisance attempts to balance the rights of property owners to use their land as they see fit and the duty of property owners to use their land so as not to unreasonably interfere with the public and their neighbors' right to use their land as they see fit.

The law of nuisance can be divided between public nuisances and private nuisances. Public nuisances are unreasonable activities which injure the community generally and which are contrary to a public good (the public health, morals, safety or general welfare), regardless of the activity's effect upon another's ability to use his or her land. On the other hand, private nuisances are those activities which constitute an unreasonable use of one's land which substantially interfere with another individual's use of his or her land.

The law of nuisance becomes even murkier when one adds in that private nuisances can be divided between nuisances *per se*, and nuisances in fact. Nuisances *per se* are those activities which are so unreasonable that they are unreasonable under any circumstances. The problem is that most activities which rise to the level of a nuisance *per se* are also public nuisances. Common examples of nuisances *per se* are uses which are illegal, uses which a landowner engages in out of malice towards a neighboring landowner, and uses which are patently contrary to public norms. Activities which fall within these categories usually constitute a public nuisance. The significance of this overlap between public nuisances and private nuisances *per se* is that, as a general rule, only the government may enjoin a public nuisance. Individual citizens may not enjoin a public nuisance unless they can show extraordinary interference with the use of their land.

As applied to the facts of the problem, however, the subtleties of the difference between a public nuisance and a private nuisance *per se* are irrelevant because operating a computer is neither. Properly built and maintained, computers are a lawful activity which provide many useful services. The issue is whether Thelma and Louis's computers constitute a nuisance in fact.

The doctrine of nuisance in fact is particularly unwieldy. As its name implies, the essence of the doctrine is simply that *under these particular facts*, the use complained of constitutes a nuisance. A use may not be a nuisance under certain facts, yet is a nuisance under other facts. So when is a use a nuisance? Whenever a court decides that the use unreasonably and substantially interferes with a surrounding landowner's ability to use his or her property. Although the law of nuisance, especially what constitutes "unreasonable use", is extremely fact sensitive, the courts and commentators have tried to put some guidelines on the doctrine. In assessing the reasonableness of the defendant's activity, the Restatement (Second) of Torts recommends that the courts consider: (1) the social value of the defendant's conduct, (2) the suitability of the defendant's conduct to the locality, and (3) the defendant's ability to avoid the interference. In addition, in assessing whether the harm to the plaintiff is "substantial," the Restatement (Second) of Torts recommends that the court consider: (1) the duration and degree of the harm, (2) the character of the harm, (3) the social value of the plaintiff's enjoyment, (4) the suitability of the plaintiff's use to the locality, and (5) the burden to the plaintiff to avoid the harm. Moreover, the courts have ruled that the magnitude of the harm should be assessed from the objective perspective of a reasonable person, not one hyper-sensitive to the defendant's use. The key elements of the law of nuisance are obviously very soft, nebulous elements: unreasonable interference, substantial interfere, contrary to public good. Because of the nature of the doctrine, its application is extremely fact sensitive.

Thelma and Louis' strongest argument is that Billie-Bob's use constitutes a hyper-sensitive use. There is no evidence that any of the other surrounding businesses are affected by the radiation leak from their computers. The argument is that Billie-Bob's television displays constitute a hyper-sensitive use which skews the effect of the radiation leak. If the defendant's use constitutes a hyper-sensitive use, i.e., if a normal person in the locality would not consider the defendant's use a nuisance, then there is no nuisance. The problem is that the omnipresence of television sets makes it difficult to argue that using a television set is a particularly sensitive use. It is unlikely that a court would find using a television set to be a hyper-sensitive use. (The omnipresence of television sets is what distinguishes this scenario from the classic drive-in theater scenarios.)

In assessing all the relevant factors, Thelma and Louis' computers arguably constitute a nuisance in fact. Although Billie-Bob's being there first is not controlling, it is a factor is assessing the pros and cons of the conduct of the respective parties. Billie-Bob was there first, and he is engaged in a lawful and important activity - the sale of appliances. Thelma and Louis and also engaged in lawful and important activity - providing travel services, but their method of providing services is substantially and unreasonably interfering with Billie-Bob's ability to sell televisions. In trying to resolve the conflict between the conflicting uses, the controlling factor arguably is that the technology exists to minimize the radiation leakage. Thelma and Louis are in a better position to minimize the conflict between the respective uses in the most efficient manner. Thelma and Louis' computers constitute a nuisance in fact as long as they emit radiation which disrupts Billie-Bob's television reception.

Answer (A) is incorrect because although who was there first is a factor to consider, it is not a determining factor. The court has to balance the competing interests and uses of the respective parties. Being there first does not automatically mean that any subsequent use which interferes with the first in time use will constitute a nuisance. Such a doctrine would unreasonably impede productive use of surrounding lands. **Answer (C) is incorrect** because the facts do not support the conclusion that Billie-Bob's use constitutes a hyper-sensitive use. Although the magnitude of the harm should be assessed from the objective perspective of a reasonable person, a reasonable person would probably consider using a television set to be an ordinary use, not a hyper-sensitive use. **Answer (D) is incorrect** because a nuisance does not turn on the degree of care exercised by the defendant. Nuisance is a condition, not an act or failure to act. A nuisance in fact may exist despite the fact that the person has used the highest degree of care to prevent or minimize the effect - though failure to take steps to minimize the effect may be relevant to the analysis of which party is in the best position to avoid or minimize the problem. **Answer (E) is incorrect** because the mere fact that a use is permitted by local zoning laws does not insulate it from a claim that it constitutes a nuisance in fact.

- **Additional references**: *See* 9 RICHARD J. POWELL, POWELL ON REAL PROPERTY ch. 64, §§ 64.01[1], 64.02[2]-64.04[2], 64.05[2], 64.05[6] (Patrick J. Rohan ed. 1999); 11 THOMPSON ON REAL PROPERTY, SECOND THOMAS EDITION §§ 67.02(a), 67.03(a)-(b)(3) (2002 & Supp. 2006); WILLIAM B. STOEBUCK & DALE A. WHITMAN, THE LAW OF PROPERTY § 7.2 (3rd ed. 2000); Page County Appliance Center v. Honeywell, Inc., 347 N.W.2d 171 (Iowa 1984).

ANSWER SHEET

	A B C D E		A B C D E		A B C D E		A B C D E		A B C D E
1	① ② ③ ④ ⑤	6	① ② ③ ④ ⑤	11	① ② ③ ④ ⑤	16	① ② ③ ④ ⑤	21	① ② ③ ④ ⑤
2	① ② ③ ④ ⑤	7	① ② ③ ④ ⑤	12	① ② ③ ④ ⑤	17	① ② ③ ④ ⑤	22	① ② ③ ④ ⑤
3	① ② ③ ④ ⑤	8	① ② ③ ④ ⑤	13	① ② ③ ④ ⑤	18	① ② ③ ④ ⑤	23	① ② ③ ④ ⑤
4	① ② ③ ④ ⑤	9	① ② ③ ④ ⑤	14	① ② ③ ④ ⑤	19	① ② ③ ④ ⑤	24	① ② ③ ④ ⑤
5	① ② ③ ④ ⑤	10	① ② ③ ④ ⑤	15	① ② ③ ④ ⑤	20	① ② ③ ④ ⑤	25	① ② ③ ④ ⑤

	A B C D E		A B C D E		A B C D E		A B C D E		A B C D E
1	① ② ③ ④ ⑤	6	① ② ③ ④ ⑤	11	① ② ③ ④ ⑤	16	① ② ③ ④ ⑤	21	① ② ③ ④ ⑤
2	① ② ③ ④ ⑤	7	① ② ③ ④ ⑤	12	① ② ③ ④ ⑤	17	① ② ③ ④ ⑤	22	① ② ③ ④ ⑤
3	① ② ③ ④ ⑤	8	① ② ③ ④ ⑤	13	① ② ③ ④ ⑤	18	① ② ③ ④ ⑤	23	① ② ③ ④ ⑤
4	① ② ③ ④ ⑤	9	① ② ③ ④ ⑤	14	① ② ③ ④ ⑤	19	① ② ③ ④ ⑤	24	① ② ③ ④ ⑤
5	① ② ③ ④ ⑤	10	① ② ③ ④ ⑤	15	① ② ③ ④ ⑤	20	① ② ③ ④ ⑤	25	① ② ③ ④ ⑤

ANSWER SHEET

	A	B	C	D	E		A	B	C	D	E		A	B	C	D	E		A	B	C	D	E		A	B	C	D	E
1	①	②	③	④	⑤	6	①	②	③	④	⑤	11	①	②	③	④	⑤	16	①	②	③	④	⑤	21	①	②	③	④	⑤
2	①	②	③	④	⑤	7	①	②	③	④	⑤	12	①	②	③	④	⑤	17	①	②	③	④	⑤	22	①	②	③	④	⑤
3	①	②	③	④	⑤	8	①	②	③	④	⑤	13	①	②	③	④	⑤	18	①	②	③	④	⑤	23	①	②	③	④	⑤
4	①	②	③	④	⑤	9	①	②	③	④	⑤	14	①	②	③	④	⑤	19	①	②	③	④	⑤	24	①	②	③	④	⑤
5	①	②	③	④	⑤	10	①	②	③	④	⑤	15	①	②	③	④	⑤	20	①	②	③	④	⑤	25	①	②	③	④	⑤

	A	B	C	D	E		A	B	C	D	E		A	B	C	D	E		A	B	C	D	E		A	B	C	D	E
1	①	②	③	④	⑤	6	①	②	③	④	⑤	11	①	②	③	④	⑤	16	①	②	③	④	⑤	21	①	②	③	④	⑤
2	①	②	③	④	⑤	7	①	②	③	④	⑤	12	①	②	③	④	⑤	17	①	②	③	④	⑤	22	①	②	③	④	⑤
3	①	②	③	④	⑤	8	①	②	③	④	⑤	13	①	②	③	④	⑤	18	①	②	③	④	⑤	23	①	②	③	④	⑤
4	①	②	③	④	⑤	9	①	②	③	④	⑤	14	①	②	③	④	⑤	19	①	②	③	④	⑤	24	①	②	③	④	⑤
5	①	②	③	④	⑤	10	①	②	③	④	⑤	15	①	②	③	④	⑤	20	①	②	③	④	⑤	25	①	②	③	④	⑤

ANSWER SHEET

	A B C D E		A B C D E		A B C D E		A B C D E		A B C D E
1	① ② ③ ④ ⑤	6	① ② ③ ④ ⑤	11	① ② ③ ④ ⑤	16	① ② ③ ④ ⑤	21	① ② ③ ④ ⑤
2	① ② ③ ④ ⑤	7	① ② ③ ④ ⑤	12	① ② ③ ④ ⑤	17	① ② ③ ④ ⑤	22	① ② ③ ④ ⑤
3	① ② ③ ④ ⑤	8	① ② ③ ④ ⑤	13	① ② ③ ④ ⑤	18	① ② ③ ④ ⑤	23	① ② ③ ④ ⑤
4	① ② ③ ④ ⑤	9	① ② ③ ④ ⑤	14	① ② ③ ④ ⑤	19	① ② ③ ④ ⑤	24	① ② ③ ④ ⑤
5	① ② ③ ④ ⑤	10	① ② ③ ④ ⑤	15	① ② ③ ④ ⑤	20	① ② ③ ④ ⑤	25	① ② ③ ④ ⑤

	A B C D E		A B C D E		A B C D E		A B C D E		A B C D E
1	① ② ③ ④ ⑤	6	① ② ③ ④ ⑤	11	① ② ③ ④ ⑤	16	① ② ③ ④ ⑤	21	① ② ③ ④ ⑤
2	① ② ③ ④ ⑤	7	① ② ③ ④ ⑤	12	① ② ③ ④ ⑤	17	① ② ③ ④ ⑤	22	① ② ③ ④ ⑤
3	① ② ③ ④ ⑤	8	① ② ③ ④ ⑤	13	① ② ③ ④ ⑤	18	① ② ③ ④ ⑤	23	① ② ③ ④ ⑤
4	① ② ③ ④ ⑤	9	① ② ③ ④ ⑤	14	① ② ③ ④ ⑤	19	① ② ③ ④ ⑤	24	① ② ③ ④ ⑤
5	① ② ③ ④ ⑤	10	① ② ③ ④ ⑤	15	① ② ③ ④ ⑤	20	① ② ③ ④ ⑤	25	① ② ③ ④ ⑤

ANSWER SHEET

	A	B	C	D	E		A	B	C	D	E		A	B	C	D	E		A	B	C	D	E		A	B	C	D	E
1	①	②	③	④	⑤	6	①	②	③	④	⑤	11	①	②	③	④	⑤	16	①	②	③	④	⑤	21	①	②	③	④	⑤
2	①	②	③	④	⑤	7	①	②	③	④	⑤	12	①	②	③	④	⑤	17	①	②	③	④	⑤	22	①	②	③	④	⑤
3	①	②	③	④	⑤	8	①	②	③	④	⑤	13	①	②	③	④	⑤	18	①	②	③	④	⑤	23	①	②	③	④	⑤
4	①	②	③	④	⑤	9	①	②	③	④	⑤	14	①	②	③	④	⑤	19	①	②	③	④	⑤	24	①	②	③	④	⑤
5	①	②	③	④	⑤	10	①	②	③	④	⑤	15	①	②	③	④	⑤	20	①	②	③	④	⑤	25	①	②	③	④	⑤

	A	B	C	D	E		A	B	C	D	E		A	B	C	D	E		A	B	C	D	E		A	B	C	D	E
1	①	②	③	④	⑤	6	①	②	③	④	⑤	11	①	②	③	④	⑤	16	①	②	③	④	⑤	21	①	②	③	④	⑤
2	①	②	③	④	⑤	7	①	②	③	④	⑤	12	①	②	③	④	⑤	17	①	②	③	④	⑤	22	①	②	③	④	⑤
3	①	②	③	④	⑤	8	①	②	③	④	⑤	13	①	②	③	④	⑤	18	①	②	③	④	⑤	23	①	②	③	④	⑤
4	①	②	③	④	⑤	9	①	②	③	④	⑤	14	①	②	③	④	⑤	19	①	②	③	④	⑤	24	①	②	③	④	⑤
5	①	②	③	④	⑤	10	①	②	③	④	⑤	15	①	②	③	④	⑤	20	①	②	③	④	⑤	25	①	②	③	④	⑤

ANSWER SHEET

	A B C D E		A B C D E		A B C D E		A B C D E		A B C D E
1	① ② ③ ④ ⑤	6	① ② ③ ④ ⑤	11	① ② ③ ④ ⑤	16	① ② ③ ④ ⑤	21	① ② ③ ④ ⑤
2	① ② ③ ④ ⑤	7	① ② ③ ④ ⑤	12	① ② ③ ④ ⑤	17	① ② ③ ④ ⑤	22	① ② ③ ④ ⑤
3	① ② ③ ④ ⑤	8	① ② ③ ④ ⑤	13	① ② ③ ④ ⑤	18	① ② ③ ④ ⑤	23	① ② ③ ④ ⑤
4	① ② ③ ④ ⑤	9	① ② ③ ④ ⑤	14	① ② ③ ④ ⑤	19	① ② ③ ④ ⑤	24	① ② ③ ④ ⑤
5	① ② ③ ④ ⑤	10	① ② ③ ④ ⑤	15	① ② ③ ④ ⑤	20	① ② ③ ④ ⑤	25	① ② ③ ④ ⑤

	A B C D E		A B C D E		A B C D E		A B C D E		A B C D E
1	① ② ③ ④ ⑤	6	① ② ③ ④ ⑤	11	① ② ③ ④ ⑤	16	① ② ③ ④ ⑤	21	① ② ③ ④ ⑤
2	① ② ③ ④ ⑤	7	① ② ③ ④ ⑤	12	① ② ③ ④ ⑤	17	① ② ③ ④ ⑤	22	① ② ③ ④ ⑤
3	① ② ③ ④ ⑤	8	① ② ③ ④ ⑤	13	① ② ③ ④ ⑤	18	① ② ③ ④ ⑤	23	① ② ③ ④ ⑤
4	① ② ③ ④ ⑤	9	① ② ③ ④ ⑤	14	① ② ③ ④ ⑤	19	① ② ③ ④ ⑤	24	① ② ③ ④ ⑤
5	① ② ③ ④ ⑤	10	① ② ③ ④ ⑤	15	① ② ③ ④ ⑤	20	① ② ③ ④ ⑤	25	① ② ③ ④ ⑤

ANSWER SHEET

	A B C D E		A B C D E		A B C D E		A B C D E		A B C D E
1	① ② ③ ④ ⑤	6	① ② ③ ④ ⑤	11	① ② ③ ④ ⑤	16	① ② ③ ④ ⑤	21	① ② ③ ④ ⑤
2	① ② ③ ④ ⑤	7	① ② ③ ④ ⑤	12	① ② ③ ④ ⑤	17	① ② ③ ④ ⑤	22	① ② ③ ④ ⑤
3	① ② ③ ④ ⑤	8	① ② ③ ④ ⑤	13	① ② ③ ④ ⑤	18	① ② ③ ④ ⑤	23	① ② ③ ④ ⑤
4	① ② ③ ④ ⑤	9	① ② ③ ④ ⑤	14	① ② ③ ④ ⑤	19	① ② ③ ④ ⑤	24	① ② ③ ④ ⑤
5	① ② ③ ④ ⑤	10	① ② ③ ④ ⑤	15	① ② ③ ④ ⑤	20	① ② ③ ④ ⑤	25	① ② ③ ④ ⑤

	A B C D E		A B C D E		A B C D E		A B C D E		A B C D E
1	① ② ③ ④ ⑤	6	① ② ③ ④ ⑤	11	① ② ③ ④ ⑤	16	① ② ③ ④ ⑤	21	① ② ③ ④ ⑤
2	① ② ③ ④ ⑤	7	① ② ③ ④ ⑤	12	① ② ③ ④ ⑤	17	① ② ③ ④ ⑤	22	① ② ③ ④ ⑤
3	① ② ③ ④ ⑤	8	① ② ③ ④ ⑤	13	① ② ③ ④ ⑤	18	① ② ③ ④ ⑤	23	① ② ③ ④ ⑤
4	① ② ③ ④ ⑤	9	① ② ③ ④ ⑤	14	① ② ③ ④ ⑤	19	① ② ③ ④ ⑤	24	① ② ③ ④ ⑤
5	① ② ③ ④ ⑤	10	① ② ③ ④ ⑤	15	① ② ③ ④ ⑤	20	① ② ③ ④ ⑤	25	① ② ③ ④ ⑤

	A	B	C	D	E			A	B	C	D	E			A	B	C	D	E			A	B	C	D	E			A	B	C	D	E
1	①	②	③	④	⑤		6	①	②	③	④	⑤		11	①	②	③	④	⑤		16	①	②	③	④	⑤		21	①	②	③	④	⑤
2	①	②	③	④	⑤		7	①	②	③	④	⑤		12	①	②	③	④	⑤		17	①	②	③	④	⑤		22	①	②	③	④	⑤
3	①	②	③	④	⑤		8	①	②	③	④	⑤		13	①	②	③	④	⑤		18	①	②	③	④	⑤		23	①	②	③	④	⑤
4	①	②	③	④	⑤		9	①	②	③	④	⑤		14	①	②	③	④	⑤		19	①	②	③	④	⑤		24	①	②	③	④	⑤
5	①	②	③	④	⑤		10	①	②	③	④	⑤		15	①	②	③	④	⑤		20	①	②	③	④	⑤		25	①	②	③	④	⑤

	A	B	C	D	E			A	B	C	D	E			A	B	C	D	E			A	B	C	D	E			A	B	C	D	E
1	①	②	③	④	⑤		6	①	②	③	④	⑤		11	①	②	③	④	⑤		16	①	②	③	④	⑤		21	①	②	③	④	⑤
2	①	②	③	④	⑤		7	①	②	③	④	⑤		12	①	②	③	④	⑤		17	①	②	③	④	⑤		22	①	②	③	④	⑤
3	①	②	③	④	⑤		8	①	②	③	④	⑤		13	①	②	③	④	⑤		18	①	②	③	④	⑤		23	①	②	③	④	⑤
4	①	②	③	④	⑤		9	①	②	③	④	⑤		14	①	②	③	④	⑤		19	①	②	③	④	⑤		24	①	②	③	④	⑤
5	①	②	③	④	⑤		10	①	②	③	④	⑤		15	①	②	③	④	⑤		20	①	②	③	④	⑤		25	①	②	③	④	⑤